Visions of Justice

Handbook of Oriental Studies

Handbuch der Orientalistik

SECTION EIGHT

Uralic and Central Asian Studies

Edited by

Nicola Di Cosmo

VOLUME 24

The titles published in this series are listed at *brill.com/ho8*

Visions of Justice

Sharīʿa *and Cultural Change in Russian Central Asia*

By

Paolo Sartori

BRILL

LEIDEN | BOSTON

Cover illustration: "Triangle Comedy", *Mushtum* 23 (1937): 11.

Library of Congress Cataloging-in-Publication Data

Names: Sartori, Paolo, 1975– author.
Title: Visions of justice : Sharia and cultural change in Russian Central Asia / by Paolo Sartori.
Description: Leiden ; Boston : Brill, 2016. | Series: Handbook of oriental studies. Section eight, Uralic and Central Asian studies ; Volume 24 | Includes bibliographical references and index.
Identifiers: LCCN 2016034428 (print) | LCCN 2016035432 (ebook) | ISBN 9789004330894 (hardback : alk. paper) | ISBN 9789004330900 (e-book) | ISBN 9789004330900 (E-book)
Subjects: LCSH: Law—Asia, Central—History—19th century. | Muslims—Legal status, laws, etc.—Asia, Central—History—19th century. | Islamic law—Asia, Central—History—19th century. | Muslims—Legal status, laws, etc.—Russia—History—19th century.
Classification: LCC KLA477 .S27 2016 (print) | LCC KLA477 (ebook) | DDC 340.5/90957—dc23
LC record available at https://lccn.loc.gov/2016034428

Typeface for the Latin, Greek, and Cyrillic scripts: "Brill". See and download: brill.com/brill-typeface.

ISSN 0169-8524
ISBN 978-90-04-33089-4 (hardback)
ISBN 978-90-04-33090-0 (e-book)

This book is printed on acid-free paper and produced in a sustainable manner.

Contents

Acknowledgments

This book has been long in the making, and, along the way, I have accumulated many debts to people and institutions. Without their help, this project would have never seen the light of the day. I owe debts of gratitude to the Gerda Henkel Foundation, the Volkswagen Foundation, the Austrian Science Fund (FWF), the German Research Fund (DFG), the French Institute for Central Asian Studies (IFEAC, Tashkent), the Central Asia and Caucasus Research and Training Initiative of the Open Society Foundations (CARTI, Budapest), and the Austrian Academy of Sciences for providing material support for research in Europe, Russia, and Central Asia.

The seeds of this book were planted in 2007 when a Volkswagen Foundation fellowship allowed me to spend four years at the Martin Luther University of Halle-Wittenberg, in Germany. There I had the unique privilege to work with Jürgen Paul. His erudition and passion for things Central Asian have been one of my greatest intellectual inspirations over the years. Volker Adam, Bekim Agai, Ildikó Beller-Hann, Johann Büssow, Jeanine Dağyeli, Ralf Elger, Kurt Franz, Chris Hann, Asma Hilali, Christian Müller, Francesca Petricca, Nader Purnaqcheband, Philipp Reichmuth, Christina Turzer, and Wolfgang Holzwarth made my stay in Halle an exciting and collegial experience. Thank you for your generosity and patience.

A visiting professorship to the École des Haute Études en Science Sociales, in Paris, in spring 2012 allowed me finally to see the contours of this book. I am grateful to Alain Blum, Randy Deguilhem, Isabelle Ohayon, Alessandro Stanziani, and Julien Thorez for convening the research seminars where I presented a dry run of the materials which then evolved into chapters two, four, and five. An incentive to complete this book came from the many invitations I received over recent years to present my work in universities and research institutes. Audiences at Leiden University, the University of Liverpool, the Institute of Ismaili Studies (London), the Nehru Memorial Museum & Library (New Delhi), the Ben-Gurion University of the Negev, the Uzbek Academy of Sciences (Tashkent), the University of Exeter, Harvard University, and Indiana University have heard and commented on versions of some of these chapters.

The Institute of Iranian Studies at the Austrian Academy of Sciences has been a wonderful place to work over the last few years. I am deeply grateful to the Director, Florian Schwarz, for giving me the opportunity to focus on my research and creating a vibrant and stimulating academic setting where Central Asianists can feel at home. I am also thankful to my colleagues for being supportive of my work and generous in sharing their input, advice, and a healthy dose of laughter.

Over the many years of research and writing that have gone into this book, many friends and colleagues have helped me, and I would like to thank them here for their assistance: Sergei Abashin, Bakhtiyar Babajanov, David Brophy, Alfrid Bustanov, Jeff Eden, Allen Frank, Rozaliya Garipova, Rebecca Gould, Daniele Guizzo, Michael Kemper, Alberto Masoero, Nasriddin Mirzaev, Alexander Morrison, Beatrice Penati, James Pickett, Danielle Ross, and Uktambek Sultonov all contributed astute comments on various aspects of the questions addressed here. While telling a story about tossing a copy of Nabokov's *Lolita* out of the window or sharing a startling comment over the latest issue of *The New Yorker*, Ulfat Abdurasulov and Tom Welsford read the entire manuscript several times, challenged me with their probing criticism, and listened to incessant monologues. They also opened a world of friendship to me. I also want to thank Devin DeWeese, Niccolò Pianciola, Ido Shahar, and Sanjay Subrahmanyam for pushing me, either by design or inadvertently, to reach beyond the usual frontiers of academic conventions. A special word of recognition is due to Svetlana Jacquesson. Between Halle, Istanbul, and Bishkek I learned from her more than I can easily summarize.

I want to thank Nicolette van der Hoek, my editor at Brill. Her capable collaboration has made the production of this book a pleasant experience. The reports of two anonymous referees of Brill Publishers were useful in revising the manuscript, and I am naturally grateful to them. Special thanks are due to Alan Hartley for careful copyediting and to Bettina Hofleitner for the maps. I thank Cambrige University Press for permission to reprint sections in the Introduction from my article "Constructing Colonial Legality in Russian Central Asia: On Guardianship," *CSSH* 56/2 (2014): 419–47. I also thank Brill for allowing me to reproduce in Chapter 2 parts of my article "Authorized Lies: Colonial Agencies and Legal Hybrids in Tashkent, c. 1881–1893," *JESHO* 55/4–5 (2012): 688–717.

The greatest debts are owed, of course, to my family. Special thanks to my parents Gildo and Giovanna Sartori for their unfailing and unconditional support and care. Caterina came into this world just as I started work on the manuscript. Together with this book she travelled many places and faced an itinerant life with her big smile. The late Edda Benetti Plafoni helped keep my sometimes flagging spirits high with her memorable dinners. It is to Barbara Plafoni Sartori that I dedicate this book for her witchcraft, big heart, and dreams.

Note on Transliteration and Nomenclature

For Islamic names and terms, I adopt the transliteration system for Arabic used by the *International Journal of Middle East Studies*. In so doing, I opted for a simple one-to-one correspondence between grapheme (in the original Arabic script) and phoneme (in the Latin). I have avoided rendering the presumed pronunciation of words in Persian and Chaghatay (Central Asian Turki) and introducing any artificial phonetic distinction between front and back vowels characteristic of the Turkic languages spoken in Central Asia. My transcription of Russian follows the *Chicago Manual of Style* with a few exceptions: *iu, ia* instead of *yu* and *ya*.

One complicating factor for the transliteration system that I employ is the variety of orthographic forms for certain names (e.g. Murād, Murat). In the attempt to avoid a normative approach to rendering such variations, I render names in the form in which they appear in whatever text is under discussion. For the sake of clarity and uniformity, however, I did not follow this rule when dealing with Islamic terms appearing in Russian sources. I thus give no account of how they are rendered in Russian and opt instead to transliterate them from their *presumed* Arabic-script rendering (e.g. *mulk* and *sharīʿa* instead of *miulk* and *sharigat*).

Most of the unpublished material on which the chapters of this volume are based comes from post-Soviet archives, and the citation of the archival material thus follows the standard system used in Russian studies. The archival collection, the inventory, the file, and the folio are indicated respectively with the following Russian abbreviations: f. (*fond*), op. (*opis'*), d. (*delo*), and l., ll. (*list, listy*), ob. (*oborot*).

Throughout this book I refer frequently to Central Asian historical actors as "Muslims." The adjective "Muslim" here refers to the population and is employed mostly as an emic category. It does not reflect any ascription to religiosity or politics. Nor do I understand "Muslims" as a population inhabiting a clearly defined and self-contained sociocultural domain. As the reader will see, this book includes cases reflecting substantial variations among Muslims' beliefs and behavioral patterns that would complicate any essentialist vision of things Muslim. The same approach applies to the terms "Russians" and "colonizers."

Abbreviations

Archives

AMIKINUz	Arkhiv muzeia istorii, kul'tury i isskustva narodov Uzbekistana, Samarqand
FBKOANRUz	Fundamental'naia biblioteka karakalpakskogo otdeleniia Akademii Nauk Respubliki Uzbekistan, Nukus
IQM	Ichan Qal'a Muzei, Khiva
IVRAN	Institut vostochnykh rukopisei Rossiiskoi Akademii Nauk, St. Petersburg
NBUz	Natsional'naia biblioteka Uzbekistana im. Alishera Navoi, Tashkent
ObAKh	Oblastnoi arkhiv Khodzhenta, Khujand
TsGARUz	Tsentral'nyi gosudarstvennyi arkhiv Respubliki Uzbekistan, Tashkent
TsVRUz	Tsentr vostochnykh rukopisei im. Abu Raikhana Beruni pri Tashkentskom gosudarstvennom institute vostokovedeniia, Tashkent

Journals and Reference Works

AHR	*American Historical Review*
AHSS	*Annales. Histoire, Sciences Sociales*
AS	*Asiatische Studien*
BSOAS	*Bulletin of the School of Oriental and African Studies*
CAS	*Central Asian Survey*
CAC	*Cahiers d'Asie centrale*
CMR	*Cahiers du Monde russe*
CSSH	*Comparative Studies in Society and History*
DI	*Der Islam*
EIr	*Encyclopœdia Iranica.* London and New York: Routledge & Kegan Paul, 1985–
EI2	*Encyclopaedia of Islam*, 2nd ed. Leiden: Brill, 1960–2004
HLJ	*Hastings Law Journal*
GAL	Brockelmann, Carl. *Geschichte der arabischen Literatur.* Leiden: Brill, 1996 [1st ed. 1943], 5 vols (vols. G.I–II and S.I–III)
GLR	*Griffith Law Review*

IESHR	*The Indian Economic and Social History Review*
IJMES	*International Journal of Middle East Studies*
ILS	*Islamic Law and Society*
IS	*Iranian Studies*
JAS	*The Journal of Asian Studies*
JESHO	*Journal of the Economic and Social History of the Orient*
JFGO	*Jahrbücher für Geschichte Osteuropas*
JIS	*Journal of Islamic Studies*
JLP	*Journal of Legal Pluralism*
JMMA	*Journal of Muslim Minority Affairs*
JOAS	*Journal of the American Oriental Society*
JPS	*Journal of Persianate Studies*
JRAI	*Journal of the Royal Anthropological Institute*
JRAS	*Journal of the Royal Asiatic Society*
Kritika	*Kritika: Explorations in Russian and Eurasian History*
LHR	*Law and History Review*
LSI	*Law and Social Inquiry*
LSR	*Law and Society Review*
MAS	*Modern Asian Studies*
ONU	*Obshchestvennye nauki v Uzbekistane*
MSR	*Mamluk Studies Review*
PP	*Past and Present*
SLR	*Sidney Law Review*
SVR	*Sobranie vostochnykh rukopisei Akademii Nauk Uzbekskoi SSR.* Tashkent: Fan, 1952–87, 11 vols
TS	*Turkestanskii sbornik: Sobranie sochinenii o Turkestanskom krae voobshche i sopredel'nykh s nim stran Srednei Azii*, ed. V.I Mezhov. St. Petersburg: Tip. Valasheva, 1868–1917, 594 vols
TV	*Turkestanskie Vedomosty*
WDI	*Die Welt des Islams*
ZDMG	*Zeitschrift der Deutschen Morgenländischen Gesellschaft*
ZGUP	*Zhurnal grazhdanskogo i ugolovnogo prava*

List of Maps and Illustrations

Maps

Illustrations

MAP 1 *Central Eurasia in the early 19th century.*
© BETTINA HOFLEITNER

MAP 2 *Central Asia prior to Russian colonization.*
© BETTINA HOFLEITNER

MAP 3 *Russian Central Asia.*
© BETTINA HOFLEITNER

Introduction

In the summer of 1936 the Uzbek writer Abdulla Qahhor (1907–68) published a short story in the satirical journal *Mushtum* ("The Fist").[1] Titled "The Thief," the story recounts the behavior of the average Muslim population of Central Asia encapsulated in the pursuit of redress under tsarist rule. "The Thief" is a morality tale of an elderly little man who struggles against the colonial bureaucracy to recover his property, a stolen ox, and gets lost in the interstices of local power relations. The plot is simple. An old woman, "rising at dawn to knead dough," inspects her household and finds that an ox has disappeared. Summoned by her cries, her husband, Qobil Bobo, soon realizes that the animal has been driven away through a hole in the barn. Inquisitive neighbors come in and crowd the scene. Among them is a striking figure, a neighbor whose deformed face lacks a nose; he holds the position of "fiftier" (*ellikboshi*), which is to say a local notable who had authority over fifty households. It is through this persona that we can begin to discern the contours of the colonial system of justice. A conversation with the *ellikboshi* is enough for us to sense that Qobil Bobo's hopes of recovering his property rest on the support of a cohort of officials, both native and Russian, and their willingness to listen to his trivia. The following excerpts illustrate an ordinary experience of a colonial subject seeking redress in Russian Turkestan:[2]

> Then the neighbor of Qobil Bobo came in, the noseless *ellikboshi*. Going into the barn, he examined the hole and the post to which the ox had been tied. For some reason, he shook the post all over. Then, he summoned Qobil Bobo and with a nasal voice said: "Your ox isn't going anywhere: we'll find it!" That the *ellikboshi* entered the barn to inspect the scene gave some hope to Qobil Bobo, who was delighted with his words. As the old man began to cry, "May God be magnanimous with you … my ox was piebald," the people dispersed. They all debated how, when, and with which instrument the thief had broken in, which direction the ox had gone, and in which market it would be sold. The noise abated. The wife of Qobil Bobo stopped crying and left, praying for the *ellikboshi* as she went.… The *ellikboshi* again inspected the hole where the thief had entered. Arms folded, Qobil Bobo, weeping, followed him. "Don't cry,

1 Abdulla Qahhor, *Asarlar* (*6 tomlik*) (Tashkent: Ghofur Ghulom Nashriyoti, 1967), 1: 59–62.

2 Throughout the book I use Russian Central Asia and Russian Turkestan as synonyms.

> I say, don't cry! If your ox has not left the land of the White King,[3] we can find it without fail." The *ellikboshi* spoke with confidence, as though it were a matter of simply going right out and finding the ox. "One must give something to this man, may God help him, for all his travails. Even a cat does not come out in the sun for free. Has he perhaps spent some money to become *ellikboshi*? To one county administrator [*mingboshi*, lit. "thousander"] alone he brought seven hundred bundles of clover and a one-year-old colt. And besides, he's not receiving a salary from the treasury!" Qobil Bobo shook his wallet and handed to the *ellikboshi* all that was in it. Having accepted the offering, he promised to report the incident immediately to the bailiff [*amin*]. In the evening, Qobil Bobo decided to go to the *amin*. A dry spoon can wound the mouth, they say. How much money to take to the *amin* now? For those who give, one is much, but for those who take, ten is little. After consulting with the old woman, Qobil Bobo decided that this would be his last expense, on which depended the return of the loss. Does it make sense to be skimpy here? When Qobil Bobo appeared before him, the *amin* belched loudly then guffawed so that his fat chin trembled. "So a cow disappeared, you say? No... not a cow... an ox, a piebald ox... An ox?! Ah, it was an ox! Um, a piebald ox? Ah, so... It is the only thing I have... the ox." The *amin* stuck half of his small finger into his nose and laughed.

"The Thief" was published on the cusp of the anti-colonial campaigns in early Soviet Central Asia[4] and, as such, it is shaped as a fragment of a bygone age. In opening this satirical piece with the expression "from the past" (*o'tmishdan*), Abdulla Qahhor, who had spent his childhood in tsarist-ruled Kokand, attempted to render a cultural atmosphere that had begun to fade away after the October Revolution. Indeed, the story echoes many of the common assumptions about colonial justice that had circulated widely in Russian Central Asia and that, by the time "The Thief" was published, had become literary motifs. It offers a medley of greedy and careless administrators; it opens a window on a Kafkaesque bureaucratic system that obliged appellants to go back and forth from one official to another; it describes bailiffs, police chiefs, and translators as individuals with discretionary power to act however they wished. Reading the story, one would think that justice in Russian Central Asia was all about bribery:

---

3 *Oqposho* in the text. Central Asians used the term "White King" to refer to the tsar.

4 For an overview on such campaigns, see D. Northrop, *Veiled Empire: Gender and Power in Stalinist Central Asia* (Ithaca: Cornell University Press, 2003).

A week passed. During this week, to identify the suspect, the old woman went to a fortune teller [*azaiimxon*] whose prayer was powerful enough to take a castle. She laid out half a sack of *jiida* berries,[5] three large cups of corn, and two skeins of thread. Nothing happened. On the eighth day Qobil Bobo went back to the *amin*, whose hair stood on end with rage. "You what? Should *I* drive your ox to your house, or what? After all, you should go and appeal [*axir, borilsin, arz qilinsin-da!*]: the subject who comes with a request confers honor upon the authorities [*fuqaroning arzga borishi arbobning izzati bo'ladi*]." Qobil Bobo consulted with friends: what to take to the police chief, if not money? Everyone knows that, before you reach him, your back will break from bowing. Even if Qobil Bobo can deliver [only] three chickens, one of them a mother hen, this is what he has. The neighbors, instead, collected one hundred eggs, but he [Qobil Bobo] was unable to get past even the translator with this offering. The translator took the entire gift and promised to explain the case immediately to the police chief. Qobil Bobo began to lose hope. Then he enraged, but, of course, that was in vain. Don't mess with the authorities: you'll lose no matter what! [*o'ynashmagil arbob bilan—seni urar har bob bilan*]. Now that he was well acquainted with the case, the police chief took his two best chickens and three rubles. Fortunately for Qobil Bobo, he did not say, "I will report immediately to the commandant" but told him instead to apply again to the *amin*. The *amin* said: "Go to the *ellikboshi*!" Seeing Qobil Bobo, the *ellikboshi* became angry: "Tell yourself who the suspect is! I don't make miracles [*avlio emasman*]![6] How could I know who stole your ox? And I suppose that it was butchered long ago. Instead of complaining here, I would go to the best tanners and look at the pelts. However, if it went to a tanner, it is now just a skin. And from this very skin they must have made a pair of galoshes that are now in the market. "Oh, God, what grief! My poor little head," whispered the wretched old man. "Are you a child, or what? Why do you cry? You are an adult. If this was the only ox in the whole world, it would be another matter. God willing, your loss will be reimbursed. So be it: I will tell my father-in-law, and he will lend you one of his oxen. Is one ox worth the blood of a man?" The next day the *ellikboshi* took Qobil Bobo to his father-in-law, a cotton trader named Egamberdi. The merchant sympathized with the old man and at the time of plowing gave him not one ox but two. But with a "minor" condition. Qobil Bobo will find out about that in autumn. . . .

5 *Jiida* denotes a plant belonging to the genus *Elaeagnus* (silverberry, oleaster).

6 Lit. "I am not a saint."

There is, of course, much that these fictional fragments neglect: institutions, forms of behavior, notions, and cultural practices that we shall discover as we progress through the pages of this book. But there are two elements in "The Thief" that anticipate much of what the reader will find in the cases on which this study is based. There is, first of all, a strong sense of the ordinary in the way Muslims make use of the legal instruments that the Russian Empire put at their disposal. Indeed, turning to Russian authorities was for Central Asians an ordinary course of action, not only because Muslims often employed the appellate system introduced by Russians but also because Muslims experienced colonial justice as part of their own culture. It is not by coincidence that Abdulla Qahhor renders the bailiff's invitation to turn to Russian authorities with the Uzbek *arz*: this is a term that has a long historical pedigree in Islamic Central Asia and was used to denote the procedure of appealing to Muslim rulers, that is, the khans (see Chapter 1).

Secondly, the story of "The Thief" revolves around the idea that justice resides with the individuals in power, not in the court. That is, redress depended less on an institutionalized system of adjudication than on a web of interpersonal power relations. The "rule of law" paradigm with which students of colonialism are all too familiar is conspicuous by its absence in "The Thief." I am aware of the risk of collapsing law into power relations, and I am aware that it would be useful, instead, analytically to disaggregate law from power. I therefore pay great attention in this book to how Muslims followed, interiorized, and manipulated the *rules* of the colony. In Russian Central Asia, however, legal culture emanated from the relationship between the people and the men in power. As we shall see, it was in communicating with military officials, police chiefs, translators, and local headmen that Muslims learned about the law, its rules, and the moral world that it governed. Thus, the Russian administration was the main venue in which Muslims were initiated into colonial legality.

How did local subjects regard law in this colonial context? What was the legal consciousness of Muslims under Russian rule and how was it constituted? How did Russian colonialism change Muslims' sense of justice and legal entitlements in Central Asia? It is these questions that *Visions of Justice* primarily attempts to answer. This book is thus part of a broader historiographical project that aims at rethinking the ways in which the history of law and colonialism in Central Asia has been written so far.

Over the last few decades, scholarship on the history of nineteenth- and early-twentieth-century Central Asia has generally been aligned more closely with Russian imperial and Soviet studies than with Islamic and Persian studies. This largely Russo-centric approach has given rise to many misleading assumptions and dominant narratives about the legal institutions, formal and informal, that populated the Islamic juridical field of the Central Asian khanates before the Russian conquest, in 1865. The same interpretive disposition has led to a misreading of the regional manifestations of Islamic legality and Muslim morality. In this study, I therefore aim to revisit the field of Central Asian Islamic legal history.

More importantly, by studying legal materials produced in nineteenth-century Central Asia, we are able to tackle several important wider questions in the field of law, colonialism, and imperial history. The last thirty years have witnessed a flourishing of scholarship in this area. An entirely new set of interpretive paradigms has been established and is now readily available to those historians of law and colonialism who focus on the history of the Islamicate world. The interpretive paradigms that I have in mind arise from various fields, such as post-colonialism, global history, and legal pluralism, which I will discuss shortly. Their deployment does not, however, always lead to satisfactory interpretations. Their adoption is conducive to narratives that cannot accommodate most of the regional specifics that are reflected in material originating, in the case of this book, in Central Asia. This study is thus an invitation to discover law as experienced by Central Asian Muslims under tsarist rule and to reflect on the interpretive possibilities to study law in a situation of colonialism.

The Russians' penetration of the southern regions of Central Asia (Transoxiana) began in 1865, when they besieged Tashkent. They then progressed further south, into the Khanate of Kokand and by taking Samarqand and the Zarafshan Valley, which had belonged to the Emirate of Bukhara. The next step was Bukhara and Khiva, which fell in 1868 and 1873. Thus, in the second half of the nineteenth century, the Russian Empire ruled most of Central Asia. It did so directly through the Governorship-General of Turkestan, established in the 1867 on the basis of a civil-miltary administration, that is, a bureaucracy charged with operating indigenous institutions and staffed largely by the military and representatives of the "natives" (Russ. *tuzemtsy*). As we shall see, the Russians followed a strategic course of action to ensure a certain degree of continuity with the past and thus "preserved" such institutions as *sharīʿa* courts, local administrative units, police forces, and charitable endowments. The Russian Empire also governed the region indirectly through the protectorates of Khiva and Bukhara, where it devolved sovereignty to native rulers, members of the Qunghrat and Manghit dynasties, respectively.[7]

---

7 For an introduction to the study of Russian colonialism in Central Asia, see A. Morrison, *Russian Rule in Samarkand, 1868–1910: A Comparison with British India* (Oxford: Oxford University Press, 2008).

The main argument of this study is that Russian colonialism affected Muslims' legal consciousness and effected changes in the way Central Asians understood their entitlements and interpreted legal action. Such changes manifest themselves at the level of institutions as well as in the domains of imagination and morality. First of all, with Russian subjugation, Muslims learned to navigate a normative space that differed substantially from the juridical field typical of the Muslim polities ruling the region. As we shall see in Chapter 1, the dispensation of justice according to *sharīʿa* was, before the Russian conquest, in the hands of Muslim royal courts and judges (*qāḍī*s) who acted mainly on their behalf. To be sure, *sharīʿa* might not have been enforced in a consistent manner, the resolution of conflicts depended on various agents, and notions of "practice" might have differed from locale to locale. Nothing in our sources, however, suggests that, before colonization, the local population understood such variations as constituting different bodies of law. Under Russian rule, things changed significantly. Central Asians learned to profit from legal diversity and choose among legal institutions operating under different legal systems. In Russian Central Asia, there were "native courts," which applied *sharīʿa* for the settled population and customary law (*ʿādat*) for the nomads. There were also courts presided over by Russian justices of the peace and Russian military officials. Colonial bureaucrats, too, especially the military, tried cases. This is a situation typical of legal pluralism based on institutional arrangements that favored the idea that a Muslim subject could pick the most suitable venue to which to bring his affairs. This situation affected the way in which the locals formulated their visions of justice and their convictions about entitlements, because, in dealings with these courts, they became exposed to different, even diametrically opposite, notions of morality. What was impermissible according to *sharīʿa* could be licit, sanctioned, and ultimately favored by the laws of the Russian Empire. Behavior changed also. To call a Muslim judge corrupt, ignorant, and incompetent, for example, became the norm among Central Asians when filing a complaint with Russian authorities. But we observe important changes also in the field of land tenure, charity, and guardianship—legal domains that were important to the conduct and everyday life of the local population.

In this introduction I will discuss the advantages and pitfalls of several different approaches to the study of Muslim legal culture in a situation of colonialism. I thus review the literature relevant to the study of *sharīʿa* and its encounter with Western empires. For this purpose, I discuss two interpretive paradigms, "legal pluralism" and "law and society." It is here that I elaborate my own approach that focuses on "legal consciousness." In the following sections of this introductory chapter I illustrate certain limitations to the study of

Muslim law and colonialism from a comparative perspective. I do so by examining the literature on global legal history and on Russian imperial history.

1 Law and Colonialism

Law is central to colonialism. Historical reflections on a wide array of themes, such as governmentality, forms of communal organization, behavior, and cultural production, have demonstrated this phenomenon. It is thus natural that many students of colonialism have been given pause concerning the cultural significance of law, but there is a problem in this historiographical output. Most of the studies on law and colonialism have been at pains to escape a narrative of binaries. Scholarship in this field tends to follow two, only apparently opposed, interpretive strands: either it describes the ideological and institutional forms in which colonial legal governance, the tension towards the rule of law, and coercion manifested themselves, or it dissects the agency of colonized subjects.[8]

When applied to Muslim-majority regions, the first approach focuses on *sharīʿa* and the transformative process that molded it into codes and statutes.[9] Transformation in the Islamic juridical field under colonial rule is manifest.[10] Western empires, for example, claimed exclusive right over violence, thereby restricting the jurisdiction of *qāḍīs* to the so-called personal-status law, itself a colonial legal category. There is also an institutional arrangement common to many colonial situations whereby Muslim legists were organized into a jural hierarchy and made subject to judicial review. Such an arrangement affected the moral standing of *qāḍīs*, whose rulings became more easily quashed on account of judicial malpractice, either purported or actual. Many have also argued that the codification of *sharīʿa* by means of the translation and massive publication of a narrow selection of juristic sources had lasting effects that rigidified the understanding of *sharīʿa* and overhauled

8 This is noted also in E. Kolsky, "Introduction." *LHR* 28/4 (2010): 973.

9 L. Buskens, "Sharia and the Colonial State." In *The Ashgate Research Companion to Islamic Law*, ed. R. Peters and P. Bearman (Farnham: Ashgate, 2014): 209–21; A. Layish, "The Transformation of the Sharīʿa from Jurists' Law to Statutory Law in the Contemporary Muslim World." *WDI* 44/1 (2004): 85–113.

10 For an overview, see P. Sartori and I. Shahar, "Legal Pluralism in Muslim-Majority Colonies: Mapping the Terrain." *JESHO* 55/4–5 (2012): 637–63.

its governing principles.[11] There were changes also at the semantic level. One such change is the transformation of agrarian systems from a regime of usufruct to one of ownership, that is, from status to contract; another is the possibility of freeing up property that once constituted a *waqf* asset;[12] yet another is the hybridization of certain legal practices, such as the Islamic procedure of oath-taking before Russian justices of the peace.[13] Finally, notions of rupture and displacement are also borne out by the testimony of Muslim intellectuals who lived through and reflected upon the effects of colonialism and the impact that the latter had on Islamic legal culture. The spread of Salafism and the corresponding call for independent legal reasoning (*ijtihād*) and hermeneutic eclecticism (*takhayyur*) are eloquent manifestations of the reaction of Muslim thinkers to colonialism.[14] The process of decolonization too, with its purported reenactment of *sharīʿa*, attests to the structural changes taking place in the colonial period, which had long-lasting effects on the way local jurists came to view *sharīʿa*. Sub-saharan Africa, especially, is a case in point. The reintroduction of Islamic law courts in Nigeria, for example, and the ensuing debates on their jurisdictional boundaries reflect an understanding of the difference between criminal and civil law that were introduced under British rule.[15] Brinkley Messick has called the product of this process of transformation "colonial *sharīʿa*," an expression capturing a point of no return in a narrative of subordination. According to such a narrative, Muslim legal actors are passive spectators against which the imperial institutional forces and the

11 Wael Hallaq has termed this process "entexting." See *Sharīʿa: Theory, Practice, Transformations* (Cambridge: Cambridge University Press, 2009): 547–8; J. Strawson, "Revisiting Islamic Law: Marginal Notes from Colonial History." *GLR* 12/3 (2003): 362–83; E. Giunchi, "The Reinvention of *Sharīʿa* under the British Raj: In Search of Authenticity and Certainty." *JAS* 69/4 (2010): 1119–42; and R.D. Crews, *For Prophet and Tsar: Islam and Empire in Russia and Central Asia* (Cambridge, MA: Harvard University Press, 2006): 25, 192.

12 C. Gazzini, "When Jurisprudence Becomes Law: How Italian Colonial Judges in Libya Turned Islamic Law and Customary Practice into Binding Legal Precedent." *JESHO* 55/4–5 (2012): 746–70.

13 V. Martin, "Kazakh Oath-Taking in Colonial Courtrooms: Legal Culture and Russian Empire-Bulding." *Kritika* 5/3 (2004): 483–514.

14 Layish, "The Transformation of the *Sharīʿa* from Jurists' Law to Statutory Law in the Contemporary Muslim World"; N.J. Brown, "*Shariʿa* and State in the Modern Muslim Middle East." *IJMES* 29/3 (1997): 359–76.

15 A. Christelow, "Islamic Law and Judicial Practice in Nigeria: An Historical Perspective." *JMMA* 22/1 (2010): 185–204.

epistemic machinery of Orientalism are deployed.[16] The work of Wael Hallaq is exemplary of this approach. Conceiving of *sharīʿa* as a bundle of institutions and doctrinal knowledge, his studies usually omit the ethical dimension of the law as it was lived by Muslims in general, not only by its most erudite practitioners.[17] This is a *choix du domaine*, one would say, but also one that views the colonial encounter as a fist fight in which *sharīʿa* always loses.

The second approach, instead, is informed by the idea of legal pluralism, here broadly defined as a school of thought that assumes that "state law is not the only source of recognized social order."[18] By putting greater emphasis on the interlocking of law and society and concentrating on the fissures of empires, studies that adopt this approach have elaborated a vision of Muslims' subaltern agency against a backdrop of colonial constraint. Agency has been, in this context, detected in several ways. Generally speaking, followers of this approach hold that colonial subjects operated within an autonomous cultural sphere. We have seen recently a more temperate evaluation of what the subalterns can and cannot do in the colonial legal field. Lauren Benton has made important observations on the uncertainties and incompleteness of imperial legal systems and invited us to reflect on the blank spots and loopholes in the imperial judicial system. Her work offers rich illustrations of how the gaps in imperial law offered to the subalterns enough space to accommodate their sense of justice and to pursue redress. This phenomenon has long been the subject of academic commentary. Significantly, however, Benton has provided compelling arguments on how the colonized unwillingly contributed to the development of the jurisdictional policies of empires. They did so by shopping for legal forums ("legal jockeying," Benton would call it) and emphasizing the notions of legal difference on which such policies were premised. Others, of course, have noted the subalterns' predisposition to forum shopping, but here Benton's contribution to studies of law and the culture of colonialism

16 B. Messick, *The Calligraphic State: Textual Domination and History in a Muslim Society* (Berkeley: University of California Press, 1993): 58–66.

17 Hallaq, *Sharīʿa: Theory, Practice, Transformations.*

18 F. Pirie, *The Anthropology of Law* (Oxford: Oxford University Press, 2013): 11. Legal pluralism has been a topic of extensive research, especially in the field of legal anthropology. See two recent syntheses and reviews of the literature with regard to early modern and modern history: L. Benton and R.J. Ross, "Empires and Legal Pluralism: Jurisdiction, Sovereignty, and Political Imagination in the Early Modern World." In *Legal Pluralism and Empires, 1500–1850*, ed. L. Benton and R.J. Ross (New York: New York University Press, 2013): 1–17; Sartori and Shahar, "Legal Pluralism in Muslim-Majority Colonies: Mapping the Terrain."

seems particularly significant. She explains jurisdictional regulation less as an imposition than as the outcome of a conversation between the colonizers and the colonized, a conversation to which the latter gave a meaningful stimulus. There are further refinements of Benton's approach. Mitra Sharafi, in particular, has considered the phenomenon of failed attempts to alternate between legal jurisdictions and illustrated the extent to which repeated legal action ("legal lottery," in her terms) was ephemeral.[19] Others have highlighted instead the normative agency of the subalterns in their interaction with the European administrations. Some, in particular, have demonstrated how legal encounters in the colony led to instances of deep hybridization, which are usually considered unintended consequences of colonization and the extension of the rule of law to the areas under imperial control.[20]

In one way or another, however, studies on colonialism, law, and culture have necessarily converged on the same conclusion: in manipulating legal jurisdictions and shopping for different forums, subaltern subjects reified the same cultural premises on which colonialism was built and thereby reinforced its predicaments. If one looks for the agency of colonial subjects, in both the jurisdictional and the normative spheres, one finds that their courses of action are yet another evidence of colonial hegemony, but there is a problem in this approach. To measure the conduct of the subalterns in colonial terms is to adopt a circular thinking: one examines the way in which the subaltern operates within a colonial system of signification only to discover that her courses of action are informed and, therefore, ultimately constrained by precisely that system. It seems plain that the interpretive choices offered by this approach are limited: subalterns as subalterns have an agency of sorts, which escapes the system of signification imposed by the colonizers, and subalterns as subalterns can only reinforce the system of signification of the colonizers. Either way, a narrative of cultural difference emerges from such studies,[21] for difference is both a premise and a conclusion of their approach.[22]

---

19 M. Sharafi, "The Marital Patchwork of Colonial South Asia: Forum Shopping from Britain to Baroda." *LHR* 28/4 (2010): 979–1009.

20 I. Hussin, "The Pursuit of the Perak Regalia: Law and the Making of the Colonial State." *LSI* 32/3 (2007): 759–88; P. Sartori, "Authorized Lies: Colonial Agency and Legal Hybrids in Tashkent, c. 1881–1893." *JESHO* 55/4–5 (2012): 688–717.

21 K.M. Parker, "The Historiography of Difference." *LHR* 23/3 (2005): 685–95.

22 On the limitations of the paradigm of resistance and domination, see S. Falk Moore, "Certainties Undone: Fifty Turbulent Years of Legal Anthropology, 1949–1999." *JRAI* 7/1 (2001): 103–106.

Sensitive to the risk arising from the "theoretical exhaustion"[23] that I have just outlined, John Comaroff observes widespread doubt among scholars as to whether there is "anything more to say on the topic" of law, colonialism, and culture.[24] Comaroff, however, rejects such defeatism, arguing that there remains a great deal more to say, if one reflects on four foundational coordinates of colonial legal regimes: first, "that 'colonial law' refers to an irreducibly diverse ensemble of practices and institutions"; second, "that cultures of legality were *constitutive* of colonial society"; third, "that colonies were prime sites of sociolegal experimentation"; and fourth, "that the tensions of empire were regularly mediated by means of law."[25]

Comaroff has, however, been criticized for outlining an agenda that consists of accumulating mere ethnographic illustration without pursuing further conceptual exploration. According to Bill Maurer, it would be more useful to consider what binds law *and* society (or law *and* culture). Many have noted that law and culture are mutually constitutive, suggests Maurer, but this observation, in itself, does not help us clarify the processes that govern their mutuality. Sally Engle Merry observes that, "once the interconnectedness of law and culture are acknowledged, the concept of mutual constitution does little analytic work in disentangling the important questions of power and change. These include the relative power of forms of law, law enforcement, legal consciousness, and legal regulation in forming cultural practices and the power of cultural practices to influence and channel legal regulations."[26]

But are such observations not, *mutatis mutandis*, an invitation to reflect on sociocultural change, itself an angle from which historians have often contemplated the past? Isn't the very call for unpacking the interconnectedness of law and culture an encouragement to focus on the transformations taking place within a society, the push-and-pull prompting the reiteration of certain practices, and, ultimately, the way in which a set of notions, values, and postures gain currency and become traditions in a given era? To answer these questions, I propose to start from the simple observation that the colonial encounter, like any other, always brings about certain permutations. Its elusive, serendipitous, and fragmentary character notwithstanding, social and cultural changes thus lie at the heart of colonialism.

When tackling a topic as vast and indeterminate as "change" in a situation of colonialism, however, one cannot avoid dealing with the notion of

23 B. Maurer, "The Cultural Power of Law? Conjunctive Readings." *LHR* 38/4 (2004): 843.

24 J.L. Comaroff, "Colonialism, Culture, and the Law: A Foreword." *LSI* 26 (2011): 307.

25 Ibid.: 314.

26 S.E. Merry, "Comments on Comments." *LSR* 38/4 (2004): 861–66.

acculturation that has been current since the 1970s and has recently evolved into more sophisticated, though not necessarily sharper, characterizations such as hybridity and (transcultural) transfer. Here, following the arguments of Sanjay Subrahmanyam, I would argue that the notion of acculturation (and its derivative vocabulary) is unhelpful in our discussions of change, assuming, as it does, the preexistence of reified cultures.[27] For our purposes, it is more useful to proceed instead from the premise that cultural encounters depend on the need for and the disposition of parties to mutual understanding. Sanjay Subrahmanyam's reflections are particularly instructive for our purposes:

> Time and again we are forced to come to terms with situations that do not represent mutual indifference, a turning of backs, or deep-rooted incomprehension, but rather show shifting vocabularies and changes wrought over time by improvisation that eventually themselves become part of a received tradition.[…] State and empires were very rarely ships that passed in the night of incommensurability.[…] Rather, what usually happened was approximation, improvisation, and eventually a shift in the relative position of all concerned. The British, once they had conquered India, did not remain—even a single generation afterward—the same British who had conquered it.[28]

Having thus established that sociocultural change cannot be imagined as one-way traffic—still less historicized and explained as the mere product of hegemonic colonial imposition—we need to consider how one might go about identifying *change* in the legal sphere. In other words, what has changed and how? Legal anthropologists and historians sympathizing with the social sciences would most probably refer to the law-and-society paradigm in search for a solution in that field.[29] They would, for example, take stock of the forms of reification of colonialism and consider how objects embody the mutuality

27 S. Subrahmanyam, *Courtly Encounters: Translating Courtliness and Violence in Early Modern Eurasia* (Cambridge, MA: Harvard University Press, 2012): 25.

28 Ibid.: 29–30.

29 The law-and-society paradigm is born from sociolegal studies in the 1970s as a reaction to earlier scholarship that treated law as a juristic topic with a predilection for functionalism. It argues that law and society are mutually constitutive and therefore that law should be studied as part of the complexity of social life. For a history and critical assessment of this paradigm, see C. Tomlins, "What is Left of the Law and Society Paradigm after Critique? Revisiting Gordon's 'Critical Legal Histories.'" *LSI* 31/1 (2012): 155–66.

of law and culture. It is here, Maurer claims, that the "and" in "law *and* culture" more clearly manifests itself.

2 Legal Consciousness

If studies of law and colonialism have struggled to eschew the binaries of "difference," one wonders whether there is a third way to historicize change in the juridical field. One possible solution would be to adopt what anthropologists usually term "the emic perspective," the attempt to see the world of a historical agent in his or her own terms, in the same way in which s/he saw it. Of course, an epistemological skeptic might suggest that any such attempt is absurd, in the absence of any sure way of knowing. Historians, after all, work with texts that are artifacts, not windows opened onto the past. Documents do not usually say what an historical actor thought or said at a given moment, and, if they do, we cannot know whether or not this actually happened. My advocating the adoption of the emic perspective, however, has less to do with the relationship between reality and written records than with the need to reflect on the epistemes that inform the way we approach the study of colonialism. In other words, if one wants to understand the historical actors and the cultural practices that populate the colonial archives, one should attempt to disentangle the stories of such actors and such practices from the colonial genres in which they have been accommodated. To oblige ourselves to think first in emic terms allows us to venture into new heuristic possibilities. The advantage is significant because one can, in principle, avoid superimposing assumptions about cultural difference on the historical material at hand.[30] As we shall see, Muslims pursued their own interests pragmatically, often by taking legal action against the integrity of Islamic institutions.

The purpose of this work is not, of course, to deny difference, either socially or culturally defined, especially when we refer to situations of colonialism, and still less to postulate that difference is irrelevant to the study of law and colonialism. Those familiar with Uzbek literature may remember the passage of Cho'lpon's 1936 novel *The Night*, in which the young Zebi is brought before the Russian military court for having poisoned her husband. The Russian military official presiding over the tribunal asks her to lift the black veil that covers her face (*paranji*) so that he may ascertain her identity. As the translator explains

30 I am here following the method exemplified in the work of V. Narayana Rao, D. Shulman, and S. Subrahmanyam, *Textures of Time: Writing History in South India 1600–1800* (New York: Other Press, 2003).

the request, Zebi resolutely objects, explaining that she would prefer to die than to show her face to strangers (*voy, o'la qolay! Shuncha nomahramning oldida yuzimni ochamanmi? Undan ko'ra o'lganim yaxshi émasmi?*).[31] Further explanations that the removal of the veil was among the requirements of the tribunal are of little avail, and, in the end, only a mullah is able to persuade her. He explains that there is no difference between Russians and dogs, for the former are unbelievers and it would thus be licit for her to unveil her face before the Russians as she would do before a dog (*kofir bilan itning farqi yo'q. Itdan qochmaysizmi? Shunday bo'lsa, kofirdan ham qochmasangiz bo'ladi. Bu joiz?*).[32] Portraits such as this must have populated the imagery of many Central Asians who lived under Russian rule. If cultural difference amounts to this, however, it cannot overwrite efforts to glean larger cultural shifts in the legal sphere, which is precisely what this study sets out to uncover.

The emic approach affords us an even greater advantage. The adoption of an emic perspective obliges the historian to ponder a network of practices reflecting the worldview of the historical actors under observation. That is, the emic perspective offers an approximation to the conceptual schemas informing the behavior of the agents that inhabit the basis of our sources. Translated into the legal domain, this approach advocates the exploration of the commonsense meanings of law. The advantage is a shift of heuristic perspective: law is not simply acting upon society but is something emerging from social action. My emphasis on the emic perspective is close to what sociologists Patricia Ewick and Susan Silbey call "legality":

> As a constituent of social interaction, the law—or what we call legality—embodies the diversity of the situations out of which it emerges and that it helps structure. Because legality is embedded in and emerges out of daily activities, its meanings and uses echo and reasonate with other common phenomena, specifically bureaucracies, games, or "just making do." Legality is not sustained solely by the formal law of the Constitution, legislative statuses, court decisions, or explicit demonstrations of state power such as executions. Rather, legality is enduring because it relies on and invokes commonplace schemas of everyday life.[33]

31 Cho'lpon, *Kecha va kunduz* (Tashkent: Sharq, 2000): 264.

32 Ibid.: 265.

33 P. Ewick and S.S. Silbey, *The Common Place of Law: Stories from Everyday Life* (Chicago: University of Chicago Press, 1998): 17.

The astute reader may note that I am setting out to reflect on the subjectivity of legal actors. To put it slightly differently, I want to explore the phenomenon of what we may term "legal consciousness," what it was and how it may have changed over time. By "consciousness" I do not mean here a critical consciousness, the kind of interpretive disposition that we often find among intellectuals who operate self-reflexively.[34] Rather, by "legal consciousness" I mean instead people's understanding of right or wrong when they took legal action, their sense of legal entitlements, the moral underpinnings that prompted their pursuit of redress, the way that they interpreted the moral world they lived in. "Legal consciousness" is thus understood here as "what people do as well as say about law."[35] This work is based on a substantial number of cases that illustrate how people articulated their beliefs and sensitivities in the sphere of justice.

Some may well object that, to explore the consciousness of historical agents, is, for the historian, an undertaking doomed to fail: it is one thing to collect people's stories about law that are recounted "in their own words"; it is an entirely different thing to read sources against (or with) the grain in search of the hidden voices of those who spoke about the law. While the sociologist may record a voice and replay it, the historian has to dissect voices that were, more often than not, merely ventriloquized and thus content herself with murmurs rather than statements fully articulated. But if we concede that hermeneutics can help us understand the intended meaning of *The Prince* or its "uptake," as Quentin Skinner would have it,[36] there is a chance that one can also infer ideas from behavior (patterned or not) and surmise the sense of entitlements that prompted legal actions. I do not conceive of texts as a kind of fiction, nor do I imagine them as representative of oppressive epistemic forces alone. I see little advantage in such epistemologically defeatist approaches. Instead, I propose that a linguistically and contextually informed hermeneutic effort may help us intercept the intended meaning of both a text and an action. Interception is not always possible, but it is worth pursuing.

Taking the emic perspective, this study addresses two questions central to our understanding of legality in Russian Central Asia. The first is, why did

---

34 This was the intended meaning of the term "consciousness" in Jean and John Comaroff, *Of Revelation and Revolution: Christianity, Colonialism, and Consciousness in South Africa* (Chicago: University of Chicago Press, 1991): passim.

35 S. Silbey, "Legal Consciousness." In *New Oxford Companion to Law*, ed. P. Cane and J. Conaghan (Oxford: Oxford University Press, 2008): 695–6.

36 Q. Skinner, *Vision of Politics*, vol. 1, *Regarding Method* (Cambridge: Cambridge University Press, 2002): passim.

Muslims come to certain understandings about law in one particular way or another? The second is, how did their sense of right and wrong change over time? Again, it is not useful to think in terms of imposition and still less of acculturation, because to do so necessarily posits Muslims' behavior in a teleological narrative of adherence to foreign values, a concession to external agents, and an ultimate submission to colonialism. Hegemony and its denial cannot be the only lessons that we derive from historicizing colonialism. It seems to me more useful to evaluate Muslims' behavior on its own terms, at least to the extent that linguistic conventions make that possible. I therefore want to start from the commonsense observation that, in the face of the presumed cultural fixity of Islam, many Muslim legal actors regarded ethical fluctuations in their behavior as a perfectly legitimate thing, and their conduct was not viewed by their coreligionists as a departure from—and still less a betrayal of—*sharīʿa*. Ultimately, a Muslim was no less a Muslim when he was put in prison for drinking alcohol or fined for gambling. *Visions of Justice* is based on cases that illustrate how Muslims experienced the law in a colonial society and regarded the legal system of the colony as a source of opportunities on various levels. I do not want to downgrade the experience of colonialism as one governed only by pragmatism. Muslims certainly had ideas, values, and notions to which they referred when doing what they did. At any rate, Muslim contemporaries were not preoccupied with the cultural permutations that they themselves experienced. Therefore, this study is not governed by such a preoccupation.

3 Comparisons

In colonialism and law, there was a strong similarity between Russian Central Asia and other colonial enterprises that established a plural legal regime and ostensibly subsumed indigenous bodies of law. Russians took a twofold course of action to deal with legal diversity. Like their counterparts in other regions of the Muslim world, they blended the purported preservation of the status quo with a broader vision of institutional and social change. On the one hand, they claimed to have maintained nearly intact the core of indigenous judicial institutions ruling according to *sharīʿa*,[37] which were presided over by *qāḍīs*

37 Throughout the book, I purposefully adopt the term *sharīʿa* as an emic category. I thus view "Islamic law" as a domain that includes the jurists' modes of reasoning as well as the cultural perceptions of the uninitiated. For a similar approach, see J. Scheele, "Councils without Customs, Qadis without State: Property and Community in the Algerian Touat." *ILS* 17/3 (2010): 351 fn. 3.

(Muslim judges); on the other, they effectively reformed the procedure of appointment to the position of judge by establishing a system of popular elections: where *qāḍīs* had once been designated by the head of a Muslim principality, "native judges" (*narodnye sud'i*) were, under Russian rule, to be chosen by voting representatives of local communities.[38] Furthermore, Russians restricted severely the jurisdiction of Islamic law courts, thus removing, for instance, murder cases and highway robbery from their purview.

Changes in the very definition of the office of *qāḍī* did not, however, include the latter's powers of law enforcement. First, in precolonial Central Asia the enforcement of law was a prerogative of the ruling principality; there are countless cases illustrating how the subjects of a Central Asian khanate could simply dismiss the authority of a court (or a jurist, i.e., a mufti) and ask that their case be heard at the khan's chancellery (see Chapter 1). Second, under Russian rule Central Asian *qāḍīs* not only could still count on attendants and community elders (*āqsaqāl*) to provide police services, but they also had unprecedented latitude to punish any behavior they deemed contrary to *sharīʿa*. While in precolonial Central Asia *qāḍīs* would have requested the intervention of the ruling principality (see Chapter 1), under Russian rule they could sentence people, for instance, to a month's detention for consumption of alcohol (*ʿarāq wa pīwū* < Russ. *pivo*, "beer") and illicit behavior (*bītartīblīk*).[39] In sum, *qāḍīs* were still in place in tsarist Central Asia, but that wider Islamic juridical field that we may term *sharīʿa* and in which their courts had hitherto been embedded no longer existed, because institutions of arbitration and mediation, which were alternative or complementary to the *qāḍīs*, had, in the meantime, disappeared or changed substantially.[40]

It is one thing to alert ourselves to the general constraints—and, as we have seen, the possibilities—that Russian statutory law imposed on the jurisdiction of *qāḍīs* but quite another to determine how colonial forms of governance changed Islamic judicial practices and juristic reasoning and to what extent such changes affected Muslims' legal consciousness in Central Asia: this is an entirely different story, and one which has hitherto been largely untold. In tackling this vast field of study, I hope to challenge the prevailing approach adopted by scholars of law and colonialism and legal pluralism, who are concerned almost exclusively with detecting institutional and procedural

38 P. Sartori, "Judicial Elections as a Colonial Reform: The Qadis and Biys in Tashkent, 1868–1886." *CMR* 49/1 (2008): 79–100.

39 06.05.1909, TsGARUz, f. I-365, op. 1, d. 85, l. 117ob, 12.01.1908, f. I-366, op. 1, d. 95, l. 12.

40 I have explored this idea in "The Evolution of Third-Party Mediation in *Sharīʿa* Courts in 19th- and Early 20th-Century Central Asia." *JESHO* 54/3 (2011): 311–52.

changes in the domain of indigenous law. This book deals primarily with the history of legal behavior among Muslims in Russian Central Asia rather than with the policies on Islamic law developed in a colony of the Russian Empire. As such, it is integral to the study of global legal regimes in the age of colonialism as well as the Russian legal history of the post-Great Reforms period.

The global-history approach to the study of European empires postulates that the assertion of legal hegemony in the colony was effectively dependent on the initiatives of the colonial subjects who manipulated jurisdictions to achieve their own purposes. Global historians have repeatedly demonstrated the irony that, through playing across jurisdictions, subaltern subjects actually ended up reinforcing the colonial regimes and thus unwittingly helped accelerate institutional change.[41] It is striking that the matter of how new constructions of legality and cultural meaning of law[42] became dominant among the subjects of the colony tends to escape sustained attention. In other words, if studies of colonialism and world history have presented law as a discursive[43] as well as an institutional[44] resource with which colonial subjects might interact with the state, they are at greater pains to explain how the colonized came to view themselves as legal subjects of the empire and thus personified colonial notions of law.[45] It is by looking at the techniques of personification that one can hope to disentangle cases of cultural change from the wider texture of colonialism and thus shed light on the social dynamics which sustained colonial legal constructions.[46]

---

41 Sharafi, "The Marital Patchwork of Colonial South Asia: Forum Shopping from Britain to Baroda."

42 I draw here on S.S. Silbey, "After Legal Consciousness." *Annual Review of Law and Social Sciences* 1 (2005): 360.

43 E. Newbigi, L. Denault, and R. De, "Introduction: Personal Law, Identity Politics and Civil Society in Colonial South Asia." *IESHR* 46/1 (2009): 2. See also the articles in the "Forum: Maneuvering the Personal Law System in Colonial India," in *LHR* 28/4 (2010).

44 J. Saha, "A Mockery of Justice? Colonial Law, the Everyday State and Village Politics in the Burma Delta, c. 1890–1910." *PP* 217 (November 2012): 187–212.

45 *European Expansion and Law: the Encounter of European and Indigenous Law in 19th and 20th Century Africa and Asia*, ed. W. Mommsen and J. de Moor (Oxford and New York: Berg, 1992); B.Z. Tamanaha, "Understanding Legal Pluralism: Past to Present, Local to Global." *SLR* 29 (2007): 381–6.

46 A. Riles, "Law as Object." In *Law and Empire in the Pacific: Fiji and Hawai'i*, ed. S.E. Merry and D. Brenneis (Santa Fe: School of American Research Press, 2004): 187–212; D.R. Peterson, "Morality Plays: Marriage, Church Courts, and Colonial Agency in Central Tanganyika, ca. 1876–1928." *AHR* 111/4 (2006): 983–1010; N. Chatterjee, "Muslim or Christian? Family Quarrels and Religious Diagnosis in a Colonial Court." AHR 117/4 (2012): 1101–22.

Historians of the Russian empire, in particular, seem generally to agree that, under tsarist rule, Central Asian Muslims could easily access the services of the "native courts," which remained broadly untouched in the wake of the Russian conquest.[47] In specific domains of Islamic law such as the notarization of property rights,[48] there were no substantial changes, but these continuities should not lead us to assume that, under Russian rule, Muslims lived in an unchanging preserve of "differentiated jurisprudence"[49] nor that their conceptions and practice of Islamic law and constructed cases remained unchanged from the time before the conquest.

What I hope to demonstrate is that the deeper one looks into jurisdictional politics in colonial Central Asia, the less amenable are such stories to integration into the "grand narratives"[50] of the Russian empire, let alone of "global legal regimes."[51] Historians of the Russian empire and global history may still want to telescope stories collected here and there and mold them into a few cohesive narratives on the law and the empire or patterns of structuring legal authorities across the world. I suspect, however, that this method risks crafting stories which are less revealing than prescriptive and that misidentify, misinterpret, or simply miss altogether the social significance of the changes that Russian colonization established in the sphere of legal consciousness among Muslim communities in a particular region.[52]

In resisting the temptation to confer greater historical salience on the cohesive forces behind Russian legal history and the global history of law and colonialism, I do not attempt to "recover the 'decentered' narratives of people without power,"[53] nor do I aim to discern among Central Asians the traits of cultural resistance and counter-hegemony. In what follows, I do not advocate a Marxist reading of Central Asian material. Instead, I want to suggest that, by

47 For a review of the relevant literature see the next section.

48 P. Sartori, "Colonial Legislation Meets *Sharīʿa*: Muslims' Land Rights in Russian Turkestan." *CAS* 29/1 (2010): 43–60.

49 J. Burbank, "An Imperial Rights Regime: Law and Citizenship in the Russian Empire." *Kritika* 7/3 (2006): 412.

50 See the manifesto-like piece by the editors of *Kritika*, "The Imperial Turn." *Kritika* 7/4 (2006): 706.

51 L. Benton, *Law and Colonial Cultures: Legal Regimes in World History: 1400–1900* (Cambridge: Cambridge University Press, 2002): 3.

52 A move back from "the global" to the "regional" has recently been advocated by G. Balachandran, "Claiming Histories beyond Nations: Situating Global History." *IESHR* 49/2 (2012): 267, and J. Scheele, *Smugglers and Saints of the Sahara: Regional Connectivity in the Twentieth Century* (Cambridge: Cambridge University Press, 2012): 12.

53 C.A. Bayly, *The Birth of the Modern World, 1780–1914: Global Connections and Comparisons* (Malden, MA: Blackwell, 2004): 8.

focusing on the social fragments of Central Asia, we can hope to chart new genealogies and correlations in the field of colonialism and law[54] and thus complement the interpretations that present-day Russianists and world historians adopt in the field of Islamic law.

The reader may object that, in developing my argument as I do in conversation with historians of both Russian and global history, I am needlessly adding further complexity to a picture which is already somewhat multifarious. Anyone who explores social and cultural change in law in a Muslim colony under Russian rule must necessarily engage the domains of imperial and world history. While one may still want to keep world history and imperial history as separate disciplinary entities, it is becoming increasingly difficult to situate the chronology of modern empires outside of global historical connections.[55]

3.1 *Global Legal Regimes: The View from Central Asia*

The historiography of law and empire in the age of colonialism is increasingly a historiography of global legal regimes. This analytical move consists of viewing jurisdictional conflicts as constitutive of a transimperial legal order; it also connects detailed histories of legal encounters in the colonies with an enhanced vision of world history and international law, one that is necessarily more fluid and fractured than structured around institutional patterns.[56] One of the recurring ideas implied by this approach is that empires established layers and hierarchies of jurisdiction in response to increasing tension in the colonies. It thus appears that the colonial legal systems did not simply reflect an assertive imperial project to impose a new set of institutions in an area of conquest. Rather, the tendency is now to view empires asserting "greater legal hegemony"[57] as the result of the intensification of jurisdictional politics involving both the imperial governments and their subjects in the colonies: on the one hand, the jockeying for jurisdiction over colonial disputes pushed the hierarchies of power to compete against each other; on the other, the institutional arrangements of the state offered a forum within which the colonial subjects might pursue their own claims and achieve their petty purposes.[58] Lauren Benton claims, correctly, that jurisdictional politics is constitutive

---

54 For an insightful illustration of this approach, see E.B. Lewis, "Frontier as Resource: Law, Crime, and Sovereignty on the Margins of Empire." *CSSH* 55/2 (2013): 241–72.

55 D. Ghosh, "Another Set of Imperial Turns?" *AHR* 118/3 (June 2012): 772–93.

56 Benton, *Law and Colonial Cultures*: 3.

57 L. Benton, "Law and Empire in Global Perspective: Introduction." *AHR* 117/4 (October 2012): 1094.

58 Benton, *Law and Colonial Cultures*: 3.

of colonial cultures[59] because, in adopting specific strategies and profiting from the legal services provided by the state, colonial subjects reinforced precisely the cultural predicaments of imperial governments.[60] This argument is pushed to the extreme when one observes, as Benton does, that the creation of specific institutional arrangements such as the constitution of native courts or the application of the *terra nullius* doctrine "responded to the conditions and peculiar conflicts surrounding legal administration in the colonies."[61] In just this way, the Dutch, for example, established native courts in Cape Colony in the wake of the adjudication of a homicide case in which a settler murdered a native woman. It appears that, by pursuing redress, the locals contributed, albeit involuntarily, to the imposition of colonial hegemony.[62]

This approach reminds historians of the ostensibly cohesive character of imperial legal cultures, one that is expressed in political theories and a juristic literature often detached from the dispensation of justice on the ground. Pamphlets, feuilletons, and statutory laws may well fail to reflect the institutional fractures of empires, which often become visible only in the day-to-day *practice* of law. Favoring the extension of property rights might be a rewarding thing to do in the metropoles, but it could be difficult to reconcile with the oppressive character of economic exploitation in the colonies (see Chapter 3). This approach thus calls for greater care in handling stories coming from the colonies, suggesting that the latter might not represent what philosophers, lawmakers, and politicians advocated as best for their empires. There might be some echoing between colony and metropole, but imperial regimes might also be characterized often by a complete absence of communication between the various layers of imperial administrations. This approach may lead us to cast a critical gaze on the project of "governmentality" that supposedly underlay the actions taken by colonial officials.

It is only when looking at the practice of law across several imperial polities that we can single out similar patterns of institutional arrangements that we might otherwise regard as specimens of some kind of cultural exceptionalism. In this respect, Benton's work is particularly instructive, as it urges students of colonialism not only to look for similar policies enacted by imperial governments in the colonies but also to remember that "patterns of political reordering inside polities correspond to efforts by emergent states […] to achieve

59 Ibid.: 13.

60 Ibid.: 148–9.

61 Ibid.: 168.

62 Ibid.: 180–2.

recognition as legitimate international actors."[63] Benton thus emphasizes the international context in which imperial polities not only competed for power but also cited the legal practices of one another as precedents for their own course of actions. The microhistories of jurisdictional politics in the colonies may become more comprehensible if we do not keep empires as fixed points of reference and attempt instead to follow the variable geometries of global history. Joining the dots among the legal cases retrieved from colonial archives does not necessarily lead us to reproduce the cultural geography of empires; the resulting picture may become exemplary only if projected upon a study of cases in international law.

One is left to wonder whether this global-history approach is more suggestive than conclusive and whether it may create more misconceptions than it claims to debunk. It is one thing to observe that, in the colonies "the rule of law" is followed out of necessity and through trial and error rather than according to a grand plan designed in the metropole;[64] it is an entirely different thing, however, to assign agency only to those indigenous elites who would appear to be those who favored (and had vested interests in) the jurisdictional arrangements of the colonies. One is reminded of cases such as that of Lagos under British rule, when the colonial authorities rejected calls for the formal recognition of Islamic courts.[65] In 1894 the British in Nigeria adopted the pragmatic expedient of avoiding any engagement with Islamic law courts. A few years later, in 1912, Muslim *originaires* (natives) in the Malian cities of Kayes and Medine were faced with a decree that made Africans subject to courts of customary law, thereby depriving them of the right to take their civil matters to *qāḍīs*.[66] In both Lagos and Mali, the formal denial of recognition to a body of law was equally a statement of institutional hegemony, suggesting that colonial polities could react to procedural ambiguities by eliminating rather than securing the rights of subordinate jurisdictions.[67]

There are other stories of tension that produced no substantive change in the way justice was dispensed in the colonies. Laura Stoler recounts a case of homicide in East Sumatra, a region where laborers (mostly ethnic Gayos and

---

63 Benton, "Law and Empire in Global Perspective: Introduction": 1098.

64 Benton, *Law and Colonial Cultures*: 168. Comaroff, "Colonialism, Culture and the Law."

65 A.'K. Makinde and P. Ostien, "Legal Pluralism in Colonial Lagos: The 1894 Petition of the Lagos Muslims to Their British Colonial Masters." *WDI* 52 (2012): 51–68.

66 R. Shereikis, "From Law to Custom: The Shifting Legal Status of Muslim *Originaires* in Kayes and Medine, 1903–13." *Journal of African Studies* 42 (2001): 261–83.

67 The fate of *qāḍīs* in Punjab under British rule is another example; see R. Ivermee, "*Shariʿat* and Muslim Community in Colonial Punjab, 1865–1885." *MAS* 47/5 (2013): 1–28.

Malays) were subject to systematic maltreatment. One of the civil servants involved in investigating the murder in question, Assistant Resident Frans Carl Valck, noted in a report that the laborers "not knowing where to demand justice, probably took the law into their own hands and took revenge by killing."[68] In reconstructing the case of a personal feud, Valck inadvertently exposed the culture of brutality of the Dutch planters. The quest for truth cost him his career; his reports were then scattered and forgotten in the archives in The Hague, and the assassination was portrayed as the action of a political mob prompted by Muslims from Aceh. Presumably, if the Gayos and Malays took up arms against their colonial masters instead of bringing their grievances before the district officer, it was because they were deterred by the planters' power and their own lack of trust in "the rudimentary judicial system."[69] In fact, as Valck reported, when the Malays complained that a planter had kicked them, they were advised to look to the district officer for redress.[70] When the laborers attacked the planters, they must thus have been wary of the legal alternative to violence as well as the consequences that a murder of a settler might later have had them.

If the colonial subjects were compelled to choose between appealing to foreign authorities and taking up arms against their masters, as was the case with the Malays, wasn't the assertion of colonial hegemony in the end inevitable, if not clearly predetermined by the institutional script of colonial rule? Could Europeans rely on anything more penetrating and pervasive than a free-standing claim to authority and jurisdiction over their colonial subjects? Western powers did so by retaining the prerogatives of judicial review in all the Muslim-majority regions, where they had the power to assess the conduct of Muslim judges. Polities had instruments to strengthen their power by running the courts of second instance rather than by granting to the colonial subjects a space of differentiated jurisprudence. The establishment of native courts in a colony may thus be a bureaucratic expedient for processing the paperwork that would otherwise pile up in poorly-staffed colonial offices and a tool conferring jurisdictional authority to adjudicate cases involving the natives, who otherwise would not be tried because of blind spots and loopholes in the legal apparatus of the colony. It is important to consider histories that account for the contribution of the colonized to the colonial legal regimes

---

68 A.L. Stoler, *Along the Archival Grain: Epistemic Anxieties and Colonial Commonsense* (Princeton: Princeton University Press, 2009): 215–6.

69 Ibid.: 209.

70 Ibid.

and to bear in mind the institutional asymmetry on which such regimes were organized and the forms of domination sustained by them.

I also hesitate to see patterned behaviors in the colonies in light of the transfer of administrative knowledge from one empire to another. In almost every Muslim region under colonial rule, Western officials referred to specific manuals of Islamic law available in translation, for example, the *Mukhtaṣar* of Khalīl ibn Ishāq, a juristic compendium of the Maliki legal doctrine adhered to by most Muslim communities in the Maghreb (Libya and Tunisia) and in sub-Saharan Africa (Mali and Mauritania). From the 1850s on, the French produced various annotated translations of the *Mukhtaṣar*, which were employed several decades later by the Italian Court of Appeals in Libya when ruling on cases of Muslim personal-status law; the French translation of the *Mukhtaṣar* later became an official legal source also in Tripolitania under Italian rule.[71] That French justices shared the translations of this legal manual with their Italian neighbors does not imply that, on matters of jurisprudence, the two colonial polities followed similar patterns: "unlike the French," argues Claudia Gazzini, "the Italians in Libya never embarked on a codification project, because their previous attempts to do so in earlier enterprises in Eritrea had failed and possibly also because they lacked the local expertise to do so."[72] This would suggest that, for empires and their colonial polities, the gathering of information within their own administrative borders amounted to more than simply following the lead of other international actors. In addition, bureaucrats often referred to authoritative precedents in order to acquire legitimacy in the eyes of their superiors or the public opinion. The fact that Russians, for instance, translated the Islamic legal manual that British officials had chosen as a juristic reference for hearing cases involving Muslims in India—*al-Hidāya*[73]—does not mean that the activities of Central Asian jurists were bound to this text alone,[74] nor does it prove that Russians ever used this primer (or its

71 F. Renucci, "Le juge et la connaissance du droit indigène. Eléments de comparaison entre l'Algérie et la Libye aux premiers temps de la colonization." In *Le juge et l'Outremer*, vol. 3, *Médée ou les impératifs du choix*, ed. B. Durand and E. Gasparini (Lille: Centre d'Histoire Judiciaire, 2007): 211-26.

72 Gazzini, "When Jurisprudence Becomes Law: How Italian Colonial Judges in Libya Turned Islamic Law and Customary Practice into Binding Legal Precedent": 749.

73 On the promotion of this particular text for the codification of Anglo-Muhammadan law, see R. Travers, *Ideology and Empire in Eighteenth-Century India: The British Bengal* (Cambridge: Cambridge University Press, 2007): 123; Giunchi, "The Reinvention of *Sharīʿa* under the British Raj: In Search of Authenticity and Certainty."

74 While *al-Hidāya* was no doubt part of the "traditional" curriculum of Islamic learning in Central Asian madrasas, there were dozens of Islamic references which, for the local

translation) for judicial review. In such a fragmented picture of colonial legal politics, where cause-and-effect relationships are difficult to establish, it is unclear whether the promotion of one manual affected the output of Islamic law courts[75] or simply allowed a stricter interpretation of *sharīʿa* by colonial judges and lawyers.[76] To think in terms of global regimes may simply confuse a picture in which projects of transformation are still far from being clarified.

The history of nineteenth-century Central Asia, one of the most populous colonies of the Russian empire, is resistant to any such attempt to integrate it into a history of global legal regimes. When they conquered the Kazakh steppe, the Russians championed a doctrine of land tenure that was similar to the *terra nullius* regime; like the British in Australia, tsarist authorities claimed that the pastoral groups inhabiting the steppe did not own the land on which they lived. Though this doctrine was known to have a flimsy basis, it proved crucial in helping to reform the patterns of land tenure among the Kazakhs and undermine a class of landowners. In designing a doctrine that conferred upon Kazakhs and pastoral groups in general only usufruct rights,[77]

---

jurists, bore equal weight and relevance. *Al-Nuqāya,* otherwise known as the *Mukhtaṣar al-wiqāya fī masāʾil al-Hidāya* written by ʿUbaydallāh b. Masʿūd Ṣadr al-Sharīʿa al-Thānī (d. 1346) became so popular that its commentary (*sharḥ*) was translated into Persian in early modern Central Asia; see A. Idrisov, A. Muminov, and M. Szuppe, *Manuscrits en écriture arabe du Musée regional de Nukus (République autonome du Karakalpakstan, Ouzbékistan). Fonds arabe, persan, turkī et karakalpak* (Rome: Istituto per l'Oriente C.A. Nallino, 2007): 108–9.

75 According to Ghislaine Lydon, for example, the *Mukhtaṣar* of Khalīl ibn Isḥāq was the legal manual most often cited in the Muslim tribunals of Senegal under French rule. See her "Droit islamique et droits de la femme d'après les registres du Tribunal Musulman de Ndar (Saint-Louis du Sénégal)." *Canadian Journal of African Studies* 41/2 (2007): 298.

76 In Niger, "the preference for codified law among French administrators tended to shift the legal discourse of the region towards the Mālikī law already available as a resource," B.M. Cooper, *Marriage in Maradi: Gender and Culture in a Hausa Society in Niger, 1900–1989* (Portsmouth, NH: Heinemann, 1997): 38. According to Benjamin Soares, such processes also occurred under colonial rule in present-day Mali: "The Attempt to Reform Family Law in Mali." *DWI* 49/3–4 (2009): 403.

77 *Polozhenie ob upravlenii v stepnykh oblastiakh.* In I.I. Kraft, *Sbornik uzakonenii o kirgizakh stepnykh oblastei* (Orenburg: Tip. P.N. Zharinova, 1898): 103, 108 (arts. 119–20, 125); *Materialy po kirgizskomu zemlepol'zovaniiu. Syr-Dar'inskaia oblast'. Aulieatinskii uezd* (Tashkent: Tip. V.M. Il'ina, 1915): 54–55; *Materialy po kirgizskomu zemlepol'zovaniiu raiona reki Chu i nizov'ev reki Talasa Cherniaevskogo i Aulieatinskogo uezdov Syr-Dar'inskoi oblasti* (Tashkent: Tip. V.M. Il'ina, 1915): 100. See also I.W. Campbell, "Settlement Promoted, Settlement Contested: the Shcherbina Expedition of 1896–1903." *CAS* 30/3–4 (2011): 425.

tsarist officials acted independently by creating their own ethnographic and administrative knowledge rather than by emulating other colonial polities.

Neither did the land law that tsarist officials introduced in the settled regions of Russian Central Asia refer to juristic literature circulating in the networks of the colonial legal regimes. Contrary to the opinion of Ekaterina Pravilova,[78] the statutory laws that nominally secured peasants' usufruct rights alone were the product of home-grown Russian Orientalism. Rather than the translation of the Ottoman Code (*Mejelle*) and the handbooks by German Orientalists, such laws reflect a selective reading of Islamic juristic literature and information gathered in situ from individuals acquainted with the administrative practices of the khanates that constituted the informational basis of the officials in power in Turkestan (see Chapter 3).[79]

The jurisdictional layering that Russians introduced among settled communities in Muslim Central Asia by confirming the office of *qāḍī* and retitling it as "native judge" was not imported from French Algeria. The Russians did not follow the French in this case, even if the former claimed to be closely monitoring the latter and occasionally exchanged intelligence.[80] It was instead an institutional arrangement deep-seated in Russian administrative practices, which was first tested in Crimea and later adopted in the Caucasus.[81] None of the requests addressed by Central Asians to the tsarist authorities on matters regarding indigenous legal institutions were ever satisfied. On the contrary, as we shall see in Chapter 2, Russian officials sought the juristic support of muftis nearly every time they sought to introduce an institutional innovation, and such support was generally forthcoming.

---

78 E. Pravilova, "The Property of Empire. Islamic Law and Russian Agrarian Policy in Transcaucasia and Turkestan." *Kritika* 12/2 (2011): 361–6.

79 Russian statutory laws refer to the land that belonged to the former Muslim principalities of Central Asia as *amliak* land, where *amliak* is a calque from *amlāk*—a term borrowed from the administrative jargon of the Bukharan Emirate used to denote "state land" (see Chapter 3). Had the officials who drafted the statute had in mind the Ottoman *Mejelle*, they would have employed other terms (such as *miri* or *arazi-i memleket*); see Martha Mundy and Richard Saumarez Smith, *Governing Property, Making the Modern State: Law, Administration and Production in Ottoman Syria* (London: I.B. Tauris, 2007): passim.

80 P. Werth, "Changing Conceptions of Difference, Assimilation, and Faith in the Volga-Kama Region, 1740–1870." In *Russian Empire: Space, People, Power, 1700–1930*, ed. J. Burbank, M. von Hagen, and A. Remnev (Bloomington: Indiana University Press, 2007): 178; S. Haule, "'... us et coutumes adoptees dans nos guerres d'Orient.' L'expérience colonial russe et l'expédition d'Alger." *Cahiers du Monde russe* 45/1–2 (2004): 292–320.

81 N. Dingel'shtedt, "Zametki. Sudebnoe preobrazovanie v Turkestane." *ZGUP* 9 (1892): 5.

3.2 *The Imperial Rights Regime*

If the global history of law complicates our understanding of nineteenth-century Central Asia, the imperial background in which the history of the region is usually accommodated is probably no less complicated. Although the question of legal diversity has long preoccupied legal historians and students of colonial history, it is only recently that people have begun to study the legal history of the peripheries of the Russian empire and, most notably, its colonies.[82] Only a few studies on Central Asia are available, and their accounts of the Russian imperial project in indigenous law connect stories of erratic and cautious accommodation with instances of gradual impact. Robert Crews sees, in the Russian administration of Islamic law, a way for the colonial authorities to seek out "continuities with earlier practice"[83] and avoid "introducing institutional innovations that might provoke Muslim resistance."[84] He argues that Russians emulated their Muslim predecessors (the *khān*s and *amīr*s)—as the arbiter of religious disputes.[85] Though correct in its outlines, this interpretation obscures important discontinuities with pre-colonial legal practices in a narrative of static and benevolent inclusion. In particular, Crews perilously overlooks the fact that Russians did not think in quite the same way as the khans and that the interactions between Russian colonial authorities and their subjects were based on the assumption that the legal system that existed before the conquest was irremediably corrupt. This premise clearly influenced the idiom in which locals expressed their ideas of justice, as becomes evident especially if one considers that exchanges among Central Asians and Russians could not necessarily replicate the same discursive patterns in which communications between Muslim principalities and local communities used to take place. Central Asians could now directly address the authorities without following that heavily codified notarial etiquette employed by the scribes in the old days of the khans. Copying templates for warrants, deeds, and letters—an activity integral to the preservation and transmission of knowledge in the madrasa—engraved the language of "scribes" (*munshī*s)

82 V. Martin, *Law and Custom in the Steppe: The Kazakhs of the Middle Horde and Russian Colonialism* (Richmond, UK: Curzon, 2001); V.O. Bobrovnikov, *Musul'mane Severnogo Kavkaza: Obychai, pravo, nasilie* (Moscow: Vostochnaia Literatura, 2002); A. Jersild, *Orientalism and Empire: North Caucasus Mountain Peoples and the Georgian Frontier* (Montreal: McGill-Queen's Press, 2002); M. Kemper, *Herrschaft, Recht und Islam in Daghestan: Von den Khanaten und Gemeindebünden zum ǧihād-Staat* (Wiesbaden: Harrassowitz, 2005); R.D. Crews, *For Prophet and Tsar: Islam and Empire in Russia and Central Asia* (Cambridge, MA: Harvard University Press, 2006).

83 Crews, *For Prophet and Tsar*: 273.

84 Ibid.: 258.

85 Ibid.: 259.

with formulae and stock-phrases that kept communication between the khan and his subjects terse and highly formalized. Such conventionalized literary practices were less appropriate under the tsarist administration, whose information gatherers were eager for detail and color.[86] New scripts and tropes[87] were thus provided, which made it easier for locals to cater to Russians' distaste for indigenous forms of legalism.

Central Asians were aided by a new class of go-betweens, people who, like most of the native representatives of the colonial administration (the so-called "living wall"),[88] inhabited a liminal cultural space—not yet like the colonizers but above the average Muslim population in respect to administrative knowledge and bureaucratic resourcefulness. Indeed, locals could now hire for themselves Russian lawyers who were conversant in imperial law. Individuals such as Anton Glaz were famous in the region for their shrewd maneuvering between jurisdictions and playing with the legal status of those he assisted. Representing the interests of one Fayzibai Batibaev for an unpaid debt, Glaz was about to lose the case when he appealed the ruling issued by a native court, claiming that his client was a Christian Kazakh and that he was, as a non-Muslim, subject to the jurisdiction of the imperial courts. When summoned to the provincial chancellery, Fayzibai acknowledged the truth, that he was a Muslim-born Uzbek (*sart*) who followed *sharīʿa*.[89] The military officials who had occasion to observe Glaz's artful practices concluded that "as he [the lawyer] was unable to win the case legally[...], he opted for an illegal way to draw it out to a great length." Little surprise that, being wary of the challenges posed by such individuals, military officials discussed whether to allow them to represent locals in cases to be heard in native courts.[90]

There was also a cohort of translators, as depicted vividly in the short story of Abdulla Qahhor, who played the crucial role of mediator between various Central Asian appellants and Russian officials. The colonizers' defective knowledge of Central Asian languages and their heavy reliance on the *perevodchiki* (Russ., "translators") placed a heavy burden on the affairs of the imperial

86 It does not follow, however, that local rulers did not have an equally good reason to want accurate information about the world they ruled. See P. Sartori, "Seeing like a Khanate: On Archives, Cultures of Documentation, and 19th-Century Khorezm." *JPS* 8/2 (2016): 228–57.

87 On British scripts followed by colonial subjects, see Peterson, "Morality Plays."

88 Morrison, *Russian Rule in Samarkand, 1868–1910: A Comparison with British India*: 149.

89 Commandant of the Kurama district to the Syr-Daria provincial chancellery, August 1885, TsGARUz, f. I-17, op. 1, d. 4082, ll. 31–31ob.

90 Ibid., l. 30.

administration.[91] Both European observers and locals often seized the occasion to expatiate on translators' misconduct to complain about the failings of the colonial bureaucracy, but this might also have functioned as a commonplace motif deployed to cater to the tastes of specific audiences that disliked the idea of imperial rule sitting on the shoulders of indigenes and would have preferred a more robust bureaucracy intruding into the mundane affairs of local institutions.[92] In fact, in the everyday regimen of a scriptural polity such as the Governorship-General of Turkestan, it is common to find military officials' appreciating the aid of their translators. As we shall see in Chapter 4, their notes in the margins of their translations were often essential for the military officials to understand the context, often extremely legalistic, of the correspondence that they reviewed. This makes it easy to explain the careers of many such cultural brokers.[93] For example, Aleksander Kuhn,[94] the discoverer of the "Archive of the Khans of Khiva," owed his knowledge about the courtly culture of the Qunghrat Khanate—and many other things Khorezmian—to his native assistant and translator, Mīrzā ʿAbd al-Raḥmān. Sifting through hundreds of petitions, one has the impression that many Russian officials survived the avalanche of paperwork,[95] eloquently termed *kantseliarizm* by Arendarenko,[96] thanks to many others like Mīrzā ʿAbd al-Raḥmān who took good care of most of the routine translations from Chaghatay and Persian to Russian.[97]

---

91 Morrison, *Russian Rule in Samarkand, 1868–1910: A Comparison with British India*: 148–50.

92 N.S. Lykoshin, "Kazii (Narodnye sud'i): Bytovoi ocherk osedlogo naseleniia Turkestana." In *Russkii Turkestan: Sbornik 1. Prilozhenie k gazete "Russkii Turkestan"* (Tashkent: Tipografiia "Russkii Turkestan," 1899): 95–6.

93 One such case was Mirza Radzhab Abduzhabbarov, who spent his whole working life as translator for the chancellery of the commandant in Jizzakh. He was decorated several times, including with the order of St. Anne. See his service records (*posluzhnoi spisok*) in TsGARUz, f. I-17, op. 1, d. 2850, ll. 31–32.

94 Aleksander Ludvigovich Kuhn, is the Orientalist to whom we owe the "discovery" of the Archive of the Khans of Khiva during the Russian siege of Khiva in 1873 as well as fine studies on property relations and fiscal practices in the oasis of Khorezm under the rule of the Qunghrats. See further A. Azad and O. Yastrebova, "Reflections on an Orientalist: Aleksandr Kuhn (1840–88), the Man and His Legacy." *IS* 48/5 (2015): 675–94.

95 In his *Pol zhizni v Turkestane. Ocherki byta tuzemnogo naseleniia* (Petrograd, 1916): 33–4, 38, Nil Lykoshin suggests that the police chiefs (*pristavy*), for example, were simply overwhelmed by petitions (6,000–12,000 papers to process per year).

96 G.A. Arendarenko, *Dosugi v Turkestane, 1874–1889* (St. Petersburg: Tipografiia M.M. Stasiulevich, 1889): 174.

97 Some local translators were recruited from among those who attended Russian schools. See, for example, the file of one Sait Akbergenov, which includes his grades from the

In addition, indigenous calls for the application of imperial law became detrimental to the traditional institution of Islam in first place; the annulment of charitable endowments and the circumvention of the Islamic law of inheritance pursued by the natives are glaring examples. Despite what Crews says, Muslims in Central Asia seem to have seen the Russian administration less as a "House of Islam" than as a sorry set of individuals to manipulate as they saw fit. As I hope to show, Russians did not replace the khans and assume the responsibility for justice in order simply to preserve the institutional setting they found. They did so because it allowed them to base their view on Muslim justice and thus shape the way that Muslims understood legality in general.

Alexander Morrison has, in contrast, put greater emphasis on the reform of the Muslim judiciary and the way this intervention sparked litigiousness among local communities. Morrison situates his account of this reform in a broader institutional picture of the colony populated by state representatives voicing discontent with *sharīʿa* courts and recommending that their system be dismantled altogether. By doing so, he seeks to show that, in Central Asia, the military ruled with a healthy dose of pragmatism and that the Russians ended up retaining even those legal systems that they profoundly disliked. Characterizing the policy adopted by Russians in Central Asia, including in matters of Islamic law, Morrison speaks of "inadvertently benevolent neglect."[98] This interpretation too calls for a corrective. In various realms of Islamic legal practice, from specious casuistry to routine notary practices, little change may be immediately visible, but a colonial project to transform Islamic law can surely be seen to have been in place when, for instance, Russians substituted legal institutions populated by *qāḍīs*, trustees, and bailiffs with "native courts" in which Muslim judges operated either alone or deprived of the crucial contribution of other mediatory agents. If, before the conquest, *sharīʿa* courts were embedded in an institutional setting—the chancellery (*dīwān*) and the offices of the trustees (*yasāwuls*, *amīns*, *maḥrams*)—that protected *sharīʿa*, this did not remain the case under Russian rule, where *qāḍīs* and other legal experts found themselves spending much of their time dodging malicious—and often unfounded—accusations of bribery and malpractice.[99]

Pedagogical Institute in Perovsk, 1912, TsGARUz, f. I-17, op. 1, d. 2059; see also the service record of Isym Askarov, who completed his studies at the Tashkent *gorodskoe uchilishche* (municipal school) in 1912, TsGARUz, f. I-36, op. 1, d. 6083, l. 2.

98 Morrison, *Russian Rule in Samarkand, 1868–1910: A Comparison with British India*: 291.

99 See Chapter 2.

A strikingly different picture emerges from the work of Virginia Martin on customary law among the nomads of the steppe. Martin's main contention is that Russian lawmakers and administrators were enthusiastic supporters of the colonial tenet of the "rule of law," who believed that the creation of "civic-mindedness" (*grazhdanstvennost'*)[100] among the indigenous peoples of the empire rested on the rapprochement (*sblizhenie*)[101] of an inferior body of law in local use—"custom" (*obychai*)—with the empire's superior legal system—"*the* law" (*zakon*). Martin accords particular attention to the civilizing goal of Russians and the transformation of local legal practices, which should be achieved without using force to introduce imperial law. Russian lawmakers imagined that, once they came into contact with the tsarist legal system, the people in their colonies would one day abandon their primitive ways and embrace the imperial law. Besides stressing the imperial idealistic call to rule "by example," Martin also argues that Russians actually promoted a change in the application of customary law as they involved Central Asians in codifying their mores. She argues that setting customary laws down in writing implied changing much of their social significance. However, in emphasizing the much trumpeted doctrine of rule by example and according attention solely to the process of legal codification, she overlooks the fact that Russians interfered directly in the arbitration of disputes among the locals, thereby affirming their own views on justice. To date, there is no clear attestation of how such codes were employed in judicial proceedings and how they may have actually changed the daily practices of the courtroom.[102]

Contradictions begin to emerge when one couples narratives of continuities and benevolent neglect with Martin's claim that changes, though slow, were to be expected in the field of procedural laws, as the empire was applying pressure for legal change. Jane Burbank, by contrast, blends the antinomies of conciliatory compromise and profound transformation in a narrative of inclusive state legal pluralism. Her synthesis presents the image of a polity—the

100 Martin, *Law and Custom in the Steppe*: 4, 43; see also Werth, "Changing Conceptions of Difference, Assimilation, and Faith in the Volga-Kama Region, 1740–1870": 170, 184–5.

101 On the concept of *sblizhenie*, see Morrison, *Russian Rule in Samarkand, 1868–1910: A Comparison with British India*: 35, 98, 284.

102 Kazakhs, following a request by the Russians, produced summaries of their rulings to serve as legal precedents, but such legal compendia were apparently drafted to be read, understood, and, perhaps, employed by outsiders alone, that is, the Russians. At any event, there is to date no evidence that Kazakhs resorted to these codes when applying customary law. I briefly consider this question in my "Murder in Manghishlaq: Notes on an Instance of Application of Qazaq Customary Law in Khiva." *DI* 88/2 (2012): 217–57.

Muscovite autocracy—that spread its wings over Eurasia and provided ethnic groups and religious communities with spaces of differentiated jurisprudence. In her words, "the Russian imperial rights' regime, founded on the state's assignment of rights and duties to differentiated collectivities, created conditions for including even lowly subjects in basic practices of governance. [...] Russia's system of ascribed collective rights provided imperial subjects with a legal framework of connection to the polity, empowered them to engage in basic social functions under the protection of the law, and enabled them to decide some matters of local but significant importance with the sanction of the state."[103]

The notion on which Jane Burbank's thesis of differentiated jurisprudence is centered is the concept of "custom," a residual category comprising any body of laws outside of imperial law and a term that is ubiquitous in the vocabulary of statutory laws of Russia.[104] The assumption is that the official recognition of customary laws—that is, indigenous bodies of law—in the Caucasus, Siberia, and Central Asia secured the existence of a separate collective legal field. In the Russian imperial vision of a house for all the people who had their own customs, collectives of differentiated jurisprudence could administer their lives as they were guarded by the all-encompassing reach of the autocracy. This seems to have been the great advantage in becoming a citizen of the Russian empire after all: as soon as the state associated a subject with labels of identification such as estate (*soslovie*) and confession, this person would be entered into one category of citizenship and thereby attached to one jurisprudence collective: Russian peasants were expected to bring their grievances before the township courts, as were the indigenous Siberians who enjoyed rights of landholding according to their customs, and as Muslims in the Caucasus and Central Asia were left to refer to the *qāḍīs*.

The history of the Russian empire shows that its formation as a multiple legal regime is owed in large part to the Realpolitik that guided the expansion of the polity to the south and the east. Inclusion was a sine qua non for officers and governors who aimed to establish their rule over non-Orthodox peoples. To allow the local peoples to manage their own governance and thereby affirm established legal practices was instrumental in asserting power, extracting revenues, and keeping the hinterland relatively peaceful.

In Chapter 2, I shall target certain aspects of Burbank's argument. I contend that this imperial policy was applied only temporarily in Russian Central

103 Burbank, "An Imperial Rights Regime: Law and Citizenship in the Russian Empire": 400.

104 A revealing parallel is the French treatment of customary law in North Africa; see J. Scheele, "A Taste for Law: Rule Making in Kabylia (Algeria)," *CSSH* 50/4 (2008): 895–919.

Asia. This becomes clear when we examine how the state waded progressively into the realm of Islamic law. There too it was obliged to sponsor a regime of legal pluralism. The judicial system was regulated by statutory laws that reflected confessional distinctions: Russians were to follow the general laws of the empire, the indigenous settled population was expected to access the legal services provided by *sharīʿa* courts, and the nomads were to follow the rulings of the courts of customary law.

Russians did not, however, simply endow Muslims with "self-justice" (*samoupravlenie*). The entire history of the colonization of Central Asia is, in fact, punctuated by official calls for intervention and reforms. The apex of this trend was reached in 1913, when a project for the dissolution of the native courts proposed that *sharīʿa* courts be replaced by justices of the peace.[105] At that time, assimilation (*assimilatsiia*) was the buzzword for those Russians officials who were unhappy with a pluralistic legal regime.[106]

I shall not use the paper trail left by the commissions proposing that *sharīʿa* be dissolved to challenge the argumentation of the imperial legal-rights regime; after all, the Russians never succeeded in doing away with *sharīʿa* in the empire. Instead, I want to draw attention to some of those practices of legalism that show how the Russian bureaucracy dealt with Islamic law and tried to change its policies. There were two levels of colonial intervention in Islamic law in Russian Central Asia. One such level was imposed ex officio, and it introduced the first set of changes at the institutional and jurisdictional level. Russian policy established an asymmetry between the laws of the empire and Islamic law, first by defining the boundaries of application of *sharīʿa*. Statutory laws enacted in Turkestan proclaimed that the imperial law courts had exclusive jurisdiction over a wide array of penal and civil cases involving the Muslim population, consisting principally of crimes against state authorities, Russians, and the Christian faith. But the imperial law courts were also expected to hear cases against individuals—murder, abduction, and rape—and to deal with crimes against the property of individuals, cases of usurpation, arson, raids, robbery, damage to state property, and forgery of legal documents. These regulations reduced dramatically the range of authority of *sharīʿa* courts, as they were to hear only matters of personal-status law and only a few cases of penal law, such as theft, assault, and cursing. The issue of jurisdiction became more important as Muslims learned to operate within different legal arenas

105 Anonymous [Maḥmūd Khwāja Bihbūdī], "Qāḍī wa bīlār ḥaqqīnda lāyiḥa." *Āyina* 5 (1913): 106–8.

106 *Proekt uprazdneniia narodnykh sudov v Turkestanskom krae*, 1913, TsGARUz, f. I-36, op. 1, d. 6009, l. 166ob.

and to insist that their cases be heard according to imperial law. This also happened in cases of personal-status law, as in matters of inheritance and disputes concerning charitable endowments.

Russian intervention in Islamic law was not limited to a contraction of the jurisdiction of the Islamic judge. Colonial authorities also attempted to change *sharīʿa* at the level of procedural laws by stepping directly into the adjudication of disputes. One crucial such innovation saw the colonizers introduce a system of judicial review. Under the provisions of this new system, Muslims were entitled to appeal the judgments of *sharīʿa* courts by addressing their grievances to the district chancellery (*uezdnoe upravlenie*). The judgments would be reviewed by an assembly of Muslim jurists, but the process of revision would be overseen strictly by Russian bureaucrats. It is in the practice of legal commentary, paper-pushing between chancelleries, and the exercise of forensic skepticism that Russians sought to change the meanings of right or wrong according to Islamic law.

To bring about substantial changes in the administration of justice among the Muslims of Central Asia meant also to influence Muslims' view of Islamic law. This was an enterprise in which the Russians distinguished themselves: if they accomplished anything, it was to convince Muslims that they could express their ideas about justice and injustice. The Russians pushed Muslims hard to do so by letting the local populace know that their stories of *qāḍī*s' malpractices and court misconduct did matter to the colonial government. The Russians took seriously any claim of injustice coming from Muslims, in the hope that an appeal would provide evidence to undermine Islamic law.

Reviewing the activity of Islamic law courts was a matter more of day-to-day bureaucratic practice than of theorizing from afar. Nor did such practices always reflect a consistent or clear vision as to what constituted good and bad *sharīʿa*. Divergences and frictions are therefore visible within the colonial administration of Turkestan, especially with regard to the future of Islamic law in the region. However, the practice of reviewing *qāḍī*s' judgments inevitably led people to consider the possibility of revoking them and of questioning the native judiciary's competence to adjudicate. It was precisely while reviewing *qāḍī*s' activity that the two main bureaucratic apparatuses of the administration of the colony went head to head with one another: the district chancellery sought to affect directly the activity of the *sharīʿa* courts, while the provincial chancellery (*oblastnoe upravlenie*) usually defended the autonomy of the *sharīʿa* courts. It was usually the provincial chancellery and its head, the military governor, that succeeded in this battle. Substantial hesitation among officials prevented the final dissolution of the *sharīʿa* courts, which a few military governors (of Syr-Darya and Ferghana) considered premature (*prezhdevremenno*), while others (those of Semireche and Samarqand) advocated aloud. Even those officials who avoided the final closure of *sharīʿa* courts were in favor of radical reforms: indeed, they proposed that military district (*okrug*) courts become a judicial level of second instance for appeals involving Muslim parties.[107] The governors were probably aware that, when military justices had, in the past, reviewed Muslims' appeals, they had overturned 95% of the *qāḍīs*' judgments.[108] This proposal signals that the two governors had great respect for the experience that Russian officials had accumulated while reviewing the activity of Islamic law courts up to 1913. In their view, the knowledge that the colonial bureaucrats had accumulated on *sharīʿa* should not have been allowed to dissipate.

4 Sources

Students of law, colonialism, and the Islamicate world tend to view *qāḍī* courts as the unique site of application of the law, the place where one should look to find changes (or the lack thereof) in a given legal culture. In choosing the courts as a revealing site of colonial legal domination, however, historians might reasonably have sought to create a reliable basis of information. Situations of legal diversity often called for the imposition of state law on alternative systems deemed indigenous, the creation (and repeated negotiation) of jurisdictional boundaries, and the enactment of procedural links between competing jurisdictions; it is thus perfectly conceivable that one might want to confer on court cases a particular exemplarity.[109] I do not claim that this is an entirely misleading approach but that, in focusing so closely on *qāḍī* courts, one risks assuming that *qāḍīs* exercised a similar monopolistic function in the exercise of justice in the years before colonization.

As I will show in Chapter 1, the situation in Central Asia during the Russian conquest was substantially different. It is during that period that we observe a distinct hierarchy of authority, whereby Muslim principalities concentrated all jurisdiction in their hands, while *qāḍīs* worked for them in the humbler capacity of legal advisors. In the first half of the nineteenth century, in the Uzbek khanates, *qāḍīs* did not dispense justice autonomously as an independent

107 TsGARUz f. I-36, op. 1, d. 6009, ll. 163ob–164; 169ob.

108 Morrison, *Russian Rule in Samarkand, 1868–1910: A Comparison with British India*: 269.

109 This approach is exemplified throughout *Muslim Family Law in Sub-Saharan Africa: Colonial Legacies and Post-Colonial Challenges*, ed. Shamil Jeppie, Ebrahim Moosa, and Richard Roberts (Amsterdam: Amsterdam University Press, 2010).

judiciary but heard a case only after receiving instructions from the central chancellery to which they were expected to report. In such a system, the justice dispensed by the ruler was more authoritative than that of the *qāḍīs*, whose activity might be contested. In the following case, a female victim of assault appealed first to the district governor (*ḥakīm*) of Khwāja-Īlī (in present-day Qaraqalpaqstan). The governor instructed an attendant to bring the two parties before the *qāḍīs* of the city. As the defendant admitted the assault, the judges proceeded to appoint a woman trustee to examine the body of the claimant and assess the degree of injury. As the examination disclosed various instances of harm, the *qāḍīs* consulted with a mufti, who ruled in favor of a corporal punishment for the defendant. When the *qāḍīs* were about to execute the ruling of the jurist, the defendant questioned the authority of the jurors and left the hearing. Following is the text of the judicial report [Fig. 1], in translation:

> Let it be known to the pivot of glory, Yasāwul-Bāshī Aqā, may his power increase, that a certain woman called Ḥanīfa Bīka, from the Shīrīn mosque community in [the district of] Khwāja-Īlī appealed to the governor and claimed that her husband, a certain Ṣādiq, unlawfully assaulted her, causing injury. [The governor thus instructed] a *yasāwul* to go to [the locality], find the husband and deliver the two parties to us [the *qāḍīs* of Khwāja-Īlī]. Later, when we questioned the man, he acknowledged the assault; then we appointed a faithful and pious woman as trustee to examine [the body of] the aforementioned [claimant], and this trustee informed us that indeed [Ḥanīfa Bīka] showed signs of bodily harm in various parts. Then, we decided that the [issue] of this woman should be treated as a judicial case. As we were executing the ruling of the mufti and thus intended to punish [the defendant] according to *sharīʿa*, he stood up and said, "No!" and then left [the hearing]. This alone is what occurred before us; no financial issues [were discussed]. The event was recorded.[110]

The dispensation of justice in precolonial Central Asia was thus centered on a petitioning system that brought the populace together with the royal court and its representatives on the ground. This suggests that, at least in Muslim-majority colonies, the people would be perfectly equipped to address their grievances to the colonial masters, and this is the reason that

110 The report can be dated inductively to the beginning of the twentieth century. TsGARUz, f. I-125, op. 1, d. 498, l. 29.

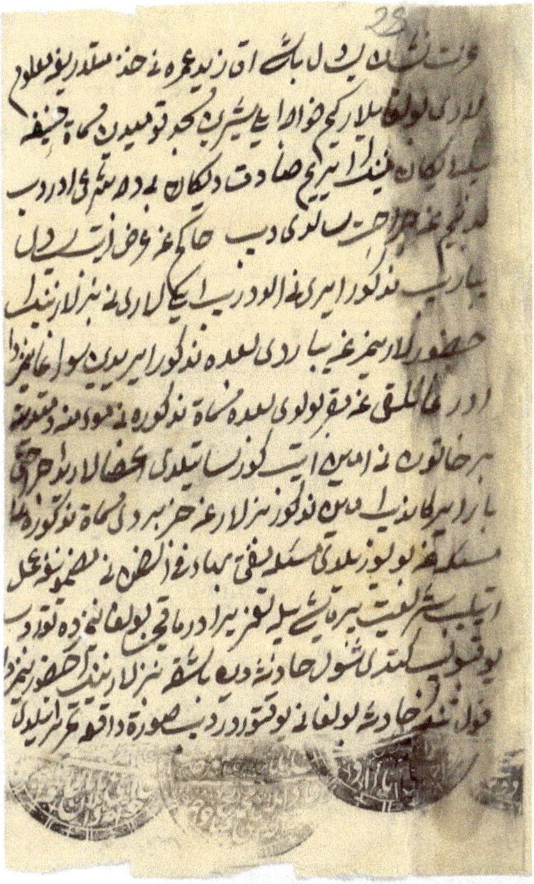

FIGURE 1 *Khwāja-Īlī* qāḍīs' *report to the office of the Yasāwulbāshī, TsGARUz, n.d., f. I-125, op. 1, d. 498, l. 29.*
COURTESY OF THE CENTRAL STATE ARCHIVE OF UZBEKISTAN

the archives of the colonial polities are filled with appeals filed by locals.[111] It thus becomes clearer that substantive changes in Muslims' legal consciousness become more visible and less readily neglected when one looks for them in the mundane activity of the colonial bureaucracy and of mid-level institutions

---

111 This disputes the presumption that colonial courts, rather than the bureaucratic apparatus of the colony, was where locals filed their grievances; see Merry, "Colonial Law and Its Uncertainties": 1068.

rather than in the registers of *sharīʿa* courts. It is here that experience is more freely articulated and less constrained by the *qāḍīs*' legalese. It is therefore to such a source basis that I turned to write this study. The sources I use in this book, however, amount to the output of the colonial administration in its broadest sense, because the administration included "native" institutions such as law courts, charitable endowments, schools, and neighborhoods, which left ample documentation (mostly of a legal nature) in Chaghatay and Persian. In addition, I draw on sources crafted from the sixteenth to the early nineteenth century for comparative purposes. This material is mainly in Arabic and Persian. I discuss these sources in greater detail in the following chapters.

In this book I have made extensive use of Islamic legal texts such as deeds, fatwas, judgments, and reports. In doing so, I make no assumption that texts written in Arabic-script languages are intrinsically more "useful" than those written in Russian by virtue of their reflecting local writing practices. They are no doubt crucial to understanding a local system of knowledge, but "indigenous" sources are not endowed with greater authenticity than any other texts, including those written by non-Central Asians. One script hardly makes a text more or less authentic than do others. Nor, in principle, are there sources that can speak more authoritatively of the past and those who lived it. In addition, legal documents, regardless of their language, do not open windows on the past. Therefore, whenever and wherever possible, I *combined* sources in Russian alongside texts in Arabic, Persian, and Chaghatay in an effort to consider together different visions of justice that, in my view, represent the world of colonial Central Asia.

5 Outline of the Book

This book is both an experiment and a methodological compromise, for it attends to two tasks at once: by reconstructing the institutional setting, the legal procedures, and the patterns of consumption of law in the region before colonization, it attempts to trace changes in Muslim legal consciousness in Russian Central Asia.

Chapter 1 sets the stage and, in drawing from Pierre Bourdieu, presents *sharīʿa* as a juridical field, that is, a space in which operated various institutions and officials, at the center of which stood the royal court of the local khans. Chapter 2 shows how Russian intervention in the *sharīʿa* juridical field led to an institutional and discursive overhaul. It is here that I illustrate how Central Asians interiorized the colonial visions of Islamic law as a despotic system of justice, acquiesced to the view of *qāḍīs* as irremediably corrupt, and, by doing so, contributed to delegitimizing *sharīʿa* as the sole source of Muslims' legality. In this chapter, I also show how Muslims adapted rapidly to the moral reorientations suggested by the Russians. Locals repeatedly became legal players and thus conversant with the practice of filing lawsuits driven by malice. Chapter 3 offers a thorough reevaluation of the law of property under Russian rule. It portrays the transition from a regime of usufruct to one of landed property in which the Islamic vocabulary of property acquired new meanings. As a segue to a discussion on property relations, Chapter 4 demonstrates that changes in legal consciousness consisted also of taking legal action against the integrity of Islamic institutions as important for communal forms of organization as charitable endowments (*waqf*s). In Chapter 5 I deal with the legal genre of fatwas. I illustrate that the colonization of the Islamic juridical field was a fragmented experience for Muslims and one in which different legal sensibilities overlapped. By examining the issuance of fatwas in its various bureaucratic contexts, I will show the coexistence of former and new juristic practices that led to competing and sometimes contrasting definitions of *sharīʿa* as a moral world.

CHAPTER 1

The Islamic Juridical Field in Central Asia, ca. 1785–1918

Introduction

Before the Russian conquest, Central Asian rulers played a central role in the dispensation of justice according to *sharīʿa*. This phenomenon has long been overlooked, because studies of dispute resolution in the Islamic world, especially in Central Asia, tend to assign greater importance to the legists than to the state—that is, the Muslim ruler and his representatives in court. Students of Islamic law usually hold that the settlement of disputes in Muslim-majority areas depended on *qāḍī*s and *ḥakīm*s who, respectively, adjudicated[1] and arbitrated[2] cases independently or facilitated reconciliation by means of mediation, either judicial or extrajudicial.[3] In the resulting narrative, the state is pushed to the margins of jurisprudence.[4] Every new monograph on the subject of Islamic law shows that the state provided either a court of second instance, by offering a *maẓālim* appellate system,[5] or a mechanism of governance

---

1 J. Schacht, *Introduction to Islamic Law* (Oxford: Clarendon Press: 1965): 188–98; W.B. Hallaq, *The Origins and the Evolution of Islamic Law* (Cambridge: Cambridge University Press, 2005): passim; M. Khalid Masud, R. Peters, and D. Powers, "*Qāḍīs* and Their Courts: An Historical Survey." In *Dispensing Justice in Islam: Qadis and Their Judgements*, ed. M. Khalid Masud, R. Peters, and D. Powers (Leiden: Brill, 2006): 1–44. A notable exception to this trend is the work of Mathieu Tillier; see, e.g., his "Judicial Authority and *Qāḍīs*' Autonomy under the Abbasids." *Al-Masaq: Journal of the Medieval Mediterranean* 26/2 (2014): 119–31.

2 On arbitrators, see A. Othman, "'And Amicable Settlement Is Best': *Ṣulḥ* and Dispute Resolution in Islamic Law." *Arab Law Quarterly* 21 (2007): 64–90; W.B. Hallaq, *Sharīʿa: Theory, Practice, Transformations* (Cambridge: Cambridge University Press, 2009): 159–64.

3 I. Tamdoğan, "*Ṣulḥ* and the 18th Century Ottoman Courts of Üsküdar and Adana." *ILS* 15/1 (2008): 55–83; P. Sartori, "The Evolution of Third-Party Mediation in *Sharīʿa* Courts in 19th- and Early 20th-Century Central Asia." *JESHO* 54/3 (2011): 311–52.

4 On this approach, see F. Pirie, *The Anthropology of Law* (Oxford: Oxford University Press, 2013): 97–103.

5 On *maẓālim*, see J.S. Nielsen, *Secular Justice in an Islamic State: Maẓālim under the Baḥrī Mamlūks, 662/1264–789/1387* (Leiden: Brill, 1985): 9. On the role of the state in conflict resolution in the Ottoman period, see Y. Ben-Bassat, *Petitioning the Sultan: Protesters and Justice in Late Ottoman Palestine* (London: I.B. Tauris, 2013): 24–8.

DOI 10.1163/9789004330900_003

that affected legal hermeneutics,[6] by which it ultimately constrained juristic independence.[7] This narrative creates an artificial opposition between the Islamic state and *sharīʿa*, an opposition predicated on the notion of Islamic law as the exclusive preserve of Muslim legists (*ʿulamāʾ*)—that is, as a self-contained juristic domain inaccessible to the uninitiated. Materials from nineteenth- and early-twentieth-century Central Asia call into question this binary interpretive model, shedding light on an Islamic legal system in which Muslims brought their affairs to state officials because they had the power to coerce parties to achieve a settlement and enforce a decision, either formal or informal. A clear sense of hierarchy rather than a notion of jurisdiction informed Muslims' choices to take legal action. Indeed, in the Islamic legal system reflected in the records originating from local Muslim chancelleries, *qāḍī*s rarely adjudicated, acting, instead, primarily as notaries and legal assessors, while responsibility for the resolution of conflicts fell on the rulers and the governors. Individuals appealing and adjudicating did not see two different legal standards (the Islamic state and *sharīʿa*). The same personnel resolved all types of problems, and there is little, if any, specific reference to specialized legal texts. When they adjudicated disputes, *qāḍī*s acted mostly at the request of the royal court (*ark-i ʿālī/darbār-i ʿālī/dargāh-i ʿālī*).

Interpreting the legal history of nineteenth-century Central Asia requires that we avoid assuming that the institutional arrangements and the judicial systems current elsewhere in the Islamic world were adopted also in this region, before the establishment of Russian rule. If one keeps, for instance, the Mamluks or the Ottomans as some kind of Archimedean points to tackle the history of *sharīʿa* in the modern period, one will regard the Central Asian case as aberrant. This is not, however, a particularly helpful approach, because it leads us to believe that there are some stages in the evolution of Islamic law that are more representative than others and that there are cases that may speak more authoritatively about what we term *sharīʿa* than other cases regarded as less integral to the tradition of Islamic law. As the reader will see, there was little in common between how conflicts were solved in Bukhara under the Manghits and, say, Ottoman Egypt and Qajar Iran, aside from the obvious commonalities in Islamic legalese, that is, in the vocabulary employed mostly by Muslim jurists.[8] Although institutions may seem similar at first, a closer look

6 G. Burak, "The Second Formation of Islamic Law: The Post-Mongol Context of the Ottoman Adoption of a School of Law." *CSSH* 55/3 (2013): 579–602.

7 Hallaq, *Sharīʿa: Theory, Practice, Transformations*: passim.

8 I owe this idea to F.H. Stewart, "False Friends: Overlapping Terminology in Arab Customary Law and in Islamic Law." Paper delivered at the 6th Conference of the International Society for Islamic Legal Studies, Exeter, 13 July 2009.

at the administrative practices, the language, and the legal literature employed suggest that there are fewer similarities than differences. While comparisons open up interesting possibilities to establish connections and a world of shared cultural references, they also lead one to confer normative value on one of the two comparators. If, say, one considers Ottoman agrarian history, practices in property relations in the Persianate world will always be examined in the light of the lessons we have learned from studying, say, Anatolia or Syria, thereby risking our misinterpreting the specific attributes of the Central Asian cases in hand. My approach here is different. Rather than focusing on reified Islamic legal *institutions* as such, I offer an exploration of *practices* of dispute settlement in a specific region of the Islamicate world. The legal history of nineteenth-century Central Asia, a region where, for example, rulers did not avail themselves of *maẓālim*, differed considerably from the histories of Islamic law in other regions.

While my study is firmly grounded on material originating almost exclusively from southern Central Asia, it also addresses the cumulative experience of a wider academic enterprise that began more than two centuries ago to write the history of Islamic law. In assuming that law was a privileged domain of professional legists, historians of Central Asia commonly echo an assumption integral to the tradition of Islamic legal studies in the West. For obvious reasons, Central Asia has been relegated to the margins of the discipline. In what follows I want to suggest that it also offers a stepping stone to rethinking the way we read (and write) the history of *sharīʿa* in the post-Mongol period, especially in wider Persianate history. This study is based primarily on sources from nineteenth- and early-twentieth-century Central Asia. These sources were produced in the chancelleries of the local Muslim polities before the Russian conquest and during the period in which the Bukharan emirate and the Khivan khanate fell under Russian protectorate. Further explorations in materials from earlier periods will probably show that the legal culture that I illustrate here existed in the region before the establishment of the three Uzbek khanates and, perhaps, in other regions of the Islamicate world as well.

Imagining a legal system in which the ruler and his chancery exercise legal authority and dominate legists, arbitrators, and mediators requires the application of an inclusive concept, a spatial metaphor allowing for the inclusion of a plurality of legal actors. I find one such concept in Pierre Bourdieu's notion of "juridical field." In his understanding, a juridical field "is determined by two factors: on the one hand, by the specific power relations which give it its structure and which order the competitive struggles (or, more precisely, the conflicts over competence) that occur within it; and on the other hand, by the internal logic of juridical functioning which constantly constrains the range of possible actions and, thereby, limits the realm of specifically juridical solutions."[9]

This notion is not entirely without problems. Bourdieu conceives of the juridical field as a system of power relations as well as a discursive space that is shaped exclusively by individuals who have judicial authority, that is, the legal experts. In other words, he assumes that nonexperts can be only passive recipients of legal supply and excludes the possibility that laymen too may partake in the conflicts over competence and thus affect the quality of legal services. My employment of the notion of "juridical field" differs from that of Bourdieu. I believe that people have expectations when they approach legal institutions, that they make assumptions about their entitlements, and that they thus have clear ideas about the truth of the claims that they present, originating, as these do, from the experience and knowledge that they accumulate during their lives. When I speak of the juridical field, I imagine a space in which the law—at the level of both imagination and patterned behavior—is the outcome of the relations between individuals endowed with legal authority *and* those who seek redress. The juridical field thus becomes a spatial metaphor to embrace law and society.

Richard Terdiman, who translated the work of Bourdieu into English, has noted that the notion of the "juridical field" becomes particularly effective if we can imagine "a magnet exerting a force upon all those who come within its range."[10] As I argue throughout this chapter, in Central Asia the magnet may be seen in the royal court, which animated a constellation of legal actors and judicial venues and pulled its subjects towards the seats of power, that is, Bukhara, Khiva, and Kokand. When examining behavior, social interactions, and order in this region before the Russian conquest, we see what might be termed a *sharīʿa*-informed juridical field, in which many turned to the ruler for redress or approval. This juridical field was a cultural space in which the ruler was perceived, in accordance with the Perso-Islamicate theory of kingship, as guarantor of the just application of *sharīʿa*. The Perso-Islamicate theory of kingship demanded that rulers embody an ideal of Islamic justice (*ʿadālat*) and be always accessible to the populace. The Orientalist Aleksander Semenov, who served for several years in the Russian residency in Kagan (a settlement

9 P. Bourdieu, "The Force of Law: Toward a Sociology of the Juridical Field." *HLJ* 38 (1986–87): 816.

10 Ibid.: 806.

located few kilometers southeast of Bukhara) and therefore had access to the chancellery of the Bukharan Protectorate[11] noted that:

> In spite of his [the emir's] inaccessibility to his people and his vast governing apparatus consisting of bureaucrats and officials of different ranks, who, as it would seem, could fulfill their functions independently within the limits of their competencies, in fact nothing was done without the sanction of the emir. At least, they would account to him nearly every trivia of ordinary administration and everyday life. [...] For among the duties of the Emir, as a just and independent ruler, was not only to ensure the enforcement of punishments, but also the administration of justice [*otpravlenie pravosudiia*], the Emir himself received appeals and hear cases.[12]

In applying the concept of an Islamic juridical field, I attempt to move away from the theory, discussed in the introduction, of "legal pluralism." Legal pluralists assume that, while modern states claim for themselves legislative prerogatives and try to impose normative standards on societies, behavior reflects the interactions within a semi-autonomous social field and conveys notions of justice that are often at odds with state law.[13] This approach is no doubt helpful when we study colonial and postcolonial situations and Western societies where more than one body of law is in effect, jurisdictions are delimited, and formalism is a given. It is less useful when we consider societies in the past, which either did not fall under the direct control of a state[14] or were ruled by dynasties lacking any legislative powers and that did not distinguish between various bodies of law (for example, Islamic law vs. customary law) or different legal doctrines (sing. *madhhab*). Nineteenth-century Central Asia presents one such case, because *sharīʿa* was not the emanation of the legislative will of the khanates, and the people taking legal action did not seem to

---

11 B.A. Litvinskii and N.M. Akramov, *Aleksandr Aleksandrovich Semenov (nauchno-bibliograficheskii ocherk)* (Moscow: Nauka, 1971): 43–44.

12 A.A. Semenov, *Ocherk ustroistva tsentral'nogo administrativnogo upravleniia Bukharskogo khantsva pozdneishego vremeni* (Stalinabad: Izdatel'stvo Akademii Nauk Tadzhikskoi SSR, 1954): 24, 32.

13 F. Pirie, "Legal Autonomy as Political Engagement: The Ladakhi Village in the Wider World." *LSR* 40/1 (2006): 77–103.

14 J. Scheele, "Rightful Measures: Irrigation, Land, and the *Sharīʿah* in the Algerian Touat." In *Legalism: Anthropology and History*, ed. Paul Dresch and Hannah Skoda (Oxford: Oxford University Press, 2012): 198.

have perceived different legal institutions as representing legal diversity. They did not understand *sharīʿa* in opposition to customary law. The subjects of the khans could and did shop for different legal forums—that is, they brought their affairs to different institutions such as the ruler (his court), the governor, the *qāḍī*s, or the local notables—but they did not regard such institutional actors as embodying diverse bodies of law, nor did they seem to regard existing procedural differences as particularly important in choosing among the existing legal venues. In spite of different procedural attributes, people perceived such institutions as representing the totality of the parts that constituted *sharīʿa.*

Legal pluralists may disapprove of my approach, by arguing that I am overlooking the fact that the legists and the scholars distinguished between *sharīʿa* and *ʿurf, ʿādat, dastūr* ("custom") and *taʿamul, ʿamal* ("practice"); that such distinctions could have informed laymen's understanding of legal practice; and that such notions about procedural differences may also have informed their choices. While I do not want to rule out this possibility, I have used a different methodology in this book. I have employed local legal notions as they appeared in my sources without projecting on my information any preconceptions about Muslim legal practice. Nothing in my sources suggests that, in precolonial Central Asia, Muslims navigated the Islamic juridical field by keeping in mind notions of legal diversity, thereby creating an opposition between customary norms, local practice, and Islamic law. When appealing to a local governor, for example, a subject of the khanate might have known that a governor could resort to violence (*siyasat*) in order to extort a confession; equally, this appellant might have been aware that it would have been unlikely that a *qāḍī* would use violence against parties to a dispute. Does this represent a case of legal diversity? The answer must be "no," because our sources tell us that both the governor and the *qāḍī* solved disputes according to *sharīʿa* and did not distinguish between, say, the law of governors and that of judges. Islamic legal sources are "aspirational," one would say, because they make resolutions to conflicts appear as though they were always achieved in compliance with *sharīʿa,* thereby effacing substantial differences. However, rather than interpreting the aspirational character of Islamic legal sources as an obstacle to our unveiling a world of assumed legal diversity, I suggest instead that we reflect on the fact that our sources originate from a juridical field informed by an inclusive notion of *sharīʿa*—a juridical field that could accommodate multiple legal authorities and institutions, which, as we shall see, often displayed overlapping jurisdictions and shared many legal functions. If this is what the available sources indicate, one wonders what would be the interpretive advantage of superimposing upon them a reading that downplays the significance of such inclusiveness.

The fact that, in precolonial Central Asia, the local population shopped for different legal forums actually indicates a situation of multiple jurisdictions and, therefore, a case of legal pluralism. From this perspective, one would understand legal pluralism more as a "jurisdictional web" than as interlocking normative orders.[15] This approach is a useful reminder of the complexities and contradictions of what we usually term "state law". As we shall see in greater detail in this chapter, in the 19th century, Central Asian khanates relied on various legal institutions to dispense justice. We should, however, be careful not to conflate jurisdictional plurality with legal diversity, for the two are different. Indeed, while in Central Asia Muslim dynasties created a plurality of legal institutions, such institutions were not substantially diverse because they all aspired to implement Islamic law.

The process of unpacking the ideological underpinnings of such a juridical field becomes particularly important as we set out to appreciate the discontinuities and the changes that Central Asian Muslims experienced in the wake of the Russian conquest. We must look critically at the conceptual repertoire of studies on law, colonialism, and globalization. It has been argued that, "when the Russians formed the governor-generalship of Turkestan there between the 1860s and early 1880s, they encountered Muslim communities [...] who had long made temporal authorities central actors in the mediation of these disputes."[16] As we shall see, this observation requires further clarification. Central Asian Muslim subjects did not regard emirs and khans as merely "temporal authorities," nor did they conceive of *sharīʿa* as a legal system informed by theology alone. As I hope to show, Central Asian rulers exercised Islamic judicial authority with little apparent concern for the presumed divine origin of *sharīʿa*.

Another idea that has gained some currency is that locals turned to rulers, hoping "to challenge the judgments of Islamic law court judges."[17] This view too is confusing, because there is little evidence of the use of judicial review in precolonial Central Asia. In conferring utility on this interpretation, one

15 This approach to the study of legal pluralism has been elaborated in L. Benton, *Law and Colonial Cultures: Legal Regimes in World History: 1400–1900* (Cambridge: Cambridge University Press, 2002) and L. Benton and R.J. Ross, "Empires and Legal Pluralism: Jurisdiction, Sovereignty, and Political Imagination in the Early Modern World." In *Legal Pluralism and Empires, 1500–1850*, ed. L. Benton and R.J. Ross (New York: New York University Press, 2013): 3–7.

16 Crews, *For Prophet and Tsar*: 250. A similar interpretation has been articulated in *Russian Rule in Samarkand, 1868–1910: A Comparison with British India*: 246, where Morrison uses the expression "secular authorities."

17 Crews, *For Prophet and Tsar*: 251.

lends credit to a colonial cultural construction that considered the royal court only as a site of appeal. As we shall see, Central Asians usually brought their cases before the rulers, not just when they intended to complain about *qāḍīs*' malpractice.[18]

I thus want to take categories such as "state law" or "non-state law" less as a given than as reflecting modern Western forms of governance. The question I pose in this chapter is, how can we account for a centralised administration of *sharīʿa* in the region without recourse to the usual interpretative paradigm of "modernization"? I will propose an answer to this question by arguing that, in the Central Asian khanates, the administration of *sharīʿa* constituted legal sovereignty, thus reflecting what we may term a "*sharīʿa* rule of law." By introducing the notion of the rule of law, I want to emphasize the lived experience of law rather than legal theory. The *sharīʿa* rule of law manifests itself less in the theory of the ruler's integrity[19] than in the commoners' belief that justice emanates from the royal court. This is something different from consent or obedience. I will try to account for the existence of a state of order in which behavior conforms to the law and forms of legal consciousness are "created by plebeians' own encounter with [...] occasional just outcomes."[20]

1 The Islamic Juridical Field in Nineteenth-Century Central Asia

1.1 *Rulers and Judges*

We start with a few considerations regarding the institutional arrangements that made possible the practice of *sharīʿa* in Central Asia. First of all, the appointment to legal offices depended, as a general rule, on the sovereign[21] and

18 My approach here differs from that in Crews, *For Prophet and Tsar*: 250, and Morrison, *Russian Rule in Samarkand, 1868–1910: A Comparison with British India*: 246.

19 R. Murphey, "Mustafa Safi's Version of the Kingly Virtues as Presented in His Zübdet'ül Tevarih, or Annals of Sultan Ahmed, 1012–1023 A.H./1603–1614 AD" In *Frontiers of Ottoman Studies,* ed. C. Imber and K. Kiyotaki (London: I.B. Tauris, 2005): 1:5–24.

20 L. Benton, "Not Just a Concept: Institutions and the 'Rule of Law.'" *JAS* 68/1 (2009): 119.

21 That appointment to the office of *qāḍī* depended on the ruler is a constant feature of Sunni legal history; see M.I. Calero Secall, "Ruler and Qāḍīs: Their Relationship during the Naṣrīd Kingdom." *ILS* 7/2 (2000): 235–55. This opened up several issues, among them that, in Sunni judicial theory, the validity of the judicial activity of judges appointed by the de facto political power is a sine qua non, even if that power is illegitimate; see Schacht, *Introduction to Islamic Law*: 187. In practice, the ruler might rely indirectly on public opinion to check the qualifications of a candidate; see U. Rebstock, "A *Qāḍī*'s Errors." *ILS* 6/1 (1999): 1–37.

entailed choosing among a pool of competing candidates. It was customary during the tenure of the Bukharan emir ʿAbd al-Aḥad (1885–1910), for example, that appointees to judicial positions were selected from among the offspring of Bukharan scholarly families (*makhdhūm-zādigān*), while governors and *waqf* administrators were chosen from among the ruler's allies (*aqribāʾ*).[22] Nineteenth-century Bukharan jurists looked favorably on the fact that *qāḍīs*' investiture (*taqallud*) depended on the ruler (*al-sulṭān*), regardless of whether the ruler was just, cruel, or infidel.[23]

Appointments followed established patterns of reciprocity embedded in a culture of gift exchange. An individual could be rewarded with a designation to office either for his merits or, more often than not, for his display of loyalty and generosity to the emir. A local observer of these practices, Ḥamīd Khwāja b. Baqā Khwāja, who was born to a Bukharan family of *ʿulamāʾ*, provides an interesting account of the grand celebrations (*tūy*) that the local legists organized in honor of the emir. The rule for such events in Bukhara was that the bigger a celebration was, the better the chance that the ruler would confer an office upon its organizer. Ḥamīd Khwāja was proud, for example, that his father, Baqā Khwāja, the Bukharan chief judge (*qaḍī kalān*), could organize one such *tūy* for the emir ʿAbd al-Aḥad that lasted more than a month.[24] Ḥamīd Khwāja illustrates with humor how his father's acolytes, especially the mullahs, joined the event "to inspect the service at the celebrations" (*ba-tūy mutaraṣṣid-i khidhmat shudand*). This is, no doubt, the author's ironic twist alerting us to the scholars' obsequiousness towards the chief judge. Ḥamīd Khwāja took particular pains to explain that all the mullahs attended the event in the hope of royal favor: "nobody knows if the [benevolent] eye of the emir falls [on someone] and satisfies [his] wish [for appointments]" (*mabādā ki chashm-i amīr āftāda pursish ḥāl kunad*), he tells us.[25] And the shrewdest among these celebrations' attendees could necessarily capitalize a lot: Ḥamīd Khwāja noted that some of his

---

22 Ḥamīd Khwāja, *Tanzīl al-imthāl fī dhikr bayān al-aḥwāl*, MS Tashkent, TsVRUz, no. 602: 254b.

23 The opinion is to be found in a Bukharan legal miscellany titled *Majmūʿa wa taʾrīkh-i Mullā-zāda*, MS Tashkent, TsVRUz, no. 9767: fol. 37b. This opinion quotes a fifteenth-century juristic authority, saying "The judicial investiture from an equitable and despotic ruler is licit. But his [the judge's] equitable nature must be manifest" (*taqlīd-i qaḍā az sulṭān-i ʿādil wa jābir jāʾiz ast ammā az ʿādil-i khwud ẓāhir ast*), Ikhtiyār al-Dīn b. Ghiyāth al-Dīn al-Ḥusaynī, *Mukhtār al-ikhtiyār ʿalā al-madhhab al-mukhtār*. MS Tahskent, TsVRUz, no. 5438: fols. 13b; MS Bodleian, Frazer 239: fols. 4b–5a. The *Mukhtār al-ikhtiyār* devotes an entire section to appointment (*taqlīd*) to and removal (*ʿazl*) from the office of *qāḍī*.

24 Ḥamīd Khwāja, *Tanzīl al-imthāl fī dhikr bayān al-aḥwāl*: 255b.

25 Ibid.

sharp-elbowed contemporaries benefited much more than he did. While the chief judge received from the emir a courier and a golden stirrup, our author could amass nothing more than a robe of honor.[26] Little wonder that some, by entering the emir's inner circle and organizing ever larger celebrations, managed to secure appointment to the most celebrated judicial position. This was the story, for instance, of Mullā Burhān al-Dīn. This man was *ra'is* ("chief, market inspector") of Bukhara from 1900 until 1910, when he was accused of having instigated Sunni-Shi'i clashes in the city.[27] He then fell into disgrace and was demoted to the office of judge in the southwestern province of Chahār Jūy (present-day Charjuy, in Turkmenistan).[28] By exploiting his friendship with the emirate's "treasurer" (*khazīnachī*), he secured permission from the emir in 1913 to hold a new celebration including more invitees,[29] the cost of which, interestingly, would be borne by the chief judge, Baqā Khwāja. The outcome of this display of extravagance proved successful: Mullā Burhān al-Dīn was sent back to Bukhara on account of his skills in squandering the emir's money.[30] Indeed, Ḥamīd Khwāja sardonically reports that his father alarmed another Bukharan legist, saying, "With this feast Mullā Burhān al-Dīn is going to eat either my head or yours! Unfortunately, in the following days it became manifest that he was appointed chief judge."[31] Mullā Burhān al-Dīn's appointment to chief judge brought about the demotion of Baqā Khwāja to the rank of *shaykh al-Islām*, which was, at that time, only an honorary office.

One should, of course, situate this disparaging account offered by Ḥamīd Khwāja in the latter's personal history—that is, the history of someone who, like others in the emirate,[32] attempted unsuccessfully to get hold of an administrative post. As we shall see later, such positions provided for a stable income stream, not only because they often involved prebends of various sort (as well

26 Ibid.: 256b–257a.

27 This episode is recounted briefly in *The Personal History of a Bukharan Intellectual. The Diary of Muḥammad Sharīf Ṣadr-i Ziyā*, trans. R. Shukurov and ed. E. Allworth (Leiden: Brill, 2004): 299. For more on Sunni- Shi'i clashes, see A. Khalid, "Society and Politics in Bukhara, 1868–1920." *CAS* 19/3–4 (2000): 367–96.

28 *The Personal History of a Bukharan Intellectual*: 257.

29 Ḥamīd Khwāja, *Tanzīl al-imthāl fī dhikr bayān al-aḥwāl*: fol. 257a.

30 Ibid.: 257b–258a. This episode is recounted briefly in *The Personal History of a Bukharan Intellectual*: 299.

31 Ḥamīd Khwāja, *Tanzīl al-imthāl fī dhikr bayān al-aḥwāl*: fol. 258a.

32 For another (unedifying and far less detailed) story of repeated attempts to climb the ladder of the judicial hierarchy, see Mīr Sayyid Muḥyī al-Dīn b. Mīr Sayyid Ḥabībullāh Fatḥābādī, *Khāṭirāt*, MS Tashkent, TsVRUz, no. 328/IV.

as estates and fiscal privileges) but also because of the gifts (*tārtīq/pīsh-kash*) that appointees received in exchange for their services. Little surprise that most local scholars longed to be appointed to such a position. In fact, the last decades of Manghit rule over Bukhara saw a strong outburst of factionalism between two groups of scholars, referred to in the local lore as "mountaineers" and "the urbanized" (*kuhistānī/khaṭlānī* and *tūmānī*) according to their place of origin, who competed with each other for supreme authority and for a monopoly on the money-making possibilities of offices.[33] There is little doubt that the alternate fortunes of this or that scholar reflected personal ties to the emir as well as the latter's strategies.[34] Ḥamīd Khwāja was—together with other individuals of distinguished pedigree such as Ṣadr-i Ḍiyā, whom we shall encounter later—among those who had often to endure the ruler's changing will.

The person and office of ruler played an important role also in the ritual whereby powers were conferred upon judicial appointees. The conferral of powers to a judicial post usually occurred according to a strongly ritualized protocol in which officeholders were entrusted with a diploma (*yārlīq/manshūr*) in front of other court attendants. While all these records share a formulaic nature, they show the extent to which ruling houses defined the jurisdiction as well as the specific duties of its judicial personnel. The royal courts not only determined the fees that judges could charge their clients, but they could also, at times, confer on the new appointees particular powers. If *qāḍīs*, for example, could enforce retaliation or other punitive offenses, it would be made explicit in the diploma of appointment. It did not follow, however, that *qāḍīs* always enjoyed such powers. Indeed, the reader will not find the same attributes among those enumerated in other diplomas issued for the post of judge (see Appendix 1). Making explicit specific judicial attributes was probably a response to social circumstances and fluctuations in judges' authority in a given locale. We shall see later that, in their areas of jurisdiction, legists often encountered resistance to their judicial functions, and the official endorsement of the royal court may thus have proved necessary in order to secure obedience.

---

33 The first to offer a clear, if brief, account of this struggle was S.A. Dudoignon, "Les 'tribulations' du juge Ziyā. Histoire et mémoire du clientélisme politique à Boukhara (1868–1929)." *AHSS* 59/5–6 (2004): 1095–135.

34 This is clearly exemplified by the various accounts of appointment and dismissal of judicial officials in *The Personal History of a Bukharan Intellectual*: passim.

Appointment as judge consisted, above all, in the ceremonial conferral of these diplomas. The new officeholder would kiss the diploma of appointment, rub it on his eyes, and then stick it in his turban.[35] The physical attributes of such records suggest that they were designed for display. More often than not, especially in cases of appointment to judicial posts in important urban contexts, diplomas were partially adorned with illuminated lettering and stamped with the seals of the ruler (see Fig. 2).

During this public performance the attendants prayed for the wellbeing of the ruler, and the people could meet the newly appointed legist. The subjects were thus, in general, probably fully aware of changes in legal offices, and such appointments were probably perceived by the populace as reflective of a political statement and the reconfiguring of new power relations: this judge is the man close to the ruler, not the one who has been removed from office. Sources tell us that jurists in disfavor were more likely to be packed off to the less attractive areas, such as the Turkmen steppe, than to Bukhara. The famous Muḥammad Sharīf-Jān Makhdūm, alias Ṣadr-i Ḍiyā' (1867–1932)—himself a jurist born into a family of Ersari Turkmens that had fled from the Charjuy province to Bukhara and there found its fortunes[36]—refers to the appointment to the post of chief judge of Mullā Ṣadr al-Dīn b. Bayḍā, a mullah from the mountainous region of Kulab (in present-day Tajikistan, hence his *nisba* Khaṭlānī, "mountaineer").[37] This

35 Qāḍī Muḥammad Wafā Karminagī, *Tuḥfat al-khānī*, MS Tashkent, TsVRUz, no. 16: fol. 264b (*ināyat-nāma-yi shahriyār-ra bar sar-i ū nishānda*). My thanks to Andreas Wilde for this reference. It was the *parvānachī*—yet another among various administrative figures whom we could term "chamberlain"—who usually stuck the diploma in the new appointee's turban; see N.V. Khanykov, *Opisanie Bukharskogo Khanstva* (St. Petersburg: Tip. Imperatorskoi Akademii Nauk, 1843): 185. See also Ṣadr al-Dīn 'Āynī, *Bukhārā inqilābīning ta'rīkhī*, ed. S. Shimada and S. Tosheva (Tokyo: Dept. of Islamic Area Studies, Center for Evolving Humanities, Graduate School of Humanities and Sociology, University of Tokyo, 2010): 22 (*amīrnīng yārlīghīnī bāshīgha sūqūb*). Sticking a diploma in the appointee's turban applied to several officeholders, tax collectors (*amlākdār*) included; see TsGARUz, f. I-126, op. 1, d. 746, l. 83.

36 [Ṣadr-i Ḍiyā'], *Tarjuma-yi aḥwāl-i Qāḍī 'Abd al-Shakūr*, MS Tashkent, TsVRUz, no. 1304/IV: fol. 98b.

37 For more on this person and the impact his appointment is presumed to have had on the office of chief justice in the cultural environment of Bukhara, see *The Personal History of a Bukharan Intellectual:* 105 fn. 81.

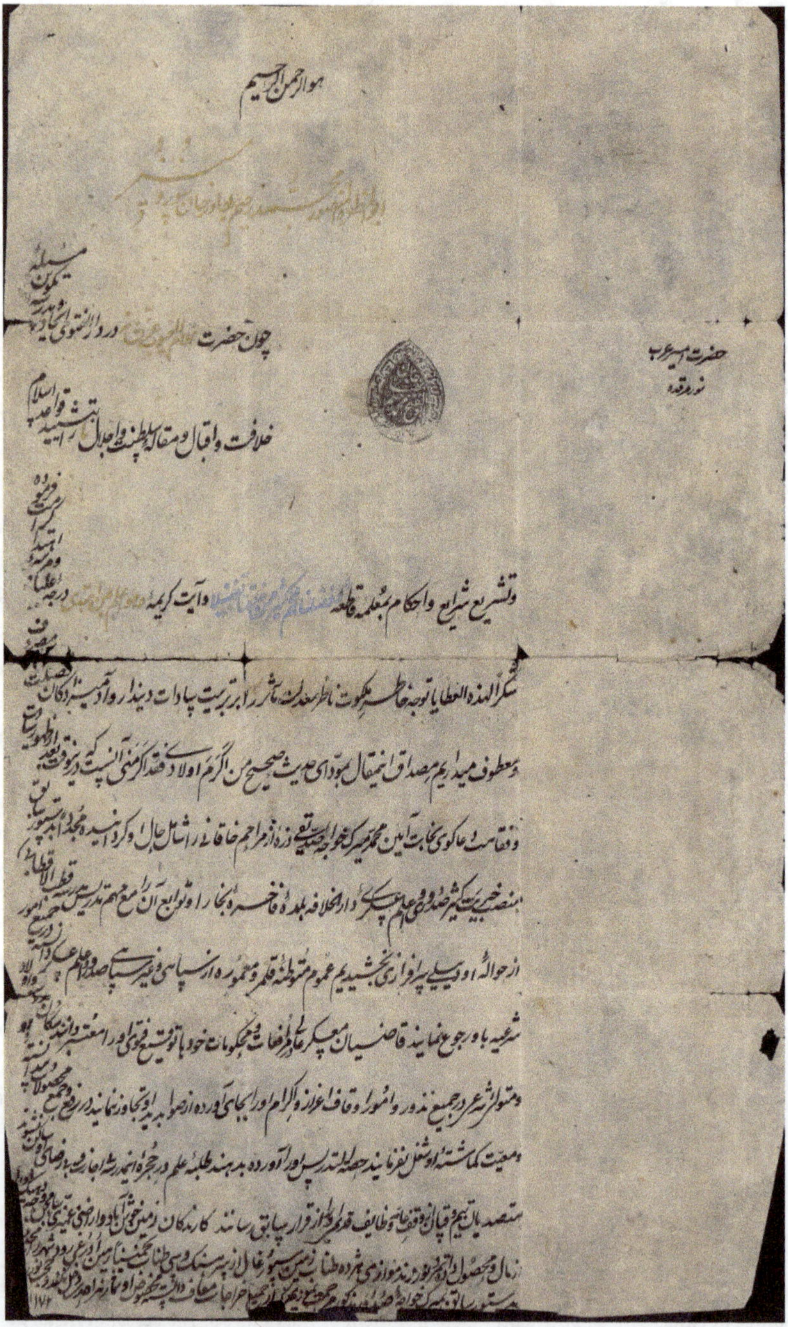
هو الرحمن الرحيم

FIGURE 2 *Diploma of appointment to the position of senior jurist for the military* (ṣudūr/aʿlam-i ʿaskarī) *issued by Muḥammad Raḥīm Khān, Bukhara, 1172/1758–9. TsGARUz, f. R-2678, op. 2, d. 177, unnumbered folio.*
COURTESY OF THE CENTRAL STATE ARCHIVE OF UZBEKISTAN

appointment was followed by the subsequent removal of eighteen officials (including his father) from other legal posts and their reappointment to judicial positions in the countryside (*az Bukhārā ba wilāyāt wa tūmānāt qāḍī kunānīda*).[38] The account of Ṣadr-i Ḍiyā' indicates how such dismissals were often loaded with political meaning for networks of scholars in the emirate. Ṣadr-i Ḍiyā' also glosses at length the decision as one affecting directly the way in which justice was dispensed and even how law was taught in the institutes of higher learning.[39]

In addition to conferring powers on candidates for the post of *qāḍī*, the ruler stood atop the judicial hierarchy. In the wake of a homicide case, for instance, Qāḍī 'Abd al-Shakūr (1817/8–1889),[40] the father of Ṣadr-i Ḍiyā', informed Emir Muẓaffar al-Dīn (r. 1860–86) of his decision to proceed with a sentence of retaliation (*qiṣāṣ*), which consisted of the corporal punishment of the murderer. Before approving the decision, the cautious emir submitted it to the chief judge in Bukhara, Qāḍī 'Abd al-Shakūr's archenemy, the aforementioned Ṣadr al-Dīn. The two *qāḍī*s stood in a hierarchical relation: the chief judge had the monopoly over homicide cases.[41] The *qāḍī kalān* quashed the ruling of retaliation and recommended that his sovereign order the payment of blood money (*diyat*). Notified of this decision, Qāḍī 'Abd al-Shakūr vehemently protested and rallied other jurists in the city. Two rulings on the same case were now brought before the emir: persuaded by the urban judicial community, the ruler rejected the sentence of compensation and upheld that for retaliation. Once he received the confirmation from Bukhara, the judge in the countryside was happy to enforce a legal order according to *sharī'a*.[42] If law is about choosing between right or wrong, however, we should also note that, in several cases, it was the ruler, not the *qāḍī*, who ultimately imposed the judgment. Such cases may well have involved disputes on more mundane affairs than homicide cases, such as those involving property rights and fiscal privileges. It was common, for example, for Bukharan rulers at the beginning of the nineteenth century to issue rulings (*ḥukm-i 'āli*) conferring on someone ownership rights

38 *Tarjuma-yi aḥwāl-i Qāḍī 'Abd al-Shakūr*: fol. 101a–b.

39 Ibid.: fol. 101b.

40 *The Personal History of a Bukharan Intellectual*: 85 fn. 5.

41 See Appendix 1.

42 *Tarjuma-yi aḥwāl-i Qāḍī 'Abd al-Shakūr*: fol. 102a–b.

over a certain amount of land after court attendants had carried out inquiries into disputes.[43]

1.2 *Appealing to the Royal Court* (ʿarḍ)

It is conventionally assumed that the job of *qāḍīs* was always to adjudicate disputes, but surprisingly few sources provide information about the exact nature of their responsibilities. Starting in the early Soviet period, a vast number of Islamic legal records stemming from the post-Timurid period has been published or described in catalogues. To date, however, records illustrating the process of adjudication and delivery of a ruling (*ḥukm*) are extraordinarily rare.[44] In Central Asian Islamic legalese, such records are called *sijill*, and they serve a specific documentary purpose. They were usually issued to the parties to a dispute and were treated as a written attestation of the outcome of a litigation and the entitlements that the latter generated.[45] Thus, in nineteenth-century Central Asia the understanding of the word *sijill* was closer to that of the term used under the Mamluks, and it should not be conflated with the Ottoman

---

43 Mīrzā Ṣādiq Munshī Jāndārī, *Munsha'āt wa manshūrāt*, MS Tashkent, TsVRUz, no. 299: fol. 124a.

44 Only two specimens of such legal texts have been published so far, though more are known to have existed and have been occasionally catalogued; see *Samarkandskie dokumenty XV–XVI vv. (O vladeniiakh Khodzhi Akhrara v Srednei Azii i Afganistane)*, ed. O.D. Chekhovich (Moscow: Nauka, 1974): docs. 14 and 15, 303–10. I have located similar texts in TsGARUz, f. I-125, op. 1, d. 602, ll. 1–10b and TsVRUz, *Khiva qozilik khujjatlari* (Aklia Aliakbarova's collection), doc. 16a, 71, 583, 645, 675, 685. The latter were described briefly, under the same numeration, in *Katalog Khivinskikh kaziiskikh dokumentov (XIX–nach. XX vv.)*, ed. A. Urunbaev et al. (Tashkent and Tokyo: Department of Islamic Area Studies, 2001).

45 Ol'ga Chekhovich renders *sijill* as "deed of attestation' (*podtverzhdaiushchii dokument*) in *Samarkandskie dokumenty XV–XVI vv. (O vladeniiakh Khodzhi Akhrara v Srednei Azii i Afganistane)*: 305. The term *sijill* is also to be found among the stipulations of endowment deeds (sing., *waqfīya* or *waqf-nāma*). The term refers to a document attached to endowment deeds as a result of a fictitious claim for the recovery of property that the endower filed against the endowment. Thus, such a document too functions as a written attestation of the outcome of a dispute. On such fictitious claims and stipulations of Central Asian endowment deeds, see K. Isogay, "A Commentary on the Closing Formula in the Central Asian Waqf Documents." In *Persian Documents*, ed. N. Kondo (London: RoutledgeCurzon, 2003): 3–12. See also *Bukharskii vakf XIII v.* Faksimile. Izdanie teksta, perevod s arabskogo i persidskogo, vvedenie i kommentarii A.K. Arendsa, A.B. Khalidova, O.A. Chekhovich (Moscow: Nauka, 1979): 24, where it is glossed as "deed of official confirmation' (*akt ofitsial'nogo utverzhdeniia*) and M.E. Subtelny, *Timurids in Transition: Turko-Persian Politics and Acculturation in Medieval Iran* (Leiden: Brill, 2007): 150, where it is translated as "endorsement."

usage as "*qāḍī* register".[46] Indeed, Central Asian *qāḍīs* did not keep registers before colonization—or, at least, not a single register from a period preceding the Russian conquest is known to have survived.[47]

Sijills appear infrequently, and, when they do, it is usually in private collections. For some reason, they pertain most often to cases involving animal theft. The fact that *qāḍīs* in the nineteenth century apparently issued *sijills* only within a narrow range of circumstances seems to reflect the restriction of the judicial powers of *qāḍīs*' under the rule of the three Uzbek khanates that were established at the end of the eighteenth century. The extent to which their powers became limited in this period becomes apparent by comparing fifteenth- and sixteenth-century Central Asia Islamic notary manuals with those written in the nineteenth century.[48] While the former point to the fact that a substantial share of *qāḍīs*'s output consisted of *sijills*, the latter clearly indicate that *sijills* were requested only in cases of animal theft. Notary manuals show

---

46 The Central Asian *sijill* did not include the witnessed record of the contents of a claim as in earlier periods, but only the ruling; cf. W.B. Ḥallaq, "The *Qāḍī*'s *Dīwān* (*Sijill*) before the Ottomans." BSOAS 61/3 (1998): 420; M.K. Masud, R. Peters, and D.S. Powers, "*Qāḍīs* and Their Courts: An Historical Survey": 21. For an insightful discussion of record-keeping practices of Ottoman *qāḍīs*, see G. Burak, "Evidentiary Truth Claims, Imperial Registers, and the Ottoman Archive: Contending Legal Views of Archival and Record-Keeping Practices in Ottoman Greater Syria (Seventeenth–Nineteenth Centuries)." BSOAS 79/2 (2016): 233–54.

47 We know of four *qāḍī* registers that were produced in Khiva between 1893 and 1912, that is, during the period of the Russian protectorate. Their composition, however, was probably prompted by new bureaucratic norms introduced by the Russians, which regulated record-keeping practices and would facilitate communication between the Khivan chancellery and the governor of the Amu-Darya Department based in Petroaleksandrovsk; see A. Shaikhova, "O Khivinskoi kaziiskoi knige iz fondov Instituta vostokovedeniia An UzSSR." ONU 6/8 (1982): 53–57. Catalogues of Central Asian Islamic legal documents usually render *sijill* as "register," which is misleading. See A. Urunbaev, G. Dzhuraeva, and S. Gulomov, *Katalog sredneaziatskikh zhalovannykh gramot iz fonda Instituta vostokovedeniia im. Abu Raikhana Beruni Akademii Nauk Respubliki Uzbekistan* (Halle/Saale: Orientwissenschaftliches Zentrum der Martin-Luther-Universität Halle-Wittenberg, 2007): doc. 18, 22, 23, 68, 69; T. Welsford and N. Tashev, *A Catalogue of Arabic-Script Documents from the Samarqand Museum* (Samarkand and Istanbul: IICAS, 2012): docs. 422, 423.

48 For an important specimen of a fifteenth-century Islamic notary manual, see Ikhtiyār al-Dīn b. Ghiyāth al-Dīn al-Ḥusaynī, *Mukhtār al-ikhtiyār ʿalā al-madhhab al-mukhtār*, MS Bodleian, Frazer 235: fol. 16a and passim. For early sixteenth-century material, see ʿAlī b. Muḥammad-ʿAlī b. ʿAlī b. Maḥmūd al-Mukhtārī al-Khwārazmī al-Kubrawī, *al-Jawāmiʿ al-ʿalīya fī al-wathāʾiq al-sharʿīya wa al-sijillāt al-marʿīya*, MS Tashkent, TsVRUz, no. 9138. On this manuscript and its author, see Subtelny, *Timurids in Transition*: 222.

that *qāḍīs* crafted only two types of *sijills*. One such document (*pusht-i maḥḍar sijill*[49]/*sijill-i ashtār, asb wa murakkab*[50]/*wathīqa-yi khaṭṭ-i sijill-asb*[51]) was given to claimants to solemnize the recovery of their property.[52] The respondents, too, had a potential interest in receiving a *sjill* in order to be able to claim later the restitution of the money from the individual who had sold him the stolen animal. This type of *sjill* was called *qahqarī*.[53] That juristic manuals lithographed in Bukhara included these two types of *sijills* only[54] is further evidence of the fact that, in the nineteenth century, *qāḍīs* probably issued rulings mostly on such cases. Does this mean that *qāḍīs* heard *only* cases involving animal theft? Or that animal theft was the most common among the cases heard by *qāḍīs*? There is no way to answer these questions, but the fact that notary manuals did not include the templates for other types of rulings suggests that

49 *Majmūʿa-yi wathāʾiq wa murāsalāt*, MS Tashkent, TsVRUz, no. 8958: fol. 15a–b (early twentieth century). The expression *pusht-i maḥḍar sijill* refers to the fact that a plaintiff could acquire a *sijill* notarized on the verso side of a protocol of claim. For one such common practice, see TsGARUz, f. R-2678, op. 2, d. 90, l. 1–10b, which refers to a case of recovery of property consisting of one horse by a certain Muḥammad Saʿīd Khwāja in Nasaf (present-day Qarshi) in 1884.

50 *Munshaʾāt-i Mirzā Bahādir Khwāja b. Ḥusayn Khwāja Pīrmastī*, MS Tashkent, TsVRUz, no. 2667: fol. 86b–87a (early twentieth century).

51 *Wathāʾiq-i mutafarraqa*, MS Tashkent, TsVRUz, no. 6057/1: fol. 5a (mid-nineteenth century); *Wathāʾiq*, MS Tashkent, TsVRUz, no. 4594/II: fol. 44a-b (late nineteenth century); *Wathāʾiq*, MS Tashkent, TsVRUz, no. 8072: fol. 1b. For the Chaghatay translation of a model document (*sijill khaṭṭ nuskhasī*), see *Majmūʿa-yi wathāʾiq*, MS Tashkent, TsVRUz 7799: fol. 53a–55a (early twentieth century, Khazarasp, Khorezm oasis).

52 I have discussed the stipulations of such documentary forms in "The Birth of a Custom: Nomads, *Sharīʿa* Courts and Established Practices in the Tashkent Province, ca. 1868–1919." *ILS* 18/4 (2011): 319.

53 *Majmūʿa-yi wathāʾiq wa murāsalāt*, MS Tashkent, TsVRUz, no. 8958: fol. 15b (here *wathīqa-yi qahqarī*); *Munshaʾāt-i Mirzā Bahādir Khwāja b. Ḥusayn Khwāja Pīrmastī*, MS Tashkent, TsVRUz, no. 2667: fol. 87b (here *sijill-i qahqarā-yi asb wa ashtar wa murakkab*); *Wathāʾiq-i mutafarraqa*, MS Tashkent, TsVRUz, no. 6057/1: fol. 5b (here *wathīqa-yi khaṭṭ-i sijill*); *Wathāʾiq*, MS Tashkent, TsVRUz, no. 4594/II, fol. 44b–45a (here *wathīqa-yi qahqarī*); idem, in *Wathāʾiq*, MS Tashkent, TsVRUz, no. 8072, fol. 5a; *Formuliarnik iuridicheskikh dokumentatsii XX v. na tadzhikskom iazyke, arabskim grafikom* [*1910 g.*], TsGARUz, R-2678, op. 2, d. 244, l. 10a (here *sijill-i qahqarī*). See the Chaghatay translation of the same type of document (*khaṭṭ-i qahqarīnīng nuskhasī*) in *Majmūʿa-yi wathāʾiq*, MS Tashkent, TsVRUz 7799, fol. 56b–58b.

54 Naẓrallāh Bāy b. Qāyil Bāy and Mullā Sulṭān b. Mullā Ṣābir, *Jung-i fatāwā wa maḥḍarāt* (Bukhara: 1325/1907–8): 473–474 (here, respectively, *sijill-i awwal* and *sijill-qahqarī*).

*qāḍī*s did not need to keep sight of such templates because they issued most probably such records only rarely.[55]

Without the vested interests of the disputants, where else could one find traces of the judicial activities of the *qāḍī*s? Most of the records that are usually termed "*qadi* documents" are actually texts that belong to private collections. Parties to disputes did not acquire texts reflecting the process of adjudication, unless they might prove useful for the substantiation of some future claim. If we exclude the few *sijill*s I mentioned, evidence of *sharīʿa* courts resolving disputes would be feeble at best. Indeed, the limitations to *qāḍī*s' judicial powers become even more apparent when one realizes that their actual role in conflict resolution amounted mostly to the notarization of amicable settlements (*ṣulḥ*).[56] More often than not, settlements were reached with the mediation of a third party, usually local notables, who decided also the stipulations of the agreements.

If *qāḍī*s and other judicial personnel left behind little evidence of judicial activities, it probably means that we have to look beyond the judges for attestations of instances of conflict resolution and records of the implementation of *sharīʿa*.

From the end of the eighteenth century, we begin to find evidence of a process of bureaucratization and centralization of the Islamic legal system. The Manghit ruler Shāh Murād (r. 1785–1800) appears to have been the first ruler to set this process in motion. The richest account of such "legal reforms" comes from a Bukharan court chronicler, Mīrzā ʿAbd al-Aẓīm Sāmī. In his "Royal Gift," a chronicle with which he intended to exalt the accomplishments of the Manghit dynasty, Sāmī wrote:

> The royal court [*bār-i mulukāna-yi dawlat*], which had been maintained since the times of Chingīz Khān, was dissolved; in lieu thereof, he [the

55 TsVRUz *Khiva qozilik khujjatlari* (Aklia Aliakbarova's collection), docs. 16a 71, 583, 645, 675, 685 refer to disputes over property rights on land and water that occurred in Khorezm in the second half of the nineteenth and early twentieth century.

56 Indeed, there are many certificates of acquittal (*ibrāʾ*) in such private collections. These records too may refer to the outcome of a dispute. When parties agreed on a settlement, *sharīʿa* courts usually notarized certificates that solemnized the stipulations of the amicable settlement, but we also encounter the opposite case. That is, certificates of acquittal could be produced following conflicts that were settled outside of the court; see my "Murder in Manghishlaq: Notes on an Instance of Application of Qazaq Customary Law in Khiva." *DI* 88/2 (2012): 217–57. We also observe cases in which such records were purposely crafted in the absence of disputes, in order to deter adversaries from taking legal action.

> emir] established the tribunal of justice [*maḥkama-yi ʿadālat*]. Forming an assembly along with forty *ʿulamāʾ*, he heard the petitions of the people [*ʿarāyiḍ-i mardum rā pursīda*] and, in the presence of the scholars, made decisions according to the religious law. Holding this assembly mostly on Fridays and Mondays, he gave no credence to the word of the claimant until the defendant appeared [*tā muddaʿā ʿalayh ḥāḍir nashawad qawl-i muddaʿī rā iʿtibār nakardī*]. There was no help for anyone to escape the justice of his tribunal: the mean and the noble, chiefs and poor people, all were equal before this rule. Even the [most miserable] servant could drag his master before this court of justice [*banda mī tawānist khwāja-yi khwud rā dar maḥkama-yi ʿadālat ba murāfaʿa kashad*].[57]

We learn from this stylized representation that Shāh Murād presided over a tribunal of justice in which people filed their claims by means of petitions. It might be objected that this excerpt is reminiscent of the mirror-for-princes genre. It is true that works belonging to this genre conventionally cite "justice" (*ʿadālat*) as the attribute that Muslim rulers should possess in order to govern the country and ensure stability;[58] Central Asian works are no exception in this respect. Several sources from that period praise the reign of Shāh Murād as one under which *sharīʿa* prospered,[59] but I see little reason to consider mirrors for princes, treatises on kingship in general, and court historiography as sources providing only *models*, unreflective of social reality.[60] If these genres insist that the ruler should possess the attributes of the just person, it was precisely because it was common knowledge that a ruler should hear cases and be involved in the

---

57 Mīrzā ʿAbd al-ʿAẓīm Būstānī [Sāmī], *Tuḥfa-yi shāhī*, ed. N. Jalālī (Tehran: Anjuman-i Āthār wa Mafāhir-i Farhangī, 1388sh/2010): 53.

58 A.S. Lambton, "Justice in the Medieval Persian Theory of Government." *Studia Islamica* 5 (1956): 91–119; eadem, "Islamic Mirror for Princes." In *Atti del covegno internazionale sul tema, La Persia nel Medioevo (Roma, 31 marzo–5 aprile 1970)* (Rome: Accademia Nazionale dei Lincei, 1971): 419–42; M.E. Subtelny, "A Late Medieval Persian Summa on Ethic: Kashifi's *Akhlāq-i Muḥsinī*." *IS* 36/4 (2003): 601–14.

59 O.D. Chekhovich, "K istorii Uzbekistana v XVIII v." In *Trudy Instituta Vostokovedeniia* 3 (1954): 62; A. von Kügelgen, *Die Legitimierung der mittelasiatischen Mangitendynastie in den Werken ihrer Historiker, 18.–19. Jahrhundert* (Istanbul: Ergon, 2002): 285.

60 I am here taking a position that differs from R.P. Mottahedeh, *Loyalty and Leadership in an Early Islamic Society*, 2d ed. (London and New York: I.B. Tauris, 2001): ix. For a position close to mine, see Y. Karev, "From Tents to City. The Royal Court of the Western Qarakhanids between Bukhara and Samarqand." In *Turko-Mongol Rulers, Cities and City Life*, ed. D. Durand-Guédy (Leiden: Brill, 2013): 124.

adjudication of disputes:[61] "If we do not appeal to the ruler [in cases regarding] blood money, water [rights, cases of] injustice, and other matters, then what is the emir good for?," wrote the nineteenth-century Bukharan polymath Aḥmad Dānish in reflecting on the duties of the Manghit emirs.[62]

The passage I quoted from Sāmī suggests that, before Manghit rule, the royal courts of Transoxiana provided some kind of legal service; to represent the latter as a survival of Chinggisid political tradition, however, is obviously an authorial action taken by Sāmī to sketch pre-Manghit legal practices in disparaging terms in order to magnify his master. It is also be possible that Shāh Murād was not the great innovator that Sāmī wants us to think. There are several precedents in the early-modern history of the Persianate world in which people could bring their complaints to the royal courts of Muslim principalities, such as those of Shāh ʿAbbās (r. 1588–1629)[63] and Sulṭān Ḥusayn Bāyqarā in Herat (r. 1469–1506).[64]

But nineteenth-century sources allow us to describe more than mere compositional conventions on men of government inhabiting the ideal type of the just ruler. Local chronicles, for example, offer vivid accounts of Central Asian rulers touring their domains to hear the grievances of their subjects—the dispensation of justice by peripatetic rulers:

> During the entire expedition his majesty entertained himself with various kinds of falconry and hunting and, at the same time, would inquire

61 M. Alam, "*Sharīʿa* and Governance in the Indo-Islamic Context," In *Beyond Turk and Hindu: Rethinking Religious Identities in Islamicate South Asia*, ed. D. Gilmartin and B.B. Lawrence (Gainesville, FL: University Press of Florida, 2000): 220.

62 *agar mā az wajh-i khūn wa āb wa sitam* [*wa*] *ghayr ba-sulṭān ʿarḍ na-kunim ba-mā amīr ba-cha muhimm ba-kār ast?*, Aḥmad Makhdūm Muhandis-i Bukhārī, alias Aḥmad-i Kalla, *Tarjimat al-aḥwāl-i amīrān-i Bukhārā-yi sharīf*, MS Tashkent, TsVRUz, no. 1987: fol. 54b. "Blood money" (*khūn*) denotes a restitutional payment, rather than a punitive one.

63 R. Matthee, "Was Safavid Iran an Empire?" *JESHO* 53/1–2 (2010): 247.

64 Niẓām al-Dīn ʿAbd al-Wāsiʿ Niẓāmī [Bakharzī], *Manshāʾ al-Inshāʾ*, comp. Abū al-Qāsim Shihāb al-Dīn Aḥamd Khwāfī, ed. Rukn al-Dīn Ḥumāyūnfarrukh, vol. 1 (Tehran: Intishārāt-i dānishgāh-i millī-yi Īrān, 1357sh/1978): 212, which includes a copy of a diploma appointing Khwāja Majd al-Dīn Muḥammad Khwāfī to the office of *parwāna*. The appointee was expected to report to the sultan (*ba mawqif ʿarḍ rasānīda*) every kind of petition (*har nawʿ-i ʿariḍa-dāsht*), including legal disputes (*qaḍāyā-i sharʿī*) or incidents related to custom (*waqāyiʿ-i ʿurfī*), and reply in written form. As we shall see, this workflow is similar to what is reflected in nineteenth- and early-twentieth-century sources. My reading here differs substantially from that of Subtelny, *Timurids in Transition*: 84 fn. 48.

> every day about the affairs of the subjects and the poor, catching their hearts, like game, with the falcon of his kindness.[65]

> At times he [ʿAbd al-Ahad] went to the provinces of Qarshi and Shahrisabz to hear the petitions of the people [*ʿarāyiḍ-i fuqarā*].[66]

It might be objected that these are not vivid accounts of the dispensation of justice, given that such vignettes appear in poetry and paintings [Fig. 3] and thus may be read as compositional motifs.[67]

However, because it has been established that court chroniclers made extensive use of archival records,[68] it would make little sense to regard chronicles as less authoritative than legal records, the more so because there are several travelogues that refer to Central Asian rulers holding public audiences to hear their subjects' claims:

> The people who are in charge of the dispensation of justice [*sudoproizvodstvo*] in the khanate [of Khiva] are those at the head of the administration and the *qāḍīs*. The khan is expected to issue rulings publicly to those who address him with an appeal [*arz*].[69]

> Every day, around two o'clock, [the khan] goes to court to hear cases and complaints [*razbirat' dela i zhaloby*]. In summer quarters, court is held right in the courtyard, in which are arranged earthen couches; the khan

65 Shir Muhammad Mirab Munis and Muhammad Riza Mirab Agahi, *Firdaws al-Iqbal (History of Khorezm)*, trans. Y. Bregel (Leiden: Brill, 1999): 456–7.

66 Mīrzā ʿAbd al-ʿAẓīm Sāmī, *Taʾrīkh-i salāṭīn-i manghitīya (Istoriia Mangytskikh gosudarei)*, ed. L.M. Epifanova (Moscow: Izdatel'stvo vostochnoi literatury, 1962): 109a.

67 On the relationship between hunting and justice in the Mughal period, see E. Koch, *Dara-Shikoh Shooting Nilgai: Hunt and Landscape in Mughal Painting* (Washington, DC: Freer Gallery of Art, Arthur M. Sackler Gallery, Smithsonian Institution, 1998).

68 Muḥammad Riḍā Mīrāb Āgahī, *Jāmiʿ al-wāqiʿāt-i sulṭānī*, ed. N. Tashev (Samarkand and Tashkent: IICAS, 2012): xx; Fayḍ Muḥammad Kātib Hazārah, *The History of Afghanistan: Fayz Muḥammad Kātib Hazārah's Sirāj al-tawārīkh*, vol. 1, *The Sādūzāʾī Era 1747–1843*, trans. and ed. R.D. McChesney (Leiden: Brill, 2013): xciii–xcv.

69 "Iz knigi V.I.Mezhova 'Khivinskii pokhod 1873 g.' s izlozheniem svedenii o khivinskom khanstve v administrativnom i voennom ustroistve." In S.K. Kamalov, *Khoziaistvo karakalpakov XIX v.*, MS Nukus, FBKOANRUz, no. R-90: [6]. The author of this text was not Mezhov. This text does not correspond to "Khivinskii pokhod v 1873 godu (po ofitsiial'nym istochnikam)." *Voennyi Sbornik* 1873 (1911), which figures among the works of S.K. Kamalov, *Karakalpaki v XVIII–XIX vekakh: K istorii vzaimootnoshenii s Rossiei i sredneaziatskimi khanstvami* (Tashkent: Fan, 1968).

FIGURE 3 *Sultan Sanjar and the Old Woman, mid-18th century. Oil on canvas, 36 × 35 in. (91.4 × 88.9 cm). Brooklyn Museum, Bequest of Irma B. Wilkinson in memory of her husband, Charles K. Wilkinson, 1997.108.4.*

sits on one of these, on a velvet pillow, leaning on his hand for greater comfort, and hears complaints.[70]

70 "Seid-Mukhamed-Rakhim, khivinskii khan, i ego priblizhenie." *Vsemirnaia illustratsiia* n. 243, reprinted in *TS* 42 (1873): 120. Also, a vivid account of the Bukharan emir hearing the grievances of his subjects can be found in *Zapiski o Bukharskom khanstve* (*Otchety P.I. Demezona i I.V. Vitkevicha*), trans. V.G. Volvnikov and Z.A. Tsomartova (Moscow: Nauka, 1893): 51.

> As at this hour there were almost every day an *Arz* (public audience), the principal entrance, as well as the other chambers of the royal residence traversed by us, were crowded with petitioners of every class, sex, and age. They were attired in their ordinary dresses, and many women had even children in their arms, waiting to obtain a hearing; for no one is required to inscribe his name, and he who has managed to force his way first is first admitted.[71]

One of the most vivid accounts of the procedure of petitioning the ruler in Khiva comes from the Russian officer and Orientalist Nil Sergeevich Lykoshin. When, in 1912, he drafted this description, Lykoshin was the head of the Amu-Darya Department and thus a man endowed with privileged knowledge about the functioning of the legal system in the country:

> About six o'clock in the evening, the usually deserted courtyard, decorated with tall columns in the Moorish style, suddenly perked up.... Sometime later, the harem door opened, whence Isfandiyār Khān Bahādur proceeded to the place where he sits to mete out judgment and punishment. Not far from the only entrance into the courtyard there is a small stone platform, covered with a large felt mat. The khan sits on the dais in Asian style, and before him they lay out an ancient gun in its case and a small hatchet, also old; these are the insignia of power. The khan wears an expensive gold-trimmed saber of the Asian type, and on his head, in place of the usual fur hat, he has an equally large hat of lamb fur, but with a red top; this hat is the equivalent of a crown. By the khan's hand they place a kettle of green tea and a cup. Even before the khan's entrance, a *maḥram*[72] takes up a position not far from the khan's dais and stands perfectly still, with his head bare. From time to time, these *maḥrams* are silently replaced by others newly entered into the courtyard. The old man Yūsuf Yasāwulbāshī begins the ceremony.... The time for parsing the people's complaints has come....

---

71 A. Vámbéry, *Travels in Central Asia: Being an Account of a Journey from Teheran across the Turkoman Desert of the Eastern Shore of the Caspian to Khiva, Bokhara, and Samarcand* (London: John Murray, 1864): 126–7.

72 A *maḥram* was a proxy for the khan who carried out his personal instructions. According to Tarrāh, among the numerous *maḥrams* who served at court, a special position was occupied by the so-called *ʿarḍ-khāna maḥramlarī*, who were responsible for preparing the reception room for the daily ceremony and were at the khan's disposal for its duration; see Bobojon Tarroh-Khodim, *Khorazm shoir va navozandalari*, ed. A. Otamurodova and O. Abdurahimov (Toshkent: Tafakkur qanoti, 2011): 30.

> The khan's subjects complain to him about each other and ask for the restoration of rights violated by others of his subjects. The petitioner, having entered through the door, stops at the entrance, quite far from the khan, so his complaint is pronounced in a very loud voice, the supplicant almost yelling, as if he hopes to prove the severity of his grievances and to penetrate the soul of the khan with his cries. The khan, having allowed the supplicant to finish his brief complaint, says only one word, turning to the Yasāwulbāshī. This is probably an order to sort out the case. The petitioner exits, another enters.[73]

The involvement of the royal court in the local populace's petty disputes is best illustrated in the paper trail produced by the Manghit and the Qunghrat chancelleries. The records preserved by the agencies in Bukhara and Khiva show that individuals who wanted to take legal action against others had to come first to the gates of the citadel (*ba-darwāza-yi ark-i ʿālī āmada*) and submit an appeal (*ba-ʿarḍ-i ʿālī rasānīd*). If the appeal was accepted, the royal court instructed an officeholder to deal with the case. That is, only a small fraction of the disputes filed with the royal court were actually heard by the ruler and resolved by him: sultanic justice was usually administered by someone authorized by the ruler to do so.

In Central Asia, appeals (*ʿarḍ*, lit., "petition") were not submitted in writing. Taking legal action before the royal court was an oral procedure. To be sure, however, no one forbade appellants from providing additional textual support, which usually took the form of a protocol of claim (*maḥḍar*). *Maḥḍar*s were usually compiled by jurists' scribes (*muḥarrir*) and bore the seal of a mufti for which the applicant paid a fee (*muhrana*).[74] Such texts served the specific purpose of translating a complaint into a full-fledged legal case. They thus consisted of a brief description of the offense, a claim (*daʿwā*), and a request for redress. They also included a quotation from texts of substantive law (*furūʿ al-fiqh*), which served as precedents to show how the case referred to a specific point of law on which Islamic scholars had already ruled. Such texts were

---

73 N.S. Lykoshin, *Zapiska Amu-Dar'inskogo otdela Polkovnika Lykoshina o sovremennom sostoianii Khivinskogo khanstva, 1912 god*, TsGARUz, f. I-2 op. 1 d. 314, ll. 15–16 ob.

74 The structure and formulas typical of the protocol of claims have been studied preliminarily by K. Isogay, "Seven Fatwa Documents from Early 20th-Century Samarqand: The Function of the Mufti in the Judicial Proceedings Adopted at Central Asian Islamic Court." *Annals of Japan Association for Middle East Studies* 27 (2011): 259–82. On the basis of a collection of protocol of complaints and fatwas, Isogay attempts to reconstruct the adjudication procedure. He infers that, before colonization, plaintiffs filed their claims with the *qāḍī* by providing a protocol of claim. In the present study, I suggest that this was not the case, because *maḥḍar*s were, more often than not, presented to the royal court.

encoded in vernacular legalese and peppered with Islamic legal formulae, and they left little room for the claimant's voice.

1.3 *The Royal Court*

The royal court usually opted for a resolution of the conflict without recourse to adjudication by the *qāḍī*. As the correspondence between the khans and their attendants shows, the prime concern of the royal court was to streamline the provision of reparation of an offense. The royal court was, however, aware of the possibility that defendants might object to the solution offered to them. The court therefore instructed its addressees that, if the defendants denied the claim, the case should be passed to a *qāḍī* for adjudication.

In the following example, Emir Ḥaydar (r. 1800–26) addresses a letter (*maktūb*) to a local governor, instructing him to deal with the case directly, unless the parties to the dispute request the application of the adjudication's procedure:

> Let the refuge of glory, the repository of the emirate, and the choice of the khans, Muḥammad Ḥakīm Bī Mihtar, know that [some] villagers [*fuqarā*] have assaulted and dishonored a certain ʿĀlim Bābā. The aforementioned [parties] must be summoned and the honor taken [from ʿĀlim Bābā] be restored. Should they respond in legal terms [*agar ānhā ḥarf-i sharʿī gūyand*], they must be referred to the *qāḍī*, who will hear the conflict between the parties [*muddaʿī muddaʿā ʿalayh murāfaʿa kunand*]. Let be peace upon you![75]

This is how Emir Ḥaydar reacted to the cases brought before him. Other Bukharan rulers proceeded in a similar fashion. Emir Naṣrallah (r. 1827–60), for example, instructed Bī Muḥammad Ḥakīm Bī Kul Qūshbīgī to deal with a case of insolvency in the following way:

> Let the refuge of the vizirate, the repository of the emirate, a man of noble rank and position, Bī Muḥammad Ḥakīm Bī Kul Qūshbīgī, know that a certain Qurbān Bāy, an Arab, is debtor [*qarḍdār*] of Khān Bahādur Afghān. Although he owns a plot of land, as reflected in a deed, he does not want to exchange it for a just price in order to resolve a debt. You must summon him and look into the matter [*bāyad ki ḥāḍir karda bīnīd*]. Should it really be as reported, you must have his land handed over to

75 *Maktūbāt-i Amīr Ḥaydar*, MS Tashkent, TsVRUz, no. 5412: fol. 3a (*maktūb* v). The letter is a copy bearing the date 1215/1800–1.

> the proxy, Mullā Dhū al-Fiqār, for its just price. Should [he respond] in legal terms, you have to support the law [*agar ḥarf-i sharʿī wāqiʿ shawad ḥāmī-yi sharʿ shawīd*].[76]

It is striking that, in the two passages above, the individuals asked to resolve disputes did not hold judicial office. Emir Ḥaydar wrote to his *mihtar*, while Naṣrallah involved the *qūshbīgī*.[77] Under the rule of Emir Muẓaffar, appeals were frequently transmitted to Sayyid Mīrak, who held the office of *yasāwul-i ʿulamāʾ*. Such appeals included all sorts of claims under both criminal and civil law. We read, for instance, that, one day in Muḥarram 1282/May-June 1865, Sayyid Mīrak was informed by the royal court that a certain Qurbān Bāy had committed a double homicide. He had killed his wife and his younger brother after he had seen them engaged in illicit intercourse (*kār-i nā-mashrūʿ*). The woman's mother, together with other trustworthy individuals (*ādamān-i khāliṣ*), offered a different version of the case. They said that the two men had argued on their way home and on that occasion Qurbān Bāy killed his brother; then he moved on to his home and murdered his wife. The royal court thus instructed Sayyid Mīrak to make an inquiry, ascertain the truth, and report back. He was further instructed that, if the *yasāwul-i ʿulamāʾ* established that Qurbān Bāy had indeed killed the two because he had seen them during illicit intercourse, Sayyid Mīrak should resolve the case by enforcing the payment of blood money, which, we may infer, would lead to the notarization of a contract of peaceful settlement. If the circumstances of the murder were different, the *yasāwul-i ʿulamāʾ* was expected to proceed instead according to the adjudication procedures.[78] This was a case of homicide. Sayyid Mīrak was

---

76 *Majmūʿa-yi maktūbāt-i Sayyid Amīr Naṣrallah Bahādur Khān ba Muḥammad Ḥakīm Bī Kul Qūshbīgī*, MS Tashkent, TsVRUz, no. 1998: fol. 131b (*maktūb* 441).

77 On the office of *qūshbīgī*, see W. Holzwarth, "The Uzbek State as Reflected in Eighteenth Century Bukharan Sources." *Asiatische Studien* 60/2 (2006): 334–5.

78 *bāyad ki taḥqīq karda ḥaqīqat-i ū rā dānista ʿarḍ kunīd ki agar ba-kār-i nā-mashrūʿ dīda qaṭl karda bāshad khūnash hadr mīshawad wa illā muwāfiq-i sharʿ-i sharīf ba-qaṭʿ mīrasad*, *Maktūbāt-i Amīr Muẓaffar ba-Sayyid Mīrak wa ʿarāyiḍ-i Sayyid Mīrak*, MS Tashkent, TsVRUz, no. 1740: fol. 32a [sic! 23a] (Oriental pagination), doc. 432. The manuscript has been described in *Sobranie vostochnykh rukopisei Akademii Nauk Uzbekistan. Istoriia*, ed. D.Iu. Iusupov and R.P. Dzhalilov (Tashkent: Fan, 1998): 411–12. The instructions *bāyad ki taḥqīq karda ḥaqīqat-i ū rā dānista ʿarḍ kunīd* are doubtless formulaic expressions employed also in the instructions that the royal court sent to the judges.

usually instructed to resolve more mundane cases, such as the usurpation of *waqf* properties[79] or matters concerning guardianship.[80]

Read literally, these instructions suggest that the royal court functioned as a court of equity, that is, a legal venue that resolved conflicts by avoiding the more formalistic system of adjudication followed by the *qāḍīs*. As we have seen in the preceding section, the royal court either resolved disputes directly during hearings presided over by the ruler or directed parties to the authority that would resolve them. Indeed, the royal court often instructed its attendants to refer the parties to the *qāḍīs* in case of the denial (*inkār*) of a claim. The royal court's representatives (attendants, governors, notables) and the *qāḍīs* represented a sort of dualism: the former was a quicker way to achieve the resolution of a conflict; the latter was a more elaborate procedure of adjudication. It would be wrong, however, to suggest that they represented a case of legal diversity. Certainly, it was not so in the eyes of those who sought redress at the royal court, because the court did not follow a law different from *sharīʿa*. This is best reflected in those cases in which the royal court transferred to *qāḍīs* the resolution of claims that were filed directly with the royal court. It is to these cases that we now turn.

1.4 Qāḍīs *as Prosecutors*

The procedure of appeal to the royal court could lead to the involvement of members of the judicial body. Judges, regardless of their rank, were often assigned to hear a case only following the royal court's agreement to make inquiry into an appeal.[81] As in the case of Sayyid Mīrak, the royal court advised the judges on how to deal with lawsuits—for example, by suggesting the enforcement of restitution of money or the prohibition of slander.[82] In Bukharan bureaucratese,

79 *Maktūbāt-i Amīr Muẓaffar ba-Sayyid Mīrak wa ʿarāyiḍ-i Sayyid Mīrak*, MS Tashkent, TsVRUz, no. 1740: fol. 23b, doc. 438.

80 Ibid.: fol. 25b, doc. 471.

81 See the royal warrants addressed to the chief judge (*qāḍī kalān*) Mullā Mīr Ṣadr al-Dīn, AMIKINUz, untitled collection of Arabic-script documents: collection series no. 396a and 398. Cf. Welsford and Tashev, *A Catalogue of Arabic-Script Documents from the Samarqand Museum*: doc. 190, 197. The biography of Mullā Mīr Ṣadr al-Dīn, "one of the most influential figures in the Bukharan legal establishment from the early 1860s until the early 1880s," is outlined in ibid.: doc. 85, fn. 2.

82 AMIKINUz, untitled collection of Arabic-script documents: collection series no. 396a: *wāqiʿan chunīn bāshad ḥaqīqat-i ū rā taḥqīq karda dānista tanga-yi māndagī-yi ū rā girifta dāda*; 398: *maʿlūm shawad bāyad ki taḥqīq karda* [text damaged] *manʿ namūda ʿār-i ū rā* [text damaged].

such instructions were referred to as *amr-i ʿālī*, that is, a direction delivered by the royal court, with which the appointees, regardless of their office, were obviously expected to comply. The communication of such a command to the office holder followed the procedures of a public ceremonial in which the royal warrant was entrusted to the recipient. The latter would, as in the case of the diploma of appointment, kiss it, rub it on his eyes, and wear it in his turban (*tabarruk-nāma-yi kirāmī rā būsīda ba-chashmānam mālīda tāj-i sar namūda*). He would literally "wear it as a crown around its head." This procedure applied also to the *qaḍī*s when, as we shall see, they were instructed to adjudicate a case, and it symbolized clearly that the recipient greatly esteemed being entrusted such an order.[83] The following example illustrates in detail such a procedure and situates it in a specific legal case. It shows how women could take legal action by appealing directly to the ruler and how *qāḍī*s proceeded in the manner of a prosecutor, according to the instructions of the royal court.

> A certain Tūy Bībī from Ūstī[84] appealed and let us know [*ʿarḍ-i ʿālī*] that Sulṭān Murād and Jumʿa Bāy, who are wicked men, together with Shāh Nazar, Ḥūr Bībī, and Nūr Sulṭān, attacked her integrity, assaulted her, and caused her much distress. [You ordered me] to look [into this matter] and, if this is what happened, to restore her honor. In case [the defendants object], [you advised me] to hear the case. Oh, you, seat of the world, [let it be known that] this supplicant who strives to please [you] took the royal warrant with his two hands of politeness, kissed it, and rubbed it on his eyes. I summoned Sulṭān Murād and Jumʿa Bāy to the bazaar of Khwāja Kanfī and questioned them. They said that they did not assault the woman and denied [*munkir*] the claim. The impartial local notables [*āqsaqālān*[85] *wa kadkhudāyān-i khāliṣ*] intervened and prayed endlessly for my great Lord and said that Sulṭān Murād and Jumʿa Bāy brought a royal warrant

83 TsGARUz, f. I-126, op. 1, d. 20, ll. 47, 91; I-126, op. 1, d. 22, l. 58.

84 It is unclear whether "Ūstī" refers here to a settlement (*mawḍiʿ*) or a province (*wilāyat*) southwest of Bukhara; see *Naselennye punkty Bukharskogo émirata (konets XIX–nach. XX vv.). Materialy k istoricheskoi geografii Srednei Azii*, ed. A.R. Mukhamedzhanov (Tashkent: Universitet, 2001): s.v.

85 For the position of *āqsaqāl*, see A. Wilde, "Creating the Façade of a Despotic State: On Āqsaqāls in Late 19th-Century Bukhara." In *Explorations in the Social History of Modern Central Asia (19th-Early 20th Century)*, ed. P. Sartori (Leiden: Brill, 2013): 267–98.

> showing that they had filed a claim for their rights of inheritance against Tūy Bībī. For this reason, they had a controversy over self-interest. They [the local notables] took 800 *tanga*s from Tūy Bībī and gave them to Sulṭān Murād and Jumʿa Bāy. The latter stated that they withdrew their claim on the inheritance and gave a certificate [*wathīqa*] to Tūy Bībī. The woman, too, said that she relinquished her claim for slander and entrusted to the two men a certificate of complete discharge of obligation [*khaṭṭ-i wathīqa-yi ibrāʾ-i ʿāmm*]. The parties reconciled, and [the dispute] was resolved.[86]

Looking at the case of Tūy Bībī has, I hope, clarified the marginal role played by the *qāḍī* in the resolution of disputes. He no doubt acted on behalf of the state, when the emir instructed him to look into a conflict, but, as soon as the defendants denied the accusation, an action that would have made the production of evidence incumbent on the claimant, a third party intervened and arranged an amicable settlement.[87] In the resolution of the conflict, the *qāḍī*'s role was thus confined to that of a notary: he solemnized the discharge of obligations on each side and reported the settlement to the ruler.[88]

Having established that, in the *sharīʿa* field in nineteenth-century Bukhara, the judicial personnel often acted at the instigation of the ruling house, we should note that, in certain cases, parties to a dispute referred to *qāḍī*s of their own volition and that, in doing so, they were presumably not appealing to the emir. Sporadically, we find petitions to the ruler in Bukhara or his closest acolytes in which we can discern that complainants approached a *qāḍī*, prayed for the well-being of the emir, and filed directly with the judge a claim against suspects.[89]

In these cases too, however, *qāḍī*s appear not to have had a monopoly on Islamic justice nor to have acted independently within their own territorial

---

86 Judicial report (*ʿariża-dāsht*) to the emir, n.d., TsGARUz, f. I-126, op. 1, d. 1761, l. 3. Stamp of a Bukharan *qāḍī* seal glued to the text.

87 I have illustrated at length this procedure of mediation in my "The Evolution of Third-Party Mediation in *Sharīʿa* Courts in 19th- and Early 20th-Century Central Asia." *JESHO* 54/3 (2011): 311–2.

88 For dozens of such cases, see TsGARUz, f. I-126, op. 1, d. 1761–65.

89 TsGARUz, f. I-126, op. 1, d. 1762, l. 15: report addressed by Qāḍī Mullā Fayḍullāh Khwāja to the emir (undated and unstamped); TsGARUz, f. I-126, op. 1, d. 1762, l. 21: report addressed by Qāḍī Mullā Saʿdallāh Ṣudūr to the emir of Bukhara (undated and unstamped); TsGARUz, f. I-126, op. 1, d. 1762, l. 23: report addressed by Qāḍī Mullā Imānallah Khwāja to the emir (undated and unstamped); TsGARUz, f. I-126, op. 1, d. 1762, l. 24: report addressed by Qāḍī Mullā Mīr Qudratallāh Raʾis to the emir (undated and unstamped).

jurisdiction. From the nature of their correspondence with the administrative center of the emirate, it appears that *qāḍīs* took pains to provide regular reports of what they did. Individuals holding the official post of judge were held accountable for the way they conducted preliminary investigations and for the way they performed adjudication in their court. In sum, every step of their judicial activity, as well as involvement in conflict resolution, was duly reported to the center. This seems to be a general rule in both criminal and civil cases, although in the emirate offenses were not necessarily perceived as falling into such different categories.

Let us consider cases of murder. We sometimes find that the heirs of murder victims went to judges to file claims of homicide against the suspects. In such cases, the judge usually sent his attendant (*mulāzim*) for a preliminary investigation. Before taking such a step, he would demonstrate before the chancellery of the emir that he was legally justified in doing so by asserting that he was following an established practice among the judges of the region (*muwāfiq-i taʿāmul-i qāḍīyān ba mawḍaʿ-i madhkūr*). The court attendant would gather local notables and respected representatives of the local community and inspect the corpse for evidence of foul play. Should the attendant conclude that the deceased had indeed been murdered, the *qāḍī* would summon the suspects. If the suspects denied the accusation, the *qāḍī* would not adjudicate the case but would instead write a report to the emir in which he informed him deferentially that a person had been murdered, that the corpse had been buried, and that there was an heir to the deceased who had filed a claim of murder.[90] The *qāḍī* would proceed to hear the case only if instructed by the emir to do so. This bureaucratic procedure often placed the judge in the awkward position of communicating to the emir his willingness to hear a claim (*murāfaʿa-yi ānhā rā mī pursida bāsham*) in order to receive permission to rule on a case of homicide.[91]

Reporting to the emir did not only reflect the mechanics of a local bureaucratic system. Indeed, there were cases in which *qāḍīs* referred to the emir to secure approval for judicial procedures that might otherwise have been considered unorthodox. The Bukharan *qāḍī* Mullā Muḥammad Amīn wrote a report to the emir informing him of a case of battery and uxoricide and the subsequent detention of the murderer after confession (*iqrār*). The emir instructed the *qāḍī* to make a formal inquiry. As the judge proceeded to summon the

90 *īn duʿāgūy murda-yi madhkūra rā dafn kunānīda daʿwāgar būdan-i Mullā ʿAbd al-Ḥamīd-i madhkūr-i wārith-i munḥaṣir-i way ṣūrat-i ḥāditha maʿlūm-i mawlāyam shawad gufta az rū-yi ghulāmī wa riḍā-jūy ʿarḍ-i bandagī namūdam*, cf. TsGARUz, f. I-126, op. 1, d. 1762, l. 16.

91 TsGARUz, f. I-126, op. 1, d. 1761, l. 15.

parties, the culprit subsequently denied the accusations of murder, and the four heirs to the victim relinquished gratis the claim against him. In the face of this unexpected outcome, the *qāḍī* did not notarize the statement of relinquishment (*pusht-i maḥḍar nā karda*) and instead wrote to the emir explaining that the emir alone should decide this issue and that the *qāḍī* would act accordingly.[92]

As I argued earlier, the recurrent impression while reading *qāḍī*s' correspondence with the emir and his ministers is that legists always felt obliged to report to the center. For example, judges recounted how they dealt with testimony as a probative procedure and thus reported the outcome of witnesses's credibility test. The procedure would entail the *qāḍī* informing the emir's closest minister (*qūshbīgī*) that a party produced testimony during a hearing. The Bukharan chancellery would then instruct another judge[93] (including, on occasion, the *qāḍī kalān*)[94] to proceed with testing the credibility (*tazkīya*) of the testimony.[95] The latter judge would make an inquiry into the probity of the witnesses and report to the Bukharan administration.[96] The *qāḍī* holding the hearing would then wait for further instructions from the center of the emirate.

One may wonder whether all this back and forth between the *qāḍī*s and the emir's chancery was simply empty theater, in which legists made scrupulous play of their deference to the ruler while in practice simply proceeding unimpeded with their assigned job. This would be misleading. It would be difficult to account for so much ink spilled and paper wasted. Given the overwhelming number of records left by the Muslim chanceries at the time of the Russian conquest, such an idea should be dismissed outright. What is important, instead, is that the available archival evidence points not only to the increasing restrictions on the *qāḍī*s' autonomy but also to the existence of a system of prosecutorial justice according to which judges' investigations and other judicial activities were, more often than not, instigated by the state. Khorezm perhaps demonstrates this tendency most clearly. In 1910, after a particularly

---

92 Ibid.: l. 19.

93 See the report of Mullā ʿAbd al-Ḥamīd Khwāja Ṣadr Raʾis addressed to the emir, n.d., TsGARUz, f. I-126, op. 1, d. 1796, l. 14, in which the author explains that he received the instructions to test the credibility of two witnesses on account of a petition that the chief judge, Mullā Mīr Badr al-Dīn, had transferred to the chancellery. The *qāḍī kalān* had alerted the emir that, during the hearing, the claimant had produced the testimony of two men to corroborate his claim.

94 Ibid.: l. 6.

95 Mīrzā Ṣādiq Munshī Jāndārī, *Munshāʾāt wa manshūrāt*, MS Tashkent, TsVRUz, no. 299: fol. 123.

96 TsGARUz, f. I-126, op. 1, d. 1796, ll. 5, 12.

meager harvest,[97] Sayyid Islām Khwāja, grand vizier under Isfandiyār Khān (r. 1910–18), addressed the *qāḍī*s in Astana, a town 16 kilometers east of Khiva, with instructions explaining that they should not, for example, attach their seals to certain records concerning cotton and grain. They were also instructed to redirect applicants to the royal court for matters regarding the allotment of agricultural produce and thus refrain from looking into such cases without prior authorization (*bī rukhṣat*).[98]

1.5 *Trustees*

The individuals who appealed to the royal court had another instrument at their disposal. In filing a complaint with the emir's court, they could request to be assigned somebody who would act in the capacity of trustee to oversee the investigation (*az barāy-i ḥaqīqat-i ān amīn ṭalab shuda*).[99] Texts refer to this appointee in various terms, such as *amīn*,[100] *maḥram*, and *yasāwul*. Despite this variation in terminology, the trustee was always appointed from among the court personnel (*az ghulāmān-i darbār-i ʿālī*)[101] and therefore acted on behalf of the royal court. Such individuals were usually instructed to join (*hamrāh*) other officeholders and hold, with the latter, an official inquiry (*taḥqīq*). In this latter case, *qāḍī*s, for example, were officially informed about their appointment by the same trustee. The royal court entrusted to the trustee a missive of instruction addressed to the *qāḍī*. This could be a text summarizing the case, or simply a short note on the verso side of the protocol of claim. The latter would include the statement "a trustee was requested" (*amīn ṭalab shuda*). On the verso, the addressee could also find a set of instructions. One such instruction reads as follows:

97 Khivan sources indicate that the harvest was so bad that it impoverished the population and obliged the royal court to take the financial situation of the country under direct control; see Isfandiyār Khān to Nil Lykoshin, 19.08.1912, TsGARUz, f. I-2, op. 1, d. 289, l. 140.

98 TsGARUz, f. I-125, op. 1, d. 579, l. 2.

99 AMIKINUz, untitled collection of Arabic-script documents: collection series no. 385. For a description of the record, see Welsford and Tashev, *A Catalogue of Arabic-Script Documents from the Samarqand Museum*: doc. 239.

100 The *amīn* apparently specialized as assessor of bodily injuries. For a case in Bukhara, see TsGARUz, f. R-2678, op. 2, d. 4, l. 1.

101 These individuals were otherwise referred to as "the men of the pen" (*ahl-i qalam*), that is, those officeholders who were in charge of fiscal duties and resolving claims and disputes (*ahl-i qalam barāy-i jamʿ-i māl wa qaṭʿ-i duʿāwī wa nizāʿ*), Aḥmad Makhdūm Dānish, alias Kalla, *Nawādir al-waqāyiʿ*, MS Tashkent, TsVRUz no. 4266: fol. 52 (Western pagination).

> Let it be known to the chief judge, the refuge of the law and glory, Mullā Ṣadr al-Dīn Qāḍī Kalān, that a certain plaintiff has filed a claim against a certain claimant by producing a protocol of claim. We instructed ʿAbd al-Rasūl Mīrzā Bāshī Yasāwul to reach [the parties] and resolve the conflict [*farmūdīm rasīda qaṭʿ rasānīda*].[102]

The division of labor between the trustee and the *qāḍī* is uncertain. While we see reports emphasizing the role of judges and restricting trustees to ancillary functions,[103] we know of other cases in which the two seem to have held inquiries together and together reached the resolution of a conflict.[104] There is yet another variation in the relationship between them: the trustee settled the dispute, while the *qāḍī*s solemnized the amicable settlement[105] and reported to the court the outcome of the dispute. We find an example of such procedure in the following case [see Fig. 4]:

> A certain Sarwar Āy from the rural settlement of Qara-Bāsh-Sarmast requested a trustee [*amīn*]; she came to the gates of the royal citadel and prayed in favor of my Lord. She informed [the chancellery] that a certain Fayḍullāh who comes from the same settlement entered her house during the night with evil intentions. He cut the hair of her daughter Gawhar Āy and left. The people followed him and apprehended him. For this reason, from among the servants of the royal court of justice [*darbār-i maʿdalat-madār-i ʿālī*], Sayyid Pahlawān was appointed by royal decree. He came and summoned the parties and held a trial [*āmada tarafayn rā ba-murāfaʿa-yi sharʿīya ḥāḍir gardānīd*]. [Sarwar Āy], the aforementioned

102 TsGARUz, f. R-2678, op. 2, d. 178, l. 4. On the same folio is the notarization of the defendant's delivery of money to the claimant and the latter's relinquishment of the claim.

103 TsGARUz, f. I-126, op. 1, d. 759, l. 5.

104 *Ẓarīf Khwāja Ḥisābchī Maḥram* […] *ba-masjid-i Farr āmada mubārak-nāma-yi ʿālī rā bar āwarda ba-Qāḍī Mullā Fayḍullāh Khwāja duʿā-gūyishān dād ki duʿā-gūyishān mubārak-nāma-yi ʿālī rā dīda būsīda ba-chashmān-i khwud mālīda fawran hamrāh-i maḥram-i madhkūr bar āmada mawḍaʿ-i Mīrzā Qul raft ba-masjid-i Farr āmada fuqarāyān-i mawḍaʿ-i madhkūr wa aṭrāf-i jawānib rā jamʿ karda muwāfiq-i amr-i ʿālī aḥwāl-i Sayyid Mukhtār wa Sayyid Murād wa Sayyid rasūl nām az ānjā būda rā taḥqīq karda pursīda dīdand*; cf. ʿAbd al-Wahhāb Mīrshab, n.d., TsGARUz, f. I-126, op. 1, d. 1796, l. 4.

105 Welsford and Tashev, *A Catalogue of Arabic-Script Documents from the Samarqand Museum*: docs. 144b.i and 144b.ii. The trustee was, in this case, someone who had the title of "Yasāwul." For other such cases in which the emir Muẓaffar al-Dīn appointed *yasāwul*s to the office of trustees to achieve the settlement of disputes that would later be notarized by *qāḍī*s, see TsGARUz, f. R-2678, op. 2, d. 178, l. 4, 43.

> claimant, [admitted that she] did not see Fayḍullāh with her own eyes and was [therefore] in doubt [*gumān*]. [At that point], the *āqsaqāls* advised her to relinquish her claim gratis. [So she did]. She made a relinquishment, and the conflict was resolved. According to the established practice [*muwāfiq-i taʿāmul*], the *āqsaqāls* took 15 *tangas* [from the parties] and handed them over to the trustee [*yasāwul*] as his travel allowance [*farsakh pulī*].[106]

The report recounts the trial as if it were held by the servant (*ghulām*) of the royal court rather than by the *qāḍī* who attached his seal to the verso of the text. Nor is the trustee who held the trial said to be assisted by any judge. It is clear, though, that the *qāḍī* was the same who notarized the relinquishment of claim. The presence of a *qāḍī*'s seal on the verso of the report suggests, however, that the application of the law by the royal court was in perfect accordance with the *sharīʿa*. If so, it seems that judicial attributes were not a requisite for hearing cases according to Islamic law. For the parties, it was irrelevant that Sayyid Pahlawān represented *sharīʿa* by virtue of a specific judicial title. They were more interested that the representative of the state and its prosecutorial judicial system be fully involved in their dispute.

In nineteenth-century and early-twentieth-century Bukhara, one could file a lawsuit with the royal court and avail oneself of a trustee to adjudicate his/her case *without* necessarily involving the judges. Following is an illustration of this procedure:

> A certain Manṣūr Bāy came to the gates of the glorious citadel and prayed to our Lord. He said that he had entrusted to the custody [*amānat*] of his uncle Ṣābir Bāy one *ṭanāb*[107] [of land] of his own, tax exempt [*milk-i ḥurr*], two *ṭanābs* of garden land [*chahār bāgh*], and one courtyard (*ḥawīlī*). [All these properties can be found] in the locality of Būkhūn Pīr. When [Manṣūr Bāy] demanded [the restitution of his wealth, Ṣābir Bāy] disobeyed. A trustee [*amīn*] was requested; [accordingly] Raḥmatallāh Bīk was appointed [to this office]. He brought the diploma of noble rank, greeted and thanked [us], and immediately instructed a man to summon the defendant, together with the respected people of the locality

---

106 Excerpt from TsGARUz, f. I-126, op. 1, d. 1762, l. 11. The verso side bears the seal of Qāḍī Mullā Muḥammad Idrīs Khwāja, 1293 [1876].

107 The *ṭanāb* was a unit of land measurement in Central Asia of approximately 0.4 hectares. See E. Davidovich, *Materialy po metrologii srednevekovoi Srednei Azii* (Moscow: Nauka, 1970): 128.

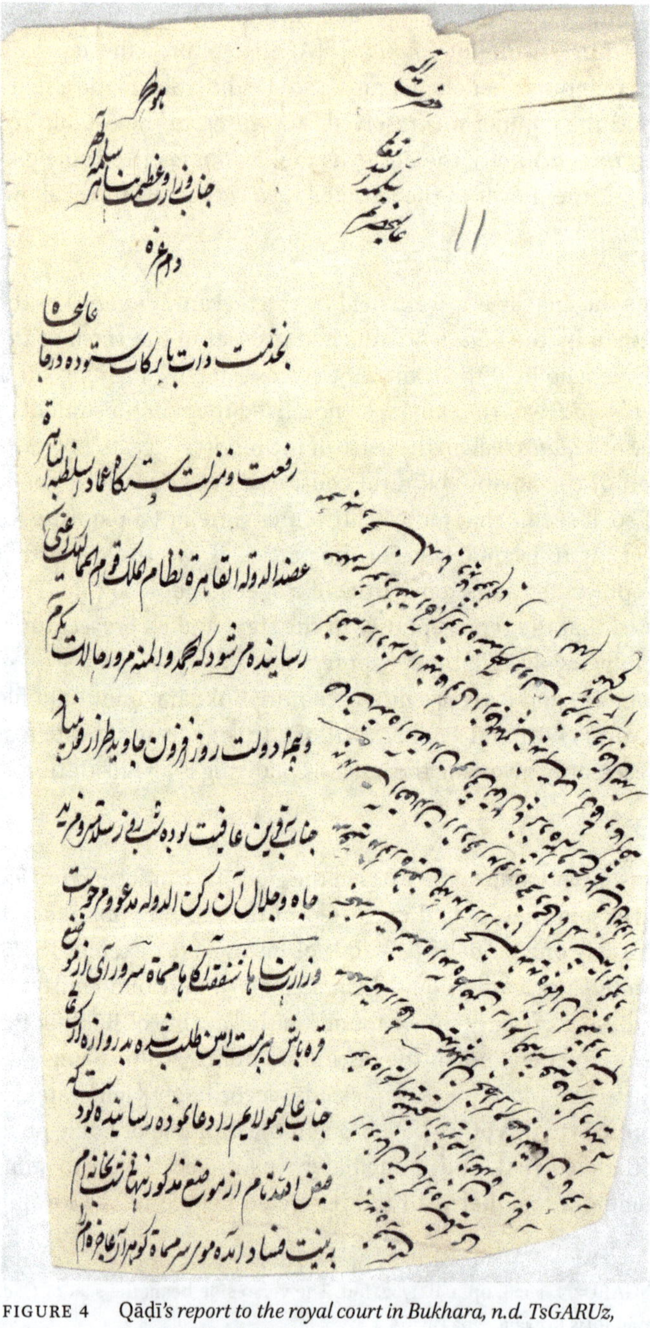

FIGURE 4 Qāḍī's *report to the royal court in Bukhara, n.d. TsGARUz, f. I-126, op. 1, d. 1762, l. 11.*
COURTESY OF THE CENTRAL STATE ARCHIVE OF UZBEKISTAN

> [*maʿ kalān-shawandigān-i mawḍaʿ*]. He [then] heard the conflict according to the noble law [*ʿalā ḥasbu ʾl-sharʿ-i sharīf*]. [Assisted by] virtuous *āqsaqāl*s, he relinquished the plaintiff's claim in exchange for one hundred current *tanga*s and thus reconciled the two parties. He paid to this man of noble rank [the trustee] a travel allowance for the service he had provided, according to local custom and practice [*az rū-yi ʿurf wa taʿāmul farsakh pulī-khidhmatāna girifta dāda*].[108]

The royal court followed this procedure in overseeing all sorts of civil lawsuits, which could involve disputes between individuals,[109] such as the one we have examined, or larger constituencies of people, such as pastoral and tribal groups who came into conflict over the delimitation of property rights. One such case was a dispute between the Yūqāqchī and the Kazakhs, which involved garden land and a small piece of tax-privileged land. When the plaintiffs filed the lawsuit before the royal court, they produced a protocol of claim and requested a trustee. A certain Sulaymān Bīk was appointed to the office. The record relates that he came in person to the place of the dispute, summoned the two parties, and held an inquiry according to Islamic law (*bar wafq-i sharʿ-i sharīf pursīda*). During the hearing the *āqsaqāl*s reconciled the parties, and the plaintiff relinquished his claim in return for ten *ṭanāb*s of land liable to the payment of the tithe. The parties paid for the service (*khidhmatāna*).[110]

Submitting a formal request for a trustee was a way to ensure that the royal court would be fully involved in hearing the claim, whatever its nature. The royal court did not react only to financially significant cases, nor did it assist individuals whose standing would require that the men in power pay particular attention to them. The royal court did not discourage claimants from bringing unedifying stories of petty brawls, nor did Bukharan officials refrain from intruding into marital discords and personal grief. Reviewing the following case may serve to illustrate the degree to which the people of the Bukharan emirate were aware of the services provided by the royal court and

108 Excerpt from report to the Qūshbīgī, TsGARUz, f. I-126, op. 1, d. 1003, l. 22.

109 See the case of repayment of a debt (*qarḍ*) of 14,000 *tanga*s involving a certain Shādī Murād Tarāzūdār from the locality of Bāgh Ḥaydar against "a few Muslims" (*chand nafar musulmān*). The case was adjudicated by ʿAbd al-Raḥman Bīk Chihra Āqāsī after the plaintiff had appealed to the royal court and requested the appointment of a trustee (*amīn*); see report to the Qūshbīgī dated 1318/1900–1, TsGARUz, f. I-126, op. 1, d. 967, l. 10.

110 See anonymous report to the Dīwānbīgī dated 1318/1900–1, TsGARUz, f. I-126, op. 1, d. 1003, l. 28.

made extensive use of them. A certain Sharīfa Bīgīm from Kumūsh Kent—in the Kāmāt district, close to present-day Vobkent, north of Bukhara—claimed approximately 16 *ṭanāb*s of land, one courtyard, one building for agricultural tools (*amlāk-khāna*), and four thousand *tanga*s in cash against her husband, a certain Luṭfullāh. She went to the royal citadel, prayed for the wellbeing of her Lord, and requested the appointment of a trustee (*amīn ṭalab shuda*). The court accordingly issued a diploma designating Shāh Murād Bīk as trustee. Shāh Murād Bīk went to the place with an attendant, summoned the parties, and questioned them according to Islamic law (*ṭarafayn rā ba-murāfaʿa-yi sharʿīya ḥāḍir kunānīda bar wafq-i sharʿ-i sharīf pursīdam*). We learn from the record of the adjudication that Luṭfallāh agreed to divorce his wife irrevocably (*yak ṭalāq-i bāyin ḥarām gardānīda*) in return for five hundred *tanga*s and a half *ṭanāb* of land. The parties expressed satisfaction, and the conflict was resolved. Shāh Murād Bīk was paid for his service according to local custom (*az rū-yi taʿāmul*). So reads the case in the rescript sent to the emir's chancellery.[111]

Why did Sharīfa Bīgīm go to the royal court? The fees the *qāḍī*s charged their clients were certainly not the reason for Sharīfa Bīgīm to prefer the trustees. In fact, referring to the royal court cost no less than adjudication. People regularly complained that trustees charged more than the norm,[112] and we find that the Bukharan administration had, on more than one occasion, to regulate their tariffs.

People were free to pick a court in order to maximize their own investment and gain an advantage. It would thus be fair to assume that the royal court represented, in the eyes of the appellants, an institution different from the *qāḍī*s' court. Indeed, judicial summons issued in Khorezm, for example, inform their addressees that they should resolve their conflicts either before the *qāḍī*s (*sharīʿatgha kīlīb*) or by requesting a trustee from the royal court (*khāndīn yasāwul*).[113] Such petitions to the ruler seem to attest to "forum shopping."[114]

111 Anonymous report addressed to the Qūshbīgī in 1321/1903–4, TsGARUz, f. I-126, op. 1, d. 1003, l. 23.

112 *ba-dawlat-khāna masmūʿ shuda ast ki ba-tūmānhā az wajh-i janjāl wa murāfaʿa-yi fuqarā ba-qāḍīkhānahā pul bisyār az fuqarāyān pursīda kharj wa kharājāt bisyār shuda maḥrām wa māʾmūr khidhmatān*[*a wa*] *kharājāt pulī rā bisyār mīgirifta-and*, TsGARUz, f. I-126, op. 1, d. 754, l. 3; *az wajh-i janjāl wa murāfaʿa-yi fuqarā ba-qāḍī-khānahā pul-i bisyārī az fuqarāyān bar āmad shuda chand rūz janjāl wa murāfaʿa ṭūl yāfta*, ibid.: l. 4.

113 TsVRUz, *Khiva qozilik khujjatlari*, docs. 426, 657, 789. See the description of these documents in *Katalog Khivinskikh kaziiskikh dokumentov* (*XIX–nach. XX vv.*): same numeration.

114 K. von Benda-Beckmann, "Forum Shopping and Shopping Forums: Dispute Processing in a Minangkabau Village." *JLP* 19 (1981): 117–59.

Observing that people were free to choose the most convenient site of redress, however, does not mean that royal and *qāḍī* courts were mutually exclusive sites of adjudication nor that they applied fundamentally different procedural laws. Evidence like that cited above points to the trustees' following substantive legal doctrines or antecedents that were deep-seated in the local traditions of Islamic law. As we have seen, reports to the ruler suggest that both trustees and *qāḍī*s heard cases according to Islamic law—or, at least, that is what sources would lead us to believe. Conventional legal formulas appear indiscriminately in the records they produced. There was a tendency among trustees and *qāḍī*s to solemnize extrajudicial mediation achieved by a third party, thereby avoiding confrontation and the passing of judgment. We also find many cases in which trustees and *qāḍī*s cooperated. Though the royal trustees and the *sharīʿa* court of the *qāḍī*s may well have been perceived by the people as different legal resources, the Islamic juridical field in fact included both, as both were answerable to the state. The main difference between them, therefore, was less procedural than logistical. *Qāḍī*s operated within convenient reach, as they were appointed to regional locales; enjoying the services of the trustees, on the other hand, required one to travel to Bukhara or Khiva, file a claim there, and cover the trustees' expenses during their investigation.

In general, bringing one's grievance to the emir or the khan was a means of limiting judicial discretion. In other words, filing a lawsuit in Bukhara or in Khiva was a rejoinder to some local *qāḍī* and a means of shifting the case away from local power holders. In this sense, resorting to the ruler or the local governor[115] rather than a *qāḍī* reflected a general recognition of forms of social control. The ordeals of Baqā Khwāja, another scholar whom we encountered earlier, are paradigmatic for our purposes. It seems that, in the wake of his appointment in Kerki (an important trading post of the emirate on the Amu-Darya, now in Turkmenistan), during the time of Emir Muẓaffar al-Dīn (r. 1860–85), he found it difficult to come to terms with the customs of the Turkmens. Disapproving of how local notables welcomed him with gifts of carpets, he obstinately rejected their offerings by packing them back on the shoulders of his visitors and chasing them away. Appalled at how the majority of the Turkmens were engaged in what he regarded as bribery (*ʿādat-i akthar-i turkmānīyān pāra-khwur wa rishwat-khwur*) he complained about the matter before the local governor who, however, sided with the locals and wrote to the Emir accusing Baqā Khwāja of malpractice. The story relates that the royal court sent an envoy (*taḥqīqchī*) and that the subsequent investigation led to

115 Fatwa in which someone is said to have appealed to the governor, Tashkent 1865, TsGARUz, f. I-164, op. 1, d. 13, l. 5.

Baqā Khwāja's removal from office.[116] It appears, therefore, that the Turkmens were thus able to avoid being subjected to a new judicial regime and got rid, at least this time, of the Bukharan jurist. The story should alert us to just how far the fortunes of a *qāḍī* depended on the favor of the populace.

Complainants knew that no appointee to the position of judge could enjoy full institutional exclusivity. Materials from early-twentieth-century Bukhara indicate that Muslims brought their affairs to state officials because they had the power to coerce parties to achieve a settlement and enforce a decision, either formal or informal. Reports such as the following show provincial governors expanding their powers in the legal sphere:

> Our servant and his sons, who were assigned to the districts of Mīr and Tātkint, interfered [*dākhil*] with the work of the judges [*qāḍī wa ra'is*]. They assigned their own man to [oversee] every dispute [*har janjāl*], and they did not refer to the *qāḍīs*. They themselves held inquiries [*murāfaʿa pursīda*], attached their seals to certificates of relinquishment and acknowledgement [*ba-khaṭṭhā-yi ibrāʾ wa iqrārī muhr karda*], and reconciled [the disputing parties]. I went to visit your servant on Saturday. I told him that His Majesty and the governors of the provinces defer all the affairs of their subjects to the *qāḍīs* and refer to the noble law. They do not let the established practice of the governor and people of authority [*taʿāmul-i ḥākim* [*wa*] *shawandigān*] affect the work of the judges. Your servant said, "The established practice in this province is such that, if the people come to me [with their disputes], I solve them. I do not send them to you. If they come before you [with their problems, then] you solve them. This is not my business." This was his answer.[117]

Personal relations had a bearing on the way people chose to solve their problems. Parties would always prefer to try their luck in the court of the emir or the local governor if, in doing so, they were able to avoid some legal functionary for whom they had little sympathy. When a *qāḍī* was not familiar to the community, for instance, people were often suspicious that he might cause oppression (*jabr wa nafsānīyat*) by neglecting their corporate interests.

---

116 Ḥamīd Khwāja, *Tanzīl al-imthāl fī dhikr bayān al-aḥwāl*, MS Tashkent, TsVRUz, no. 602: fol. 90b–91a.

117 TsGARUz, f. I-126, op. 1, d. 759, l. 8. For another case of a local governor resolving disputes without referring the cases to the judges, see TsGARUz, f. I-126, op. 1, d. 759, l. 33.

In one such case, petitioning the royal court allowed the community to have a local mullah appointed as deputy judge (*nā'ib-i qāḍī*).[118]

Litigants were free to refer directly to the *qāḍī*s when they could predict the outcome of a case or more simply instrumentalize judicial procedures as they saw fit. In what follows, the celebrated Bukharan intellectual Ṣadr al-Dīn ʿAynī recounts a dispute initiated by a certain Yahyā Khwāja (a pious scholar known in the city for scolding the official clergy and the court attendants for their laxity) against a mullah, a certain Qārī Samīʿ, who used to parade his piety with a large rosary and made a living exploiting the people's credulity. Yahyā Khwāja forged a set of legal documents (*ḥujjathā-yi sākhta-yi sharʿī*) with reference to which he accused Qārī Samīʿ of usurping his courtyard, and "dragged him to a *qāḍī* court". The dispute made it to the office of the chief judge, who ruled that Qārī Samīʿ should pay 15,000 *tanga*s in exchange (*badal*) for the courtyard. But Yahyā Khwāja agreed to the notarization of an amicable settlement (*ṣulḥ-nāma*) between the parties, on condition that Qārī Samīʿ deliver the sum in cash before the *qāḍī*. The defendant complied with this condition and brought the cash to court. When the judge was about to notarize the relinquishment (*ibrā'*) of the claim and the delivery (*taslīm*) of the sum, the plaintiff asked him not to attach the seal. Yahyā Khwāja explained that he would temporarily return the money to the defendant in trust (*be-ṭarz-i amānat*) and therefore asked the *qāḍī* that he be given back the deeds he had forged. He thus explained to the judge that, if Qārī Samīʿ promised not to wave his rosary at people and perpetrate any deceit, he would withdraw his claim; otherwise, should Qārī Samīʿ again indulge in fraud (*ḥarakathā-yi farībgarāna*), Yahyā Khwāja would file the same claim and request compensation by means of a settlement (*badal-i ṣulḥ rā ṭalab khwāham kard*).[119] There is little doubt that, before filing the claim directly with the *qāḍī*, Yahyā Khwāja could foresee what would happen and thus manipulate the judge.

2 On the Public Dimension of Law

To rethink the contours of the Islamic juridical field of Central Asia requires that one count the populace among the legal actors operating in such a field. They were those who took legal action and thus activated the legal system

118 Ibid.: l. 42.

119 Ṣadr al-Dīn ʿAynī, *Yāddāshthā*, ed. Jaʿfaruf (Stalinabad: Matbaʿa-yi Wizārat-i Madaniyat RSS Tājikistān, 1959): 3:12–14.

that I have described. They were the recipients of justice. They were, most certainly, not part of the legal profession and, as such, they had to rely on the legists and the *ʿulamāʾ* for expert knowledge. They knew something, however, and that was enough to push them to take legal action and pursue redress. It informed people's assumption about their entitlement and about what they thought was right or wrong. We may term this "common knowledge."

Speaking of assumptions about legality inevitably leads us to discuss what people know and what the "ways of knowing" are. How do we do that? Some would follow a commonsense approach and attempt to disambiguate information from knowledge, as did Peter Burke in *A Social History of Knowledge*. Burke noted that "We [...] need to distinguish knowledge from information, 'knowing how' from 'knowing that,' and what is explicit from what is taken for granted, [...] what is relatively 'raw, specific, and practical' [...] [from] "what has been cooked, processed, or systematized by thought.'"[120]

The utility of such an approach is questionable, because usually, for all intents and purposes, individuals become informed about things as elaborate as taxation, recipes, or witchcraft that had been already reflected upon by other people and that were the outcome of a cognitive process in someone else's head.[121] A more practical way of approaching the problem would be to adopt the conception of knowledge as used by the anthropologist Fredrik Barth. By "knowledge," Barth means "feelings (attitudes) as well as information, embodied skills as well as verbal taxonomies and concepts: all the ways of understanding that we use to make up our experienced, grasped reality."[122] Knowledge, according to this understanding, consists less of a corpus of disconnected information than of dispositions for interpretation: "knowledge provides people with materials for reflection and premises for action."[123]

---

120 P. Burke, *A Social History of Knowledge: From Gutenberg to Diderot* (Cambridge: Blackwell Publishers, 2000): 11.

121 I am drawing here on S. Subrahmanyam, "Between a Rock and a Hard Place. Some Afterthoughts." In *The Brokered World: Go-Betweens and Global Intelligence, 1770–1820*, ed. S. Schaffer et al. (Sagamore Beach, MA: Watson Publishing International, 2009): 432.

122 Fredrik Barth, "An Anthropology of Knowledge." *Current Anthropology* 43/1 (2002): 1.

123 Ibid. Barth's definition of knowledge is close to what Jay Smith calls "interpretive disposition," that is "a set of disparate beliefs and assumptions whose cumulative effect produces a general moral sense and a particular view of the world." J.M. Smith, "Between *Discourse* and *Experience*: Agency and Ideas in the French Pre-Revolution." *History and Theory* 40 (2001): 141–2.

In nineteenth-century Central Asia, common knowledge about law was part of what Daniel Lord Smail termed a "public archive":[124] a common knowledge about the law existed simply because certain legal practices were performed in public and because people's memory about such practices was relevant to the preservation of local traditions. One wonders how otherwise to explain the existence, for example, of so many private collections of Islamic legal deeds in Central Asia. It must have been common knowledge that, if one wanted to safeguard one's rights, one should keep at the ready pieces of evidence to deploy in court and that to safeguard said rights (to a plot of land, for example) required the acquisition and preservation of those documents in which those rights were attested.[125] There is presumably nothing particularly difficult about learning the basics of the Islamic law of evidence as it was practiced in Central Asia: a plaintiff would first be asked to produce testimony (*bayyina*) in support of a claim; written attestation to certain rights would serve the same purposes in court. In a legal culture that accorded preeminence to oral testimony, there were jurists who, in the nineteenth and early twentieth centuries, recognized the probative value of deeds.[126] The following fatwa illustrates such a phenomenon:

> [Question:] We invoke blessing in the name of the supreme Lord. What do the imams of Islam—may God be pleased with them all—have to say on the following question? The matter is as follows. It happened that Mulla Mīr Bābāy Muftī had a sound and legal debt [*dayn*] for a certain amount of money that constituted the financial obligation of Bābā Bāy. In the condition that allows the acknowledgment and the execution of all the usufructs, the aforementioned Bābā Bāy legally acknowledged before a community of Muslims the aforementioned debt and had a legal deed [*khaṭṭ-i wathīqa-yi sharʿī*] notarized with the seal of a *qāḍī* of Islam, which deed he entrusted to Mullā Mīr Bābāy Muftī. In this case according to the Sunna of Muḥammad and his legal doctrine [...] and the school

124 D.L. Smail, *The Consumption of Justice: Emotions, Publicity, and Legal Culture in Marseille, 1264–1423* (Ithaca, NY: Cornell University Press, 2003): 211.

125 This is well exemplified in T. Welsford, "Fathers and Sons: Re-Readings in a Samarqandi Private Archive." In *Explorations in the Social History of Modern Central Asia (19th–20th Century)*, ed. P. Sartori (Leiden: Brill: 2013): 299–323.

126 Consider the following legal opinion: "Isn't it the case that the deed (*wathīqa*) in possession of the aforementioned purchaser and which was drawn in accordance with the ruleds, is relevant, binding, and applicable? Yes." *A Catalogue of Arabic-Script Documents from the Samarqand Museum*: doc. 375. The use of deeds in court may help a respondent to deny a claim; ibid.: 493, 496, 512.

> of law [*madhhab*] of Ḥanīfa, if the aforementioned Bābā Bāy denied the claim [*munkir*] for the said sum of money or if he says that he has already delivered said sum of money, then this deed should be considered a piece of evidence [*īn khaṭṭ-i wathīqa-yi madhkūra ḥujjat bāshad*] that the aforementioned sum [needs to be paid], isn't that true? Explain and be concise.
>
> [Answer:] Yes, it is, and God knows best.[127]

Popular knowledge expanded beyond the functionality of deeds. People were acquainted also with certain juristic principles. A Bukharan subject evidently knew that, if the dead body of his wife was found together with the corpse of the man who purportedly cuckolded him, he would stand a good chance of avoiding retaliation because the killing would be understood as a heat-of-the-moment action. The following example introduces us to the details of one such homicide case: a Bukharan notable (*bāy*)[128] was accused of having killed his wife and a man under two different circumstances and having adjoined the corpses so as to give the impression that he had killed them after having found them during the sexual act. The aggrieved party held that he had manipulated the murder scene so that this double murder would be treated as a case of manslaughter (*hadr*), that is, unintentional homicide.[129] If so, he would have been held accountable only for the payment of blood money and thus avoided retaliation or the payment of a larger sum [see Fig. 5]:

127 Anon., *Jung*, MS Tashkent, TsVRUz, no. 6102: fol. 331b. The opinion can be dated inductively on the basis of various seals, as about mid-nineteenth century.

128 It is current among students of Central Asian history to translate *bāy* as "wealthy landowner" or "rich man." This is problematic, because such a definition is based on Soviet bureaucratese of the 1930s and does not take account of the fact that, in Khorezm, *bāy* was an official administrative position. This we learn from a series of diplomas retrieved in the province of Urgench, which show that individuals holding the title of *bāy* (along with *katkhudās*, "steward") enjoyed fiscal privileges (*tarkhān/suyūrghāl*) because they worked in some official capacity for the royal court (*dawlat-khwāh khādim wa kār-āgāh mulāzimlārīmīz*). I have consulted deeds of fiscal immunity now held in the private collection of Komiljon Xudoybergenov.

129 A. Layish, *Legal Documents from the Judean Desert: The Impact of the Sharīʿa on Bedouin Customary Law* (Leiden: Brill, 2011): 40.

> On 8 Muḥarram 1306 [14.09.1888] Aḥmad Bāy from the [jural] community [*jamāʿa*][130] [called] Īskī came before ʿAbd al-Sattār Bīk Tūqsabā and Qāḍī Sayyid Mullā Jalāl Raʾis. He prayed for [the well-being of] the ruler and reported: "I saw a certain Khidhīr Bāy in my household at midnight together with Tūkhta Āy, my wife. One [was lying] over the other, and I killed them." [...] In light of his confession, we arrested the man, and we ordered two of our men, together with five or six men from among the notables of the province, [to inspect the murder scene]. They went and ascertained that the two persons assassinated were naked, that one was [lying] on the top of the other as though they had had intercourse [*ba haʾiyat jamāʿ mikardagī*]. The [members of the jural] community to which the two assassinated belonged, say that: "The murderer was in fact unacquainted with Khidhīr Bāy, that they had an altercation [*khuṣūmat*] and that one murdered the other; then he [Aḥmad Bāy] took [the corpse] from there and put it over his wife after he had murdered her. [The man and the woman killed] are not guilty [*bī-gunāh*]. The blood money for the murdered persons found in one place is less than if they had been killed in two [different] places; [in this case, however,] the blood money should be higher." After one night and one day, the [jural] community of the two murdered persons came and said that [they saw] blood traces more than seven *ṭanāb*s[131] from the household of the murderer and that traces of a scuffle were also visible.[132]

This case of a doctored murder scene is not unique among homicide cases in Bukhara.[133] In the wake of a judicial report to the royal court, for instance, the emir ordered one of his attendants to solicit from a jurist a legal opinion addressing the possibilities of double murder. The mufti held that "if the two were murdered in one place and their blood was spilled there, their blood money should be of an amount appropriate to compensation for manslaughter

130 It appears that the author of the text confers on the term "community" (*jamāʿa*) specific attributes of communal organization that I do not understand. It is clear, however, that the community as a legal entity could produce evidence on behalf of its members. On the jural community, see F.H. Stewart, "Customary Law among the Bedouin of the Middle East and North Africa." In *Nomadic Societies in the Middle East and North Africa: Entering the 21st Century*, ed. Dawn Chatty (Leiden: Brill, 2006): 242.

131 It is unclear why here the author employs *ṭanāb* as a measure of lenghth, while the term is usually defined as a measure of area.

132 See TsGARUz, f. I-126, op. 1, d. 1761, l. 4.

133 Another such case in which two dead bodies were placed together, apparently to diminish the amount of blood money, can be found in TsGARUz, f. I-126, op. 1, d. 1761, l. 6.

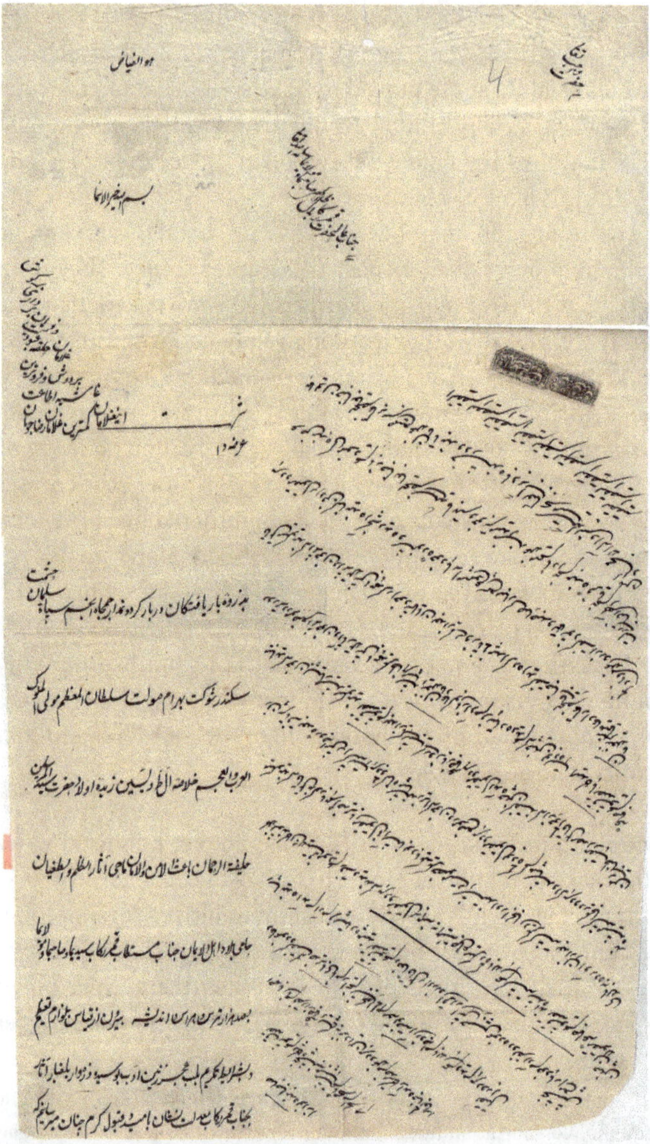

FIGURE 5 *Judicial report to the royal court in Bukhara, n.d. TsGARUz, f. I-126, op. 1, d. 1761, l. 4.*
COURTESY OF THE CENTRAL STATE ARCHIVE OF UZBEKISTAN

[*khūn-i ānhā hadr mībāshad*]. Therefore, nothing is incumbent on the murderer [*ba-qātil-i madhkūr chīzī lāzim namīshavad*]. Should the heirs to the murder victim hold that they were killed unjustly [*ba-nā ḥaqq kushta*], they should file a claim, and the [accused] murderer should swear an oath."[134]

If members of a jural community from the back of nowhere were cognizant of such juristic proscriptions and their consequences, it would be fair to assume that there was a space of shared knowledge in which the populace could learn about proscriptions from the specialists. Central Asian records account for legal actions, in a mixture of legalese and local parlance, that reflect a meshing of cultural practices blending the professional exercises of jurists with the lay comments made at the teahouse: in cities such as Samarqand, Bukhara, and Khiva, where madrasas covered much of the urban landscape, we can assume that people from all backgrounds shared a minimum knowledge of the law.

I am not arguing in any way against the legists fulfilling the role of the legal experts: as we have seen, in diplomas of appointment to various legal offices we find that *qāḍīs* and muftis alone should fulfill specific duties and enjoy prerogatives on account of their profession. Among nomads, too, the person performing judicial duties enjoyed a monopoly on violence in cases of deviation from Islamic law.[135] What I suggest is different. It is a matter of fact that ordinary people, too, monitored carefully the boundaries of the law and denounced deviations from what was deemed local or customary practice.

The records produced by the chancellery of the Bukharan emirate or the Khivan khanate show that categories of justice and morality, as well as notions of procedure, were intelligible to ordinary people: a woman could thus categorize a domestic beating as an offense before the jurist translated it into a case of battery.[136] One wonders how otherwise to explain the fact that women filed cases of assault without the intervention of jurists. Consider, for example, the case of a certain Yakhshī Murāt who had assaulted his wife Saʿādat Bīka

134 See ibid.: l. 25. For the application of this procedure, see ibid.: l. 7: the perpetrator of a double murder was apprehended and questioned. He stated that he saw his wife during illicit intercourse with a man and killed both of them. He swore an oath (*sawgand khūrda*). The legists entrusted to him a certificate of manslaughter (*khaṭṭ-i hadr*), which would probably have favored the payment of blood money.

135 "Let him punish those who opposed the command of the noble law" (*sharʿ-i sharīf amrīgha mukhālifat qīlghānlārgha taʿzīr ūrūb*). This sentence is found in a diploma from the royal court of Khiva, which conferred the appointment of a man to the office of judge and moral inspector (*qāẓī-raʾīs bi ʾl-istiqlāl*) among the Khiṭāy, a tribal group (*ṭāyfa*) of the Qaraqalpaq confederation (*ūlūs*). Shawwāl 1255/December 1839. Private collection of Abdusalim Idrisov, Nukus, Qaraqalpaqstan.

136 See the report addressed by the governor of Gürlen to the chamberlain (*yasāwulbāshī*) in Khiva, Rabīʿ al-Awwāl 1335/January 1917, TsGARUz, f. I-125, op. 1, d. 498, l. 28.

and consequently left the conjugal dwelling. Niyāz Bīka, the mother of the injured party, appealed directly to the royal court in Khiva. No doubt Niyāz Bīka recognized fully the legal resources available to her, as she must have sensed that bodily harm (*majrūḥ*)[137] constituted a legal category for which one could pursue redress.

The acquisition of legal categories and the formation of certain assumptions about right and wrong were all inevitable for the populace because the law had a public dimension. First of all, law was practiced in public. Hearings, for example, were held in the open, in the presence of bystanders. Legal deeds were notarized in front of several individuals. I speak here not of professional witnesses (*ʿudūl*), nor those individuals authorized to give testimony (*guwāh*), but of the requirement in Central Asian Islamic legal deeds that documents be notarized before a gathering of people in court (*ḥuḍḍār-i majlis*) [See Fig. 6].[138] The people in question were presumably local notables, but their presence created a bond between the court and the wider populace, ensuring that what took place in court could later be recounted elsewhere in public. When a person died, the wealth to be divided among her heirs would usually be described in a list (*rūykhaṭṭ*)[139] in front of the neighborhood (*jamʿ-i kasīr ḥuḍūrīda*).[140] This public practice contributed to creating entitlements and, more generally, a sense of how a family wealth should be divided among the heirs.

People knew that what they said had a bearing on inquests. Everywhere, rumors and hearsay will provide circumstantial evidence.[141] A certain course of action acquired a particular legal force if done in public. If someone, for example, stated in front of others that he owed money to another person, the acknowledgment of such a debt would be inscribed in the memory of the local community, and the people who witnessed such a statement must have known the implications of this admission.[142]

---

137 *Jarḥ*, in Layish, *Sharīʿa and Custom in Libyan Tribal Society*: Glossary 292.

138 See, e.g., the division of the inheritance of one Qilich Bāy notarized by a *qāḍī* in Khiva in 1864. At least three people in addition to the witnesses were present at the notarization; see *Katalog Khivinskikh kaziiskikh dokumentov*: doc. 587.

139 For a description of one such case in Bukhara, see Ḥamīd Khwāja, *Tanzīl al-imthāl fī dhikr bayān al-aḥwāl*: fols. 100b–101a.

140 *Katalog Khivinskikh kaziiskikh dokumentov*, doc. 236. I checked the document at TsVRUz, *Khiva qozilik khujjatlari*: doc. 236. See also TsGARUz, f. 1-125, op. 1, d. 486, l. 124.

141 Gürlen *qāḍīs*' notification to the *yasāwulbāshī* in Khiva, 6 Rabīʿ al-Thānī 1335/30.01.1917, TsGARUz, f. 1-125, op. 1, d. 498, l. 75. The elders provide circumstantial evidence based on hearsay in a case of disputed property between private individuals and the endowment of a mosque community.

142 *A Catalogue of Arabic-Script Documents from the Samarqand Museum*: doc. 69.

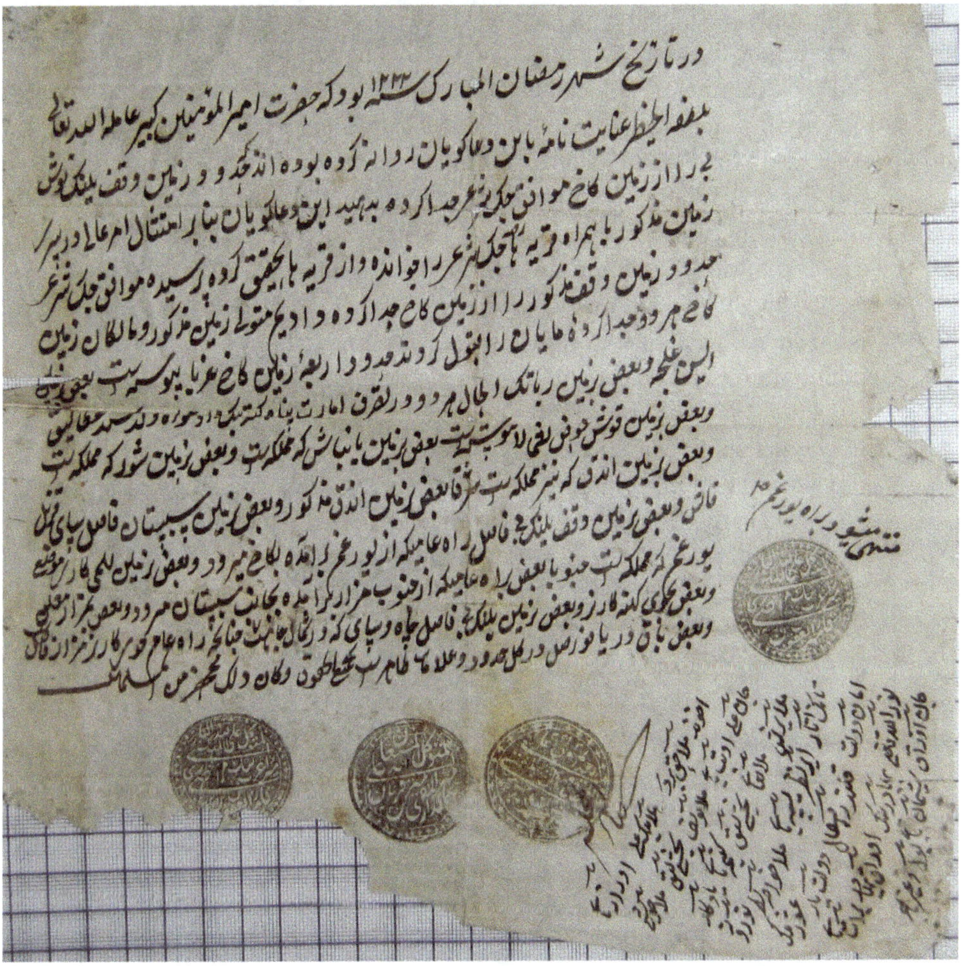

FIGURE 6 *Rescript addressed to the royal court of Emir Ḥaydar (1807). Three legists notarized the demarcations of* waqf *land in Kākh. Twenty-nine individuals participated in the notarization as* ḥuḍḍār-i majlis.[143]
COURTESY OF THOMAS WELSFORD

The fate of a culprit depended also on the public's disposition towards him. The choice between entrusting a culprit to a guarantor (*kafīl*) and jailing him required one to consider his reputation and determine the consequences of such a decision for the social relationships of the parties and the

143 The document is described in Welsford and Tashev, *A Catalogue of Arabic-Script Documents from the Samarqand Museum*: doc. 415.

community to which they belonged. After a robbery somewhere in Khorezm,[144] for example, the victim followed the trail of the thieves, caught one of them, and took him before a local governor (*ḥākim*). The latter threatened to use violence (*sīyāsat*) against him. Under threat, the suspect confessed (*iqrār*) his crime and provided the names of his two associates. As the latter were found and it was ascertained that the three men had indeed perpetrated the crime (*jināyat*), the case was settled by the official representatives of a local community who arranged for monetary compensation to the victim. The governor thus notified the royal court and asked for further instructions. In so doing, he asked whether the thieves should be detained or sent to Khiva. But there was a third option available, handing the culprits over to a guarantor. Because the guarantor was responsible for the culprits' behavior, the guaranty placed a burden on the entire community that the *kafīl* represented. It was often the local notables holding official administrative positions (*āqsaqāl/kathkhudā/nā'ib*) who acted in this capacity and thus provided "donative liability"[145] to individuals who confessed to felonies such as murder and robbery.[146]

3 Colonialism, Orientalism and the Study of *Sharīʿa*

From the first years of Russian rule in Central Asia, it was widely claimed that *sharīʿa* there had always functioned as a legal domain controlled exclusively by the legists. As we shall see in the next chapter, military officials, bureaucrats, and scholars all had reason to claim that the *qāḍī*-centric *sharīʿa*, as observed under Russian rule, was an exact continuation of what had existed before the conquest of Central Asia. Writing in 1909, Privy Councillor Count Pahlen described imperial policy as follows:

> When we subjugated Turkestan, the Russian government adopted the principle of preservation [*polazhila printsip sokhraneniia*] with regard to

144 Muḥammad Yūsuf Bāy ibn Pahlavān Maḥram to the *yasāwulbāshī* in Khiva, 25 Dhū al-Qāʿda 1334/23.09.1916, TsGARUz, f. I-125, op. 1, d. 498, ll. 57. It proved impossible to establish the location of the robbery, because the victim is not identified by his place of origin or residence, but as belonging to a community (*qawm*) called Sārt Ālācha and administered by an *āqsaqāl*.

145 I here employ the terminology of Hallaq, *Sharīʿa: Theory, Practice, Transformations*, 258.

146 For instructive cases in which *āqsaqāl*s and *kathkhudā*s acted in the capacity of "guarantors," see the following reports of conflict resolution in Khorezm: Muḥammad Yūsuf Bāy b. Pahlavān Maḥram to the *yasāwulbāshī* in Khiva, 12 Dhū al-Qāʿda 1336/19.08.1918, TsGARUz, f. I-125, op. 1, d. 498, l. 87–87ob; Muḥammad Yaʿqūb Bāy b. Jabbār Qulī Maḥram to the *yasāwulbāshī* in Khiva, 22 Jumādī al-Thānī 1335/15.02.1917, ibid.: l. 111.

> the native courts of the indigenes and introduced those changes from which the population would benefit and which would diminish their fanaticism, thereby allowing for a merger with the Russians.[147]

Russians molded the juridical field of *sharīʿa* into the system of "native courts" (*narodnyi sud*), that is, courts presided over by Muslim legal scholars who would enjoy access to this position through elections via ballot. In this way, the colonial administration retained only Muslim jurists, while it overhauled the larger legal context and web of power relations in which such jurists were formerly embedded.[148]

By operating this way, the Russians not only stripped local rulers of their legal powers but also denied that Muslim rulers had ever been qualified to administer justice. The imperial enterprise of reconstructing the mechanics of *sharīʿa* in colonial Central Asia was, on the one hand, useful for a project of cultural transformation[149] and, on the other, integral to an edifice of knowledge that was predicated on the assumption that law was the domain of the professional legists alone. Much of the colonial staff was engrossed in the mundane occupations of administration and was thus not absorbed in Central Asian legal history. Russian imperial administration was not monolithic, as officials everywhere spoke in many voices, but, when colonial masters at times conceded that, in earlier periods, local rulers did intervene in judicial affairs, they usually held that local power-holders could practice justice only "in an arbitrary way."[150]

When they did not caricature Muslim rulers' prominent role in the juridical field, colonial officials merely ignored its importance. One eloquent illustration is provided by the unpublished work of the famous Orientalist Vladimir

147 *Otchet po revizii Turkestanskogo kraia po Vysochaishemu poveleniiu Senatorom Gofmeisterom Grafom K.K. Palenom. Narodnye Sudy Turkestanskogo Kraia* (St. Petersburg: Senatskaia Tipografiia, 1909): 6.

148 [Aleksandr K. Geins], *Sobranie literaturnykh trudov Aleksandra Konstantinovicha Geinsa* (St. Petersburg: Tipografiya Stasyulevicha, 1898): 1:466; N.S. Lykoshin, "Kazii (Narodnye sud'i): Bytovoi ocherk osedlogo naseleniia Turkestana." In *Russkii Turkestan: Sbornik 1. Prilozhenie k gazete "Russkii Turkestan"* (Tashkent: Tipografiia "Russkii Turkestan," 1899): 53.

149 W.B. Hallaq, "On Orientalism, Self-Consciousness and History." *ILS* 18/3–4 (2011): 404.

150 N.A. Khalfin, *Rossiia i khantsva Srednei Azii (pervaia polovina XIX veka)* (Moscow: Nauka, 1974): 12; I.F. Kostenko, *Sredniaia Aziia i vodvorenie v nei Russkoi Grazhdanstvennosti* (St. Petersburg.: Tip. B. Bezobrazov, 1871): 63. For British India, see R. Singha, *A Despotism of Law: Crime and Justice in Early Colonial India* (New Delhi: Oxford University Press, 1998): 27.

Viiatkin, which is devoted to the cultural history of the Shibanid empire[151] and includes a section on the local judicial system.[152] Viiatkin probably did not know that royal courts in Bukhara, Khiva, and Kokand had administered justice. His study is based on an unknown text on Islamic judicial ethics (referred to vaguely as *adab al-qāḍī*) and three early-modern notary manuals: the copybook of a late sixteenth-century Samarqandi *qāḍī*;[153] the *Mukhtār al-ikhtiyār ʿalā al-madhhab al-mukhtār* by Ikhtiyār al-Dīn b. Ghiyāth al-Dīn al-Ḥusaynī, who was *qāḍī* in Herat under the rule of the Timurid Sulṭān Ḥusayn Bāyqarā;[154] and the otherwise unidentified *Shurūṭ-i arangī*. The system of conflict resolution, which Viatkin calls *shariat*, shows the *qāḍī*s and the muftis as the only officials who performed judicial duties under the rule of the khans.

Russians presented the establishment of the native courts of justice as a twofold achievement: first, the purported preservation of the status quo and, second, the creation of a more rational legal system freed from discretionary powers of the local rulers over justice.[155] Orientalists were fully implicated in

---

151 The Shibanid/Abulkhairid dynasty ruled Central Asia throughout the sixteenth century; see R.D. McChesney, "Shībānī Khān and Shībānids." In *EI2* vol. IX: 426 ff. and 428 ff.

152 V.L. Viiatkin, *K voprosam izucheniia uzbekov v Srednei Azii* (*XVI vek*) (written in Samarkand 1932), unpublished manuscript (150 folios), TsGARUZ, f. R-2773, op. 1, d. 1103, ll. 1–37.

153 *Majmūʿa-yi wathāʾiq*, MS Tashkent, TsVRUz, no. 1386. The text is a formulary manual consisting of 737 copies of legal texts notarized between the years 996/1588 and 999/1591 at the court of Mawlanā Ṣiddiq al-Ḥalwāʾī, the deputy of the chief judge. It was entrusted to Viatkin by the *qāḍī* of Urgut in 1907. A few of Viatkin's translations were published as *Kaziiskie dokumenty XVI veka*, ed. R.R. Fitrat and K.S. Sergeev (Tashkent: Komitet Nauk Uzbekistana, 1937). A selection of texts from the *Majmūʿa-yi wathāʾiq* appeared in Uzbek translation as *Vasiqalar to'plami.* (*XVI asrining ikkinchi iarmi Samarkand oblastidagi iuridik dokumentlar*), ed. B. Ibrohimov (Tashkent: Fan, 1982). The manual has been used also by Rozaliia Galievna Mukminova for her *Sotsialnaia differentsiatsia naseleniia gorodov Uzbekistana v XV–XVI vv.* (Tashkent, Fan: 1985). Muzaffar Alam has noted correctly that some of Mukminova's translations of texts from the *Majmūʿa-yi wathāʾiq* are defective. See his "Trade, State Policy and Regional Change: Aspects of Mughal-Uzbek Commercial Relations, c. 1550–1750." *JESHO* 37/3 (1994): 202–27, ns. 3, 14, 15.

154 Muzaffar Alam, *The Languages of Political Islam: India, 1200–1800* (Chicago: University of Chicago Press, 2004): 52. Alam lists only one manuscript copy preserved in Patna, though an earlier one is held in the Bodleian Library; see Fraser 234, 235, 239. This manual seems to have been used widely in Central Asia, up to the early twentieth century: other copies of this work (including the one examined by Viiatkin) have recently been discovered in the manuscript library of the Institute of Oriental Studies in Tashkent. One of them was probably inspected by Ol'ga Chekhovich, who translated a few passages, TsGARUz, R-2678, op. 1, d. 379.

155 See Chapter 2.

this cultural project. This is clearly visible in Russian imperial and early Soviet Central Asia, where experts in vernacular languages and the history of Islamic culture wrote on *sharīʿa* by creatively extrapolating from what they saw in the "native courts." One such case is provided by Nil Sergeevich Lykoshin (1860–1922), who devoted an entire work to the *qāḍī*s in Russian Central Asia, which was based on his participating observation as police chief (*pristav*) in the Muslim-majority neighborhoods of Tashkent. Lykoshin explains that the native courts among the settled population of Turkestan replaced (*smenil*) the earlier legal system, which consisted exclusively of *qāḍī*s, on whose will the life of the people depended. He emphasizes that the institutional changes introduced by the Russians in Islamic law amounted merely to restricting the competencies of the former *qāḍī*s: a few offenses were subsumed by other legal jurisdictions, and corporal punishment was abolished.[156]

In other cases, we observe Orientalists pushing their informants to recount a story precisely according to their preferred themes. During field work in Bukhara, a group of Soviet academics led by the famous ethnographer and linguist Mikhail Andreev[157] approached a former expert of the Islamic law of inheritance (*tarīkachī*), who had worked as attendant at the royal court, and asked him to write down the duties of the chief judge or market inspector (*raʾīs*).[158] Their questions were invariably based on the assumption that the late-Manghit judiciary exercised a monopoly over the articulation and execution of justice.[159] Little wonder, then, that the insider's account was accommodated within a set of conceptions foreign to local judicial practices.[160] By contrast, an account of the judicial system in Khiva under the Qunghrats—the

156 See his "Kazii (Narodnye sud'i): Bytovoi ocherk osedlogo naseleniia Turkestana": 53.

157 K.F. Akramova and N. Akramov, *Vostokoved Mikhail Stepanovich Andreev (nauchno-biograficheskii ocherk)* (Dushanbe: Irfon, 1973). I owe this reference to Ulfatbek Abdurasulov.

158 *Tarjuma-yi aḥwāl-i Qāḍī Kalānhā-yi darūn-i Bukhārā*, TsGARUz, R-2678, op. 2, d. 251, 60b–4. The informant was a certain Qārī Aḥmad, who had assisted Bukharan judges.

159 N. Fioletov, "Sudoproizvodstvo v musul'manskikh sudakh (sudy kaziev) Srednei Azii." *Novii Vostok* 23–24 (1928): 204–17.

160 One of the results of this ethnographic expedition to Bukhara was the monograph by M.S. Iusupov, *Sud v Bukhare. Sudoustroistvo i sudoproizvodstvo v Bukharskom emirate v kontse XIX i nachale XX v.v.* (written in Samarkand, 1941) (unpublished manuscript, 305 folios), MS Samarqand, AMIKINUz, no. 828. Though Iusupov notes in passing that the emir himself decided on the appeals of his subjects and on the reports (ll. 15–16), he did little to investigate the procedures according to which Bukharans filed their claim with the royal court and focused, instead, on the *qāḍī*s and their courts.

production of which was not, apparently, prompted by Soviet academics—conferred on the royal court a central role in the resolution of conflict.[161]

One should avoid generalizations in speaking of Orientalists and Islamic legal studies. Many experts in Islamic law who were "educated in the textualist, mostly German, philological tradition"[162] advocated the study of doctrinal texts and thus understood *sharīʿa* as a law of jurists. In their view, *sharīʿa* was a legal doctrine whose evolution depended solely on the *muftīs* as legal theorists, while *qāḍīs* were merely technicians responsible for reconciling doctrine with the extralegal circumstances of the moment. The Orientalist scholarship on Islamic law circulating in the Russian Empire, most of which in the colony was of European origin, is no exception.[163] It had little impact, however, on the way Russians conceived of the "native courts." For them it was the *qāḍī* who was primarily accountable for the implementation of *sharīʿa*.

---

161 Bābājān Safaruf [Babadzhan Safarov], *Khwārazm taʾrīkhī (1864–1934)*, MS Tashkent, TsVRUz, no. 10231, in particular the section entitled "Practices of solving disputes submitted to the rulers, the office holders and the governors" (*khān ʿamaldārlār ḥākimlārnīng birgāndān* [?] *daʿwā janjāllārnī muḥākama qīlīsh ʿādatlārī*), fols. 21–23. The author was born at the end of the nineteenth century in Khiva, studied in a local madrasa, and worked as mufti under the Qunghrats. See *Sobranie vostochnykh rukopisei Akademii Nauk Uzbekistan. Istoriia*, ed. D.Iu. Iusupov and R.P. Dzhalilov (Tashkent: Fan, 1998): 236. That he served in some juristic capacity can be inferred from a request for a legal opinion that he sent to Bukhara in 1919; see B. Kazakov, *Bukharan Documents: The Collection in the District Library, Bukhara*, trans. J. Paul (Berlin: Klaus Schwarz, 2001): 44.

162 I. Agmon and I. Shahar, "Theme Issue: Shifting Perspectives in the Study of Shariʿa Courts: Methodologies and Paradigms." *ILS* 15/1 (2009): 4.

163 For an overview of the available literature at the beginning of the twentieth century, see A.E. Krymskii, "O posobiiakh dlia izucheniia musul'manskogo prava." In *Istoriia musul'manstva. Somostoiatel'nye ocherki, obrabotki i dopol'nennye perevody iz Dozi i Gol'dtsiera*, ed. A.E. Krymskii (St. Petersburg: Tipogr. V. Gattsuk, 1904): part II, 28–38. As late as 1912, the Orientalist Nikolai Ostroumov noted that, "with regard to Islamic studies and most notably to the study of Islamic jurisprudence, the Russian scholarship (*russkaia pechat'*) deserves to be reproached. It is impossible to rule 20 millions of Muslims, not only without knowledge of *shārīʿa* but also without acknowledging the latter's necessity"; see his *Islamovedenie. 4. Shariat po shkole (mazkhab) Abu-Khanify* (Tashkent: Tip. Pri Kants. Turk. Gen.-Gub, 1912): 19. On Ostroumov, see B. Babajanov, "'How Will We Appear in the Eyes of *Inovertsy* and *Inorodtsy*?' Nikolai Ostroumov on the Image and Function of Russian Power." *CAS* 33/2 (2014): 270–88. Babajanov here overlooks the fact that, in spite of his misuse of the word "code" for *sharīʿa*, Ostroumov clearly understood that the application of Islamic law depended on the interpretive role of the jurists (muftis); hence, it is to Ostroumov that we owe the first comprehensive list in Russian of authoritative juristic sources employed by local muftis: Ostroumov, *Islamovedenie. 4*: 9–18.

4 *Sharīʿa* and the Governing Authorities

Another problem we may face in examining scholarship in Islamic legal studies and *sharīʿa* in precolonial Central Asia is the assumptions we bring to the concept of governing authorities or "the state." Considering a region of the Muslim world such as Central Asia in the nineteenth century may lead us to situate the local khanates in a wider history of modernization and a narrative of cultural change in which Muslim polities translated their encounter with the West into their own experiences of modernity. This may risk our assuming that modernizing trends current—for example, in the Ottoman Empire during the Tanzimat period—prevailed also in Khiva, Bukhara, and Kokand. Central Asian legal history is completely different. The Muslim polities that governed there did not display the sorts of reforms or the cultural orientations that were current in the Ottoman Empire in the second half of the nineteenth century: we find few attempts at the formalization and proceduralization of judicial activities, and we cannot cite instances of codification similar to the *qānūn-nāmas* and legal transplantation of, say, Western legal texts.[164] In Central Asia we do, however, see forms of "corporate identity" and "a public welfare apparatus," as well as "a universal administrative and bureaucratic control"[165] and instruments of "surveillance, discipline, and punishment," all features that Wael Hallaq considers intrinsic to the model of the modern nation state, under the rule of which *sharīʿa* lost its pristine functions and was eclipsed.

According to Hallaq, modernizing trends in the Muslim world began in the Ottoman Empire as an endemic process of centralization—itself a measure to counteract the military and economic power of the West—and then affected much of the Muslim-majority colonies. Under these conditions, *sharīʿa* became subjected progressively to the legislative ethos of states that imposed their own juristic views. The modern state and *sharīʿa* are, in Hallaq's view, incompatible, because both represent two "machines of governance" that tolerate no external infringements aimed at "determining the substance of law."[166]

There are two problems with the way Wael Hallaq approaches the study of *sharīʿa* in the modern period. First, he leads us to view the centralization of

164 See A. Rubin, *Ottoman Nizamiye Courts: Land and Modernity* (New York: Palgrave MacMillan, 2011).

165 W.B. Hallaq, "Islamic Law: History and Transformation." In *The New Cambridge History of Islam*, vol. 4, *Islamic Cultures and Societies to the End of the Eighteenth Century*, ed. Robert Irwin (Cambridge: Cambridge University Press, 2010): 143.

166 W.B. Hallaq, *Sharīʿa: Theory, Practice, Transformations* (Cambridge: Cambridge University Press, 2009): 361.

the judicial apparatus as a centripetal force, by which *sharīʿa* is driven from the landscape it originally inhabited. The idea that *sharīʿa* was centrifugal to the state is misleading for the legal history of Central Asia and the wider Hanafi world. Muzaffar Alam has shown how attempts to rethink the relationship between *sharīʿa* and the state are visible in Herat under Shāhrukh in the first half of the fifteenth century and later under Bābur (r. 932–37/1526–30).[167] This became an even stronger phenomenon in the late eighteenth century and throughout the nineteenth—or at least we have more sources that attest to it. This phenomenon has nothing to do with the encounter with the West. More than a century before Awrangzeb (r. 1068–1118/1658–1707) solicited the compilation of the collection of legal opinions called *al-Fatāwā al-ʿĀlamgīrīya*, the first ruler of the Abū ʾl-Khayrids in Bukhara commissioned the compilation of the *al-Fatāwā al-Shībānīya* in Persian, which would have been easily intelligible to the local populace.[168] A few decades later, Shāh ʿAbbās commissioned the imposing *Jāmiʿ-i ʿAbbāsī* to popularize the Shiʿi legal literature in the vernacular, so the Persianate world witnessed, between the sixteenth and seventeenth centuries, several attempts by sovereigns to define the Islamic legal domain.[169]

The other problem is that, in distinguishing between the state, as a preserve of legal authority, and the judiciary, one makes an a priori distinction between two entities that are actually of the same substance: most of the people who staffed the chancellery of the khanates—the administrative apparatus of local Islamic polities—had the same background as the jurists who were appointed to the post of *qāḍī* or worked as muftis. Rulers themselves, for example, were often jurists or were surrounded by legists such as the *yasāwul-i ʿulamāʾ*. *ʿUlamāʾ* staffed the chancelleries of the khanates and taught in the madrasas established by local dynasts. The state and whatever legalistic knowledge emanates from it should not necessarily be regarded as different from or opposed to the production of the *ʿulamāʾ*. Drawing an artificial boundary between the state and the *sharīʿa* (or the *ʿulamāʾ*) risks applying the notions of legal diversity to a juristic field that contained only one body of law. In Central Asia,

167 Alam, *The Languages of Political Islam: India, 1200–1800*: passim.

168 *ammā baʿd: chunīn gūyad al-faqīr* [followed by the name of the author, P.S.] *ki bāʿith bar taḥrīr-i īn kalamāt wa taqrīr-i īn maqālāt ān-ast ki ḥaḍrat-i ṣāḥib-qirān-i nādir-zamān īn faqīr-i shikasta-yi durust-iʿtiqād rā amr kard ki kitābī bar bāb-i masāyil-i sharʿīya-i farʿīya nawīsad ki qarīb ba-fahm wa maʿmūla bihi bāshad tā bar jamīʿ-i mustafīdān-i ān āsān bāshad*, ʿAlī b. Muḥammad ʿAlī b. ʿAlī b. Maḥmūd al-Mukhtārī al-Khwārazmī al-Kubrawī, *al-Fatāwā al-Shībānīya*, MS Tashkent, TsVRUz, no. 6112/1: fols. 7a–7b. Described in SVR VIII: 290.

169 R. Jurdi Abisaab, *Converting Persia: Religion and Power in the Safavid Empire* (London: I.B. Tauris, 2004): 58.

the subjects of the khanates distinguished between the royal court and the *qāḍīs* as different legal venues. But they did so only on account of an asymmetry of powers of enforcement rather than because of procedural differences.

The literature on the state's legal administration is narrow, and nearly all of it is surprisingly similar: the justice of the royal court is either substantively different from *sharīʿa* as it deals with the reparation of offenses that do not fall within the jurisdiction of the *qāḍīs*, or it is referred to as *maẓālim*, which serves as a court of second instance.[170] To the best of my knowledge, a recent work by Yossef Rapoport is unique in having approached the relationship between the royal court and *sharīʿa* from a different perspective. In a study addressing the purported deterioration of the Islamic legal system under the Mamluks, Rapoport has argued that "the *maẓālim* courts of the pre-Mamluk classical tradition [...] were [...] transformed into courts of wide jurisdiction, parallel to the *sharīʿah* courts of the *qadis*. These new institutions were called *siyāsah* courts, because of their emphasis on equity at the expense of the formalism of the *sharīʿah*. [...] The *siyāsah* courts of the fifteenth century had jurisdiction over cases that had little direct effect on public policy, such as reclamation of debts and matrimonial cases."[171] Rapoport's contribution in opening new lines of inquiry into the entanglement of *sharīʿa* with the justice emanating from the royal court is twofold: he shows that the *qāḍīs* and the magistrates of the ruling principalities were complementary, and he demonstrates an increasing tension between the two as the establishment of the institutions of "*siyāsah* courts" signaled a centralization of legal administration that culminated in the interference of the rulers in the way *qāḍīs* resolved disputes. The centralized Ottoman administration is usually held up as the sole case in which such tension was resolved by the ruler by means of the *qānūn*, that is, a medium for reconciling *sharīʿa* to the ruler's law.

Elaborating further on Rapoport's argument, I propose that the justice of the royal court and *sharīʿa* are not merely complementary but are one and the same thing. First, we have seen that, in nineteenth-century Central Asia, Islamic law was not administered only by a professional judicial body. I hope to have shown that, after the fall of the Ashtarkhanids and the Abū 'l-Khayrids (1747) and the subsequent establishment of the three main ruling principalities, the administration of law underwent bureaucratization and centralization that led to a greater involvement of the royal court in people's private affairs. The archives of the Manghit (r. 1753–1920), Ming

170 Ben-Bassat, *Petitioning the Sultan: Protesters and Justice in Late Ottoman Palestine*: 24–8.

171 Y. Rapoport, "Royal Justice and Religious Law: *Siyāsah* and Sharīʿah under the Mamluks." *MSR* 16 (2012): 75.

(r. 1798–1876), and Qunghrat (r. 1770–1920) bureaucracies suggest that *qāḍīs* more often than not served in the humble capacity of legal advisors and were thus held accountable for every decision they took. If we move away from records produced only for patterns of private consumption—which, according to the Soviet academic taxonomy, are usually termed "*qadi* documents")[172]—we see that Central Asians living under the rule of the Muslim principalities accessed the legal services provided by the royal court, which may or may not have required the legal expertise of *qāḍīs*.

Second, the fact that nineteenth-century jurists issued opinions that conferred legitimacy on the view that *qāḍīs* should submit to the will of the local ruler means that manifestations of dependence on the ruling house were becoming an established feature of the Islamic juridical field in Central Asia.[173] That opinions were issued on this point of law also suggests that the dependence of the *ʿulamāʾ* on the rulers was disputed among legal experts.[174]

5 On Customary Law

In examining the historiography of law in post-Mongol Central Asia and considering the state, we have to deal with an additional complication that requires a specific, though cursory, treatment. It is often assumed that Central Asian khanates occasionally operated in a legal field different from *sharīʿa*, which somehow represented the cultural legacy of the Mongols. Chinggis Khan is known, among other things, for having been a lawgiver who introduced a body of customary laws called the *yasa* (*jasaq*). There is no way to establish what the *yasa* was during Chinggis Khan's time, because the available sources referring to his regulations were produced centuries later.[175] Things are no easier in the Timurid period in attempting to evaluate the *törä*, a term Maria Eva

172 A translation of the Russian *kaziiskie dokumenty* (Uzbek, *qozi hujjatlari*).

173 J. Pickett, *The Persianate Sphere during the Age of Empires: Islamic Scholars and Networks of Exchange in Central Asia, 1747–1917*. PhD diss. (Princeton University, 2015): chap. 5.

174 For an argument against the submission of the *ʿulamāʾ* to the Manghit ruling house, see Ahmadi Donish, *Navodir-ul-vaqoe"*, ed. A. Devonaqulov, 2 vols. (Dushanbe: Donish, 1988–9): 2:53–4.

175 R.G. Irvin, "What the Partridge Told the Eagle: A Neglected Arabic Source on Chinggis Khan and the Early History of the Mongols." In *The Mongol Empire and Its Legacy*, ed. R. Amitai-Press and D. Morgan (Leiden: Brill, 1999): 10; D. Morgan, "The 'Great Yasa of Chinggis Khan' Revisited." In *Mongols, Turks, and Others: Eurasian Nomads and the Sedentary World*, ed. R. Amitai and M. Biran (Leiden: Brill, 2005): 305–7.

Subtelny explains as the "Turko-Mongolian custom as practiced by Temür, his descendants, and their Chaghatay[-speaking] followers," which "overlapped and complemented the Chinggisid *yasa*."[176] One of the elements connecting the Timurid *törä* directly to Chinggisid customary law is said to be the *yārghū*, the "court of investigation," which Subtelny describes as "the chief instrument of enforcement of the *yasa*."[177] References to the *törä* and the *yārghū* in Timurid sources, however, convey rather a perceived tension between the latter and the *sharīʿa*[178] than a reflection of how the *yasa* and the *törä* actually functioned. By the nineteenth century, *yārghū* had acquired a completely different meaning and was applied to punishments meted out by the royal court.[179]

Thomas Welsford has made a strong case that the Mongol *yasa* and the Timurid *törä* were nothing other than instruments to invoke Chinggisid traditions, "however contextually understood. Because there was no authoritative record dating back to Chingīz's own rule, people knew of a 'Chingizīd tradition' only in the form of its various late avatars, each articulating a world-view somewhat different from the next."[180] This interpretation holds true also for later periods. As Anke von Kügelgen has noted, Manghit historiographers repeatedly praised their patrons for having abolished "Chinggisid innovations" (*bidʿathā-yi chingīzī*) which consisted largely of forms of taxation other than those sanctioned by *sharīʿa*.[181] The Khivan chroniclers Munīs and Āgahī do

176 Subtelny, *Timurids in Transition*: 15–16.

177 Ibid.: 21. Another sympathizer with this view is Jürgen Paul, in *Zentralasien* (Frankfurt am Main: Fischer, 2012): 317.

178 Subtelny, *Timurids in Transition*: 25; İ. Togan, "Uluğbek zamanında Yasa ve Şeriat Tartışmaları." *Tarih Çevresi* 1 (1994): 9–16; İ.E. Binbaş, "The Anatomy of a Regicide Attempt: Shāhrukh, the *Ḥurūfīs*, and the Timurid Intellectuals in 830/1426–27." *JROAS* 23/2 (2013): 33.

179 Aḥmad Makhdhūm Dānish Muhandis-i Bukhārī, alias Aḥmad-i Kalla, *Tarjimat al-aḥwāl-i amīrān-i Bukhārā-yi sharīf az Amīr-i Dānyāl tā ʿaṣr-i Amīr ʿAbd al-Aḥad*, MS Tashkent, TsVRUz, no. 1987: fol. 15b; *Maktūbāt-i Amīr Ḥaydar ba Muḥammad Ḥakīm Bī*, MS Tashkent, TsVRUz, no. 2120: fol. 304a (*yasāwul rā ʿafw farmūdīm bāyad ki taḥṣīldārān az way yarghū ṭalab nasāzand*); Semenov, *Ocherk ustroistva tsentral'nogo administrativnogo upravleniia Bukharskogo khantsva pozdneishego vremeni*: 13. Jürgen Paul claims that the *yārghū* continued to exist after Shāhrūkh, although he provides no evidence in support of this statement, *Zentralasien*: 317.

180 T. Welsford, *Four Types of Loyalty in Early Modern Central Asia: The Tūqāy-Tīmūrid Takeover of Greater Mā warā al-Nahr, 1598–1605* (Leiden: Brill, 2012): 85.

181 Von Kügelgen, *Die Legitimierung der mittelasiatischen Mangitendynastie in den Werken ihrer Historiker*: 270–2.

the same, when they recount how Eltüzer Khān Qunghrat abrogated similar "unlawful innovations" in taxation in Khorezm.[182]

It follows that, if there was in early-modern Central Asia a legal field that might have been different from Islamic law and fallen under the jurisdiction of the ruling house alone, it must have been the *yārghū*, which disappeared, however, with Shāhrukh, if we are to credit the reconstruction made by Subtelny. By contrast, starting in the sixteenth century, texts occasionally refer to "Chinggisid" legal practices that deviate from Islamic law. It does not necessarily follow that such practices represented a Turko-Mongolian customary law or a kind of justice administered by the state.

In the attempt to move away from a statist perspective, historians of Islamic law (most notably students of Ottoman history) have sought to show not only that the courts applying *sharīʿa* enjoyed a certain degree of autonomy from the state but also that their judicial operations were effectively informed by principles of "collective responsibility and self-government."[183] In emphasising, instead, close ties between *sharīʿa* courts and the state, my argument might be accused of resurrecting an interpretive paradigm that was abandoned long ago. Against this objection, I should note that my study develops the idea that Central Asian khanates did not claim legislative prerogatives for themselves. They never legislated on matters of *sharīʿa* law, nor did they attempt to codify it. By promoting forcefully a theory of justice that rested on the defense of *sharīʿa*, the khanates drew upon notions of local practice, custom, and collective responsibility. This inclusive aspect of the state rests uncomfortably on a narrative of opposition between legal centralism and autonomous legal fields. I thus situate the state in a juridical field in which all legal actors use *sharīʿa* as a common set of legal values to translate the particular into the universal. Judges, along with cultural brokers, saints, and people endowed with local knowledge, were all expected to act according to *sharīʿa*. The khanate watched and held everyone accountable.

---

182 Shīr Muḥammad Mīrāb Mūnis and Muḥammad Rizā Mīrāb Āgahī, *Firdaws al-iqbāl: History of Khorezm*, trans. Y. Bregel (Leiden: Brill: 1999): 183–84. There is a striking similarity, however, between Shah Murād, Eltüzer Khān and Shāhrukh, who are all praised for having restored *sharīʿa* by abrogating unlawful forms of taxation (*qālanāt*); see M.E. Subtelny, "The Sunni Revival under Shār-Rukh and Its Promoters: A Study of the Connection between Ideology and Higher Learning in Timurid Iran." In *Proceedings of the 27th Meeting of Haneda Memorial Hall Symposium on Central Asia and Iran August 30, 1993* (Kyoto: Institute of Inner Asian Studies, 1993): 20.

183 B.A. Ergene, *Local Court, Provincial Society and Justice in the Ottoman Empire: Legal Practice and Dispute Resolution in Çankırı and Kastamonu (1652–1744)* (Leiden: Brill, 2003): 24.

It may be useful to revisit, briefly, the meaning of customary law in the Russian period, especially because we shall come across this category in the following chapters. Received wisdom on law and colonialism holds that the Europeans "invented" customary law by requesting that indigenous experts commit to writing down the laws that they followed locally and that had previously existed only in oral form. Colonial "invention" of customary law took other forms also. Russian officials, for example, were directly engaged in their collection and recording and thereby acted as legal anthropologists. In the Caucasus, Russians assembled books of village rules, in Arabic, and in Central Asia they compiled digests of customary laws, mainly in Russian (*erezhe/ sbornik obychaev*). In both cases, the "invention" of customary law amounted to a purposeful disambiguation of certain norms from a larger system of legal signification in which they had previously been entangled.[184] In both the Caucasus and Central Asia, the compilation of books of customary law and their extended commentary in the Russian press was integral to an imperial policy aimed at disempowering *sharīʿa* among specific Muslim communities in the hope that it would facilitate their subjugation. Virginia Martin observes that:

> The diverse collections of rules and principles that were presented for government use or published in the periodical press were identified collectively as the "customary law" (*obychnoe pravo*) of the Kazakhs. In this way, Russian officials and scholars "invented" Kazakh customary law and gave it claim to universality. They produced a body of written customs that may have captured many of the judicial practices of a particular kinship group or region at a particular time, but once recorded[,] the oral customs ceased to accurately reflect changing, everyday practices.[185]

184 R. Roberts and K. Mann, "Law in Colonial Africa." In *Law in Colonial Africa*, ed. K. Mann and R. Roberts (Portsmouth, NH: Heinemann, 1991): 4; M. Chanok, "Paradigms, Policies, and Property: A Review of the Customary Law of Land Tenure." In ibid.: 61–84. M. Kemper and M. Reinkowski, "Einleitung: Gewohnheitsrecht zwischen Staat und Gesellschaft." In *Rechtspluralismus in der Islamischen Welt. Gewohnheitsrecht zwischen Staat und Gesellschaft*, ed. M. Kemper and M. Reinkowski (Berlin and New York: De Gruyter, 2005): 2–3; B.M. Cooper, "Injudicious Intrusions: Chiefly Authority and Islamic Judicial Practice in Maradi, Niger." In *Muslim Family Law in Sub-Saharan Africa: Colonial Legacies and Post-Colonial Challenges*, ed. S. Jeppie, E. Moosa, and R. Roberts (Amsterdam: Amsterdam University Press, 2010): 183–218. A. Guerin, "Racial Myth, Colonial Reform, and the Invention of Customary Law in Morocco, 1912–1930." *The Journal of North African Studies* 16/3 (2011): 361–80.

185 Martin, *Law and Custom in the Steppe: The Kazakhs of the Middle Horde and Russian Colonialism* (Richmond, UK: Curzon, 2001): 4.

Any process of codification is an attempt to fix specific norms, to confer normative value on them, and, probably, to exclude other norms deemed unsuitable under changing social circumstances. This is not characteristic only of colonial governmentality. Muslim jurists, too, produced books of substantive law, such as collections of fatwas and abridged legal manuals (*mukhtaṣar*),[186] in order to endow with authority specific modes of juristic reasoning and certain judicial procedures, with the effect that they gave the latter claim to universality.[187] The use of terms such as *dastūr* and *ʿurf*, which we often find in vernacular deeds in Central Asia, is no less a cultural construction—that is, an ex post facto categorization adopted to confer on a given practice, whether well established or not, the force of custom.

Also, Paul Dresch[188] and Judith Scheele[189] cite the need to distinguish between invented custom and nonstate forms of legalism manifesting themselves in the colonial period that cannot be reduced to colonial "inventions" and Western impositions. Both have argued that emphasis on the invention of customary laws does more to obscure than to clarify the meaning of the laws or normative orderings that we call "customary." I agree with Dresch and Scheele that little has been done so far to understand how Kazakh customary law functioned and how its practitioners and consumers conceived of it.

There are two aspects of customary law in colonial Central Asia that should be addressed further. First, it seems that, for Kazakh arbitrators (*bīs*), it was of little concern that they operated in courts established by the Russians to dispense justice under a legal system that today we tend to dismiss as a colonial "invention." Either they considered irrelevant what they recorded in court registers and thus catered to the expectations of the Russian administration, or, more likely, they were perfectly at ease with the new institutional arrangement of the customary law courts and thus believed that they were operating according to a normative system that ought to be called *ʿādat*. Kazakh arbitrators may well have regarded with favor the institutional innovation of the native courts in light of their own personal interests. The clientele of the new

---

186 M. Fadel, "The Social Logic of *Taqlīd* and the Rise of the *Mukhataṣar*." *ILS* 3/2 (1996): 193–233.

187 A. Fekry Ibrahim, "The Codification Episteme in Islamic Juristic Discourse between Inertia and Change," *ILS* 22/3 (2015): 157–220.

188 P. Dresch, "Legalism, Anthropology, and History: A View from Part of Anthropology." In *Legalism: Anthropology and History*, ed. P. Dresch and H. Skoda (Oxford: Oxford University Press, 2012): 1–37.

189 J. Scheele, "A Taste for Law: Rule Making in Kabylia (Algeria)." *CSSH* 50/4 (2008): 895–919.

customary-law courts represented a source of income and, as such, clearly increased their power. Some Kazakhs may, however, have viewed customary law less as a colonial invention than as an expression of their own legal culture.

Second, and more significantly, the *bīs* who adjudicated according to customary law among a specific Muslim community could also, if needed, easily change legal hats and act in the capacity of *qāḍīs* who would rule according to *sharīʿa*.[190] We observe this curious phenomenon in various places in Russian Central Asia.[191] This originates from the fact that the incorporation of this region into the Russian Empire brought about an "Islamic revival," which manifested itself in the proliferation of institutions of Islamic higher learning (*madrasa*), where more Muslim students could study and practice *sharīʿa*. As a result, we observe, along with procedural differences, a significant overlap of Islamic stock phrases between *ʿādat* and *sharīʿa* courts under Russian rule.[192]

Taken together, these two aspects suggest that Russian imperialism in Central Asia changed the meaning that people gave to custom and ultimately affected their legal consciousness.

Conclusion

Subjects of the khan filed their claims with the royal court for many reasons. According to a widely shared perception, agencies in Bukhara, Khiva, or Kokand were more powerful than provincial officeholders—for example, a *qāḍī*— and the royal court's sanctioning of a ruling would ensure its execution. Materials from early-twentieth-century Central Asia, especially from Khorezm, indicate that *qāḍīs* lacked even the power to summon parties, as demonstrated by the following record indicating that a respondent used violence against a court attendant:

> Mullā Muḥammad Panāh, the husband of Bībī Bīka, who is the sister of Mullā Jumʿa Niyāz from Khiva, opened her [wife's] chest with a key and stole leather galoshes and valuable clothes. Moreover, he beat the

190 Sartori, "The Birth of a Custom: Nomads, *Sharīʿa* Courts and Established Practices in the Tashkent Province, ca. 1868–1919": 312.

191 Allen J Frank has noted the same phenomenon, which he terms "an overlap between qadis and biys" among the Kereys of Petropavlovsk. E-mail communication, 26 February 2015.

192 P. Sartori, "Murder in Manghishlaq: Notes on an Instance of Application of Qazaq Customary Law in Khiva (1895)." *DI* 88/2 (2012): 235–40.

> aforementioned Bībī Bīka for no reason and made her suffer. For this reason, the *qaḍī īshān* appointed Mullā Sayyid Muḥammad as trustee [*yasāwul*] and sent him [to the place]. [Mullā Muḥammad Panāh, however,] beat him too and insulted him. Therefore, the above mentioned [Mullā Jumʿa Niyāz] has a claim against Mullā Muḥammad Panāh. Let them come to the royal court of his majesty—may his rule last forever—together with the attendant, Raḥman Birgān Bājbān, who is the guard [*nawkar*] of Muḥammad Yaʿqūb Bāy Yasāwulbāshī, and resolve the case. They should pay two *tanga*s for each parasang to the attendant. This instruction was written on 6 Rabīʿ al-Thānī in 1336 [19.01.1918].[193]

Disputing parties who traveled to the seats of power made significant financial investments to file their claim with the authorities. There may have been other reasons for such investments: a desire to shift the case away from local power struggles, to attract the maximum possible publicity for one's case in order to restore public credibility,[194] or out of distrust for local officeholders. Our sources suggest that local subjects enjoyed the right to request that their cases be transferred to Khiva, for example, even during trials held at the office of a governor or in a *qāḍī*'s court.[195] The prerogative of subjects living in localities far from center of the khanate to lodge a lawsuit with the royal court thus belonged to a "culture of justice."

In nineteenth-century Central Asia, as elsewhere in the Islamicate world, most claims were heard and resolved informally. My argument—the royal court's prominent role in the resolution of conflicts—accounts for only a fraction of what occurred in villages and provinces, away from the centers of power, where local notables and elders regularly settled disputes. Deeds of acquittal and amicable settlement notarized by *qāḍī*s, common as they were in Central Asia, probably attest to the resolution of conflicts that first were treated informally, without the aid of a state representative. Informal settlements were integral to the local legal "system," but this observation does not detract from the argument that power relations among state officials affected the practice of Islamic law. Muslims would not bring their affairs to a

193 TsGARUz, f. I-125, op. 1, d. 633, l. 90. A parasang (*farsakh*) is approximately 5½ kilometers.

194 I draw on Daniel Lord Smail's notion of publicity in *The Consumption of Justice: Emotions, Publicity, and Legal Culture in Marseille, 1264–1423*.

195 TsGARUz, f. I-125, op. 1, d. 498, ll. 44; 56–56ob.

judge unless ordered to do so by the royal court or a governor.[196] The local populace knew that *qāḍīs* acted mostly as notaries and legal assessors, and their rulings may, in fact, attest to trials held at the request of a governor or the royal court.

The Central Asian royal courts no doubt devoted attention to the mundane affairs of their subjects while ignoring established judicial practices that were followed in other regions of the Islamicate world, because appeal to the royal court (*ʿarḍ*) served to relieve social tensions. More importantly, however, it gave the central government the opportunity to monitor local affairs in a regular fashion and thus to make timely adjustments in response to changing social circumstances.

---

196 TsGARUz, f. I-125, op. 1, d. 509, l. 145. This rescript of the *dīwānbīgī* to the khan demonstrates the extent to which Khivan authorities could instruct *qāḍīs* on how to proceed in civil-law cases. This is a case of debt: the *dīwānbīgī* writes to a *qāḍī*, orders him to appoint a trustee (*amīn*), and sends him with a guard to a locality to sell certain possessions to the creditors (14.11.1916).

CHAPTER 2

Native Judges into Colonial Scapegoats

Introduction

In the nineteenth century the Russian Empire extended its domains into the Kazakh steppe and Transoxiana. Russian legal planners and officials had to secure social order in the new territories that fell within the state's purview. Both the absorption of local bodies of law into the structure of imperial governance and the official recognition of indigenously enshrined local rights and obligations were seen as necessary "to keep the peace, in return for tribute and taxes."[1] The Russian Empire thus established a pluralistic legal regime. It introduced courts (military and civil) presided over by Russian justices and native courts presided over by *qāḍīs* with a view to preserving *sharīʿa*—or at least what Russians thought *sharīʿa* amounted to before the conquest. Some features of Islamic legal culture were profoundly transformed, while others remained intact. This chapter looks at one such rupture. It shows that the legal structure of the colony required that native judges (*qāḍīs*) be depicted as corrupt, even as it encouraged many false accusations against them to be filed by Muslims with the colonial administration of Russian Turkestan.

The forms of governance that the Russians adopted in the realm of law differed little from other Western instruments of domination in Asia. St. Petersburg's civilizing mission presumed an asymmetry between imperial law and the various forms of indigenous justice. Russians believed that bringing "civic-mindedness" (*grazhdanstvennost'*)[2] to the peoples of the Kazakh steppe and Transoxiana rested on the rapprochement (*sblizhenie*)[3] between an inferior body of law locally in use, "custom" (*obychai*), and the empire's

1 J. Burbank, "An Imperial Rights Regime: Law and Citizenship in the Russian Empire." *Kritika* 7/3 (2006): 402.

2 V. Martin, *Law and Custom in the Steppe: The Kazakhs of the Middle Horde and Russian Colonialism* (Richmond, UK: Curzon, 2001): 4, 43; see also P. Werth, "Changing Conceptions of Difference, Assimilation, and Faith in the Volga-Kama Region, 1740–1870." In *Russian Empire: Space, People, Power, 1700–1930*, ed. J. Burbank, M. von Hagen, and A. Remnev (Bloomington: Indiana University Press, 2007): 170, 184–5.

3 On the concept of *sblizhenie*, see Chapter 1, fn. 101.

superior legal system, "*the* law" (*zakon*). In their view, this transformation of local practices could be achieved without using force to introduce imperial law. Russian authorities thus allowed colonial subjects to present cases before local legists in "native courts" (*narodnye sudy*), but they hoped, with time, to impress upon them the greater desirability of operating within the imperial legal system.[4]

The institutional arrangements that were established in Central Asia, however, differed significantly from the solutions that had been applied in other Muslim-majority regions of the empire. In 1788 Catherine the Great established the Muslim Spiritual Administration, in the form of a muftiate in the Ural town of Ufa, to supervise the local mosque communities of European Russia, as well as to appoint and control their imams; another task of the muftis was to issue fatwas and regulations that would legitimize state policy and legislation from an Islamic point of view. It is usually held that Islamic law became confined, in daily practice, largely to issues of personal status, that is, registering births, marriages, and divorce and dealing with issues of inheritance.[5] These were the fields that the tsarist administration left largely to the imams of the local mosque communities. Other important aspects of Islamic law, however, such as charitable endowments (*waqfs*) to finance mosques and schools, were, in the Volga-Urals, often left in a gray area, without official recognition. In the region under the purview of the muftiate, Muslims could, and did, bring their affairs to "communes" (Russ. *zemstvo, pl. zemstva*) and jury trials, at least after Alexander II's (r. 1855–81) reforms of the judiciary. This was not the case in Russian Central Asia, where communes did not exist and judicial powers were, instead, in the hands of the military.[6] As we shall see, when Muslims appealed to the Russian government, their grievances were actually heard by military officers who deliberated with wide discretion on points of law specific to *sharīʿa*. It is thus common to find officers seconded to Turkestan who had not been initiated into the rudiments of Islamic law and who deliberated creatively on *waqf* law, property rights, customary dowry, the law of evidence, and so forth. This situation had serious unintended consequences for the practice of law in general, and, more specifically, for the legal culture of the colony. Military officers most often resolved conflicts by applying both imperial law and Islamic law, thereby

4 E. Schuyler, *Notes of a Journey in Russian Turkestan, Khokand, Bukhara, and Kuldja*, 5th ed., 2 vols. (London: Sampson Low, Marston, Searle, and Rivingston, 1876): 1:168.

5 R.D. Crews, "Empire and the Confessional State: Islam and Religious Politics in Nineteenth-Century Russia." *AHR* 108/1 (2003): 76 fn. 94.

6 A.S. Morrison, "Metropole, Colony, and Imperial Citizenship in the Russian Empire." *Kritika* 13/2 (2012): 329.

hybridizing procedures in forms that are typical of colonial situations. Central Asia represents, from this point of view, an exception in which the rule of law, as imagined by legal planners in the imperial metropole, was suspended. Such an arrangement made the region institutionally different from those areas under the rule of the Muslim Spiritual Administration.

Although the watchword among Russian lawmakers was "preservation" (*sokhranenie*),[7] the formal incorporation of local customs into the body of the imperial law in fact brought about *new* legal cultures. Imperial legal taxonomies distinguished between laws for settled communities of Muslims and laws for nomads. Such a distinction reflected a widespread assumption that the nomads were only superficially Islamized: "the Kazakhs are Muslim only in name" (*musul'manin Kirgiz—musul'manin tol'ko nominal'nyi*), noted one colonial officer.[8] In the eyes of the Russians, the legal culture of the nomads made a case for absolute indigeneity. Kazakhs were thus regarded as subjects of a legal order called *adat* (Ar. *ʿādat*), which was deemed less articulate than Islamic law proper:

> The main difference between *sharīʿa* and *ʿādat*, that is the legal system according to the native customs of the Kazakhs, is that *sharīʿa* distinguishes criminal from civil offenses. *ʿĀdat*, does not, however, conceive of penal offenses and includes the latter without any distinctions in the category of civil misdemeanors, which are sanctioned with material compensations for the offended party or her kinfolk.[9]

The colonizers not only disambiguated customary law from *sharīʿa* on the basis of procedural differences. They also conceived of laws as mirroring the varying nature of the peoples inhabiting the region. Russians thus held that the Kazakhs qua nomads followed a legal system different from *sharīʿa* because they were naturally unsuitable for a normative order based on Islam. From the Russian point of view, *sharīʿa* courts simply could not exist (*sushchestvovat' ne mozhet*) among the Kazakhs,[10] whose law "was based on customs that are harmless for the people and for the government, while the legal system of the *qāḍīs* is based on the laws of Muḥammad (*Magomet*), develops fanaticism, and places the people in a restricted space that does not permit intellectual

---

7 *Ob ustroistve sudebnoi chasti v Turkestanskom krae*, chap. 3, *Ustroistvo suda*, 1881, TsGARUz, f. I-1, op. 27, d. 68, l. 1.

8 Ibid.: l. 14ob.

9 Ibid.: l. 3.

10 Ibid.: l. 10b.

growth."[11] Consequently, in the Hobbesian world of Russian planners and officials, members of settled communities would have to refer to native courts presided over by *qāḍīs* who applied Islamic law, while nomads were expected to resolve their conflicts before a native judge called, in Russian, *biy* (Chaghatay, *bī*) who was said to apply customary law.

Given that the term *bī* appears repeatedly in this study, it is worth clarifying its historical meaning and its evolution after the Russian conquest of Central Asia. Numerous contemporary Russian observers stated that *bīs* had traditionally filled a voluntary office and that their authority to arbitrate in disputes had been contingent upon the consent of both opposing legal parties.[12] In contrast to this view, outside the Governorship-General of Turkestan, *bīs*' legal authority reflected their powers as tribal leaders, which were conferred upon them by the local ruler.[13]

To begin to grasp how *sharīʿa* and *ʿādat* became essential components of a state-sponsored regime of legal pluralism, let us imagine a single day in a town somewhere in colonial Central Asia. A certain Būra Bāy appears before an Islamic judge in pursuit of redress. He has initiated legal action against a certain Mullā Bāy, whom he accuses of stealing his horse. After the *qāḍī* has

11 Ibid.: ll. 3–30b.

12 "Although the term *biy* is most often translated as judge, it is wrong to associate the position with a formal court of law, such as one would find in the reform-era legal system in Russia proper. That is, traditionally, the *biy* owed his title neither to formal training, nor to appointment to a post. Rather, he accepted the honor of being called a *biy* by virtue of his knowledge of Kazakh *ʿādat* and of his ability to mediate a situation fairly. In general, a *biy* was any person to whom disputants turned to help them resolve disputes." Martin, *Law and Custom in the Steppe*: 27. The same view can be found in R.D. Crews, *For Prophet and Tsar: Islam and Empire in Russia and Central Asia* (Cambridge, MA: Harvard University Press, 2006): 216 "Kazakhs assume the title *biy* on an informal basis."

13 See the diplomas for the appointment of *bīs* among the Qaraqalpaqs under the rule of the Qunghrats, which were published in *Dokumenty arkhiva khivinskikh khanov po istorii i étnografii karakalpakov*, ed. Iu. É. Bregel' (Moscow: Nauka, 1967): 297–98, 431, 530. On the appointment of *bīs* among the Kazakhs (*qazaqīya ūlūs*) in the Dasht-i Qipchaq, see Muḥammad Bahādur Khān's diploma in favor of Shāh Murād b. Sārī Qul, who was appointed to govern the Mehdiqulī branch (*tīra*) of the ʿĀlim clan (*khalq*) in 1856, TsGARUz, f. I-125, op. 2, d. 14, l. 1. For other examples, see TsGARUz, f. I-125, op. 2, d. 12, l. 1; d. 9, l. 1. Although among the Kyrgyz of the Tian Shan, the title *bī* was acquired by succession, it clearly had an imperial dimension, as appointments to office required the issuance of diplomas by Qing agencies. See D.G. Prior, "High Rank and Power among the Northern Kirghiz: Terms and Their Problems, 1845–1864." In *Explorations in the Social History of Modern Central Asia (19th–20th Century)*, ed. P. Sartori (Leiden: Brill, 2013): 142–3.

ruled in his favor,[14] Būra Bāy leaves the judicial chamber and walks past a man named Tura Bāy, who is about to enter a courtroom applying Kazakh customary law. Tūra Bāy's son was murdered by members of his clan (*urūgh*) a few days earlier. At first, it seemed that the murder would result in retaliation, but influential individuals successfully mediated between the parties, persuading Tūra Bāy to relinquish his claim in return for a consideration.[15] While the contract of amicable settlement is being recorded, a certain Sayyid Ghazīkhān is in the office of Georgii Lamzdorf, a Russian notary. Ghazīkhān intends to circumvent the application of the Islamic law of inheritance. He wants to secure, according to Russian personal-status law, the legal entitlements of his daughters, who, according to *sharīʿa*, would be entitled to receive only a smaller share. Lamzdorf solemnizes Ghazīkhān's will, which stipulates that, on his death, his estate is to be divided equally among his heirs.[16] The notary stays on late in his office, and it is dark when he finally manages to put away his papers and leave the building. On his way out, he hears angry shouting from a neighboring courtyard, where Khāl Muḥammad and his associates have just broken into the house of Tūlaghān Āy, Khāl Muḥammad's divorced wife, and a quarrel over marital obligations is coming to blows. The next morning, assisted by her son, Tūlaghān Āy will file charges of assault and battery against her former husband in the Russian imperial court.[17]

This is a bricolage of judicial records of several legal proceedings at different times and in different places in Russian Central Asia. In connecting these stories, I have attempted to illustrate how events analogous to these could have occurred simultaneously in many cities in the region: the documentation produced by the Russian civil-military administration leaves little doubt of this. The cases I have pieced together from various records might, with a little latitude, be seen as a snapshot of a routine day in an urban Central Asian courtroom during the period of Russian rule: an urban Muslim notable obtaining a ruling from the judge of a native court applying *sharīʿa*; a case involving Kazakhs in the room next door being determined according to customary law; and a variety of other indigenous legal protagonists requesting that their cases be heard under Russian civil and penal law.

14 *Sharīʿa* court register (Beshagach district, Tashkent), entry no. 3, 25.04.1882, TsGARUz, f. I-36, op. 1, d. 2170, l. 2.

15 Certificate of amicable settlement (*ṣulḥ*) produced by Kazakh arbitrators (*bīlār*) in Tashkent, 07.07.1868, TsGARUz, f. I-36, op. 1, d. 434, l. 11. I translated it and commented on it in "The Birth of a Custom: Nomads, *Sharīʿa* Courts and Established Practices in the Tashkent Province, ca. 1868–1919." *ILS* 18/3–4 (2011): 304–305.

16 TsGARUz, f. I-365, op. 1, d. 94, ll. 2–30b.

17 TsGARUz, f. I-21, op. 1, d. 59.

Nothing in the examples I provide departs substantially from what had been envisaged by Russian planners. The statutory laws (*polozhenie*) applied in Central Asia specified that indigenous city dwellers and nomads should apply their own "custom"—Islamic law or customary law, respectively—and could also, if they wished, bring cases in the Russian imperial courts or take their grievances directly to the colonial administration.

Imagined between St. Petersburg and Tashkent, this was the legal order of an empire's colony into which new paradigms of legality were to be introduced. The legal system was designed to draw the indigenous population closer to the sphere of influence of imperial law and encourage Central Asians to adopt new, more "civilized" patterns of conduct. In this respect, the Russians were pursuing an ambitious project of cultural engineering, one element of which sought to transform the ways their colonial subjects could seek and achieve legal redress. Underlying this project lay an unquestioned faith in the cultural superiority of imperial law to local customs, well articulated in the words of Virginia Martin: "in order to effect change and promote progress [...] toward abidance by the rule of law (*zakonnost'*), Russian officials would rule their subjects by example, with 'benevolent guidance' not force or imposition."[18]

Russians no doubt regarded native courts as temporary institutions[19] that would soon be replaced by imperial judicial institutions called "justices of the peace" (*mirovoi sud*). The colonial legal project was based on the idea that local legal cultures would one day give way to new ideas of civic mindedness and that the cultural diversity between the colonizers and their subjects would be eliminated in favor of the introduction of the rule of law: "[native courts] can be tolerated under certain restrictions only. Leaving this system in place [...] will bring about a decrease of its importance, while our legal system will conquer the trust of the people."[20] The introduction of imperial law was, however, constantly deferred.[21] Several governors-general and other officials did attempt to do away with the native courts but, as happened in other colonial judicial settings, such projects were not brought to fruition. By retaining the native courts until the last days of the empire, the Russians never came close to achieving that universalizing governmentality to which they had long aspired.[22] Far from achieving universality, they reinforced difference. This does not mean, however, that the Russians failed to extend imperial law among the Muslim communities of Central Asia. Contrary to the view that only rarely

18 Martin, *Law and Custom in the Steppe*: 36.

19 Crews, *For Prophet and Tsar*: 268.

20 TsGARUz, f. I-1, op. 27, d. 68, ll. 3–3ob.

21 Crews, *For Prophet and Tsar*: 292.

22 J.L. Comaroff, Colonialism, Culture, and the Law: A Foreword." *LSI* 26 (2011): 306–7.

did Central Asians bring their grievances before the justices of peace,[23] locals often did ask that their cases be heard according to Russian law.[24] Admittedly, this generally happened in unusual situations in which Muslims found themselves unable to negotiate their grievances within the Muslim community and had to appeal to an alternative court. Muslims most probably brought far fewer legal actions before imperial forums than they did before the native courts. Regardless of the frequency of such actions, however, appeals by Muslims to the colonial administration reveal the force of the imperial episteme, reinforcing, as they did, the logic behind the civilizing mission of the Russian Empire.

In adopting, as I do, the imperial term "native court" (*narodnyi sud*), I want to suggest that we are dealing with an institution designed for the colony and, consequently, with an institutional innovation. This is not to suggest, of course, that the Russians invented the office of *qāḍī* nor that they made up Islamic law. Even a cursory comparison of the notarial output of *qāḍī*s before and after the establishment of Russian rule allows us to appreciate the persistence of many formulaic expressions. Continuities in the formulaic character of Islamic notarial output reflect the degree to which *qāḍī*s' legalese was a conservative language that remained stable throughout the centuries[25] and was scarcely susceptible to adaptations. If, however, one had to read the social history of the native courts from the point of view of their notary activity, one would misidentify the changes that occurred in the practice of Islamic law. By embedding *sharīʿa* in the colonial institutional edifice, Russians necessarily changed many of the attributes of Central Asian Islamic judicature. In the eyes of the colonizers, a *qāḍī* was now a "native judge" (*narodnyi sud'ia*), that is, a local official who served the empire and, as such, could receive rewards for his labor and was entitled to a retirement pension.[26] Central Asians, by contrast, regarded *qāḍī*s as the guarantors of Islamic law in Russian Turkestan but did not find in them the same men who had represented the traditional legal regime that operated under the khans' rule. Continuities with the past were observable more in theory than in practice. The courts presided over by *qāḍī*s, which once were accountable directly to the royal courts and to governors and which were regularly visited by bailiffs and mediators, became under Russian rule, "*qāḍī* courts" (*kaziiskie sudy*) that were answerable only to the Russians.

---

23 Crews, *For Prophet and Tsar*: 261.

24 See Chapter 4.

25 Ol'ga Chekhovich wrote a magnum opus on this subject, which remains unpublished. See her *Istoriia razvitiia aktov iuridicheskogo oformleniia feodal'nykh otnoshenii v Srednei Azii XII-XVI vv.* (written in Tashkent 1979), unpublished manuscript, TsGARUz, f. R-2678, op. 1, d. 60.

26 TsGARUz, f. I-1, op. 2, d. 1023.

Needless to say, *qāḍīs* were now operating in a juridical field that was substantively different from the one in which they used to live and which I outlined in Chapter 1.

In this chapter, I will show that the establishment of native courts entailed both advantages and disadvantages for local legists. I shall do so by eavesdropping on the life of a Tashkent "native judge," Muḥyī al-Dīn Khwāja. A man of distinguished juristic pedigree—his father, Muḥammad Ḥakīm Khwāja Īshān, had served as chief judge (*qāḍī kalān*) in Tashkent under the rule of Khoqand—Muḥyī al-Dīn Khwāja was one of the most prominent personalities, not only in the colonial juridical field but also in the wider public space of colonial Tashkent. His Russian-language obituary, by the famous Orientalist Nikolai Ostroumov,[27] leaves little doubt about the importance of the role that Muḥyī al-Dīn Khwāja played as cultural broker (*posrednikom mezhdu etoi vlast'iu i narodom*) at the heart of the Governorship-General. Ostroumov's recollections about Muḥyī al-Dīn Khwāja are almost exclusively enthusiastic, praising the Muslim legist for implementing the new laws of the empire and his exemplary conduct that persuaded others to come closer (*k sblizheniiu*) to the Russians. Ostroumov knew many things about Muḥyī al-Dīn Khwāja, especially his dealings with imperial officials. Not only does Ostroumov tell how Muḥyī al-Dīn Khwāja attended events of great significance both in the metropole and the colony and describe his two decorations with the orders of St. Stanislav and St. Anna; he also recounts how Muḥyī al-Dīn Khwāja was somehow "spoiled" (*izbalovanny*) by the exceptional degree of attention that Russian officials, including many generals and military governors, accorded him. Despite his defective knowledge of Russian, the Muslim legist became an insider also in the sometimes hostile spheres of the imperial bureaucracy.

If Ostroumov's obituary opens a window on a few important aspects of Muḥyī al-Dīn Khwāja's world, his apparel, and lifestyle—including a "special room" (*osobaia komnata*) that he had fashioned in the style of a Russian house in order to welcome European guests—it also suppresses many other facets of his personality. The repeated elections to the position of *narodnyi sud'ia* offered Muḥyī al-Dīn Khwāja many chances to accrue wealth as a landowner in both the city and the garden belt outside the walls of Tashkent. At his death, he left an impressive paper trail that documents his various transactions designed to increase his wealth in land and cash. Most of his properties followed the

27 Reprinted in N.P. Ostroumov, *Sarty. Ėtnograficheskie materialy* (*obshchii ocherk*), 3rd ed. (Tashkent: Tip. Gazety "Sredneaziatskaia Zhizn'," 1908): 125–31.

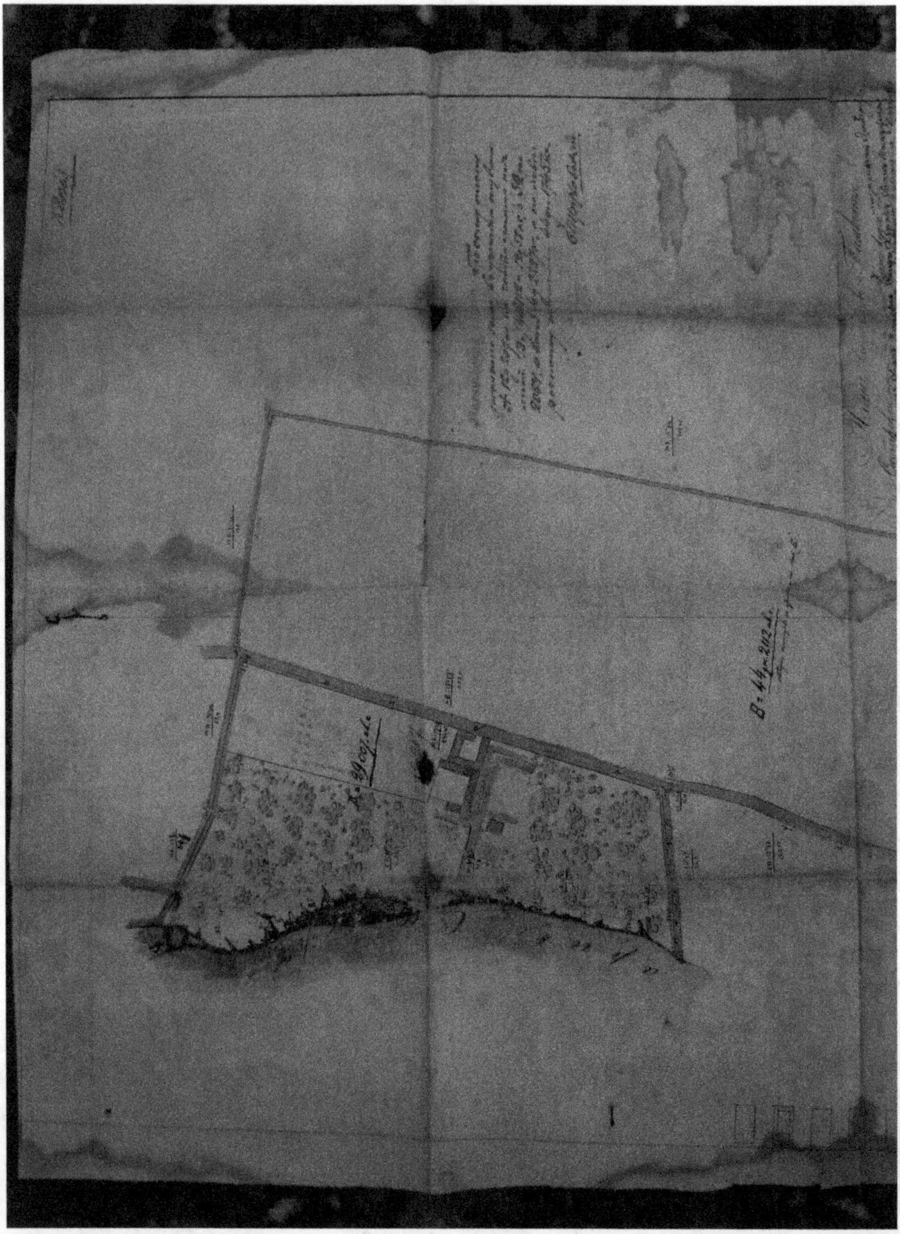

FIGURE 7 *Detail of a map illustrating Muḥyī al-Dīn Khwāja's possessions in the vicinity of the Anhor canal, Tashkent.*
COURTESY OF VOLIDA AHROROVA AND HAMIDULLO QABULNIYOZOV

rules of devolution of the Islamic law of inheritance, the traces of which we today find scattered in the Central State Archive of Uzbekistan and the private collections of the offspring of his niece, Vosila Ahrorova.[28]

By serving the empire as a *qāḍī*, he also often acted in the capacity of guardian for underage children, having at his disposal large amounts of cash that allowed him to operate somewhat freely as a money lender.[29] His role as go-between is also important for the character of Muḥyī al-Dīn Khwāja. As we shall see in Chapter 5, his juristic output, especially that which he produced in conversation with Russian officials, combined Islamic writing traditions, such as fatwas and juristic tracts, with extended reflections on Russian statutory laws and bureaucratic practices.

As his patrimony and influence grew, however, so did the number of his enemies among both the locals and Russian officials. Tashkentis repeatedly accused him of bribery, judicial malpractice, and abuse of power. Imperial bureaucrats spied on him and concocted stratagems to remove him from office. He had to step down only once, in the wake of the 1892 "cholera riot," which has beautifully reconstructed Jeff Sahadeo.[30] The figure of Muḥyī al-Dīn Khwāja is both exceptional and exemplary of the biographies of many other native judges, who could exploit bureaucratic and political resources to amass considerable wealth;[31] who enjoyed unprecedented leeway in levying fines and other sanctions;[32] and who ultimately were subjected to increased criticism with respect to both their morality and their skills as legists.

28 Vosila Ahrorova (b. 10.01.1926) is the daughter of Muḥyī al-Dīn Khwāja's youngest son, Sayyid Ahrār Khān. The latter must have inherited most of the codices and lithographs that constituted Muḥyī al-Dīn Khwāja's private library, while his deeds probably went to his other two sons. The Central State Archive of Uzbekistan acquired a significant number of such deeds in 1939 from a certain Zafar Alimov. See the introduction to the description, called *Tashkentskii Kazi Kalian*, of the two inventories (*opisi*) that describe the collection I-164.

29 I have discussed this in "Constructing Colonial Legality in Russian Central Asia: On Guardianship." *CSSH* 56/2 (2014): 419–47.

30 J. Sahadeo, *Russian Colonial Society in Tashkent, 1863–1923* (Bloomington: Indiana University Press: 2007): 94–107, esp. 104–5.

31 G.A. Arendarenko, *Dosugi v Turkestane, 1874–1889* (St. Petersburg: Tipografiia M.M. Stasiulevich, 1889): 169.

32 *Otchet po revizii Turkestanskogo kraia po Vysochaishemu poveleniiu Senatorom Gofmeisterom Grafom K.K. Palenom. Narodnye Sudy Turkestanskogo Kraia*. This is noted in Crews, *For Prophet and Tsar*: 268.

1 Reforms

The incorporation of local bodies of law into the legal system of the empire was designed in accordance with imperial legal planners' notion of "reform." *Reforma* was the key word used by Russian officers and administrators when they drew up regulations to make the application of Central Asian law more efficient and to make sure that the legal practice of local communities complied with imperial standards.[33] From the following discussion, however, it will be clear that such reform amounted to redrawing the scope of the jurisdiction of the *qāḍīs*. Procedural law, too, necessarily underwent a profound transformation. But such transformation was less proclaimed than subtly labored during the endless back-and-forth between the offices of the colonial administration. The changes of day-to-day notarial and judicial practice in Islamic law did not respond only to the will of Russian legal planners.

The establishment of Russian rule in Central Asia coincided with the drafting of the Provisional Statute (*Proekt Polozheniia*), a set of temporary regulations issued in July 1867. It was, however, the 1886 Statute[34] (partially amended in 1901) that provided colonial authorities with guidelines for regulating the life of local peoples. With regard to the practice of law, the major difference between the 1867 and the 1886 statutory laws consisted in the latter's replacement of imperial tribunals, once exclusively staffed by the military, with justices of the peace. It took at least two decades to separate the judicial from the administrative powers. Predictably, many administrative-military personnel did not like such a rearrangement, which endowed Russians officials and Muslim subjects with the same legal standing in a public court.[35] Despite resistance from parts of the colonial elite, beginning in 1886 justices of the peace in Turkestan began work. In the absence of the communes, however, the justices serving in these courts were not elected by the local communities but were appointed directly by the ministry.[36]

The 1886 statute (§ 117) stated that there were, in general, three instances of justice in Russian Turkestan: the justice of the peace, who operated at

33 N. Frideriks, "Turkestan i ego reform." *Vestnik Evropy* 6 (1869): 691–712.

34 *Polozhenie ob upravlenii Turkestanskogo kraia.* (*2 iiunia 1886 g*). In *Materialy po istorii politicheskogo stroia Kazakhstana* (*so vremeni prisoedineniia Kazakhstana k Rossii do Velikoi Oktiabr'skoi sotsialisticheskoi revoliutsii*). ed. M.G. Masevich (Alma-Ata: Izdatel'stvo Akademii Nauk Kazakhskoi SSR, 1960): 1:352–79.

35 N. Mordvinov, *Zapiska k proektu o sudebnoi reforme v Turkestanskom krae*, 1891, TsGARUz, f. I-18, op. 1, d. 139, ll. 2–5ob.

36 J. Baberowski, "Law, the Judicial System, and the Legal Profession." In *The Cambridge History of Russia*, vol. 2, *Imperial Russia, 1689–917*, ed. Dominic Lieven (Cambridge: Cambridge University Press, 2006): 358.

the district (*uezd*) level, a court in each province (*oblast'*), and the senate (*senat*).[37] These institutions had jurisdiction over the entire population of the Governorship-General of Turkestan (§ 140). They ruled on crimes perpetrated against the government, the Orthodox Church, the fiscal system, and the public (for example, deceit, treason, incitement of opposition to the government, damage to telegraph lines, murder, usurpation, and robbery) (§ 141), and they had jurisdiction over every kind of crime or tort perpetrated by a native against a Russian (§ 142). In addition to these courts presided over by Russian officials, there were native courts, which acted "on the basis of existing customs" (*na osnovanii sushchestvuiushchikh* [...] *obychaev*) (§ 208), where "custom" was a notion broad enough to include *sharīʿa*. These courts could hear only cases in which the parties came from the indigenous population. In the native courts, legal proceedings were conducted in accordance with either Islamic or tribal customary law. A court was chaired by a single judge operating within a clearly delimited territorial jurisdiction. This was not an innovation, as territoriality had long been a characteristic of the office of *qāḍī*.[38] What was new, however, was the notion that "the jurisdiction of civil actions is determined by the place of residence of the defendant, while for penal cases it is defined by the place in which the crime has been perpetrated" (§ 212), that is, what is often referred to in legal language as *actor sequitur forum rei*.[39] A consultative judicial body (Russ., s"*ezd*) with several judges represented a tribunal of appeal whose decisions were definitive (§ 240). In addition, the colonial rulers introduced norms that interfered with local legal systems: 1) if both parties agreed, Muslims could bring a case to a justice of the peace or to an *oblast'* court (§ 213); 2) by lodging a complaint in the chancery of the district commandant, a Muslim could appeal a decision of a people's court (§ 243). These regulations were drafted to enable the colonial government to become directly involved in administering justice over its subaltern subjects but might also disrupt the extension of the rule of law to the colony: though statutory laws hinged on a separation of powers many conflicts were, as we shall see, resolved directly by having the military

37 In Russian Turkestan, a *uezd* denoted a district with a population of 250,000 or more; an *oblast'* was a province ruled by a governor and having a population of up to one million; cf. Morrison, *Russian Rule in Samarkand, 1868–1910: A Comparison with British India*: xxiv.

38 My opinion here differs from Crews, *For Prophet and Tsar*: 268, and from Morrison, *Russian Rule in Samarkand, 1868–1910: A Comparison with British India*: 249, who relies on L. Kostenko, *Sredniaia Aziia i vodvorenie v nei Russkoi Grazdhanstvennosti* (St. Petersburg: V. Beozobrazov, 1870): 63–64.

39 The article was not amended in the 1901 Statute but was rubricated as article 214; see *Polozhenie ob upravlenii Turkestanskogo kraia s izmenieniiami i dopolneniiami po 1-e ianvaria 1901 g.* (Tashkent: Tip. Porcevykh, 1901).

man the key offices in the administration of the Governorship-General on the basis of their own extrajudicial considerations. Such regulations were often conducive to authoritarianism, especially when military officers ruled on cases at their own discretion. This situation resembles what the Italian philosopher Giorgio Agamben terms a "state of exception,"[40] that is to say, a suspension of judicial authority that strengthens the executive powers of the state and leaves its subjects to face the disciplinarian whims of law.

The most noteworthy reform introduced by the Russians in Central Asia in the realm of indigenous law during nearly five decades of rule involved the method of appointment to the office of judge. The colonial government decided that native judges would be elected every three years. The system was not based on direct voting: instead, ballots were cast only by representatives of fifty households (called *īllīkbāshī*) in the communities in every defined area of settlement, such as a city district or a village. To become effective, the results of elections had to be confirmed by the colonial authorities. This applied to settled communities electing their *qāḍīs*. In the same way, nomads were to elect the judges (*bīs*) for *ʿādat*-based courts.

In general, the colonial government attempted to limit the jurisdiction of *qāḍīs* to cases of personal status, succession, and charitable endowments. Native judges, however, informally retained authority over criminal offenses such as usurpation of land,[41] assault, rape, and robbery, despite the criminal offences falling officially under the jurisdiction of the justices of the peace.[42] They also introduce a sanction-oriented provisions in order to replace the *ḥudūd* system, that is, a set of fixed punishments for offenses that are considered under Islamic law to be "violations of the claims of God (*ḥuqūq Allāh*)"[43] and over the application of which the judge has no discretion. The basic guidelines for the reorganization of the judiciary in Central Asia under the umbrella of Russian rule are to be found in the judicial reform signed by Alexander II in 1864, which called for avoiding arbitrariness, allowing oral argumentations, and holding public trials. More specifically, Russian administrators sought to introduce immediately into the Central Asian legal environment the idea that

40 G. Agamben, *State of Exception*, trans. K. Attell (Chicago: University of Chicago Press, 2005).

41 *Zhurnal soveta Turkestanskogo General-Gubernatora*, 22.11.1891, TsGARUz, f. I-717, op. 1, d. 6, ll. 495–512.

42 Martin, *Law and Custom*: 92. See, e.g., the following cases of animal theft in the Sībzār *qāḍī*-court register for the year 1899: TsGARUz, f. I-365, op. 1, d. 74, ll. 45, 77, 83, 117, 149, 155.

43 R. Peters, *Crime and Punishment in Islamic Law: Theory and Practice from the Sixteenth to the Twenty-First Century* (Cambridge: Cambridge University Press, 2005): 7.

judges should be independent, being elected by the members of their community.[44] This marked an epochal change: under the rule of the khans, judges and anyone else providing legal services used to be appointed directly by the royal court. An observer contemporary with the Russian reforms noted that the introduction of elections to the native judge's office, the establishment of judicial assemblies as tribunals of second instance,[45] and the abolition of corporal punishments ultimately shattered the previous *qāḍī* courts (*sobstvenno govoria, sovershenno unichtozhil prezhnii kaziiskii sud*).[46]

What the colonizers termed "judicial reforms" amounted, then, more to the restriction of the jurisdiction of the native courts than a complete refashioning of legal tradition. The Russians in Central Asia never pursued this more ambitious latter goal, framing their juridical reforms instead in that larger strategy of noninterference (*ignorirovanie*) that sought to avoid stirring up local feelings of discontent. "To exert violence upon the people is to ignite that spark that will light a fire,"[47] declared an official supporting the idea that criminal offenses such as animal theft and murder should be left in the purview of *ʿādat* courts. We could call this a pragmatic solution. Understaffed as it was, the colonial government in Turkestan would not, in any case, have had the means to introduce the rule of law by force. But there was more. The colonizers believed that, in the long run, introducing new legal practices and integrating them with existing ones would lead the local population to lose respect for their

44 Baberowski, "Law, the Judicial System, and the Legal Profession" 344–68.

45 Russian officers often claimed that consultative judicial bodies (§ 240) were an institution that already existed in precolonial Central Asia. One of the most eloquent advocates of this view was the state counsellor (*deistvitel'nii statskii sovetnik*) Ivan Ivanovich Kraft (1861–1914). In his work on the legal system in Russian Turkestan, he held that "[people] who were dissatisfied by the rulings of the *qāḍīs* appealed to the governor upon whose order cases were transferred to consultative judicial bodies" (*ne dovolnye resheniiami kaziev prinosili appeliatsii beku, po rasporiazheniiu kotorogo dela peredevalis' na reshenie s"ezda kaziev*); cf. I.I. Kraft, *Sudebnaia chast' v Turkestanskom krae i v stepnykh oblastiakh* (Orenburg: Tipo litografiia N.N. Zharinova, 1898): 61. This was plainly false. Just a few decades after the publication of Kraft's work, the Soviet Orientalist Aleksander A. Semenov explained that the local judicial system did not include appellation or cassation; see his *Ocherk ustroistva tsentral'nogo administrativnogo upravleniia Bukharskogo khanstva pozdneishego vremeni* (Stalinabad: Izdatel'stvo Akademii Nauk Tadzhikskoi SSR: 1954): 31–2.

46 *Otchet po revizii Turkestanskogo kraia po Vysochaishemu poveleniiu Senatorom Gofmeisterom Grafom K.K. Palenom. Narodnye Sudy Turkestanskogo Kraia* (St. Petersburg: Senatskaia Tipografiia, 1909): 8.

47 TsGARUz, f. I-1, op. 27, d. 68, l. 15.

mores and choose the purportedly more civilized imperial tribunals.[48] This belief was based on the idea that the native judges' corruption (*podkupnost'*) would inevitably undermine the credibility of *sharīʿa* to the advantage of the imperial tribunals.[49] Establishing native courts was thus seen as a temporary concession to the local subjects to gain their trust.

Measuring the extent of the reordering of the indigenous legal systems is important not only for discerning the motives of the legal reforms but also for recognizing their unintended consequences. Judicial reforms, though important and substantive, stopped at the threshold of procedural law. Fine-grained Russian-language treatises devoted to the mechanics of Islamic law were conspicuous by their absence. After decades of experience in Central Asia, lawmakers' intentional avoidance of engaging with *qāḍīs*' hearings suggests a particular vision of colonial intervention in the realm of indigenous law. Russians' plans of legal reforms apparently did not envisage codification. Codification was a performative representation of cultural domination as well as a successful tool for transforming Islamic law from a jurists' law into a statutory law. Statutory law consisted of a clear set of rules, a code, that we see applied in other Muslim-majority regions under colonial rule and that, in general, helped to make *sharīʿa* a consistent and predictable legal system.[50] With the sole exception of the attempt made by Count Pahlen at the beginning of the twentieth century, the codification of *sharīʿa* was long disregarded as an instrument of rule in Russian Turkestan.[51]

2 Elections

Electing their own judges (and tax officials) was, for Muslims in Central Asia, a break with the past.[52] In precolonial times the centralized administration of

---

48 G. Zagriazhskii, "O narodnom sude u kochevago naseleniia Turkestanskago kraia, po obychnomu pravu (zan')." In *Materialy dlia statistiki Turkestanskago kraia*, ed. N.A. Maeva (St. Petersburg: Tip. Transhelia, 1876): 4:190; Kraft, *Sudebnaia chast' v Turkestanskom krae i v stepnykh oblastiakh*: 92.

49 TsGARUz, f. I-1, op. 27, d. 68, l. 30b, 4.

50 A. Layish, "The Transformation of the *Sharīʿa* from Jurists' Law to Statutory Law in the Contemporary Muslim World." *WDI* 44/1 (2004): 85–113.

51 A. Morrison, "Creating a Colonial Shariʿa for Russian Turkestan: Count Pahlen, the Hidaya and the Anglo-Muhammadan Law." In *Imperial Cooperation and Transfer, 1870–1930: Empires and Encounters*, ed. V. Barth and R. Cvetkovski (London: Bloomsbury, 2015): 127–49.

52 *Otchet po revizii Turkestanskogo kraia po Vysochaishemu poveleniiu Senatorom Gofmeisterom Grafom K.K. Palenom. Narodnye Sudy Turkestanskogo Kraia*: 8.

the khanates had appointed its representatives (*ʿamaldār*), even at the village level. The appointment to a certain administrative position was conceived as a means of establishing reciprocity between the state and its representatives, based on an exchange of favors: if an administrator proved loyal to the state, he would enjoy certain benefits, the most common being tax exemption.[53] This meant that, behind an appointment made by the local ruler or representatives of the state, there were often factions lobbying for an official administrative position. As an endorsement from a local governor usually involved fiscal privileges, these benefits were probably redistributed among the group who supported a candidature.[54] We have seen the ritualized repertoire of conferral of appointments to judicial offices in the Bukharan emirate and in Khorezm. The situation was similar in Tashkent under Khoqandi rule, where diplomas of appointment to the position of *qāḍī* were issued up to the eve of the Russian conquest.[55] Local groups lobbied to have their members appointed directly to some judicial capacity until the introduction of the Provisional Statute in 1867.[56]

Introducing the electoral process for the appointment of native judges among the Muslim population marked a first important event that would test the strength of the Russian government. At the beginning of 1868, a special commission was given the task of explaining to the locals the main traits of the Provisional Statute.[57] The commission that was created to mediate

53 R.N. Nabiev, *Iz istorii kokandskogo khanstva* (*Feodal'noe kkhoziaistvo Khudoiar-Khana*) (Tashkent: Fan, 1973): 242 and passim. Such fiscal privileges could be bestowed as a *tarkhān* status granting immunity mainly "to religious figures such as prominent Sufis or members of sacred lineages," W. Wood, *A Collection of Tarkhan Yarliqs from the Khanate of Khiva*. Papers on Inner Asia 38 (Bloomington: Indiana University Research Institute for Inner Asian Studies, 2005): 29–30. This is true also for other regions of precolonial Central Asia, such as the Ferghana Valley; cf. A. Juvonmardiev, *XVI–XIX asrlarda Farghonada er-suv masalalariga doir* (Tashkent: Fan, 1965): docs. 18/42, 105/71, 6/81. A state appointment to an official post did not, ipso facto, imply the privileges described.

54 A. Wilde, "Creating the Façade of a Despotic State: On *Āqsaqāls* in Late 19th-Century Bukhara." In *Explorations in the Social History of Modern Central Asia* (*19th–Early 20th Centuries*), ed. P. Sartori (Leiden: Brill, 2013): 267–98.

55 Copy of a diploma for the appointment of Abū al-Khayr Khwāja Ẓāhir to the office of *qāḍī* for the city of Turkestan and the Kazakh tribal groups (*īlāt*) of the province, March-April 1865, TsGARUz, f. I-336, op. 1, d. 14, ll. 129–30.

56 Naẓar Khwāja Shaykh al-Islām to Cherniaev, with a request to appoint a certain Mullā ʿAbd al-Ṣamad Qāḍī to office, n.d., TsGARUz, f. I-336, op. 1, d. 14, l. 128; see another petition of local residents and notables to appoint Mullā ʿUmar Qāḍī, n.d., TsGARUz, f. I-336, op. 1, d. 14, l. 131ob.

57 F. Azadaev, *Tashkent vo vtoroi polovine XIX veka. Ocherki sotsial'no-ekonomicheskoi i politicheskoi istorii* (Tashkent: Izdatel'stvo Akademii Nauk Uzbekskoi SSR, 1959): 96.

between the Russians and the local population on issues pertaining to elections included Tashkenti *ʿulamāʾ* such as Ḥakīm Khwāja, who had served as *qāḍī kalān* (chief judge) under the rule of Khoqandi, other *qāḍī*s such as ʿAzīzlār Khwāja, and other notables such as the merchants Sayyid ʿAẓīm Bāy and ʿAẓīm Āqsaqāl. Needing to implement institutional changes, the Russians obviously relied on the local elite, which included a learned hierarchy (mullahs and *makhdhūms*) and individuals claiming the status of the descendants of saints (*sayyids*, *khwājas*). But the distinguished titles attached to personal names leave little doubt that the commission consisted chiefly of the old Tashkenti establishment: *qāḍī, muftī, aʿlam, bāy*, and *āqsaqāl* are titles of status attached to the names of the members of the commission and reminiscent of older power relations. They also chart a space of moral authority that the Russians had yet to invade.[58] The colonial masters soon became aware of the challenges posed by the constituency on which they relied. Besides indulging in the usual Orientalist tropes in characterizing their local interlocutors—for example, "apathetic" (*apatichnym i vialym*) and "underdeveloped" (*po nerazvitosti svoei*)—Russians noted how difficult it would be to break the older bonds of reciprocity and unfold all instances of machination against them. They also sensed that the members of the commission were, as go-betweens, less concerned with the commission's proclaimed goals than with the necessity of pleasing colonial officials and the *ʿulamāʾ*.[59] Reviewing the following passage[60] from the records of the 1868 electoral commission will help us appreciate the complicated nature of what the Russians sought to achieve:

> The chairman [of the commission] asked whether they [members of the commission] know what [the ballots] are collected for, what the elections are, and what depends on them. The population should know that they do not have to hesitate to elect whom they want; the administration hopes that good people will be elected. The populace must keep in mind that, under the former governments, it was the rulers who appointed [judicial] officials who did not care about the people, oppressed [the locals], extorted illegal fees, and abused their power. The current government, on the contrary, cares about its subjects and deems it necessary that officials be elected by the people and approved by the people's superiors, for people know better who are the good individuals and who can

58 See the charts of local representatives of the Tashkent city district, TsGARUz, f. I-1, op. 16, d. 66, ll. 12–13.

59 Ibid.: l. 65ob.

60 Ibid.: l. 36.

> be useful. Elections for these positions will take place every three years, and the people cannot change [elected] officials before their three-year term is up. If they find anything [wrong about such appointees], let them bring a complaint to the commandant of Tashkent. As they listened to all the things the chairman had to say, the members [of the commission] answered that they understood everything. They thanked the authorities for their care and expressed the belief that good people would be chosen, given that the elections would affect their own well-being. The chairman then explained the electoral procedure. Everyone entitled to elect [a native judge] should write the name of one candidate on a note and drop it in a box. Those who are illiterate should apply to Ibragimov, one of the translators. When all select a name and drop their ballots into the poll, the box will be opened in the presence of all the electors: he who receives the most votes will be elected to the post.

When the commission touched on the issue of the election of the native judges, it was objected by a Tashkent clique that the electoral procedure contravened *sharīʿa*. The commission responded to this objection in a way that would later become standard for collaborations among the colonizers and the *ʿulamāʾ*. They tried to find a solution from within the Islamic juristic tradition and requested a fatwa to answer the following questions: could Muslims, where the ruler is not a Muslim, still perform their prayers on Friday and during major festivities? And could they appoint a *qāḍī*?[61] In response to these questions, the jurists concluded that Muslims can join in assembly (*jamāʿa*) and reach an agreement (*ittifāq*) to appoint to the office of judge (*qāḍī-yi Islām*) a man knowledgeable in Islamic law. Formulating this opinion amounted to little more than glossing in Persian and Chaghatay what could be found in such established collections of legal opinions as the thirteenth-century *Fuṣūl al-ʿImādī*[62] and the fifteenth-

61 TsGARUz, f. I-1, op. 16, d. 66, ll. 7–6. Text unstamped.

62 This is a work also known as *Fuṣūl al-iḥkām fī uṣūl al-aḥkām*, compiled in Samarkand by ʿImād al-Dīn Abu al-Fatḥ ʿAbd al-Raḥīm Zayn al-Dīn b. Abū Bakr al-Samarqandī (d. ca. 1271). See *GAL* SI: 382 (656). It was a text widely used by Muslim jurists in Central Asia and is quoted extensively in the opinions issued by the jurists and in the lists of books left by local scholars; cf. *Isāmī-yi kitābhā-yi mawjūda ba dast-i faqīr az manqūlāt-i bahr al-manāfiq*, MS Samarkand, Library of the Historical Museum of Samarkand, 4089/9, fol. 3r. The list bears the seal of Mullā Abū al-Qāsim Muftī, which is dated 1322/1904–5; see also N.P. Ostroumov, *Islamovedenie. Shariat po shkole (mazkhab) Abu-Khanify* (Tashkent: Tip. Pri Kants. Turk. Gen.-Gub: 1912): 17; A. Idrisov, A. Muminov, and M. Szuppe, *Manuscrits en écriture arabe du Musée regional de Nukus (République autonome du Karakalpakstan,*

century *Jāmiʿ al-fatāwā*.[63] The colonial innovation of the elections had, in this way, survived the permissibility test of Islamic law.[64] It was neither an attempt to comply with Islamic "orthodoxy" nor a pretext to draw new boundaries around the attributes of the *qāḍī*. Soliciting this fatwa was simply a way for the commission to rebut objections to the innovation of the elections.

The introduction of the new regulation reflected a pragmatic approach to the deregulation of judicial authority. In the early 1860s, the colonizers did not know much about Central Asia and feared the traditional patronage system of the khans. They therefore hoped that the locals would, if granted the right to vote, choose the most respectable person among their peers (*bolee pochitaemoe litso*), a person whose moral virtues would also guarantee that he would be skilled in administrative work. Colonial officers could thus avoid, they thought, the risk of choosing the wrong person, as this was no longer their responsibility.[65] Russians, however, retained the power to confirm the results of the elections. In this way, they had, in principle, the last say on every elected candidate. In some cases, the Russians certainly used such power to appoint to office jurists who, they thought, would best serve their interests. Here is one such case:

> Commandant of Tashkent
> to the Military Governor of Syr-Darya Province
> April 8–9 1874
>
> Report
> According to the regulations of your Excellency dated 22 September 1873 no. 6904, I have organized the election of *qāḍī*s […] for the next triennium. Consequently, I have the honor to request the approval of […] the individuals elected to the aforesaid positions, whose names I here enclose. In this case, I consider it necessary to report that I thought to confirm ʿAẓīm Khān in the post of *qāḍī* in the Besh-Agach district, even though [he received] fewer votes. He has already served two to three years [in the same capacity] and has proved himself capable of continuing this activity not only in a way that does not cause any harm to our

---

Ouzbékistan). *Fonds arabe, persan, turkī et karakalpak* (Rome: Istituto per l'Oriente C.A. Nallino, 2007): 82.

63 A work by Qirq Emre al-Ḥamīdī al-Ḥanafī (d. 1475), see *GAL* SII: 226 (316).

64 TsGARUz, f. I-1, op. 16, d. 66, l. 3.

65 Ershov, "Neskol'ko slov o vyborakh." *TV* 75 (1908): 105. In 1885, the commandant of the Perovsk District noted that the natives should blame themselves (*vina samogo naroda*) for their inability to elect skillful candidates, TsGaRUz, f. I-17, op. 1, d. 4082, l. 19.

> interests but also, in some cases, in a manner that is very helpful to us. Meanwhile, the majority of the inhabitants of the Besh-Agach [district], whose population consists of *īshāns* [Ṣūfī masters], has voted for 'Aẓīm-Khwāja Īshān, who, like all *īshāns*, is among the most bigoted servants of Islam. This *īshān* distinguishes himself from other citizens even by his clothes: he is always dressed in white, he walks without shoes, and in general represents, in the eyes of the ignorant crowd of their worshippers, some kind of saint. [...] I wish that our government would not allow such a fanatic to attain the office of *qāḍī*. He is the one who not only fulfills the duties of a judge among the Asiatic population but who also has very often engaged in the interpretation and explanation of the rules and regulations of the *sharī'a* to the population. Indeed, with the upcoming introduction of a new statute in the region, an official of so fanatical a disposition will be very harmful. Therefore I humbly beg and plead Your Excellency to approve 'Aẓīm Khān for the next triennium as a man already tested.[66]

In assessing the impact of the elections on the career of the legists, one should bear in mind that far more *qāḍīs* were active in Russian Turkestan than was the case under the khans: "in every hole they [the Russians] made one policeman (*mīngbāshī*), one *qāḍī*, seven trustees (*amīn*), and fourteen *īllikbāshīs*," noted the chronicler Mīrzā 'Ālim Tāshkandī in 1884, observing how, in the district of Khoqand alone, there were now twenty judges.[67] Pahlen's report indicates that, at the beginning of the twentieth century, 275 native judges were serving in Turkestan, many more jurists than were appointed as *qāḍī* before the Russian conquest. The case of Tashkent is telling: since 1868, four native judges were elected to office, one in each city district (*daha*), while under the rule of Khoqand there had been periods when one *qāḍī* was enough for the entire province, including the Qurama district, located south of Tashkent and inhabited mostly by Kazakhs.[68] Elections did not result in a continuous turnover

66 TsGARUz, f. I-36, op. 1, d. 883, ll. 31–32.

67 Mīrzā 'Ālim Tashkandī b. Dāmullā Mīrzā, *Ansāb al-ṣalāṭīn wa ta'rīkh al-khawāqīn*, MS Tashkent, TsVRUz, no. 1314/I: 170b.

68 *īlgārī zamānlārda ya'nī khānlārnī waqtlārīda Tāshkandda īkkī ūch qāḍī būlūr īdī wa gāhī bir qāḍī shahrnī tamām īshlārīn qīlūr īdī ḥattā ki bir qāḍī qūrama ūyāzīdāghī īshlārnī ham qīlūr īdī ammā Tāshkand shahrī ūrūsīya dawlatīgha tābi' būlghāndan sung ham bir nicha waqtlār tūrt dahagha bir qāḍī būlūb tūrdī*, Raḥīm Khwāja Īshān 'Alī Khwāja Īshān-ūghlī (*qāḍī* of the Sibzar district) to the Tashkent city commandant, 28.10.1893, TsGARUz, f. I-36, op. 1, d. 3494, l. 4. The information provided by the native judge is confirmed by diplomas of appointment to the office of *qāḍī* for the province (*wilāyat*) of Tashkent under the rule of the khans of Khoqand; see Dāmullā [the rest of the name is unlegible], 1822–3,

of legists as was the case under the rule of the khans and the emirs, nor did it lead to a great deal of instability: there were many judicial positions now to fill, and the electoral procedure was left in the hands of local actors. Positions were exchanged for money, and squabbles among local groups frequently followed elections to such posts.[69] Pahlen even referred to the election system as a complete failure because of bribery cases,[70] though prosecutors often found that such accusations were groundless. The colonial masters rarely overturned the outcome of judicial elections, as they were bound de jure to the will of those who voted. Nor can one discern much from the texts that voters produced to notify the colonial administration about their agreeing to the results of a particular election. Russians received a list of names with seals and signatures that looked as if it was designed to leave little room to intrude into the groups' dynamics, which led to the appointment of an individual to a post of native judge.[71] Such texts were termed "election documents" (Russ., *vyborny list*, Uzbek, *ṣāylāw khaṭṭ*),[72] but they were also termed, in local parlance, "letters of agreement" (*ittifāq-nāma*). Seldom do we recover in these documents the voices that could reveal the grubby details of the elections. In one such case, for example, we find that the selection of a candidate to a certain office was, in fact, a private enterprise arranged among a few individuals who later turned to the voters and asked them to draft a false "receipt" (*kfītānsa*, Russ., *kvitantsiia*).[73] As the voters could hide their machinations behind the succinct wording of their lists, we can assume that Russians did not have the power to reveal the truth behind such elections. The newly introduced electoral system created an atmosphere of suspicion, and enemies, as the *qāḍī* Muḥyī al-Dīn Khwāja explained:

TsGARUz, f. I-323, op. 2, d. 81, l. 1; Īshān Maḥmūd Khwāja Ẓahīr, 1810 and 1847, TsGARUz, f. I-323, op. 2, d. 89, l. 1 and d. 87, l. 1; Maḥmūd Khwāja Īshān, 1854, TsGARUz, f. I-323, op. 2, d. 88, l. 1. The situation varied from place to place. Until the end of the 1870s, Samarkand could count on just one *qāḍī*; see Arendarenko, *Dosugi v Turkestane*: 168–9; Morrison, *Russian Rule in Samarkand, 1868–1910: A Comparison with British India*: 259. The situation later changed drastically as is reflected also in the *sharīʿa*-based notary output in the province of Samarkand; see T. Welsford and N. Tashev, *A Catalogue of Arabic-Script Documents from the Samarqand Museum* (Samarkand and Istanbul: IICAS, 2012): passim.

69 See the discussions among Russian officials following the election of ʿĀdil Khwāja to the office of native judge; he had been opposed by ʿAẓīm Khwāja Īshān supported by the influential Sayyid ʿAẓīm Bāy, TsGARUz, f. I-36, op. 1, d. 883.

70 *Otchet po revizii Turkestanskogo kraia*: 11.

71 TsGARUz, f. I-164, op. 1, d. 50, l. 2.

72 TsGARUZ, f. I-36, op. 1, d. 883, l. 3.

73 Judicial report, 31.10.1892, TsGARUz, f. I-164, op. 1, d. 50, l. 4.

> To his Majesty, the Commandant of Tashkent. Appeal of the native judge of the Sibzar district of Tashkent, Muḥammad Muḥyī al-Dīn Khwāja Ishanov. 5 July 1897. Muhammad Khwāja ʿAbdū ʿAẓīm Khodzhinov sued me before the native court for a sum of more than 2,000 rubles. Because I am the respondent, the lawsuit has been transferred to the *qāḍī* of the Shaykhantaur district, who, on 14 April 1898, ruled against the claim on account of a lack of evidence. The plaintiff was dissatisfied with the decision and appealed to the assembly of native judges [*s"ezd narodnykh sudei*]. Because of the lack of personnel [...], Your Excellency has been pleased to order the appointment of new candidates to the post of judge. [...] In an attempt to safeguard not only my interests but also the interests of justice, which I have served as far as [I have been able] with honor for many years, I take the liberty of submitting to your Majesty some considerations with respect to the personnel of such judicial assembly. [...] It should be taken into account that the present case is the fruit of hatred towards me and desire for revenge, not only on the part of the plaintiff but also by the whole party hostile to me. The enmity of this party [*partiinaia vrazhda*] generates all sorts of rumors, and I would be very uncomfortable if I were to win this case: people in the city would begin to say that the composition of the assembly reflected [my] biased attitudes towards the case, as it included one who was my supporter or successor.[74]

Factionalism soon became the major result of the election system introduced by the Russians. The establishment of a tribunal of second instance (*s"ezd kaziev*) enjoying powers of judicial review, exacerbated local antipathies even further, as illustrated by the passage I have just quoted. Factionalism among the *ʿulamāʾ* was already widespread across Central Asia before colonization. The works of Ṣadr al-Dīn ʿĀynī and Ṣadr-i Ḍiyāʾ illustrate the conflicts between families and groups of scholars in Bukhara and show how the Manghit rulers exploited such conflicts for their own benefit.[75] They also illustrate how, in relating instances of factional rivalry, authors generally take a partisan view of events, sympathizing with one group against another. Ṣadr al-Dīn ʿĀynī thus depicts Badr al-Dīn, who was appointed to the position of chief judge by the Bukharan emir ʿAbd al-Aḥad, as "unrivalled in despotism and without equal in

74 Muḥyī al-Dīn Khwāja's appeal to the Tashkent city commandant, 06.02.1899, TsGARUz, f. I-36, op. 1, d. 3881, l. 11.

75 Ṣadr al-Dīn ʿĀynī, *Bukhārā inqilābīning taʾrīkhī*, ed. S. Shimada and S. Tosheva (Tokyo: Dept. of Islamic Area Studies, Center for Evolving Humanities, Graduate School of Humanities and Sociology, University of Tokyo, 2010): 54–57.

power" (*istibdādda bī-hamtā wa tadbīrda bī-mānand*).[76] Ṣadr-i Ḍiyā adopts a slightly different position, emphasizing instead how factionalism was reflected in the removal from office of individuals who had earlier been appointed by the opposing factions and the cooptation, instead, of people removed from their post. From Ṣadr-i Ḍiyā's highly colored account, we learn that, among the first institutional innovations materializing with his tenure as chief judge, Badr al-Dīn appointed to the position of madrasa instructor persons who had earlier been dismissed from the office of *qāḍī*, lacked sufficient knowledge, and were illiterate (*qāḍīyān-i maʿzūl rā ki aktharī bī-sawād wa bī-ʿilm būdand āwarda mudarris sākht*).[77]

The idiom changes significantly, however, when we turn to vernacular narratives produced during the Russian period. These works often depict elected members of the native administration so contemptuously that one wonders whether such portrayals are intended to serve some larger rhetorical purpose of critiquing colonial society. *Qāḍīs* who were elected to office under Russian rule are presented as dishonest, unqualified for judicial duties, and prone to bribery. The account offered by one of the last Khoqand chroniclers, Mīrzā ʿĀlim Tāshkandī, provides a vivid illustration of such a critical disposition towards the colonial administration and its native judges. I quote here one such passage that includes a portrayal of the new *qāḍīs* and is reminiscent of the caricatures one would find in the periodical press [Fig. 8]:

> They [the Russians] said that that they would elect [to the office of] *qāḍī* two honest men [*ba-diyānat ādam*], but they did not accept for the position of judge several honest and just mullahs who were among the scholars the wealthy [of Khoqand] had selected [as candidates]. Instead, they accepted as *qāḍī* the hopeless Makhdhūm Khwāja Kalān, who had been [previously] dismissed from office [but] who had [for the occasion] let his beard and mustache grow. Moreover, they accepted as judge also one Mullā Mīr Maʿsūm, who is the son of the [former] chief judge Dāmullā Muḥammad Yūsuf. They [the Russians] gave them a robe, and [this is how] they turned them into *qāḍīs*. [...] Some unsuitable [*nā-munāsib*] individuals [also] bribed [*pāra birīb*] native administrators [*amīn wa īllīkbāshī*] with three or four hundred rubles and became *qāḍī* in the village, while other, honest, individuals were marginalized.[78]

---

76 Ibid.: 54.

77 *Tarjuma-yi aḥwāl-i Qāḍī ʿAbd al-Shakūr*, MS Tashkent, TsVRUz, no. 1304/IV: fol. 101b.

78 Mīrzā ʿĀlim Tashkandī, *Ansāb al-ṣalāṭīn wa-taʾrīkh al-khawāqīn*: fol. 150a–152a. This passage has been paraphrased also by Bakhtiyar Babadzhanov in his *Kokandskoe Khanstvo: Vlast', Politika, Religiia* (Tokyo and Tashkent: NIHU Program Islamic Area Studies Center

QAZI SAJLAV

Qadimƣi zamanda Turkistanda „sajlav“ namida ʙir ojuncaq ʙar edi. Oşa vaqtda qazi, miꞑʙaşi, amin va elliкʙaşilar sajlaʙ qojulardi. Butun luttiʙazilik, koz ʙojavcilik, makr-hijla, paraxorlik kaʙi ʙir qanca lik-likiar ana oşa „sajlav“ icida ʙoliʙ otardi.

„Sajlav“ niꞑ tizgini ʙajlar, mulkdarlar, aƣzi kattalar qolida, kimniꞑ puli kop ʙolsa oşa sajlanadi, cunki ʙutun masalani para olgur hol qiladi. Kamʙaƣal, ʙeva-ʙecaralar ʙir cetda qaladi, gap ʙularniꞑ xajrijati ustida emas, cunki amaldarlarniꞑ hamijan taşvişi ortada kondalaꞑ ʙoliʙ turadi. 40 — 50 miꞑ somga amal satiʙ algan kşilar esa, ʙuniꞑ ornini tez vaqt icida toldiriʙ, artdiriʙ ham aladilar, ʙu ortada ʙutun şurva kamʙaƣalniꞑ ʙaşiga tokuladi.

Mana şu hangamadan ʙir ʙolagi qiliʙ, ʙiz ʙunda qazi sajlavini aldik.

Şahar a'janlari, jurt ʙela xorlari sajlav aldidan toplanişiʙ oz kandidatlarini otkaziş ucun tirişar edilar. Zahid aka kamʙaƣal ʙolgani ucun unga na ʙan, na quj uşqan edi. Qaziliqqa kandidat ucun şaharniꞑ qor — qutli mulla, ulama, eşan va mudarrislari korsatilgan, tarafdarlar har qajsisi, oziniꞑ eşani, mahsumi, damlasini maxtaʙ, keca alingan katta-katta para ʙadaliga oliʙ — teriliʙ gap ʙalmaqda edi. Pravardi iş çançalga ajlandi.

Hasan tulki, Raşid Mahsum tamanidan vakil edi, u daha ellikʙaşilariga pulni taqsimlaʙ ʙoliʙ, miꞑʙaşi Qadir duma aldiga keldi.

Eşan Mahsum çanaʙlariga kop salam ajtdilar... Hi, qoj dedi — miꞑʙaşi — Mahsum kop mumsuk adam emiş, u qazi ʙolalmajdi... Joq, dedi — Hasan tulki — Mahsum kop saxi kşi, siz ʙaşqalarniꞑ ʙahridan kecaʙeriꞑ, Hasan tulki pulni sanaj ʙaşlaganda — jaq, miꞑʙaşi şundaj dedi: Kraji qazi ʙolganga jaraşa, şundaj adam ʙoladi — da, ellikʙaşil

Ojundan oq, kesakdan ot ciqdi. Bara-ʙara iş muştlaşga ajlandi. Qij-cij şavqun arasida şu gaplar eşitilardi:

— Mirʙadal mahsumiꞑ kim, ozi? La'natil Hij, cillasi craƣ kormagan eşaniꞑga la'nat, senga tuşiʙ qalƣan gap ʙarmi? Ha, seni ʙu jerga kim karcallan qiliʙ qojdi — a?.. Usman Mahsumni kim qazi ʙolmajdi, dedi? Haj itvacca istiƣfar ajt, kafir, Raşid Mahsum kimdan kam?!..

Hasan tulki Raşid Mahsumniꞑ qazi ʙolişiga qattiq işangan va unga hakim tora ʙilan ʙoladigan muamalani ham jaxşilaʙ orgatgan edi. Sajlav kuni Raşid Mahsum şahar Hakimi aldiga peşvaz ciqdi va uniꞑ kaftiga sanaqsiz altunlarni ʙasiʙ: façaliska taqsir, dua qilaman, jana orni ʙar, dedi. Hakim kuliʙ qojdi.

Saqa taşlaşda hakim, miꞑʙaşi quti ustida turiʙ, jurt kattalariniꞑ qulaƣiƣa şeviriʙ turdilar...

Oşa kuni-jaq avaza tarqaldi: Raşid Mahsum qazi ʙolgan emiş...

FIGURE 8 *"Qāḍīs' election" under Russian rule, according to the satirical journal* Mushtum, *17–18.09.1937.*

Central Asians began to see elections as a mark of moral decay. This attitude became so prevalent in local communities that it later became a topic of satirical poetry. The Khoqandi poet ʿUbaydallāh Ustā Sāliḥ-ūghlī, alias Zawqī (1853–1921) devoted a long poem of rhyming couplets (*dāstān*) to a famous turf war between two local legists—Mullā Kamāl and Mullā Ḥakīmjān—who contended for the post of *qāḍī* in one district of the city of Khoqand in 1909. The fight between the two parties involved, as usual, the Russian authorities, especially the city's commandant, Viktor Medinskii, who, in the end, sided with Mullā Ḥakīmjān and endorsed his election. Here is the passage from the poem containing Zawqī's rendition of Mullā Ḥakīmjān's victory:

> Medinskii the governor with his attendants / came and gathered the community.
>
> He questioned everyone about the event / so he could see [for whom] the people agreed.
>
> They praised Ḥakīmjān by inflating [his name] / and cooked up the affair in this way.
>
> The opinion of the governor went in favor of Ḥakīmjān. / He said: "The office of *qāḍī* belongs here [to this man]."[79]

Many believed that one elected to the office of *qāḍī* must have been siding with the Russians and must therefore be irremediably corrupt.[80] This was how *qāḍīs* lost their moral standing in local society.

3 Judges as Scapegoats

Rather than simply an object of public contempt, the purported inclination of native judges to bribery, malpractice, and ignorance of the law became for Central Asians a resource to use to their own benefit. I say "purported" because

---

at the University of Tokyo, 2010): 560–1. Babadzhanov seems to confer on Mīrzā ʿĀlim Tāshkandī a positive epistemological status. The text, however, clearly suggests that the author had anti-Russian dispositions, for he claims that those locals who served the Russians were a bunch of thugs and that, under the colonial government, immoral behavior such as prostitution and murder became prominent (fol. 151b).

79 Gh.K. Karimov, *O'zbek adabiioti tarikhi. Uchinchi kitob* (*XIX asrning iqqinchi iarmidan XX asr boshlarigacha*) (Tashkent: O'qituvchi, 1975): 210.

80 See the poems of the Uzbek Zavqi (1853–1921) at http://zerrspiegel.orientphil.uni-halle.de/t599.html and http://zerrspiegel.orientphil.uni-halle.de/t585.html.

colonial officials, from their first appearance in the region, proclaimed their concern for the moral attributes of native judges.[81] This concern, whether sincere or not, was a cornerstone of the colonial project to replace native judges with imperial tribunals. The important aspect of such cases is not really the attempt of Central Asians to involve colonial authorities in mediating disputes.[82] This happened in the case of Russian statutory laws, and the administrative setting of the Governorship-General openly invited the colonial subjects to appeal to tsarist officials. As we have seen in Chapter 1, this was hardly an innovation, as it was customary among locals to turn to their rulers for redress. What invites reflection is instead the ability of colonial subjects to adjust their language of grievance to the idiom of colonial bureaucracy. Such an ability not only shows how receptive and responsive was the local population to new cultural patterns and changing social circumstances but also reflects a process of "legality," the culture of law and the sense of legal entitlement that people possessed as individuals or as members of a community. Fundamental to Central Asian Muslims' sense of legality during the period of Russian rule was the idea that the native judges had to be portrayed before the colonial masters as corrupt. There are too many accusations of bribery and embezzlement leveled against *qāḍīs*, inspired by malice, to support the view that native courts in Russian Turkestan were a colonial showcase of "undoubted corruption."[83] I do not mean to exclude the possibility that native judges were corrupt. Bribery is a topic as old as the Muslim world,[84] and native judges operating in Russian Central Asia are no exception.[85] In addition, their judicial duties make

81 See, e.g., I.F. Kostenko, *Sredniaia Aziia i vodvorenie v nei Russkoi Grazhdanstvennosti* (St. Petersburg.: Tip. B. Bezobrazov, 1871): 64; N. Dingel'shtedt, "Odno iz otzhivaiushchikh uchrezhdenii." *ZGUP* 7 (1892): 1–23; A. Zuev, "Kirgizskii narodnyi sud." *Zhurnal ministerstva iustitsii* 12 (1907): 161–208. Many sources also demonstrate that the Russians viewed the *qāḍīs* with suspicion and were disturbed by their moral authority over the local communities; see, e.g., TsGARUz, f. I-21, op. 1, d.s 75, 108, 113, 114, 144, 202.

82 Crews, *For Prophet and Tsar*, 268: Morrison, *Russian Rule in Samarkand, 1868–1910: A Comparison with British India*: 259.

83 Ibid.: 284.

84 M. van Berkel, "Embezzlement and Reimbursement. Disciplining Officials in ʿAbbasid Baghdad (8th–10th Centuries AD)." *International Journal of Public Administration* 34 (2011): 712–19.

85 In his memoirs, Mīr Sayyid Muḥyī al-Dīn b. Mīr Sayyid Ḥabīballāh Fatḥābādī recounts a case in which a *qāḍī* operating in the region of Khutfar (Bukharan Emirate) was found guilty of machinations (*buhtān*) in a case of extortion. See his *Khāṭirāt*, MS Tashkent, TsVRUz, no. 328/IV, fols. 113–114 (second half the nineteenth century).

qaḍīs particularly liable to public criticism and satire,[86] especially because they could deploy power that many did not have: "if your claimant is a judge, [you'd better] express your grief to God," says an Uzbek proverb.[87]

Taking accusations of corruption at face value, however, is problematic for various reasons. First, *qaḍīs*' "bribery" (*rishwa*) was a key term of the idiom of hatred that, before the Russian conquest, Muslims used to express disapproval of their conduct as legists and blacken their name. In his *Khulāṣat al-aḥwāl* (1886),[88] the Tashkent savant Abū ʿUbaydallāh refers to a dispute between his father and a "stranger" (*bīgāna wa bīrūna*) over a plot of garden land abutting the courtyard where his family lived. His father had a particular interest in the property in question, because his courtyard was, by all accounts, too small for the family, but the stranger was able to purchase the property first. When the father of Abū ʿUbaydallāh heard this, he protested before the legists of Tashkent, claiming that his right of pre-emption (*shufʿa*), as owner of property abutting the plot under question, had been overridden. But the legists dismissed the protest, because the purchaser had bribed them to do so (*chīzhā ba-ṭarīqa-yi rishwa dāda*).[89] In 1828, eleven muftis from Tashkent opined on a case in which a person who had lost a case subsequently insulted the adjudicating *qāḍī* by calling him "corrupt" (*rishwa khwur*). The jurists held that, according to Islamic law, the slanderer should be liable to punishment (*mustaḥaqq-i taʿzīr*) and explained that it was incumbent upon the *qāḍī* to give his denouncer an exemplary punishment (*taʿzīr-i balīgh*).[90] These examples would suggest that accusations of corruption reflect instances of bribery less than the accusers' antipathy toward the *qāḍīs*.

A second problem with taking accusations of corruption at face value is that it obscures the significance of a longstanding culture of gifts (*hadya*) and donations (*tārtīq*), which were regarded as marks of respect, loyalty, and

86 I have in mind here the satirical poem of Sidqii Khondailiqii (1884–1934) against the *qāḍī* of O'n Qo'rghon, whom he called ignorant (*nodon*) and corrupt (*rishva desa tashlab o'zini tomdin*). See his *Tanlangan asarlar*, ed. B. Qosimov and R. Javharova (Tashkent: Ma"naviiat, 1998): 211–13.

87 *Da"vogarning qozi bo'lsa, dardining olloga ait*, B. Sarimsoqov et al., *O'zbek khalq maqollari* (Tashkent: Fan, 1978): 190.

88 T.K. Beisembiev, *Annotated Indices to the Kokand Chronicles* (Tokyo: Research Institute for Languages and Cultures of Asia and Africa, 2008): 22.

89 Abū ʿUbaydallāh Khwāja Tāshkandī, *Khulāṣat al-aḥwāl*, MS Tashkent, TsVRUz, no. 2084: fol. 5a.

90 Anon., *Jung*, MS Tashkent, TsVRUz, no. 6102: fol. 321b.

submission in politics[91] and law.[92] In Chapter 1 we saw how the judge Barāq Khwāja strongly opposed the custom current among Turkmens from Kerki of presenting gifts to the judges. The *qaḍī*'s attitude, as it was recounted by his son, may seem perfectly logical to us. Evidently, however, the governor in Kerki regarded the practice as perfectly legitimate, and, in deciding whether the practice was right or wrong, the historian risks falling prey to his or her own unstated moral beliefs. What may seem to certain jurists perfectly normal—the payment for the bailiff's service, say, or the charging of a notary's fee—may appear to others as deplorable.[93] It is possible that the culture of gift exchange survived the conquest and the institutional reorganization of the judicial system. If so, our approach should not be informed by the fact that some contemporary observers regarded such cultural practices as forms of corruption and depravity. These reporters may well have been acute commentators, but they were perhaps not fully attuned to Central Asian culture. The American consul in Tashkent who provided one of the most outspoken accounts of the corruption of *qaḍīs*[94] was no doubt a man in the habit of making hasty judgments:

> The Tadjiks and Uzbeks are readily distinguished from each other, not only in appearance but also in character. The Tadjik is larger and fuller in person, with an ample black beard, and with an air of shrewdness and cunning. He is fickle, untruthful, lazy, cowardly, and boastful, and in every way morally corrupted.[95]

---

91 A. Wilde, *What is Beyond the River? Power, Authority and Social Order in Eighteenth and Nighteenth-Century Transoxiana* (Vienna: Press of the Austrian Academy of Sciences, 2016): 67–80; G. Arendarenko, *Bukhara i Afganistan v nachale 80-kh godov XIX veka* (Moscow: Glavnaia redaktsiia vostochnoi literatury, 1974): passim; D.N. Logofet, *Bukhara: Strana bezspraviia* (St. Petersburg: V. Berezovskii, 1909): 53; G.Iu. Astanova, "Dokumenty iz arkhivov Uzbekistana po istorii Tadzhikistana *XIX*–nachala XX veka." *ONU* (1991, no. 8): 57.

92 Anon., *Jung*, MS Tashkent, TsVRUz, no. 6102: foll. 109b; 115ob–116. See also *The Personal History of a Bukharan Intellectual. The Diary of Muḥammad Sharīf Ṣadr-i Ziyā*, trans. R. Shukurov and ed. E. Allworth (Leiden: Brill, 2004): 152–53, where Ṣadr-i Ḍiyā' refers to the donations that his uncle 'Ināyatallāh received following his appointment to the post of *ra'is* in Qarshi.

93 S.A. Dudoignon, "La question scolaire a Boukhara et au Turkestan russe, du "premier renouveau" a la sovietisation (fin du XVIIIe siecle-1937)." *CMR* 37/1–2 (1996): 143.

94 Schuyler, *Turkistan: Notes of a Journey in Russian Turkistan, Khokand, Bukhara, and Kuldja*: 1: 169.

95 Ibid.: 108.

The third point that needs to be addressed in considering accusations against *qaḍīs* pertains to elementary *Quellenkritik*. Trusting the detractors of *qāḍīs* leads to the reinforcement of the common colonial assumption that native judges always enjoyed discretionary powers.[96] This approach is misguided, and we would do well to disentangle the intentions behind each accusation of corruption leveled against *qaḍīs*. Central Asians soon came to understand that charges of bribery were a powerful way of attracting the attention of the colonial authorities. It was common knowledge that Russians were always eager to listen to the colorful details of native judges' purported dishonesty, about which we find countless extravagant stories in the archives. Let us consider the case of Tīnīq Āy, a Kazakh widow living in a "nomadic encampment" (Chag., *avīl*, Russ., *aul*) in the *raion* (district) of Jizzakh. After her husband died, she had an affair with a man and, from this relationship, gave birth to a boy. Two women of the same encampment wanted to remarry her to another man, but Tīnīq Āy did not comply with their wishes. The two women decided that Tīnīq Āy deserved to be punished: they came to her house, assaulted Tīnīq Āy and her mother, and strangled the baby in cold blood. It was probably for fear of other violent forms of retaliation that Tīnīq Āy did not file a claim against them. Instead, she turned to the colonial authorities, recounted only in passing her baby's murder, and concocted the story of being harassed by a native judge (*bī*) and giving him fifteen rubles to let her go. It did not take long for the Russians sifting through the witnesses' statements to discover that the accusations of bribery (*vziatochnichestvo*) had been made up to draw attention to the brutal murder.[97]

Most such accusations were found groundless by both Russian prosecutors and Muslim judicial assessors. Let us consider, for instance, an admission (*iqrār*) of false accusation against a native judge. The background to the text is as follows. A certain ʿAlī Khwāja had sued Muḥyī al-Dīn Khwāja for malpractice. The plaintiff's uncle, Manṣūr Khwāja, and the respondent owned several plot of lands in an area called Qizil Qurghān, east of Tashkent, which was particularly suitable for agricultural purposes because it was watered by

96 "Native judges enjoy too much power, and they often abuse their authority, especially by ruling arbitrarily against the weak (*narodnye sudy imeiut slishkom mnogo sily i neredko zloupotrebliaiut svoei vlastiu, dopuskaia proizvol' i nasilie nad slabym*)," N.S. Lykoshin, "Kazii (Narodnye sud'i): Bytovoi ocherk osedlogo naseleniia Turkestana." In *Russkii Turkestan: Sbornik 1. Prilozhenie k gazete "Russkii Turkestan"* (Tashkent: Tipografiia "Russkii Turkestan," 1899): 95.

97 TsGARUz, f. 1-21, op. 1, d. 752, ll. 2–11.

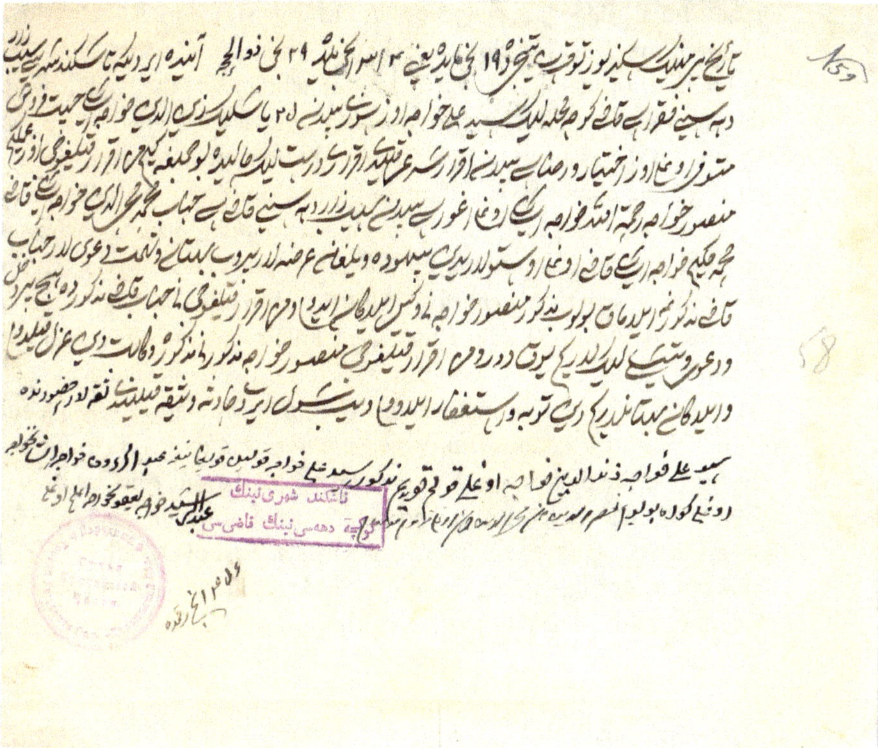

FIGURE 9 *ʿAlī Khwāja admits that his lawsuit against the* qāḍı *Muḥyī al-Dīn Khwāja was driven by malice and repents before a native court, 19.06.1897. TsGARUz, f. 1-164, op. 1, d. 7, l. 58.* COURTESY OF THE CENTRAL STATE ARCHIVE OF UZBEKISTAN

several streams.[98] Hoping that Muḥyī al-Dīn Khwāja would be dismissed from office and forced to sell part of his estates, Manṣūr Khwāja concocted a case against him and persuaded his nephew to file a claim against the *qāḍī*. The Russian administration found that the case was driven by malice. Muḥyī al-Dīn Khwāja, however, requested that the plaintiff admit that his claims were ill-intentioned. He therefore dragged him into another native court, where a *qāḍī* notarized ʿAlī Khwāja's admission of false allegations and repentance. What follows is the certificate notarized by the *qāḍī* and that Muḥyī al-Dīn Khwāja preserved in his personal archive [Fig. 9].[99]

98 TsGARUz, f. 1-164, op. 1, d. 6, l. 62.

99 TsGARUz, f. 1-164, op. 1, d. 7, l. 58.

On 29 Dhū al-Ḥijja 1314 [19.05.1897] ʿAlī Khwāja stated he is the 25-year-old son of the deceased cloth merchant Zayn al-Dīn Khwāja Īshān, citizen [*fuqarā*] of the Sibzar district [and inhabitant of] the Qāḍī Khwāja *maḥalla* [neighborhood]. Of his own will, he acknowledged in a just way that, at the instigation [*ighwāsī bīlān*] of his uncle Manṣūr Khwāja, son of Raḥmatallāh Khwāja Īshān and acting on behalf of the latter, he had submitted false petitions [*bīhūda wa yalghān ʿariḍalār*] conveying slanderous claims [*buhtān wa tuhmat daʿwālār*] against the *qāḍī* of the Sibzar [district], Muḥammad Muḥyī al-Dīn Khwāja Īshān, son of Muḥammad Ḥakīm Khwāja Īshān Qāḍī Kalān. The acknowledger has no claims against or any relationships with the aforementioned *qāḍī*. He also dismissed himself from the capacity of proxy of Manṣūr Khwāja and repented his futile actions [*tawba wa istighfār aylādūm*]. This event was registered in the presence of trustworthy people. Sayyid ʿAlī Khwāja, son of Zayn al-Dīn Khwāja signed; ʿAbd al-Ra'uf Khwāja, son of Īshān Khwāja witnessed the signature of Sayyid ʿAlī Khwāja. Naṣr al-Dīn Khān, son of Bahr al-Dīn Jān, signed. Seal: Qāḍī of the Kukcha district, city of Tashkent. Signature: ʿAbd al-Rashid Khwāja Yaʿqūb Khwāja Aʿlam-ūghlī.

4 False Appeals

Under Russian rule in Central Asia, "appeals" (Pers., *ʿarḍ/ʿariḍa*, Russ., *proshenie*) became an effective tool in the hands of the local Muslim population. Even under the khans, of course, Central Asians had been able to pursue redress by appealing directly to the central authority, thereby involving the rulers in their conflicts. With the advent of colonization, however, there was now a broad range of new means through which to reach the rulers. First, the initiatives of Muslim appellants were less restricted by the scribal rules of Islamic compositional genres. While, in the Bukharan emirate or the khanate of Khiva, petitions were usually submitted orally or, at best, translated by muftis' assistants into a protocol of claim (*maḥdar*), under colonial rule locals enjoyed ample opportunity to craft their petitions by using their imaginations. Those who were literate might draft these materials themselves; those who were not could hire a scribe or a translator to produce a petition in Chaghatay, the language in which Central Asians were expected to correspond with the colonizers. Many Muslims chose to have their appeals written directly in Russian. Producing and submitting a petition did cost money, of course, but it seems to have cost considerably less than what was usually levied under Muslim principalities to hear a case:[100] as we have seen, *muḥarrir*s charged for crafting a protocol of claim, trustees and court attendants levied fees for their services (*farsakh pulī/ khidhmatāna*), and *qāḍī*s expected a gift when they took charge of a claim. And when a claimant lived far from the seat of power and initiated a case, she often had to feed the trustee and his retainer as well as the local notables who acted as mediators.[101] Filing a petition with the Russian administration, by contrast, cost only 60 (later 80) kopeks.[102]

When evaluating the petitioning system involving Muslims in the colony, we should also consider that colonial officials were less concerned with the possibility that their petitioners lied than eager to trust accusations against judges' malpractice. This stood in stark contrast to the attitude that the khans and their courts had towards appellants whose knavery and mischief were, instead, the object of sanction. In order to appreciate this contrast in full, we should now turn to the areas of Central Asia in which colonial administrative arrangements were in close contact with the older system of the khans. One of those areas is Khorezm. Following the siege of Khiva in 1873, a treaty between the Russians and the Qunghrat dynasty led to the partition of Khorezm into two political and administrative entities: on the right bank of the Amu-Darya, the Amu-Darya Department (Amu-Dar'inskii Otdel) was established as one of the provinces of the Governorship-General of Turkestan, while in an area on the left bank of the river the khan retained the prerogatives of political independence under a formal regime of protection.

The new administrative division of Khorezm did not restrict the movement of goods and people across the Amu-Darya; legal and fiscal arrangements introduced in the Amu-Darya Department allowed the preservation of the social fabric of the region. One such arrangement regulated the resolution of disputes between citizens living on opposite sides of the river and stipulated that lawsuits filed in Petroaleksandrovsk—which involved as defendants individuals inhabiting the Khanate of Khiva—would be processed by the Qunghrat authorities. In other words, if somebody in the Amu-Darya Department filed

100 TsGARUz, f. I-125, op. 1, d. 498, ll. 65-64-64ob. A Khorezmian governor informs the royal court in Khiva about the complex and unexpected developments of a case of unpaid debts. During a hearing, the plaintiff had complained about the *qāḍī*, and the judge later expressed the desire to turn with the defendant to the royal court in Khiva. The governor tried to dissuade them from doing so because filing a lawsuit there would cost a considerable sum of money.

101 TsGARUz, f. I-125, op. 1, d. 498, l. 84.

102 Morrison, *Russian Rule in Samarkand, 1868–1910: A Comparison with British India*: 184.

a lawsuit in the chancellery of the commandant in Petroaleksandrovsk, which was the administrative seat of the Otdel, the Russian official would have this petition translated and redirected to the khan in Khiva. This precipitated a cascade of administrative events in the protectorate: the Qunghrat ruler would process the legal cases on the basis of a principle on territoriality and thus hand over the documentation to one of his provincial governors, who would involve other levels of local administrators: community leaders, tribal headmen, village elders, and so forth. The latter were required to investigate the charges against the subjects of the khanate and report to the governor, who would in turn report to the khan, who was expected to get back to the Russian official in Petroaleksandrovsk. This bureaucratic machinery is of great interest to us because it produced documentation that indicates that the Qunghrats perceived a change in legality among the Muslims who lived under Russian rule.

One of the side effects of this bureaucratic procedure was the increasing number of lawsuits, filed in the office of the Russian official, that the Qunghrats discovered to have been driven by malice. Early in the history of the partition of Khorezm, only 12 years after the siege of Khiva, we find Muḥammad Raḥīm Khān II warning the Amu-Darya Department that Muslims there were submitting false petitions (*yālghān ʿarḍlār*) and that it was difficult for the Qunghrat authorities to hear such cases because the claimants usually dismiss the authority of *qāḍīs*, do not show up in court, and even calumniate judges and governors.[103] The Russians appear not to have taken counter-measures to this new legal phenomenon, instead dismissing such warnings as irrelevant. The correspondence across the Amu-Darya River illustrates instances in which the Khivan authorities, with a dose of irony, reported to the Russians that, in listening to the words of deceivers, the colonizers were actually conferring a flimsy authority on false accusations and malign imputations. Such instances are best exemplified by cases of Muslim family law. We find, for example, that a Kazakh from Krasnovodsk filed a lawsuit against a Khivan subject, claiming that the latter had abducted his wife and his two children. The investigation in Khiva found that the woman had already obtained an irrevocable divorce from the claimant in consideration of a sum of money and that the couple had, in fact, never had children.[104] Another Kazakh petitioned the Russians seeking restitution of the dowry following an engagement to a Kazakh woman from

103 *sīzgā tabiʿ ādamlārnīng baʿḍīsī sharīʿatgha tūrmāyman dīb kītīb bārīb qāḍīlārgha wa ḥākimlārgha tuhmat qīlīb*, 02.06.1885, TsGARUz, f. I-125, op. 1, d. 29, l. 70ob.

104 TsGARUz, f. I-125, op. 1, d. 190, ll. 36–38.

the protectorate, which, he argued, had never resulted in marriage. The investigations revealed a different story: seven years earlier, the woman had engaged herself to another man before several witnesses and had been married to him for two years. The authorities in Khiva were thus adamant that the claim was slanderous (*buhtān wa yālghān*).[105] In a somewhat different story, a Kazakh claimed before a Russian official in Petroaleksandrovsk that her daughter had been abducted. According to the claimant, the abductor was someone living under the jurisdiction of the Khivans. The defendant was able to prove that the suspect had indeed kidnapped the girl and taken her to Chimbay, and there the two had contracted a legal marriage before a *qāḍī*, before a cohort of notables acting as witnesses and with the consent of the girl's parents, including the claimant! And the couple had a two-year-old daughter. Again the Khivan authorities concluded that the petition was a case of mischief (*buhtān*).[106]

One wonders whether the repeated use of the term "slander," which so often appears in the terse bureaucratese of the Qunghrats, prefigured some kind of instrumental purpose. It is one thing to qualify a claim as null but a completely different thing to assert that the statement of a claimant is injurious and defamatory. Not only do we encounter the categories of "null and void" (*fāsid wa bāṭil*) in the sites of application of *sharīʿa* and in the records written in the Islamic juristic idiom, but we also find that Khivan bureaucrats too were conversant with these notions and used vernacular equivalents such as *bīkār*[107] and *nā-rāst*[108] to replace Arabic juristic terms such as *fāsid wa bāṭil* and could thus clearly explain that certain claims were unsound. It is easy to find cases of such bureaucratic conduct. For example, in one letter of instruction (*fatak*), the Khivan royal court orders a bailiff and a retainer to escort the parties to a dispute before the khan in order that their dispute be resolved. On the verso of the *fatak*, we learn that nine days after this notification, during the hearing in Khiva, the plantiff admitted that the claim was unfounded (*daʿwāmnī būshqa qūydūm dīb iqrār*).[109]

It would thus be misleading to assume that, outside the Russian sphere of influence, Khorezmians did not petition their ruler with grievances that were later never substantiated and were therefore voided. Instead, the emphasis

105 Ibid.: ll. 13–14ob. See also TsGARUz, f. I-125, op. 1, d. 81, l. 5ob.

106 IQM, P-8, KP 3674, ll. 33–33ob: *qīzīmnī wa māllārīmnī qāwub ālīb kītdīlār dīgānī sūzī buḥtān dūr*.

107 TsGARUz, f. I-125, op. 2, d. 633, l. 93ob; 110ob; 111ob.

108 Ibid.: l. 130ob.

109 TsGARUz, f. I-125, op. 2, d. 633, ll. 95–95ob. For a similar case, see ibid.: ll. 39–39ob; ll. 98–98ob.

placed on the category of "slander" should alert us that we are here dealing with something different—that is, a moral judgment qualifying the behavior of those appellants who were purposefully submitting false petitions to the Amu-Darya Department.[110] In other words, the Qunghrats were signaling that, although the arrangements introduced by the Russians in Khorezm largely preserved the traditional institutions of equity, they also brought about a major change in Muslims' legal consciousness and hence in their morality. The Russians tolerated the locals' many false petitions. It thus seems that the Qunghrats did not limit themselves to admonishing the Russians that their subjects were submitting claims that were to be voided but that they indicated that some Muslims living on the other side of the Amu-Darya were now maliciously submitting false petitions. The Khivan authorities were pointing out the obvious limits of the new institutional arrangement that allowed such behavior.

If so, one would like to know what prompted the Muslims, mainly Kazakhs, living in the Amu-Darya Department to undertake such courses of action and indulge in practices that would have been censured in the protectorate. What was slander in Khiva had now become in Petroaleksandrovsk only a claim to be voided. This qualitative shift in interpreting false allegations must have depended on several factors. First, submitting a petition to Petroaleksandrovsk was less costly that obtaining an audience at the royal court in Khiva, for the reasons given above. Second, Muslims must have had a general perception of impunity in the areas of Russian rule; third, and most important, was the varying publicity surrounding the procedure of filing claims on the opposite sides of the Amu-Darya. For those who had made themselves a bad name, obtaining an audience at the royal court must have been difficult; even more difficult would have been to prevent their reputation from reaching the authorities involved in the application of royal justice. Things were very different in the blind bureaucratic machinery of the Russian Empire, where such factors as fame and notoriety counted for little.

5 A Strategic Alliance

We now return to Tashkent to examine another interesting aspect of the culture of lies that had spread after the establishment of colonial rule. It was often the case that the Russian colonial masters and their Central Asian subjects would make a strategic alliance to undermine the credibility of the *qāḍīs*. In doing so, the respective parties sought different goals. The colonizers pursued

110 For a local use of the term *buhtān*, see TsGARUz, I-125, op. 2, d. 633, l. 32.

a cultural project that consisted of establishing the moral superiority of their tribunals vis-à-vis the native courts. Locals, by contrast, were more concerned with pursuing financial gains.

Let us consider an episode involving an alleged forgery that occurred in Tashkent approximately fifteen years after the Russian takeover. In late December 1881, a man named Bāy Bābā Turabāy-ūghlī[111] was on his deathbed. He summoned his grandson Dhākir Jān and asked him to act on his behalf to establish a charitable endowment (*waqf*). On 25 December, the young man appeared in the native court presided over by Muḥyī al-Dīn Khwāja, who notarized a deed according to which Dhākir Jān, by virtue of his power of attorney (*wakīl*), established a *waqf*, dedicating the income from six shops to two mosques. This evidently upset several potential heirs.

There are some unconventional elements in the "endowment deed" (*vakuf-name,* Pers. *waqf-nāma*). First, it appears that the *qāḍī* was granted authority (*tafwīḍ*) to stipulate the conditions (*shurūṭ*) for administering the *waqf.* Second, the name of the administrator (*mutawallī*) who was to oversee the endowment is not given in the document. We read instead that the administrator was to be appointed by the person who had the authority to make decisions regarding the administration of the endowment (*mutawallī-yi madhkūr manṣūb bāshad az qibal-i man lahu al-wilāya*), namely, the *qāḍī.*[112] These apparently minor points are important. The inclusion of these stipulations in the *waqf* deed formally excluded the relatives of the founder from receiving a share of the revenues produced by the shops. From this point of view, the deed seems to attest to an act of piety: Bāy Bābā established a *waqf* exclusively for charitable purposes, without attempting to promote a descent group by appointing one of his descendants as administrator of the endowment,[113] but not all the members of his family praised Bāy Bābā for this display of piety. His nephew Ṣādiq Jān claimed that the *qāḍī* Muḥyī al-Dīn Khwāja, together with Dhākir Jān, had concocted a stratagem to divert Bāy Bābā's properties from his close relatives and get hold of a portion of the *waqf*'s revenues.[114]

111 In Russian, Baibaba Turabaev.

112 The endowment deed is available in TsGARUz, f. I-17, op. 1, d. 32607, l. 3.

113 More often than not, Central Asian endowment deeds stipulate that the office of administrator be assigned to the son of the founder of the *waqf* and inherited by his agnates (*awlād*), thereby favoring the creation of a "family trust." On this point, see M.E. Subtelny, *Timurids in Transition: Turko-Persian Politics and Acculturation in Medieval Iran* (Leiden: Brill, 2007): 150–1.

114 Disinheriting one's relatives might also have been perceived by many as immoral, and there is a good chance that most people in Tashkent would have been on Ṣādiq Jān's side in the dispute. See Chapter 4.

The following is an excerpt from an appeal that Ṣādiq Jān submitted to the governor-general of Turkestan at the beginning of May 1890. The document marks the beginning of the family drama:

> When he departed, my brother [sic] Bāy Bābā Turabaev left six shops in the Tashkent bazaar in the eastern part of the city. These shops belong to a *waqf*, and their revenues belong to me, because I am the heir to the endowment [*kak naslednik vakufa*]. For unknown reasons, the *qāḍī* of Sibzar[115] has appointed himself to the post of administrator [*mutavaliem*] and is exploiting the incomes generated by the endowment; he has rented the shops for twenty rubles a year for the last seven years. [In addition] I lent him 110 rubles, which I should not have given. He has kept the endowment deed [*vakuf-name*], even though he is not a relative of Turabaev and cannot fulfill the duty of administrator; according to the deed, it is I who should act in this capacity.[116]

The document was compiled in Russian and signed by Ṣādiq Jān, who was illiterate.[117] Ṣādiq Jān must, at that time, have had access to the services of a scribe. The short appeal is peppered with vernacular terms—*mutavali* (Ar. *mutawallī*) for "administrator," *vakuf-name* (Pers. *waqf-nāma*) for "endowment deed," and *kazi* (Ar. *qāḍī*) for Muslim judge. We thus assume that its author must either have been acquainted, albeit superficially, with the Islamic institutions involved in the case and/or unable to render these vernacular terms into Russian. In any event, the author of this document seems to have adopted various expedients in order to streamline the process of composition.

Be that as it may, Ṣādiq Jān probably presented himself to the scribe as one of the direct heirs of the founder of the *waqf* and stated that he was thereby entitled to the position of administrator, a position that, he claimed, had been usurped by the judge Muḥyī al-Dīn Khwāja. Had the endowment deed stipulated that the post of administrator should pass from the founder to his heirs, Ṣādiq Jān would have had good reason to emphasize his agnatic relation to Bāy Bābā. Indeed, the position of administrator entailed, along with the main duty—to safeguard and increase the wealth of the endowment—the right to

115 This was the name of the city district in which the *qāḍī* Muḥyī al-Dīn Khwāja was working.

116 *Proshenie*, 03.05.1890, TsGARUz, f. I-17, op. 1, d. 4887, l. 48.

117 In another appeal filed with the Russian administration, Ṣādiq Jān stated that he was illiterate and requested that another person sign for him (*Ṣādiq Jān Ākhūn Jān-ūghlī khaṭṭ bīlmagān ūchūn Bābā Bīk Nār Būta Bīk-ūghlī qūlūm qūydūm*); cf. *Proshenie*, 30.12.1891, ibid.: l. 20b.

a share of its revenues, that is, a salary (*ḥaqq al-tawlīya*). The expression "heir to the *waqf*" is thus clearly a misunderstanding; the scribe misconstrued the forceful argument that Ṣādiq Jān intended to use to uphold his putative rights.

Even more striking is that the appeal was submitted to a Russian administrative authority rather than to a Muslim one. The argument embedded in it presupposes that its addressee would know that, in Central Asia as elsewhere in the Muslim world, most Islamic endowments were not genuinely charitable but were instead established to circumvent the Islamic law of succession. A person who owned property and did not want it to be divided among his heirs—or dispersed, if his female relatives married—could establish a *waqf* and stipulate that it be administered by a family member. In this way, the property in question would remain under the family's influence.[118] It is unlikely that the Russian official who received the petition would have been expected to know all this and to interpret the appeal as intended.

The other allegations in the petition are plainly false. Muḥyī al-Dīn Khwāja had never acted officially as administrator: by the conditions stipulated by the founder of the *waqf*, he was empowered in his capacity as *qāḍī* to appoint a person to act as administrator of the endowment. Therefore, the accusation that he had usurped the post and squandered the *waqf* revenues was baseless. In fact, as I hope to show, he could not have done this, as he did not have direct access to the *waqf* revenues. In addition, Ṣādiq Jān was not automatically entitled to be appointed administrator, because access to the latter office was regulated instead by the *qāḍī*. Finally, as became clear later, Ṣādiq Jān had a history of bitter disputes with the Muslim judge: not long before, he had accused Muḥyī al-Dīn Khwāja of extorting money from him. That accusation proved false and driven by malice.[119] This record shows how a *qāḍī* assessed an appeal that Ṣādiq Jān had submitted to the Russian authorities accusing Muḥyī al-Dīn Khwāja of extortion. Ṣādiq Jān opted for the Russian court of appeals but was unable to produce evidence to support his charges. The report indicates that the *qāḍī* discovered that Muḥyī al-Dīn Khwāja had previously removed Ṣādiq Jān from the guardianship of his underage brother after a case of embezzlement. This

118 On this subject, see A. Layish, "The Mālikī Family *waqf* According to Wills and *waqfiyyāt*." BSOAS 46/1 (1983): 1–32; idem, "The Family *Waqf* and the *Sharīʿa* Law of Succession in Modern Times." *Journal of International Law* 4/3 (1997): 352–88; idem, "*Waqf*s of Awlād al-Nās in Aleppo in the Mamluk Period as Reflected in a Family Archive." JESHO 51/2 (2008): 287–326; D.S. Powers, "The Maliki Family Endowment: Legal Norms and Social Practices." IJMES 25 (1993): 379–406.

119 Qāḍī of Zangi-Ata to the military governor of Syr-Darya Province, 19.01.1890, TsGARUz, f. I-164, op. 1, d. 23, l. 26. See below, Appendix IV.

was apparently the reason that Ṣādiq Jān had taken legal action against Muḥyī al-Dīn Khwāja.

What prompted Ṣādiq Jān to file a groundless appeal? Why was he willing to risk making statements that could easily be shown to be false? What was he trying to obtain? As I hope to show, Ṣādiq Jān, like many Central Asian Muslims, knew that colonial officials were convinced that *qāḍī*s were incompetent and corrupt and was attempting to use this stereotype to his advantage.[120] Like many before and after him, Ṣādiq Jān was trying to appropriate the discourse on the Islamic judiciary produced by the colonial administration in order to manipulate the Russians who would rule on his appeal.

Initiating legal action against Muḥyī al-Dīn Khwāja would have been fairly easy.[121] Russian authorities had placed the *qāḍī* under intense scrutiny soon after they installed themselves in Tashkent. Like his father,[122] Muḥyī al-Dīn Khwāja had collaborated with the Russians in the aftermath[123] of the conquest, in various capacities. Most notably, under the stern rule of Governor-General Cherniaev, in 1884 he had headed a special commission established to create a spiritual administration in Turkestan on the model of the one in Ufa.[124] He had also received several awards for his positive attitude toward the colonizers.[125] As time passed, however, the Russians became increasingly concerned at the moral authority that he enjoyed among the locals, an authority that resulted in large part, they suspected, from the privileged standing that they themselves had granted him. The following is an excerpt from a

120 Morrison, *Russian Rule in Samarkand, 1868–1910: A Comparison with British India*: 272.

121 I know of at least other three instances in which investigations proved that legal actions taken against Muḥyī al-Dīn Khwāja were driven by malice and personal hatred: the report of a judgment (*ḥukm*) issued by a council of *qāḍī*s, 31.07.1886, TsGARUz, f. I-164, op. 1, d. 6, l. 73; an acknowledgment (*iqrār*) of repentance (*tawba wa istighfār*), 19.05.1897, TsGARUz, f. I-164, op. 1, d. 7, l. 58; a copy of a report from the council of *qāḍī*s to the city commandant, 1899, ibid.: 68. See also TsGARUz, f. I-17, op. 1, d. 5387, 5775, 6367, 6469.

122 *Biografiia Tashkentskogo uchenogo Seid Mukhammed Khakim Khodzha* (*Otets Kaziia Mukhitdina*), f. I-164, op. 2, d. 2a, ll. 1–15ob.

123 On Muḥyī al-Dīn replacing his father in the post of *qāḍī* in January 1870, see TsGARUz, f. I-36, op. 1, d. 725, ll. 1–3. He was appointed to the post ex officio by the Russians.

124 TsGARUz, f. I-1, op. 1, d. 326.

125 *Posluzhnoi spisok na Kaziia Sibzarskoi chasti g. Tashkenta*, n.d., TsGARUz, f. I-17, op. 1, d. 6468, ll. 143–143ob. The document was produced at the request of the prosecutor of Syr-Darya Province; see his correspondence with the Tashkent city commandant, 29 Nov. 1897, ibid.: l. 149. See also the awards issued by the chancellery of the governor-general and Alexander III in 1875 and 1891 respectively, TsGARUz, f. I-164, op. 1, d. 5, l. 8, 2.

confidential report[126] on Muḥyī al-Dīn Khwāja, which the Tashkent city commandant wrote at the request of the military governor of Syr-Darya Province:

> When the elections to the office of native judge were introduced, the inhabitants of Sibzar voted for Muḥyī al-Dīn [Khwāja], in view of the facts that he was an influential indigene among the Russians and that the title of *qāḍī* was a hereditary prerogative in [his] family. [...] The great powers that the law [*zakon*] confers on the native judge and the uncontrolled authority [the latter enjoys] in levying taxes strengthened, to a certain extent, the importance that Muḥyī al-Dīn [Khwāja] has among [his] people. [...] In the eyes of the Russians, Muḥyī al-Dīn Khwāja became a distinguished man because of the careful fulfillment of all his duties, as well as his manifest tolerance for every innovation, which inevitably changed entirely the lifestyle of the locals, who were forced to accustom themselves in one way or another to the new cultural influences [of the Russians. Be that as it may], in his milieu, Muḥyī al-Dīn Khwāja remained the strict guardian of rigid Muslim traditions: he zealously performs the religious rituals and instills in the conscience of his fellow citizens the conviction that his apparent devotion to the Russian government is stimulated by nothing but the need to render assistance to his people, defend the interests of the latter in the face of the Russian government, and hinder the Russians' efforts to change the life of the Muslims. [...] All this persuades me that the reelection of Muḥyī al-Dīn Khwaja to the office of native judge is not desirable, and it is better, in my opinion, to refuse the services provided by this undoubtedly cultivated indigenous man.[127]

This passage illustrates how the most influential representatives among the military officers of the Russian administration monitored the activity of this powerful *qāḍī*. Most notably, the author of this report had reviewed several cases in which legal action was taken against Muḥyī al-Dīn Khwāja. On one such occasion, the official acknowledged that, "[the *qāḍī*] knows how to make use of the *sharīʿa*, and he was able to acquaint himself with the norms of our [i.e., Russian] law to such an extent, that, to prove him guilty in any case of misconduct turned out to be extremely difficult; he knows how to adorn every injustice in legal dress."[128]

126 *Raport*, 24.03.1893, TsGARUz, f. I-36, op. 1, d. 3367, ll. 13–22ob.

127 Ibid.: ll. 15, 21–21ob.

128 Ibid.: ll. 20–20ob.

While it might have been possible for colonial officials to voice contempt for the *qāḍīs*, it was no easy task to convince an administrator to prosecute a specific *qāḍī* on charges of criminal malpractice. The colonial state was a multifaceted entity, and the success of an appeal depended to a great extent on the reaction of the particular administrator who had to deal with it. Those who staffed the lower levels of the administration—city commandants and the like—were used to baseless accusations and knew that many of the appeals that landed on their desks were without grounds. It is little wonder, then, that Ṣādiq Jān's appeal was quickly deemed groundless and was rejected. In the event, however, the rejection was unduly hasty. The Tashkent city commandant, Stepan Putintsev, overlooked the fact that Ṣādiq Jān's appeal contained two different complaints: one regarded the *waqf*, the other extortion. Putintsev knew that Muḥyī al-Dīn Khwāja had been acquitted, some months earlier, of extortion when Ṣādiq Jān had been found to be motivated by a desire for revenge.[129] When he saw the appeal to the governor-general, the city commandant probably thought that Ṣādiq Jān's complaints regarding the *waqf* were merely another attempt to discredit Muḥyī al-Dīn Khwāja. This is probably why Putintsev recommended that the provincial chancellery (*oblastnoe upravlenie*) dismiss the case.[130] As we shall see, Putintsev was correct, but the chancellery was not satisfied with his assessment and instructed the commandant to produce additional evidence. Consequently, at some time before the end of May 1891, Putintsev asked his assistant, Artillery Captain Nil Sergeevich Lykoshin,[131] to question everyone involved in the case.

When questioned by Lykoshin, Ṣādiq Jān declared that his uncle Bāy Bābā had called for him a few days before his death and had said, in the presence of two witnesses, that he intended to establish a *waqf* in support of two mosques, that the endowment would consist of six shops he owned, and that he wanted Ṣādiq Jān to be the administrator. Ṣādiq Jān admitted he had never seen the *waqf* deed, but he staunchly maintained that his uncle had proceeded as he had said he would. Ṣādiq Jān then went on to discuss the charges of extortion he had brought against Muḥyī al-Dīn Khwāja. He claimed the *qāḍī* had obliged him to pay 110 rubles, a demand with which Ṣādiq Jān complied for fear of Muḥyī al-Dīn Khwāja's power and influence. Russian administrators were convinced that Islamic courts were dysfunctional and corrupt, and the abuse of

129 TsGARUz, f. 1-164, op. 1, d. 23, l. 26.

130 City commandant to the provincial chancellery, 18.01.1891, TsGARUz, f. 1-17, op. 1, d. 4887, l. 49.

131 See A. Morrison, "Sufism, Pan-Islamism and Information Panic: Nil Sergeevich Lykoshin and the Aftermath of the Andijan Uprising." *PP* 214 (2012): 262–64.

power by *qāḍīs* was a leitmotiv of their view of judicial malpractice. Ṣādiq Jān was evidently playing on this by attempting to depict Muḥyī al-Dīn Khwāja as a man who had taken advantage of his position to enrich himself.

In order to verify Ṣādiq Jān's claims, Lykoshin inspected the shops that were endowed in favor of the two mosques. It turned out that the administrator of the *waqf* was a man named Maqsūm—the imam of one of the two mosques—who had been appointed to this post by the *qāḍī* in October 1890. Maqsūm had the deed establishing the *waqf*, which he showed to Lykoshin. The document stated clearly that Bāy Bābā had dedicated his six shops in favor of the two mosques and that the person who helped him to do so was his grandson, Dhākir Jān. Lykoshin was also able to clarify that the deed did not stipulate that the descendants of the founder of the *waqf* were to be appointed to the post of administrator. Lykoshin wrote, "The deed does not include any stipulation with regard to this and therefore, according to *sharīʿa*, the right to appoint the *mutawallī* belongs to the *qāḍī*, who can hold elections in the neighborhood (*maḥalla*) or consult members of the community."

The Russian official was willing to reason in the manner of a Muslim jurist in order to define what should be considered right or wrong with regard to the stipulations in the *waqf-nāma*. Apparently, notions emanating directly from the notary practice of *sharīʿa* courts shaped substantially the investigations carried out at the lowest level of the colonial administration. Lykoshin established that Muḥyī al-Dīn Khwāja had acted as he was supposed to. The previous year, in keeping with the stipulations set forth in the *waqf-nāma*, he had appointed an administrator (*mutawallī*), Maqsūm. Since then, although the revenues generated by the shops had nearly doubled, all the money had gone to refurbishing them and none to the administrator. Having established that Ṣādiq Jān's allegations regarding the *waqf* were groundless, Lykoshin became convinced that Ṣādiq Jān's claims of extortion perpetrated by the *qāḍī* were also unfounded.

Given that, Ṣādiq Jān had made similar accusations on a previous occasion, Lykoshin decided that this present claim was merely a further attempt to discredit the *qāḍī* and recommended closing the investigation. He wrote: "I am convinced that Ṣādiq Jān is not in a position to justify the lawsuit regarding the 110 rubles and is unable to support his claim that he should be appointed to the post of *mutawallī*."[132]

While his assistant was compiling this report, Putintsev decided to question Muḥyī al-Dīn Khwāja himself. During that interview, the *qāḍī* confirmed that it was Bāy Bābā who had decided to establish the endowment and that he

132 Act no. 69, 03.06.1891, TsGARUz, f. I-17, op. 1, d. 4887, ll. 42–45.

had wanted the imams of the two mosques to administer the revenues. Muḥyī al-Dīn Khwāja also argued that the allegations of malpractice regarding the *waqf* were an attempt by Ṣādiq Jān to discredit him and gain votes for another candidate in elections to choose a judge. The *qāḍī* told Putintsev that, after his reelection to office, none of the accusations had been repeated and argued that, if there had been any basis for them, the people responsible for the *waqf* would have gone to the authorities and complained about him. Muḥyī al-Dīn Khwāja also explained that Ṣādiq Jān's attempt to compromise him had begun after the *qāḍī* had found him guilty of embezzling more than one thousand rubles while acting as guardian for his minor brother and had ordered him to repay the sum. Ṣādiq Jān, who had, for unknown reasons, managed to avoid paying, had, since then, been defaming the judge.[133]

By mid-May 1891 the city commandant had collected enough evidence to argue that Ṣādiq Jān's appeals to the Russian authorities were motivated by malice and should be rejected. It was at this moment, when Ṣādiq Jān had little hope of convincing the colonial authorities to hear his case, that Mayram Bībī, Bāy Bābā's daughter and Ṣādiq Jān's cousin, addressed a petition directly to the governor-general of Turkestan. This was part of a larger plot against the *qāḍī*, so the timing of the appeal, as well as the arguments, are important. On 7 June she wrote:

> My father died ten years ago, leaving an inheritance that consists of [six shops] [...], 110 rubles, and other goods that amount to a value of 300 rubles. I am the direct heir to all this wealth. Nevertheless, I cannot make use of this inheritance because it seems that the *qāḍī* [...] has crafted a document that says that my father dedicated everything to a *waqf*, while the latter was, in fact, nearly dead. I consider this document a forgery [*vymyshlennym*] because, at the moment of its production, my father was not fully in possession of his mental faculties. He was on his deathbed, as can be attested by several witnesses. For seven years, Muḥyī [al-Dīn Khwāja] collected the revenues from the shops, and I do not know for what purpose he has used them.... Since Muḥyī has been back in office as judge, he has collected the revenues. I ask that my inheritance be restored, that the revenues equivalent to 840 rubles generated by the rent be given to me, and that the *qāḍī* be investigated for malpractice according to Russian law.[134]

133 *Bayān-nāma*, 11.05.1891, ibid.: l. 50.

134 *Proshenie*, ibid.: l. 31.

It was once again Putintsev, the humble official on the bottom rung of the ladder of colonial command, who was assigned to deal with the petition.[135] His findings were clear:

> The appeal produced by Mayram Bībī Turabaeva is a copy without additions [*bez vsiakikh izmenenii*] of the appeal filed by her cousin Ṣādiq Jān. [Evidently] the latter wishes to be appointed to the post of *mutawallī* of the *waqf* established by the deceased Bāy Bābā Turabaev in support of two mosques. With regard to the content of the *waqf* deed, Ṣādiq Jān does not have the right to hold this office. [...] With this appeal, Mayram Bībī cannot produce any information regarding Bāy Bābā Turabaev's *waqf*, which was not produced earlier by Ṣādiq Jān, whose appeal was rejected. The latter has appealed repeatedly on his behalf; he is now using, instead, the stratagem of depicting his relative Mayram Bībī as the person entitled to the property endowed to the *waqf*.[136]

Putintsev asserted that Ṣādiq Jān had understood that there was no chance that his claim would be taken seriously, so he had approached his cousin and persuaded her to submit a petition. Putintsev recommended that the appeal should not be heard, but, again, he had acted too quickly. His decision was not backed by the highest bureaucrats, who might have felt that the commandant was siding with Muḥyī al-Dīn Khwāja, thereby acting against the interests of his superiors. As we shall see in Chapter 5 with regard to cases of guardianship, opposing one's superiors could have harmful consequences.

Putintsev also overlooked the fact that Mayram Bībī was the first to claim that her father was not in full possession of his mental faculties when the endowment deed was notarized. Although her appeal was in Russian, Mayram Bībī was relying on an Islamic legal argument. In fact, before submitting her petition to the colonial authorities, she had secured a fatwa decreeing that the shops were not to be considered a *waqf* because, at the moment when he dedicated his properties to the mosques, Bāy Bābā was mortally ill (*maraḍ al-mawt*).[137] As explained by Ron Shaham, the question of mortal illness on which her argument rested is a concept developed by Muslim jurists that relies on the assumption that a person foreseeing his imminent death may be inclined to contract transactions relating to his property that prejudice the

---

135 Counsellor of the military governor to the city commandant, 24.06.1891, ibid.: l. 33.

136 City commandant to the provincial chancellery, 27.06.1891, ibid.: ll. 33ob.–34.

137 Undated legal opinion (*fatwā*), ibid.: l. 38. Four *muftīs* attached their seals to the document.

rights of his legal heirs or creditors. To defend the latter, the jurists prescribe that any donation made by a person on his deathbed in favor of a legal heir is not effective unless approved by the other heirs after the ill person's death.[138]

Mayram Bībī's fatwa thus stated that, when Bāy Bābā created the *waqf*, he was no longer in full possession of his mental faculties and was incapable of reasoning and realizing the consequence of his actions and was not in full possession of his mental faculties.[139] The muftis held that that a testator's disposition of property in such a state was inadmissible (*nā-jā'iz wa nā-muʿtabar*) and opined that Bāy Bābā's estate could not constitute a *waqf*. They suggested in their legal opinion that the shops be divided (*qismat namūda*) according to the Islamic law of inheritance, given that, "for the legal disposition [of an asset and the rights to it as well as its disposal] to be valid and effective, the reasoning ability of the person who disposes [of the substance and the rights to it] is a [necessary] precondition."[140] The fatwa was summarized in Russian and attached to Mayram Bībī's appeal.[141] Once again—as in the case of the first complaint that Ṣādiq Jān submitted to the authorities and in the report Lykoshin wrote after investigating the charges—the colonial administration was asked to make a decision on the basis of documentation that, although it was written in Russian, embodied notions of justice stemming directly from *sharīʿa*.

Bāy Bābā's alleged mental incompetence was a convincing argument. The chancellery of the governor-general accepted it, ignoring the recommendations made by Putintsev, and ruled that new evidence should be collected regarding Bāy Bābā's death.[142] It would be wrong to ascribe this decision simply to a zealous bureaucrat's determination to impose the Russian rule of law. Instead, someone in the chancellery must have been persuaded by the argumentation articulated by Mayram Bībī on the basis of the fatwa: if, at the moment of the stipulation of the *waqf-nāma*, Bāy Bābā was on his deathbed, then the endowment deed could be voided. The fact that this line of argument was accepted means that a high-ranking Russian colonial administrator wished to remove Muḥyī al-Dīn Khwāja from office.

---

138 R. Shaham, *The Expert Witness in Islamic Courts: Medicine and Crafts in the Service of Law* (Chicago: University of Chicago Press, 2010): 135.

139 *dar ḥālī-ki marīḍ ba maraḍ al-mawt būda ʿaql wa hūsh wa imtiyāz-i way bi 'l-kullīya zā'il gardīda lā yaʿqil wa maʿtūh gardīda bāshad*, undated legal opinion (*fatwā*), TsGARUz, f. I-17, op. 1, d. 4887, l. 38.

140 *dar taṣarrufāt-i sharʿīya wa ṣiḥḥat wa nufūdh-i ān ʿaql-i mutaṣarrif sharṭ bāshad*, ibid.

141 *Perevod. Vypiska iz shariatskikh knig*, n.d., ibid.: l. 39.

142 Counsellor of the military governor to the city commandant, n.d., ibid.: l. 16.

The positive response of the colonial administration to the arguments deployed by Mayram Bībī encouraged Ṣādiq Jān. The latter, however, realized that, because his previous accusations regarding Muḥyī al-Dīn Khwāja's usurpation of the post of *mutawallī* and squandering the *waqf*'s incomes had been ruled groundless, he needed to find new lines of argument. If, for example, he managed to prove that there were inconsistencies in the *waqf-nāma*, there was a good chance that the *waqf* would be annulled. It was precisely at this point that Ṣādiq Jān accused Muḥyī al-Dīn Khwāja of having forged the endowment deed (*oni utverzhdaiut, chto vakuf vovse ne byl uchrezhden Turambaevym i chto vakuf-name podlozhno*).[143] Presented with this accusation, the provincial chancellery retrieved the original *waqf-nāma* and had it translated and presented.[144] It was shown to Muḥyī al-Dīn Khwāja and Ṣādiq Jān for confirmation. When questioned, the *qāḍī* explained that, at the time of the notarization of the deed, he had affixed his seal, as had another senior mufti, Mullā ʿAbd al-Rasūl. He also pointed out that later, when ʿAzīzlār Khān was elected to the post of *qāḍī*, the latter had appointed Dhākir Jān *mutawallī* of the *waqf* and had affixed his seal (as had his son, who was also a mufti).[145]

When he was shown the *waqf-nāma*, Ṣādiq Jān raised a new argument. He claimed that his uncle had left at his disposal documents attesting to the ownership of the property at hand, that is, the shops. This proved, Ṣādiq Jān argued, that Bāy Bābā intended him to take possession of the property; had the latter truly intended to endow the six shops in the *waqf* deed, he should have attached these documents to the *waqf-nāma* itself, instead.[146] This new claim, however, was not supported by *sharīʿa*: nowhere in Islamic law is it stated that certificates proving the ownership of a given asset have to be attached to a *waqf-nāma*. In fact, Ṣādiq Jān was unable to obtain a mufti's opinion to support

143 *Proshenie*, 30.12.1891, ibid.: l. 2. Ṣādiq Jān's new attorney, Anton Glaz, was one of the most renowned Russian lawyers in Tashkent; see above, Introduction.

144 Translation, n.d., ibid.: ll. 52–54.

145 Muḥyī al-Dīn Khwāja to the city commandant, 18 Nov. 1892, ibid.: l. 29.

146 Ṣādiq Jān to the city commandant, 19 Nov. 1892, ibid.: l. 30. Ṣādiq Jān appealed to the Russian authorities once more and asked again that new probative elements be considered. This time he claimed that Dhākir Jān had never been the *mutawallī* of the *waqf* and that Dhākir Jān's father was willing to testify that he had never heard that his son had been appointed to this position. Ṣādiq Jān also stated that one of the two people named in the *waqf* deed as a witness—who had given testimony (*bayyina*) that, in drawing up the deed, Dhākir Jān had acted as a proxy (*wakīl*) for Bāy Bābā—was unknown to the people of the *maḥalla*. His last argument concerned the seals on the document: according to Ṣādiq Jān they were affixed to it some years after the *waqf-nāma* was originally produced.

this claim, and he could cite no provision in the colonial statutory law that obliged a *qāḍī* to act as he claimed was correct.

Ṣādiq Jān had tried hard to prove that the *waqf-nāma* had been altered, in order to divert the income fraudulently from Bāy Bābā's properties. As he had no evidence of this, the provincial chancellery helpfully fabricated some. While preparing documentation for the prosecutor, the officials staffing the provincial chancellery had some leeway to insert explanatory notes (*spravka*) or reformulate the arguments in petitions. They were therefore in a position to modify key information in favor of or against the *qāḍī*. This is what the Russian officials wrote in their explanatory note:

> In the translation of the original [*waqf*] document [...], there is a note explaining that it is impossible to ascertain precisely the year in which the document was compiled, as it is difficult to decipher the last numbers in the date written on the deed against which a dispute over a [case of] forgery [*o podloge*] is now under scrutiny. [In addition] we consider that [...] the declaration to the *qāḍī* of Sibzar regarding [Bāy Bābā] Turabaev's donation of the aforementioned property was made on 4 May 1881, as is stated in the document, and was not made by [Bāy Bābā] Turabaev himself, as he was ill, but by an individual named Dhākir Jān, on whom [Bāy Bābā] conferred the powers of attorney, in the presence of two witnesses. The document in question was drawn up on 25 December 1882, one year and seven months after the declaration; there are several seals on the document.[147]

This excerpt from the chancellery's attached explanatory note contains a collection of allegations of the crudest kind. First, the statement that the date of the *waqf-nāma* is impossible to read is absurd. The note made in the margin of the translation, which explains that the date on which the document was drawn up is partially illegible,[148] does not refer to the Islamic (*hijrī*) date, which is an integral part of the *waqf-nāma* and is clearly 16 Ṣafar 1299.[149] It refers, instead, to the date according to the Julian (Old Style)

147 *Zhurnal obshchego prisutstviia syr-dar'inskogo oblastnogo pravleniia*, no. 11, 30.01.1893, TsGARUz, f. I-17, op. 1, d. 32607, l. 62.

148 [*1881*] *ili v 1882 godu, tak kak tsifry na pole podlinnogo dokumenta tochno opredelit' po neiasnosti takovykh* (*odin ili dva*) *nevozmozhno. Perevodchik Aidarov*: "[1881] or 1882, the last figure on the document is unclear and impossible to decipher. The translator: Aidarov." Russian translation of the endowment deed, n.d., TsGARUz, f. I-17, op. 1, d. 4887, l. 53.

149 See the endowment deed (*waqf-nāma*), TsGARUz, f. I-17, op. 1, d. 32607, l. 3 (Fig. 10).

calendar in use in Russia, which the *qāḍī* was required to add at the top of the righthand margin of the deed to facilitate the filing of the document. Actually, the original *waqf-nāma* clearly reads *jumʿa* 25 *jadī* (Friday 25 Capricorn).[150] It is true that the last figure in the year is slightly smeared [Fig. 10], so that it could be read as either 1881 or 1882, but this a quibble on the part of the person who added the note, given that the text of the Russian translation of the *waqf-nāma* stated clearly that the document was notarized on 25 December 1881.[151]

The insertion of the note in the margin of the translation suggesting that the date was difficult to decipher is itself suspicious. While this note was signed by Aidarov, whose signature is also found at the end of the translation, there is no doubt that the translation of the deed in its entirety was the work of another person. Moreover, when Aidarov gave the translation to the provincial chancellery he attached a letter in which he stated that the translation of the *waqf-nāma* was truthful (*veren*), although he found it doubtful that a *qāḍī* could be delegated the authority to define the stipulations of the *waqf*.[152] Had the date of notarization in fact been impossible to decipher, Aidarov would have mentioned this inconsistency in his letter to the chancellery. Could it be that, after the translation was made, someone in the provincial chancellery asked Aidarov to comb the *waqf-nāma* for inconsistencies? The smear on the last figure of the Julian date was all that the translator managed to find, and he probably offered his remark about the inconsistency of the dates in order to provide the chancellery with evidence to use against Muḥyī al-Dīn Khwāja.

The Russians also argued that the endowment had been registered later than it actually was. This was another fabrication, as the entire file contains nothing indicating that the *waqf* had been dedicated before the notarization of the deed, on 4 May 1881. The Russian administrators were attempting to show that the endowment deed had been notarized later than its actual stipulation. Clearly, if this was the case, it would have meant that the *qāḍī* had exploited Bāy Bābā's illness to craft the certificate as he saw fit, that is, to his own advantage. Once again, it is striking how far the Russian bureaucrats were willing to go in their attempt to undermine the veracity of the endowment deed by introducing arguments based on the Islamic legal principle that dispositions made by a person on his deathbed could be invalidated.

150 Ibid. In Russian Central Asia, scribes often used astrological terms with some latitude in lieu of the Russian terms denoting the months of the Julian calendar; 25 *jadī* 1881 corresponds to 25 December 1881.

151 TsGARUz, f. I-17, op. 1, d. 4887, l. 53.

152 Letter accompanying the translation of the endowment deed, 24.01.1892, ibid.: l. 51.

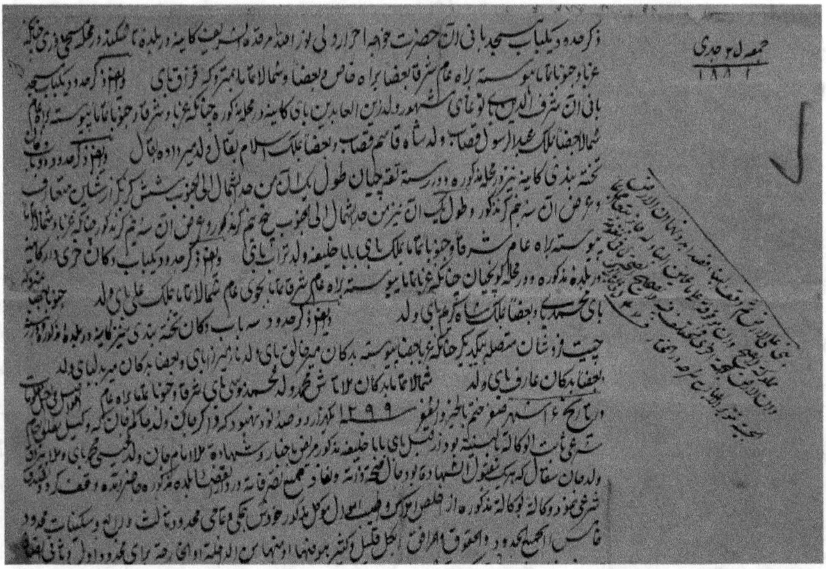

FIGURE 10 *Detail of the endowment deed of the two mosques in the Maḥsīdūzī* maḥalla, I. *TsGARUz, f. I-17, op. 1, d. 32607, l. 3.*
COURTESY OF THE CENTRAL STATE ARCHIVE OF UZBEKISTAN

Their conspiracy against Muḥyī al-Dīn Khwāja led the Russians to make much of the fact that two seals had been added to the deed after it was notarized. The administrators insisted that this was particularly damning evidence of wrongdoing, neglecting to mention that, although two seals had in fact been attached later for a completely different reason, the reason was legitimate and had nothing to do with the crafting of the original document. Muḥyī al-Dīn Khwāja explained that, when another person took over his office as *qāḍī*, the new judge appointed Dhākir Jān to the post of administrator, recorded this event directly at the end of the deed, and added his seal.[153] The last line of the *waqf-nāma*, clearly in a different hand, confirms the statement Muḥyī al-Dīn Khwāja made to the colonial officials investigating the case.[154] In order to ensure that Dhākir Jān's appointment would have *sharʿī* legitimacy, the new *qāḍī* added, "regarding the appointment [to the post of administrator, this right rests with] the aforementioned Bāy Bābā and the person he delegates,

153 *2-nchī mandīn sūng būlgān qāḍī madhkūr waqfgā Dhākir dīgān mutawallī qīlgān sababdīn waqf-nāma ākhirīgā bir khaṭṭ yāzīb muhr qīlgān īkānlār*, ibid.: l. 290b.

154 *mutawallī naṣb karda shud Dhākir Jān walad-i Ākhūnd Jān rā*, TsGARUz, f. I-17, op. 1, d. 32607, l. 3.

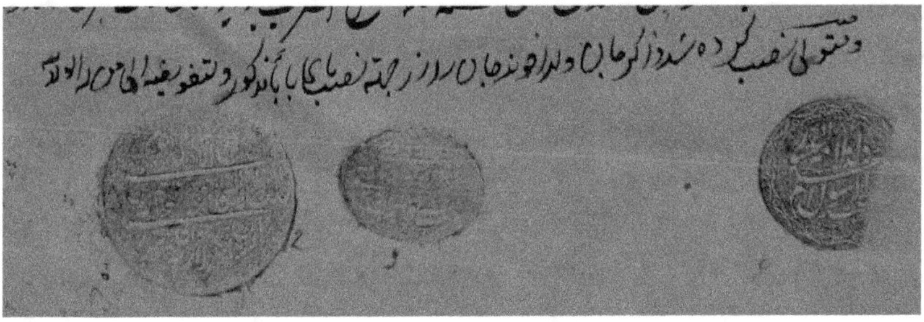

FIGURE 11 *Detail of the endowment deed of the two mosques in the Maḥsīdūzī* maḥalla, II. *TsGARUz, f. I-17, op. 1, d. 32607, l. 3.*
COURTESY OF THE CENTRAL STATE ARCHIVE OF UZBEKISTAN

who enjoys [legal] authority" (*az jihat-i naṣb Bāy Bābā'-i madhkūr wa tafwīḍihu ilā man lahu al-wilāya*). This formula is a stock phrase used in the original stipulation of the deed, which delegated to the judge the authority to choose the administrator for the *waqf* (*mutawallī-yi madhkūr manṣūb bāshad az qibal-i man lahu al-wilāya*).[155]

This episode proves that the individual who succeeded Muḥyī al Dīn Khwāja in the office of *qāḍī* considered the *waqf-nāma* and its stipulations fully in accordance with Islamic law. The Russian translation that was given to the colonial authorities confirms this reading and the inferences I have drawn.[156]

Several people in the provincial chancellery evidently wished to concoct false accusations against Muḥyī al-Dīn Khwāja and added misleading notes, inserted undocumented elements, and even manipulated the evidence at hand. However, when the gathered materials and the notes added by the chancellery were sent to the provincial prosecutor for further examination, the prosecutor ruled that the charges against the *qāḍī* were barred by statute and should be dropped. He also ruled that, if they wished, Ṣādiq Jān and Mayram Bībī could contest Bāy Bābā's will in a *sharīʿa* court.[157] While, on the one hand, this judgment is striking because it counters Russian statutory law—which gave Central Asians the right to lodge claims with the colonial administration and have cases heard in the imperial courts—on the other hand, the prosecutor's decision probably followed a simple line of argumentation: there was too

155 Ibid.

156 *nizhe sego pisano drugim pocherkom nizhesleduiushchee: Zakirdzhan Akhundzhanov mnoiu naznachen mutavalliem na osnovanii togo, chto naznachenie mutavalliia Baibaboiu predostavleno pravo "men'liakhul' viliaia," t.e. kaziiu,* TsGARUz, f. I-17, op. 1, d. 4887, l. 54.

157 Register 44, 26.01.1893, ibid., l. 65.

much Islamic law in the case for his office to handle. It was thus the provincial prosecutor who intervened to clear Muḥyī al-Dīn Khwāja of the accusations made against him. In the years that followed, ten other lawsuits for malpractice were filed by the provincial chancellery against the *qāḍī* at the request of other Muslim appellants. In 1906, thirteen years later, and well after Muḥyī al-Dīn Khwāja's death, Ṣādiq Jān tried again to have himself appointed *mutawallī* of the *waqf* his uncle had established.[158]

Conclusions

Appeals by colonial subjects to nonnative administrative authorities are one form of forum shopping that emerged under legal regimes established by imperial powers. By "forum shopping," I refer to the movement of litigants from one legal jurisdiction to another in search of the most favorable ruling. Mitra Sharafi has examined failed attempts to forum-shop among the Parsi community, which spread from colonial Bombay to the princely state of Baroda (in western India), Iran, and Britain and which resemble closely those that occurred in Russian Central Asia. The common feature shared by these two distant colonial polities is, to use Sharafi's words, the existence of "a flow of hopeful litigants". The term Sharafi uses to describe this mechanism is "legal lottery," that is, "a promise that one might win this time, even if one probably would not."[159] For the person found guilty, for example, of animal theft, it was tempting to turn to the colonial authorities with an appeal and claim that the judges who ruled against him were corrupt.[160] As we stated previously, the procedure cost little and was usually slow, and it might well happen that, while investigating, Russian authorities would find other irregularities on the basis of which to charge a native judge with malpractice.

The term "legal lottery" emphasizes the ephemeral character of many of the cases that colonial subjects asked the authorities to hear. This applies also to Central Asia, where the large majority of the complaints filed with the Russian officers consisted of false accusations that did not yield the hoped-for results. Thus, the appeals of colonial subjects may look like "acts of micro-

158 *Proshenie* of Ṣādiq Jān to the governor-general, 10.02.1907, TsGARUz, f. I-36, op. 1, d. 4364, l. 3.

159 M. Sharafi, "The Marital Patchwork of Colonial South Asia: Forum Shopping from Britain to Baroda." *LHR* 28/4 (2010): 1009.

160 TsGARUz, f. I-21, op. 1, d. 144, ll. 1–26.

scopic agency,"[161] the more so, if one evaluates them against the backdrop of the financial and emotional investments they required.

There are, however, other important aspects of the phenomenon that the concept of the legal lottery overshadows and obscures. By focusing instead, as we have done, on the relationship between local appellants and imperial authorities, we are able to shed light on the process by which the colonial legal culture was constituted through social relations. The district and provincial chancelleries of the Russian colonial administration in Central Asia were venues where the local population engaged the state in a dialogue over legal questions. It is within this institutional framework, outside the courtroom, that Russian bureaucrats and Central Asian Muslims had the scope to elaborate their notions of "lawful" and "unlawful."

Colonial subjects engaged in active discussions about the interpretation of procedural laws. On occasion, they turned to professionals and sought consultation, as in the case examined here, but their "jurisdictional jockeying"[162] did not depend exclusively on the colonial lawyers or local intermediaries who wrote their petitions. It appears that the boundaries between colonial state and local society were so indistinct as to allow the indigenous population to adopt the appropriate moral vocabulary, the discretionary powers of *sharīʿa* courts being a case in point. This happened routinely, as Central Asians filed appeal after appeal, gaining experience each time and honing their skills at dealing with colonial administrators.

The relationship between colonial state law and Muslim society was mutually constitutive: Muslims' knowledge of legal matters was significantly influenced by their dialogue with colonial officials, while Muslims' conceptions of justice structured the practices of the Russian bureaucrats who heard their appeals. By formulating their arguments in various ways, colonial subjects could determine how their appeals were handled at the various levels of the state administration. They could also influence the decision-making process of Russian officials and could ultimately shape the notions of justice and injustice according to which a particular issue was examined.

Ṣādiq Jān and Mayram Bībī laid their claims against Muḥyī al-Dīn Khwāja precisely because Russian statutory law allowed them to take their grievances to the administrative authorities. The appeals and the bureaucratic paperwork produced by Russian officials represent normative practices

161 Sharafi, "The Marital Patchwork of Colonial South Asia: Forum Shopping from Britain to Baroda": 981.

162 The terminology here is Benton's: *Law and Colonial Cultures: Legal Regimes in World History: 1400–1900* (Cambridge: Cambridge University Press, 2002): 3, 13, 29.

reinforcing colonial rule and its cultural project.[163] As they addressed their appeals to the administrative authority of the colony, Ṣādiq Jān and Mayram Bībī may, in a sense, have conferred legitimacy upon the legal authority of the colonial state. In addition, they took legal action against an Islamic institution—a *qāḍī* presiding over a *sharīʿa* court—in such a way that his alleged malpractice would be reviewed by the provincial prosecutor according to the general laws of the empire. But, by exploiting the appellate system and entwining Russian bureaucrats in their own machinations against a Muslim judge, Ṣādiq Jān and Mayram Bībī managed to draw colonial administrative authorities into the orbit of Islamic law. As Ṣādiq Jān and Mayram Bībī successfully exercised their normative agency, Russian officials made great show of referring to Islamic procedural laws in their judicial review. Such practices of legal hybridization were not among the prerogatives of the Russian administrative authorities, a fact that the provincial prosecutor immediately reinforced by redirecting the case to the jurisdiction of a *sharīʿa* court.

These unfounded accusations of judicial malfeasance and corruption did undermine *qāḍīs*' legal authority, but only partly. As above, under the institutional arrangements introduced by Russians, *qāḍīs* enjoyed unprecedented power because they could count on Russian police forces for the enforcement of their judgments. In addition, after the fall of the Muslim potentates in the areas that formerly belonged to the Khoqand khanate and the Bukhara emirate, *qāḍīs* now had a monopoly over *sharīʿa* in Russian Turkestan, that is, they did not have to compete for legal authority with governors and representatives of the royal court.

163 Ibid.: 148–9; Sharafi, "The Marital Patchwork of Colonial South Asia": 980–1, 1009.

CHAPTER 3

The Bureaucratization of Land Tenure

Introduction

How did colonial empires engage preexisting forms of land tenure and seek to influence them for their own, mainly fiscal, purposes? This question is crucial for anyone seeking to understand how empires promoted settlement policies, attempted land confiscation, and developed tools of governance to extract revenues. The question is crucial also for the historian of law, because property relations stand at the intersection of several legal domains, such as the law of contract, inheritance, and family law. Discerning how rights of land tenure were attested, secured, and defended can therefore illuminate changes and continuities in the legal culture of those Muslim communities that became subjects of a non-Islamic government in Central Asia. This chapter aims to explore the ways in which imperial statutory laws and Russian bureaucratic practices transformed property relations among Muslims in the Governorship-General of Turkestan, and the ways in which they did not. This chapter will focus on how Central Asians engaged the colonial property regime as a way of acquiring landed estates that once belonged to the treasury of the khanates. At the same time, I hope to show how colonial bureaucratic practices brought about a new, more exclusive, process of textualization of forms of land tenure. This process led to the Muslims' articulation of a narrower understanding of property.

How do we approach most usefully the study of property relations and land rights as they were expressed in a cultural domain where Russian legal and administrative practices mixed with Islamic juristic thinking and established fiscal customs? This is a particularly complex question, because most of the sources suggest that the colonization aimed at the preservation of the status quo in order to avoid discontent and therefore often claimed to have left in place existing patterns of land tenure. Several Russian officials attempted to decipher the legal and fiscal attributes of land-ownership in Turkestan with a view to securing the compliance of established practices of land tenure with new fiscal policies.[1] Others, by contrast, advocated a complete overhaul of such practices. Whether cautious with traditions or sympathetic to profound

1 B. Penati, "Notes on the Birth of Russian Turkestan's Fiscal System: A View from the Fergana Oblast'." *JESHO* 53/5 (2010): 679–711.

DOI 10.1163/9789004330900_005

reform, Russians did not operate alone. Colonial subjects played a crucial role as cultural brokers. As we shall see in detail, local scholars who were endowed with privileged knowledge of property relations were instrumental in shaping perceptions and reasoning among Russians. The available information suggests that we are dealing here with a typical colonial situation of cultural imbrications in which innovations were often formulated in vernacular languages (Persian and Chaghatay), using a vocabulary peppered with conventional and formulaic expressions derived from the specialized terminology of Islamic law. Disentangling meanings, notions, and perceptions about land rights requires that we clarify the principles and the wide array of social practices that determined the forms of land tenure in the period before the Russian conquest.

There has been substantial scholarship on this subject over the last two decades. In the growing body of literature dealing with landholding in Islamic Central Asia, however, one can discern a problem of method that keeps us from acquiring a clearer picture of precolonial property relations. First, scholarship on landholding has relied heavily on what are usually termed "documentary sources" without a firm grasp of the culture of documentation that informed the production of such sources. Most scholars have thus read "documents" as if they could speak for themselves, thereby avoiding the interpretive problems necessarily posed by eliciting meaning from these sources. It is naïve to approach texts without exploring the conceptual repertoire and the social context shaping their production. This approach to "documentary sources" is best exemplified in catalogues and calendars of legal texts that have been produced since the Soviet period and often include glaring misinterpretations.[2] This observation does not necessarily mean that such repertoires are useless. Most historians have, however, adopted a "lexical" approach to their materials—assuming, that is, that there is a consistent logical equivalence between words and things and that terms appearing in one source carry the same force in another. They have thus overlooked how meaning inheres in context. Consequently, the taxonomies of property relations that we find reflected in the glossaries of catalogues merely repeat each other, in spite of the possibility that meanings might well have changed over time or that the social circumstances behind the production of texts described therein might

2 *Katalog Khivinskikh kaziiskikh dokumentov (XIX–nach. XX vv.)*, ed. A. Urunbaev et al. (Tashkent and Tokyo: Department of Islamic Area Studies, 2001); E. Karimov, *Regesty kaziiskikh dokumentov i khanskikh iarlikov Khivinskogo khanstva XVII–nachala XX v.* (Tashkent: Fan, 2007); B. Kazakov, *Bukharan Documents: The Collection in the District Library, Bukhara*, trans. J. Paul (Berlin: Klaus Schwarz, 2001).

be completely different.[3] We should keep this in mind as we attempt to read legal deeds alongside juristic tracts.

Second, studies on agrarian history tend to confer great epistemological authority on documentary sources because of their presumed implicit proximity to reality. These studies seem to have neglected that royal warrants, diplomas, and legal deeds are, in fact, written in a formulaic language that tends, as we shall see, to be conservative and does not reflect changes in the domain of legal and fiscal reasoning. Assuming that such texts provide unmediated access to the past, scholars have trivialized the possibility that information on evolving landholding patterns might be reflected better in other sources such as juristic treatises or narrative sources. It is to the latter that I want to turn in this chapter. My source basis comes primarily from the Bukharan emirate (eighteenth and nineteenth centuries). When Russians subjugated Transoxiana, they thought that practices of land tenure in the emirate reflected broader patterns at work in Central Asia.[4] To study precolonial Bukharan juristic sources on land tenure is therefore the key to grasping what Russians understood (or thought they understood) as eminently "indigenous" and "traditional" in the field of agrarian relations.

Third, most of the sources that are usually examined to illustrate the situation before the Russian conquest actually refer to the post-1860 period and thus speak various idioms.[5] We must often rely on texts produced in Russian, written by military officials, administrators, and Orientalists, which are reminiscent of Islamic legal scholarship and interweave vernacular bureaucratese, though they do not always make their points of reference explicit. (I will discuss this colonial textual genre in Part 2.) At the same time, elements of what appears to be a purely *sharīʿa*-derived Islamicate vocabulary as found in late

3 I draw here on Florian Schwarz, who pointed out that the limitation of catalogues lies in their not reflecting the dynamics of property relations; see his "Contested Grounds: Ambiguities and Disputes over the Legal and Fiscal Status of Land in the Manghit Emirate of Bukhara." *CAS* 29/1 (2010): 53.

4 The approach of the Russians to land tenure in Central Asian was predicated on the assumption of some kind of cultural uniformity. A study by Ulfatbek Abdurasulov shows that land-tenure practices differed considerably between Bukhara and Khiva; see his "Pravovaia i fiskal'naia dinamika zemlevladeniia v Khorezme (XIX–nachalo XX v.)." *Vostok-Oriens* 4 (2015): 32–46.

5 This is exemplified by A. Morrison, "*Amlākdārs*, *Khwājas* and *Mulk* Land in the Zarafshan Valley after the Russian Conquest." In *Explorations in the Social History of Modern Central Asia (19th–20th Century)*, ed. Paolo Sartori (Leiden: Brill, 2013): 23–64. As I will show, things do not become clearer if one uses instead sources from the Timurid and Shibanid periods, such as those edited and published by Chekhovich, on the assumption that, from the Mongol conquest to Russian colonization, property relations did not change in Central Asia.

nineteenth- and early twentieth-century Chaghatay- and Persian-language sources may, in fact, reflect forms of linguistic usage shaped by colonial regulations and bureaucratic practices. Facing the difficult task of making sense of this fabric of linguistic practices—a task attempted in many colonial contexts[6]—several scholars have failed to appreciate how the definition of land rights depended on legal as much as fiscal attributes.

This chapter consists of four parts. In the first, I review the existing scholarship in light of a major shift in the meaning of landed property rights that manifested itself more clearly in the available sources from the eighteenth and the nineteenth centuries. Indeed, the term *milk* was used in that period to denote the ownership of produce, not of land. The consequence of this sematic shift was that, by means of taxation, Muslim rulers received a share of the produce and thereby acquired entitlements on private estates. This led to a situation of "co-dominion" in which the ruler, the landowner and the tenant shared the usufruct of the same land. In the second part, I trace how Russian lawmakers legislated on land tenure by purporting to build on local notions of "property" (and alleged lack thereof) and that they manipulated Central Asian juristic traditions. In the third, I show that the Russians introduced a more rigid understanding of property that depended on contractual evidence, which led to a bureaucratized understanding of agrarian relations. Finally, I examine two legal cases that exemplify how Central Asians attempted to take advantage of the new situation to seize land that once belonged to the former Muslim polities of Central Asia.

1 Forms of Land Tenure in Bukhara Before the Russian Conquest

1.1 *What Approach?*

Before trying to identify the ways in which land tenure in nineteenth-century Central Asia changed under Russian rule, as well as the ways in which it was unchanged, we need to offer a brief preliminary overview of the factors determining tenure and its forms. One way to do this is to consider the taxonomical principles according to which local jurists defined the types of land and its use. This approach allows us to gain a firmer grasp of the rules that formalized the juridical status of land tenure and provides us with the tools to understand

6 B.S. Cohn, "The Command of Language and the Language of Command." In *Writings on South Asian History and Society*, Subaltern Studies 4, ed. R. Guha (Delhi: Oxford University Press, 1985): 276–329.

how such rules informed local notary practices and were therefore reflected in deeds. Undertaking this interpretive task is essential, because deeds constitute most of the sources available to us that reflect property relations. One might be tempted to call this the "juristic" approach, but I suggest that that would be mistaken. It does not take a great leap of imagination to see that the kind of juristic sources I propose to turn to are directly informed by and therefore reflect local practices and social circumstances. Juristic sources do not represent legal theory as opposed to law in action.[7]

Others would proceed differently. Jürgen Paul, for example, proposes that any discussion of land tenure start from the idea that land has always been, in Central Asia, a commodity, and that, if one can transfer something, it must be labeled "property."[8] Attractively sensible, Paul's proposal is nevertheless problematic in its anachronistically liberal conception of property, which originates in the West after the French revolution. It is problematic also because it conceptualizes property relations exclusively within the narrow domain of transactions, according to which, if someone can transfer her rights on land, then this land must belong to her. This notion conflates several forms of land tenure that were regarded by locals as substantively different on account of their environmental components—whether, for example, the land was a pasture or an agricultural field—and its fiscal attributes. In fact, there existed in precolonial Central Asia a variety of juridical constructions that allowed landholders to dispose of, say, state land or mortmain as if it belonged to them. It is common among students of this region to read sources in which individuals and communities had room to operate as they saw fit with land belonging to the treasury or to charitable endowments. As we shall see, this was common to people who, by virtue of their longstanding relation to the land, secured rights of disposal that were passed from one generation to another. These people could sell, mortgage, and donate the property rights on improvements (*uskūna/suknīya*) such as structures or plantations that existed on the land they tilled, whether the latter was the patrimony of the state or a charitable endowment.[9]

7 A diametrically opposite reading is propounded in A.K.S. Lambton, *Landlord and Peasant in Persia: A Study of Land Tenure and Land Revenue Administration* (London: Oxford University Press, 1953): 53.

8 See his "Recent Monographs on the Social History of Central Asia." *CAS* 29/1 (2010): 126.

9 T. Welsford and N. Tashev, *A Catalogue of Arabic-Script Documents from the Samarqand Museum* (Samarkand and Istanbul: IICAS, 2012): docs. 162, 163, 330, 345, 362.

However, the deeds reflecting such transactions also specify that the land—that is, the soil—belonged to the treasury or an endowment. In other words, while the owner of the improvements might have changed, the lessor of this land—whether the ruler, a charitable endowment, or a landowner—did not lose his property rights by virtue of the various transactions initiated by the lessee. In order to make sense of such complex juridical constructions, it may be more useful to clarify the attributes of land-ownership and the reasons various juridical constructions were elaborated to favor the transactions allowing for the commodification of land. Discerning local understandings of property will also facilitate our task of reconstructing the meanings that colonial masters and subjects conferred on the vocabulary of property that they employed after the conquest.

To advocate, as I do, a close examination of legal material is not without risks. Chris Hann has noted that "the focus on property relations must not be restricted to the formal legal codes which play a major role in our own society, but must be broadened to include the institutional and cultural contexts within which such codes operate."[10] This is an invaluable warning about the temptation to impose a normative point of view on our material and on agrarian relations, but it also poses a daunting interpretive challenge. While nineteenth-century Central Asia is one such institutional and cultural context in which formal legal codes did not exist, one also finds a wide variety of juristic treatises, legal opinions, notary manuals, and established practices that shape property relations into one coherent conceptual repertoire, that is, a system. This system articulated itself in a strongly legalistic vocabulary. Eschewing the adoption of such a vocabulary is a probing task, especially if one considers that the idiom of Islamic legal deeds (Ar. *wathīqa*, pl. *wathā'iq*), which convey most land transactions, is highly formulaic and resistant to change. Taken together, however, this material actually represents a case of early-modern legalism. Despite the absence of rigid codes of law, we are dealing here with norms and normative processes that are manifestly articulated in a formalistic vocabulary.

---

10 C. Hann, "Introduction: The Embeddedness of Property." In *Property Relations: Renewing the Anthropological Tradition*, ed. C. Hann (Cambridge: Cambridge University Press, 2008): 7.

1.2 *Taking Stock of Emic Notions of Land Tenure*

Key Terms of Land Tenure

bayt al-māl: treasury
dahyak: tax amounting conventionally to one-tenth of the harvest
mamlaka: state land
mamlūk: estate
milk: ownership of produce, i.e., usufruct
kharāj: tax amounting conventionally to one-fifth of the harvest
khāṣṣa: crown land
milk-i kharājī (also *mamlūk-i kharājī*): the treasury owns one-fifth of the produce, while the private landowner owns one-tenth of it
milk-i ʿushrī (also *mamlūk-i ʿushrī*): the treasury owns one-tenth of the produce, while the private landowner owns one-fifth of it
milk-i ḥurr: the landowner owns the entire produce, i.e., tax-exempt property
tankhwāh: grant of a rent
ʿushr: tax amounting conventionally to one-tenth of the harvest

There are several important terms in the idiom of landholding in Islamic Central Asia, with which the reader may already be familiar. One is *mamlaka* (or *zamīn-i pādishāhī*), a term usually translated as "state land." As such, *mamlaka* should not be confused with the private domain of the ruler (*khāṣṣa*), though there may sometimes be substantial overlap between the two.[11] *Milk* denotes private ownership. *Mamlaka* and *milk* are basic legal concepts in *sharīʿa*.[12] There are many others that are specific to the bureaucratic language of the Central Asian chancelleries; we will encounter them in this chapter. The common assumption about *milk* among historians of nineteenth-century Central Asia is that it refers to private land-ownership. In other words, *milk* has generally been understood—by myself in the past and by other scholars—in its classical sense, as denoting property rights to land.[13] For the historian

11 I follow here the rendering of M.E. Subtelny, *Timurids in Transition: Turko-Persian Politics and Acculturation in Medieval Iran* (Leiden: Brill, 2007): 206.

12 R. McChesney, "Central Asia. XI. Economy from the Timurids until the 12th/18th Century." In *EIr* vol. V: 218–19.

13 A. Morrison, *Russian Rule in Samarkand, 1868–1910: A Comparison with British India* (Oxford: Oxford University Press, 2008): 59 and passim; P. Sartori, "Il *waqf* nel Turkestan

of nineteenth- and twentieth-century Central Asia, however, such an understanding of *milk* is misleading. As used as early as the second half of the eighteenth century, the term instead denoted rights not to the land itself but to its proceeds. We owe this revised understanding of the term to the Soviet numismatist Elena Davidovich. First in correspondence during the late 1960s with Ol'ga Chekhovich—a famous Soviet historian of agrarian relations in medieval Central Asia[14]—and later in a paper delivered at the Barthold Lectures in Moscow in 1975,[15] Davidovich observed that, at least from the fifteenth century,[16] local potentates extended their rights to private landed properties. It is unclear when, precisely, this process occurred and under what circumstances. One would be tempted to think, as Chekhovich does, of confiscation and aggressive fiscal policies as effective means of putting pressure on landowners. When Shībānī Khān, for example, conquered Herat in 1515, he divided the dominions (*mamālik*) of Khorasan among his three sons and deprived landowners of their revenues by introducing a tax called *rasm al-ṣadra*, which was equal to the tithe (*dahyak*).[17]

Whatever the policies of these potentates, the effects of this process were manifold. What used to be a private property-right to land (*milk*) was made

---

russo tra legislazione e pratica amministrativa coloniale." *Quaderni Storici* 132/3 (2009): 802; "Colonial Legislation Meets *Sharīʿa*: Muslims' Land Rights in Russian Turkestan." CAS 29/1 (2010): 43–60; Penati, "Notes on the Birth of Russian Turkestan's Fiscal System: A View from the Fergana Oblast' ": 744; Morrison, "*Amlākdārs*, *Khwājas* and *Mulk* Land in the Zarafshan Valley after the Russian Conquest": 30. Here Morrison refers to Schwarz, "Contested Grounds: Ambiguities and Disputes over the Legal and Fiscal Status of Land in the Manghit Emirate of Bukhara": 35.

14 U. Abdurasulov, "Ol'ga Chekhovich: Two Facets of a Soviet Academic." IS 48/5 (2015): 785–804.

15 E.A. Davidovich, "Feodal'nyi zemel'nyi milk v Srednei Azii XV–XVIII vv.: Sushchnost' i transformatsiia." In *Formy feodal'noi zemel'noi sobstvennosti i vladeniia na Blizhnem i Srednem Vostoke. Bartol'dovskie chtenia 1975 g.*, ed. B.G. Gafurov, G.F. Girs, and E.A. Davidovich (Moscow: Nauka, 1979): 39–62.

16 Ibid.: 50.

17 See Ghiyās al-Dīn b. Himām al-Dīn al-Ḥusaynī, alias Khwāndamīr, *Ta'rīkh-i ḥabīb al-siyar fī akhbār-i afrād-i bashar*, ed. J. Humā'ī, 2nd ed. (Tehran: Khayyām, 1333/1954): 4:383. I owe this inference to a remark found in the collection of Chekhovich notes, TsGARUz, f. R-2678, op. 1, d. 531, l. 54. On the subject of land confiscation under the Shibanids, see also R.G. Mukminova, *K istorii agrarnykh otnoshenii v Uzbekistane XVI v. Vakf-name* (Tashkent: Fan, 1966): 40–41. For similar attempts at confiscations in the history of the Islamicate world, see B. Johansen, *The Islamic Law on Land Tax and Rent: The Peasants' Loss of Property Rights as Interpreted in the Hanafite Literature of the Mamluk and Ottoman Period* (London: Croom Helm, 1998).

proportional to one's share of taxation.[18] In other words, there was a transition from a regime of property to one of usufruct, in which the meaning of "landowner" evolved into "tax farmer." This transition brought about the notion that *milk* land was a form of "co-dominion," by which is meant that the ruler and the landowner possessed different shares of what the land produced.[19] This idea will be crucial for contextualizing the knowledge that Russian officials gathered on the subject of Central Asian forms of land tenure. We shall return to the notion of co-dominion in detail later.

Davidovich's argument that *milk* in the post-Timurid era denoted a form of co-dominion draws strong support from an interesting juristic source, a treatise devoted to the study of the lands subject to taxation, titled *al-Risāla fī taḥqīq arāḍī al-ʿushrīya wa al-kharājīya*, which was compiled in 1768–9.[20] Its author was a Bukharan *qāḍī*, ʿIbādallāh b. ʿĀrif Khwāja al-Bukhārī, who included this short treatise in Arabic and Persian in a larger compendium of Hanafi law called *Jāmiʿ al-maʿmūlāt*. The treatise is better known under the title *Risāla-yi Ḥabībīya*, which the author named for his son Ḥabībullāh. While the work has been known to students of agrarian history since 1970,[21] its importance remains largely underestimated. Because the work may help us understand how legists formulated the rules that determined ownership and possession in Transoxiana a century before the Russian conquest, it is to this treatise that I now turn.

ʿIbādallāh begins his account by explaining that "state land" (*mamlaka*) is any kind of private "estate" (*mamlūk*) whose proprietors have died without heir. In such cases, ʿIbādallāh says, the "treasury" (*bayt al-māl*) subsumes these estates into state land.[22] I use the word "estate" deliberately to distinguish *mamlūk* from *milk* (property), which appear as distinct categories in the treatise.

The *qāḍī* further distinguishes estates with reference to two basic fiscal categories called *ʿushr* and *kharāj*. Private estates are thus called *mamlūk-i kharājī* and *mamlūk-i ʿūshrī*. Making sense of such categories requires us to remember

18 *uravniav ikh prava na zemliu i rentu*, Davidovich, "Feodal'nyi zemel'nyi milk v Srednei Azii XV–XVIII vv.: Sushchnost' i transformatsiia": 50.

19 Ibid.: 44.

20 This text exists in two manuscripts in Tashkent, TsVRUz, no. 6196/II and 4976/III.

21 M.A. Abduraimov, *Ocherki agrarnykh otnoshenii v Bukharskom khanstve* (Tashkent: Fan, 1970): 8. See also *SVR* XI: 307–8. The entry devoted to a description of the *Risāla* refers to unpublished translations produced by two other Soviet Orientalists, A. Vil'danova and A. Javonmardiev (in Russian and Uzbek, respectively).

22 *arāḍī-yi mamlaka ān-ast ki … mālik-i ān fawt shuda wa az way wārithī nay mānda wa bayt al-māl shuda ast wa mamlaka ḥaqq-i ʿāmma-yi muslimīn gardīda ast.*

a basic rule that our author has tacitly followed while compiling his treatise: the sultan extracts 30% from the yield produced on state land,[23] leaving the remainder to the landholder. The taxes generated are further divided into three parts: one-third of the taxation is called *ʿushr*, the remaining two-thirds *kharāj*.[24] The *kharāj* is thus twice the size of the *ʿushr*. It follows that *ʿushr* is one-tenth of the entire produce, while *kharāj* is one-fifth, calculated on the entire harvest. These are conventional calculations that, however, informed the compilation of the *Risāla-yi Ḥabībīya* and that are useful to keep in mind as we read the treatise and review the colonial documentation. An interesting addition to the category of *ʿushrī* estates is when:

> Upon order of the Islamic ruler someone brings to life [*iḥyāʾ*] land left fallow without proprietor [*zamīn-i mayta bilā mālik*] and turned into state land and cultivates it with *ʿushrī* water; this land becomes an *ʿushrī* [estate], according to the doctrine of Imām Muḥammad [Shaybānī]. But, according to the doctrine of Abū Yūsuf (peace be upon him!), it becomes *ʿushrī* only if the surrounding estates consist of land left fallow without a proprietor; if the lands around it are *kharājī*, this fallow land without proprietor will become *kharājī* after being brought to life. According to the doctrine of the Imām Abū Yūsuf (peace be upon him!), this land, by virtue of its restoration upon order of the Islamic ruler becomes the private property [*milk*] of that person from whom the Islamic ruler takes the tithe [...] and gives it to his partners, who are the commons. Until the day of resurrection, this land, after the death of these conquerors, remains among their heirs or by virtue of sale will belong to someone else [*ba-sabab-i bayʿ-i īshān ba-dīgarī ʿāyid shuda*].

Although this reasoning may sound convoluted and abstruse, we shall see that it shaped the approach to the systematization of local forms of land tenure taken by several Russian officials.

ʿIbādallāh is equally conventional in his account of the Islamic theory of land-ownership. The true innovation of the *Risāla-yi Ḥabībīya*, however, is in its elaboration of a supplementary category of land tenure. This category involves state land that the Islamic ruler (*pādishāh-i Islām*) sells in exchange for a Qurʾān. In this symbolic transaction, the purchaser acquires the tithe (*ʿushr*)

23 In nineteenth-century Bukhara, there were cases in which the state levied 40%; see O.D. Chekhovich, "O razmere kheradzha v Bukhare XIX veka." *ONU* (1961/3): 38–44.

24 C. Cahen, "Kharādj," *EI2* vol. IV: 1031.

levied on that land.[25] There is a simple juristic principle underpinning this procedure: the ruler disposes of all the state land as an administrator (*mutawallī-yi ʿāmma*) and is therefore entitled to receive a management fee equivalent to the tithe. By acting in this capacity, he has the power to sell this fee,[26] while he should use the *kharāj* to the benefit of all Muslims. Consequently, by virtue of this sale, the purchaser becomes the proprietor of the *ʿushr*,[27] while, at the same time, he should pay to the ruler the *kharāj* levied from his estate.[28] We observe in this context a major semantic shift in *milk* from land to proceeds. It is here that is articulated most clearly the idea that *milk* denotes ownership of a share of taxation.[29]

ʿIbādallāh states that this transaction between the ruler and his subject underlies another form of land tenure, called conventionally *milk-i ḥurr*: the landowner who purchased state land from the ruler could sell back to the latter two-thirds (*thulthān*) of the estate in return for the rent equivalent to the *kharāj* levied on the "remaining third part" of the estate (*thulth-i bāqī*). With the first transaction the landowner acquired the property of the *ʿushr*. By this sale, the landowner would now obtain also the *kharāj* of the produce originating from the estate. Consequently, his property would be called *ḥurr*, i.e. "freed" from the payment of the two types of taxation.[30] Florian Schwarz has argued that this procedure may not, in fact, have produced full fiscal exemption.[31] Instead, he proposes that the land was merely *kharāj*-exempt, and the owner would still have had to pay the *ʿushr*. This reading overlooks the fact that the creation of *milk-i ḥurr* land consisted of two transactions. In the first, the landowner purchased a plot of land from the state: this land was liable for *kharāj* though exempted from *ʿushr*. In the second transaction, the landowner sold back two-thirds of the newly purchased estate in exchange for exemption from *kharāj* on the remaining third. The result was that the landowner now

25 *ḥiṣṣa-yi ʿushr-i ān mamlūk mushtarī mīshawad*, in *Risāla-yi Ḥabībīya*, MS Tashkent, TsVRUz, no. 6196/II: fol. 262a.

26 *ḥaqq al-tawlīya-yi khwud rā ki ʿushr-i ʿān wilāyat-i bayʿ dārad*, ibid.

27 *ʿushr-i ʿān taʿalluq ba-mushtarī wa milk-i way shuda ast*, ibid.

28 *kharāj-i ānrā az barāy-i ʿāmma az mushtarī-yi madhkūr mīgīrad*, ibid.

29 Davidovich, "Feodal'nyi zemel'nyi milk v Srednei Azii XV–XVIII vv.: Sushchnost' i transformatsiia": 43.

30 *wa agar miyān-i pādishāh-i Islām wa mushtarī-yi madhkūr mubādala wāqiʿ shawad bar wajh ki thulthān-i īn arāḍī rā mushtarī-yi madhkūr bar badal-i kharāj-i thulth-i bāqī ba-pādishāh-i Islām ba-dahad maʿqabūlihi īn thulth-i bāqī milk-i ḥurr-i khāliṣ az kharāj wa ʿushr shawad, Risāla-yi Ḥabībīya*, MS Tashkent, TsVRUz, no. 6196/II: fol. 262a.

31 See his "Contested Grounds: Ambiguities and Disputes over the Legal and Fiscal Status of Land in the Manghit Emirate of Bukhara": 36.

owned a plot of land the produce of which was exempt from both *ʿushr* and *kharāj*.[32] The jurist thereby formalized a form of fictional exchange allowing the landowner to purchase from the state a complete fiscal exemption that would allow him to receive three-tenths of the produce generated by the land he possessed.[33]

1.3 *The Semantic Shift of* Milk

The creation of *milk-i ḥurr* is reflected in many deeds dating back at least to the second half of the fifteenth century, which have been the subject of extensive commentary.[34] Elena Davidovich,[35] in particular, has reached the revealing conclusion that I anticipated above: non-tax-exempt *milk*, which is called, in the *Risāla-yi Ḥabībīya, mamlūk-i kharājī*, is a form of "co-dominion"[36] between

32 *Risāla-yi Ḥabībīya*, MS Tashkent, TsVRUz, no. 6196/II: fol. 265a.

33 On this point, see also Davidovich, "Feodal'nyi zemel'nyi milk v Srednei Azii XV–XVIII vv.: Sushchnost' i transformatsiia": 41; Subtelny, *Timurids in Transition*: 222.

34 *Dokumenty k istorii agrarnykh otnoshenii v Bukharskom khanstve*, vol. 1, *Akty feodal'noi sobstvennosti na zemliu XVII–XIX vv.*, ed. O.D. Chekhovich (Tashkent: Fan, 1954): xix. Subtelny notes that there are templates for the compilation of such deeds in fifteenth-century formulary manuals: *Timurids in Transition*: 222. See also Morrison, *Russian Rule in Samarkand, 1868–1910: A Comparison with British India*: 99; Schwarz, "Contested Grounds: Ambiguities and Disputes over the Legal and Fiscal Status of Land in the Manghit Emirate of Bukhara": 35.

35 See her "Feodal'nyi zemel'nyi milk v Srednei Azii XV–XVIII vv.: Sushchnost' i transformatsiia."

36 The publication in which she first used this expression is "Usilenie feodal'noi razdroblennosti. Zhizn' tadzhikov v Bukharskom khanstve v XVII i pervoi polovine XVIII v." In *Istoriia tadzhikskogo naroda*, vol. 2, *Pozdnyi feodalizm* (*XVII v.-1917 g.*), ed. B.I. Iskandarov and A.M. Mukhtarov (Moscow: Nauka, 1964): 37. Jürgen Paul has characterized Davidovich's idea of co-dominion as "her own construction" because "she does not produce evidence in Central Asian Muslim legal thinking about such a thing." He also suggested that "it could be said that she is overextending her evidence on a particular point", "Recent Monographs on the Social History of Central Asia": 126. Paul is correct in noting that Davidovich never mentioned the *Risāla* in her work. Nor does Ol'ga Chekhovich make use of it in her various studies in the subject, though she translated excerpts of it in 1963. It is unclear why scholars have not profited from this source as one would expect, as many deeds, which Chekhovich had published, belong to the eighteenth century, precisely the period in which the *Risāla* was composed. Chekhovich and Davidovich's purposeful decision not to deal with the treatise must have depended on rivalries among academics in Uzbekistan working in the field of agrarian history and claiming an intellectual monopoly of some sort over specific topics and sources. It is clear, for example, that, already by the end of the 1960s, Elena Davidovich was encouraging her colleague Chekhovich to produce a magnum opus on the subject of *milk*. If ever Chekhovich had made plans for such a

the ruler and the landowner, who co-own the produce of a certain land. Her work shows that, while the landowner and the ruler divided among themselves a share (about 30%) of the produce originating from a certain estate, they disposed of the same land as an undivided estate. This is easy to prove, so to speak. The legal procedure leading to the creation of *milk-i ḥurr*, whereby a landowner acquires from the ruler a tax-exempt piece of land, consists of a separation of estates between the ruler and the landowner, which originally constituted a larger undivided dominion. This is illustrated in the deeds notarized by *qāḍīs*, which describe the "boundaries" (*maḥdūdāt*) of the internal divisions that are drawn during the notarization of the transaction.[37] The very act of dividing the estate suggests that, before the application of this procedure, the land was not divided between ruler and landowner—hence the idea of co-dominion. But even if one were to neglect the importance of the *Risāla*, the evidence from legal deeds is overwhelming. We have already mentioned documents reflecting the creation of *milk-i ḥurr*. One should also read closely the more everyday sale deeds. The conservative character of the Islamic law of contract notwithstanding, deeds notarized in Bukhara are unique in specifying land-ownership as *milk-i kharājī*.[38] This qualification suggests that the property rights of the seller and the purchaser were implicitly determined and therefore constrained by those of the ruler (*milk-i ʿushrī*).

A second aspect that we must consider in order to appreciate the originality of Davidovich's approach is that the ruler enjoyed rights to private estates, which he could transfer to a third party.[39] Of course, one could qualify these rights as eminently fiscal, amounting to a share of the rent produced by the land equivalent to the *kharāj*. If so, we should also recognize the fact that, as the *Risāla-yi Ḥabībīya* explains, the person who possessed a private estate owned in fact only a share of the rent equivalent to the *ʿushr*. This is well illustrated in the following example:

publication, they must have been jeopardized by Abduraimov's *Ocherki agrarnykh otnoshenii v Bukharskom khanstve*. In the margins of Chekhovich's personal copy of this work, we find several notes in which she accused Abduraimov of having plagiarized her and Davidovich's work: (*doslovnoe moe; ėto zhe Davidovich!*).

37 "Feodal'nyi zemel'nyi milk v Srednei Azii XV–XVIII vv.: Sushchnost' i transformatsiia": 49; *Dokumenty k istorii agrarnykh otnoshenii v Bukharskom khanstve*, vol. 1: docs. 11, 12, 18, 19, 21, 25.

38 Welsford and Tashev, *A Catalogue of Arabic-Script Documents from the Samarqand Museum*: docs. 34, 68, 97, 161, 162, 248b.ii, 254, 259, 260, 262, 264, 266, 267, 312, 327, 331, 344, 346, 354, 369, 376.

39 "Feodal'nyi zemel'nyi milk v Srednei Azii XV–XVIII vv.: Sushchnost' i transformatsiia": 47.

> He [is the Lord]. An eminent ruling prescribed that the tithe [*dahyak*][40] of the locality of Tābān would be the property of Muḥammad Zamān Khwāja, [while the locality itself] would become a tax-farming grant [*tankhwāh*] of Walad-i Jaq Jaq. The latter has died, and we have now bestowed the locality as a tax-farming grant on the aforementioned [Muḥammad Zamān Khwāja]. Let the officeholders of the chancellery take notice of this [change] in the register [*daftar*] and let them not overlook [this royal order]. Year 1036 [1626–27] Imāmqulī Bahādur Khān.[41]

The deed—a royal warrant issued by the chancellery of the Bukharan emirate—suggests that Muḥammad Zamān Khwāja possessed a private estate (*milk/ mamlūk-i kharājī*) by virtue of his owning one-tenth of the taxation.[42] It likewise shows that the ruler could grant his own fiscal rights, that is *milk-i ʿushrī*, to the same land first to other individuals.

One might observe that to regard *milk* as a form of co-dominion is to apply a narrow understanding of property that is contingent on the notion of fiscal exemption. I would object to this because, if a private landed property (such as the estate belonging to Muḥammad Zamān Khwāja) could be made a grant (*tankhwāh*) and consequently transferred to a tax farmer, this constitutes a meaningful transformation in the local understanding of property.[43] At the center of this semantic shift lies the idea that land (*arāḍī*) can be exchanged

---

40 On *dahyak* meaning "tithe" and as a synonym of *ʿushr*, see *Risāla-yi Ḥabībīya*, MS Tashkent, TsVRUz, no. 6196/II: fol. 268b. It was also used for a tax levied on certain land devoted to benefit charitable endowments, see TsGARUz, f. I-126, op. 1, d. 689, l. 1; M.N. Rostislavov, *Ocherk vidov zemel'noi sobstvennosti i pozemel'nyi vopros v Turkestanskom krae* (St. Petersburg: Tip. Brat. Panteleevykh, 1879): 336; *Dokumenty k istorii agrarnykh otnoshenii v Bukharskom khanstve*: 240 fn. 114; M.A. Abduraimov, "O nekotorykh kategoriiakh feodal'nogo zemlevladeniia i polozhenii krest'ian v Bukharskom khanstve v XVI–nachale XIX veka." *ONU* (1963/7): 36; Schwarz, "Contested Grounds: Ambiguities and Disputes over the Legal and Fiscal Status of Land in the Manghit Emirate of Bukhara": 35.

41 *Dokumenty k istorii agrarnykh otnoshenii v Bukharskom khanstve:* 13 (doc. 4). More references can be found in "Feodal'nyi zemel'nyi milk v Srednei Azii XV–XVIII vv.: Sushchnost' i transformatsiia": 47–48.

42 This formulation is in accordance with the notions articulated, two centuries later, in the *Risāla*.

43 The complexity of overlapping meanings of property is also the basis of conflicts between landowners (*milkdār*) and *tarkhān* grantees, which flared up every time the latter prevented the former from obtaining their share of revenues. TsGARUz, f. I-126, op. 1, d. 759, ll. 4, 5.

for taxation (*bar badal-i kharāj/dar ʿawaḍ-i kharāj*).[44] Davidovich again was the first to note this semantic shift, when she suggested that *ʿushr* and *kharāj* should be regarded as rent[45] rather than as taxes, because the land is only nominally occupied by the purchaser in exchange for regular payments. Most of the landowners—that is to say, the individuals who held *kharājī* estate in co-dominion with the ruler—did not live on the land, which was, instead, rented out to peasants. The following text illustrates that point:

> All of us gave our plots—*mulk*s, bought by us for money, assembled through much sacrifice—in rent to farmers, and they perform work, from the receipts they paid us out of four *batmans*,[46] one *batman*, and the other three *batman*s they used themselves. This order (law) has existed since ancient times; none of our rulers has interfered with it, and we cultivated this land ourselves. From last year until the present, the tax-collectors [*sarkār*] have been using what ought to be used by us; the remainder is used by the farmers themselves, and nothing comes to us. Having lost both land and money, we have become poor. We have turned a few times with petitions to our *ḥākim*s and have received the answer that the senior governor is coming, who will return your plots, and make you happy. [...] Now you have happily come into your domain and have taken into your own hands all the affairs and hearts of us inhabitants. We turned to you about this matter, but you would not permit us and, leaving, now leave us poor people with uneasy hearts. We await this from your Excellency: that you, in cherishing us, poor folk, and showing us, the inhabitants, your love, will restore to us the ancient law and return to us our *mulk*s, so that we may not lose our welfare and property, and we

---

44 See, respectively, *Risāla-yi Ḥabībīya*, MS Tashkent, IVANRUz, no. 6196/II: fol. 262a, and *Dokumenty k istorii agrarnykh otnoshenii v Bukharskom khanstve:* docs. 11 (p. 50), 12 (59), 18 (91), 19 (95), 21 (102), 25 (119).

45 *Postepennoe preobrazovanie naloga... v rentu-nalog, po mere obrazovaniia gosudarstvennykh kategorii zemel'noi sobstvennosti i milkov v izvestnoi pozdnee forme.* See Ol'ga Chekhovich's "notes on Davidovich's letters" (*po pis'mam o milke E.A. Davidovich*), n.d., TsGARUz, f. R-2678, op. 1, d. 531, l. 78. Davidovich wrote two letters to Chekhovich in which she addressed directly the issue of the transformation of forms of land tenure. She sent the first from Lithuania (Poselok Nida) in July 1968 and the second from Dushanbe in August 1968. See TsGARUz, f. R-2678, op. 1, d. 531, ll. 76, 77.

46 *Batman* (also *man/mann*) was a non-standard measure of weight, which differed substantially from one region to another.

> would pray for the White Tsar and the senior governor-lord, and occupy ourselves with our own affairs.[47]

In this petition addressed to the Russian authorities, a group of landowners lamented that they had rented out their possessions to tenants and that, after the conquest, the tax collectors began to raise the land tax imposed by the newcomers directly from the peasants. The tax-collectors consequently deprived the landowners of the share they had been receiving since ancient times, as they put it. This example is important for our purposes because it shows that landowners did not always live on the land they owned.[48] These landowners should therefore be regarded as tax farmers who, rather than considering land a commodity, were interested primarily in the extraction of its revenues. This is an important point of departure for subsequent reflections on property relations and agrarian history in the region under study.

1.4 *A New Model of Property Relations?*

The correspondence between the Bukharan chancellery and the officeholders of the emirate in the first half of the nineteenth century further attests to the changing nature of the lexicon of property relations. Letters of instruction and simple communications illustrate how the bureaucratic center of the emirate regarded *milk* as tax-exempt landed property alone (what legal deeds call *milk-i ḥurr*), considering everything else the patrimony of the state. In October 1813, in a missive addressed to his vizier, Muḥammad Ḥakīm Bī Ināq, the Manghit ruler Emir Ḥaydar (r. 1800–26) lamented that the emirate had been negligent in the survey and registration of tax-exempt properties (*milkhā*) and that it had become increasingly difficult to discover who were the owners. The ruler referred to the case of a certain Muḥammad Amīn Khwāja, who had issued a complaint concerning the malpractice of fiscal assessors who had levied taxes from him, despite the fact that his land was, he said, tax-exempt. When the emir asked someone to verify whether his fiscal status had indeed been recorded in a register (*daftar*), it turned out that Muḥammad Amīn Khwāja did not, in fact, enjoy any fiscal privileges. In his letter to the vizier, the emir was concerned with the possibility that other people had been infringing on state lands (*zamīn-i bisyārī az musulmānān dākhil-i mamlaka shuda-st*). Emir Ḥaydar had a remedy for this untenable state of affairs: no one should levy

---

47 I here quote from Morrison, "*Amlākdārs, Khwājas* and *Mulk* Land in the Zarafshan Valley after the Russian Conquest": 52.

48 "Ownership did not always imply possession," McChesney, *Central Asia: Foundations of Change* (Princeton: Darwin Press, 1996): 59. Such was the case also with *tankhwāh* grantees.

taxes on the land that Muslims have, from time immemorial, been enjoying as their property (*ba-ṭarīq-i milkīyat taṣarruf karda*). Fiscal assessors should, instead, tax those lands on which people had in the past paid taxes (*az qadīm kharāj dada bāshad az ānjā gīrand*).[49] In writing to his minister, the ruler had in mind a clear opposition between the estates on which taxes were due and which he regarded as state land, and anything else that was exempt from taxation and that he considered private property.

We find precisely the same distinction half a century later in a warrant that Emir Muẓaffar sent to the Bukharan *qāḍī* Muḥyī al-Dīn. In his correspondence with the *qāḍī*, the Bukharan ruler referred to a complex situation around the village of Rāst Bādanī Kāmāt, northeast of Bukhara, in what is today the district of Vobkent. The area in question included 150 *ṭanāb*s of privately owned land subject to taxation (*milk-i kharājī*), land under a tax-farming grant (*tankhwāh*), and tax-exempt property. The entire village of Rāst Bādanī Kāmāt amounted to 105 *ṭanāb*s and had been granted to the proprietors of the neighboring lands subject to taxation. The village was taken back by the state and was made an asset of the treasury (*ba-mamlaka taʿlluq yāfta*). After the confiscation, the emir rented out this area to the local residents at a fixed rate. He also ordered that the landowners pay a tax on the estates newly converted into state land. This is when the problems began. First, some landowners neglected the new tenancy contract[50] of the residents of Rāst Bādanī Kāmāt and attempted to keep the rent for themselves.[51] Other landowners paid the treasury less than stipulated.[52] Things worsened when a tax collector began to operate in ignorance of the new fiscal measures. Every time the landowners, the tenants, or the local notables complained about the worsening situation, the emir instructed the *qāḍī* to make inquests (*taḥqīq*). The chancellery of the emirate, however, ascribed little importance to the legal status of the various estates in question. Instead, it was crucial for the state primarily to distinguish whether a given area was subject to taxation and, if so, what fiscal rate was applied to it. The following warrant illuminates the pragmatic approach of the Bukharan chancellery toward the issue of property relations: for Manghit bureaucrats,

---

49 *Maktūbāt-i Amīr Ḥaydar ba Muḥammad Ḥakīm Bī*, MS Tashkent, TsVRUz, no. 2120: fol. 32b–33a.

50 In the Bukharan emirate, tenants and sharecroppers (*muzāriʿīn*) could work on state land (*mamlaka*) on the basis of rent contracts (*ijāra*). See ibid.: fol. 286b [04.05.1890]. The notarization of rent contracts, however, was not required of tenants.

51 *Mubarak-nāmajāt-i Amīr Muẓaffar ba Qāḍī Muḥyī al-Dīn*, MS Tashkent, TsVRUz, no. 407: fol. unnumbered [42a].

52 Ibid.: [49a].

milk denoted tax-exempt land, while *milk-i kharājī* was merely another type of land generating taxable revenues. Hence, it was not referred to as property (*milk*) but simply as *kharājī*:

> Let Mullā Mīr Muḥyī al-Dīn, the refuge of virtue and the shelter of legal knowledge, know that Ṣāḥib Naẓar Āqsaqāl and ʿUmar Qulī Āqsaqāl, from the locality of Rāst Badanī Kāmāt, brought to the attention of His Majesty that, in that area they have six hundred and six *ṭanāb*s, [which consists of] temporarily tax-exempt land [that is now] left fallow, taxed land, and tax-exempt land [*zamīn-i tankhwāh-i bāzyāft wa kharājī wa milk*]. The notable Āta Bāy is the [tax] collector. [But] he has not collected taxes on the improvements and on the land according to [our] practice, that is, in the established amount. He collected too much. We hope that this [request] will be approved so that you will forbid [this behavior], amend those [practices] so that they will be lawful, and report [back to us]. 1293 [1876].[53]

Those who owned land subject to taxation could transfer their assets at they pleased and regarded themselves as proprietors. Nothing, however, prevented the tenants from thinking the same way. By working on state land to improve it and by paying to the state a tax on the structures they erected or the plantations that they established (*uskūna pulī*), tenants could secure quasi-property-rights.[54] The latter, as we have noted, would ensure that tenants could bequeath to their offspring the land according to the Islamic law of inheritance,[55] but they would also be able to transfer the property rights to the land's improvements to other individuals by virtue of legal transactions notarized before a *qāḍī*, thereby disposing of the land as if it effectively belonged to them. With this in mind, one could expand Davidovich's argument and argue that *milk* in nineteenth-century Transoxiana reflected not a form of co-dominion between the ruler and the landowner but a web of property relations in which the entitlements of the ruler, the landowner, and the tenant overlapped. Of course, none of these actors regarded his entitlements to a share of the produce as a form of co-dominion. What mattered for each was to be able to dispose of a share of the produce rather than to own the land.

53 Ibid.: [122a].

54 McChesney, *Central Asia: Foundations of Change*: 59.

55 Welsford and Tashev, *A Catalogue of Arabic-Script Documents from the Samarqand Museum*: doc. 345.

We have considered so far a flexible system of property relations that is determined by the fiscal status of land. In this system, usufruct was the eminent attribute of tenure, which led to the creation of property rights—hence, the frequent expression "proprietary usufruct" (*taṣarruf-i mālikāna*) in deeds. There is little doubt that, throughout the seventeenth, eighteenth, and nineteenth centuries, Central Asian jurists agreed to safeguard the integrity of such rights and regarded them as a prerogative of the tenants. Muftis issued many legal opinions showing that, upon the tacit agreement (*sukūt*) of a landowner, a tenant who cultivated and improved an estate could, with time, act as if he were a proprietor of the land and pass it on to his offspring.[56]

This was the case with the land that individuals or communities received by royal grant. The effective disposal (*taṣarruf ba-ṭarīq-i milkīyat-i dhī al-yad*) of such land "since time immemorial" (*az qadīm al-ayyām*) gave rise to property rights. One who possessed such land would thus regard it as his own (*makhṣūṣ*).[57] Rights to summer pastures are a particularly complex case. Usually situated on rain-watered mountain land, away from winter settlements (*qishlāq*) where people worked agricultural land, summer pastures were state land (*mamlaka*). The ruler would allow herdsmen who engaged in seasonal transhumance to use this land to feed their cattle. He could also transfer the revenues produced by such pastures to a third party—for example, a notable, or a *sayyid*—and thus turn it into a source of tax-farm income.[58] While the legal status of summer pastures evidently prevented them from becoming private property,[59] pastoral groups might nevertheless come to regard such land as their own property, on account of the prolonged access and rights of use they had enjoyed. Climatic instability may have made pastures attractive also for seasonal agriculture, and nomads may have erected structures such as storehouses or barns. Such groups probably attempted to infringe on the rights of the state and thus acquire

56 TsGARUz, f. I-164, op. 1, d. 13, l. 1; TsGARUz, f. R-2678, op. 2, d. 17, l. 1; TsGARUz, f. I-125, op. 1, d. 495, l. 10; Welsford and Tashev, *A Catalogue of Arabic-Script Documents from the Samarqand Museum*: doc. 679.

57 See *Materialy po istorii Ura-Tiube. Sbornik aktov XVII–XIX vv.*, ed. A. Mukhtarov (Moscow: Izdatel'stvo Vostochnoi Literatury, 1963): 49. This text is a royal warrant issued by Emir Ḥaydar in the early nineteenth century. It confirms that a *sayyid* (descendant of the Prophet) has the right to dispose of water and lands in the province of Ura-Tepe as his property. The ruler also prohibited fiscal assessors from collecting taxes from such properties. See also ibid., 15.

58 P.P. Ivanov, *Khoziaistvo dzhuibarskikh sheikhov. K istorii zemlevladeniia v Srednei Azii v XVI–XVII vv.* (Moscow and Leningrad: Izdatel'stvo Akademii Nauk SSR, 1954): 73, 75.

59 Report (*doznanie*), assistant of the commandant of the Samarqand Province, 23.01.1898, TsGARUz, f. I-21, op. 1, d. 475, l. 40b.

ownership of such land, but, their rights to pastures were regulated by the state every year through the work of its agents. It is also clear that pastoral groups seldom felt the need to secure their rights to pastures by means of notarization. Things changed considerably with the Russians, under whose rule there was a shift from a flexible system of agrarian relations based on usufruct to one based on land-ownership attested by legal deeds.

2 Russian Approaches to Landholding in Russian Turkestan

For almost two decades, from the beginning of his tenure in 1867, von Kaufman, the first governor-general of Russian Turkestan, ruled the country on the basis of provisional statutory laws drafted by the so-called Steppe Commission. At the same time, he sought to establish a new statute that would design a land policy specifically for Turkestan. He therefore constituted several commissions that collected legal deeds and treatises in vernacular languages and attempted (so it has often been reported) to describe agrarian relations and forms of land tenure in Central Asia.

2.1 *Vernacular Knowledge and its Colonial Uses*

1869 was an important year in the history of colonial legislation on land tenure in Turkestan. The chancellery of the Governorship-General received reports from the Orientalist Aleksander Kuhn (1840–88) and Colonel Mikhail Nikitich Nikolaev indicating that there had existed, before the Russians, a complex situation in which land rights overlapped with fiscal privileges. Taking stock of this information, the chancellery advised Kaufman to establish a commission to study the agrarian question.[60] At the head of this commission was Andrei Ivanovich Gomzin (d. 1885), a major general who directed the chancellery of the Governorship-General from 1869 to 1877.[61] He was assisted by the commandants of all the provinces (*oblast'*) and several local informants. The

60 A.P. Savitskii, *Pozemel'nyi vopros v Turkestane* (*V proektakh i zakone 1867–1886*) (Tashkent: Izdatel'stvo SamGU, 1963): 15–16.

61 "A man without education but who knew very well the laws and all the possible circulars, and who was a marvelous accountant," G.P. Fedorov, "Moia sluzhba v Turkestane (1870–1910)." *Istoricheskii Vestnik* 9 (1913): 809. On Gomzin's strained relationship with General Mikhail Dimitrevich Skobelev, one of the preeminent personalities of the Russian conquest of Central Asia, see B.A. Kostin, *Mikhail Dimitrovich Skobelev* (Moscow: Moladaia Gvardia, 2000).

reports that this commission produced were extremely important and will be instructive in our investigation. They will allow us to trace the genealogy of Russian legislation on landholding, as we see how the statutory laws promulgated in 1886 incorporated some of the notions of landholding formulated by the Gomzin commission. The Gomzin commission's reports will also help us see how the colonizers attempted to instrumentalize a purported continuity with the past.

To whom does the land belong? What do *milk-i ḥurr* mean and *milk-i ghayr-i ḥurr* mean? What does *waqf* mean? Is the land possessed individually or communally? Does the land belong to the individuals who possess it? Do they possess under customary law or *sharīʿa*?[62] Judging from the nature of the questions that they posed, the members of the 1869 Gomzin commission had at least a grounding in the rudiments of landholding in Central Asia. And one or more members of the commission must have been able to review legal deeds, suggesting that they had mastered Persian. The vocabulary of tax-exempt landownership (*milk-i ḥurr*) and tax-liable land-ownership (*milk-i ghayr-i ḥurr*), for example, was used only in native-language purchase deeds in which the creation of *milk-i ḥurr* was notarized.[63] This suggests that the commission had access through its local informants to Islamic juristic knowledge. Gomzin and his fellows certainly understood that acquainting themselves with the local idiom of land tenure was a key to their mission. This is clear from the three reports (*doklad*) that the commission submitted to the chancellery of the Governorship-General. Their notes show that, to explore the established forms of land tenure in the territories of Bukhara and Khoqand now conquered by the Russians, required tinkering with the *sharīʿa* and its local written traditions. The notion on which the commission structured its report was that "the basic principle of Islam, according to which the land belongs to the Muslim world, offers the possibility [...] of reducing the various regulations of *sharīʿa* on private property to one of possession and usage."[64]

62 TsGARUz, f. I-1, op. 22, d. 3, l. 86.

63 *Dokumenty k istorii agrarnykh otnoshenii v Bukharskom khanstve*: 59, 102, 119.

64 *Osnovnoe polozhenie islama, chto zemlia est' dostoianie vsego musul'manskogo mira, daet, odnako, vozmozhnost' svesti v raznoobrazniia postanovleniia shariata o pravakh chastnoi sobstevnnosti k idei pol'zovaniia ili vladenia*, TsGARUz, f. I-1, op. 22, d. 3, l. 101. Here the commission referred also to several important studies on Islamic law in Russian and French: Baron N.N. Tornau, *Musul'manskoe pravo* (St. Petersburg: Tip. Vtorogo otdeleniia sobstvennoi E.I.V. Kantseliarii, 1866); M. Perron, "La proprieté pour la loi Musulmane n'est qu une possession." In Khalil ibn Ishaq, *Précis. de jurisprudence musulmane ou principes de*

In this regard [the commission reported] another reason for the incertitude of *sharīʿa* [on property rights], which derives from the unquestionable principle of the state's ownership rights [articulated by] the authors and the commentators of *sharīʿa*. The result is that the commentaries serve to distinguish among the rights of use [*pol'zovanie*] and defense from legal attempts of individuals [to seize the property of the state] and from illegal constraints posed by the state itself. However, among those rights that the written Muslim law ascribes to individuals and communities, it is easy to discern also those that the law denies to individuals and communities and that belong to the state. So, in the books of Abū Bakr Khwāhar-zāda and the *Tafariq-i Baqqālī*[65] it is written that *milk-i ḥurr-i khālis* are called the lands on which *kharāj* and *ṭanābāna* [tax per *ṭanāb*] are not levied. The lands are the property of those who possess them, who purchased them for money and relinquished a cultivated portion of them to the treasury. [The proprietors] acquired, according to royal warrants, the right to eternal disposal. Further, in explaining the method of creating *milk-i ḥurr*, the *sharīʿa* says that everyone who wishes to turn the land that is in his possession or use into land to which he has rights of ownership and is therefore tax-exempt, he has first to purchase it for money from the ruler and, after that, to relinquish two-thirds of it to the Treasury. [In this way, he] turns one-third of it into private property and avoids paying *kharāj* and *ṭanābāna* on it. […] These norms lead to two inferences: 1) only lands that are *milk-i ḥurr* are the property of private individuals, while the others, as they were not alienated [by the treasury], belong to the state as the owner of a *votchina* (ancestral landed estate); 2) a necessary attribute [*priznak*] of private landownership is the fiscal exemption of the land. From this one can infer that all the lands on which *kharāj* and *ʿushr* is paid are state lands.[66]

---

législation musulmane civile et religieuse selon le rite malékite, trans. M. Perron (Paris: Imprimerie Nationale, 1848–54), vol. 3: 578 fn. 18.

65 This is no doubt a corruption of the title *Jāmiʿ al-tafārīq fī al-furūʿ*, a compendium of Islamic substantive law by Muḥammad b. Abū al-Qāsim al-Baqqālī al-Khwārazmī (d. 1190). The Gomzin commission took the reference to these twelfth-century juristic authorities directly from deeds for the creation of *milk-i ḥurr*. For such deeds covering the early modern period, see, *Dokumenty k istorii agrarnykh otnoshenii v Bukharskom khanstve*: 45, 55, 105, 124, 188. Such juristic references were used also for composing similar deeds in later periods. AMIKINUz, no. 1119. Cf. Welsford and Tashev, *A Catalogue of Arabic-Script Documents from the Samarqand Museum*: doc. 34.

66 TsGARUz, f. 1-1, op. 22, d. 3, ll. 101–102ob.

The members of the Gomzin commission, namely the military commandants of the various provinces, distinguished "property" (*sobstvennost'*) rights to land from "possession" (*vladenie*) and "use" (*pol'zovanie*) and regarded the latter two categories as insufficient to determine the former. More important, the reasoning reflected in the works of the Gomzin commission is strikingly similar to that in the *Risāla-yi Ḥabībīya* and in the work of Davidovich. This applies, for example, to the proposition that it was only the fiscal status of the land that determined ownership rights. In particular, it pertains to the creation of tax-exempt landed property, which required that the treasury alienate (*otchuzhdenie*) its rights to the land—hence the division (*maḥdūd*) of what was in co-dominion between the ruler and the landholder. It is particularly important that the members of the commission were careful to explain that, by virtue of creation of *milk-i ḥurr*, the landowner could finally purchase land. This is reflected clearly in the *Risāla* and in legal deeds, where taxation is exchanged (*bar badal*) for land.[67] But decisive proof of the commission's full acquaintance with Central Asian Islamic juristic literature comes from the treatment of land subject to taxation. The following excerpt shows that the members of the Gomzin commission regarded *milk-i kharājī* as "estate" (*mamlūk*), thereby suggesting, implicitly, an important parallel to the *Risāla*:

> In specifying with all exactitude the rights to the lands sold by the treasury and, as such, exempted from taxation, the *sharīʿa* categorizes all the other types of land in private use under one rubric: *mamlūk* or *milk-i ghayr-i ḥurr*. [This] means a possession that is not *ḥurr-i khāliṣ* on account of the negative preposition *ghayr*. [...] Various commentators of the Muslim world disagree on the way one should determine the factual use [*fakt pol'zovaniia*] that confers on the individual [some] rights to the land. All of them agree, however, that, with the termination of the factual use and the turning of their possession into fallow land [*mawāt*], all the rights of the individual to the land also cease. With the right to the land [...] comes also the possibility to alienate by sale or inheritance. One needs only answer the following question: does the right assigned to an individual to use fallow land lead to a termination of the right that the state had to this land? According to the rules of *sharīʿa*, the land that is *milk-i ghayr-i ḥurr* originates either from lands that are left fallow following irrigation or in other ways. [But they are] all subject to taxation, if they are not turned into *milk-i ḥurr-i khāliṣ*. The right of the individual to them can always be taken away by the state, in case of fiscal evasion or in the

67 Ibid.: l. 103.

> absence of land use, or if the land becomes fallow again. [...] From what was said, one should infer the following: 1) The holder of *milk-i ghayr-i ḥurr* is a user but not a proprietor, even if his right of use is inheritable and transferable. 2) One who becomes the possessor of land by using it does not receive ownership rights but instead loses all rights to the land with the termination of its use. 3) Land-ownership rights belong to the state also with regard to the lands that are at someone's disposal, because the state has the power to sell these lands either to their possessor or to another individual. In this way, the basic right of the individual to *milk-i ghayr-i ḥurr* land is a right of use that originates from the irrigation of the land, which is given to another person through inheritance or sale. [...] Considering what has been said, the commission has come to the conclusion that: 1) One can recognize ownership rights only to those lands that have been transferred by the state according to the principles and the stipulations determined by *sharīʿa*. One should consider these lands as [...] under private ownership [...]; the tax is a direct consequence of the land-ownership right of the state. 2) Accordingly, no other lands have any owner [*votchinnik*] other than the state. Whoever occupies these lands by establishing pastures, structures, or gardens does so merely with rights of use, which are more or less defined and limited.[68]

The Gomzin commission was adamant in its conclusions. All the lands within the boundaries of the Governorship-General belonged to the treasury and could not be the object of transactions without the permission of the Russian government. At the same time, the plots of land that were *milk-i ḥurr* and those acquired by the Russians before the new legislation were considered private property.[69] A parallel might seem to present itself here between the Gomzin commission representing the Russian government and the Bukharan Emirate under the rule of Emir Ḥaydar: but this would be misleading. True, both used fiscal categories to define forms of land tenure, thereby classifying the land into what was exempt from taxation and what was subject to it. However, the Gomzin commission sought also the legitimation of its study of local forms of land tenure in light of the Russian imperial tradition:

> This principle that it is the state that enjoys property rights to the land, which is a tenet of the Muslim legislation, belongs also to pre-Petrine Rus' and exists up to the present in the Digest of Laws [*Svod Zakonov*]

68 Ibid., ll. 103ob–105ob.

69 Ibid., l. 117.

> with regard to the great majority of lands of the Russian state. [This principle] never affected the enrichment of the people, nor did it hamper the improvement of the land. But leaving to the regent the means to direct the colonization [*napravliat' kolonizatsiiu*] [served the purpose] of defending the alien [*inorodcheskoe*] and often also its own Russian people from the unfortunate fate of land deprivation [*obezzemleniia*]. [...] Conversely, when [we] hurriedly conferred patrimonial rights [*votchinnoe pravo*] upon a population that was accustomed only to enjoy rights of use, [we] often brought about very bitter consequences for the same population. [It] created a few small landowner-exploiters and a mass of miserable, disadvantaged, abject [people] deprived of their land.[70]

It is here that we first find evidence of an attempt to instrumentalize the idea of continuity with Central Asian fiscal practices and the traditions of the Russian imperial law, but this tendency becomes even clearer in further reformulations of what the commission understood to be the local traditions of land tenure. While on the one hand, it recognized that *milk-i ḥurr* is close to the Russian notion of "ownership" (*sobstvennost'*),[71] it firmly stated, on the other, that the notion of ownership right is completely alien to Muslim law, which is, of course, a misrepresentation.[72]

The idea that there existed only one form of private property in Central Asia and that the creation of such property depended on the ruler's willingness to relinquish land in exchange for taxes lent itself to certain obvious conclusions. The first was the idea that the ruler in Central Asia was necessarily a kind of Oriental despot who owned all the lands and disposed of them as he pleased. The second was the idea that all land subject to taxation should be regarded as belonging to the treasury: many Russian officials inclined to the view that lands which were, in Bukhara, labeled *mamlaka* and *mamlūk* (*milk-i kharājī*) were part of a single domain of state land. However tempting this view, it is misleading. It is true that the state enjoyed certain rights to private estates by owning a share of the rent that was proportional to a certain amount of land. As the *Risāla-yi Ḥabībīya* made clear, however, the legal category of *mamlaka* remained distinct from *mamlūk* and *milk*.

70 Ibid., l. 115.
71 Ibid., l. 139ob.
72 Ibid., l. 138ob.

2.2 *Interpreting Russian Statutory Laws*

The conflation of private estates with state land is epitomized by the Russian interpretation of the term *amlāk*. Originally this expression was used by the Bukharan chancellery only as a synonym of *mamlaka*.[73] It did not convey a strictly legal meaning but primarily a fiscal one: state land under taxation. Russian administrators used it to denote every kind of land subject to taxation, regardless of the tax rate and thereby including private estates (*milk-i kharājī/ʿushrī*).[74] This idea became the gospel of the Kaufman administration, which, in 1873 and 1881, proposed two land-reform projects. Both proposals stipulated that land should be divided into three categories, each of which was purported to correspond to a concept stemming from Islamic law: 1) state land (*amliak*); 2) tax-exempt private property (*milk*), and 3) land belonging to charitable endowments (*vakf*). These two projects shared the major assumption that "Islamic law does not, in general, contemplate the right to

73 Abduraimov, "O nekotorykh kategoriiakh feodal'nogo zemlevladeniia i polozhenii krest'ian v Bukharskom khanstve v XVI–nachale XX veka": 36. In his *Ocherk pozemel'no-podatnogo i nalovogo ustroistva b. Bukharskogo khantsva* (Tashkent: Izd. Sredne-Aziatskogo Gosudarstvennogo Universiteta, 1929): 23, Aleksander Semenov suggests that *amlāk* denoted in Bukhara only fallow land part of which the ruler assigned to the population for irrigation and from which was levied more than was paid on the "*kharāj* lands." Semenov does not here provide any evidence other than a reference to a personal communication, and it is unclear what he means. It is difficult to know what the *ḥiṣṣat al-kharāj* levied from state land amounted to, because it was determined (*qarār*) every year.

74 N. Khanykov, *Opisanie Bukharskogo khanstva* (St. Petersburg: Tip. Imp. AN, 1843): 116–19; Fedor K. Girs, *Otchet revizuiushchego po Vysochaishemu poveleniiu, Turkestanskii krai, Tainogo Sovetnika Girsa* (St. Petersburg: Senatskaia Tip., 1884): 344–5; *Proekt Vsepoddaneishago otcheta General-Ad'iutanta K.P. von Kaufman po grazhdanskomu upravleniu i ustroistvu v oblastiakh Turkestanskogo General-Gubernatorstva. 7 noiabria 1867–25 marta 1881 goda* (St. Petersburg: Voennaia Tip., 1885): 229–30; A.I. Shakhnazarov, *Sel'skoe khoziaistvo v Turkestanskom krae* (St. Petersburg: V.F. Kirshbaum, 1908): 64. In his *Russian Rule in Samarkand, 1868–1910: A Comparison with British India*, Morrison writes that Rostislavov "appears to be the originator of the Russian understanding that *mulk* and *amlak* refer, respectively, to private and State land, stating that they were separate legal concepts." In fact, Rostislavov, who wrote in 1874 and 1879, was a late contributor to the colonial discourse about *amlāk*. In January 1869, for example, Golovachev, who was military governor, asked the commandant of Tashkent to collect all the *vakufnyie, amliakovye*, and *mul'kovye* deeds (i.e., deeds of *waqf, amlāk*, and *milk* lands), a fact suggesting that, by the year the Gomzin commission began its work, the notion that *amlāk* included both *mamlaka* and *milk-i kharājī* had already circulated among the Russians in Turkestan. See TsGARUz, f. I-36, op. 1, d. 454, l. 6.

own land [...] and only the sovereign has the right to allocate it."[75] Both projects were met with fierce criticism by the commissions that reviewed them in St. Petersburg. One argument against them was that they aimed to introduce in Turkestan a land law that reinstated juridical categories predating the law of emancipation of state peasants issued in 1861, whereas the latter regulated that "only unpopulated lands directly owned by the treasury could be considered 'state lands.'"[76] Another matter of contention between the proponents of the land-reform projects and their opponents was the category of state land (*amliak*), as used by the Kaufman administration in a sense that went far beyond the term's fiscal meaning. The Russians used *amliak* as a portmanteau term that blended juridical and fiscal categories. Thus, the notion of *amliak* actually applied to two different legal categories of landholding, state land (*mamlaka*) and private estates (*milk/mulk* in the vernacular). At the same time, however, various fiscal categories, such as state land subject to all sorts of taxation, former crown lands (*khāṣṣa, ṣulṭānī, mīrī, qūrūq*), and private estates on which were levied a wide range of taxes, such as *kharāj, ʿushr*, etc., fell under the rubric of *amliak*. The major implication of the application of the category of *amliak* was that the vast majority of cultivated land on which taxes were levied should have been considered the patrimony of the Russian Empire.

Not everyone agreed with this view. In St. Petersburg, Fedor Karlovich Girs, the leader of an official senate inspection tour in Turkestan in 1882, issued a vehement critique of the land laws proposed by Kaufman and his clique. Writing in *Turkestanskie Vedomosty*, the official newspaper of the colonial government in Tashkent, Girs stated that "the theory of the absence of property rights in Islamic jurisprudence was a purely political invention," and he added that "exacting taxes cannot continue to be an obstacle to recognizing

75 *voobshche pravo pozemel'noi sobstvennosti po musul'manskomu voprosu ne sushchestvuet* [...] *vozvyshaetsia verkhovnaia vlast' khana ili emira, kotoromu prinadlezhit pravo rasporiazheniia zemel'noi sobstvennost'iu strany*. G.[irs F.K.], "K voprosu o zemlevadenii v Turkestanskom krae II." *TV* 26–29 (1885): 66–7.

76 E. Pravilova, "The Property of Empire. Islamic Law and Russian Agrarian Policy in Transcaucasia and Turkestan." *Kritika* 12/2 (2011): 380. The review of the 1871 land-reform project found ample coverage in the press, which favored the Kaufman administration. The article "Po povodu proekta zemel'nogo ustroistva Turkestanskogo kraia," *Golos* 56 (1875), reported and commented on the main criticisms of the project. Among them: "Notoriously, the major goal of this reform [1861 emancipation] consists of turning the agricultural population of the empire into peasant-proprietors, not into possessors of state lands" (*sdelat' zemledelcheskoe naselenie imperii krest'ianam-sobstvennikami, a ne obiazatel'nymi vladeltsami zemel' pravitel'stvennykh*). The article appeared also in *TS* 152 (n.d.): 9.

property rights" and that "*sharī'a* says nothing against private ownership of land."[77] Although Girs, along with the commission that reviewed the 1873 and 1881 projects, denounced the limits of the legislation on land rights as it had been formulated up to that time, central agencies in St. Petersburg were critical of his recommendation that the government should accord the indigenous population of Turkestan full ownership rights. In 1886 the State Council in St. Petersburg approved a new statute (*polozhenie*) that contained several measures intended to resolve the question of the legal status of lands. The statute evidently accepted most of the ideas formulated in a draft proposal on land organization (*pozemel'noe ustroistvo*) produced by the Ignatev commission in 1884. The statute introduced two broad categories of subjects among the "sedentary population," viz., "rural communities" (*sel'skie obshchestva*) and "city dwellers" (*gorodskie zhitely*) and provided the normative basis for the definition of landed-property relations in the following articles:

> Article 255: The rural sedentary population retains a permanent and hereditary right to those lands (*amliak* land) that they possess, use, and dispose of [*zemly, sostoiashchiia v postoiannom, potomstvennom ego vladenii, pol'zovanii i rasporiazhenii*], on the basis of the rules defined by local custom.
>
> Article 269: Land holdings assigned to urban inhabitants that are located within the confines of the city boundaries are considered the property of the individuals in question.

Ekaterina Pravilova has argued that the statute adopted in 1886 was a compromise between the view that all Central Asian land constituted state property and the view that held that the settled rural population could enjoy private property rights to land.[78] Worded as it was, Article 255 stood somewhere between two polarized positions on colonization. Agencies in St. Petersburg and Tashkent were involved in a complex debate on plans about resettlement policies (*kolonizatsiia*) for Turkestan. Some experts, such as Girs, regarded the colonization of Central Asia as a process of integration of Turkestan into the body of the empire; they thus saw in the confirmation of land-ownership rights to Central Asian Muslims a way to help Russian settlers, when the latter finally

77 G[irs], "K voprosu o zemlevadenii v Turkestanskom krae II.": 69, 70.

78 Pravilova, "The Property of the Empire": 380.

acquired land.[79] Others, such as Gomzin, von Kaufman, and Ignat'ev instead regarded Turkestan as the patrimony of the empire and its lands as the property of the state.[80] But the matter is more complicated. Pravilova also notes that the wording of Article 255 "described the rights of the 'settled rural population' to *amliak* lands as 'possession, use and disposal,' which, of course, actually corresponded to the definition of 'property' in the Russian civil code."[81] Thus, she suggests, the effect of Article 255 (and its equivalent in the statute's 1901 revision) was to accord property rights to Central Asian peasants. This interpretation is problematic for several reasons, which we should now consider.

Breaking the article into its constituent elements may be useful but may also lead to glaring misinterpretations. When Article 255 was published, contemporary observers did not all read it the same way. The Russian officials who participated in the drafting of 1886 statute employed a lexicon of property relations that differed from the terse definition of property formulated in the Russian civil code. As we have seen, the tendency was to gloss the term *amliak* as state land. It would therefore be counterintuitive to imagine that Russian lawmakers adopted this term to denote "private property." In 1891 an article published in the *Turkestanskie Vedomosty* lamented that not even the shadow of the concept of property was present in Article 255 and suggested that the lawmakers had regarded the land of Turkestan as a *res nullius*.[82] This suggests that people at that time did not read Article 255 as Pravilova does, and, in the reports of the Gomzin commission (1869), the Russian officials involved in the study of local forms of land tenure distinguished carefully the idea of property (*sobstevnnost'*) from other notions of tenure (*vladenie*) and use (*pol'zovanie*). This attention manifests itself also in the proposal for "land organization" drafted by the Ignat'ev commission (1884), which served as the basis of the 1886 statute.[83]

Pravilova is correct in assuming that some contemporaries of the statute might have read "possession, use, and disposal" as the defining attributes of

---

79 G[irs], "K voprosu o zemlevadenii v Turkestanskom krae II": 76; Id., "K voprosu o kolonizatsii," *TV* 29 (1885): 80.

80 *Zemli Turkestanskogo kraia, za iskliucheniem sostoiashchikh na prave pol'noi sobstvennosti, ostaiutsia gosudarstvennymi*; see Art. 255 of *"Pozemel'noe ustroistvo Turkestanskogo kraia," vyrabotannyi komissiei grafa Ignat'eva*. In Savitskii, *Pozemel'nyi vopros v Turkestane*: 181.

81 Pravilova, "The Property of the Empire": 381.

82 *V zakone etom, kak vidno, o prave sobstvennosti net nikakogo nameka*, A.P., "Pravo pozemel'noi sobstvennosti v Turkestanskom krae." *TV* 18 (1891): 70.

83 See Savitskii, *Pozemel'nyi vopros v Turkestane*: 181–5. See also the comments of the Ministry of War on the proposal, ibid.: 186–95.

property, as they were in the Russian civil code.[84] However, as one Russian commentator noted in 1907,[85] the 1886 statute included other articles that restricted the scope of the rights accorded in Article 255 and complicated its interpretation. For example, Article 259 identified Central Asians' rights to the land as pertaining to "use" (*pol'zovanie*), while Article 260 specified that the locals enjoyed ownership only of plantations and structures. One is left to wonder why, if Article 255 recognized de jure property rights to land by the rural population by employing the concepts of "possession, use, and disposal," Article 269 stated that city dwellers enjoy ownership of plots of land by employing the category of "property." Evidently, the legislators attempted to preserve the attributes of and the distinction between these different notions of tenure.

Rather than superimposing onto Article 255 the idiom of the Russian civil code, it is perhaps more helpful to read the article as a whole and clarify the purposes the Russians wanted to achieve with it. The primary message conveyed was that the new government's "confirmation" (*utverzhdenie*) of the forms of land tenure existing among the local population accorded to local custom. Read in this light, the references to "possession, use, and disposal" and *amliak* land necessarily acquire a different meaning: the Russians aimed to preserve the complexity of existing land rights embedded in the term *amliak* and as understood by the local population. Key to understanding of the intended meaning of the article is appreciating that confirmation of rights to land would be achieved, in the legislator's view, by relying on local customs. As Beatrice Penati has suggested, Article 255 was a *renvoi* to Islamic law,[86] but the *renvoi* was implicit because the article does not clarify the procedures that would be required to secure the confirmation of land rights. The notarization of legal deeds would play a crucial role. Article 261 states that transactions of land between indigenes (*tuzemtsy*) would be conducted according to local customs (*sovershchaiutsia po sobliudaemym v kazhdom meste mezhdu tuzemtsami obychaiam*). At the same time, Article 235 confers on native judges the authority to notarize every type of deed and contract between locals, except for those acts that were stipulated according to the general rules of the empire. It follows that native judges, that is, *qāḍī*s, were to notarize deeds attesting to the land rights of Muslims in Russian Central

84 One of them was N. Dingel'shtedt, "Pozemel'nye nedorazumeniia v Turkestane." *Vestnik Evropy* 2 (1892).

85 A. Frei, "Zakon 10 iiunia 1900 i primenenie ego k bogarnym zemliam." *TV* 58 (1907).

86 B. Penati, "Swamps, Sorghum, and Saxauls: Marginal Lands and the Fate of Russian Turkestan." *CAS* 29/1 (2010): 61.

Asia. It is unlikely that Muslim native courts would solemnize deeds of sale of land according to the definition of property in the Russian civil code. Equally, it is improbable that the legislators overlooked the fact that the Islamic legal language employed by native courts does not distinguish between possession, use, and disposal (*vladenie, pol'zovanie,* and *rasporiazhenie*). A complicating factor in assessing the implications of the *renvoi* to Islamic law is that harmonization between Islamic and Russian laws on issues of land tenure was apparently never a major concern for the colonial administration. While one may get a superficial impression of this by comparing the legal terminology used in the notarization of land deeds before and after the Russian conquest,[87] substantive evidence comes from the Chaghatay translation of the statute. There, Article 255 is rendered without reference to the notion of *amliak*:

> [The government confirms] as property of the sedentary population the lands that are in the permanent and hereditary use and at the disposal of the population according to the customs of the locale, Article 262, and other articles of this statute.[88]

The Chaghatay version of the statute was provided to the native officials who, like the *qāḍīs*, served the Russian administration. The translation of Article 255 seems to reflect an attempt to distinguish between rights of "use" (*taṣarruf*) and "usufruct" (*manfa'at*). Be that as it may, it confirmed property rights (*milk*) to the local population by leaving the definition of *milk* to the *qāḍīs*. This explains the continuity in the way *qāḍīs* notarized landed-property rights before and after the Russian conquest.[89]

What were Muslims' perceptions of the statutory laws on landholding? Soviet historians explained the attempt of the colonial government to produce a legislative framework leading to the creation of a patrimonial

87 I have discussed these aspects in "Colonial Legislation Meets *Sharī'a*."

88 *sārtīya fuqarālārīnīng dāymā atā bābālārīdīn mīrāth qālīb ālārnīng taṣarruflārīda kīlgān wa ālār manfa'atlānīb tūrghān mulk yirlār ūshbū jāynīng rasm wa 'ādatlārīgha wa ham ūshbū niẓāmnīng min ba'd kīlādūrghān 262-nchī wa bāshqa mas'alalārīgha muwāfiq ūz mulklārī īkānlīghīgha mustaḥkam qīlīb bīrīlādūr*, TsGARUz, f. 1-36, op. 1, d. 4008, l. 270b. The Chaghatay translation of the statutory law was published in lithograph as *Turkistān wilāyatīdaghī ḍabt wa rabṭ qīlmaq ya'nī bāshqārmāghīnīng niẓāmī* (Tashkent: Tip. Portsevikh, 1901). Article 255 is on p. 39.

89 As shown in my "Colonial Legislation Meets *Sharī'a*."

state,[90] but this ideological claim remains unproven.[91] Alexander Morrison has suggested that the Russians did away with a landed aristocracy that, before the conquest, either owned tax-exempt land (*milk-i ḥurr*) or temporary fiscal grants (*tarkhān*).[92] He has convincingly shown that former Bukharan and Khoqandi officials, such as tax collectors, lost their privileges after the consolidation of Russian rule. However, we know of no substantive disturbances caused by dispossessed landowners, a concern that, significantly, preoccupied the Ministry of War during the review of the proposal of the Ignat'ev commission, which included an article stating that the Russian government would not confirm the fiscal privileges originating from *milk-i ḥurr*. At the request of Governor-General Kaufman, the article was expunged from the statute.[93] Considering that, in several districts of Samarqand Province, *milk-i ḥurr* comprised the majority of the area under agriculture,[94] it is unlikely that this class of land aristocracy would have accepted the large-scale appropriation of its holdings without making a fuss. Indeed, members of this class seem to have moved with alacrity to defend their interests whenever these came under threat:

> The residents of Panjshanba to the governor. We poor and miserable people appeal to you in hope of your mercy. In the wake of the conquest of Katta Kurgan, our notables went to the city in order to subject themselves to our White Tsar. [At that time], you promised us that our *mulk* will remain *mulk* and so will [our] *waqf*s. Now our *mulk*s have been turned into *amlāk*, and for this reason we poor and miserable people are deprived of our tranquility. In the hope that you will redirect this request to the governor.[95]

In this appeal written in Chaghatay, the notables of Katta Kurgan explained that colonial officials had reassured them that fiscal privileges on *milk-i ḥurr*

---

90 S.I. Il'iasov, *Zemel'nye otnoshenii v Kirgizii v kontse XIX–nachale XX vv.* (Frunze: Izdatel'stvo Akademii Nauk Kirgizskoi SSR, 1963): 80.

91 Sartori, "Colonial Legislation Meets *Sharīʿa*"; Penati, "Notes on the Birth of Russian Turkestan's Fiscal System: A View from the Fergana Oblast' "; Pravilova, "The Property of the Empire."

92 Morrison, "*Amlākdārs*, *Khwājas* and *Mulk* Land in the Zarafshan Valley after the Russian Conquest": 23–64.

93 Savistkii, *Pozemel'nyi vopros v Turkestane*: 190.

94 Copy of a list of *milk* land drafted by a former Bukharan official under Emir Muẓaffar, at the request of the Orientalist Aleksander Kuhn, 1870, TsGARUz, R-2678, f. 1, d. 381, 1–3.

95 TsGARUz, f. I-1, op. 14, d. 28, l. unnumbered.

and charitable endowments would be left untouched under Russian rule. The speakers seem to have understood *amlāk* as land from which taxes are levied; certainly, it is that way that the translator, a certain Ibragimov, glosses the word in Russian (*zemlia s koei postupaet podat' v kaznu*).[96]

There is little doubt that Russian statutory laws were, in principle, less advantageous for those who possessed *milk-i ḥurr* land. Some people also imagined that the implementation of Article 255 would create a situation in which former proprietors of estates subject to taxation (*milkdār*) would be demoted to tenants on a par with those who had worked on *mamlaka* land under the ruler of the emir and the khans.[97] Regarding these specific points, a certain Mullā Kamāl al-Dīn, the first Samarqandi jurist to become a native judge under Russians rule,[98] recounts a revealing anecdote. In an account of his attempt to regain the office of native judge from which he had been removed, Mullā Kamāl al-Dīn reports several conversations he had with colonial officials. In one such conversation with a certain Lieutenant Savinkov, he was asked to illustrate the existing landholding situation in Turkestan. This is Mullā Kamāl al-Dīn's answer:

> The landowners [*mulkdār*] have been suffering severely [in recent years]." Later they [Savinkov] asked: "Is there any way to resolve this problem by taking into account the types of land?" I said: "*Mulk* land is of three types: one is *mulk-i ḥurr*, another is *mulk-i ʿushrī*, and another is *mulk-i kharājī*. The meaning of *mulk-i ḥurr* is such that the person who tills the land does not pay anything to the treasury [*khazīna*], whereas he pays the *kharāj* on the proceeds to the landowner. *Mulk-i ʿushrī* means that, from the proceeds of the land, one-tenth goes to the treasury and two-tenths to the landowner. The meaning of *mulk-i kharājī* is this: from the proceeds of the land two-tenths go to the treasury and one-tenth to the landowner. This makes three-tenths. Now they pay one-fifth of the proceeds from their ownership to the treasury. The rest of the proceeds go to the peasants who can take it for themselves. This law [*niẓām*]

96 Ibid.: l. 8.

97 Rostislavov, *Ocherk vidov zemel'noi sobstvennosti*: 7.

98 Mullā Kamāl al-Din compiled this text after his dismissal from the office of native judge in 1871. On him, see Morrison, *Russian Rule in Samarkand, 1868–1910: A Comparison with British India*: 254–55.

> has become [a source of] serious suffering for landowners, because they had invested a great deal of money to acquire this *mulk* land.[99]

At first sight, this account suggests that landowners had no means of preserving their fiscal privileges, while peasants were able to enjoy a larger share of the produce—but matters are not so simple. First, Mullā Kamāl al-Dīn points out correctly that, under colonial rule, owners of *milk-i ḥurr* land would pay one-fifth to the government. They therefore lost the absolute fiscal exemption they had enjoyed under the Bukharan emir and were lowered to the status of those who, before the conquest, owned *milk-i kharājī*. However, Mullā Kamāl al-Dīn's account wrongly assumes that peasants would not hand over to their landowners the rent required by their contractual obligations of tenancy. This reflects the assumption that landowners had no means of enforcing contracts. We have already seen that landowners did not hesitate to take their affairs to the colonial administration, and there is no reason to imagine that Russians would deliberately side with the peasants in every case. The bureaucratization of land tenure put greater emphasis on the importance of documents. Thus, any written attestation of tenancy obligations would ensure that landowners received what was due to them. Local landowners may well have had to pay something to the Russian government, but it would be misleading to assume that the Muslim landed aristocracy, as a class, was eradicated—in fact, the opposite was true. Notwithstanding the less favorable conditions for owners of *milk-i ḥurr*, the *qāḍī* Muḥyī al-Dīn Khwāja was able, under the new fiscal rules introduced by the Russians, to amass a fortune in landed estates in Qizil Qurghān, outside Tashkent. These lands were rented out to tenants.[100]

Second, one should not underestimate the key role played by native judges in helping to preserve, where possible, preconquest forms of land tenure. In notarizing transactions, native judges were bound to specify exactly what people owned, whether improvements or the soil itself. In this way, they disambiguated land-ownership from mere possession, that is, the condition of a tenant. The same applies to temporary fiscal exemptions for, say, the descendants of saints. Private collections show how such groups used documentation in the

---

99 *Risāla-yi Mullā Kamāl al-Dīn*, MS St. Petersburg, IVRAN, S-1690: fols. 49a–49b. The manuscript is described in L.V. Dmitrieva and S.N. Muratov, *Opisanie tiurkskikh rukopisei instituta vostokovedeniia* II (Moscow: Nauka, 1975): 117, no. 70.

100 Gh. Karimov, P. Sartori, and Sh. Ziyodov, *Sebzor dahasi qozisi faoliiatiga oid khujjatlar* (Tashkent: O'zbekiston, 2009): doc. 117–23.

vernacular to ensure the preservation of their privileges.[101] This implied that such groups had instruments for enforcing the stipulations of deeds beyond the obvious recourse to the Russian administration. This scenario excluded the situation in which peasants could expropriate landowners.

Third, and more significantly, the bureaucratization of land tenure triggered a fierce competition to acquire land that had, before the conquest, belonged either to the treasuries of local potentates or to the crown. Muslim groups attempted to acquire such land by leveraging on the colonial bureaucratic regime that conferred higher probative force on legal deeds. If peasants had been better off than landowners, there would have been no such attempts to expand landed property. It is to this phenomenon that we now turn.

3 Living Off the Fat of the Land

It is unclear what was the fate of the land that belonged previously to the Muslims rulers (khans, emirs) or was considered state land (*mamlaka*) and as such counted as property belonging to the treasury (*bayt al-māl*) of the khanates.

When the Russians conquered Central Asia, much of the land belonging to the Khoqand khanate and the Bukharan emirate was occupied by the local population who cultivated it and enjoyed usufructuary rights. Locals were not just tenants. The populace could and did acquire the right to install themselves permanently (*ḥaqq al-qarār*) on state land by purchasing the improvements, which included plantations and buildings. This situation generated entitlements that were often subsequently formalized as quasi-property rights, but both individuals and communities acquired property rights exclusively on improvements, thereby leaving to the state the ownership of the bare substance (*raqaba*) of the land.

One is tempted to assume that, as the local rulers lost their powers, the population tilling state lands found themselves in a favorable position to attempt to persuade the Russians that they were the owners of the land they tilled, but matters were complicated. As the Russians established their rule in the country, they introduced a bureaucratic regime that conferred definitive probative value on deeds.

101 T. Welsford, "Fathers and Sons: Re-Readings in a Samarqandi Private Archive." In *Explorations in the Social History of Modern Central Asia (19th–20th Century)*, ed. P. Sartori (Leiden: Brill, 2013): 299–323.

Under Kaufman, the first governor-general, various commissions were created to inquire into the land rights and fiscal status of the native population. We know that these commissions faced severe problems in assessing the information they gathered from the natives, and it is not clear how land-ownership was actually verified on the basis of vernacular documents.[102] A project of land-assessment reorganization (*pozemel'no-podatnoe ustroistvo*) became one of the ambitious undertakings of the Russian administration already under the first governor-general. Government agencies (*organizatsionnye raboty*) were set up to prepare land assessments.[103] They began in Tashkent Province (*uezd*) and moved on to Samarqand and Ferghana. These agencies were instrumental in establishing cadastral offices, which could provide detailed information on, for example, who tilled the land, the crop sown, and a calculation of the tax to be levied from the fiscal units. In case of the data yielded by these agencies, Penati claims that, at least in Ferghana, the land that had belonged to the members of khan's family was registered as belonging to the treasury (*kazennaia*).[104]

In other provinces of Russian Turkestan, by contrast, the fate of the land of the Bukharan emirate and the Khoqand khanate seems to have been far more complicated than in Ferghana. It appears, for example, that, in Samarqand Province, *sharīʿa* courts continued to observe the distinction between private land-ownership (*mulk*) and state land (*mamlaka*) that had existed before the Russian conquest, under the rule of the Bukharan emir. They did so by notarizing zealously all transactions of property rights pertaining to improvements of state land.[105] In most cases, these transactions involved buildings and plantations on land of agricultural significance. Had the Russian state converted land formerly belonging to the emirate (*mamlaka*) into treasury land (*kazennaia*), the individuals who acquired property rights on the improvements of such land (as sanctioned by *sharīʿa* courts) would have been lessees of the Russian government. Lacking any other evidence, it is difficult to say what kind of certification of lease the Russian administration could issue in favor of these individuals. These people were installed on land of agricultural significance, that

---

102 Penati, "Notes on the Birth of Russian Turkestan's Fiscal System: A View from the Fergana Oblast'": 744.

103 Land assessments, however, were made on the basis of cadastral surveys that had no legal force. See TsGARUz, f. I-17, op. 1, d. 30291/23.

104 Penati, "Notes on the Birth of Russian Turkestan's Fiscal System: A View from the Fergana Oblast'": 759.

105 Welsford and Tashev, *A Catalogue of Arabic-Script Documents from the Samarqand Museum*: doc. 131, 461a, 463, 464, 465, 467, 468, 470, 498, 501, 515, 525, 534, 547, 568, 598, 599, 600, 616.

is, in rural settlements. Had these rural areas been surveyed by the land-assessment agencies, the people in question would probably have come to belong to a rural community (*sel'skoe obshchestvo*).

The rural community was a fiscal entity that was copied from the Russian "commune" (*mir*). Rural communities were responsible for the apportionment (*raskladka*) of the land tax, which was calculated "on a sampling of local yields, multiplied by the average market price of that produce for the five previous years."[106] While land assessments were in the hands of the Russian military-civil administration, decisions on who paid what were made by the headmen of the rural communities. The *sel'skoe obshchestvo* was a colonial creation that had no counterpart in local parlance or in that of the native courts. Members of such communities thus continued to secure their rights to land through notarization in the native courts.[107] Individuals exchanged plots of land not only within rural communities but also across community boundaries, but deeds issued by native judges were insufficient to sanction land-ownership in the rural communities. The amendments of 1900 to the statute allowed individuals to leave rural communities. The procedure that led to the assignment of a plot of land in a rural community was called *vydel'* and consisted of acquiring a certificate of possession (*vladenie*). This certificate was called a *dannaia*.[108] There is no apparent connection, however, between the legal deeds that members of the rural communities acquired from native courts and the *dannye* that they received from the colonial administration. The overlapping rights reflected in these two different genres of bureaucratic text created a chaotic situation. It required only knowledge and expediency for the locals to take advantage of this situation to pursue their own goals.

While there were *qāḍīs* who, under Russian rule, acted as the watchdogs of the land formerly belonging to the emirate and the khanate, there were other local actors who attempted to take advantage of the blind-spots in the land surveys to take possession of state land. I hope to show that local groups had an

---

106 B. Penati, "The Cotton Boom and the Land Tax in Russian Turkestan (1880s–1915)." *Kritika* 14/4 (2013): 747.

107 Native judges notarized sales of plots of land within rural communities by omitting the plots' cadastral numbers. This is reflected in a collection of deeds pertaining to plots of land in Mahram County, in the district of Khoqand, where transactions took place in 1909. See *Kollektsiiai fondi shaxsii Mullomuhammad Sharif ibni Abduzalil* [*sic!—Mullā Muḥammad ʿAẓīm Mullā Muḥammad Sharīf-ūghlī*]: *qozii volosti Mahram*, ObAKh, f. I-145, op. 1, d. 58, ll. 1–20.

108 On the *vydel*, see Sartori, "Colonial Legislation" and B. Penati, "Beyond Technicalities: On Land Assessment and Land-Tax in Russian Turkestan." *JFGO* 59/1 (2011): 1–27.

interest in the nonirrigated ("marginal") lands such as pastures (*yaylāw*) and regarded it an advantage to turn it into private property.[109]

3.1 *Case Study: Partners in Profit*

Let us turn now to a revealing legal dispute over land belonging to the treasury of the former Bukharan emirate. The case pertains to competing claims to an area of one hundred *ṭanāb*s of rain-watered land (*zamīn-i lalmī-kār*) that had, before the Russian conquest, belonged to the Bukharan emirate. The contested land was situated in Kalta-Sāy, in the lower valley of the Shīrāz district (*tūmān*), in the region of Samarqand. Although its origins can be traced back to the mid-1850s, the dispute intensified only after the Russian conquest, when the territory in question came under colonial administration.

The earliest evidence available indicates that in March-April 1856, in the *sharīʿa* court of the Shīrāz district, the Tuyāqlī Mullā-Kīk community (*jamāʿa*) acknowledged the receipt of a spring in a place called Lāy Chashma, in the aforementioned locality, for the irrigation of 50 *qūsh*[110] of land. They also declared that they had dug the spring, canalized its water, and irrigated the surrounding land according to their established practices (*ba-qadr-i rasm-i khwudhā*). The representatives of the Tuyāqlī Mullā-Kīk community also acknowledged before the *qāḍī* an agreement that they had reached with their fellow kinsmen from the Tuyāqlī Jangal community. This consisted of the transfer (*taslīm*) of possession of a spring in Ūzūn-Sāy, in the aforementioned lower valley, for the irrigation of 20 *qūsh* of land. The transfer had been made so that the Tuyāqlī Jangal community could dig the spring in Ūzūn Sāy, irrigate the land with its water, and develop certain forms of agriculture (*gasht wa zarāʿat*). Apparently, two Tuyāqlī communities divided among themselves the state land in Kalta-Sāy, by allotting the rights to two neighboring springs, one in Lāy Chashma, the other in Ūzūn-Sāy. The Islamic legal record makes clear that the two parties did

---

109 As marginal lands, pastures received special fiscal treatment by the Russians. According to the 1886 statutory law, taxes on rain-watered land were levied at the rate of 10% of the actual yield of the harvest; after the amendments brought of 1900, taxes were instead calculated in proportion to area. It is unclear whether this change in fiscal policy was instrumental in instigating native attempts to seize marginal lands; the evidence so far collected does not give a consistent picture.

110 *Qush* is the Chaghatay rendering of the term *juft*. It signifies the amount of land that can be tilled using a single pair of oxen (*juft-i gāv*). See Semenov, *Ocherk pozemel'nogo-podatnogo ustroistva b. Bukharskogo khanstva*: 53. On the *qush* as a variable variable measure of land area, see E. Davidovich, *Materialy po metrologii srednevekovoi Srednei Azii* (Moscow: Nauka, 1970): 122–23.

not own the land there but that they had only received the springs and their water to use in cultivating the surrounding land.[111]

This was the situation when the Russians came to Central Asia. The situation evidently deteriorated in 1897, when three members of the Tuyāqlī Mullā-Kīk community—Bigīm Qul Mīrzā Bāy, Qul Bigīm, and Ḥasan Naẓar—sold 68 *ṭanāb*s of the rain-watered land in the locality of Ūzūn Sāy to several people belonging to the Turk community.[112] As Ūzūn Sāy was known to have belonged to the Bukharan state, the native court certified not the sale of the land itself but only of its improvements, that is, the cultivated land. In other words, this legal record shows that Bikīm Qul Mīrzā Bāy, Qul Bigīm, and Ḥasan Naẓar sold only their usufructuary rights to the land. Nearly one month after the issuance of the *sharīʿa* court record,[113] however, the three vendors persuaded the headman (*volostnoi upravitel'*) of Tuya-Tartar County and a local notable (*āqsaqāl*) to aver that the 68 *ṭanāb*s of land mentioned in the legal record were their own property (*mulk*).[114]

At the end of 1897, twenty-two residents of the Inichka settlement (*qishlāq*), in Chashma-Āb County of Jizzakh Province, petitioned the military governor of the Samarqand region. The residents were all members of the Tuyāqlī Jangal community who claimed that, from time immemorial, they had had the use of about 400 *ṭanāb*s of rain-watered land (*bahārī-kārlīk*), which they had inherited from their forefathers (*qadīm al-ayyāmdān āta-bābālārmīzdān*). They did so by referring to a legal certificate in their possession, which attested to their rights. They also explained to the Russian authorities how they used the land. They said that every year, in spring, they cultivated it and lived off its produce. Problems began when Bigīm Qul and Qul Bigīm, who were residents of Bīdāna, sold about 100 *ṭanāb*s to the Turk community, residents of Usmat-Qatartar County. The sale was apparently solemnized by the native court in Shīrāz, which issued a legal certificate.[115] The residents of Inichka asked the Russian authorities in Samarqand to come to their assistance and help them ascertain the truth about the case.

Lieutenant Kolchanov, head of the suburban area (*prigorodnyi uchastok*) of Samarqand Province, was put in charge of the preliminary investigation of the case. He checked the native court records that the claimants mentioned

---

111 TsGARUz, f. I-21, op. 1, d. 475, l. 5.

112 30.06.1897, ibid.: l. 6.

113 27.07.1897, ibid.: l. 6ob.

114 *ūshbū wathīqa ichīda yāzīlgān 68 ṭanāb yir wajhīdān taftīsh qīldūm ūshbūnī ichīda maḍkūr Bigīm Qul* [. . .] *ḥaqq wa mulkī īkān*, ibid.

115 Ibid.: l. 9.

in their petition and found that the "indigenous document" (*tuzemnyi dokument*) proved that "the land in the localities of Lāy Chashma and Ūzūn-Sāy (20 *qūsh* of land) was allocated to a community [*priznan za obshestvom*] of the Tuyaqli clan [*rod*]. To this latter clan belonged both the parties to the dispute." Kolchanov added that the 20 *qūsh* appeared to belong partly to the residents of Inichka and partly to the residents of another settlement, called Bīdāna. It seemed to the Russian official that the residents of the latter settlement had sold their shares of rain-watered land long ago and that they tried to appropriate the shares belonging to the Inichka residents. They did so by selling secretly nearly 100 *ṭanāb*s to the Turk community.

Kolchanov seems to have received little help from his translators. His report shows that he misunderstood much of the content of the *sharīʿa* court record provided by the Inichka residents. Kolchanov held that the land in Ūzūn Sāy was "shared" by the residents of Inichka and Bīdāna. In fact, the record indicates that people from Inichka had rights to the land in Ūzūn Sāy, whereas the other party—the Bīdāna residents, members of the Tuyāqlī Mullā-Kīk community—had usufructuary rights to Lāy Chashma. Kolchanov's faulty knowledge of the vernacular languages also prevented him from reconstructing properly the sequence of the documents and thus grasping the stratagem concocted by Bigīm Qul and Qul Bigīm, together with the county headman and the *āqsaqāl*, to sell state land as if it were their private property. When Kolchanov questioned the *qāḍī* who had notarized the sale deed, the latter answered that he had agreed to issue the deed because the county headman and the *āqsaqāl* had confirmed that the land belonged to the sellers. Apparently, Kolchanov could make no sense of the documents in Persian and in Chaghatay and thus overlooked a major discrepancy between them: in the native court record, the object of the transaction was the improvements on rain-watered land, whereas the affirmations produced by the county headman and the head of the rural community showed that the object of sale was private land.[116]

The end of this story reveals that Russians could not always prevent the indigenous population from seizing what was, before the conquest, state land. The Russian authorities ruled that the dispute should be adjudicated by an extraordinary assembly of *qāḍī*s. The latter gave a concise report of the hearing, stating that, when the claim of the agent of Inichka residents for the usurped land was denied, the *qāḍī*s asked the plaintiffs to produce testimony of their claim. Interestingly, it seems that they did not review the *sharīʿa* court record, which had been issued in the precolonial period. Instead, as the plaintiff could not provide the requested probative evidence, the judges asked the defendants

116 Ibid.: ll. 4–4ob.

to swear an oath. At this point, a third party intervened and suggested settling the dispute amicably, and the defendants paid 1,500 *tangas* for the land in question.[117] As we shall see, settlements would be a successful instrument in the hands of the locals in securing land-ownership rights to estates they attempted to seize.

3.2 *Case Study: Troubles in Jalayir*

> On 5 January 1887, I reached Qara Quduq early in the morning, together with ʿAbd al-Sattār, who had formerly served as *qaḍī*, and Mullā Birdī Bāy, a *qaḍī* [presently on duty]. The head of Zaamin County, Mullā Darwīsh, and forty notables [*pochetnye*] [also were with me]. [I was also followed by] Balabanov, a translator, and two guards [*jigit*s] in the service of the provincial chancellery. As soon as we reached the place, [a crowd of] nearly a hundred individuals gathered [before us]. They were Uzbeks belonging to the Turk and Jalayir clans [*rod*]. We found there barns for the cattle and cultivated fields. The *qāḍī*s and others told me that [the premises] were built last year. While facing the crowd, I read aloud the decision of the Muslim judicial assembly and your order [instructing that those improvements be torn down]. As soon as I finished [reading it], Mullā Rustam yelled at me that, as long as he lives, nobody would ever touch those buildings. After that, he took out a knife and threw it before my feet. He then laid his head on the ground and began to shout at me, asking that I chop off his head with that knife. When the headmen of Zaamin County climbed on the roof of one building in order to execute [the removal of the buildings], the Fayḍullāh brothers, their relatives, and even their wives took measures to counter my orders. They tried to spread chaos and to get the county headmen down from the roof. The crowd [was all around and] pushed me. I could not move. The two guards heard that somebody was calling on the people to pull out their knives in order to defend Mullā Rustam. In the end, [I was able to] arrest him and his brothers. I immediately dispatched them to Jizzakh, awaiting your command. During many years of service, I have never experienced anything resembling this event, and I felt anxious and frightened [*vzvolnovan i potresen*]. As I was leaving, the Jalayirs began to beat up the Turks.

117 13.01.1899, copy of the decision, ibid.: l. 38.

> I cannot say who beat whom, because everybody was fighting. The Turk people mounted their horses and rode away.[118]

This was the end of the story of one family trying to get hold of state land in a mountainous area of Jizzakh Province, which had, before the Russian conquest, belonged to the Bukharan emirate. The story is not one of heroic resistance by subaltern subjects against domination by Russians in Central Asia. Rather, it is the last act of a drama that centered on local communities who were asserting emotionally their aspirations concerning land rights, of which they had no proof.

The story can be traced back more than twenty years. For at least a generation, two communities (*jamāʿat*), the Jalayir and the Turk, had been involved in a competition over water and land resources along a stream called Jalayir. The stream runs from south to north, nearly 20 kilometers east of Zaamin, in a poorly irrigated area. There was a rural settlement (*mawḍaʿ/qishlāq*) and a summer pasture (*yaylāw*), both named after the stream. The confrontation between the Jalayir and the Turk led to blows, when one community usurped the summer pasture attached to the settlement, cultivating it for themselves and refusing others access to it. At this point, the story becomes more complicated, as a third community asserted rights to the pasture. But let us start from the beginning.

The earliest evidence available in the records collected by the Russians on this case is a document from May 1861. At this time, a few years before the Russian conquest, twenty-four people appeared before a *qāḍī* in Ura-Tepe, which was, at that time, a small semi-autonomous principality, highly unstable politically,[119] seemingly under the formal control of the Bukharan emirate. These individuals intended to register a substantial change in the way they had been sharing the water of the Jalayir stream. Until that time, the water had been accessible and was distributed on the basis of a sequence of twenty daily shares according to an old custom of the local populace (*mushtamal bar dawra-yi bīst shabāna rūza ba rasm-i qadīm-i ahālī*). The group of people owning (*mālikīn*) the water decided to seek the notarial services of the *qāḍī* in Ura-Tepe in order to add another three shares to their water allotment. Accordingly, they transferred the ownership (*tamlīk*) of one share of water (*yak āb*) to three individuals, Rajab ʿAlī Bāy, Subḥānqulī, and Sawīr Qulī Bāy. The latter handed over 14,000 *tangas* to the most prominent member of the group, one Mūsā

118 Report, Captain Rybushkin to the commandant of Jizzakh Province, 06.06.1888, TsGARUz, I-21, op. 1, d. 56, l. 58.

119 *Materialy po istorii Ura-Tiube. Sbornik aktov XVII–XIX vv.*: 4.

Dīwānbīgī, thus extinguishing an earlier debt.[120] As his title "Dīwānbīgī" suggests, Mūsā must have held a prominent administrative office as tax surveyor in the emirate.[121] He must have exerted his authority and requested that his three fellow group members pay that considerable sum of money to be entitled to ownership rights to the water. A few months later, Mūsā Dīwānbīgī appeared before the same *qāḍī* and acknowledged that he had a duty to perform, consisting of paying to Rajab ʿAlī Bāy, Savīr Qulī Bāy, and Mullā Rustam (brother of the aforementioned Subḥānqulī) exactly the same sum of money as he had received. We do not know why he had to return the money to its former owners. This course of action, however, is noteworthy because it marks the rise of a smaller group among the Jalayir community. The latter's internal balance of power shifted in favor of the offspring (*awlād*) of a certain Fayḍullāh. Two of his sons, Mullā Rustam and Subḥanqulī, each owned two shares of water. A few years later, the latter and their seven brothers secured ownership (*mulk*) of 200 *manns*[122] of land in the settlement of Jalayir. This portion abutted another ancestral undivided estate (*mushāʿ*) belonging to Fayḍullāh's sons who were thus expanding their possessions.[123]

Fayḍullāh's offspring, notably Mullā Rustam, did not conceal their ambition to get hold of the land belonging to the Jalayir settlement. They revealed their intentions clearly after the Russian conquest, when they seized an area in the mountainous locality of Qara Quduq. When this happened, the people from Jalayir, notably a group around a certain Ibrāhīm, complained that this land had been traditionally kept as summer pasture and that only part of it was used for small-scale agriculture. In early 1884 Mullā Rustam and other six individuals were accused by another group of having usurped the land and prevented the Jalayir residents from accessing it. Mullā Rustam's opponents brought the case to the attention of the Russians. They argued that they possessed approximately 1,000 *batman*s of land, inherited from their forefathers, which consisted of arable land and summer pastures (*takhmīnan mīng batmānlīk yir qadīm al-ayyāmdān āta-bābāmīzdān qīlghān īkīn wa yaylāw jāylārimīz īdī*). The

120 TsGARUz, I-21, op. 1, d. 56, l. [8].

121 Mīrzā Badīʿ al-Dīvān, *Majmaʿ al-Arqām* (*Predpisaniia Fiska*). (*Priemy dokumentatsii v Bukhare XVIII v.*), ed. A.B. Vil'danova (Moscow: Nauka, 1981): 54, 97.

122 *Mann* (or *man*, from *bātman*) is usually employed as a measure of weight. Davidovich, *Materialy po metrologii srednevekovoi Srednei Azii*: 85–94. It was also used, as in this case, to denote the area that could be sown with a specific quantity of seeds. See Kh.A. Kaiumova, *Narodnaia metrologiia i khronologiia Tadzhikov Karategina, Darvaza i Zapadnogo Pamira XIX–nachala XX vv.* Synopsis of PhD diss. [*avtoreferat*] (Khojand, 2009): 16 and 18.

123 TsGARUz, I-21, op. 1, d. 56, l. 90b.

appellants informed their Russian addressee that Mullā Rustam and his affiliates were spreading the rumor that they had purchased (*ṣātīb āldūk dīb*) the land in Qara Quduq. This piece of information, whose crucial importance we recovered only after the fact, is instrumental in situating the following course of events in the context of Russian legislation: could Mullā Rustam and his men buy that land?[124] This appeal led to an inspection showing Mullā Rustam's muscular behavior with the purpose of acquiring land-ownership. This was a war waged with documents rather than with weapons. The number of documents grew, along with the fortune he was amassing.

Captain Rybushkin, assistant to the commandant of the Jizzakh *raion*, led the investigation. He concluded that the land had never been made arable and that it was, instead, a summer pasture belonging to the Jalayirs. If this land were to be made arable, the nomads (*kochevniki*) would lose their summer pastures. Both parties were forbidden to turn this land into arable land, argued Rybushkin, whereas it was perfectly lawful for the Jalayirs to use it as pasture. The Russian officials therefore ruled that the cultivation of the land in question should be forbidden to both the parties, according to resolution no. 2674 of the governor-general, dated 22 April 1882, until the land-tax assessment should be carried out; the Jalayirs should be accorded the right of using that land as summer pasture and bringing their flocks there.[125]

Ibrāhīm and his community were not satisfied with this decision. A few months later, they complained that the new prohibition of plowing those lands affected their finances substantially by reducing greatly the production of the land. Accordingly, he and his fellow clan members asked to be allowed to till the land that belonged to them (*prinadlezhashii nam*).[126] This argument attracted the sympathy of Pankratov, the head of the Jizzakh *raion*, in whose eyes Ibrāhīm seemed to be defending the interests of a group of poor against the party of the rich led by Mullā Rustam. Pankratov was convinced that the request of Ibrāhīm was just (*spravedlivo*) and concluded that it would be reasonable to allot to his party some of the pasture for conversion into arable land.[127] Pankratov's superior, the commandant of the Khojand Province, agreed in principle with his observations but noted a glaring contradiction between Pankratov's recommendations and the information that he had gathered on

124 Ibid.: l. 1.

125 Ibid.: l. 3–4.

126 N.d., ibid.: l. 13. Similar petitions were submitted on 31 July 1884 and 22 August 1884, respectively, ibid.: l. 14 and 15–15ob.

127 24.08.1884, ibid.: l. 16.

the land in question:[128] the land had never been tilled and had always been used by nomads (*v pol'zovanii kochevnikov*). "Therefore", asked the commandant of Khojand Province, "if some of [the Jalayirs] till this land, would this act not contravene [the idea that the land] is the summer pasture of these nomads? If this is not the case and the nomads have enough land for their summer pasture, then I ask you to allow the poor party to till it."[129] It was natural for the Russians to assume that the people who used pastures were nomads.

As in the preceding case of Ūzūn Sāy, the parties to the dispute resorted to a native court to settle their conflict amicably. Mullā Rustam, acting on behalf of forty households, acknowledged a settlement of the dispute between the people they represented and the party of Ibrāhim over the land of Qara Quduq, which consisted of fallow and pasture land (*zamīn-i būz-i marʿāt wa yaylāw*). In exchange for the release of the previous claims, a substantial portion of land in Qara Quduq became the shared property of Mullā Rustam and his brother Ḥasan and the community on whose behalf they acted (*ba māyān wa jamāʿa-i muʿakkalīn makhṣūṣ gardānīda*).[130]

By filing a claim against a fellow member of a community, one could acquire rights to a pasture and notarize them as a deed of amicable settlement. With a certificate issued by a native court, which solemnized such rights, it would be easy to persuade the Russians that one's position was sound. The Jalayirs were clearly aware that the bureaucratization of property relations was instrumental to seizing pasture. Mullā Rustam had just received a copy of this document when two members of his community again petitioned the Russians:

> This year, the assembly of *qāḍīs* issued a decision on the land in Qara Quduq. The *qāḍīs* gave two copies of the decision, one to our group, that is, forty households, and one to the party of Ibrāhim, of sixty households. Now, when we suggest dividing the land between our forty households and cultivating it, Mullā Rustam claims that the [*qāḍīs*'] decision involves him alone and does not concern us. In order to avoid further conflicts, we ask you to order that our land be divided.[131]

An *āqsaqāl* of Zaamin was immediately dispatched to make an inquest. Reporting to the authorities in Jizzakh, he explained that, as a consequence

128 Ibid.: l. 40b.

129 Ibid.: l. 160b.

130 January–February 1885, ibid.: l. 20b.

131 Bīk Kīldī Muḥammad Khwāja-ūghlī and Bābā Āqsaqāl Aḥmad Ṣūfī-ūghlī to Pankratov, 20.11.1885, ibid.: l. 250b.

of the conflict over Qara Quduq, the residents of the Jalayir settlement were divided into two groups. The first comprised sixty households, the second forty. The former claimed that they intended to cultivate the land. Mullā Rustam and his forty households argued that the land should not be cultivated and should be retained as summer pasture. But Mullā Rustam lied:

> As he and his men took the water from a small river nearby and plowed and cultivated an area, Mullā Rustam claimed that the land in question belongs to him [*yirīm ḥaqqīm*]. They cultivated an area of six *puds* of barley [a *pud* could produce about 100 kg of barley]. They cultivate another five *puds* of barley in a place called Īlānlī, a pasture above Qara Quduq. Beside this, in a place even higher, he plowed land that measured about sixty *puds*, which [in the past] had been already tilled [*āq yir*]. Some of it is cultivated in wheat, some in barley, and the rest has been left fallow [*qūrūq*]. Above, there is also a pool [*ḥawḍ*] from which water is taken for irrigation.[132]

In order to strengthen his rights to the land he cultivated, Mullā Rustam claimed he had paid a land-tax and asked that the members of his group contribute to such expenses. Twenty-one households refused to do so and claimed, instead, their own share (*ḥiṣṣa*) of the land that they would plow independently (*zarāʿat qīlāmīz*). Mullā Rustam opposed them, requesting that they first pay a share of the tax to till the land in Qara Quduq. "Should they not be able to pay," concluded Mullā Rustam, "the twenty-one households would continue to use the land as summer pasture."

The Zaamin *āqsaqāl* was the first to understand that, if knowledge of this case were to spread, other groups might attempt to seize pastures for agricultural purposes. Indeed, he informed the Russians that there was also another community, the Turks, who had rights to the pastures of Qara Quduq, which amounted to two months in the summer of every year. He also warned the military-civil administration that, if taxes were collected from the party of the twenty-one households and the latter were allowed to cultivate the land, the Turks might advance the same claims. The *āqsaqāl* was clearly recommending that the Russians preserve the land in Qara Quduq as summer pasture to avoid conflicts and social disturbances.[133]

---

132 05.12.1885, ibid.: l. 31ob.

133 To the head of the Jizzakh *uezd*, 24.11.1885, ibid.: l. 24.

A day before the Zaamin *āqsaqāl* sent his report to the head of the Jizzakh district, the Turk community made a strategic move by appealing to the Russians:

> Even though the assembly of *qāḍī*s ruled that our land should remain summer pasture and communal property, Mullā Rustam and his community has tilled it and cultivated it, even though the two parties had reached an agreement, according to *sharīʿa,* that the land should remain pasture. Now we too want to cultivate our land and therefore appeal to you to order a trustworthy person to deal with the case in order to avoid future conflicts. We ask that our right to the land be upheld and that we be allowed to use it as we see fit, whether we want it as summer pasture or as cultivated land.[134]

The Zaamin *āqsaqāl* was dispatched again to Qara Quduq and found that it was established practice that the Turk community would every year open a well at Qara Quduq for their cattle. That year, however, Mullā Rustam with his men prevented them from doing so. The Russians decided to arrest Mullā Rustam for seven days on a charge of seizing land illegally and asked the *āqsaqāl* to take measures to prevent other landholders from restricting the access of other, less wealthy, individuals to the pasture.[135]

In the meantime, justice was served. A native court of six *qāḍī*s ruled on the dispute between the party of Mullā Rustam, his brothers, and other residents of the Jalayir settlement and the Turk community. The *qāḍī*s compared with their court register a copy of the decision, which they had issued and entrusted to the Turks. The year before, they had found that Mullā Rustam and his brother had admitted that, from ancient times, the Turks had been using the land in Qara Quduq as a summer pasture and its water and that the two had never prevented the Turks from doing so. The Turks too had acknowledged that, if Mullā Rustam and his people would agree not to prevent them from accessing the land, they would drop their claim. The conflict thus ended in an amicable settlement,[136] but Mullā Rustam took a new tack, requesting that the land in Qara Qudud be registered as the property (*milkīyat*) of his community, even though his property rights were not evident. The *qāḍī*s, however,

---

134 Raḥmān Bāy Karīm-ūghlī, Mullā Īgam Birdī Ḥasan-ūghlī, and ʿAlī Murād ʿAwaḍ-ūghlī acting on behalf of 170 households of the Turk community (*jamāʿa*), 23.11.1885, ibid.: l. 26.

135 See the Russian's decision in the right margin of ibid.: l. 31ob.

136 *ūshbū ṭarīqada ibrāʾ wa musālaḥa būyincha sāf būlghān*, 15.03.1887, ibid.: l. 36.

explained that four certificates of release (*tūrt khaṭṭ-i wathīqa-yi ibrā'*), which he had ready, did not prove that he could use the land as his own property (*mulk būlmāydūr*). In fact, Qara Quduq was, the legists explained, state land (*pādshāhlīk mamlaka*), and the two parties should use it, provided that they used it as a pasture (*īkkāwī ham yaylāw qīlīb mutaṣarrif būlmāqlārī darkār*) [Fig. 12].[137]

After the decision of the native court, the provincial chancellery issued a regulation requiring the local headmen (*illīkbāshī*) to accompany any group (*qaysī jamāʿadan būlsa*) that applied before a native court for the notarization of a transaction in land. In their absence, the *qāḍī*s should not issue documents. The Russians evidently understood that there was a danger that local power holders might expropriate land formerly belonging to the state.[138] They were right: Mullā Rustam appealed in the meantime to another native court, requesting the issuance of documents regarding a large area of land. Even though the native judges were unwilling to support him—this itself is evidence that not all *qāḍī*s were easily corrupted—Mullā Rustam did not give up on his plans. Two years later, information reached Jizzakh about a man using Qara Quduq for agricultural purposes[139] who had furthermore built some barns there.[140] Skirmishes between the party of Mullā Rustam and the Turk continued until the commandant of the Jizzakh *raion* ordered that the former be exiled.[141] The Russian official noted that Mullā Rustam was a man particularly harmful to the prestige of Russian rule in the region. He depicted Mullā Rustam as a local rich man (*bogatyi mestnyi kulak*) who failed to obey the Russian authorities. The commandant argued that, if stern measures were not taken to punish his riotous behavior, he might come to enjoy great popularity among the local population.[142]

While Mullā Rustam was attempting to seize the land in Qara Quduq, fighting Ibrāhīm and holding the Turk community at bay, he and other Jalayirs had opened another front in the conflict for irrigated land (*zamīn-i ābī-kārī*) against the Balghalis, a neighboring community. The area in question was situated around a settlement called Shahid Kutchi, on the Aq-Bulaq stream,

137 Ibid.

138 Headmen of the Jalāyir settlement to the head of the Jizzakh *uezd*, n.d., ibid.: l. 20.

139 Mullā Darwīsh reported about the fact that the buildings were not removed and that the people had been cultivating the land four months later, cf. ibid.: l. 40.

140 Commandant of the Jizzakh *uezd* to his adjutant, Rybushkin, 19.09.1887, ibid.: ll. 41–42ob.

141 15.01.1888, ibid.: l. 68.

142 Commandant of the Jizzakh *uezd* to military governor of Samarqand Province, 10.10.1888, ibid.: l. 78.

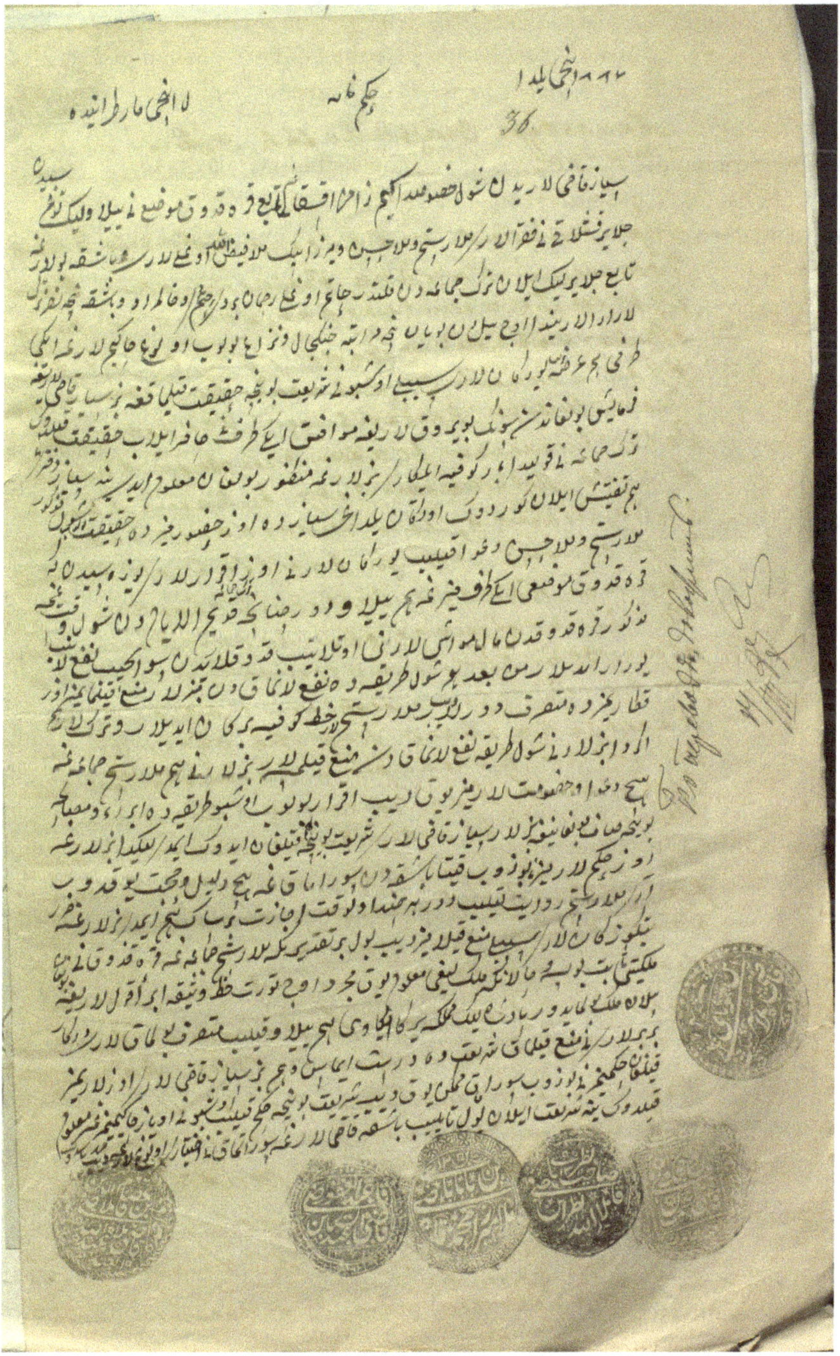

FIGURE 12 *Record of a ruling issued by the native judicial assembly of Zaamin, 15.03.1887, TsGARUz, I-21, op. 1, d. 56, l. 36.*
COURTESY OF THE CENTRAL STATE ARCHIVE OF UZBEKISTAN

a few kilometers east of the Jalayir settlement. The situation was particularly disadvantageous for the Balghalis, because the land was surrounded by areas of ancestral undivided property (*mushāʿ*) in the possession of other communities. One such community was the Jalayirs. The first round of conflict ended in 1881, when representatives of the Balghalis and the Jalayirs met at a native court in Zaamin. The parties concluded a settlement according to which half of the contested area and the corresponding water shares of the Aq-Bulaq would be counted as property (*ḥaqq wa milk-i khāliṣ*) of Mullā Rustam and Ibrahīm and the groups of Jalayirs whom they represented.[143]

The conflict between the Jalayirs and the Balghalis resumed in 1904, when the land-tax commission assessed the situation. As the two communities could not agree on the boundaries of the area, the commissar of the Jizzakh land-tax commission requested the involvement of the police chief (*pristav*) of the Zaamin *raion*. This is how the Russian official recounted the scene that unfolded as he reached the locale of Shahid Kutchi:

> On the spot, I found that the Jalayirs claimed that their land abuts the land of the Balghali settlement. So it does, on the western side, along a road. However, the residents of the Balghali *qīshlāq* contested this border and located it 1½ *verst*s further west on rain-watered land. I inspected the available documentation. […] On the basis of these deeds, I could not determine the western border. I decided to pass the case on to the native court. In my presence, two attorneys representing each side were chosen. They agreed that the case should be transferred to the competence of an assembly of judges to whom I explained the issue in detail. I ordered them to determine precisely the western border and leave untouched the cultivated lands, because the latter had already been divided by a native court in 1881. The native judicial assembly came to the spot and issued a decision based on an oath. This decision identifies the western border with the road heading to the *qīshlāq*. In this way, it includes part of the settlement and cultivated lands. […] This is not in accordance with the previous ruling. In addition, the Jalayirs received part of the settlement, which includes buildings, a mosque, and an old graveyard, together with rain-watered and pasture land and nearly all the water. […] Given the fact that the native judicial assembly did not determine the western border and notwithstanding the order not to touch the cultivated land, I, together with the residents of the two *qīshlāq*s, the commissar, and a land assessor [*zemlemer*], walked to the western side

143 Certificate of acknowledgment, five *qāḍīs*' stamps, 24.05.1881, TsGARUz, f. I-21, op. 1, d. 634, l. 27. In Persian; abridged version in Chaghatay, ibid.: l. 21.

> from the Balghali *qīshlāq*, to the Aq-Bulaq spring, and began to determine who cultivates what. In this way I wanted to determine the de facto possession [*fakticheskoe vladenie*]. The two parties began to produce evidence and indicate precisely where the cultivated lands are located. It turned out that the pasture land is used by both parties. According to the evidence on the de facto possession [*po viiasneniiu fakticheskogo vladeniia*], all the cultivated land and the entire *qīshlāq* should be considered as belonging to the Balghalis, [whereas] part of the rain-watered land and about one-half of the pasture should be considered as belonging to the Jalayirs. I, together with Captain Rubakhin and the assessor Pleger, drew a map [*glazomernyi chertezh*] on which we laid out a proposal for a redefined border between the Balghalis and Jalayirs. The Balghalis agree, but the Jalayirs insist on their evidence and express dissatisfaction with the project, as they wished the border to be identified with the road.[144]

The Balghalis thus appealed against the decision of the *qāḍīs*. The case was reviewed by the *okrug* military court in Samarqand, which collected the depositions of several people. Among them was the land-tax commissioner Captain Rubakhin, who provided a revealing insider's account of the conflict. He said that the dispute was initiated by a few immoral (*nedobrosovestnye*) residents of Jalayir, who were led by ʿAlī Bīk (son of Mullā Rustam), a former county headman who had been imprisoned for bribery (*za podkup*). Rubakhin noted that the only thing that ʿAlī Bīk had in support of his claims was the native-court record issued in 1881, which gave a terse description of the division of land between the Jalayirs and Balghalis. The commissioner also noted that the Jalayirs exploited the absence of more ample documentary evidence on the division of the land. Rubakhin, however, was adamant that the burden for this unjust decision fell on the native judicial assembly, whose

> glaring superficiality turned out to the benefit of the Jalayirs. The assembly had to define the boundaries of the rain-watered land of the Jalayirs according to *sharīʿa*. This was all they had to do. But they did not follow your order; they did check the document, [but] they did not go to the spot and did not inspect the irrigated land. For reasons unclear to me, they divided the Balghali settlement. Alfalfa fields, two shrines, one mosque, and twenty-two courtyards with buildings and plantations, which belonged to the Balghalis according to uncontested, permanent, and hereditary possession, use and disposal,[145] were assigned to the Jalayirs

144 *Doznanie*, 29.09.1904, ibid.: ll. 15–20.

145 This is the wording of Article 255.

FIGURE 13 *Land assessor's map of the contested lands in the Jalayir and Balghali settlements, Iam County, Jizzakh District, 1904, TsGARUz, f. I-21, op. 1, d. 634, l. unnumbered.*
COURTESY OF THE CENTRAL STATE ARCHIVE OF UZBEKISTAN

> on the basis of only one oath, which was sworn by a few suspicious indigenes, who had no idea whatsoever of what they were swearing. The decision was absolutely unjust, partial, and not in accordance with any rules. I consider it necessary to appeal it and file an action against the judicial assembly [...] for their superficiality, for the intentionally inadequate selection of witnesses, and for their mockery of justice [*izdevatel'stvo nad pravosudiem*].[146]

The impassioned report of Rubakhin provided scant juristic grounds for curtailing the ambitions of Mullā Rustam and his son, but it must have been easy for the Samarqand *okrug* military court to find arguments to overturn the *qāḍīs*' judgment. In reviewing the case, the military officials ruled that the native judicial assembly was in breach of the statutory law (Article 211 of the *polozhenie*) that conferred on native courts the power to hear cases among "physical" entities only, while the military court considered rural communities to be "juridical" entities. The case therefore fell under the jurisdiction of the Russian justices of the peace, and the decision of the native court was quashed.[147] This time, a certificate of settlement did not prove sufficient to seize marginal lands.

Conclusion

Russian land policy in Central Asia was centered on the alleged recognition of the existing forms of land tenure. The rationale behind such a policy was simple: reinforcing tenure would guarantee a stable fiscal income. The question of whether imperial agencies regarded such income as sufficient for financing the colonial enterprise in Russian Turkestan and in compliance with policies of resettlement (*pereselenie*) is of little concern to the present study; readers are directed instead to the excellent studies of Beatrice Penati.[148]

Of greater interest for a legal history of Russian Central Asia is the fact that colonization was conducive to the bureaucratization and subsequent modification of local perceptions of tenure. The purported preservation of indigenous notions of land tenure restricted a complex understanding of property

146 Land-tax commissioner Rubakhin to the Zaamin chief of police (*pristav*), 01.10.1904, TsGARUz, f. I-21, op. 1, d. 634, ll. 23–23ob.

147 Ruling of the Samarqand *okrug* court, 26.10.1904 [copy], ibid.: l. 40b.

148 See especially her "The Cotton Boom and the Land Tax in Russian Turkestan (1880s–1915)," and "Managing Rural Landscapes in Colonial Turkestan: A View from the Margins." In *Explorations into the Social History of Modern Central Asia (19th–20th Century)*, ed. P. Sartori (Leiden: Brill, 2013): 65–109.

relations and transformed it into a narrower, liberal notion of land-ownership. Local sources indicate that, before the Russian conquest, Central Asian rulers, landowners, and tenants viewed land less in terms of property relations than in terms of rent and usufruct. This notion is reflected in Islamic juristic sources and notarial materials in which the legal term *milk* (property) refers to produce, not to land. Land was not just a commodity that could be exchanged and monetized. Central Asians regarded land mainly in terms of its agricultural produce. Local juristic sources therefore indicate that property rights to land should be made equal to and exchanged for property rights to the produce. In other words, a peasant tilling a plot of land, say, in Marghilan, was not particularly interested in whether the land belonged legally (i.e., formally) to someone living in Tashkent, as long as he was entitled to a share of the produce. In fact, that peasant could sell his proprietary entitlements to the land by claiming to have planted trees or erected a warehouse or a barn, for instance. Hence, Islamic legal deeds tell us that individuals sold and purchased property in the form of improvements (*uskūna/suknīya*) on the land. It is unlikely that a peasant would boast the ownership of a tree, but he must have known that his share of the produce gave him rights to the land. Central Asian fatwas indicate clearly that, because peasants' usufruct generated proprietary rights (*taṣarruf-i malīkāna*), landowners could not easily evict them from peasants' own possessions.

This situation conflicted with what the Russians understood as land-ownership. As the Russian bureaucracy conferred exclusive probative value on deeds attesting to ownership rights, specifically on arable land, it necessarily disempowered individuals who enjoyed only rights of disposal to communal property and groups traditionally practicing seasonal pastoralism. Groups engaged in seasonal pastoralism rarely kept deeds at hand unless the khan and his chanceries restricted their access to the land with narrow contractual stipulations. In their understanding of land tenure, they had been able to dispose of land that belonged to them from time immemorial. Colonial bureaucracy made things easier, by contrast, for those who could document on paper their rights, either ostensible or actual, to cultivated land. The paperwork of district chanceries suggests that, in such circumstances, a battle for *milk* unfolded on many fronts. We know that local scrambles for land often ended in amicable settlements, which stipulated that one party pay the other for certain plots of land. It is no coincidence that such exchanges appear to have involved lands that belonged formerly to the treasury of the khanates. It would be hasty to conclude that such turf wars were less authentic than simulated, but it apparently did not take long for locals to understand that the Russian bureaucratic regime had become a valuable new legal resource.

CHAPTER 4

Annulling Charitable Endowments

Introduction

I will begin with an extended anecdote as a form of casual ethnographic observation. The last time I was in Uzbekistan I heard someone recollecting stories about charitable endowments (*awqāf*, sg. *waqf*); it was a sunny day in October 2014, and I was in Khorezm. I had spent the entire day with my informant, Erkinboy, inspecting private collections of Islamic manuscripts in the village of Oromobod. We were about to head home when, walking through the gate of a house I stumbled across a wire that tore the upper of my right shoe. A mixture of embarrassment and anxiety marked the face of my companion. Erkinboy decided to make a detour to the city of Khiva, the closest place that had a shoe-repair shop. As we entered the citadel and walked past a row of silent madrasas erected in the nineteenth century, my informant began to explain, in a tone of self-entitlement, that, in the distant past, a set of powerful Islamic endowments had stood behind those desolated buildings and were eventually abolished by the Soviets; as my guide began to mourn the passing of the golden epoch before the October Revolution, when *awqāf* had kept the Islamic world of Khiva alive and well, I sensed that there was something odd about these stories. I had heard similar tales years before, though narrated in other cities, such as Samarqand, Bukhara, and Tashkent, and they all centered on one plot: the Soviets alone should be blamed for closing down the Islamic endowments in the region, in spite of the fact that Soviet power was, in fact, represented by a new generation of local Muslim communists.[1] Stories like these are, however, predicated also on another assumption that makes them quixotic: Muslims should always like *awqāf*.

In this chapter I explore some of the attempts to annul *waqf* endowments in the period before and after the Russian conquest of Central Asia in 1865. I begin by examining complaints about the inequity of *waqf* provisions, particularly on the part of heirs of an endowment's founder who were not designated as beneficiaries. My exploration is necessarily tentative, because attempts to annul endowments are to be found almost exclusively in legal source-material in which details about the nature of such inequities, either

1 N. Pianciola and P. Sartori, "*Waqf* in Turkestan: The Colonial Legacy and the Fate of an Islamic Institution in Early Soviet Central Asia (1917–1924)." *CAS* 26/4 (2007): 475–98.

ostensible or actual, are scanty. These vignettes clearly suggest that opposition to the wealth-distribution mechanisms of endowments required recognition of the available legal resources. With the establishment of a pluralistic legal regime, the Russians increased the number of such resources, thus making it easier for locals to annul endowments in an effort to free up property. The analysis of this phenomenon is vital to our appreciation of the changes that took place in the domain of knowledge and its distribution among the Muslim population of colonial Central Asia.

The conventional understanding of the *waqf* holds that it is, first and foremost, an act of "charity."[2] The founding of a charitable endowment ostensibly constitutes something useful and desirable for a community of believers, and the act confers an aura of piety on the individual who dedicates his/her wealth for the benefit of a (religious) institution;[3] someone who relinquishes the usufruct of his/her properties for the benefit of, say, a madrasa or mosque or to provide funds for the recitation of the Qur'ān is worthy of mention as an example of probity.[4] This is what historiographers do when they present the Bukharan emirs Danyāl Bī (r. 1758–85), Shāh Murād (r. 1785–1800), and Ḥaydar (r. 1800–26) as just rulers (*pādishāh-i ṣāḥib-i naṣfat wa ʿadālat*) and praise them for enforcing *sharīʿa* and restoring endowments that had fallen in disuse.[5]

2 "The idea, as well as the terms *ṣadaqa jāriya* or *ṣadaqa mawqūfa*, appear in virtually every treatise on the *waqf*," M. Hoexter, "The Waqf and the Public Sphere." In *The Public Sphere in Muslim Societies*, ed. M. Hoexter, Sh. Eisenstadt, and N. Levtzion (Albany: State University of New York Press, 2002): 135 fn. 18; see also P.C. Hennigan, *The Birth of a Legal Institution: The Formation of the Waqf in Third-Century A.H. Ḥanafī Legal Discourse* (Leiden: Brill, 2004): passim; J. Krsmárik, "Das Waḳfrecht vom Standpunkte des Śarîʿarechtes nach der ḥanefitischen Schule: Ein Beitrag zum Studium des Islamischen Rechtes." *ZDMG* 45 (1891): 534.

3 Timur Kuran points out that a *waqf* confers an aura of sacredness on the properties endowed to an institution. See Kuran, *The Long Divergence: How Islamic Law Held Back the Middle East* (Princeton: Princeton University Press, 2011): 112.

4 In his *Rūz-nāma*, the Bukharan jurist Muḥammad Sharīf-i Ṣadr-i Ziyā' noted: "The third good deed was: on Fridays only one muezzin served at the *khānaqāh* mentioned above, although the power of one man's voice was often insufficient because of the multitude in the congregation. For that reason, I added one more muezzin, allotting for him as a *waqf* approximately four *ṭanābs* of a pond of reeds [*kūl-i nay-zār*] in the place of Mūliyān, in order that, on Fridays, he could recite the *adhān* together with the first muezzin and help him tidy up the additional area. God, receive [this] of us!," *The Personal History of a Bukharan Intellectual. The Diary of Muḥammad Sharīf Ṣadr-i Ziyā*, trans. R. Shukurov and ed. Edward Allworth (Leiden: Brill, 2004): 270.

5 With regard to Danyāl Bī, see A. von Kügelgen, *Die Legitimierung der mittelasiatischen Mangitendynastie in der Werken ihrer Historiker, 18.–19. Jahrhundert* (Istanbul: Ergon, 2002): 333–4; Ākhūnd Mullā Muḥammad Wafā b. Muḥammad Ẓahīr Karmīnagī, *Tuḥfat al-khānī*, MS

The concept of public utility (*maṣlaḥa*) suggests that the establishment of a charitable endowment is an act that is intrinsically praiseworthy and that will secure the donor a reward (*thawāb*) in the afterlife;[6] this applies equally to so-called "family endowments," established in response to "pietistic urges."[7]

Although endowments are generally conceptualized within a narrative web of goodwill, it does not follow that everyone regards them with the same degree of sympathy, let alone moral approval. If charitable endowments served as a means of providing for the souls of many, they also placed a heavy burden on the lives of some. While we may be inclined to depict attempts to confiscate endowment properties as instances of economic "rapacity,"[8] it may be that *waqf* administrators acted just as rapaciously towards the people who found themselves within convenient reach. Consider the case of a certain Nāṣir Jān, who owned a shop abutting a wall of the Mullā Miskīn madrasa in

---

Tashkent, TsVRUz, no. 2726/III: fol. 8a. For a description of this manuscript—a twentieth-century abridged version of the original *Tuḥfat al-khānī* written in the eighteenth century—see *Sobranie vostochnykh rukopisei akademii nauk respubliki Uzbekistan: Istoriia*, ed. D.Yu. Iusupov and R.P. Dzhalilov (Tashkent: Fan, 1998): 179. The Bukharan polymath Ahmad Makhdūm Dānish (1827–97) offered a diametrically opposed evaluation of Danyāl Bī, under whose rule, he says, madrasas and mosques in Bukhara fell into decay and "the Uzbek people took over the affairs of the government [...] and stole the bread from the endowments' stores to feed their stomachs" (*nān az unbār-i awqāf duzdīda ba-maṣraf-i shikam wa furaj-i khwud mīrasānīdand*). See Aḥmad Makhdhūm Muhandis-i Bukhārī, alias Aḥmad-i Kalla, *Tarjimat al-aḥwāl-i amīrān-i Bukhārā-yi sharīf az Amīr-i Dānyāl tā ʿaṣr-i Amīr ʿAbd al-Aḥad*, MS Tashkent, TsVRUz, no. 1987: fol. 7b; cf. the Tajik edition, Ahmad Makhdumi Donish, *Risola yo mukhtasare az ta'rikhi saltanati khonadoni manghitiia* (Dushanbe: Sarvat, 1992): 8, where the passage is rendered incorrectly. With regard to Shāh Murād and his restoration of the endowments, see ʿAbd al-ʿAẓīm [Bustānī] Sāmī, *Ta'rīkh-i Ṣalāṭīn-i Manghitīya* (*Istoriia Mangytskikh gosudarei*), ed. and trans. L.M. Epifanova (Moscow: Nauka, 1962): fol. 62b. Emir Ḥaydar not only revived endowments that had fallen into decay but also renewed their deeds (*tajdīd-i sijillāt-i ānrā farmūd*): Aḥmad Makhdūm Muhandis-i Bukhārī, *Tarjimat al-aḥwāl-i amīrān-i Bukhārā-yi sharīf az Amīr-i Dānyāl tā ʿaṣr-i Amīr ʿAbd al-Aḥad*: fol. 11a. Robert McChesney suggested that Shāh Murād ordered that endowment deeds be recopied "either as an act of piety or perhaps to ensure the government had a record of *wakf*s in Bukhārā." See his "Waḳf. V. In Central Asia." *EI2* vol. XI: 92.

6 The notion of "reward in the afterlife" (*thawāb*) is integral to the language of *waqf* deeds, and its use attests to the moral dimension of charitable endowments. See F. Schwarz, "Bargeldstiftungen im Chanat von Chiva, 1840–1922." *DI* 80/1 (2003): 86–87.

7 D.S. Powers, "The Maliki Family Endowment: Legal Norms and Social Practices." *IJMES* 25/3 (1993): 379–406.

8 G.C. Kozlowski, *Muslim Endowments and Society in British India* (Cambridge: Cambridge University Press, 1985): 20.

Samarqand.[9] Nāṣir Jān found himself involved in a dispute when the administrator (*mutawallī*) of the endowment supporting this madrasa claimed that the shop had been devoted to the madrasa's benefit. The administrator's confrontational attitude did not deter Nāṣir Jān from attempting to defend his rights. Armed with a written attestation of his ownership rights, he agreed to meet his opponent before a *qāḍī*. When the judge heard the claim, he placed the burden of proof on the administrator, who failed to produce evidence. Nāṣir Jān would have sworn an oath and thus won the case, but a small group of elders[10] who were present in court arranged a reconciliation (*muṣālaḥa*) between the parties.[11] The elders decided that Nāṣir Jān should contribute to the well-being of the endowment (*khayrīyat al-waqf*) because the shop in question occupied a plot (*ʿarṣa*) of land belonging to the *waqf*. Their intervention led to the notarization of a contract of amicable settlement stipulating that Nāṣir Jān would pay a "ground rent" fee (called *ṣulḥāna*, from *ṣulḥ*, "reconciliation") to the administrator. The shop no doubt belonged to Nāṣir Jān, but the reconciliation agreement made it obligatory for whoever possessed the building to pay a sum of money to the administrator.

This case found its way into the copybook of the administrator of the endowment supporting the Tillā Kār madrasa, one of the most important institutions of Islamic education in Central Asia.[12] For the compiler of this copybook, the particularly instructive feature of this case was the right conferred on the administrator to levy a fee on a property that was not among the assets of the endowment. Honing the skills to secure additional incomes must have been crucial for an administrator who managed the income and expenses of an endowment as prominent as the one associated with the Tillā Kār madrasa. The ground rent was one such potential source of income.

In weighing expediency, however, jurists regarded the confrontational behavior of administrators in an unfavorable light. It is instructive to consider a fatwa

---

9 The madrasa is not mentioned in the two best known historical geographies of Samarqand. Cf. *Qandīya wa Samarīya. Dū risāla dar taʾrīkh-i mazārāt wa jughrāfiyā-yi Samarqand*, ed. Īraj Afshār (Tehran: Muʾassasa-yi Farhangī-yi Jahāngīrī, 1367sh/1947–48). See Y. Bregel, "Historiography. xii. Central Asia." In *EIr* vol. XII: 395–402.

10 The term "elders" is here used to translate *āqsaqālān-i khāliṣ wa mū-safidān*.

11 On the participation of elders in judicial activity in Islamic Central Asia, see Chapter 1.

12 See *Munshaʾāt-i Mīrzā Bahādir Khwāja b. Khwāja Ḥusayn Pīrmastī*, MS Tashkent, TsVRUz, no. 2667: fol. 14a–15b; for a description of the manuscript, see *SVR* I: 166–7: no. 394. The template document is under the heading "endowment deed after reconciliation" (*waqfīyat-i ṣulḥī*) and is a model rescript addressed to the chancellery of the Bukharan emirate.

delivered in relation to a conflict between an endowment administrator and a group of sharecroppers (*muzāriʿīn*). The administrator had sued them because, he claimed, the land they tilled belonged to a *waqf*. When the parties were summoned to court, the administrator was unable to produce decisive testimony supporting his claim. The burden of the oath thus fell on the sharecroppers. As in the case involving Nāṣir Jān, the swearing of the oath was avoided and the parties reconciled on the condition that the sharecroppers pay the ground-rent fee (*ṣulḥāna*) in exchange for the administrator's waiving his claim. Later, the administrator changed his mind, refused the fee, and demanded that his respondents pay a higher share of the produce. But the mufti ruled against this unscrupulous behavior: "Any claim in support of which the administrator fails to produce testimony or written evidence should not be heard."[13]

Administrators regarded themselves as being charged to take any steps necessary to increase the value of an endowment, even if this necessitated unorthodox measures. This does not mean, however, that members of the populace welcomed the actions, unscrupulous or not, of *mutawallīs*. Presumably, it would have struck people as very aggressive, for example, to enlarge the wealth of endowments by invoking unsound claims, as did administrators in Central Asia who sought to acquire entire portions of land, regardless of the fact that the landholders claimed to have been its proprietors from time immemorial. In a case that illustrates such aggressive behavior, an administrator took legal action against several landholders, claiming that the area of land to which they enjoyed property rights belonged to his endowment. To support his claim, the administrator produced a *waqf* deed, but the boundaries of the endowment must have been changed over the years, due to various transactions. For this reason, the deed was not sufficient to ascertain the rights of the *waqf* to the area in question. To strengthen his claim and combat the landholders, the administrator produced the testimony of several witnesses (*shuhūd*). On this basis, he asked that the boundaries of the area undergo a new demarcation (*taḥdīd*), which would include it among the assets of the endowment. The procedures that the magistrate followed at this point are unclear. We know, however, that the landholders denied the claim and acquired the following legal opinion:

---

13 *Daʿwī-yi fulānī-yi khwāja-yi mutawallī-yi madhkūr waqfīyat-i zamīn-i madhkūra bidūn-i bayyina-yi muʿadala wa bidūn-i ḥujjat-i sharʿī lā tusmaʿu*; see untitled collection of fatwas copied at the beginning of the twentieth century, MS Tashkent, TsVRUz, no. 2844/II: fol. 65a. The manuscript is described in *SVR* V: 382, no. 4102.

> [Question:] We invoke blessing in the name of the supreme Lord. What do the imams of Islam, may God be pleased with them all, have to say on the following question? The matter is as follows: most of the people [living] in a certain rural settlement used a certain area of land from time immemorial as [their] property. Khālid, who is the administrator of an endowment, has produced before the ruler of the noble law a protocol of claim [*maḥḍar-i sharʿī*] against several people using [that land], who do not have the power to act in the capacity of proxies, deputies, or guardians on behalf of the majority. He [also] produced [in support of his] allegation a *waqf* deed [including] all the aforementioned area and claimed a [new] demarcation of its boundaries. In this case the claim is, according to *sharīʿa*, unsound [*nā-durust*] because it addressed only a few of the landholders. The testimony of the witnesses of the aforementioned Khālid, [who say] that the *waqf* deed includes all the aforementioned area is not to be heard according to the stipulation [of the law], is that not so? Explain and be concise.
>
> [Answer:] Yes, it is and God knows best.[14]

We do not know what the outcome of the dispute was, but we assume that the landholders preferred to face the legal expenses required to draft this fatwa than to give in to the administrator and pay a rent to the endowment. As we shall see in Chapter 5, the production of a legal opinion necessitated certain fixed expenditures, requiring payment for the service of the scribe (*muḥarrir*) and for the seals of the muftis who endorsed it.[15]

Many untold stories of frustration, discord, and revenge are entangled in the more vocal success stories of the institutions to which endowments were dedicated. The establishment of an endowment is not only an act of piety or gesture of charity but also an act of dispossession that diverts some resources from certain family members and puts these resources at the disposal of an institution and the latter's administrator. We find several cases in which mortally ill individuals attempted to endow more than one-third of their wealth, thereby violating the Islamic law of inheritance, which prescribes "if a *waqf* is made through a will or during a mortal illness (*maraḍ al-mawt*), the testator can-

14 T. Welsford and N. Tashev, *A Catalogue of Arabic-Script Documents from the Samarqand Museum* (Samarkand and Istanbul: IICAS, 2012): doc. 63.

15 M.S. Iusupov, *Sud v Bukhare. Sudoustroistvo i sudoproizvodstvo v Bukharskom emirate v kontse XIX veka i nachale XX veka*, MS Samarqand, AMIKINUz, no. 828: fols. 20–21.

not award more than one-third of his estate without the consent of his heirs."[16] The founders of these endowments clearly antagonized their direct heirs.[17] A fatwa issued in mid-nineteenth-century Bukhara relates the case of a certain Mullā Mīr Sayyid, who, though mortally ill, endowed all his land and manumitted a slave. His heirs claimed that the endowed properties exceeded one-third of his estate (*ziyāda az thulth-i māl-i matrūka-yi way*), and the jurists argued that, with regard to the remaining two-thirds, the endowment and the manumission should not be considered operative (*ghayr-i nāfiẓ bāshad*).[18]

One wonders whether these cases attest to manipulation by would-be beneficiaries of the endowment rather than the expression of an urge for charity. Although it involves piety, charity, and upkeep, the foundation of a *waqf* may well exclude people from access to accumulated wealth and from participation in a vested corporate interest. Individuals attempted to shelter what they assumed to be their share of an inheritance by creating an endowment out of a portion of an ancestral undivided property (*mushāʾ*). These individuals often found themselves pressured by relatives who requested the revocation (*rujūʿ*) of such endowments.[19]

Archival materials of a primarily legal nature will, in the rest of this chapter, show that the history of modern Central Asia (late eighteenth to early twentieth centuries) is punctuated by the voices of people expressing discontent at the establishment of endowments. Although less audible than those voices praising the self-righteous intentions of a founder, they are no less relevant to the understanding of the perception of endowments in a Muslim society. I want to suggest that the Russian colonization of Central Asia marked the beginning of a period in which legal resources were exploited by the locals to pursue the annulment of charitable endowments. In the next section, I will give voice to claims of dispossession related to the establishment of endowments in the early-modern period (sixteenth to eighteenth centuries). In the

16 J.L. Esposito, *Women in Muslim Family Law*, 2nd ed. (Syracuse: Syracuse University Press, 2001): 45. See also A. Layish, *Sharīʿa and Custom in Libyan Tribal Society: An Annotated Translation of Decisions from the Sharīʿa Courts of Adjābiya and Kufra* (Leiden: Brill, 2005): 195–6 fn. 10.

17 Welsford and Tashev, *A Catalogue of Arabic-Script Documents from the Samarqand Museum*: doc 87.

18 *Maktūbāt-i Amīr Muẓaffar ba-Sayyid Mīrak wa ʿarāyiḍ-i Sayyid Mīrak*, MS Tashkent, TsVRUz, no. 1740: fol. 51b, doc. 919. The manuscript is described in *Sobranie vostochnykh rukopisei akademii nauk respubliki Uzbekistan: Istoriia*, ed. D.Yu. Yusupov and R.P. Dzhalilov (Tashkent: Fan, 1998): 411, no. 959.

19 Anon., *Jung*, MS Tashkent, TsVRUz, no. 6102: fol. 230b.

following section, I draw on several cases in which Central Asian colonial subjects attempted, successfully or not, to annul charitable endowments.

The reader who is familiar with the subtleties of the law of *waqf* may well think that my emphasis on dispossession is trivial, because the possibility that founders of endowments were depriving some individuals of rights to property that they would otherwise have enjoyed was a concern of those Muslim jurists who wrote about endowments from the beginning of Islamic legal history. These debates took place from the seventh to the ninth century among Muslim scholars who classified (and sought the legitimacy of) endowments in the context of the Islamic law of inheritance (*ʿilm al-farāʾiḍ*).[20] That early jurists debated this point of law, however, is not my concern here, nor is it my intention to offer a history of the category of dispossession in the Islamic juristic literature devoted to endowments. To read nineteenth-century legal cases in the light of ninth-century treatises would make little sense, because my material does not refer to those treatises or to the juristic argumentations laid out in them.

My interest lies in the way in which Central Asian Muslims regarded their entitlements to the properties that were dedicated to the benefit of endowments. I want to recount the reasons adduced by the heirs of founders to achieve the annulment of endowments and make sense of the idiom that they used to pursue their interests. In other words, my objective is to take stock of the emic perspective of Central Asian historical actors (not necessarily jurists) who took legal action against charitable endowments. If common sense suggests that the establishment of an endowment is regarded by many as an act of charity,[21] one is tempted to assume that the opposite course of action (the annulment of an endowment) may have a negative connotation because it effectively anticipates the decline of Islamic institutions, such as a mosque or a madrasa, for the upkeep of which a *waqf* was created. The cultivation of moral values requires the preservation rather than the destruction of endowments. I hope to show that this assumption is invalid. The available documentation suggests that legal actors regarded the annulment of a *waqf* in terms of expediency and were little concerned with the moral underpinnings of such actions. It is thus natural that, in a situation in which individuals could deploy norms to free up property, they would make all the necessary economic investments in pursuit of such interests.

---

20 Hennigan, *The Birth of a Legal Institution*: xv–xvi, 93; N. Oberauer, "Early Doctrines on *Waqf* Revisited: The Evolution of Islamic Endowment Law in the 2nd Century AH." *ILS* 20/1–2 (2013): 32–6.

21 Hennigan, *The Birth of a Legal Institution*: xvi.

This chapter is part of a larger project to correct facile narratives about the significance for Muslim society of the establishment of Russian rule. In the attempt to revise Cold War–era historiography that once conferred great salience on Muslim opposition to the Russians, Robert Crews has located the Russian colonization of Central Asia in a narrative of instrumental conciliation and purposive alliance. His study argues that Muslims viewed Russia as a "House of Islam," regarded the colonizers as protectors of their faith, and drew Russians into their "religious disputes."[22] This interpretation has two problems. First, the claim that disputes among Muslims are "religious" is based on the assumption that faith alone informed their legal behavior. This is misleading because "faith" and "religion" played scarcely any role in the formulation of a claim regarding, say, animal theft, no matter what the language of such a claim was. One should bear in mind the possibility that the legalistic texture of my source basis might obliterate the religious stimuli that prompted legal action, but it is also the case that most of the petitions I have reviewed are less legalistic than one might expect. Elsewhere, for example, I have noted that, facing issues that fell under the rubric of guardianship, widows in Tashkent petitioned Russians officials and adopted several linguistic strategies that had little religious tenor.[23] The assumption that conflicts among Muslims drew on a conceptual repertoire that was essentially "religious" is unwarranted and is not corroborated by the material available, unless we superimpose the notion of "religious" upon anything pertaining to *sharīʿa*. It would be difficult, however, to argue that Muslims perceived offenses such as usurpation, slander, or assault as "religious."

The second problem in Crews' interpretation relates to hermeneutics. It is one thing to note that some jurists appreciated Russians' toleration of Islam,[24] but it is entirely different to suggest that Central Asians brought their grievances before the Russians *because* they regarded the latter as the guardians

22 R.D. Crews, *For Prophet and Tsar: Islam and Empire in Russia and Central Asia* (Cambridge, MA: Harvard University Press, 2006): 258, 259, 260 ("religious controversies"), 283, 317, 369.

23 P. Sartori, "Constructing Colonial Legality in Russian Central Asia: On Guardianship." *CSSH* 56/2 (2014): 419–47.

24 See, e.g., H. Komatsu, "*Dār al-Islām* under Russian Rule as Understood by Turkestani Muslim Intellectuals." In *Empire, Islam, and Politics in Central Eurasia*, ed. Tomohiko Uyama (Tokyo: Slavic Research Center, 2007): 3–21; idem, "From Holy War to Autonomy: *Dār al-Islām* Imagined by Turkestani Muslim Intellectuals." *CAC* 17/18 (2009): 449–75; B. Babadzhanov, "Russian Colonial Power in Central Asia as Seen by Local Muslim Intellectuals." In *Looking at the Coloniser: Cross-Cultural Perceptions in Central Asia and the Caucasus, Bengal, and Related Areas*, ed. B. Eschment and H. Harder (Berlin: Ergon, 2004): 75–90.

of Islamic law. This is what Crews seems to imply when he writes that colonial subjects "recognized their new rulers as potential allies in the struggle to cultivate a society based on the shari'a."[25] While Crews is certainly right in pointing out that hearing the grievances of the locals was foundational to the establishment of the Russian rule in Central Asia, he seems here to suggest that Muslims took legal action against one another solely to safeguard the standards of behavior set by *sharīʿa* rather than to pursue their own interests. There may well have been cases initiated by people who had clear ideas about Islamic morality, but it is difficult to explain other cases in which malicious claimants had recourse to lies and false accusations. Such cases, which are not negligible, require a different interpretive framework.

There is more. Central Asian Muslims sometimes filed claims with the colonial administration in order to avoid the application of *sharīʿa*. In these cases, they took legal action *against* the integrity of Islamic institutions (e.g., mosques, madrasas). We should regard this phenomenon also as reflective of Muslims' behavior and consider it as an integral part of a shared cultural experience of being Muslim in Russian Central Asia.[26] By exploring such cases, we may develop an argument diametrically opposed to that suggested by Crews: Russian colonization led to the introduction of new forms of knowledge that sustained different modes of behavior. Following Fredrik Barth, I use the term "knowledge" to refer both to the expert knowledge of the jurists and the lawyers and to the imagination of laypeople, their entitlements, and their perceptions. The broader significance of this study thus lies less in retracing institutional changes in the Islamic juridical field than in explaining how the legal consciousness of Central Asians may have changed.

1 Giving Voice to the Dispossessed

There are, to date, only a few studies dealing with endowments that have touched upon the issue of dispossession, and these all focus on the entanglement of the so-called familial endowments with the Islamic law of inheritance. The point has been summarized by Miriam Hoexter, who noted that "family endowments were found to have played an important role in generating cooperation between members of the lineal descent group, who in many cases were the exclusive beneficiaries of family endowments, but also discord,

25 Crews, *For Prophet and Tsar*: 261.

26 On the concept of "Muslimness" and the history of what it meant to be a "Muslim" in Soviet Central Asia, see S. Abashin, "A Prayer for Rain: Practising Being Soviet and Muslim." *JIS* 25/2 (2014): 178–200.

tension and conflict within the same group as well as between the lineal group and relatives who did not qualify as beneficiaries."[27]

It is now generally understood that familial endowments (*awqāf ahlī* or *dhurrī*) are one of several legal institutions created by Muslim jurists as an instrument for the devolution of property rights and that, along with gifts inter vivos (*hiba*), voluntary bequests (*waṣīya*), and ad hoc transfers of property (*taslīm*),[28] endowments were used to circumvent the compulsory laws of inheritance, usually to ensure that a property would pass down the agnatic line of a family.[29] When the creation of an endowment meant that access to family wealth was restricted to a few privileged beneficiaries, however, the less fortunate might sooner or later challenge the integrity of the endowment.

In Central Asia we find little distinction between "familial" and "charitable" endowments in local Hanafi juristic literature—the categories of *khayrī* and *ahlī* which refer, respectively, to endowments established for the benefit of an institution (and hence all Muslims) and for the benefit of the family members alone.[30]

In the regional legal parlance, charitable endowments are distinguished as to their beneficiaries. In Central Asia, charity consisted of providing for relatives.[31] Jurists from this region frequently mention the category of *waqf-i*

27 M. Hoexter, "*Waqf* Studies in the Twentieth Century: The State of the Art." *JESHO* 41/4 (1998): 478.

28 In Central Asian Islamic legal language, *taslīm* (lit., delivery) is distinguished from *hiba* (gift). See, e.g., a case of transferral between two communities (*jamāʿa*) of water rights to a spring called Lāy Chashma in the Shīrāz district (*tūmān*), in the region of Samarqand: TsGARUz, f. I-21, op. 1, d. 475, l. 5 (March-April 1856).

29 D.S. Powers, "The Islamic Inheritance System: A Socio-Historical Approach." In *Islamic Family Law*, ed. C. Mallat and J. Connors (London, Dordrecht, and Boston: Graham & Trotman, 1990): 11–29. The point has been recently (and conclusively) recapitulated by Astrid Meier, "Für immer und ewig? Befristete Formen islamischer Stiftungen in osmanischer Zeit." In *Islamische Stiftungen zwischen juristischer Norm und sozialer Praxis*, ed. A. Meier, J. Pahlitzsch, and L. Reinfandt (Berlin: Akademie Verlag, 2009): 191–212, at 204. On the means of circumventing the inheritance rules, see R. Shaham, *Family and the Courts in Modern Egypt: A Study Based on Decisions by the Sharīʿa Courts, 1900–1955* (Leiden: Brill, 1997): 207–17.

30 The reader unfamiliar with *waqf* studies may find it useful to refer to the works of Aharon Layish, which explain the devolution of property rights within family endowments established in compliance with the Maliki school of law. See his "The Mālikī Family *waqf* According to Wills and *waqfiyyāt*"; idem, "The Family *Waqf* and the *Sharīʿa* Law of Succession in Modern Times."

31 This paragraph attempts to refine earlier typological interventions on Central Asian *waqf*, most notably that of Maria E. Subtelny, *Timurids in Transition: Turko-Persian Politics and Acculturation in Medieval Iran* (Leiden: Brill, 2007): 150–51, where she tries to explain the

awlād (or *waqf-i awlādī*), which refers to endowments whose principal beneficiaries are the descendants (*awlād*) of the founder; in this case, the founder's sons and daughters qualify as beneficiaries of the revenues produced by the *waqf* properties.[32] In Bukharan bureaucratese, such entitlement is referred to as *rasma-yi awlād* or *rasma-yi sahm-i awlādī*. I have traced this terminology back to a protocol of claim from the first half of the nineteenth century. This record illustrates how the heirs of an endowment's founder filed a lawsuit against an administrator on the grounds of the latter's failure to pay the share due to descendants (*sahm-i awlādī*).[33] Similar expressions were used in texts from the early period of Russian rule. Two orders (*mubārak-nāma*) issued by the chancellery of Emir Muẓaffar Khān (r. 1860–85) instructed a judge to investigate cases of alleged mismanagement after the heirs of the endowment's founder claimed that the administrators did not provide for their share.[34]

---

absence of a clear distinction between "charitable" and "familial" *awqāf* in Central Asia by pointing to a "mixed" type of endowment. It is not clear why one should view endowments in the light of this presumption, because, as Subtelny herself puts it, "the term never occurs in the Hanafite legal handbooks pertaining to medieval Iran and Central Asia," ibid.: 151 fn. 16.

32 Cf. the following model from the late Timurid period: *wathīqa-yi waqf bar nafs-i khwud wa ba'd bar awlād-i khwud*, in Ikhtiyār al-Dīn b. Ghiyāth al-Dīn al-Ḥusaynī, *Mukhtār al-Ikhtiyār 'alā al-Madhhab al-Mukhtār*. MS Bodleian, Frazer 239: fol. 55b–56a. On this formulary manual, see Chapter 1 fn. 154. For similar model documents regarding the stipulation of a *waqf-i awlād* in the early sixteenth century, see 'Alī b. Muḥammad 'Alī b. 'Alī b. Maḥmūd al-Mukhtārī al-Khwārazmī al-Kubrawī, *al-Jawāmi' al-'alīya fī al-wathā'iq al-shar'īya wa al-sijillāt al-mar'īya*, MS Tashkent, TsVRUz, no. 9138: fol. 68b–69b. On this manuscript and its author, see Subtelny, *Timurids in Transition*: 222. See also 'Alā al-Dīn Muḥammad b. Ḥāfiẓ Darwīsh Muḥammad, *Jāmi' al-wathāyiq*, MS St. Petersburg, IVRAN, MS A-933: fol. 79b–80a. The manuscript contains model documents from the first half of the sixteenth century; it has been concisely described in *Opisanie tadzhikskikh i persidskikh rukopisei Instituta narodov Azii*, ed. N.D. Miklukho-Maklai, issue 1 (Moscow: Izdatelst'stvo Vostochnoi Literatury, 1964): 139, no. 911. Endowment deeds and chancellery rescripts also include these stipulations: in June–July 1657 a certain Mullā Sayyid Muḥammad endowed his descendants with his properties in the district of Tashkent, TsGARUz, f. I-17, op. 1, d. 32663.

33 Cf. *Asnād-i muftīyān-i Bukhārā bar asās-i asnād-i kitābkhāna-yi shakhṣī-yi Sayyid Ṣādir Ḥusaynī Ishkiwarī*, ed. Muḥammad 'Alī Bāqir-zāda (Qum: Mujma'-i dhakhā'ir-i islāmī, 1391/1971–2): 87–8 (the seal bears the date 1244/1828–29).

34 *Mubārak-nāmajāt-i Amīr Muẓaffar ba-Qāḍī Muḥyī al-Dīn*, MS Tashkent, TsVRUz, no. 407: fols. 56a (*rasma-yi awlād*) and 182a (*rasma-yi sahm-i awlādī*). For a description of the manuscript, see *SVR* I: 163, no. 386.

The term *waqf-i awlādī* can also refer to an endowment whose founder stipulates that its administrator should be chosen from among his descendants,[35] and that the administrator has the right to a management fee (*ḥaqq al-tawlīya*)—usually equivalent to a tithe (*ʿushr*) levied from the revenues—an entitlement that passes from one generation of agnates to the next until the line dies out.[36] The major difference between these two types of *awqāf-i awlādī* is that, while the first may be considered a familial endowment, the second presupposes that, in addition to providing certain descendants of the founder with an administrator's salary, the revenues will be devoted to supporting the upkeep of Islamic institutions and paying the wages of their personnel.[37] The second type of *awlādī* endowment thus had a public use that the first did not. An example is the ʿAskar Bī ʿInāq *waqf*. This endowment was established to support a madrasa and a mosque in the Qambar Bī Atālīq quarter of Bukhara in the early nineteenth century. While the deed stipulates that the position of administrator was to go to the founder's male descendants (*mutawallī-yi īn waqf az awlād-i dhukūr-i wāqif*), it also emphasizes the *waqf*'s public utility (*wa waqf kardand ḥujarāt-i madrasa rā az barāy-i ṭalaba-yi ʿilm wa masjid-i madhkūr az barāy-i ʿāmma-yi muslimīn*).[38]

Of this second type, we find examples in which the founder's agnates are excluded from the administration: a founder may dedicate his wealth to, say, a mosque and stipulate that the administrator be someone with whom he had no kinship ties whatever, for example, the imam of the mosque. The trusteeship would then be transmitted to the descendants of the *mutawallī*, and the founder's family would have no access to the revenues generated by the endowment.[39]

---

35 Welsford and Tashev, *A Catalogue of Arabic-Script Documents from the Samarqand Museum*: doc. 5.

36 Text: *wa awlād ham wa ghayr ham hīch nawʿ-i taṣarruf dar ān mawqūfāt ajr nabāshad ghayr-i wilāyat-i tawlīyat*; cf. *Samarkandskie dokumenty XV–XVI vv. (O vladeniiakh Khodzhi Akhrara v Srednei Azii i Afganistane)*, ed. O.D. Chekhovich (Moscow: Nauka, 1974): 260, doc. 11. See also Welsford and Tashev, *A Catalogue of Arabic-Script Documents from the Samarqand Museum*: doc. 82, 171, 183, 185, 187.

37 The two different meanings of *waqf-i awlādī* have been conflated into a single type of charitable endowment; cf. R.G. Mukminova, *K istorii agrarnykh otnoshenii v Uzbekistane XVI v. (po materialam "Vakfname")* (Tashkent: Nauka, 1966): 233; McChesney, "Waḳf." *EI2* vol. V: 92; Subtelny, *Timurids in Transition*: 150–1.

38 The endowment deed is preserved as TsGARUz, f. I-323, op. 1, d. 26, l. 1. If there is anything corresponding to the "mixed" type of *waqf* discussed by Subtelny, it should be this and similar cases.

39 Welsford and Tashev, *A Catalogue of Arabic-Script Documents from the Samarqand Museum*: doc. 185, 344.

Other endowments produced wealth and created entitlements whose devolution did not follow the rules of descent: Central Asian juristic sources refer to such endowments as *waqf-i ʿāmm*.[40] These were endowments for which the administrators were usually appointed by a local ruler or a member of the local Islamic judiciary (e.g., the *qāḍī*). Upon the death of the *mutawallī*, the post of administrator would be assigned to someone else, by whoever had the prerogative to confer such powers.

Other *ʿulamāʾ* (legal scholars) distinguished between *waqf-i makhṣūs*—that is, endowments established for the benefit of a specific institution, such as a madrasa, mosque, or shrine, and *waqf-i ʿāmm*, that is, endowments consisting of properties designated for public use (*ʿāmma manfaʿatī ūchūn*), such as "fountains, bridges, stations, toilets, etc.".[41]

A *waqf-i awlādī* clearly might trigger competition among the agnatic descendants of the founder. A stipulation in an endowment deed notarized at the request of the famed Naqshbandi shaykh Khwāja Aḥrār (1404–90) reads: "If a conflict occurs between the descendants and other [individuals] regarding the administration of these endowed [properties], they should refer to the law" (*agar nizāʿī dar miyān-i awlād wa ghayr ham dar amr-i īn mawqūfāt wāqiʿ shawad rujūʿ ba-sharʿ namāyand*).[42] This situation was especially clear between cognates and agnates. The fact that legal opinions addressed issues

40 Anon., *Jung*, MS Tashkent, TsVRUz, no. 6102: fol. 215. The manuscript is cursorily described in S. Gulomov, "O nekotorykh podlinnykh dokumentakh iz kollektsii rukopisnykh proizvedenii fonda IVANRUz." In *History and Culture of Central Asia*, ed. B. Babadjanov and K. Yayoi (Tokyo: TIAS: Department of Islamic Area Studies Centre for Evolving Humanities Graduate School of Humanities and Sociology, 2012): 141–2.

41 Report on endowments (*waqflār bayānīda*) to Governor-General M.G. Cherniaev, Commission for the Establishment of a Spiritual Administration in Turkestan, 20.03.1884, TsGARUz, f. I-1, op. 11, d. 326, l. 33. This latter use of the term *ʿāmma* should be distinguished from that recorded by Soviet ethnographers in Tajikistan. There the expression *waqfi omma* referred to those cases in which landowners gave a share of their revenues to an endowment. This practice was, according to Soviet ethnographers, different from the case of the *waqf-i muṭlaq*. In the latter case, proprietors dedicated all the revenues to the benefit of an endowment. See N.A. Kisliakov, *Patriarkhal'no-feodal'nye otnosheniia sredi osedlogo naseleniia Bukharskogo émirata v kontse XIX-nachale XX vv.* (Moscow: Nauka, 1962): 99; K. Shaniiazov, "Ob osnovnykh vidakh zemel'noi sobstvennosti i razmerakh kharadzha v Bukharskom khanstve v kontse XIX-nachale XX veka (po étnograficheskim dannym)." *ONU* (1962–3): 54.

42 *Samarkandskie dokumenty XV–XVI vv.*: 261. Ol'ga D. Chekhovich dates the compilation of this endowment prior to 1533 and argues that the endowment deed in question is a copy; ibid.: 45–6.

such as the right of female descendants to claim entitlements to the revenues of a *waqf-i awlādī* signals that this was indeed a disputed matter. While a nineteenth-century fatwa from Bukhara holds that it is lawful for women to access such revenues,[43] in a collection of edited legal opinions probably compiled in Bukhara in the sixteenth century we find that local jurists considered it unlawful for female descendants to claim that right (*awlād-i ināth-i wāqif rā ki dar tawlīyat-i īn waqf dakhl kunand bilā sabab-i sharʿī*).[44] It was probably to avoid turbulence among his agnates that the founder of a *waqf* would stipulate that the position of administrator be held only by his living offspring[45] or that his female descendants would be appointed to this post only after the male line was extinguished.[46] As I hope to show, however, a *waqf* whose devolution did not follow the rules of descent might result in even more aggressive behavior among the heirs of the founder, leading the latter to attempt to annul the endowment.

It is difficult to reconstruct clear instances of such aggressive behavior during the precolonial period because of the shortage of extant source material, but if one brings together evidence found in notary manuals (*shurūṭ* works), as well as collections of fatwas, one finds that the heirs of the founder often posed a serious threat to the integrity of a *waqf*. For example, an Islamic notary manual of the early sixteenth century includes a section that was compiled largely to guide the *sharīʿa* court in defending the integrity of endowments in cases of attempted usurpation. It indicates, for example, how the administrator might take legal action against individuals who claim the right to dispose (*ṣāḥib wa mutaṣarrif*) of properties belonging to a particular *waqf*. The manual stipulates that the administrator might do so only if he possesses the endowment

43 TsGARUz, f. R-2678, op. 1, d. 12, unnumbered folio. See also the following judicial reports regarding female descendants (*awlād-i ināth*) of the founder of an endowment in the province of Bukhara who claimed the right to be appointed *mutawallī*, TsGARUz, f. 1-126, op. 1, d. 667, ll. 8–9.

44 Qāḍī ʿAzīzān, *Sīzdah ganj*, MS Tashkent, TsVRUz, no. 2574/IV: fol. 416b. For a description, see *SVR* VIII: 322.

45 "The endower originally stipulated that, having deducted 10% of the rental income for his own salary, the *mutawallī* of the day should divide the remaining revenue into four, giving ¼ to the founder's descendants through the line of Muḥammad Sharīf; ½ to his descendants through the line of ʿAbdallāh Khwājah; and ¼ to his descendants through the lines of Shāh Bīgīm and Māh Bīgum. The endowment has thus become valid and legal": Welsford and Tashev, *A Catalogue of Arabic-Script Documents from the Samarqand Museum*: doc. 70.

46 Mukminova, *K istorii agrarnykh otnoshenii v Uzbekistane*: 297; see also the endowment deed of Sayyid Amīn Bāy's *waqf*, TsGARUz, f. 1-323, op. 1, d. 34, l. 1.

deed,[47] in the absence of which the founder's heirs might be able to prove their rights of ownership on the strength of witness testimony (*guwāh*). This was not an exercise in casuistry; rather, while compiling this work, the jurist apparently took stock of widespread practices that are evident in sources written in later periods. In 1862–3, for example, Bukharan authorities ruled that a certain Āyim Jān might not dispose of a courtyard that her deceased husband had dedicated to a local mosque; a deed established clear obligations concerning the endowment (*ḥawlī-yi madhkūr dar gudhar waqf būda az rū-yi waqfīya jārī shawad*).[48]

Other sources reflect more explicitly the vexations suffered by an administrator in countering claims to the endowed property made by the founder's heirs. We learn from a legal opinion issued in Tashkent in the mid-1860s that the administrator of an endowment dedicated to a mosque had decided to sell the endowed property. He may have reasoned that the *waqf* was under severe threat from the founder's relatives, who sought to acquire its properties; in this case, the jurists characterized the administrator as someone who "feared the heir" (*khawfan min al-wārith*) of the founder.[49]

The picture of endowments threatened by individuals is complemented by legal documents compiled in such a way as to thwart the claims of the founder's heirs.[50] In 1916 a certain Aḥmad Jān endowed his wealth in Bukhara (then formally a Russian protectorate) to support the recitation of the Qur'ān at a shrine associated with ʿAbd al-Qādir al-Jīlānī, the eponymous founder of the Qādirīya Sufi order; the endowment deed, which was notarized only after the death of the founder, stipulated that the administrator be an elder (*āqsaqāl*) who represented the local neighborhood. On the occasion of the notarization of the endowment deed, the founder's heirs (*waratha-yi wāqif*), who were three women, separately acknowledged in court that the endowment had been notarized according to the conditions stipulated in the deed (*ba-sharāyiṭī ki min ḥujjat al-waqf*). The notary (or the scribe who acted on his behalf) took special care to state that the three women were not being coerced but were making their statement of their own free will (*az ghayr-i ikrāh wa*

47 ʿAlī al-Khwārazmī al-Kubrawī, *al-Jawāmiʿ al-ʿalīya fī al-wathāʾiq al-sharʿīya*: fol. 177a: *badān-ki ṣūrat-i daʿwā-yi waqf ba-mażmūn-i chak-i waqf ki ba-dast dāshta bāshad. Chak-i waqf* here means "endowment deed." On *chak*, see Semenov, *Ocherk pozemel'nogo-podatnogo i nalogovogo ustroistva b. Bukharskogo khanstva*: 48 fn. 86.

48 Rescript of a Muslim judge to the Bukharan chancellery (*dīwan-khāna*): TsGARUz, f. 1-126, op. 1, d. 940, l. 5.

49 Anon., *Jung*, MS Tashkent, TsVRUz, no. 6102: fol. 225b. The legal opinion was endorsed by ʿAbd al-Rasūl Muftī walad-i Mīr ʿAshūr. The seal he attached is dated 1282/1865–66.

50 Welsford and Tashev, *A Catalogue of Arabic-Script Documents from the Samarqand Museum*: doc. 352.

ijbār); the women also appear to have asked for their acknowledgment to be included in the endowment deed (*taswīd farmūdand taswīd namūda dāda shud*). One wonders, however, about the real reason for inserting this additional information in the deed, given that no one other than the administrator had any immediate interest in it. The administrator probably regarded the formulation as an instrument to deter future claims.

Appreciating cases of perceived dispossession, either ostensible or actual, among the heirs of endowment founders becomes easier in the colonial era, when many Muslims attempted to annul specific endowments by exploiting the Russian administration and selectively deploying imperial law.

2 Russian Colonial Approaches to Central Asian *Awqāf*

2.1 *The Institutional Setting*

The cases I examine in the remainder of this chapter are mainly from Tashkent, the administrative heart of the Governorship-General of Turkestan. The available archival documentation reflects a single colonial society that provides venues in which "Muslims" and "Russians" could mingle.[51] A dense web of commercial relations between the two communities existed nearly everywhere in Central Asia. The integration of Muslims into the colony was achieved by creating an administrative setting capable of narrowing the distance between the colonized and the colonizers.[52] We have observed in the preceding chapters that one successful strategy adopted by the Russians in Central Asia was the establishment of a complex, pluralistic legal regime. Beginning in 1867, statutory laws created discrete jurisdictions for exercising the state's authority in various communities—imperial law (as it was modified and codified after the Great Reforms of the 1860s and thus involved the justices of the peace) for Russians and a system of native courts for the indigenous inhabitants. Students of imperial history will no doubt find similar institutional arrangements in other colonial situations.[53] By retaining the native courts until the final days of the empire, the Russians arguably ended up subverting precisely the form of

---

51 I draw here on Paul, "Recent Monographs on the Social History of Central Asia." *CAS* 29/1 (2010): 121–22.

52 J. Sahadeo, *Russian Colonial Society in Tashkent, 1863–1923* (Bloomington: Indiana University Press: 2007).

53 P. Sartori and I. Shahar, "Legal Pluralism in Muslim-Majority Colonies: Mapping the Terrain." *JESHO* 55/4– (2012): 637–63.

governance that promoted the introduction of the rule of law.[54] They seem to have reinforced difference. The Russians may not, however, have failed entirely to extend the imperial rule of law among the Muslim communities of Central Asia. The pluralistic legal regime did not consist of entirely separate jurisdictions; there were areas in which jurisdictions overlapped substantially. Most notably, in keeping with the objective of promoting imperial values of justice, statutory laws allowed Muslims to bring civil cases to Russian courts, if both parties agreed. In addition, locals could express their grievances by filing a complaint before a district or provincial chancellery. Such institutional arrangements allowed Russian authorities to have a say on every issue raised by local subjects. From this point of view, Russians acted as if they had replaced the Muslim rulers and could thus dispense justice on matters of Islamic law.[55] In hearing legal cases involving Muslims, however, Russian authorities referred to imperial codes, thereby contributing to the creation of a hybrid colonial law[56] and introducing norms that set new standards of behavior.[57] Though the cases I discuss here refer exclusively to *waqf* law, they clearly exemplify the extent to which Russian colonial bureaucrats (mostly military officials) participated in disputes involving a wide range of Islamic law issues. As I hope to show, locals often asked to have their *waqf*-related cases heard according to Russian law, thereby supporting the Russian colonial project.

2.2 *Fiscal Measures and Their Consequences*

Since the beginning of their rule in Central Asia, the Russians were aware that much cultivated land in the region belonged formally to Muslim charitable endowments. They also knew that *awqāf* owned other assets, such as shops and caravansaries. However, in developing a policy to extract revenues from endowments and producing a knowledge that would allow their legibility, Russians attempted to situate *waqf*s within the larger design of colonial land-surveying.

Russians thus claim to have preserved endowments "on the basis of the existing [legal and fiscal] principle[s]."[58] In purported continuity with earlier fiscal

---

54 J.L. Comaroff, "Colonialism, Culture, and the Law: A Foreword." *LSI* 26 (2011): 306–7.

55 Crews, *For Prophet and Tsar*: chap. 5.

56 See Chapter 2.

57 Sartori, "Constructing Colonial Legality in Russian Central Asia: On Guardianship."

58 *vakufnye zemli priznaiutsia russkim pravitel'stvom i sokhraniaiutsia v sile na sushchestvuiushchem osnovanii, Otchet po revizii Turkestanskogo kraia po Vysochaishemu poveleniiu Senatorom Gofmeisterom Grafom K.K. Palenom. Narodnye Sudy Turkestanskogo Kraia* (St. Petersburg: Senatskaia Tipografiia, 1909): 6: 309.

practices under the local Muslim principalities, the 1867 Provisional Statute introduced two taxes on agricultural produce: the *kharadzh* and the *tanap* (Russ. for *kharāj* and *ṭanāb*,[59] respectively). The first was equated arbitrarily to the tithe, and the second was an annual tax in cash set by the governor-general.[60] In an effort to simplify the taxation system, the 1886 statute made endowment revenues subject to a land tax (*pozemel'nyi nalog*) calculated at 10% of the average yield from a single plot of land. In fact, the system became more complicated, because the amount to be paid by each fiscal unit depended on the apportionment (*raskladka*).[61]

We now come to the 1886 statute, which introduced the following laws on the *waqf* and remained in force until the collapse of the empire, in 1917:

> § 265. Populated land belonging to a *waqf* sanctioned by the government will be held in possession [*vladenie*] by the rural community inhabiting the land, on the basis of the principles defined in articles 255–61 and 264 of this statute. Unpopulated land belonging to a private *waqf* sanctioned by the government is at the disposal of the individuals for whose benefit the *waqf* was established and for these individuals' descendants, as long as they shall continue to have heirs.
>
> § 266. The establishment of a new *waqf* is permitted only with the consent of the governor-general.
>
> §267. Provincial chancelleries retain the right to confirm *waqf* deeds, organize the administration of endowments, and control the correct use of their revenues and subject them to audits.
>
> § 286. The following are not subject to government taxation [...] b) unpopulated *waqf* land, if all profits from the land are used to fund mosques, schools, or charity homes.
>
> § 289. Unpopulated *waqf* land—of whose profits part is used to fund mosques, schools, or charity homes and part reverts to private individuals—is subject to state property-taxes on the average gross value of the profits given to the private individuals.

59 See page 73 fn. 107.

60 *Proekt polozheniia ob upravlenii semirechenskoi i syr-dar'ynskoi oblastei.* In *Materialy po istorii politicheskogo stroia Kazakhstana k Rossii do Velikoi Oktiabr'skoi sotsialisticheskoi revoliutsii.* Vol. 1, ed. M.G. Masevich (Alma-Ata: Izdatel'stvo Akademii Nauk Kazakhskoi SSR, 1976): arts. 279–85; B. Penati, "Notes on the Birth of Russian Turkestan's Fiscal System: A View from the Fergana Oblast'." *JESHO* 53/5 (2010): 744.

61 B. Penati, "The Cotton Boom and the Land Tax in Russian Turkestan (1880s–1915)" *Kritika* 14/4 (2013): 747.

> § 299. Land tax collected from populated land belonging to a *waqf* that supports mosques, schools, or charity homes will be conveyed by the treasury to the institutions for which the *waqf* was established, to the total amount of the actual revenues, if the *waqf* deeds stipulate that all money from *kharadzh* and *tanap* taxes [are to be conveyed] to such institutions. Otherwise, it is at the discretion of said institutions whether to convey to such institutions the amount of tax that corresponds to the share of *kharadzh* and *tanap* defined by the *waqf* deed. The remainder shall be conveyed to the treasury.

In an article in the *Yearbook of the Ferghana Province* on the impact of land-tax assessment (*pozemel'no-podatnye raboty*) and charitable endowments, the Orientalist Nalivkin provided a historical sketch of the institution of the *waqf* in the region. He noted that Russian statutory laws offered only fiscal instruments to regulate and intervene in the sphere of Muslim charitable endowments. Taken together, these laws provided guidelines for the application of taxation on revenues produced by *waqfs* but did not define their legal status.[62] Such provisions did, however, change the relationship between the state and the charitable endowments. As we shall see, the new legislation restricted the ability of *waqfs* to exploit land assets for their own benefit while conferring more powers, if indirectly, on the rural communities to use *waqf* land as they saw fit.

Let us review a few of the major implications of Russian statutory laws by considering the fiscal status of *waqfs* and analyzing the first part of Art. 265: "Populated land belonging to a *waqf* sanctioned by the government will be held in possession [*vladenie*] by the rural community inhabiting the land, on the basis of the principles defined in articles 255–61 and 264 of this statute." The statutory laws also ensured that the rural communities that cultivated land constituting the assets of charitable endowments would enjoy a permanent and hereditary right to the possession and use of that land.[63] In terms of fiscal practice, the outcome was predictable: instead of paying the tax on the harvest or rent to the administrator of the endowment, communities or individuals that worked rural landholdings of this kind paid a property tax

62 V.P. Nalivkin, "Polozhenie vakufnogo dela v Turkestanskom krae." *Ezhegodnik Ferganskoi oblasti* (1904): 32.

63 *Zemli pozhertvovaniia v dache Imam-Ata, kak fakticheskom vladenii naseleniia, priznat' vakufom naselennym, kak na osnovanii st. 265 Polozh. Ob Uprav. Turk Kraia podlezhat utverzhdeniiu za naseleniem*, 20.10.1903, TsGARUz, f. I-19, op. 1, d. 3498, l. 7.

(*pozemel'nii nalog*) calculated at "10% of their average earnings from a single piece of land."[64]

We now come to the second part of Article 265: "Unpopulated land that is part of a private *waqf* recognized by the government will be retained by the individuals for whose benefit the *waqf* was established and for these individuals' descendants, as long as they shall continue to have heirs." This section is crucially important for understanding the fate of *awqāf* in Russian Central Asia, for it introduced into colonial legislation the idea of "private *waqf*" (*chastnyi vakuf*), a concept ostensibly derived from local legal parlance. In fact, as we have seen in the preceding section, the vast majority of the endowments in the region were funded not for the benefit of a family. Instead, they were established for charitable purposes, to fund an Islamic institution, but on the condition that the position of administrator would be held by a descendant (*awlād*) of the founder or of the saint in whose name the foundation was created. In addition, the founder could stipulate that his descendants would be entitled to receive a share of the earnings of the *waqf*. Such conditions were included for two principal reasons, to protect the endowment from the fragmentation that might occur through inheritance or marriage and to prevent (at least in theory) the endowment from being confiscated by the sovereign.[65] It follows that, by the term "private *waqf*," the colonial authorities did not mean the endowments funded exclusively to benefit their founders' descendants but rather those in which only part of the earnings were to be given to them. It is the share pocketed by the founder's descendants that the Russians intended to tax.

In most cases, a *mutawallī*'s share amounted to the 10% (*'ushr*) of the overall yield produced by the endowment's assets. Only on rare occasions were administrators entitled to receive more. For example, the administrator of the foundation that maintained the Khwāja Aḥrār madrasa in Tashkent—who was, in this case, required to be a descendant of the founder—earned a salary that amounted to one-third of all the *waqf*'s revenues, exactly the same as the sum of money that went to pay the salaries of the madrasa's entire teaching staff.[66] At any rate, Russian officials who designed the statutory laws on *waqf* must have believed that a significant part of the revenues produced—especially the

64 *Proekt polozheniia ob upravlenii semirechenskoi i syr-dar'ynskoi oblastei*: art. 287.

65 D.S. Powers, "Orientalism, Colonialism, and Legal History: The Attack on Muslim Family Endowments in Algeria." *CSSH* 31/3 (1989): 536.

66 Petition of a certain Tūra Khān Tūra Jān-ūghlī, a descendant of Khwāja Aḥrār. The addressee is unclear, n.d., TsGARUz, f. 1-164, op. 1, d. 39, l. 1.

money paid as rent for the cultivation of land that belonged to the *waqf*—was going to a single administrator. Many of the *waqfs* in Central Asia were, in fact, conglomerates of several endowments funded to benefit different institutions. The Khwāja Ahrār and Shaykhantaur *waqfs* in Tashkent, for example, included one *waqf* for a madrasa, one for a mosque, another for a shrine, and so forth. In this way, the management of a group of endowments could require the existence of more than one administrator, one for each institution being funded. The Russians must therefore have regarded the share of *waqf* revenues that was being paid to administrators as a potentially significant contribution to the treasury.

In order to implement this fiscal policy, it was necessary that endowments be registered following examination of the existing deeds and any documentation relevant to fiscal exemption. Whoever held *waqf*-related documents was asked to entrust them to the provincial chancelleries by 1 July 1887.

In inspecting the available endowment deeds, the colonial officials attempted to ascertain if an endowment had been exempted from taxation by verifying whether any royal warrant (*yārlīq/ʿināyat-nāma*) had been issued for that purpose. Contemporary Russian observers held that endowments were distinguished, in the local parlance, according to their fiscal exemptions: "black endowments" (Uzbek *qora vaqf*, Russ. *kara vakuf*) were subject to taxation, while "white endowments" (Uzbek *oq vaqf*, Russ. *ak vakuf*) were not.[67] While there is little doubt that, before the Russian conquest, the assets of certain endowments were temporarily exempted from taxation,[68] there is, to date, no clear attestation of these expressions in pre-1865 Central Asian bureaucratic language.[69] One does find the phrase *āq yir waqfī* (lit., endowment consisting of white land) in post-1865 deeds referring to charitable endowments that were tax-exempt,[70] but it is unclear whether this formulation is a translation of a new category of fiscal exemption introduced by the colonizers or attests, instead, to local practices predating the Russian conquest.[71]

67 Nalivkin, "Polozhenie vakufnogo dela v Turkestanskom krae": 10–11; [Pahlen], *Otchet po revizii Turkestanskogo kraia*: 306.

68 See the materials in A. Juvonmardiev, *XVI–XIX asrlarda Farghona er-suv masalalariga doir* (Tashkent: Fab, 1965): passim.

69 In referring to the categories of "white" and "black" *awqāf*, Nabiev suggests that this terminology is reflected in Central Asian sources, but he fails to produce evidence in support of his assertion; see R.N. Nabiev, *Iz istorii Kokandskogo khanstva* (*Feodal'noe khoziaistvo Khudoiar-Khana*) (Tashkent: Fan, 1973): 102.

70 Ruling of the native judicial assembly of the city of Osh (Ferghana Province), 22.09.1899, TsGARUz, f. I-1, op. 12, d. 430, l. 11.

71 I owe this observation to Uktambek Sultonov, who suggested that *āq yir waqfī* appears to be a translation of the Russian expression *vakuf obelennykh zemlei*.

2.3 *Tinkering with* Waqf *Deeds*

Reviewing *waqf* deeds was a complex business. Colonial legislation is unclear about the status of rural estates that belonged, according to local informants, to endowments but whose documentation was not submitted for review to the provincial chancelleries. According to the head of the Turkestan Treasury Chamber, Nikolai Mordvinov,[72] this problem first manifested itself in 1888, during the land-tax assessment in the Tashkent district: according to statements made by the local inhabitants, four plots of land that were registered as a fiscal unit belonging to the people of Khan Abad and Khalybek Kurgan were *waqf* lands. Because *waqf* deeds relating to these plots had not been submitted for review to determine the fiscal status of the land, the local population decided that they should not be counted as part of their unit. In reviewing the case, the council of the Governorship-General ruled that any rural estates that could not, according to the law (*po zakonu*), be considered as belonging to endowments and that the population relinquishes to the treasury, should be counted as lands without a proprietor and therefore appropriated by the state. Major General Aleksandr Iafimovich, the military governor of Samarqand Province,[73] disagreed with this decision. He presented the case to the minister of war and requested clarification of matters regarding unregistered endowments in light of the legislation (*raziasneniia v zakonodatel'nom poriadke*). When he asked the ministry to rule on the status of the assets of those endowments that had not been registered (*kakoe naznachenie dolzhny poluchit' te vakufnye imushchestva, za kotorymi vakufnoe pravo ne budet priznano?*), he suggested that Russian authorities also register as "endowments" those rural estates for the attestation of which deeds had not been submitted for review in time. Iafimovich based his opinion on two principles. First, Article 255 of the statutory laws stated that "the rural sedentary population retains a permanent and hereditary right to those lands that they possess, use, and dispose of, on the basis of the rules defined by local custom." Second, he noted that articles 286 and 289 suggest that the purpose of the review of endowment deeds at the provincial chancellery was to preserve the privileges of the endowments with regard to the payment of the land tax, not to confiscate (*sekvestrovat'*)

72 The discussion of the status of rural estates belonging to endowments and their confiscation by the treasury is based on a report (*doklad*) submitted by Mordvinov to the military governor of Ferghana Province on 10 March 1893. See TsGARUz, f. I-19, op. 1, d. 33346, ll. 2–7. On this individual, see Penati, "The Cotton Boom and the Land Tax in Russian Turkestan (1880s–1915)": 751.

73 A. Morrison, *Russian Rule in Samarkand, 1868–1910: A Comparison with British India* (Oxford: Oxford University Press, 2008): 296.

waqf land. A few officials[74] were apparently taking action against the council of the governorship-general, which attempted to use the review of the deeds to annul endowments and seize rural estates for the benefit of the treasury. Mordvinov noted:

> There is little doubt that, according to our local legislation [*s tochki zreniia nashego mestnogo zakonodatel'stva*], not every endowment can enjoy fiscal privileges; only those whose deeds were submitted for review [may be exempted from taxation]. However, the objectives of our intervention [*meshchatel'stvo*] in the domain of endowments are regulated by articles 6, 13, and 15 concerning the introduction of the land-tax organization, on the basis of which the provincial chancellery should only accept or reject 'the so-called *waqf* right' [*tak nazyvaemoe vakufnoe pravo*], which consists of a fiscal privilege with regard to the payment of the state land-tax.[75]

Most of the Russian officials were unclear as to what sorts of rights the endowments enjoyed. In 1904 an animated discussion developed among the members of a special commission established to review the *waqf* question in Russian Central Asia when they attempted to clarify what exactly a *waqf* was. Disagreement centered on two opposing interpretations of the expression "*waqf* rights" (*vakufnoe pravo*). Some interpreted it as the sum of those rights to a certain thing designated for the benefit of an endowment, which can be defined according to Islamic law. Others considered it the right to fiscal exemptions (*podatnye l'goty*) as stipulated in statutory law. The commission preferred the latter view, on the grounds of a ruling of the State Council that, "in order to solve the question of land-tax organization in Turkestan, one needs, above all, to avoid all the theoretical considerations based on the interpretation of Islamic law and on the mentality of the followers of Islam." Others opposed this view. A certain Ipatov, for example, disagreed with the State Council on the principle of excluding *sharīʿa* from the legal resources available in ruling the country. He noted that the statutory laws state that the region should be administered "on the basis of the existing [legal and fiscal] principle[s]" and "according to custom." He also observed that nowhere did the State Council forbid examination of the legal status of the subjects in the light of Islamic law and that it merely indicated that referring to *sharīʿa* is not nec-

74 Report, the military governor of Ferghana Province to the governor-general of Turkestan, 21.09.1893, TsGARUz, f. I-19, op. 1, d. 33346, ll. 10–11; "Minority Report" (*Osoboe Mnenie*) of S. Ipatov, assistant to the head of the Turkestan Treasury Chamber, 05.06.1904, TsGARUz, f. I-1, op. 25, d. 107, ll. 8–11ob.

75 TsGARUz, f. I-19, op. 1, d. 33346, l. 4ob.

essary in reviewing deeds submitted to the provincial chancelleries. In other words, Ipatov noted that, in principle, Russian officials could, if they wanted, use Islamic juristic literature in attempting to clarify the legal and fiscal status of an endowment: "The State Council stated that [...] it is only the term *sharīʿa* that should not find its way into the text of the Russian law. [...] In reviewing endowment deeds, it is impossible to avoid the law of *waqf* and one should consider nothing but *sharīʿa*," concluded Ipatov.[76]

Despite this and similar calls to regulate the procedure for reviewing endowment deeds and to improve the Russian legislation on endowments, the colonial bureaucracy could easily undermine the existence of *waqf*s. This happened, for example, in the case of an endowment established for the benefit of the Sar Bibi shrine in Tashkent, which received one-tenth of the earnings of a nearby caravansary. Because its documentation was submitted three weeks after the deadline, the provincial chancellery refused to confirm its existence.[77]

Statutory laws conferring probative value on *waqf-nāma*s and deeds of fiscal exemption (arts. 286, 289, and 299) were invariably invoked to undermine the integrity of the endowment. When Russian officials performed land-tax assessments in the region and found that an endowment was "dubious" (*somnitel'nym*), they registered *waqf* lands as belonging to rural communities. Instead of paying rent to the *mutawallī*s, these communities were required to pay the state land-tax.[78] Likewise, when unpopulated *waqf* lands were included in the apportionment of rural communities following land assessments and thus counted within a fiscal unit (*dacha*), rural communities requested, interestingly, that such land be counted as treasury assets and thus that *awqāf* be divested of their properties.[79]

Aleksandr Ivanovich Gippius, the last military governor of Ferghana Province, astutely pointed out that Russians failed to understand that the tenants' rent was itself evidence that the land they tilled belonged to a *waqf*. If people cultivated a plot of land on a lease contract, they did not, of course, own the land. Despite the alleged preservation of the status quo, Russian statutory

76 TsGARUz, f. I-1, op. 25, d. 107, l. 90b.

77 Syr-Darya provincial chancellery to the Tashkent city commandant, 16.06.1888, TsGARUz, f. I-36, op. 1, d. 2976, ll. 30–31.

78 S.I. Il'iasov, *Zemel'nye otnoshenii v Kirgizii v kontse XIX-nachale XX vv.* (Frunze: Izdatel'stvo Akademii Nauk Kirgizskoi SSR, 1963): 108. Il'iasov here refers to the land assessment in the district of Osh (Ferghana Valley) carried out in 1903.

79 Military governor of the Ferghana province to the governor-general, 10.08.1900, TsGARUz, f. I-1, op. 12, d. 44, l. 1-ob. This case refers to a large area of cultivated land in the Margilan district, which was close to a Russian artillery base. The military governor observed that it would be desirable for the treasury to requisition this land for the artillery's use in training.

laws led to a complete overhaul of the relationship between endowments and the communities farming their land (*my srazu zhe prekratili vsiakiia neposredstvennyia* [sic] *sviazi vakufnykh uchrezhdenii s arendatorami ili voobshe s naseleniem*).[80] Following the same reasoning, Count Pahlen noted that the Russians' approach to the registration of endowments and to fiscal exemption was overly cautious. He alerted agencies in St. Petersburg that the definition of agrarian relations depended not only on the examination of endowment deeds but also on the assessment of the legal attributes (*priznaki*) of such relations, something that most Russian officials involved in the land-tax assessments clearly avoided doing.[81]

The state land-tax soon became an instrument that made it possible for tenants to avoid paying rent to the administrators. On 29 February 1896, for instance, a certain ʿAbd-Karīm Jān appealed to the Tashkent city commandant against the administrator of the ʿIsā Khwāja Qāzī Kalān endowment. He complained that the administrator had demanded that he pay a harvest tithe because the land that he tilled belonged to the *waqf*.[82] When the appeal reached the chancellery of Syr-Darya Province, the authorities there stated that the tenants of the ʿIsā Khwāja Qāzī Kalān endowment had been exempted from payment of rent because they paid the imperial state as well as the city land-tax.[83] The Russian authorities ruled, therefore, that the ʿIsā Khwāja Qāzī Kalān land was not part of a *waqf*, because the tenant had to pay only the government and not the *mutawallī*. The state had apparently accounted the land as privately owned; for the tenants, this represented an attractive change in land rights (and perhaps also some kind of fiscal benefit).

The confirmation of new endowments after 1886 proved equally difficult. Though Article 266 required that a new *waqf* receive the authorization of the governor-general, an administrator would, in many cases, first have the endowment notarized before a native judge and only later seek authorization from the colonial authorities. In reviewing such requests, Russian officials sometimes discovered that a particular endowment failed to meet the criteria for registration.[84]

80 *Zapiska A.I. Gippiusa o vakufakh* (Tashkent, 1906), MS Tashkent, NBUz, no. 10564: fol. 6.

81 [Pahlen], *Otchet po revizii Turkestanskogo kraia*: 306, 328–9.

82 Syr-Darya provincial administration to the Tashkent city commandant, 29.02.1896, TsGARUz, f. I-36, op. 1, d. 3587, ll. 81–81ob.

83 *vse arendatory vakufa Kazy Kalian, kak platiashchie gorodskie i gosudarstvennye* [*nalogy*], *osvobozhdeny ot uplaty deneg za arendovanii imi vakufnykh uchatskov*, Syr-Darya provincial administration, 29.07.1896, TsGARUz, f. I-36, op. 1, d. 3587, l. 40b.

84 Consider e.g. the request for confirmation of the endowment of the Zar Gildak-Ata shrine, Syr-Darya provincial administration to the Tashkent city commandant, 06.04.1888, TsGARUz, f. I-36, op. 1, d. 2976, ll. 17–17ob; 19. The enforcement of Article 266 encoun-

Contemporary observers noted that the statutory laws sanctioned, in principle, the existence of charitable endowments by subjecting them to a favorable fiscal policy.[85] This might hold true only for the initial measures that were intended to reduce taxation, but the 1886 provisions changed agrarian relations among the individuals who operated within the orbit of charitable endowments. Colonial statutory laws both restricted the ability of administrators to exploit land assets for their own benefit and allowed the state and tenants to usurp those assets. In addition, the Russian administration in effect turned Muslim evidentiary requirements against Muslim legal practice. The reliance of imperial authorities on endowment deeds as evidence represented a clear break with local practices, because agrarian relations were not always solemnized in written contracts. Agrarian relations were the product of a consensus among members of a large community; it was common sense that documents could be lost or destroyed. If, before colonization, one needed to determine whether a given area belonged to a *waqf*, he would ask the people endowed with privileged knowledge. In the absence of the required documentation, the word of individuals of recognized authority carried the same probative weight as the documents of a *sharīʿa* court.[86]

3 Muslim Voices and Russian Ears

I will now analyze several attempts to annul individual endowments in Tashkent under Russian rule. These cases reflect a common pattern among

tered considerable resistance from the locals. The most striking example is a Tashkent *qāḍī* of the Beshagach district who, in spite of the new regulation, continued to notarize certificates attesting to the establishment of endowments. By the end of 1887, there were so many of these certificates that the city commandant was obliged to speak personally to the judge and ask him to provide a reasonable explanation for having issued these documents. See city commandant to the *qāḍī*, 19.05.1888, ibid.: l. 55.

85 Nalivkin, "Polozhenie vakufnogo dela v Turkestanskom krae": 32.

86 Notification to the royal court, stamped by five *qāḍīs* from Gürlen (Khorezm): TsGARUz, f. I-125, op. 1, d. 498, l. 75. The royal court had instructed the judges in Gürlen to hold an inquiry about a plot of land that was at the center of a dispute between private individuals and the endowment. In the absence of documentation other than the endowment deed, the testimony of elders (*akhbār wa shahādat*) was crucial for ascertaining whether the plot in question belonged to the *waqf*. See also Welsford and Tashev, *A Catalogue of Arabic-Script Documents from the Samarqand Museum*: doc. 183. On testimony (*shahādat*) as a legal instrument for confirming the existing stipulations of an endowment, see P. Reichmuth, "'Lost in the Revolution': Bukharan *Waqf* and Testimony Documents from the Early Soviet Period." *DWI* 50/3–4 (2010): 362–96.

founders' heirs: when they realised that the family wealth would be dedicated to a charitable endowment, they took steps to annul the endowment, by ignoring the institution for whose benefit these endowments had been established.

The first case centers on a dubious endowment deed that was notarized after the founder's death in 1879.[87] According to this document, the four widows—and sole heirs—of a certain Ḥājjī ʿAlī Īrānī ("the Iranian"), acknowledged that their deceased husband had dedicated all his wealth to the shrine of Shaykhantaur in Tashkent; at the same time, the document says, the four widows waived all their rights and claims to a share of the inheritance (*mīrāth*). The rule that one can endow only one-third of one's property in a *waqf* did not come into play here. Sometime later, the endowment's administrator paid a visit to the women and explained that, according to this deed, they were now required to pay rent to the shrine, because they were living in two houses that now belonged to the endowment. An illiterate fellow-member of the Iranian community in Tashkent acted in the capacity of attorney for the women and appealed to the Russian authorities; the latter scrutinized the case and ruled that the court document was void and that the properties should therefore be treated as inheritable wealth. Of interest here is the legal behavior of the women. It seems unlikely that a wife would agree willingly that the entire wealth amassed by her husband be dedicated to a charitable institution, thus depriving her of any support. This case suggests that someone must have got these four women into the courtroom by exploiting their husband's piety, while they were totally unaware of what was going to be written in the record of that court session. Their reaction was not only legally justified but also signals that they believed that the endowment exploited their personal resources.

The second example, which dates from the 1890s, was an unsuccessful attempt to annul a *waqf* on the grounds of judicial malpractice. Because I have already described the case in detail in Chapter 2, I limit myself here to a brief recapitulation. The claim relates to a mortally ill man who designated his grandson as his legal proxy. The grandson then dedicated six shops for the benefit of two mosques located in a neighborhood of Tashkent called Maḥsīdūzī. Like the charitable endowment in the previous case, this was a *waqf-i ʿāmm* because no one among the founder's agnates was entitled to a share of the revenues that were dedicated to the mosques. The administrator was to be appointed by a local *qāḍī* who was authorized to choose anyone he considered qualified for the post.[88] The nephew of the founder took repeated legal action against the endowment on the grounds that he was a close blood relative of

87 TsGARUz, f. 1-36, op. 1, d. 2049, unnumbered folio [l. 22].

88 The deed of this charitable endowment can be found in TsGARUz, f. 1-17, op. 1, d. 32607, l. 3.

the founder and thus, he argued, "heir to the [assets] of the endowment."[89] Unable to sway the Russian colonial authorities, the appellant sought the involvement of his cousin, the daughter of the founder, who appealed to the Russians, claiming that, when the endowment deed was recorded, her father was not in full possession of his mental faculties.[90] By making this claim, the daughter was attempting to prove that, when the endowment deed was formulated, the founder was not legally competent and that the judge who drafted the document had concocted a scheme to divert the properties for fraudulent purposes. In support of her claim, she secured a fatwa that called for the application of the compulsory laws of inheritance (*farāʾiḍ*) under the theory of deathbed illness (*maraḍ al-mawt*):[91] the assets of the founder, the mufti ruled, should be divided among his heirs because soundness of mind is a precondition for disposing legally of one's assets.[92] This argument failed to convince the Russians to annul the endowment. Some years later, the founder's nephew managed to secure for himself the post of administrator with the assistance of a sympathetic judge who appointed him to the office; the charitable endowment prospered until the day when the imams of the two mosques sued him for embezzlement and asked that he be removed from his post. He attempted to persuade the colonial authorities that he, more than anyone else, deserved this appointment and that he had been given this post because he was "the closest heir to the endowment's assets" (*kak samyi blizkii priamoi naslednik oznachennogo imushchestva*).[93]

Another contested *waqf* was established by a certain Yūsuf ʿAlī Khwāja Inʿām Khwāja-ūghli. The endowment consisted of two shops that were dedicated to the upkeep of a mosque. The *waqf* was established in 1875 and, for the first nine years, the founder served as administrator. Upon his death, his son, Khidīr ʿAlī Khwāja, and his father (i.e., Khidīr ʿAlī Khwāja's grandfather) went to a *sharīʿa* court to confirm the validity of the endowment, to declare that the original endowment deed had been lost, and to apply for a new one with the help of the residents of the neighborhood (*maḥalla*). Khidīr ʿAlī Khwāja and his grandfather also stipulated that the position of administrator should be held by a non–family member appointed by the *qāḍī*, although they would retain some control over the properties. They included the stipulation that, together with the neighborhood community, Khidīr ʿAlī Khwāja and his grandfather would

89 Appeal, 03.05.1890, TsGARUz, f. I-17, op. 1, d. 4887, l. 48.

90 Appeal, 07.06.1891, ibid.: l. 31.

91 Undated legal opinion (fatwa): ibid.: l. 38; four muftis attached their seals thereto.

92 *chūn-ki dar taṣarrufāt-i sharʿīya wa ṣiḥḥat-i nufūdh-i ān ʿaql-i mutaṣarrif sharṭ bāshad*, TsGARUz, f. I-17, op. 1, d. 4887, l. 38.

93 Appeal to the governor-general (*proshenie*): 10.02.1907, TsGARUz, f. I-36, op. 1, d. 4364, l. 30b.

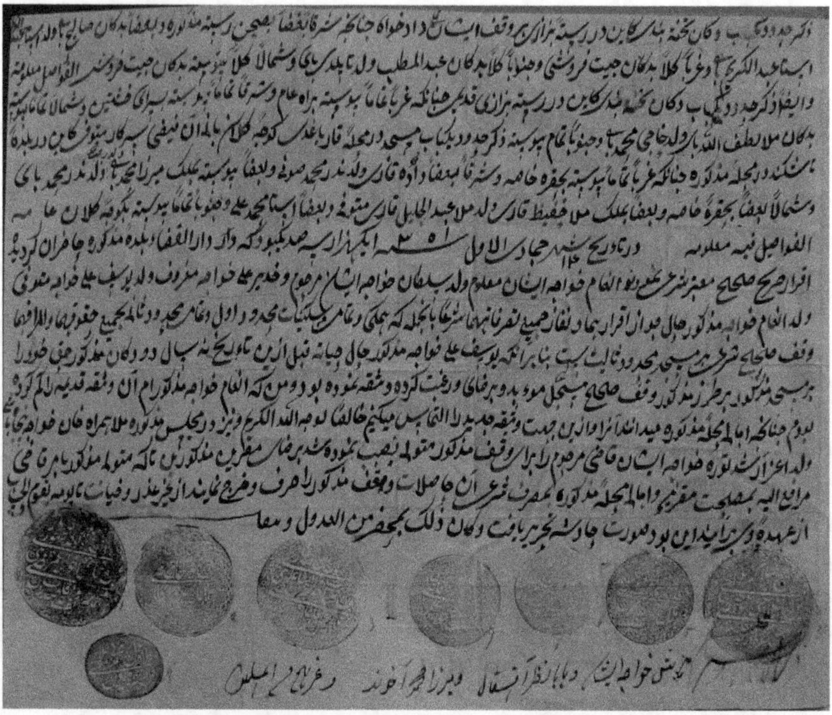

FIGURE 14 *Deed confirming the validity of an endowment, Tashkent 12.03.1884. TsGARUz, f. I-17, op. 1, d. 32597, l. unnumbered* [2].
COURTESY OF THE CENTRAL STATE ARCHIVE OF UZBEKISTAN

advise the administrator about how best to administer the *waqf*.[94] They thus secured the notarization of a record that would prove useful if requested to produce evidence in support of the validity of the endowment [Fig. 14].

From the fact that the *sharīʿa* court was prepared to rely on what residents of the neighborhood had to say in order to draft a new endowment deed, it is apparent that the people living there were well acquainted with the circumstances in which the endowment had been established. Indeed, an elder (*āqsaqāl*) witnessed the notarization of the document.[95] The validity of the

---

94 *ba-maṣlaḥat-i muqarrīn wa ahālī-yi maḥalla-yi madhkūra ba-maṣraf-i sharʿī ān ḥāṣilāt-i waqf-i madhkūr rā ṣarf wa kharj namāyand*, TsGARUz, f. I-17, op. 1, d. 32597, l. unnumbered [2].

95 Participation of "elders" was common in the notarization of legal documents in post-Mongol Islamic Central Asia, *Dokumenty k istorii agrarnykh otnoshenii v Bukharskom khanstve*, vol. 1, *Akty feodal'noi sobstvennosti na zemliu XVII–XIX vv.*, ed. O.D. Chekhovich (Tashkent: Fan, 1954), 204.

endowment was secured by the participation of an impressive number of Muslim jurists (six *qāḍīs* and two muftis) who notarized the record.[96] This must have been an unusual practice for an endowment with modest assets, and one wonders why it was necessary to mobilize so many officials to confer legal force on this deed. The Russian authorities knew about this endowment: three years after its creation, the record was passed on to the provincial chancellery and scrutinized by the military governor himself. The Russians knew that this was not an original endowment deed and disapproved of the absence of many stipulations that such a contract should have included.[97]

We lose sight of the *waqf* for nearly thirty years, until 15 February 1914, when Khidīr ʿAlī Khwāja was accused of having seized the two shops belonging to the endowment and appeared before a *qāḍī*. The native judge ruled in favor of the plaintiff, the administrator, relying on two main pieces of probative evidence. The plaintiff brought to court the record mentioned above, in which Khidīr ʿAlī Khwāja and his grandfather confirmed the validity of the endowment. The *qāḍī* authenticated this record after identifying the abovementioned seals, which he treated as legal evidence (*ḥujjat-i sharʿī*) of the soundness of the endowment. The second piece of probative evidence was the account book in which previous administrators of the endowment had duly noted the revenues generated by the rental contracts (*ijāra*); the two shops were apparently leased out to tenants. Among those who signed the register in his capacity as administrator was the self-same defendant—Khidīr ʿAlī Khwāja—who had been collecting the rent payments for the two shops. Strangely, when the *qāḍī* questioned the defendant and asked him to explain why he had seized the two shops and prevented the administrator from disposing of their usufruct, Khidīr ʿAlī Khwāja responded that ownership of these shops had never been conveyed to a religious endowment and that they had been left to him as an inheritance by his father (*atāmdīn mirāthgha qālghāndūr waqf īmas dīb*).[98]

The story of this *waqf* overlaps with another one: exactly three weeks after Khidīr ʿAlī Khwāja was summoned to the *sharīʿa* court, a Russian justice-of-the-peace court (*mirovoi sud*) declared him insolvent in the matter of a debt of two thousand rubles and ordered that his possessions be sold at public auction. At this point, Khidīr ʿAlī Khwāja granted his wife power of attorney, and

96 The eight seals were apparently attached when the document was notarized.

97 TsGARUz, f. 1-17, op. 1, d. 31916, l. 59: on 10 June 1888 the military governor noted that the document he had received from the administrator did not prove that the assets were *waqf* properties.

98 Report to the Tashkent city commandant, 26.04.1914, TsGARUz, 1-36, op. 1, d. 6864, l. 19. Here, the *qāḍī* of the Shaykhantaur district informs the city commandant about a hearing that took place on 16 February 1914.

she and the bailiff went to the bazaar to determine the location of the two shops, their status, and their market value. The woman obviously had no evidence to prove that her husband owned the shops, but the bailiff listed them among his possessions (*na pravakh sobstvennosti*) and confirmed that Khidīr ʿAlī Khwāja had inherited the two shops from his father and that they were his private property.[99]

Khidīr ʿAlī Khwāja struck back. As soon as he received the inventory lists from the bailiff, he challenged the ruling of the native court by appealing to the Russian authorities:

> [The] two shops [...] are my property. I inherited them from my father, and they are worth at least three to four thousand rubles. These shops were my father's property. I have owned these buildings since he died more than thirty years ago, without interruption and without dispute. In such conditions—at least, so it would appear—I should be able to consider myself safe from claims by third parties against the shops, and I should have no need to fear that what belongs to me can ever be taken from me. And yet the very opposite has happened. The [...] [*qāḍī*]—only God knows for what reasons and on what legal basis—considers these shops to be [property belonging to] a *waqf*.[100]

This narrative may strike the reader as a tale of personal misfortune intended to arouse pity, but, as we shall see, what happened next is more serious. Khidīr ʿAlī Khwāja attached to this appeal a copy of the inventory showing that the shops were his property. At the same time, he argued that cases involving "Mohammedan spiritual institutions" (*magometanskie dukhovnye uchrezhdeniia*) fall under the jurisdiction of Russian courts according to Article 1282 of the Regulation of Civil Proceedings (*ustav grazhdanskogo sudoproizvodstva*) and a deliberation that the governing senate (*pravitel'stvuiushchii senat*) issued in 1904. In support of his argument, he referred also to previous cases in which the court of the Tashkent military district had ruled on the annulment of endowments in 1912 and 1913.[101] Khidīr ʿAlī Khwāja was manipulating the legal resources of the colony just as a Russian lawyer would have done.

The city commandant, who apparently knew nothing about the colonial laws regarding endowments, requested that the *qāḍī* clarify the matter in a report. The *qāḍī* reported on his previous decision but added two important points: first, he explained that he viewed as a mere legal stratagem (*ḥīla*) Khidīr

99 The inventory lists can be found at ibid.: ll. 15–18ob.

100 Appeal to the Tashkent city commandant, 17.03.1913, ibid.: ll. 13–14ob.

101 Ibid.

ʿAlī Khwāja's appointment of his wife as proxy and persuading the Russian bailiff to record the shops as his property. Second, the *qāḍī* probably sensed that the involvement of Khidīr ʿAlī Khwāja in the *waqf*'s management and, especially, that his current financial interests needed to be fully disclosed to the Russians. The Muslim judge reported that he had questioned the residents of the neighborhood and that they had stated that Khidīr ʿAlī Khwāja had served as administrator of the *waqf* for nineteen years, after which the position was taken over by the imam of the mosque and, finally, by a person appointed directly by the neighborhood.[102] Apparently, the *qāḍī* was explaining to the Russian authorities what they did not want to see: as long as Khidīr ʿAlī Khwāja had been involved in the affairs of the endowment, he never tried to seize the property; now, having been excluded from the administration of the *waqf* and in dire straits because of an unpaid debt, he sought to annul the endowment, according to Russian law, on the basis of far-fetched claims.

The chancellery that oversaw the case could not reconcile itself to the idea that a Russian courtroom should try a *waqf* case. Thus, the colonial officials returned the file to the same native court with the following instructions: "the case is yours!" (*delo Vam podsudnoe*).[103] In sum, the file was reviewed three times, twice by the same judge[104] and finally by a council of *qāḍīs*. All found that Khidīr ʿAlī Khwāja should be prevented from seizing the shops.

But Khidīr ʿAlī Khwāja was determined.[105] He appealed again, vehemently, arguing that, according to the imperial civil code and the statutory laws, the *sharīʿa* court had no jurisdiction over *waqf*-related cases.[106] This time Khidīr ʿAlī Khwāja succeeded, and the file was sent to the Russian military district court (*okruzhnoi sud*),[107] which held in favor of the defendant and struck down the Islamic court's ruling.[108] The endowment was thus divested of its property and annulled by a founder's heir.

Khidīr ʿAlī Khwāja's recognition of the available legal resources clearly originated from a social milieu in which colonial subjects shared their knowledge of the mechanics of imperial law. His emphasis on problems of jurisdiction

102 Report to the Tashkent city commandant, 26.04.1914, ibid.: l. 19.

103 Instruction to the native court, 26.06.1914, ibid.: l. 20.

104 Report to the Tashkent city commandant, 02.08.1914, ibid.: l. 26. The *qāḍī* informs the Russian authorities of a hearing that took place on 17 June 1914.

105 Appeal to the Tashkent city commandant, 24.07.1914, ibid.: l. 37.

106 Appeal to the Tashkent city commandant, 08.10.1914, ibid.: ll. 29–29ob.

107 Appeal to the prosecutor of the Tashkent military district court, ibid.: l. 45.

108 Ruling of Tashkent military district court, 31.12.1914, copy, TsGARUz, f. 1-36, op. 1, d. 6487, l. 12.

is of interest. Khidīr ʿAlī Khwāja argued that his opponent was an administrator who acted on behalf of an endowment consisting of shops belonging to a mosque. As such, these shops represented "the property of a Mohammedan spiritual institution" (*imushchestvo magometanskogo dukhovnogo uchrezhdeniia*) that fell under the administration of the imperial treasury. Moreover, the appellant held that a *waqf* is a legal institution, while native courts had authority only over juridical persons: "Article 211 of the local statutory law [...] refers to disputes between natives as individual physical persons [*mezhdu tuzemtsami, kak otdelnymi fizicheskami litsami*] but not to disputes between institutions, even if the latter are to be considered native."[109] There is little doubt that Khidīr ʿAlī Khwāja (or the person who helped him to prepare his appeals) was familiar with these subtle points of law and that they had been invoked in previous cases in which the Russian military district court had ruled against the integrity of endowments.

Precedents mattered. The mother of all such controversies, which had occurred a few years earlier, involved a certain Ivan Alekseev and the *waqf* administrator of the ʿĪsā Khwāja Qāḍī Kalān madrasa. The case was ordinary enough to bolster the administrator's legal action: Alekseev held a plot of land belonging to the endowment under a contract of tenancy but had failed to pay the rent for three years. In 1908 the administrator sued him before a justice of the peace, who ruled that Alekseev should be evicted from the plot. Alekseev then resorted to a Russian lawyer named Reiser, who appealed the ruling on the ground that the *waqf* was a "Mohammedan spiritual institution." The lawyer explained that, according to Article 1282 of the Regulation of Civil Proceedings, cases involving such institutions could not be examined by justices of the peace, suggesting that the ruling on the eviction of Alekseev had to be quashed. In December 1913 the Russian military district court considered this argument favorably and dismissed the case.[110]

In the eyes of the colonial subjects, this decision must have opened up new possibilities for freeing up property belonging to endowments. Khidīr ʿAlī Khwāja and others regarded this precedent as a particularly powerful resource for removing endowment cases from the jurisdiction of *qāḍīs*. In June 1913, for example, the administrator overseeing the *waqf* of the Qiyāt mosque appealed to the military governor, protesting that a certain Nūr Muḥammad Ḥājjī Karīm Birdī Bāy-ūghlī had usurped a piece of land belonging to the endowment and begun there the construction of a few shops and other buildings. He did so without permission and failed to pay the rent for several years. The admin-

109 TsGARUz, f. I-36, op. 1, d. 6864, l. 29.

110 18.02.1913, TsGARUz, f. I-36, op. 1, d. 6487, l. 84–84ob.

istrator asked that the Russian authorities order the suspension of construction until Nūr Muḥammad honored his tenancy contract. The administrator also asked the notarization of a new contract stipulating that Nūr Muḥammad pay rent to the endowment also for the buildings he had constructed.[111] Nūr Muḥammad was summoned to court, where a *qāḍī* ruled in favor of the administrator.[112] Like Khidīr ʿAlī Khwāja, Nūr Muḥammad tried to overturn the judgment, claiming that he had inherited the land on which the shops had been built from his deceased brother, who had donated the land to the *waqf*. He also explained that he had deeds attesting to his renovation of the already existing shops in compliance with the regulations of the Tashkent municipality. Nūr Muḥammad emphasized that he could produce evidence of his rights to the shops according to both Islamic and imperial law (*sharīʿat būyincha wa ham niẓāmgha muwāfiq dalīl wa ḥujjatlār*) and asked that a council of judges review the previous judgment.[113] Three weeks after this appeal was filed, Nūr Muḥammad took action again. This time, someone wrote in Russian on his behalf. Among the reasons he adduced in his own favor, Nūr Muḥammad explained, as had Khidīr ʿAlī Khwāja, that native courts have jurisdiction only over individuals, while the administrator who had taken legal action against him in this case represented a "Mohammedan spiritual institution." He also referred to the stipulation of the imperial civil code that such institutions should be administered by the treasury and that cases involving them fell under the authority of the military district court. Finally, Nūr Muḥammad referred to the case of the ʿĪsā Khwāja Qāḍī Kalān *waqf* as a precedent for the application of these rules.[114] The assembly of *qāḍī*s reviewed the previous decision of the native court and upheld it,[115] but this confirmation proved to avail the administrator little. The Tashkent city commandant transferred the case to the military district court, which ruled in his favor, thus divesting the endowment of its land.[116]

Interestingly, Nūr Muḥammad's second appeal landed on the desk of the Tashkent commandant with an explanatory note (*spravka*) added in its margin by a local translator, a certain Shakirdzhan Ishaev, who worked in the city

---

111 Appeal to the military governor of Syr-Darya Province, 03.06.1913, ibid.: l. 76.

112 The ruling was issued on 13.09.1913. See the *qāḍī*'s report to the Tashkent city commandant, 22.09.1913, ibid.: l. 79.

113 20.09.1913, ibid.: l. 85. Someone else signed the appeal, as Nūr Muḥammad Ḥājjī Karīm Birdī Bāy-ūghlī was illiterate (*khaṭṭ bīlmagān ūchūn*).

114 10.10.1913, ibid.: ll. 80–80ob.

115 Assembly's report to the Tashkent city commandant, 10.03.1914, ibid.: l. 93.

116 29.05.1914, ibid.: ll. 66–66ob.

chancellery and who, significantly, also wrote the appeal of Nūr Muḥammad (who was illiterate). Ishaev was probably exceptional among his colleagues. His service record (*posluzhnoi spisok*) indicates that he was born in Tashkent in 1859 and that he began working with the Russians at the age of 25. He had no official madrasa training and he had attended no Russian school (*vospitanie poluchil domashchnee*). He had, however, received a silver medal for diligence and a bronze medal for his contribution during the imperial census (*vseobshchaia perepis' naseleniia*) in 1897.[117] When Ishaev crafted the appeal of Nūr Muḥammad, he was 54 years old, with 29 years' experience as translator.

In writing the explanatory note, Ishaev reminded his superior that there were no Mohammedan spiritual institutions in the Governorship-General of Turkestan (*v Turk. Krae magometanskikh dukhovnikh uchrezhdenii net*), therefore Article 1282 of the Regulation of Civil Proceedings did not apply to disputes among local subjects on matters of *waqf* law. Ishaev also opined that the ruling on the ʿĪsā Khwāja Qāḍī Kalān *waqf* addressed a specific issue of a failure to pay rent, while Nūr Muḥammad was being sued for the usurpation of *waqf* assets. The translator suggested that these were two completely different cases. The ruling of the Russian military district court on the case of the ʿĪsā Khwāja Qāḍī Kalān *waqf* could therefore not be regarded as a precedent for transferring the case from a native to a Russian court (*opredelenie okruzhnogo suda ne mozhet sluzhit' osnovaniem k iz'iatiiu ot narodnogo suda dela*).[118] If Ishaev objected in principle to the essence of Nūr Muḥammad's appeal, the question arises who, if not the appellant himself, was insisting that the appeal include such arguments. Nūr Muḥammad was not assisted by lawyers, although he might have been advised by others with similar experiences, but local appellants were no doubt exposed to bureaucratic practices and a culture of legal precedents that may well have affected their knowledge and legal consciousness.

The dispute over the ʿĪsā Khwāja Qāḍī Kalān *waqf* precipitated a cascade of lawsuits in which Muslims invoked imperial law in an effort to seize properties donated to endowments.[119] In the absence of similar precedents, however, divesting an endowment of its properties was not always easy. The Russians were clearly unsympathetic to requests to annul *waqfs*, which originated

117 TsGARUz, f. I-17, op. 1, d. 35430, ll. 1–30b.

118 TsGARUz, f. I-36, op. 1, d. 6487, l. 800b.

119 Another case involved the assets of the Arpa-Pāy *waqf* in Tashkent. By referring to the ruling that charitable endowments were to be considered "Mohammedan spiritual institutions," the Tashkent military court quashed a previous judgment issued by a native court, thus divesting the *waqf* in question of a bathhouse. See the ruling of the Tashkent military court no. 73 (copy): 17.10.1915, TsGARUz, f. I-36, op. 1, d. 6864, l. 103.

merely from the desire to seize their properties and were thus based on accusations driven by malice.[120]

We find similar attempts to annul endowments elsewhere in the Governorship-General of Turkestan. In 1904, for example, a certain Mikhail Ivanovich Raikov, acting on behalf of Mullā Mīr ʿUmar, requested that the authorities in Khujand not treat two particular plots of land as *waqf*. Twelve years earlier, Mullā Mīr ʿUmar's father, Khwāja Mīr Salīm, had built a madrasa in the same city and designated some land as an endowment for the benefit of this institution. He stipulated that the land revenues would support the madrasa and pay the salary of the administrator and the teacher and fund a bursary for the students. To make the endowment legal, Khwāja Mīr Salīm turned to a native court, but a *qāḍī* refused to notarize the *waqf-nāma* because, as we have seen, statutory laws required the permission of the Russian administration. At this point, Khwāja Mīr Salīm drafted himself one and acted as a *mutawallī* until he died in 1904. Just before his death, he appointed his son, Mīr ʿUthmān Khwāja, the younger brother of Mullā Mīr ʿUmar, as his successor as administrator. Unhappy with his father's decision, Mullā Mīr ʿUmar requested the annulment of the endowment and the recognition of the land as his property.[121]

Conclusion

When they took legal action against endowments, Central Asian Muslims must have known that the colonial administration had transferred the powers of judicial review to the prosecutors of the military district courts.[122] They also must have realized that prosecutors looked favorably on the invalidation of *qāḍīs*' rulings.[123] Moreover, the jurisdiction of Russian courts extended to conflicts over *waqf* properties, according to a resolution of the senate in 1904.

120 Military governor of Ferghana Province to the chancellery of the governor-general, 30.10.1904, TsGARUz, f. I-1, op. 12, d. 430, ll. 5–5ob.

121 Military governor of Samarqand Province to the chancellery of the governor-general, 13.05.1906, TsGARUz, f. I-1, op. 12, d. 900, ll. 2–3. His appeal was, however, rejected on account of a paradoxical loophole: the endowment did not exist de jure, as the Khojand *qāḍī* had not notarized the *waqf* deed and the Russian authorities had not confirmed the endowment. It was impossible to annul a nonexistent *waqf*.

122 [Pahlen], *Otchet po revizii Turkestanskogo kraia po Vysochaishemu poveleniiu*: 103–5.

123 *Russian Rule in Samarkand, 1868–1910: A Comparison with British India*: 269–70.

Colonial subjects such as Khidīr ʿAlī Khwāja (and the Russian lawyers who assisted them) were no doubt aware of such favorable circumstances.[124]

The reliance of Central Asians on legal notions deriving from Russian imperial civil code, statutory laws, and precedents, as demonstrated in the cases I have examined, may strike the reader as exceptional. In fact, these and other examples reflect a juridification of the Muslim communities of Central Asia after the Russian conquest, by which I mean an increase in legal services that is met by an increased demand for regulation.[125] By the beginning of the twentieth century, Muslims under tsarist rule had been acquainted with Russian bureaucracy for decades, with the result that they acquired an understanding of imperial legal terminology. This allowed locals to engage assertively in forum shopping.

In Russian Central Asia, Muslims regarded pragmatically access to legal services, whether from a *sharīʿa* court or an imperial law court. If we concede that justice in Central Asia, as in Europe, was a public performance that involved a "principle of publicity,"[126] then, in earlier times, one might argue, the heirs of a founder might have desired to challenge the validity of a *waqf*. They would not, however, pursue legal actions against an endowment unless they had the legal resources to ensure a successful outcome of the dispute and thus avoid "bad *fama*."[127]

Under Russian rule, things changed. First, with the enactment of statutory laws, the validity of endowments became more precarious. Registering endowments required following bureaucratic procedures that made it easier for Muslims to question the trustworthiness of an endowment deed or to usurp the assets of a *waqf*. The colonial bureaucracy must have contributed to the creation of an atmosphere in which the status of endowments became more uncertain. Second, the cases presented here show how new jurisdictional arrangements allowed colonial subjects to have recourse to legal venues in which Islamic law was not applied. The colonial institutional setting evidently favored "repeat players." When it amounted to repeating their claims, individuals such as Khidīr ʿAlī Khwāja had little to lose by attempting to annul a *waqf*.

---

124 Appeal to the prosecutor of the Tashkent military district court, 29.09.1915, TsGARUz, f. I-36, op. 1, d. 6864, ll. 116–116ob.

125 L. Ch. Blichner and A. Molander, "Mapping Juridification." *European Law Journal* 14/1 (2008): 36–54.

126 D.L. Smail, *The Consumption of Justice. Emotions, Publicity, and Legal Culture in Marseille, 1264–1423* (Ithaca: Cornell University Press, 2003).: 22.

127 On *fama*, see M. Vallerani, *Medieval Public Justice*, trans. Sarah Rubin Blanshei (Washington, DC: Catholic University of America Press, 2012): 108–12.

While legal institutions and behavior changed, however, pursuing the annulment of an endowment still hinged on notions of morality. Reporting to his superiors on the Tashkent bazaar and the traders operating in it, Nil Lykoshin,[128] the officer in charge of the "Asiatic" quarter of Tashkent, explained that:

> there are also small private endowments supporting this or that mosque, which do not have any documentation and rely, instead, only on a promise given in the presence of [a few] witnesses. In times of prosperity the founders of these small endowments become generous and promise [to pledge] their shops' revenues to the benefit of [the local] mosque. If, because of unforeseeable circumstances, their income decreases and becomes insufficient, then nothing but a sense of shame [*nichto, krome nekotorogo styda*] before their community can make these founders of endowments swallow their own words and become again the proprietors of their own assets.[129]

Along with the institutional innovations I have just mentioned, there was a change in the legal consciousness of Muslims. In earlier times Muslims had sought redress on the basis of their assumptions about what they thought was right or wrong. This was the case also under Russian rule, but with a significant difference. Appellants now lived in a situation of "juridification," in which the possibilities of meeting people who had access to privileged knowledge increased dramatically. Tashkent was full of translators, lawyers, and other such figures acting as cultural brokers or go-betweens. It is thanks to such cultural brokers that we possess the appeals of individuals such as Khidīr 'Alī Khwāja, but this does not exclude the possibility that, as is sometimes the case when we seek the advice of our own tax advisors, people such as Khidīr 'Alī Khwāja might learn something new and thus change their ideas on their own entitlements.[130]

---

128 On this person, see A. Morrison, "Sufism, Pan-Islamism and Information Panic: Nil Sergeevich Lykoshin and the Aftermath of the Andijan Uprising." *PP* 214 (2012): 262–64.

129 Report to the military governor of Syr-Darya Province, 05.11.1894, TsGARUz, f. I-36, op. 1, d. 3708, l. 40ob.

130 I draw here freely from S. Subrahmanyam, "Between a Rock and a Hard Place: Some Afterthoughts." In *The Brokered World: Go-Betweens and Global Intelligence, 1770–1829*, ed. Simon Schaffer et al. (Sagamore Beach, MA: Science History Publications, 2009): 432.

CHAPTER 5

Fatwas for Muslims, Opinions for Russians

Introduction

Affiliation with the Hanafi school of law (*madhhab*) is key to Muslim identity in present-day Central Asia.[1] Such an affiliation is seen today as part of a deep historical process that connects current developments to the early-medieval history of Transoxiana.[2] This is not just a post-Soviet phenomenon. The Hanafi legal doctrine has long been endowed with greater authority in the region and has thus enjoyed a preeminence over other schools of law, and Central Asian jurists have, for centuries, situated themselves in a chain of clearly recognizable interpretive traditions: attestations of how local *ʿulamāʾ* perceived themselves as close followers of, say, Abū Ḥanīfa can be found in materials dating from throughout the Islamic history of the region.[3]

Although references to Hanafi hegemony are ubiquitous in the Central Asian legal literature, little has so far been done to describe Hanafi jurisprudence and its mechanics during the rules of the Uzbek khanates of Bukhara, Khiva, and Khoqand. What characterized Central Asian Hanafism when the Russians conquered the region? What kind of changes did local jurists experience in their doctrinal sphere during the tsarist era? What does the output of jurists tell us about changes in people's understanding of law? These are the questions I seek to address in this chapter, in order, first, to help us situate Central Asia within a wider Hanafi ecumene and, second, to establish whether that form of Islamic jurisprudence as practiced in Central Asia can be distinguished from other regional legal practices that are usually referred to as

---

1 Shaykh Muhammad Sodiq Muhammad Yusuf, *Ikhtiloflar, sabablar, yechimlar* (Tashkent: Sharq, 2011): 12–13.

2 K. Kehl-Bodrogi, *"Religion Is Not So Strong Here": Muslim Religious Life in Khorezm after Socialism* (Berlin: Lit, 2008); I. Hilgers, *Why do Uzbeks Have to Be Muslims? Exploring Religiosity in the Ferghana Valley* (Berlin: Lit, 2008); J. Rasanayagam, *Islam in Post-Soviet Uzbekistan: The Morality of Experience* (Cambridge: Cambridge University Press, 2011).

3 W. Heffening-[J. Schacht], "Ḥanafiyya." *EI2* vol. III: 162–4; Y. Ro'i, *Islam in the Soviet Union: From the Second World War to Gorbachev* (New York: Columbia University Press, 2000): 56–7; A. Khalid, *Islam after Communism: Religion and Politics in Central Asia* (Berkeley: University of California Press, 2007): 28; A.J. Frank, *Bukhara and the Muslims of Russia: Sufism, Education, and the Paradox of Islamic Prestige* (Leiden: Brill, 2012): 2.

DOI 10.1163/9789004330900_007

"Hanafi." These are questions of fundamental importance not just for those interested in the comparative history of colonialism and the modern Islamicate world. In order to understand the long process of adaptation and change that occurred in the history of Islamic jurisprudence in Central Asia we need first to consider what exactly a fatwa was and how muftis functioned in the region before and after colonization. Only then can we begin to understand that, contrary to what Islamic juristic scholarship produced in Uzbekistan today would have us think,[4] the practice of issuing fatwas in present-day Central Asia is far removed from that in the period before colonialism, reflecting, as it does, modes of reasoning that came into existence only under Soviet rule.

In spite of representing a complex juristic genre, fatwas are key to detecting changes in Muslims' legal consciousness. Fatwas were not produced exclusively for elite consumption.[5] Fatwas were routinely acquired by the populace as devices that allowed them to take legal actions and pursue redress. They preserved fatwas as we today preserve a document to attest to our entitlements. By exploring the mechanics of colonial-era fatwa-issuance (*iftā'*), we begin to grasp just how deep was its impact, not only on juristic practices but also on people's legal consciousness more generally.

Two institutional arrangements allow us to examine jurists' output under Russian rule and identify continuities and changes in the way jurists operated. The colonizers did little, if anything, to affect the powers of the mufti; they simply ignored them. Colonial statutory laws that regulate the jurisdiction of Muslims' native courts do not even mention the office of mufti.[6] By avoiding any interference with that office, the colonizers effectively safeguarded the integrity of muftis' writing practices. There are important continuities between fatwas compiled in Russian Central Asia and those issued under the Muslim principalities before the conquest. Colonialism also marked

4 Shaykh Muhammad Sodiq Muhammad Yusuf, *Zikr ahlidan so'rang 1* (Tashkent: Sharq, 2011): 13–14.

5 I here disagree with Adeeb Khalid, *Making Uzbekistan: Nation, Empire, and Revolution in the Early USSR* (Ithaca and London: Cornell University Press, 2015): 11.

6 Neither the Provisional Statute of 1867 nor the Statute of 1886 defined the position of muftis in native courts, because native courts were thought of as operating in parallel with the imperial courts, thus ignoring the utility of Muslim jurists in Islamic legal practice. The reaction of the Muslim judiciary was prompt. In early March 1868 the Tashkent *qāḍīs* appealed to the colonial authorities with the request to allow muftis to be included in the staff of the native courts. The Russians agreed and delegated to the *qāḍīs* the choice of the legal experts that would work alongside them in court; cf. TsGARUz, f. 1–36, op. 1, d. 452, ll. 1–3, although all appointments of muftis had to be confirmed by the colonial authorities. See, e.g., the appointment of muftis in Tashkent in 1884, TsGARUz, f. 1–36, op. 1, d. 2396, ll. 1–5.

a new age of bureaucratization and accountability that increased the overall output of legists. That is, native judges were held accountable to the colonial bureaucracy for all the procedures used in the trials they held. In apparent contrast to the former practice of reporting to the royal courts, *qāḍīs* were now obliged to record judicial proceedings in special ledgers (*daftar/kaziiskaia kniga*) provided by the Russian administration. *Qāḍīs* thus produced a deluge of records that shed light on the review process of fatwas brought to court by disputing parties.

While there are clearly continuities in the crafting of legal opinions, interactions between the colonial administration, the Muslim population, and local jurists led to substantive innovations. Such innovations are manifest mostly in the opinions that muftis had to deliver on specific points of law at the request of colonial officials. This happened every time Muslim parties disputed the interpretive authority of the native legists and appealed to the Russians for judicial review. Colonial officials would consequently turn to indigenous legal experts to clarify exactly how *sharīʿa* ruled on a particular subject. In doing so, they often overlooked the fact that Islamic law could actually accommodate divergent views on a single point of law. It is in the answers to the queries of the Russian officials that we can detect the birth of a new legal genre. Muslim jurists in such contexts articulated their arguments in an idiom that was far more expressive than that in the fatwas drafted according to the established compositional traditions and that was much more accessible to the uninitiated. Accountability to the colonial administration, however, inevitably undermined their interpretive independence. In principle, muftis did issue divergent opinions on the same subject matter. This divergence of opinion was, however, of little use to the Russians, who sought to eliminate such interpretive discord between Muslim jurists, thus emphasizing certain legal notions over others. The Russians never managed, however, to establish a single Islamic orthodoxy, nor did they manage to codify *sharīʿa*.

When approaching the study of Islamic jurisprudence in nineteenth-century Central Asia and its place in the wider Hanafi ecumene, we should keep two precautions in mind. First, established practices of textual consumption usually inform the way we read texts. That is to say, a single text can be read differently in different places and in different times according to different interpretive traditions. We get a sense of these different traditions from the numerous differing commentaries to be found on the various juristic compilations to which muftis refer, such as *al-Hidāya*, the *Mukhtaṣar al-Wiqāya*, and the *al-Fatāwā al-ʿĀlamgīrīya*. These are texts that represent long-standing Hanafi legal traditions in regions as culturally diverse as the Middle East and Central and South Asia. Cultural differences (especially in the legal sphere) notwithstanding, students of colonialism have often observed certain policies that are common to particular imperial administrations. One common such policy consisted of promoting the translation of certain Hanafi texts, chosen almost arbitrarily to serve as standard manuals, in hopes of facilitating colonial officials' understanding as well as the simplification and rationalization of Islamic legal practice. A famous example was *al-Hidāya*,[7] which appeared first in English translation in British India and then in Russian in colonial Central Asia.[8] Notwithstanding *al-Hidāya*'s wide circulation in India and Central Asia, however, it is evident, from the wide variety of commentaries on the text, that Muslims in Central and South Asia read the work in very different ways. When thinking of Hanafism as a common body of juristic knowledge, we should therefore remember that, while there was a shared textual knowledge from Hyderabad to Semipalatinsk and from Herat to Kayseri, jurists might nevertheless draw very different inferences from these texts and might deliver very different opinions on specific questions. Even within one region, Muslim jurists did not always share the same opinion on these standard texts, nor did they always use it in the same way. We know, for instance, that scholars as distinguished as the Bukharan jurist ʿAbd al-Shakūr, the father of Ṣadr-i Ḍiyā', turned to *al-Hidāya* every time they wanted to examine candidates for the office of mufti,[9] and we find in the work of Aḥmad b. Ḥāfijiz al-Dīn al-Barāngawī (1877–1930), a Tatar mullah who studied in Bukhara between 1901 and 1905, an account in which *al-Hidāya* is cast in a demeaning light. Al-Barāngawī in the following passage ventriloquizes a Kazakh inhabiting the Bukharan Emirate:

> On his camel, Nārāṭ Bāy addressed me, "Hey Mullah, do you read the book up on the camel?" I said, "What book is that?" He interrupted and said, "You don't know it?" When I asked my companion, he said that it was *al-Hidāya*. He said, "There was a student like us who, when he traveled with the Kazakhs, read *al-Hidāya* on a camel. When a Kazakh asked what book that was, he answered, "The book you read on a camel!"[10]

---

7 A. Khalid, *The Politics of Muslim Cultural Reform: Jadidism in Central Asia* (Berkeley: University of California Press, 1998): 70; A. Morrison, *Russian Rule in Samarkand, 1868–1910: A Comparison with British India* (Oxford: Oxford University Press, 2008): 275–6.

8 The Russian rendering of *al-Hidāya* was based on Charles Hamilton's English translation published in 1791; see *Khidaia: Kommentarii musul'manskogo prava*, vols. 1–4 ed. and trans. from the English by N.I. Grodekov (Tashkent: 1893).

9 On the examination to ascertain whether a person was fit to be appointed to the position of mufti, see TsGARUz, I-126, op. 1, d. 11, l. 5.

10 This excerpt from the *Taʾrīkh-i Barangawī* (1914) appeared in translation in A. Frank, "A Month among the Qazaqs in the Emirate of Bukhara: Observations on Islamic

As Muslim scholars sharing the same educational background may have divergent opinions on the same text, it is important to account for such divergences and find out why their opinions differ, rather than basing our interpretations on a purported commonality of interpretive dispositions.

Second, Muslim governments are usually credited with having promoted the Hanafi doctrine as the dominant legal school in Transoxiana. Stephen Dale, for example, notes that "in the Timurid century both Samarqand and Herat [...] attracted internationally known Hanafi scholars."[11] A policy of promotion of Hanafism is discernible also in the governance of the Abū'l-Khayrids: Muḥammad Shībānī Khān (r. 1501–10), for instance, commissioned the compilation of the imposing *al-Fatāwā al-Shībānīya* by ʿAlī al-Khwārazmī.[12] We see a similar pattern a century later, under the Ashtarkhanids: Mīr Ḥabībullāh's magisterial collection of responsa titled *Wāqiʿāt-i dīn-i jalālī* is dedicated to Subḥān Qulī Muḥammad Bahādur Khān (r. 1680–1702).[13] The shape of such a policy becomes much clearer in a later period. In the nineteenth century, the source basis is overwhelming: diplomas tell us that the appointment to the position of the mufti was at the discretion of local rulers.[14] There is also a progressive "canonization" of legal texts, mainly of positive law (*furūʿ al-fiqh*), through translation into Persian or Chaghatay.[15] But what is it

---

Knowledge in a Nomadic Environment." In *Explorations in the Social History of Modern Central Asia (19th–Early 20th Century)*, ed. Paolo Sartori (Leiden: Brill, 2013): 255.

11 S. Dale, "The Later Timurids c. 1450–1526." In *The Cambridge History of Inner Asia: The Chinggisid Age*, ed. Nicola di Cosmo et al. (Cambridge: Cambridge University Press, 2009): 207.

12 See Chapter 1 fn. 168. See also R. McChesney, *Waqf in Central Asia: Four Hundred Years in the History of a Muslim Shrine, 1480–1889* (Princeton, NJ: Princeton University Press, 1991): 5.

13 MS Tashkent, no. 9019, described in *SVR* VIII: 329.

14 T. Welsford and N. Tashev, *A Catalogue of Arabic-Script Documents from the Samarqand Museum* (Samarkand and Istanbul: IICAS, 2012)

15 The *Mukhtaṣar al-wiqāya fī masāʾil al-Hidāya* (otherwise known as *al-Nuqāya*) by ʿUbaydallāh b. Masʿūd b. Tāj al-Sharīʿa al-Maḥbūbī al-Bukhārī was taught in madrasas and thus circulated widely in Transoxiana. It became so popular that Khorezmian rulers requested that its commentary (*sharḥ*) be translated into the vernacular. Under the rule of Abū al-Ghāzī Bahādurkhān (r. 1644–63) the commentary of a certain Dāmullā Muḥammad Ṣalāḥ (fl. sixteenth century) was rendered into Persian. Muḥammad Raḥīm Khān Firūz (r. 1864–1910) ordered the translation into Chaghatay of the commentary of ʿAbd al-ʿAlī b. Muḥammad al-Ḥusayn al-Birjandī (d. 1525). See A. Ėrkinov, N. Polvonov, and H. Aminov, *Muhammad Rahimkhon II Feruz Kutubkhonasi Fehristi* (*Khorazmda kitobat va kutubkhonachilik tarikhidan*) (Tashkent: Yangi Asr Avlodi, 2008): 208, and

that is specific to Central Asian legal history, given that we observe the same course of events throughout the larger Hanafi world? Under the Ottomans and the Mughals, the Hanafis enjoyed precedence over other legal scholars.[16] In the Middle East and in South Asia muftis could be appointed by the state,[17] and there too the imprimatur of the ruler conferred on texts an aura of authority.[18]

In light of these similarities, Guy Burak has argued that the evolution of the Hanafi school of law in the post-Mongol period across the Middle East and Central Asia was shaped by dynasties that regulated the school's structure and doctrine.[19] In making that argument, Burak assumes that muftis were constrained in their juristic interpretations by princely authority. This assumption may be true of the Ottoman Empire, where "the Hanafi doctrine [...] was molded into an unequivocal body of rulings ready to be applied by the qadis,"[20] but it is more difficult to substantiate in the legal history of Central Asia, where there is little reason to assume that the mechanics of Hanafi jurisprudence reflected the monopolistic vision of the ruling dynasty. Rulers did occasionally

---

A. Idrisov, A. Muminov, and M. Szuppe, *Manuscrits en écriture arabe du Musée regional de Nukus (République autonome du Karakalpakstan, Ouzbékistan). Fonds arabe, persan, turkī et karakalpak* (Rome: Istituto per l'Oriente C.A. Nallino, 2007): 108–9. We know of another *fiqh* work in translation in Khorezm. The manuscript library of the Institute of Archeology and Ethnograhy of the Qaraqalpaq branch of the Uzbek Academy of Sciences holds the *Risāla al-mashrūʿat wa ghayr mashrūʿat* (otherwise known as *Maṭalib al musallī* or *Fiqh al-Kaydanī*), a fourteenth-century treatise in Arabic with interlinear translation in Chaghatay (MS R-320). A Persian commentary is extant in another manuscript library in Nukus. See *Manuscrits en écriture arabe du Musée regional de Nukus*: 134.

16 W. Hallaq, *An Introduction to Islamic Law* (Cambridge: Cambridge University Press, 2009): 80.

17 J.R. Walsh, "Fatwä II. Ottoman Empire." In *EI2*.

18 On Mughal India, see M. Alam, "*Sharīʿa* and Governance in the Indo-Islamic Context." In *Beyond Turk and Hindu: Rethinking Religious Identities in Islamicate South Asia*, ed. D. Gilmartin and B.B. Lawrence (Gainesville: University Press of Florida, 2000): 216–45; M. Khalfoui, "Together but Separate: How Muslim Scholars Conceived of Religious Plurality in South Asia in the Seventeenth Century," *BSOAS* 74/1 (2011): 87–96.

19 G. Burak, "The Second Formation of Islamic Law: The Post-Mongol Context of the Ottoman Adoption of a School of Law." *CSSH* 55/3 (2013): 579–602.

20 R. Peters, "What Does It Mean to Be an Official Madhhab? Hanafism and the Ottoman Empire." In *The Islamic School of Law: Evolution, Devolution, and Progress*, ed. P. Bearman, R. Peters, and F.E. Vogel (Cambridge, MA: Harvard University Press, 2006): 147.

commission[21] and/or compile fatwa collections—for example, Shāh Murād (r. 1785–1800) and his *Fatāwā-yi ahl-i Bukhārā* and Emir Ḥaydar (r. 1800–26) and his *al-Fawā'id al-alfīya*.[22] But the overwhelming majority of fatwa collections were assembled by jurists working autonomously[23] or in consultation with colleagues.[24] In both cases, it was the jurists' initiative, not their rulers', that led to the production of these collections.

As further evidence of governmental intrusion into the affairs of the jurists, Burak notes that, beginning in the Timurid period, appointments to judicial offices reflected a hierarchy at the apex of which stood the *shaykh al-Islām*[25] who had "authority to inspect and examine the competence and knowledge of their appointed jurists."[26] There is an Ashtarkhanid-era diploma that indicates that, in Samarqand, the position of *shaykh al-Islām* involved the supervision of juristic affairs in the city,[27] but there is little evidence that in later periods

---

21 Emir Ḥaydar was apparently especially fond of the *Mabsūṭ* commissioned from copysts in Khorezm. See *Maktūbāt-i Amīr Ḥaydar ba Muḥammad Ḥakīm Bī*, MS Tashkent, TsVRUz, no. 2120: fol. 20a, 26b, 31b.

22 Amīr Ḥaydar b. Amīr Shāhmurād, *al-Fawā'id al-alfīya*, MS Tashkent, TsVRUz, no. 2434/IV. See *SVR* VI: 457.

23 *jamī'-i riwāyāt-i ma'mūla rā jam' karda-and wa ghayr-i ma'mūla rā ḏikr na-karda-and wa na-āwarda-and*, cf. Qāḍī 'Azīzān, *Sīzdah ganj*, MS Tashkent, TsVRUz, no. 2574/IV: fol. 357a. The anonymous work is dated to the first half of the sixteenth century, during 'Ubaydallāh Khān's rule (1533–39), *SVR* VIII: 322.

24 *ba'ḍī az khullān wa dustān az īn kamīna iltimās kardand ki jam' karda shawad dar 'ilm-i fiqh ba'ḍī az masāyil-i mutadāwila rā binābar multamas-i īshān jam' karda shud ba'ḍī az wāqi'āt-i zamān-i khwud rā mubtanī ba-riwāyāt-i mu'tamida az kutub-i mu'tabara wa tasmīya karda shud ānrā ba-fawāyid-i samarqandī tā mubtadiyān az ū fāyida gīrand*; see Muḥammad b. Bābā' al-Samarqandī, *al-Fatāwā al-samarqandīya*, MS Tashkent, TsVRUz 3132/I: fol. 4b. The work dates to 1023/1614, see *SVR* VIII: 320.

25 See Mīrzā Badī' Dīvān, *Majma' al-arqām ("Prepisanie fiska")* (*Priemy dokumentatsii v Bukhare XVIII v.*), ed. and trans. A.B. Vil'danova (Moscow: Nauka, 1981): 87a. The reliability of this source has been questioned vigorously by Y. Bregel in *The Administration of Bukhara under the Manghits and Some Tashkent Manuscripts*. Papers on Inner Asia 34 (Bloomington, IN: Research Institute for Inner Asian Studies, 2000).

26 Barack, "The Second Formation of Islamic Law: The Post-Mongol Context of the Ottoman Adoption of a School of Law": 592.

27 *wa riwāyāt ki muftīyān mī-nawīsand ba-tawaqqu'-i ū rasānad*, A. Urunbaev, G. Dzhuraeva, and S. Gulomov, *Katalog sredneaziatskikh zhalovannykh gramot iz fonda Instituta vostokovedeniia im. Abu Raikhana Beruni Akademii Nauk Respubliki Uzbekistan* (Halle/Saale): Orientwissenschaftliches Zentrum der Martin-Luther-Universität Halle-Wittenberg, 2007): doc. 101.

the individuals bearing this title reviewed and censored the opinions issued by other jurisconsults. Discussing the office of *shaykh al-Islām* for the later Timurid period Beatrice Forbes Manz notes that, "there is little indication that this office furthered the influence of the dynasty in any direct way. It was an honorary position."[28] This is true also for the period immediately preceding the Russian conquest. In Tashkent, for example, a *shaykh al-Islām* would act as the chief administrator of the charitable endowments (*mutawallī-bāshī*) in the province, but he would not be assigned any juristic task.[29] *Sharīʿa*-court records show that disputing parties regularly acquired legal opinions from muftis of their choice and thus maneuvered in a juristic space in which the state had little means of imposing norms of behavior. For a clearer sense of how Hanafi jurisprudence worked, we should look into the more mundane activities of the muftis, rather than merely gesturing at practices of cultural patronage.

The present chapter consists of several parts. Part 1 is a sketch of the major compositional rules that a jurist followed in crafting a fatwa. Part 2 offers an overview of the institutional setting in which litigants might (or might not) be able to acquire fatwas. Part 3 exemplifies the possible uses of the fatwas. Part 4 illustrates how fatwas were reviewed in court for purposes of adjudication. Part 5 examines the birth of a new juristic genre, namely, the written opinions on specific points of Islamic law that were issued for the colonial administration.

1 How to Write a Fatwa

In nineteenth-century Central Asia, before the Russian conquest, parties to a dispute generally acquired legal opinions (fatwas) and produced them in court during trials. As elsewhere in the Islamic world,[30] the office of the mufti in Central Asia was integral to adjudication.[31]

---

28 B. Forbes Manz, *Power, Politics and Religion in Timurid Iran* (Cambridge: Cambridge University Press, 2007): 214.

29 TsGARUz, f. I-164, op. 1, d. 1, l. 7. Khoqandi diploma dated 1279/1862–3, for the appointment of Īshān Āy Khwāja.

30 U. Heyd, "Some Aspects of the Ottoman Fetvā." *BSOAS* 32/1 (1969): 56.

31 A diploma for the appointment to the position of *ṣudūr* and *aʿlam-i ʿaskarī* in Bukhara, which was issued by Abū al-Fatḥ Muḥammad Raḥīm Khān in 1758–59, orders the *qāḍīs* of the royal army always to refer to the fatwas of the new appointee while adjudicating disputes (*qāḍīyān-i muʿaskar-i ʿālī dar murāfaʿat wa maḥkūmāt-i khwudhā tawqīʿ-i fatwā-yi ū rā muʿtabar dānand*), TsGARUz, f. R-2678, op. 2, d. 177, l. 25.

Why would litigants come to court with a fatwa? When a dispute reached the court of a *qāḍī*, parties were required to produce a legal opinion to corroborate their claims. Parties had to comply with this demand within a short period, usually three days.[32] For this purpose, they referred to a person versed in Islamic jurisprudence who was willing to support their case. The task of this individual was complex. He had to translate the position of his client into a legal case (Ar. *mas'ala*); he then formulated a doctrinal question (Ar. *istiftā'*) and proposed a view of the matter by quoting authoritative juristic references. In the regional legal parlance, the resulting text was called *riwāyat* ("quotation") and consisted of two parts: the first, in Persian (or Chaghatay), included the case and the question; the second provided quotations from juristic authorities, usually in Arabic. At this point, the litigant would submit the *riwāyat* to several muftis[33] and ask them to respond to the question. If they found that the proposed view was based on established juristic quotations, the muftis would attach their seals and write their opinion, that is, the fatwa proper: "let it be so" (Pers. *bāshad*, Chaghatay *bulūr*) (see Fig. 15).

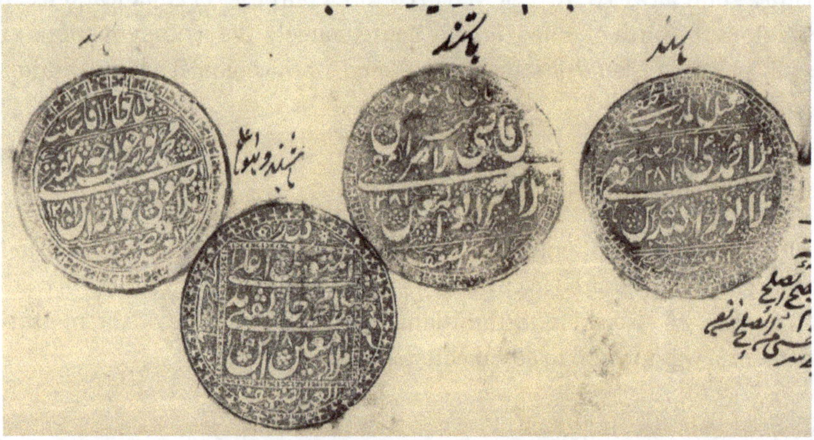

FIGURE 15 *Detail of a fatwa: seals and responses* (bāshad), *1864. TsGARUz, f. R-2678, op. 2, d. 126, l. 1.*

32 Legal opinion on a case of delayed production of a fatwa in court, TsGARUz, f. I-126, op. 1, d. 1729, l. 8. I owe this reference to James Pickett.

33 *rivaiat pisal Mulla Khodzha Agliam po initsiative Khodzhibek Makhzuma Mulla Salikhbekova, kotoryi raznosilsia po domam agliamov i muftiev, dlia prilozheniia pechatei,* Report to the military governor of Syr-Darya Province, 01.08.1883, TsGARUz, f. I-36, op. 1, d. 2273, l. 2.

With this fatwa in hand, the party would return to court and submit the text to the *qāḍī* for his perusal and that of the other jurists. The outcome would look something like Fig. 16:

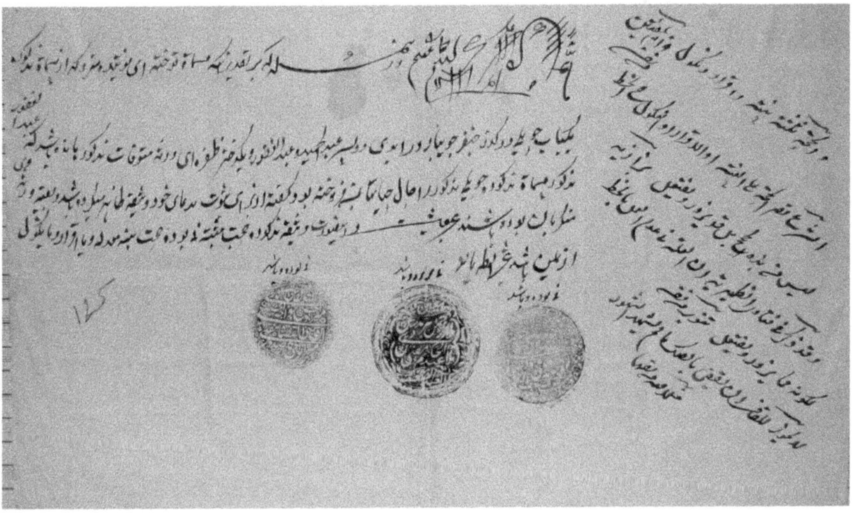

FIGURE 16 *A fatwa.*
COURTESY OF THOMAS WELSFORD[34]

[Question:] We invoke blessing in the name of the supreme Lord. What do the imams of Islam—may God be pleased with them all—have to say on the following question. The matter is as follows: at her death Tūkhta Āy left an estate [*matrūka*], which consisted of one courtyard in the neighborhood of Khanfar-i Jūybār, to her heirs [*waratha*]: her two sons,

[1] "and evidence is threefold: testimony, admission, and retreat", *Khizānat al-muftīyīn*.[35]

[2] "and the strength of the law is the evidence that consists of testimony, admission, and retreat; a document is not as powerful as evidence, for it can be falsified and fabricated", *Bazzāziya*.[36]

34 The document is described in Welsford and Tashev, *A Catalogue of Arabic-Script Documents from the Samarqand Museum*: doc. 146.

35 *Khizānat al-muftīyīn fī al-furūʿ* by al-Ḥusayn b. Muḥammad al-Samʿānī al-Ḥanafī (d. 1339), *GAL* SII: 163 (204).

36 *Fatāwā al-Bazzāzīya*, also known as *Jāmiʿ al-wajīz*. This is a collection of fatwas and *wāqiʿāt* written by Ḥāfiz al-Dīn Muḥammad b. Muḥammad al-Bazzāzī al-Kardarī (d. 1424). See *GAL* SII: 225 (316).

'Abd al-Ḥamīd and 'Abd al-Ghafūr, and her daughter Muẓaffara Āy. 'Abd al-Ghafūr claims that his mother sold the courtyard to him when she was alive; he produced a deed [*wathīqa*] as a certification of his claim [*az barāy-i thubūt-i mudda'ā-yi khwud*]. The other heirs denied the claim [*munkir*]. According to *sharī'a,* in this case such a document is not established evidence [*ḥujjat-i mutha-bbata nay būda*]; evidence [*ḥujja*] should be a just testimony [*bayyina-yi mu'addila*], an admission [*iqrār*], or a retreat from one's oath [*nukūl az yamīn*]; isn't that so? Explain and be concise.

[Answer:] Yes, [the deed] is not [established evidence]

[3] "As mentioned in the *Fatāwā al-Ẓahīrīya* itself, the reason for not entering into evidence a document is that it can be falsified and fabricated", *Tanwīr*.[37]

[4] "It is not permissible for the *qāḍī* to rely on a document without the testimony of witnesses", *Khulāṣat* [*al-fatāwā*].[38]

The text in the left-hand column provides a summary of the case discussed in court. Three individuals inherited from their mother the property of a courtyard. One of the heirs claimed to be the only owner of the courtyard because he had purchased it from his mother before her death. Summoned to court, the *qāḍī* invoked the Islamic laws of evidence and asked the claimant to produce evidence in support of his claim. He did so by producing a purchase deed. The respondents denied the claim and questioned the authenticity of such a deed. At this point, the judge asked the parties to produce a legal opinion. The text that I present here in translation is the *riwāyat* that the respondents produced in court. The legal opinion was drafted in their favor, stating that deeds lack probative value in court and that *qāḍī*s should rely only on testimony. The right-hand column includes four quotations cited in support of the juristic reasoning articulated in the left-hand column.

Fatwas comprise a distinct compositional genre. As such, their crafting is determined by an evolving discourse on the etiquette of compilation. The

37 *Tanwīr al-abṣār wa jamī' al-biḥār* otherwise known as *Tīmūrtāshī* is a work by Shams al-Dīn Muḥammad al-Timurtāshī al-Ghazzī al-Ḥanafī (d. 1595). See *GAL* SII: 311 (427).

38 A work by Ṭahir b. Aḥmad b. 'Abd al-Rashīd al-Bukhārī Iftikhār al-Dīn (d. 1147), see *GAL* SI: 374 (640–41).

most prominent role in this discourse is played by the jurist, who is able to select the authoritative sources that are needed to address a given question. The selection of such sources is subject to a system of classification of doctrinal authority (*taṣnīf*) that is centered on the idea of the preponderant view (*tarjīḥ*). In other words, to issue a fatwa requires that a mufti establish the most suitable opinion among those transmitted down to his era. How should one do that, especially considering the growing body of literature available in the nineteenth century? There was a hierarchy of juristic texts to follow, but that was not enough. When facing differing opinions on the same point of law, a mufti had to search for the preponderant view. He would do so by examining the attribute (*maʿlama*) that earlier jurists conferred upon opinions within an established chain of authority.[39] That is, the crafting of a "good" fatwa depended on the ability of the mufti to identify the preponderant view on a given issue and quote it in the proper manner. We should not, however, underestimate the interpretive task and juristic effort of those who compiled *riwāyats*. Their duty was not simply to select the correct quotations but to identify the doctrinal principle that might help to resolve—to the benefit of the petitioner, of course—the concrete case they were asked about.

The Bukharan *qāḍī* ʿIbadallāh b. Khwāja ʿArif al-Bukhārī, whom we encountered in Chapter 3 as the author of the *Risāla-yi Ḥabībiya*, illustrates the method in the following way.[40] He imagined a jurist who had to be taught how to discern an authoritative opinion from among many. He writes:

> If a quotation [*riwāyat*] displays the phrase "[this is] the adopted opinion" [*ʿalayhi al-fatwā*] or "this is sound" [*huwa al-ṣaḥīḥ*] or "[this is] the accepted opinion" [*huwa al-māʾkhūdh al-fatwā*] or "[this is] the opinion being advocated on it" [*bihi yuftā*] or anything like that, the jurisconsult is not allowed [*muftī rā jāyiz nīst*] to choose a different [*khilāf*] quotation, for he would then be a sinner [*athīm wa gunāhkār*]. If a quotation displays instead the phrase "this is sounder" [*huwa al-aṣaḥḥ*] or "this is the principal [opinion]" [*huwa al-awlī*] [...] or anything with that meaning, the jurisconsult is allowed to deliver an opinion that contradicts that one quotation [*chīzī ki mukhālif-i ān az riwāyāt fatwā dahad*].[41]

39 "An attribute is a sign of preponderance" (*maʿlama ʿalāmat-i tarjīḥ ast*), Mīr Rabīʿ b. Mīr Niyāz Khwāja al-Ḥusaynī, *Risāla-yi raḥmānīya*, MS Tashkent, TsVRUz, no. 9060/XII: fol. 405a.

40 *Jāmiʿ al-maʿmulāt*, MS Tashkent, TsVRUz, no. 6196/I.

41 Ibid.: fol. 5a.

'Ibadallāh explains that there is a hierarchy of authoritative texts that the mufti should consider in issuing an opinion:

> First [come] the collections of legal opinions, and the first and most distinguished among them is the *Khulāṣat* [*al-fatāwā*],[42] after which comes the *Fatawā-yi Imām Qāḍī Khān*,[43] then the *Muḥīṭ*,[44] then the *Dhakhīra* [*al-fatāwā*],[45] then the *Khizānat al-muftīyīn*,[46] then the *Multaqaṭ*,[47] and then the *Qunya*.[48] Let it be so, because the mufti should give an answer by quoting the *Khulaṣat* [*al-fatāwā*] for every question that is found therein and for which the [*Fatāwā*] *Qāḍī Khān* offers a different opinion that lacks the character of a fatwa; and he should proceed according to the aforementioned order.[49]

By explaining the hierarchy of legal texts from which muftis were expected to extract a legal opinion, 'Ibadallāh was indicating the rules that governed the authoritative chain of transmission of legal opinions in his time. Such rules excluded the possibility that late-eighteenth-century muftis could quote directly from the Sunna or the first jurists of the Hanafi legal school (Abū Ḥanīfa, Abū Yūsuf, and Muḥammad Shaybānī).[50] 'Ibadallāh thus assumed

42 See fn. 38.

43 The author of the *Fatāwā Qāḍī Khān* is Fakhr al-Dīn al-Ḥasan b. Manṣūr al-Uzjandī al-Farghānī (d. 1196). See *GAL* SI: 376 (643–44).

44 Otherwise known as *Muḥīṭ al-Burḥānī*, a work of Burḥān al-Dīn Maḥmūd b. Aḥmad b. al-Sadr al-Shahīd al-Bukhārī b. al-Māzah (d. ca. 1174). See *GAL* SI: 375 (642).

45 This work is an abridgment of the *Muḥīṭ al-Burḥānī* by the same author, see *GAL* SI: 375 (642). See also Welsford and Tashev, *A Catalogue of Arabic-Script Documents from the Samarqand Museum*: doc. 56; Idrisov, Muminov, and Szuppe, *Manuscrits en écriture arabe du Musée regional de Nukus (République autonome du Karakalpakstan, Ouzbékistan). Fonds arabe, persan, turkī et karakalpak*: 58.

46 See fn. 35.

47 *Multaqaṭ fī al-fatāwā al-Ḥanafīya*. The author of this work is Nāṣir al-Dīn Abū al-Qāsim Muḥammad b. Yūsuf al-Samarqandī al-Ḥusaynī al-Madanī (d. 1258). See *GAL* SI: 381 (655–56).

48 *Qunyat al-fatāwā* by Najm al-Dīn Mukhtār b. Maḥmūd b. Muḥammad al-Zāhidī al-Ghazmīnī (d. 1260). *GAL* SI: 382 (656).

49 *awwal kutub-i fatwā wa afḍal wa awwalī-yi ān Khulāṣa wa ba'd az ān Fatāwā-yi Imām Qāḍī Khān ba'd az ān Muḥīṭ ba'd az ān Dhakhīra ba'd az ān Khizānat al-muftīyīn ba'd az ān Multaqaṭ ba'd az ān Qunya bāshad bar īn-wajh ki har mas'ala ki dar kitāb-i Khulāṣa būda bāshad ki khilāf-i ān mas'ala dar kitāb-i Qāḍī-Khān wa muzayyil ba-ma'lama-yi fatwā nay būda bāshad wa mufti bāyad ki jawāb ba-riwāyat-i Khulāṣa ba-dahad ān-chunīn ba-tartīb ki madhkūr shud*; see *Jāmi' al-ma'mulāt*: fol. 5b.

50 Ibid.: fols. 11a–11b.

that a mufti was a legal interpreter who followed the established opinion of his legal school. In line with this reasoning, a certain Mīr Rabīʿ b. Mīr Niyāz Khwāja al-Ḥusaynī explained a century later that the term "mufti" should be glossed as a "follower" (*muqallid*) of the eminent jurists of his school of law. For this reason, in issuing fatwas, a mufti should follow the established chain of juristic authority and therefore avoid assembling or using new collections of fatwas (*jung*).[51] In other words, Central Asian jurists such as ʿIbadallāh and Mīr Rabīʿ categorically excluded the possibility that local muftis could issue legal opinions on the basis of independent legal reasoning (*ijtihād*).[52]

2 How to Acquire a Fatwa?

Acquiring a *riwāyat* was relatively easy in nineteenth-century Central Asia, because the drawing up of such texts was among the services offered by individuals trained in madrasas. The text itself was usually composed by a scribe (*muḥarrir*), assisting either the judiciary in court or a mufti. The scribe's task consisted of translating the position of his client into a legal case and formulating a rhetorical question that would elicit a positive answer. He therefore included also the quotations in the margins of the text. The muftis were merely to attach their seals, should they agree with the juristic position expressed. Figure 17 exemplifies this process. This illustration reproduces a working copy of a *riwāyat* collected in Bukhara during an academic expedition headed by the ethnographer and linguist Mikhail Andreev in 1940,[53] which lacks muftis' seals. For reasons unknown to me, the copyist added an unanticipated but revealing sentence: "Īshān Ākhūnd wrote this *riwāyat* on the basis of a copy provided by the scribe [*az nuskha-yi muḥarrir*]. Īshān Ākhūnd attached his seal to the *riwāyat* for Mullā Fūlād and entrusted it [to him]."[54] From this addition, we know that the production of a *riwāyat* was indeed the routine and repetitive work of a clerk rather than the unique juristic output of a mufti.

---

51 Mīr Rabīʿ b. Mīr Niyāz Khwāja al-Ḥusaynī, *Risāla-yi raḥmānīya*, MS Tashkent, TsVRUz, no. 9060/XII: fol. 404a–404b. The term *jung* has been used since the seventeenth century to refer to legal miscellanies that, along with fatwas, contain all sorts of juristic genres (mainly as copies), such as protocols of claims (*maḥḍars*) and tracts (*risālas*). They often look like scrapbooks; it is unclear how they were used by jurists.

52 For more information on this subject, see my "*Ijtihād* in Bukhara: Central Asian Jadidism and Local Genealogies of Cultural Change." *JESHO* 59/1–2 (2016): 193–236.

53 K. Akramova and N. Akramov, *Vostokoved Mikhail Stepanovich Andreev* (*nauchno-biograficheskii ocherk*) (Dushanbe: Irfon, 1973): 154.

54 TsGARUz, f. R-2678, op. 2, d. 177, l. 17a.

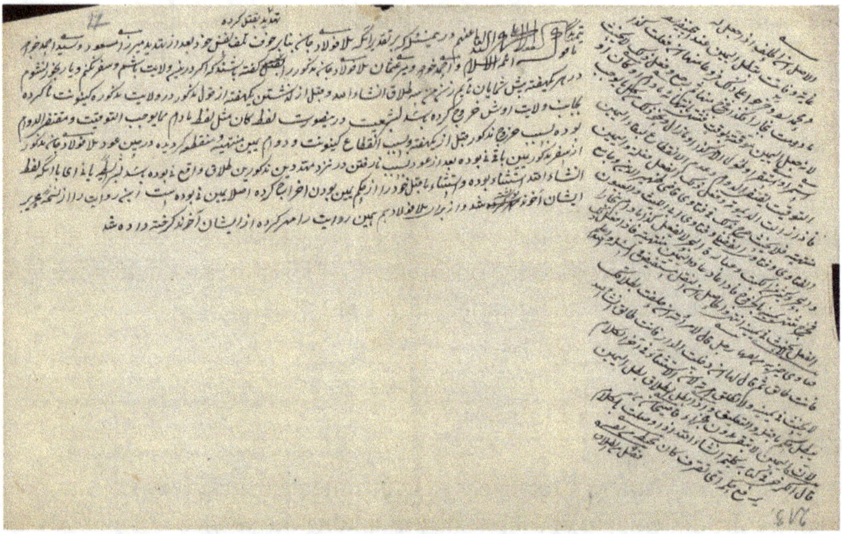

FIGURE 17 *Draft of a* riwāyat*, TsGARUz, f. R-2678, op. 2, d. 177, l. 17a.*
COURTESY OF THE CENTRAL STATE ARCHIVE OF UZBEKISTAN

Bukharan sources tell us that muftis often entrusted their *muḥarrir*s with papers stamped with their seals, which simply needed to be filled in with the requested *riwāyat*.[55] This service had a price, two *tanga*s for the formulation of the text (*mirzāyāna*) and five *tanga*s for the seal (*āq muhr*).[56] Seals evidently conferred legal force on the *riwāyat*; the more seals, the better the chance of winning a case. Seals also reflected the existing power relations among the jurists in town. In nineteenth-century Nasaf (present-day Qarshi), for example, established practices (*ba-dastūr-i qadīm*) ensured that all the muftis would initially submit their *riwāyat*s to the senior jurist (*aʿlam*) and that the *qāḍī*

55 Ṣadr al-Dīn ʿĀynī, *Bukhārā inqilābīning taʾrīkhī*, ed. S. Shimada and S. Tosheva (Tokyo: Dept. of Islamic Area Studies, Center for Evolving Humanities, Graduate School of Humanities and Sociology, University of Tokyo, 2010): 53.

56 M.S. Iusupov, *Sud v Bukhare. Sudoustroistvo i sudoproizvodstvo v Bukharskom emirate v kontse XIX veka i nachale XX veka (Samarkand, 1941)*, MS Samarqand, AMIKINUz no. 828: fols. 20–21. For a forceful critique of this practice as an unlawful innovation (*bidʿat*), see Muḥammad Ikrām Muftī, *Risāla dar bayān-i bidʿāt-i mashhūra maʿ ḥikāyāt-i ʿarabīya* (Bukhara: Qārī ʿAbd al-Wāhid Bukhārī, 1330/1911), MS Tashkent, TsVRUz, no. 3144 (lithog.): fol. 53: *āq muhr-i muftīyān ki ba-kāghadh-i safīd-i bī-khaṭṭ wa bī-ḥukm wa bī-daʿwā muhr mīkunand agar mīgūyand ki īn muhr kardan ḥukm nīst bas īn muhr chīst wa agar gūyand ḥukm ast ḥukm ba-chīst wa ba-kīst.*

would consider for review only *riwāyat*s bearing his seal.[57] Given the ubiquity of the term *aʿlam* in Central Asia,[58] we can assume that the practice of submitting legal opinions first to the senior jurists existed outside of the Bukharan emirate. Records produced in the period before the Russian conquest show that the endorsement of senior jurists was widely considered a prerequisite for a succesful fatwa. The following diploma for the appointment of an *aʿlam* in Bukhara may help us understand the instrumental force of the *aʿlam*'s seal. The reader will note the extent to which the royal court could determine the hierarchy of jurists in the Islamic juridical field:

> All the *qāḍī*s of Islam and all the magnificent heirs of the Prophet and the splendid nobles and all the residents, especially all the muftis and scribes [*muḥarrirān*] of the Bukharan court [*maḥkama*], should consider [this man] a full *aʿlam*. Therefore, when they draft *riwāyat*s and protocols of claims [*maḥḍar*s], they should submit them to him and have him stamp them [*ba-muhr-i aʿlam rasānīda*]. The deputies of the judges [*nayibān-i quḍḍāt*] should not enforce the *riwāyat*s without his seal.[59]

A litigant might be unable to secure a *riwāyat* stamped with the seals of the eminent jurists of the city. Especially when one sued a locally prominent legist, it was difficult to persuade the latter's peers to side with the claimant. One such case is reflected in a ruling issued by an assembly of judicial assessors who reviewed, for the colonial administration, the development of a lawsuit against Muḥyī al-Dīn Khwāja. This case was referred to in Chapter 2 as one driven by malice that ended with the claimant repenting before the court. The account offered in the ruling suggests that, although the claimant was able to acquire a *riwāyat* and produce it in court, this legal opinion lacked the stamps of the town's jurists. This unendorsed document obviously had less legal force than the *riwāyat* produced by the other party. Here is how the Tashkent jurists explain the case:

---

57 TsGARUz, f. R-2678, op. 2, d. 177, l. 27. Royal order (*ḥukm-i humāyūn*) issued by an emir of Bukhara. Seal illegible; probably second half of the nineteenth century. Yusupov argues that the seal of an *aʿlam* would accord legal force to a *riwāyat* on punishment; see his *Sud v Bukhare*: 34.

58 In the year 1865 in Tashkent alone operated more than a dozen "senior jurists" (*aʿlam*), TsGARUz, f. I-164, op. 1, d. 3, l. 2.

59 *aʿlam-i Bukhārā-yi sharīf*, n.d., Mīrzā Ṣādiq Munshī Jāndārī, *Munshāʾāt wa manshūrāt*, MS Tashkent, TsVRUz, no. 299/I: fol. 38b–39b. This collection of model documents includes copies of texts dealing with Bukharan chancery practices dating to the first half of the nineteenth century. See *Sobranie vostochnykh rukopisei akademii nauk Uzbekistan. Istoriia*, ed. D.Iu. Iusupov and R.P. Dzhalilov (Tashkent: Fan, 1998): 412.

> On 31 July 1886, in the supreme court of Tashkent presided over by the judges of Islam, there occurred the following event: the plaintiff, ʿAbd al-Karīm Jān, together with the defendant, Mullā ʿAbd al-Khāliq, attorney to Īshān Mullā Muḥammad Muḥyī al-Dīn Khwāja Īshān, were summoned to the court of second instance [*maḥkama-yi atīya*]. [Let it be known that] in the court of first instance [*maḥkama-yi awwal*], the aforementioned parties were asked to produce a *riwāyat*. They did so, and their legal opinions were examined. On account of the iniquity [*fasād wa buṭlān*] of the plaintiff's claim against the defendant, all the jurists [*aʿlam wa muftiyān*] appointed in the Tashkent district agreed to issue a fatwa and stamped their seal on the *riwāyat* of the defendant [for the text is] in accordance with the case. No one among the *ʿulamāʾ* issued a fatwa in favor of the plaintiff nor attached his seal to the latter's *riwāyat*, given that [the text] is not in accord with the case.[60]

Presented with ʿAbd al-Karīm Jān's blank *riwāyat*, the Tashkent jurists doubtless inquired about the identity of the other litigant. When they heard that it was Muḥyī al-Dīn Khwāja, the muftis declined to attach their seals to the text. A similar case occurred a decade later, when a certain ʿĀlīya Pācha attempted to seize from Muḥyī al-Dīn Khwāja the powers of guardian over her minor children. It proved impossible for her to have the lawsuit heard by native judges, because, as she complained before the Russians, "no jurist would impress his seal on our *riwāyat* because they all fear Muḥyī al-Dīn Khwāja."[61] It is here that we see how Central Asian jurists read *riwāyat*s: without the muftis' positive answer (which in the previous quotation is termed "fatwa") and their seals, a *riwāyat* had little legal force in court.

In this section, I have illuminated the mechanics of issuing fatwas, but there are still many questions to answer: in such a system, how did someone become a prominent jurist, acquire a reputation, and increase his authority? Only by governmental decree. But how? Through juristic disputes? I also explained that, when fatwas were used for judicial purposes, only senior jurists could attach their seals to them. If so, on what occasions did "common" muftis write their own fatwas? Only when assembling their own collection of opinions and legal miscellanies (*jung*)? What happened if the plaintiff and the respondent presented to court opposing *riwāyat*s that were endorsed by senior jurists?

60 TsGARUz, f. I-164, op. 1, d. 6, l. 73. Stamped with the seals of four Tashkent *qāḍīs*.

61 *na nash rivaiat ni odin agliam, ni odin muftii pechati svoei ne prilozhili iz boiazni ot Mukhitdina Khodzhi*, appeal to the Tashkent city commandant, 02.07.1896, TsGARUz, f. I-17, op. 1, d. 6226, l. 34ob.

The preference of the court for the one mufti or the other had far-reaching consequences for the reputation of the muftis. Here again, we can appreciate how the state, or state-appointed functionaries, influenced the Islamic juridical field.

3 Who Needs Fatwas?

Let us now consider briefly the circumstances in which groups and individuals in nineteenth-century Central Asia might wish to solicit legal opinions. This will help us illuminate certain patterns of textual consumption that characterized fatwas as a compositional genre. Space prevents us from considering the entire range of possibilities for issuing fatwas, but I hope to offer some insights into the uses to which fatwas might be put.

3.1 *Descent Groups*

The work of recent scholars has brought to light a growing number of private manuscript collections in Uzbekistan, including, among a wide variety of genres, family trees (called *shajaras* or *nasab-nāmas*) and fatwas.[62] In a significant number of cases, legal opinions were produced at the instigation of descent groups that initiated the writing of family trees or inherited them. Material from the Ferghana Valley has recently been published that includes deeds now among the possessions of a community claiming descent from Qutayba Ibn Muslim, a commander of the Abbasid forces that conquered Transoxiana in the early eighth century. These deeds comprise a *shajara* accompanied by several legal opinions.[63] The latter were clearly produced for

62 Y. Kawahara, *Private Archives on a Makhdūmzāda Family in Marghilan* (Tokyo: Department of Islamic Area Studies, Center for Evolving Humanities, Graduate School of Humanities and Sociology, University of Tokyo, 2012).

63 The documents are briefly described in *Mazar Documents from Xinjang and Ferghana (Facsimile)*, vol. 1, ed. J. Sugawara and Y. Kawahara (Tokyo: Research Institute for Languages and Cultures of Asia and Africa, Tokyo University of Foreign Studies, 2006). They are discussed more fully in B. Babadzhanov *Kokandskoe Khanstvo: Vlast', Politika, Religiia* (Tokyo and Tashkent: NIHU Program Islamic Area Studies Center at the University of Tokyo/Institut Vostokovedeniia Akademii Nauk Respubliki Uzbekistan, 2010): esp. pp. 691–95. In my brief comment on the production of these fatwas, I have drawn largely from Babajanov but have added my own evaluations. I take issue with some preliminary evaluations Babajanov offered on these documents. First, on p. 692, he refers to a *ḥadīth* translated into Persian, which appears at the end of a family tree, WT-QM-01. He presents this quotation as a *riwāyat*, meaning "a document with quotations from famous juristic

more than one reason. First, they were viewed as an instrument to be used to uphold the legal validity of the *shajara* by arguing that the family tree should be treated as legal evidence. This served the purpose of obliging the neighboring Muslim population to respect the descent group.[64] Second, the fatwa aimed to ensure that the descent group would be granted tax-farming rights and obliged the local power-holder to accord the descent group such rights.[65] Such legal opinions may have proven crucial, especially in time of political change, when the descent group had to persuade the new ruler to reinstate former fiscal privileges.[66] Third, such documents legitimize, from the perspective of *sharīʿa*, the practice of receiving the offerings (*nadhūrāt/ṣadaqāt/*

---

collections," that is, a fatwa, but this quotation was not instrumental in the issuance of a legal opinion. In this case, there is no question (*istiftāʾ*), and no answer is extant. Instead, it should be read as a general, established, formula calling attention to the fact that the genealogy of the descent group is valid and that it is therefore obligatory for Muslims to respect them (*dar āncha sayyid-i ṣaḥīḥ al-nasab rā bar jamīʿ-i musalmānān ikrām wa iḥtirām-i īshan wājib-ast*). Compare with WT-QM-02-9 (p. 97) and WT-QM-03-3 (p. 84). With regard to document WT-QM-01, he indicates the existence of a *qāḍī*'s ruling, but we could not find it. On p. 693, Babajanov confuses with a fatwa the notarization of the family tree, to which are attached eight seals but on which no legal opinions are expressed. In *Kokandskoe Khanstvo: Vlast', Politika, Religiia*: 693 fn. 1, Babajanov asserts that, reading these documents, one has the feeling that someone has attempted to "imitate" (*podrazhat'*) fatwas. There is no reason, however, to consider these legal opinions less legal or more artificial than any other legal artifact produced by a Muslim notarial office.

64 *shajara-yi madhkūra bar īn-maḍmūn ḥujjat-i sharʿīya būda ʿizzat wa iḥtirām tawqīr wa ikrām-i sādāt-i madhkūrīn bar kāffa-yi inām lāzim bāshad*, *Mazar Documents from Xinjang and Ferghana (Facsimile)*, vol. 1: 84 [WT-QM-03-3]. The use of fatwas was apparently instrumental in encouraging the respect of the readers. *Shajaras* often open with a legal opinion that argues that those who fail to show respect for men of noble lineage should be punished (*taʿzīr*) with 39 stripes of the lash. See *Mazar Documents from Xinjang and Ferghana (Facsimile)*, vol. 3 ed. A. Muminov, N. Abdulahatov, and Y. Kawahara (Tokyo: Research Institute for Languages and Cultures of Asia and Africa, Tokyo University of Foreign Studies, 2007): 150 (WT-MS-01-06) and 157 (WT-MM-01-06) and Welsford and Tashev, *A Catalogue of Arabic-Script Documents from the Samarqand Museum*: doc. 668. The Samarqandi fatwas contain a larger body of citations from juristic references than do the Ferghani fatwas.

65 *wa nīz īshan muṣrif-i kharāj bāshand wājib bāshad bar man lahu al-wilāya ki kharāj-i arāḍī-yi īshān rā ba-īshān gudhārand*, *Mazar Documents from Xinjang and Ferghana (Facsimile)*, vol. 1: 84 (WT-QM-03-3) and 96–97 (WT-QM-02-9/10).

66 J.E. Dagyeli, "By Grace of Descent: A Conflict between an *Īšān* and Craftsmen over Donations," *DI* 88 (2012): 279–307.

hadāyā) presented to the shrine of the saint.[67] This fatwa thus clearly prevents the use of critical judgment against the descent groups. It was common for descendants of the saints who made a living as guardians of shrines to ask the faithful for money, and some Central Asian jurists considered the act of giving votive offerings to the shaykhs administering the more pedestrian affairs of the shrines as an illicit course of action, because people made such offerings in the hope that shaykhs would intercede with the saints or God. Whether this was permissible or not has been debated by jurists from earliest times, but the clearest attestation of the nature of such a debate comes at the beginning of the twentieth century, when offerings to shaykhs seem to have become a matter of public concern. Between 1915 and 1917,[68] several requests for legal opinions reached *al-Iṣlāh*, a journal published in Tashkent by a group of local jurists. In 1916, for example, a mufti from Khojand asked, "If the descendants of the saints (*khwāja wa tūra*) and the Sufi masters (*shaykhs*) ask their disciples (*murīds*) for offerings (*nadhrs*) and if the latter make the offerings with the hope of salvation (*najāt*), is this right?"[69] The editors of the journal published the following fatwa:

> In authoritative texts, particularly in the *Khulāṣat al-fatāwa*,[70] in the chapter devoted to fasting, it is written [...] that if offerings [*nadhr*] are not made to God, they are illicit [*ḥarām*]. More precisely, if the offerings are made to God, they must be used to benefit the indigent, as are ritual and voluntary alms [*zakāt wa ṣadaqa*]. It therefore follows that the descendants of the saints [*khwāja*], teachers [*mashāyikh*], and many others must be indigent. [...] Let it be known that the offerings to the dead that are made by most people and things such as money and candles that

67 *Mazar Documents from Xinjang and Ferghana (Facsimile)*, vol. 1: 88 (WT-QM-02-18), 72 (WT-QM-03-15), and 68 (WT-QB-02). This latter legal opinion is an original document, not a copy added to the scroll of the family trees.

68 A.Ḥ.D., "Mas'ala: Sū'āl-Jawāb," *al-Iṣlāḥ* 5 (1915): 146–7; "Chīmkintlīk Mullā Īrgash Ṣāliḥ Naẓar-ūghlī-dan sū'āl." *al-Iṣlāḥ* 16 (1915): 291–2; "Namangāndan Niẓām al-Dīn Khwāja Sayf al-Dīn Khwāja-ūghlī ṭarafindan sū'āllār." *al-Iṣlāh* 5 (1916): 153.

69 In Russian Turkestan the question was first raised in the work *'Ibrat al-Ghālifīn* (1311/1893–4), in which the famous Dukchī Ishān denounced the descent groups (*khwāja, tūra*, and *sayyid*) for "disciple hunting" (*shikār-i murīd*) in order to extort money. See B.M. Babadzhanov, "Dukchi Ishan i Andizhanskoe vosstanie 1898 g." In *Podvizhniki islama: kul't sviatykh i sufism v Srednei Azii i na Kavkaze*, ed. S.N. Abashin and V.O. Bobrovnikov (Moscow: RAN, 2003): 257.

70 See fn. 38.

> are donated to sanctuaries to draw nearer [*qurubat hāsil ītmāq ūchūn*] to the saints [*awliyā'*]—for example, by turning to Ghawth al-Aʿzam[71] to alleviate pain or satisfy a certain wish—are futile and illicit acts [*bātil wa ḥarām*]. Because making an offering is an act of devotion [*ʿibādat*], being devoted to a creature is not right [*durust īmās*]; moreover, the dead will never receive the offerings made to them. In the case of offerings to the dead, if one believes [*iʿtiqādda būlsa*], failing to consider God, that being bountiful with the dead is for [the benefit of] the people, this is, for God, misbelief [*kufr*]. When one makes an offering, one [usually] says, "Oh God, in all justice I offer thee this gift; if thou wilt alleviate my suffering, if thou wilt grace me with what I lack, or if thou wilt fulfill my wish, then I will feed the poor that live near the sepulcher of these saints, I will bring prayer rugs to the mosques, and there I will light candles or give money." If things like these, which are offerings made to God, are then used to benefit the indigent that live near the tombs of the masters and honor their memory, then the offering is lawful [*jāyiz*]. If, instead of being made to the tombs of the masters, to the mosques, and to the needy who inhabit the sanctuaries [*mujāwir*], the offerings are given to other poor wretches, this, too, is a lawful thing; [as] it is not necessary that offerings be used for the masters or for the descendants [*awlād*] of the saints. If it should happen that there were no needy people, bestowing offerings on the wealthy, those of noble rank, or on men of learning would not be lawful. Because it is a fact that offering gifts to creatures is illicit, bestowing goods on wealthy people is not contemplated by the *sharīʿa*. [Certainly] similar acts have [been committed and accordingly they have] come down to us, yet it is not necessary to commit them [*adāsī wājib ūlmaz*], given that they are illicit. Serving a master on whom gifts have been bestowed [*mandhūr ūlmīsh shaykh*] is not licit, while it may be so if the master is needy or married or has children unable to work; in this case [an action of this sort will be considered] as being the same as ritual alms. Unless the person offering gifts affirms that his objective is to draw nearer to God, accepting his gifts and bestowing them on the needy is a loathsome act and is forbidden (*makrūh wa taḥrīm*).[72]

We have so far examined a case concerning offerings made to a descent group, which were probably regarded as yet another resource for the upkeep of a

---

71 The author refers here to ʿAbd al-Qādir Gīlānī (d. 1166), the putative founder of the Qādirīya Sufi order.

72 Khāl Muḥammad Tūra Qūlī, "Khujandlī afandī Tūra sū'āllārīna jawāb." *al-Iṣlāḥ* 13 (1 July 1916): 399–403.

charitable endowment.[73] The *waqfs* and the direct involvement of descent groups in their administration are yet another social field that stimulates legal thinking and the output of muftis. It is not uncommon to find fatwas issued to reinstate the stipulations (*shurūṭ*) of a *waqf*. For instance, the appointment of a member of the descent group to the office of administrator (*mutawallī*)—a stipulation commonly found in *waqf* deeds—could be endorsed by jurists by means of a fatwa that added supplementary legal weight.[74] Likewise, the *shaykh* who oversaw a shrine complex would seek in a fatwa confirmation of the rights to dispose of the produce yielded by the lands attached to the *waqf*.[75] This last observation on the pattern of the use of fatwas by the people leads us to address more directly the relationship between legal opinions and contracts.

3.2 *Fatwas for Contracts*

Contracts, here broadly understood, represent by far the largest of the legal genres to be found in private collections in Central Asia. In this region, contracts, drawn up according to the rules of formulary manuals in Persian or Chaghatay, are extremely common and are found in places as remote as the rural provinces of Qaraqalpaqstan. Their legal force was subjected to extensive juristic commentary: contracts, like other legal documents, can be acquired easily if one has the financial means to pay a scribe. Cases of forgery are, therefore, not rare. The approach of the Muslim jurists to contracts is also complicated by the fact that Islamic law originally conferred greater probative weight on the testimony (*bayyina*) of witnesses than on written evidence (*ḥujja*).[76] Jurists in the formative period of Islamic law held that the status of written documents was uncertain and therefore regarded documentary evidence as inferior to oral evidence. We know that, in practice, *qāḍīs* everywhere in the Islamicate world, including Central Asia, accepted legal documents as valid proof (*dalīl/burhān*)[77] but there is an authoritative juristic tradition that

73 Document WT-QB-02 refers explicitly to the *waqf* and, in particular, to the office of administrator (*tawlīyat*) of the *waqf* as a prerogative of the descent group (*awlād*).

74 *Mazar Documents from Xinjang and Ferghana (Facsimile)*, vol. 3: 99 (WT-KT-17).

75 Ibid.: 100 (WT-KT-16).

76 J. Schacht, *An Introduction to Islamic Law* (Oxford: Oxford Unversity Press, 1982): 18, 82.

77 The frequent recourse to documents in *sharʿī* judicial proceedings is described in H. Gerber, *State, Society and Law in Islam: Ottoman Law in Comparative Perspective* (Albany: State University of New York Press, 1994): 177–78; A. Layish, *Sharīʿa and Custom in Libyan Tribal Society: An Annotated Translation of Decisions from the Sharīʿa Courts of Adjābiya and Kufra* (Leiden: Brill, 2005): passim. For a discussion of legal documents, see A. Layish, "*Shahādat al-naql* in the Judicial Practice in Modern Libya." In *Dispensing Justice in Islam: Qadis and Their Judgements*, ed. M. Khalid Masud, R. Peters, and D. Powers

questions recourse to written texts in judicial contexts. I will now review three cases that exemplify the uses of fatwas in judicial contexts with special reference to the law of contract.

The first case illustrates how a legal opinion could be used to defend the validity of existing contracts, to protect them from attempts to breach them, and to make them binding. One Aḥmad Bīk had rented half of a rice market, which he held on a royal lease (*musta'jar az pādshāhī-yi khwud*), to a certain Tilū Bāy for 1,750 *tangas* for six months. In his capacity as lessee, Tilū Bāy had been receiving the emoluments of the said rented property for two months. Without any legal impediment (*az ghayr-i ʿudhr-i sharʿī*), Tilū Bāy decided to breach the aforementioned rent contract (*ijāra-yi madhkūra rā faskh mīnamāyam*) and refused to hand over the equivalent of the rent. It is safe to assume that this situation led Aḥmad Bīk to sue Tilū Bāy. The plaintiff brought to court the following opinion:

> [Question:] [...] According to Islamic law, the said rent is, in this case, a binding contract [*ʿaqd-i lāzim*], and tenant cannot violate it if there were no legal impediments.[78] Given the agreement of the aforementioned two contracting parties,[79] the equivalent of the rent is due to be paid by the lessee.[80] [Therefore,] the statement of the aforementioned lessee constitutes damage [*ḍarar*] under the terms of the contract. [For this reason, the statement] "I breach [the contract]" is, in the absence of legal support, unworthy of consideration:[81] is that not so?
>
> [Answer:] Yes, it is not [worth consideration].[82]

The native judge who examined the case must have discerned particular legal force in this fatwa and in the position of Aḥmad Bīk. It would otherwise be difficult to explain why Tilū Bāy acknowledged his debt to the lessor for the lease of half of the rice market. On this occasion, the lessee also undertook to pay the sum of money in four installments: 300 rubles for three months and

(Leiden: Brill, 2006): 496–99; B. Ergene, "Evidence in Ottoman Courts: Oral and Written Documentation in Early-Modern Courts of Islamic Law." *JAOS* 124/3 (2004): 471–91.

78 *mar musta'jir-i madhkūr rā az ghayr-i aʿdhār-i sharʿīya wilāyat-i faskh nay.*

79 *az rū-yi qarār-i muʿtāqidayn-i madhkūrīn.*

80 *badal-i ijāra bar mustā'jir-i madhkūr lāzim.*

81 *faskh mīnamāyam bī sanad-i sharʿī lā yuʿtabar.*

82 Welsford and N. Tashev, *A Catalogue of Arabic-Script Documents from the Samarqand Museum*: doc. 452a.

250 rubles on the fourth month.[83] To secure the binding force of the rental contract, Aḥmad Bīk asked the *qāḍī* to issue a ruling (*ḥukm*) on the legal validity (*ṣiḥḥat*) of the rent on the basis of the aforementioned acknowledgment (*az rū-yi iqrār*) and the legal opinion (*az rū-yi riwāyat*).[84]

The second case deals with underage individuals selling their property rights to improvements (*sukniyāt*). The object of sale consisted "of a coach house comprising three large pavilions and four fixed-structure shops,"[85] located in the great market of the Khwāṣī quarter in Samarqand. The sale was made by the guardian (*waṣī*) of the underage persons. The same *qāḍī* notarized the sale twice within four months, before the same witnesses.[86] There is, however, a major difference between the two deeds of sale. On the right margin of the second deed, the *qāḍī* added the following fatwa:

> [Question:] Is the aforementioned sale by Mullā Ūrūn Bāy on behalf of the aforementioned minors, Nadhrī Qulī and Sharāfat Āy, legally valid for their benefit according to the splendid Law of the Prophet? [Answer:] Yes, and God knows best.

Apparently, the contracting parties decided to confer on the deed supplementary legal value, asking that such a legal opinion be attached to the document in order to prevent any claim against its validity.[87] Another relative might lodge a suit against the parties on the grounds that the sale was not made for the benefit of the minors. Two citations from the *Fatāwā Qāḍī Khān* were chosen to void this case:

> [1] "When immovables are shared between minors and adults, they can be the object of a complete sale".
> [2] "The guardian is the person whose acts are entirely for the benefit of the minors."

The third case also deals with guardianship. A guardian refused to sell the undivided shared property belonging to certain underage individuals for a particular price, preferring to sell it to his own son for a higher price. The payment was, however, deferred for one year, and the purchaser undertook to pay

83 Ibid.: doc. 452b.i.

84 Ibid.: doc. 452b.ii.

85 Ibid.: doc. 456a.

86 Ibid.: docs. 456a and 457.i.

87 Ibid.: doc. 457.ii.

only a smaller sum in the intervening period. The sellers asked whether the sale should be considered valid under Islamic law. The answer is positive:[88]

> [Question:] The property, a house with a courtyard, is the estate [*mushtarak bi 'l-irth*] of the late Jūrah Bāy, shared between his widow, Chīnnī Āy, daughter of ʿĀbid Bāy, and all his minor children, Tāsh Muḥammad, Ikrāma Āy, and Dādra Āy. The property in question was damaged, and some of the structure was demolished. Entrusted with the upkeep of said property, Tilū Bāy, guardian of the aforementioned children, and Chīnnī Āy (the latter through the agency of her attorney, Jumʿa Bāy) have rejected offers by several just [*ʿudūl*] Muslims to purchase the property for 5,000 or 5,500 *tangas*. They have opted instead to sell it to Birdī Murād, for 7,000 *tangas*, which is more than its fair price [*qīmat-i ʿadl*], and the sale is complete, operative, binding, and legal [*bayʿ-i bātt batāt-i nāfidh-i lāzim-i sharʿī*]. The payment of this aforementioned sum has been deferred [*tāʾjīl*] for a year, but the purchaser has granted the aforementioned children a sum of 1,500 *tangas* to cover their costs for the intervening period. According to Islamic law, in this case, is the sale and the purchase by the aforementioned attorney and guardian legally sound and valid [*durust wa mujauwaz-i sharʿī*]? [Answer:] Yes.

On the verso of the fatwa is certification of the sale of the property in question performed by the guardian and another agent on behalf of the minors. The document states twice that the sale is valid on account of the aforementioned legal opinion. This addition indicates that the contract was actually notarized only after the fatwa was issued:

> [This is the] demarcation of the boundaries of the dwellings having one internal and external courtyard, located in Samarqand's Qarā Bāy Āqsaqāl quarter. The four boundaries [are as follows:] The dwellings abut: on the west partly a courtyard belonging to Ustā Qanbar Bāy, the barber, and partly a courtyard belonging to Rustām Khwāja, son of Sayyid Khwāja, on the north partly a blocked thoroughfare and partly a courtyard belonging to Mullā Muḥammad ʿĀqil Muftī, son of Mullā Bābā Jān, on the east partly a courtyard belonging to Ḥākim Pahlawān, son of Bāy Malik, and partly a courtyard belonging to Mullā ʿAbd al-Ṣamad, son of Mullā ʿAbd al-Qādir, and on the south a public thoroughfare. All the features [of the boundaries] are completely known. On 20 Dhū al-Qaʿda 1312

88 Ibid.: doc. 459a.

> [15 May 1895] Tilū Bāy son of Muḥammad Ṣābir Bāy, aged 43, who acts as guardian [*waṣī*] to Tāsh Muḥammad, Ikrāma Āy, and the minor Dādra Āy, children of Jūra Bāy, and Jumʿa Bāy son of ʿĀbid Bāy, aged 26, who acts as proxy [*wakīl*] on behalf of his sister Chīnī Āy, daughter of ʿĀbid Bāy, appeared before the Samarqand *wilāyat* court. In the condition that legally allows an acknowledgment and the execution of all the usufructs, [Tilū Bāy] acknowledged that, on the basis of a legal opinion written on the back [confirming that the contract is] for the benefit of the minors, they sold to Mullā Birdī Murād b. Ḥājjī Tilū all the dwellings on the courtyard with all the rights and appurtenances; this is the property (*ḥaqq wa milk*) of the individuals represented by the guardian and the agent. The sale, for 7,000 *tanga*s, is complete, operative, binding, and conclusive and was made by the exchange of goods of equal value, [with the] legal warranty for default in ownership, in the absence of fraud or voiding conditions. [The contract was notarized] with the confirmation [of the beneficiaries]. This happened in the presence of Muslims. And the sale was allowed, [as considered to be for] the benefit of the minors on the basis of the legal opinion [written] on the back [of this document] [*wa būd jawāz bayʿ-i madhkūr khayrat al-ṣighār az rū-yi riwāyat*]. [The names of the witnesses follow].[89]

3.3 *Fatwas as Deterrents*

We now turn to a case showing how a legal opinion could become instrumental in persuading a party to a dispute to drop his claim. The waiver of the claim has been notarized on the back of the legal opinion:

> [Question:] Akram Khwāja, Mukarram Khwāja, and Bahādur Khwāja sell to Qurbān Badal Makhdūm a perfume shop that they have inherited from Aḥmad Khwāja. [This happens after] they have performed the division of the inheritance among themselves; [the perfume shop goes to them], whereas the other heirs [have received another] portion [of the inheritance consisting] of one plot of [bare] land and one plot of garden land. The sale occurs to the satisfaction [*ba-riḍā*] of the remaining heirs; [it is] complete and conclusive, made by the exchange of two things of equal value. Said purchaser then sells the perfume shop, which he has just acquired, to Barnā Khwāja. The sale is complete and conclusive and made by the exchange of two things of equal value, as is illustrated by a legal certificate that is held by Barnā Khwāja. Later, Bahādur Khwāja, acting on

89 Ibid.: doc. 459b.

> his own behalf and, as attorney, for his mother and sisters, revokes his former acknowledgment [*az iqrār-i madhkūrash rujūʿ namūda*] and lodges a claim against Barnā Khwāja for said property. According to Islamic law, in this case, the shop is now the property [*ḥaqq wa milk*] of his purchaser, Barnā Khwāja, and Bahādur Khwāja's claim is not valid [*nā durust*]. If the *qāḍī* does not hear the claim, he will be rewarded, will he not? [It is so] because the predominant opinion [*ghālib ẓann*] was to rely on said certificate, and it was thus necessary [*wājib*].
>
> [Answer:] Yes, it was.[90]

This fatwa rules favorably on the perceived probative force of a deed of sale. A *qāḍī* might consider the latter insufficient to rule against Bahādur Khwāja, but by virtue of this fatwa, Barnā Khwāja was able to discourage his opponent from pursuing his claims any further and to convince him to withdraw his demands:

> On 28 Jumādī al-awwal 1304 [22.02.1887] Bahādur Khwāja, acting on his own behalf and as attorney for his mother and sisters, made, in front of the *qāḍī* who attached the seal to this document, a valid and legal acknowledgment declaring that he has no right, pretension, or claim [*hīch ḥaqq wa dakhlī wa daʿwā nadāram*] against Barnā Khwāja, son of Fatḥullāh Khwāja, for the aforementioned shop. He also acknowledged that, regarding the price of the shop, he will refer to the heirs of Qurbān Badal Makhdūm. And all this happened in the presence of Muslims.[91]

3.4 *Fatwas for Rulers*

The last type of fatwa comprises legal opinions solicited by the ruling dynasty and its chancellery. We have found examples of such fatwas in the history of Khorezm. The first legal opinion was solicited by a Qunghrat ruler who clearly had an interest in seizing the possessions of officeholders who were accused of embezzlement:

> The question is as follows: by the supreme order of the ruler, the refuge of Islam, somebody was appointed [to the office of] tax collector and inspector [*zakātchī wa mushrif*] to collect the goods of the Muslim treasury. This person remained in office for some years and accumulated

90 Ibid.: doc. 512a.

91 Ibid.: doc. 512b.

> [wealth in] land, houses, and slaves. According to Islamic law and in the manner of the leaders and the guides of ʿUmar—the blessing of God be upon him—if the ruler, the refuge of Islam, leaves to the person in question the wealth he had before he reached that office, while he confiscates, transfers to the treasury, and employs for the necessities of the Muslims all the wealth that proceeded from his office of tax collector and inspector, beside his salary, without the consent of this person, will he find sublime reward before God? If you answer, recompense is found.[92]

Sayyid Qāsim Khwāja Aʿlam, the jurist who ruled in favor of confiscation, addressed an additional explanatory letter to the ruler:

> The purpose of this record and the issue of this statement is that, if the ruler, the refuge of Islam, has appointed one person to the post of tax collector or to any other legal royal office and that person had spent some time in that duty [but] has since deviated from his original position in such a way that he amassed houses, land, and slaves; this [behavior] is a sign of fraud. This should be sufficient [reason] for the ruler, the refuge of Islam, [to order] that the wealth that this man possessed before his appointment be left [to him]. [Otherwise, the proceedings of] his fraud should be assessed, confiscated, and transferred to the treasury. For this reason, he will find sublime reward and plentiful recompense. God knows best and justly.[93]

Qunghrat rulers acquired other similar legal opinions that awarded dignitaries temporary fiscal grants by allowing them to collect taxes from crown lands in certain localities.[94] The production of this text was probably prompted by a Qunghrat ruler who had just ascended to the throne and inquired whether such a practice of granting prebends would be in keeping with established

---

92 TsGARUz, f. I-125, op. 2, d. 608, l. 2.

93 TsGARUz, f. I-125, op. 2, d. 608, l. 1. The document has been transcribed and translated by Y. Bregel, *Documents from the Khanate of Khiva (17th–19th centuries)*. Papers on Inner Asia 40 (Bloomington, IN: Research Institute for Inner Asian Studies, 2007): 54. Bregel has, however, overlooked the fact that such a text served as an "accompanying letter" to clarify the content of the fatwa that ruled favourably on the confiscation of the estates of civil servants (cf. TsGARUz, f. I-125, op. 2, d. 608, l. 2).

94 TsGARUz, f. I-125, op. 2, d. 612, l. 1; the text has been transcribed and translated in *Documents from the Khanate of Khiva (17th–19th centuries)*: 55, though Bregel does not note its value as precedent.

customary practices. Qunghrats also solicited the production of legal opinions that made it licit for the ruler to levy taxes from the land that belonged to a dignitary, should his heirs be unable to produce evidence substantiating their property rights.[95]

4 How Not to Write a Fatwa

Legal treatises warn that things can go wrong in the issuance of a fatwa. From at least the sixteenth century to the beginning of the twentieth, Central Asian Hanafi output is punctuated by calls for distinguishing fatwas that are applicable from those that are not.[96] Local jurists appear to be promoting an affirmative practice of selection and edition of opinions that they deem established (*maʿmūla*) and correct (*muṣīb*); at the same time, they openly deprecate the fatawa collections of their contemporaries and advise that their legal opinions not be applied (*iḥtiyāt ast ki ʿamal nakunand*).[97] The parties to a dispute were usually asked to provide the court with legal opinions, which the jurists in court were asked to compare. Those based on sound juristic quotations (*riwāyat-i saḥīh alayhi al-fatwā*) were generally preferred to those that were seldom applied (*ghayr-i maʿmūla riwāyat*).[98] It is not rare to find on the verso of fatwas the note, "Let it be known to the judges of Islam and the respectable rulers that this *riwāyat* is trustworthy and established."[99] This note served to indicate that, after examination in court, a *qāḍī* had accepted this legal opinion and had dismissed the one produced by the other litigant.

How then to situate the work of a mufti beyond the opaque juristic categories of "correct" and "incorrect," "established" or "not established"? Let's imagine that a mufti issues a fatwa which is later considered incorrect by another jurist. It does not mean that the mufti in question was not skillful enough in the hermeneutic activity of deriving an opinion from authoritative sources. On the contrary, he might, in crafting his fatwa, have followed principles other

---

95 TsGARUz, f. I-125, op. 2, d. 612, l. 6; unstamped and undated note.

96 Qāḍī ʿAzīzān, *Sīzdah ganj*, MS Tashkent, TsVRUz, no. 2574/IV: fol. 357a.

97 Mīr Rabīʿ b. Mīr Niyāz Khwāja al-Ḥusaynī, *Risāla-yi raḥmānīya*, MS Tashkent, TsVRUz, no. 9060/XII: fol. 406b.

98 TsGARUz, f. I-36, op. 1, d. 2396, l. 92ob.

99 *maʿlūm quḍḍāt-i Islām wa ḥukkām-i dhawī al-iḥtirām būda bāshad ki riwāyat fī al-ḍimn muʿtabar wa maʿmūla ast*, AMIKINUz, untitled collection of Arabic-script documents: collection series no. 441b. This document is not described in Welsford and Tashev, *A Catalogue of Arabic-Script Documents from the Samarqand Museum*. In Khorezm, such an endorsement would be formulated as *riwāyat-i muʿallama huwa al-saḥīḥ*, TsGARUz f. I-125, op. 1, d. 495: passim.

than strictly juristic: the latter could be simply the social conditions, the moral concerns, and the personal motivations of the individual who applied for a fatwa; the mufti might also have found himself under coercion or simply in a position in which he could not evade the pressure of a given inquirer. A jurist might thus deliver an answer on a disputed matter of doctrine while trying to persuade his readers about a partisan view on that doctrinal issue.

4.1 *Case One:* Riwāyats *and Familial Hatred*

I now want to attempt to reason like the jurists who reviewed for the *qāḍīs* the fatwas that litigants brought to court. The purpose of this exercise is to explain the principles according to which muftis would deem a *riwāyat* unsuitable, even though other jurists had stamped their seals on it and written positive fatwas (Pers. *bāshad*).

Mullā ʿAbd al-Raḥmān b. Mullā ʿAẓīm, known in Samarqand as the Ṣūfī, died in May 1898, leaving a considerable inheritance, which was divided among his widows Bībī Rabīʿa Āy and Bībī Mu'mina, three sons (ʿAbd al-Qayyūm, Mullā ʿAbd al-Wāḥid, and ʿAbd al-Hāshim), and six daughters (Ḥikāyat, Khadīja, Marḍīya, Maghfirat, Maʿrifat, and Istam Āy).[100] It appears that in dividing the estate of Mullā ʿAbd al-Raḥmān, his eldest son ʿAbd al-Wāḥid took an advantageous position. Sometime in 1905, Maʿrifat Āy and Istam Āy sued Mullā ʿAbd al-Wāḥid for the restitution of their shares of inheritance consisting of a house with a courtyard. They did so, as we shall read in the judicial ruling, by granting a man their power of attorney and asking him to apply to a native court and make sure that the claim be recorded in a protocol. This document reflects the women's attempt to safeguard their rights from usurpation by their brother. Mullā ʿAbd al-Wāḥid responded with a counterclaim.[101] He argued that the claim made against him by the attorney for a share of his late father's estate was null and should not be heard (*bāṭil wa ghayr-i masmūʿ*). Mullā ʿAbd al-Wāḥid objected that his sisters had already taken possession (*qabḍ kard*) of half of the courtyard house; he also argued that, as far as the remaining estate was concerned, they had received (*akhdh*) a sum of 250 *tanga*s and consequently discharged him from any obligations regarding the inheritance. The jurist (or the jurist's scribe) who assisted Mullā ʿAbd al-Wāḥid employed a set of established formulae to articulate his intentions in the language of a counterclaim. The jurist affirmed that the contract by means of which Mullā ʿAbd al-Wāḥid had been relieved of his obligation, was explained to the claimants, who accepted it. Nevertheless, according to the counterclaim, Maʿrifat Āy and

---

100 Welsford and Tashev, *A Catalogue of Arabic-Script Documents from the Samarqand Museum*: doc. 548.

101 Ibid.: doc. 554.

Istam Āy took legal action against Mullā ʿAbd al-Wāḥid. They did so illegitimately (*ba-ghayr-i ḥaqq*) and should waive the claim, but they stubbornly held their position. The jurist requested formally that the *qāḍī* proceed accordingly and convince the claimants to withdraw their claim. Mullā Sayyid ʿAbd al-Majīd, the mufti who attached his seal to this protocol of counterclaim, added in the right-hand margin of this document a quotation from an important juristic reference of Hanafi doctrine, the *Kitāb al-ashbāh wa al-naẓāʾir ʿalā madhhab Abī Ḥanīfa al-Nuʿmān* by the famous Ottoman scholar Zayn al-Dīn b. Ibrāhīm b. Muḥammad b. Nujaym al-Miṣrī (1519–63). The quotation reads, *lā tusmaʿu al-daʿwā baʿd al-ibrā al-ʿāmm*, "a claim ought not to be heard after a complete waiver." This quotation will appear again in the documentation arising from the legal case.

The lawsuit lodged by the two women made its way to a "native court" in Samarqand. We have available a copy of the ruling that the *qāḍī* recorded in his ledger. The ruling opens by introducing the parties to the dispute and identifying (*taʿrīf*) their attorneys: it appears that the sisters had at their side one brother (ʿAbd al-Hāshim) and their mother, Bībī Muʾmīna, who had, in the meantime, expressed their own grievances against ʿAbd al-Wāḥid and set forth their own claims on the inheritance. The *qāḍī* diligently described the elements of the estate—a house with a courtyard, garden land, and cash and formulated the plaintiffs' demand as follows: "ʿAbd al-Wāḥid has been enjoying the usufruct of the entire estate and now refuses to provide his fellow heirs with their shares." As the judge questioned the defendant, the latter responded that "he had already given all that is due to them." The *qāḍī* reproduced at length the declarations made by the respondent. We read that ʿAbd al-Wāḥid stated that the property that previously belonged to his father was now a possession he himself had acquired (*ūz zar-kharīd mulkim dūr*), by virtue of a transaction notarized in a set of deeds, for which he provided all the information relating to their registration. He admitted, however, that ʿAbd al-Hāshim Bāy did have some rights to the garden land (*ḥaqqī bāghgha bār*) and confirmed that both Istam Āy and Maʿrifat Āy had the right to claim half of the garden land and a portion of courtyard house. Notwithstanding these latter admissions, ʿAbd al-Wāḥid refused (*munkir būldī*) the demand of the plaintiffs, who wished to enjoy a larger share of the estate. He declared that he had already handed over 250 *tangas* to the two women for their rights to the garden land and other properties. He held that their waiver was to their satisfaction. The report of the judicial hearing then took a significant turn: once the parties had been heard, the *qāḍī* appears to have left center stage in the trial, leaving the courtroom to the jurists. The parties are said to have referred (*rujūʿ*) directly to some jurists (*ʿulamāʾ*), probably outside of the court, and subsequently to have produced quotations from juristic authorities (*riwāyat*) to prove that their declarations were valid. The jurists in court were then requested to weigh the two contending positions. They preferred the arguments produced by the two sisters.[102] According to the judicial ruling, the jurists found that ʿAbd al-Wāḥid's statement about his sisters' waiver should be considered void and null[103] and that the rights to the inheritance had been recorded in deeds and that the latter should be used as the main basis on which to proceed with the claim. The jurists thought it necessary (*lāzim*) not to confer authority on ʿAbd al-Wāḥid's answer because of its pernicious nature (*fāsidligī*) and to rule (*ḥukm qīlsa kirāk*), instead, that he should hand over to the plaintiffs their due shares. The preference of the jurists (*tarjīḥ-i ʿulamā yūzasīdan*) proved instrumental in leading the *qāḍī* to reach his decision. In the final section of the ruling, he returned to the scene and ordered that the shares of Istam Āy and Maʿrifat Āy be taken from Hāshim Bāy's property—that is, from half of the courtyard and the garden—and be handed over to them.

I infer from this deferred rendering of the proceedings that the *qāḍī* must have had serious reasons to endow the muftis in court with powers to decide the case. When he accounted for the jurists' work, however, the judge overlooked much of what had happened in the courtroom. We do not know, for example, what had really puzzled him. He was certainly facing a case of alleged usurpation of inheritance complicated by a counterclaim, but we cannot say precisely what procedural issue confused him. There is no indication in the judicial report that it had been suggested that the parties access the services of the jurists in the city of Samarqand before the trial occurred and ask to appear before the judge with "quotations [from juristic authorities]" in hand.

Also omitted from the report is the entire process of weighing the arguments of the disputing parties, a task that fell to the muftis in court. It is thus by reading the documents that the parties produced in court that we can hope to reconstruct, albeit partially, the reasoning of the jurists and the making of their legal opinions. We should recapitulate how *riwāyat*s were written. Parties turned to a mufti's scribe (*muḥarrir*) with their own account of their dispute. The scribe would proceed as a modern lawyer would, translating that account into a legal case and emphasizing a point of law related to the case. In this way, he would support the position of his client and dismantle the legal edifice of

102 *muddaʿī wa muddaʿā ʿalayhi ʿulamāgha rujūʿ qīlīb sūzlārīnī rāstlīgīgha riwāyat ālīb kūrsātdīlār ki īkkī ṭarafnī riwāyatlārīnī tarjīḥgha buyūrganda ʿulamālār muddaʿīnī riwāyatīnī tarjīḥ qīldīlār*, ibid.: doc. 557.

103 *muddaʿā ʿalayhi nī aytgān jawābī iqrār wa ibrā-i aʿyān-dan dūr wa ibrāʾ ʿiyān nīrsa-dan bāṭil wa bīkār-dūr*, ibid.

his client's opponent. To achieve this, the scribe would examine a given point of law by formulating a legal question (*istiftā'*) in such a way as to answer in favor of the party who requested the legal opinion. In other words, he would formulate a rhetorical question.

Such a rhetorical question occupied the main body of the document. The quotations from juristic references were written in the margins of the document. As they provided justification for the view implicitly embedded in the question, such quotations should be suited to answering (positively) the question in the main body of the text. The party who requested the service of the scribe received a *riwāyat*, that is, a question-and-quotations text. The litigant would show the *riwāyat* to a mufti and ask that the latter endorse it. The mufti would weigh the correlation between the quotations and the case in hand. If he found that they were correlated, he would attach his seal and deliver his fatwa by writing "let it be so, and God knows best" (*bāshad wallahu a'lam*). In this way he would endorse the position of the litigant who requested the fatwa. Otherwise, he would not attach his seal and would write nothing.

Istam Āy and Ma'rifat Āy submitted to the court the following fatwa:[104]

[Question:] We invoke blessing in the name of the supreme Lord. What do the imams of Islam—may be God pleased with them all—have to say on the following question. The matter is as follows: according to *sharī'a*, to make a counterclaim was the right of the counterclaimant; waiving a claim was the right of those who made it, and that was sound. [However,] the counterclaimant does

[1] "[one has] the right to solicit [the oath] and to remain silent if satisfied", *Qā'idīya*.[105]

[2] "[the defendant] should not be required to swear an oath if this is not requested; this applies to both the parties and was also [the opinion of Abū Hanīfa and Imām Muḥammad] Abū Yūsuf", *Jāmi' al-Rumūz*.[106]

---

104 Ibid.: doc. 555.

105 Unidentified work.

106 Otherwise known in Central Asia as *Sharḥ-i nuqāya*, a work by Shams al-Dīn Muḥammad b. Ḥusām al-Dīn al-Quhistānī (d. 1554), which is a commentary on the *al-Nuqāya* (or *Mukhtasar al-wiqāya fī masā'il al-Hidāya*) of 'Ubaydallāh b. Mas'ūd Ṣadr al-Maḥbūbī

not wish that the *qāḍī* require an oath of the two plaintiffs, Maʿrifat Āy and Istam Āy. If [the judge] repeatedly makes the counterclaimant, Mullā ʿAbd al-Wāhid, swear an oath with regard to the issue at stake and the latter refuses to swear and [the *qāḍī*] rules in favor of the plaintiffs, [the *qāḍī*] should be rewarded; isn't that so? Explain, and then you will be rewarded.

[3] "the advantage of swearing an oath is to show the truth [that is hidden] when one refuses to take an oath; to refuse to take an oath is [equivalent to] making an acknowledgement", *Sharḥ-i Durar al-Biḥār*.[107]

[Answer]. Yes, let it be so.

We surmise from this text that evidence must have been the controversial issue during the hearing. This is probably what prompted the judge to cede the initiative to the muftis. Who had to produce evidence? This was the procedural issue on which the parties disagreed. Mullā ʿAbd al-Wāhid responded to his sisters' lawsuit with a counterclaim. He therefore received precedence, and the judge consequently asked him to produce proof that would support his counterclaim, but Mullā ʿAbd al-Wāhid failed to do so. He had no testimony of witnesses nor any documentation. The *qāḍī* then requested the sisters to swear an oath,[108] but Mullā ʿAbd al-Wāhid disagreed with this categorically. At this point, the *qāḍī* had no choice but to turn again to Mullā ʿAbd al-Wāhid and ask him to swear an oath, but the latter refused this solution also. The fatwa produced in court by the two women reminded the *qāḍī* that refusing to take an oath (*nukūl*) is the same as making an admission and that he would do well to rule against Mullā ʿAbd al-Wāhid.

We now come to the legal opinion of Mullā ʿAbd al-Wāhid. Here is the full text:

---

al-Sharīʿa al-Thānī (d. 1346), see Idrisov, Muminov, and Szuppe, *Manuscrits en écriture arabe du Musée regional de Nukus (République autonome du Karakalpakstan, Ouzbékistan). Fonds arabe, persan, turkī et karakalpak*: 95. The *al-Nuqāya* is a commentary on the *Wiqāyat al-riwāya*, a summary of the *al-Hidāya*, by Maḥmūd b. Aḥmad al-Mahbūbī Ṣadr al-Sharīʿa al-Awwal (d. 1274). See also *GAL* SI: 378 (647–48).

107 "A work by Shams al-Dīn Yūsuf al-Qūnawī (1315–86)", Welsford and Tashev, *A Catalogue of Arabic-Script Documents from the Samarqand Museum*: doc. 552b.

108 This procedure is described clearly in L. Rosen, *The Anthropology of Justice: Law as Culture in Islamic Society* (Cambridge: Cambridge University Press, 1989): 32–4.

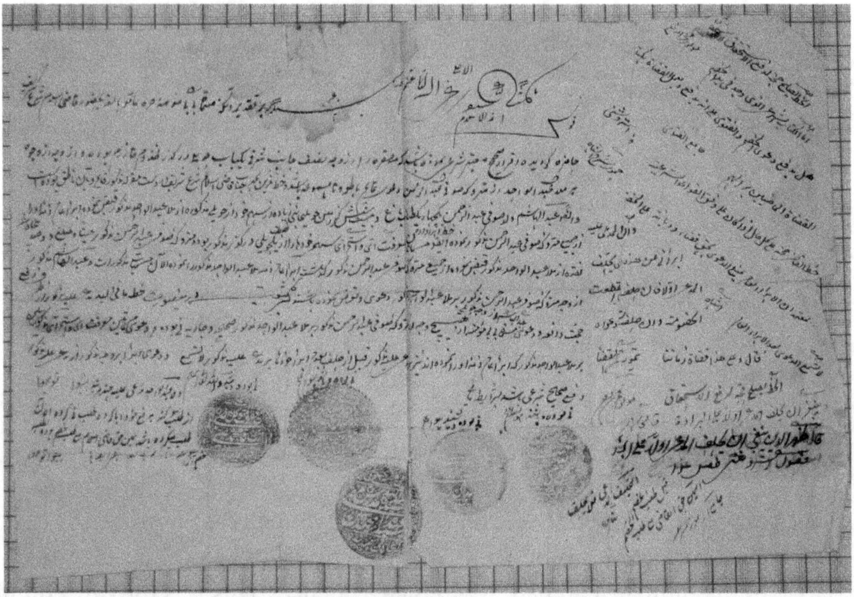

FIGURE 18 *Mullā ʿAbd al-Wāhid's fatwa, 1902–03.*
COURTESY OF THOMAS WELSFORD

[Question:] We invoke blessing in the name of the supreme Lord. What do the imams of Islam—may be God pleased with them all—have to say on the following question. The matter is as follows:

[a] Bībī Mu'mina had appeared before the *sharīʿa* court and made a sound, trustworthy, and legal acknowledgment that her previous claim against Mullā ʿAbd al-Wāḥid for one-half of

[1] "A certificate of settlement [serves] as evidence in case of recovery of property", *Mawlawī Fakhr al-Dīn.*[109]

[2] "Can a legal certificate that is at the disposal of the disputant [be sufficient] to deny or counterclaim a claim? Yes, a legal opinion [can be used] in a counterclaim, and the judges can apply the certificates issued by previous judges", *Jāmiʿ al-fatāwā.*[110]

109 "A work by Mawlawī Fakhr al-Dīn Maḥmūd b. Ilyās al-Rūmī (15th century), composed in 851/1447 as a commentary on the *Mukhtaṣar al-Wiqāyah*", Welsford and Tashev, *A Catalogue of Arabic-Script Documents from the Samarqand Museum*: doc. 452b.

110 See Chapter 2 fn. 63.

one courtyard house (from the eastern side) situated in the Makhdhūm Khwārazm quarter, which relates to the estate of Ṣūfī ʿAbd al-Raḥman, should be voided and should not be heard [*bāṭila wa nā-masmūʿa bāshad*]. The document stamped by a *qāḍī* is in the possession of the beneficiary, and he referred to the court about that.

[b] ʿAbd al-Ḥāshim, son of Ṣūfī ʿAbd al-Raḥman, had received from Mullā ʿAbd al-Wāḥid one-quarter of one *ṭanāb* of a garden and 26 *gaz* of the courtyard, which is a larger share of the aforementioned courtyard. He [ʿAbd al-Ḥāshim] completely relieved the latter [Mullā ʿAbd al-Wāḥid] of his obligations [*ibrāʾ-i ʿāmm*] with regard to the whole of the estate of Ṣūfī ʿAbd al-Raḥman; the document of relief of obligations has been produced [to the court];

[c] Maʿrifat Āy and Istam Āy had received their share of the aforementioned courtyard, together with 250 *tangas* from Mullā ʿAbd al-Wāḥid.

[3] "The certificate produced by the judge [can be applied] in all the situations, if it is in accord with the rules of the law", *Fuṣūl-i Ustrūshanī*.[111]

[4] "And the reliable [view is] that the person who waived his claim cannot make that claim anew. This claim should be upheld by the judge and relies on the integrity of the jurist", *Hamawī sharḥ-i Ashbāh*.[112]

[5] "A claim ought not to be heard after a complete waiver" (*Ashbāh*);[113]

[6] "And if the defendant says that [the claimant] has already waived the claim completely, it is the claimant who first swears, for he swears the dispute is solved; and this is what the judges of this era [should apply]", *Tīmūrtāshī*.[114]

[7] "A certificate of settlement [serves] as evidence in cases of the recovery of property", *Mawlawī Fakhr al-Dīn*.

111 *Fuṣūl al-Ustrūshanī* (or *Kitāb al-fuṣūl fī muʿādalat*), a work by Muḥammad b. Maḥmūd b. al-Ḥusayn b. Aḥmad al-Ustrūshanī (d. 1234); see *GAL* S1: 380 (653).

112 "[Otherwise know as *Ḥamawī sharḥ-i Ashbāh* or *Ghamz ʿuyūn al-baṣāʾir*]: a work by Shahāb al-Dīn Abū l-ʿAbbās Aḥmad b. Muḥammad Makkī al-Ḥusaynī al-Ḥamawī (d. 1098/1687). This is a commentary on the *al-Ashbāh wa-l-Naẓāʾir* by Ibn Nujaym al-Miṣrī (1519–63)", Welsford and Tashev, *A Catalogue of Arabic-Script Documents from the Samarqand Museum*: doc. 106.

113 *Kitāb al-ashbāh wa al-naẓāʾir ʿalá madhhab Abī Ḥanīfa al-Nuʿmān*, a work completed in 1561 by the famous Ottoman scholar Zayn al-Dīn b. Ibrāhīm b. Muḥammad b. Nujaym al-Miṣrī al-Ḥanafī (d. 1563). See *GAL* SII: 311 (425).

114 See fn. 37.

They [consequently] relieved Mullā ʿAbd al-Wāḥid of his obligation with regard to the whole of the estate of Ṣūfī ʿAbd al-Raḥman.

Now Maʿrifat Āy, Istam Āy, and ʿAbd al-Ḥāshim claim the [restitution of the] estate against Mullā ʿAbd al-Wāḥid. According to *sharīʿa*, the document in possession of the defendant in this case constitutes evidence for a counterclaim;[115] the claim of ʿAbd al-Ḥāshim for the courtyard and the one of Muʾmina Bībī for the inheritance against Mullā ʿAbd al-Wāḥid were not sound nor in force [*ṣaḥīḥ wa jāriya nay būda*]; Maʿrifat Āy and Istam Āy had already relieved Mullā ʿAbd al-Wāḥid completely of his obligation. [Therefore], in the absence of the certification of disavowal, the claim against the defendant ought not to be heard at all before one swears an oath;[118] the defendant's claim that a relief of obligation regarding the aforementioned matters [has already occurred] should be [considered] a valid and legal counterclaim.[119] Isn't that so?

[Answer:] Yes, [the claim] was not [sound].

[8] "In case of [a previous] relinquishment, it is up to the claimant to be the first to swear an oath", [*Fatāwā*] *Qāḍī Khān*.

[9] "Ẓuhr al-Dīn says: 'In case of [a previous] relinquishment, it is the claimant who should first swear an oath'", *Fuṣūl-i Ustrūshanī*.

[10] "To swear an oath is the right of the claimant; one should not swear before the individual who initiates the dispute", *Nihāya*.[116]

[11] "[To order someone to swear] an oath is the right of the judge and of the individual who initiates the dispute", *Jāmiʿ al-Rumūz*.[117]

---

115 *khaṭṭ mā fī al-yad-i muddaʿā ʿalayhi-i madhkūr az ṭaraf-i dafʿ ḥujjat-i dāfiʿ*, Welsford and Tashev, *A Catalogue of Arabic-Script Documents from the Samarqand Museum*: doc. 552.

116 *al-Nihāya*, a commentary on al-Marghīnānī's *Hidāya* by Ḥusām al-Dīn Ḥusayn b. ʿAlī al-Ṣighnāqī (d. 1310). See GAL SI: 644.

117 See fn. 106.

118 *daʿwā* [...] *qabl az ḥalf ba-ʿadam-i ibrāʾ-i khwudhā bar muddaʿā ʿalayhi-i madhkūr lā tusmaʿu.*

119 *daʿwā-yi ibrāʾ bar wajh-i madhkūr az muddaʿā ʿalayhi-i madhkūr dafʿ-i ṣaḥīḥ-i sharʿī bāshad.*

[Question] Mullā ʿAbd al-Wāḥid the defendant repeatedly refused to ask [the plaintiffs] to swear an oath with regard to his counterclaim; now he wishes to do so. [Requiring] the exculpatory oath is the right of both the *qāḍī* and the individual who instigates the dispute; the latter [the counterclaimant] can ask them [the plaintiffs] to swear. Isn't it so? Explain, and then you will be rewarded.

[Answer:] [Missing from the text][120]

This fatwa differs substantially from that produced by Maʿrifat Āy and Istam Āy. First, it includes two questions. Only the first question, however, received an answer, and it is only this one that is interesting for our purposes. The second question was reformulated and answered positively on the verso of the document.[121] The question was not reviewed by the muftis in court, so we need not discuss it.

The first question consists of two parts. The first part provides three premises against the three lawsuits lodged against Mullā ʿAbd al-Wāhid. It holds that the widow Mu'mīna Bībī already declared that her previous claim was void, because she had received a payment from Mullā ʿAbd al-Wāhid. That was also the case with ʿAbd al-Hāshim, the brother of the defendant. He too had already disavowed any claim to said property in consideration for a larger share of the estate. The legal opinion, however, asserts also that the sisters Maʿrifat Āy and Istam Āy were in the same position as the other claimants because they had relieved Mullā ʿAbd al-Wāhid of his obligations regarding their shares of the estate in exchange of a sum of money. The second part of the legal question can be summarized as follows: if a litigant is unable to provide evidence of a waiver, is it licit for him to make a counterclaim based on that waiver?

---

120 Welsford and Tashev, *A Catalogue of Arabic-Script Documents from the Samarqand Museum*: doc. 553a.

121 Ibid.: doc. 553b: "At request of the counterclaimant, it has been ruled that the onus of oath falls on the two claimants, Maʿrifat Āy and Istam Āy; if the *qāḍī* puts the two claimants under oath with regard to the counterclaim of the defendant and the latter refuses to swear the oath and he rules to postpone the oath-taking, [this decision] should not be considered an impediment to the aforementioned counterclaim; isn't it so? [Explain, then you will be rewarded]." [Answer]. Yes, it should not be [an impediment]."

The scribe who compiled the fatwa, however, did not opt for such a forthright formulation. He first wrote an affirmative sentence: "the defendant's claim [...] should be [viewed] as a valid and legal counterclaim." The question comes only after this assertion, as the question tag "isn't that so?" (*yā nay?*). It was a rhetorical question that favored the view that the counterclaim of Mullā ʿAbd al-Wāhid was sound. The scribe proceeded in this way, even though he knew that the defendant had failed to provide evidence to support his counterclaim (*ba-ʿadam-i ibrāʾ*). Had this fatwa persuaded the court, the claim against Mullā ʿAbd al-Wāhid would not have been heard. The scribe must have been fully aware of the purely rhetorical aspects of the text he was composing. If his text had any chance to persuade the court, it did not reside in the quotations from the juristic authorities he provided, of which only some supported the opinion that he was suggesting (1–7): they stated that, if a discharge of obligation has been granted, the defendant should not be asked to swear an oath, and they asserted that reconciliation is evidence for a counterclaim against the recovery of property. Other quotations (8–11) were clearly added later, as they referred to the second question. But there are no quotations that suggest that a counterclaim based on a previous waiver does not require documentation of that waiver to be considered sound. Instead, the jurist translated from Arabic into Persian a quotation from a famous Ottoman juristic work, the very same quotation that was included in Mullā ʿAbd al-Wāhid's protocol of claim. However, the scribe reworked the meaning of the original. The quotation written in the margin of the document reads: *lā tusmaʿu al-daʿwā baʿd al-ibrā al-ʿāmm*, "a claim ought not to be heard after a complete waiver." The Persian version of this quotation in the body of the document becomes: *daʿwā... ki ibrāʾ-i ʿāmm ... namūdand... ba-ʿadam-i ibrā... lā tusmaʿu*, "after a waiver, in default of the latter, a claim is not to be heard." This glaring misconstrual notwithstanding, five Samarqandi muftis stamped the *riwāyat* with their seals and endorsed it with a positive answer (*bāshad*). While such endorsements could be bought, the fatwa did not pass the court's test. The jurists who examined the legal opinion could not overlook its deceptive argumentation and therefore ruled that the line of argumentation was defective and suggested to the *qāḍī* that he rule in favor of the sisters. Had it not been for the judicial ruling that the *qāḍī* copied in his ledger, we would have found it very difficult to see that something had gone wrong with the fatwa.

5 Opinions for Russians

What we have so far established is that fatwas were the product of the interaction of two social groups, muftis (and their scribes) and their Muslim clients.

The latter comprised various social groups, including the ruling Muslim dynasty. The establishment of Russian power in Central Asia added a new layer of complexity to such interactions. Colonial officials often turned to local jurists and requested that they provide their opinion on a specific point of law. Russians usually did so while reviewing Muslims' appeals to the colonial administration, which shed light on cases of alleged legal malpractice. The Russians' main objective in requesting this service from the muftis was to clarify what *sharīʿa* prescribed on a certain legal matter. They thus seem to have disregarded the possibility that legal hermeneutics favor a plurality of nonbinding opinions. Russians often asked the assembly of judicial assessors (*s"ezd kaziev*) to deliver an expert opinion (*zakliuchenie/raz"iasnenie*) on a given subject, which they would regard as conclusive and treat as unalterable evidence against which to measure someone's conduct. In this way, Russians were creating their own knowledge of Islamic law in order to cope with the absence of a *sharīʿa* code of law. Whether this was an attempt to crystallize certain notions of *sharīʿa* and commit to the creation of an "Orthodox Islam" is difficult to say. Russians despised the fact that there was little predictability in the hermeneutic activity of the muftis and used the appellate mechanisms to hammer this home. Russians did not systematize the legal opinions they collected from muftis into a comprehensive body of knowledge that could eventually be used by colonial officials and assessors to review the proceedings of native courts. While muftis delivered a legal opinion at the request of, say, a city commandant or a prosecutor, the Russians need not have relied on that same legal opinion to rule on a different legal case, though it involved the same point of law. Colonial knowledge was fragmented, so there were unintended consequences arising from colonial fatwas. Russians pushed local jurists forcefully to deliver opinions in a new way, which obliged muftis to articulate conclusively their views on certain points of law and thus deviate considerably from the established practices of Central Asian fatwas. To illustrate this, I shall turn to a case of disputed inheritance.

5.1 *Case Study: Ḥāmida Bībī vs. Muhyī al-Dīn Khwāja*

In the autumn of 1890, in Tashkent, a certain Muḥammad Riḍā Bāy died, leaving two widows, Ḥāmida Bībī and Nāẓira Bībī. The latter had given him two children, a girl and a boy, Anzirat Bībī and the mentally disabled Hāshīm Jān. They were both underage when Muḥammad Riḍā Bāy died. The deceased also had an older brother, Ḥākim Jān. On 3 January 1891, Ḥāmida Bībī informed the Russian authorities that something had gone wrong in the division of her deceased husband's inheritance.[122] The man's estate had undergone public

122 03.01.1891, TsGARUz, f. I-17, op. 1, d. 4784, ll. 17–17ob.

appraisal. Muḥyī al-Din Khwāja, a *qāḍī* with whom the reader is now familiar, had, along with other witnesses, described during a public meeting his possessions and his credits in an inventory. It appears that there was little cash available, because Muḥammad Riḍā Bāy had given out most of his wealth in loans.[123] The deceased left no will, so the *qāḍī* decided to divide everything, loans included, among his heirs. He charged a notarial fee (*taqsīmāna*) of 1,200 rubles for his services and one of 95 rubles for the muftis. Ḥāmida Bībī argued that this violated Islamic law.[124] She also complained that Ḥākim Jān, the older brother of Muḥammad Riḍā Bāy, had sued all the heirs and subsequently received 8,600 rubles in exchange for a waiver. She blamed Muḥyī al-Din Khwāja for this, too. Ḥāmida Bībī appealed to the Russians to express her dissatisfaction (*nārāḍīlīk*) with the conduct of the *qāḍī* and asked that the truth be ascertained.

Ḥāmīda Bībī could not write the appeal herself, because she was illiterate,[125] but she was assisted by someone who understood her interests very well. First, the appellant did not confine herself to asking the commandant to ascertain the truth about the case. She also dared to suggest that he do so by relying on the testimony of four individuals. She named four men who had acted as witnesses during the hearing on the division of the inheritance.[126] She seems to have known that, should they be summoned before a court of appeals, these men would side with her. Second, the style of the appeal says much about the reason for its crafting. The prime concern of its author was the meager sum of cash that was divided among the heirs. She presumably hoped that the creditors would pay what was due to the departed, that the *qāḍī* would get less, and that the brother of the deceased should not receive payment in exchange for a waiver. By appealing the division, she hoped that the judicial assembly might divide the estate differently. In other words, Ḥāmīda Bībī hoped with this appeal to increase her share of inheritance.

The appeal reached Nil Sergeevich Lykoshin, one of the finest Orientalists in the service of the Russian Empire in Turkestan, whom the district chancellery

123 *īrim-dān qālgān har kīmnī dhimmasīgā māl wa pullārnī rūy-khaṭṭ qīlīb qūydī rūy-khaṭṭ qīlghān waqtda kūb naqd pul chiqmadī hammasī wīksil thubūt bīla har kimnī dhimmasīda īkān madhkūr adamlār dhimmasīdagī nisbat pullārnī warathalārgha taqsīm qīlīb*, ibid.: l. 17.

124 *ʿulamāʾlārdān sūrāsām būl ṭarīqa ālmāq taqsīmāna hīch sharīʿatda yūq dīb maʿlūm qīldīlār*, ibid.

125 *khaṭṭ bīlmagān ūchūn*, TsGARUz, f. I-17, op. 1, d. 4784, l. 17ob.

126 Cf. ibid. to TsGARUz, f. I-17, op. 1, d. 4784, l. 41ob.

held accountable for the Muslim-majority part of the city of Tashkent.[127] As prescribed in the statutory laws, Lykoshin transferred the appeal to the assembly of judicial assessors. Interestingly, he also asked the native court of appeals to review Muḥyī al-Dīn Khwāja's conduct according to Islamic law (*sleduet obsudit' spravedlivost' po shariatu*). He also requested a specific report on the amount of money that a native judge was entitled to ask as a fee for the notarization of a division of inheritance. Such a report, said Lykoshin, should include references to Islamic law books (*so ssylkami na knigi shariata*).[128] The *qāḍīs*' answer was prompt.[129] They ruled that Muḥyī al-Dīn Khwāja should not have counted the debts still owed to the deceased when he calculated the latter's inheritance and that he applied a fee higher than what was usually considered fair according to Islamic law (*bol'she opredelënnogo shariata*). This answer left Lykoshin dissatisfied: it was too superficial.[130] He requested a new legal opinion with detailed juristic references. Following is the way the assembly of judicial assessors complied with the task, a fine example of what we may term a "fatwa for the Russians":[131]

> Five sources say that, if the substance of the inheritance is absent, that is, if the cash constitutes somebody's obligations or, in case of landed possessions, the latter are located in another dominion, it is not right to perform a division and levy a fee: the book of Mullā Shams Muḥammad; *Fatāwā-yi Ḥāmidīya*;[132] *Bahr al-Manāfi'*;[133] *Tātārkhānī*;[134]

127 See A. Morrison, "Sufism, Pan-Islamism and Information Panic: Nil Sergeevich Lykoshin and the Aftermath of the Andijan Uprising." *PP* 214 (2012): 262–64.

128 04.01.1891, TsGARUz, f. I-17, op. 1, d. 4784, l. 18.

129 09.01.1891, ibid.: l. 19.

130 Lykoshin on behalf of the city commandant, 17.01.1891, ibid.: ll. 25–26.

131 08.02.1891, ibid.: l. 22.

132 Ḥamīd 'Alī Ibrāhim 'Abd al-Raḥīm 'Imād al-Dīn al-'Imādī, *Mughnī al-mustaftī 'an su'āl al-muftī (al-Fatāwā al-Ḥamīdīya)*. See M. Mundy and R. Saumarez Smith, *Governing Property, Making the Modern State: Law, Administration and Production in Ottoman Syria* (London: I.B. Tauris, 2007): 290.

133 A work in Arabic and Persian by Niyāz Muḥammad Muftī al-Bukhārī (late eighteenth century); see Welsford and Tashev, *A Catalogue of Arabic-Script Documents from the Samarqand Museum*: doc. 375.

134 *al-Fatāwā al-Tātārkhānīya*, a work by 'Ālim b. 'Alā' al-Dīn al-Ḥanafī, dedicated to Tātār Khān, a regent of Fīrūz Shāh Tughlūq (d. 1388). See *GAL* SII: 432 (643).

ʿĀlamgīrī.[135] Five sources say that a *qāḍī* is entitled to levy one two-hundredth when he performs the division of an estate among the heirs and notarizes such division in legal deeds:[136] *Bahr al-manāfiʿ*;[137] *Khulāṣat al-fatāwā*;[138] *Mukhtār al-ikhtiyār*;[139] *Jawāhir al-fatāwā*;[140] *Khazīnat al-fatāwā*.[141] From time immemorial in our region, [*qāḍīs*] have recourse to established practices (*taʿāmul*). The collections of fatwas that clearly indicate that it is binding on the judges of this region to apply such practices are:[142] *Ashbāh*;[143] *Chalabī*;[144] *Majmaʿ al-aḥkām*;[145] *Ṭaḥāwī*;[146] *Adab al-muftīyīn*;[147] *Tātārkhānī*;[148] *Fuṣūl-i ʿImādī*;[149] *Khulāṣat*;[150] *Kabīrī*;[151] *Birjandī*;[152]

---

135 *al-Fatāwā al-ʿĀlamgīrīya* otherwise known as *al-Fatāwā al-Hindīya*, a work commissioned by the Mughal Emperor Awrangzib ʿĀlamgīr (1659–1707). See *GAL* SII: 417 (604).

136 *naqd wa māllārnī ūlgān ādamnī warathalārīgha taqsīm qīlīb wa qīlghān taqsīmīgha wa qīlghān khaṭṭ-wathīqalārīgha ḥaqq ālmāq tughrīsīdān*, TsGARUz, f. I-17, op. 1, d. 4784, l. 22.

137 See fn. 133.

138 See fn. 38.

139 See Chapter 1 fn. 154.

140 A collection of fatwas compiled by Muḥammad b. ʿAbd al-Rashīd b. Naṣr b. Muḥammad b. Ibrāhīm b. Isḥāq Abū Bakr Rukn al-Dīn al-Kirmānī (twelfth century), see *GAL* SI: 374 (641). See also Welsford and Tashev, *A Catalogue of Arabic-Script Documents from the Samarqand Museum*: doc. 459.

141 Unidentified work.

142 *har wilāytnī taʿāmulīgha ʿamal qīlmāq ūshal wilāyatnī qāḍīsīgha lāzim dūr*, TsGARUz, f. I-17, op. 1, d. 4784, l. 22.

143 See fn. 113.

144 Unidentified work.

145 Unidentified work.

146 Probably *Mukhtaṣar al-Ṭaḥāwī*, a work by Abū Jaʿfar Aḥmad b. Muḥammad b. Salāma al-Ḥajrī al-Ṭaḥāwī (d. 933), see *GAL* SI: 173 (293).

147 Unidentified work. See T. Welsford and N. Tashev, *A Catalogue of Arabic-Script Documents from the Samarqand Museum*: doc. 668.

148 See fn. 134.

149 See Chapter 2 fn. 62.

150 See fn. 38.

151 Unidentified work.

152 Unidentified work, most probably a commentary (*sharḥ*) on the *Mukhtaṣar al-wiqāya fī masāʾil al-Hidāya* (*al-Nuqāya*, see fn. 15) a work by the Ottoman polymath ʿAbd al-ʿAlī b. Muḥammad al-Ḥusayn al-Birjandī (d. 1525), see A. Ėrkinov, N. Polvonov, and H. Aminov, *Muhammad Rahimkhon II Feruz Kutubkhonasi Fehristi* (*Khorazmda kitobat va kutubkhonachilik tarikhidan*) (Tashkent: Yangi Asr Avlodi, 2008): 22, 208. Excerpts of a legal work by Birjandī are also mentioned by Idrisov, Muminov, and Szuppe, *Manuscrits en écriture arabe du Musée regional de Nukus* (*République autonome du Karakalpakstan, Ouzbékistan*). *Fonds arabe, persan, turkī et karakalpak*: 82.

> *Zubdat al-Uṣūl;*[153] *Dhakhīra;*[154] *Ṣadr al-Shahīd.*[155] It is not right to put into effect an opinion that deviates from these books.[156] Before us, previous judicial assemblies have followed the practice as indicated by these books and issued regulations for the royal [tsarist] chancellery.[157]

Now that the colonial agencies in Tashkent had finally secured a few clear juristic guidelines to assess the behavior of Muḥyī al-Dīn Khwāja, the Tashkent city commandant could ask Muḥyī al-Dīn Khwāja himself to explain the fees he had charged. As Lykoshin had done before him, the commandant asked Muḥyī al-Dīn Khwāja to base his explanation on references to the books of *sharīʿa* (*podkrepiv svoi ob'iasneniia so ssylkami na podlezhashchie knigi shariata*). Understandably, the commandant wanted to find out whether Muḥyī al-Dīn Khwāja's conduct deviated from the regulations suggested by the judicial assessors. I quote here the report (*bayān-nāma*) on the case of Muḥyī al-Dīn Khwāja:[158]

> All five heirs attended the division of the inheritance: his mother [i.e., of the deceased], ʿĀliya Bībī, daughter of Nādir Muḥammad; his wife, Nāẓira Bībī, daughter of Sarīmsāq Bāy; his second wife, Ḥāmida Bībī, daughter of Mū'min Jānbāy; one underage boy, Mīr Hāshim Bāy; one underage daughter, Anzirat Bībī. The underage children and their mother consulted each other and agreed to appoint a merchant, Mullā Sayyid Aḥmad Bāy, son of Mīr Fayḍ Bāy, as guardian [*waṣī*]. I performed the division in the presence of many impartial individuals [*kūb khāliṣ ādamlār ḥuḍūrīda*] and discussed with them what decision would be most advantageous for the underaged. The heirs were satisfied with the terms of the division. They accepted it and signed the documents [I presented to them]. I performed the division according to Islamic law [*sharīʿatgā muwāfiq*], as

153 Unidentified work.

154 See fn. 45.

155 The text probably refers here to the famous *al-Muḥīṭ al-Burhānī* by Burhān al-Dīn Maḥmūd b. ʿAlī b. al-Ṣadr al-Shahīd (d. 1174), see *GAL* SI: 375 (642).

156 *ūshbū kitāblārnī khilāfīdāgī mas'alagha ʿamal qīlmāghī durust īmās dūr*, TsGARUz, f. I-17, op. 1, d. 4784, l. 22.

157 *ham bīzlārdīn muqaddam īlgārīgī būlūb ūtmīsh ḥurmatlīk siyāz qāḍīlārī ham ūshbū sharīʿat kitāblārīnī masʿalasīgha ʿamal aylāb dastūr al-ʿamal qīlīb maḥkama-yi pādshāhīda yāzīb qūyūbdūrlār*, ibid.

158 26.02.1891, ibid.: ll. 39–40ob.

it is discussed in the following texts: *Fuṣūl-i ʿImādī;*[159] *Radd al-Muḥtār;*[160] *ʿUqūd-i durrīya.*[161] Much of the wealth left by the departed consisted of [obligations that are attested by] deeds of credit and debt. If we proceed with the division only after the completion of their collection, the underage will not be paid.[162] It was therefore suggested that each [heir] should act in his own benefit and have custody of every asset to which he or she is entitled according to the documentation.[163] In the current division, the two underage [children] were entitled to 46,618.36 rubles. There are, at the disposal of the guardian of the minors, 29,706.16 rubles. The mother of the departed ʿĀlīya Bībī received 2,977 rubles, Ḥāmida Bībī 2,100 rubles, Nāẓira Bībī 697 rubles, along with 585 in utensils [*asbāb*]. The older brother [of the deceased], Ḥakīm Jān, son of Tāsh Muḥammad, made claims against the heirs for the undivided [*sharīklīk*] property of 24,600 rubles. The heirs denied the claim. Ḥakīm Jān brought to the court some trustworthy merchants who testified [in support of his rights to] the undivided property. I questioned them, and they testified that the two [brothers] were partners. Therefore, it was ordered that the dispute be resolved with an amicable settlement.[164] Out of 8,949 rubles, the amount of money that was determined by the settlement, the brother received 8,749 in cash and one plot of land valued at 200 rubles. If one considers that the cash available was 45,429.16 rubles, without such a reconciliation he would have received (together with the expenses for the witnesses) 24,600 rubles. This amicable settlement does not deviate from any book illustrating the rules of Islamic law.[165] Beside the cash, the

159 See Chapter 2 fn. 62.

160 *Radd al-muḥtar ʿalā al-durr al-mukhtār*, a work by the famus Ottoman jurist Muḥammad Amīn Ibn ʿĀbidīn (d. 1836). This is a commentary on the *Durr al-mukhtār*, a work by ʿAlāʾ al-Dīn al-Ḥaskafī (d. 1677). H. Gerber, *Islamic Law and Culture, 1600–1840* (Leiden, Boston, Köln: Brill, 1999): 27.

161 *al-ʿUqūd al-durrīya fī tanqīh al-fatāwā al-ḥamīdīya*, Muḥammad Amīn Ibn ʿĀbidīn (d. 1836).

162 *hammasīdīn qālādīgān nimarsanī kūbī ālādīgān bīrādīgān ḥujjat dūr wa har kīm-dīn ālādīgān ḥujjatlār ūnūb tamām būlgān-dan sung taqsīm qīlmak būlgān waqtda wārithlār arāsīdagī ṣaghīrlār ḥaqqī bārī yūq būlūb tamām būlādūr*, TsGARUz, f. 1-17, op. 1, d. 4784, ll. 39–40ob.

163 *ḥujjatlīk nimarsalār har bīrīgā taʿalluq būlsa ūl waqtda har bīrī ūz manfaʿatī ūchūn taraddud qīlīb sar-anjām qīlādūr*, ibid.

164 *ṣulḥ bīla bitmākgā būyūrīldī*, ibid.

165 *būl ṣulḥ sharīʿat ḥukmīnī har bir bayān qīlādūrgān kitābda khilāfī yūq rawshan yūl dūr*, ibid.

> documented property in Tashkent amounted to 3,184 rubles, whereas that in Ura-Tepe amounted to 1,724 rubles, making altogether a sum of 50,922. That property and the money were divided according to *sharīʿa*: a property of 200 rubles was given to the brother Ḥakīm Jān; the rest of what was in Ura-Tepe was given to those who had come from there: ʿĀliya Bībī and Ḥāmida Bībī. What is in Tashkent was given to Nāẓira Bībī and her underage children. The remaining 24,827.80 rubles was certified by bills [*wīksīl* < Russ. *veksel'*] and promissory notes. The documents attesting to the payments, which were pending, were likewise verified and divided among the heirs. The debtors were present in court, [and] they acknowledged according to the documents that they will be paying the guardian of the minors.[166] All the heirs were satisfied, and they signed. Had they found the proceedings not to their satisfaction, they had two weeks to appeal, according to Russian statutory law [*niẓāmgā muwāfiq*]. None of them did. I levied a fee of 1,200 rubles, according to Islamic law.

Muḥyī al-Dīn Khwāja's report has so far provided a detailed account of the division of Muḥammad Riḍā Bāy's inheritance and the transfer of estate to the heirs. He has provided little evidence for the way he proceeded with the fees that he had charged. It is only at this point that the *qāḍī* explained that his conduct was in keeping with Islamic law. He did so by fulfilling the request of the commandant, by disclosing the juristic reasoning behind his choice to charge those fees:

> The most excellent among the jurists [*mujtahids*]—Imām-i Aʿẓam [Abū Ḥanīfa] and the most imitated among the jurists, Yūsuf, may God have mercy upon him and upon all the jurists who hold his words above anyone else's word, such as Abū Naṣr; Abū Laylā; Abū Jaʿfar; ʿUmar; Abū Jaʿfar Kabīr; Abū al-Ḥasan Karḍī; Sarakhsī; Abū Layth Samarqandī; Imām Khwāhar-zāda; Abū Ḥafḍ-i Kabīr Bukhārī, may God have mercy upon them (they are the leaders of our religion)—have explained the rules of *sharīʿa* in such a way that, with regard to the issue of division, there are [three rates:] one-twentieth, one-fortieth, one-half of one percent. However, they prescribed that, for the benefit of the people who have to pay, the one-twentieth rate should be excluded. They also ruled that, for the benefit of the person who is to receive the fee [*taqsīm ḥaqqī*], the rate of one-half of one percent should be excluded. The aforementioned

166 *qarḍdārlār ham ūzlārī ḥāḍir būlūb ḥujjatgā muwāfiq iqrār qīlīb ṣaghīrlārnī waṣīsīgā birmak būldīlār*, ibid.

> [jurists] considered the one-fortieth rate, which is equal to the *zakāt*, and ruled that [such a fee] is to the benefit of both parties. They confirmed this view with the expressions "[this is] the opinion being advocated on it" [*bihi yuftā*], "[this is] the adopted opinion" [*ʿalayhi al-fatwā*] and "this is the selected [opinion]" [*huwa al-mukhtār*]: it is not possible to apply a different opinion when [there is already a fatwa] labeled with such expressions. Not a single *qāḍī, aʿlam,* or mufti can claim the right to do that. And with regard to the view that a fee could be calculated at the one two-hundredth rate, this does not pertain to the division of inheritance and has to do, instead, with the notarization of contracts and other deeds. This is explained in the *Fatāwā-yi ʿAlīya*,[167] in the *Fatāwā-yi Qanawī*,[168] in the book of Fasīḥ al-Dīn, in the *Muḥīṭ*,[169] *Tīmūrtāshī*,[170] *Khulāṣa*,[171] *Jāmiʿ* [*al-fatāwā*],[172] *Bahr al-manāfiʿ*.[173] Some say that it is better for the *qāḍī* not to levy any fee, and some say that it would be better for the judge not to levy anything. This, however, regards the *qāḍī*s who receive for their duties a salary from the treasury, which is enough for themselves and their families. This view is not about prohibition; it simply suggests that it is better not to levy a fee than to levy one. By the way, Article 226 of the statute allows native judges to levy a fee according to Islamic law [*qāḍīlārgā tīgishlī ḥaqqnī sharīʿatgā muwāfiq ālīnādūr*].[174]

Muḥyī al-Dīn Khwāja here disclosed to the Russians how a Muslim jurist should solve the question regarding the fee to apply for the division of inheritance. His approach is situated squarely within the local Hanafi tradition: all his references come from the Hanafi school of law. And the way he determined what legal opinion to follow is in keeping with traditional practices: he looked for an established opinion in works of *furūʿ al-fiqh*. By doing so, he followed a traditional mode of reasoning, which was articulated a century earlier in ʿIbadallāh's *Jāmiʿ al-maʿmūlāt*. There is, however, an unexpected and innovative feature to this text: Muḥyī al-Dīn Khwāja crafted a chain of juristic authorities who endorsed the legal opinion he had extracted from fatwa collections, which he

167 The text here refers to the collection of fatwas by the Ottoman *shaykh al-Islām* ʿAlī Efendi Çatalcali (d. 1692). The work has been printed several times in lithograph.

168 Unidentified work.

169 See fn. 44.

170 See fn. 37.

171 See fn. 38.

172 See Chapter 2 fn. 63.

173 See fn. 133.

174 Art. 226: *narodnye sud'i poluchaiut voznagrazhdenie na osnovanii sushchestvuiushchikh po semu predmetu obychaev.*

here explained to the Russians. He termed such juristic authorities *mujtahids*, a term used of Muslim legal experts who exercised independent juristic reasoning, usually in the pre-Mongol history of *sharīʿa*. He did so to confer additional legal force on his reasoning, but the product is a text that reveals what fatwas usually hide. As we have seen, fatwas provided only references to *furūʿ al-fiqh* works, most of which were written after the thirteenth century. Local scholars thus believed that several questions had already been discussed conclusively by earlier jurists who had reflected directly on the Qurʾān and the Sunna. If one needed to discuss such a question in the nineteenth century, he simply had to follow (*taqlīd*) the preferred view adopted by earlier jurists—hence the local understanding that a mufti was a *muqallid*, a follower of established juristic traditions.[175]

Lykoshin may have appreciated all these details and must have been impressed by Muḥyī al-Dīn Khwāja's willingness to clarify his doings, but the case also involved underaged children and therefore involved issues of guardianship. Russian statutory laws required that such issues fall within the jurisdiction of the *qāḍīs* and be reviewed by judicial assessors.[176] Lykoshin therefore passed the case to the Tashkent *s"ezd kaziev*,[177] who held that Muḥyī al-Dīn Khwāja was wrong. They explained that his decision to divide the inheritance, including debts and promissory notes, was not supported by authoritative legal literature and should thus be considered void.[178] They also noted that the amicable settlement between Hakīm Jān and the other heirs had been reached without a formal registration of the claim, without documents, and without witnesses.[179]

Muḥyī al-Dīn Khwāja must have been informed about the *qāḍīs*' report, because he turned again to the Russian authorities and requested that the

---

175 Mīr Rabīʿ b. Mīr Niyāz Khwāja al-Ḥusaynī, *Risāla-yi raḥmānīya*, MS Tashkent, TsVRUz, no. 9060/XII: fol. 404a.

176 See arts. 252 and 253 in the 1886 statutory laws: *Polozhenie ob upravlenii Turkestanskogo kraia*. In *Materialy po istorii politicheskogo stroia Kazakhstana (so vremeni prisoedineniia Kazakhstana k Rossii do Velikoi Oktiabr'skoi sotsialisticheskoi revoliutsii)*. Vol. 1, ed. M.G. Masevich (Alma-Ata: Izdatel'stvo Akademii Nauk Kazakhskoi SSR, 1960): 372. The articles were left unchanged in the 1901 revision of the laws.

177 Lykoshin on behalf of the Tashkent city commandant to the assembly of *qāḍīs*, 08.03.1891, TsGARUz, f. I-17, op. 1, d. 4784, l. 37.

178 *īn pullārnī yaʿnī ghāyib pullārnī taqsīm qīlīb birgānlārīgha rawshan iqrār qīlīb dūrlār sharīʿatimīzda jamʿī kitāblārīda wa hamma imāmlārnī muqarrar qīlgānlārīgha qarāgānda madhkūr sībzār qāḍīsīnī ūshbū qīlghān taqsīmlārī bi 'l-kullīya bāṭil dūr durust dīgān yūl hich bir kitābda yūq dūr*, 11.03.1891, TsGARUz, f. I-17, op. 1, d. 4784, l. 41.

179 Ibid.

case be transferred to a Russian prosecutor.[180] He questioned the impartiality of the judicial assembly, because, as he claimed, they had already made false accusations against him. Their first correspondence to Lykoshin, he said, illustrated their antagonistic attitude towards him: even if the Russians had only requested that they illustrate what Islamic law applies to the fees charged by *qāḍīs*, they had, in fact, seized the occasion to accuse him of malpractice. He also argued that the transfer of his file to the assembly of judicial assessors occurred according to articles 252 and 253 of the statutory laws, which deal with guardianship, while the case actually involved the division of inheritance. Muḥyī al-Dīn Khwāja also doubted that Ḥāmīda Bībī could have written the appeal that was submitted to the city commandant under her name. He suggested that the appeal had been crafted by individuals concocting stratagems in order to harm him (*zhelaiushchim povredit' mne svoimi intrigami*). He knew that she was satisfied with the division.

Muḥyī al-Dīn Khwāja and people whom he could mobilize to his own benefit deployed a critical mass of paperwork. It must have been easy for him to persuade the guardian of the two minor children of Nāẓira Bībī to warn the Russians that the entire lawsuit had been concocted without his direct involvement. Nāẓira Bībī had already alerted the commandant's chancellery that some deceitful individuals driven by malice had appealed in her name against Muḥyī al-Dīn Khwāja.[181] In that case, Nāẓira Bībī wrote in Chaghatay. Now the guardian wrote in Russian and explained that the appeal, on which the entire legal action against Muḥyī al-Dīn Khwāja was based, was fictitious (*na fiktivnom proshenii*), because it was written not by the appellant herself but by other people. He asserted that the division was just, that it satisfied him and the heirs, and that it was in keeping with Islamic law (*byl sdelan pravil'no i soglasno shariata*). He submitted his opinion to the chancellery of the city commandant[182] and to the office of the public prosecutor.[183] This was another instance of a lay person who, although not a legal expert, dared to affirm her view on Islamic law.

---

180 23.03.1891, ibid.: 46–50ob.

181 *bir nicha khiyānatgar ādamlār yulghāndīn manga nisbat bīrūb sībzār qāḍīsī wa waṣīsī ūstīlārīdīn 'arḍ bīrūb-dūr manī āyimnī yāzūb būl 'ariḍa yulghān-dūr man hīch waqt mūndāq 'ariḍa birgānīm yūq*, 14.01.1891, ibid.: l. 27. A few years later, Naẓīra Bībī herself accused Muḥyī al-Dīn Khwāja of embezzling her children's money. See my "Constructing Colonial Legality in Russian Central Asian: On Guardianship."

182 21.03.1891, TsGARUz, f. I-17, op. 1, d. 4784, l. 43.

183 23.03.1891, ibid.: l. 52–52ob.

Muḥyī al-Dīn Khwāja took the initiative and wrote to the prosecutor [Fig. 19]:

> To the worshipful prosecutor. At the Sibzar court in Tashkent, there occurred in July 1890 the division [*taqsīm*] [of an inheritance]. Ḥāmida Bībī Mū'min Jān Bāy-qīzī, [wife of] the deceased Muḥammad Riḍā, remained in Ura-Tepe; on her behalf, her older brother and attorney signed all the documents pertaining to the issue during the division. On 31 December, the aforementioned Ḥāmida Bībī submitted via post an appeal to the commandant. [The appeal was] driven by malice [*yulghān-dīn*] [and it conveyed a claim] against this judge with regard to the event that had taken place. It brought into question the division I had conducted by claiming that it contravened Article 243 of the statute [*niẓām*] and the rule of Islamic law [*sharīʿatgā mukhālif*]. I intend to show you that what I did in relation to the division was in full accordance with Islamic law and to explain what sources and points of law I followed. [...] They said that I took 1,200 rubles out of 75,749 [as a fee for] the division, and that contradicts Islamic law. Their words exemplify their falsity and deceitfulness [*ulārnī sūzīnī bīhūdalīgī wa yulghānlīgī bayānī*]. On page 16, the *Fatāwā-yi ʿAlīya* offers a quotation from Imām Abū Yūsuf, the sayings of other great imams, and a legal question [the answer to which] is labeled "[this is] the opinion being advocated on it" [*bihi yuftā*], "[this is] the adopted opinion" [*ʿuluyhi al fatwā*]. These quotations sanction [my opinion]; no one can act against those prescriptions; the *qāḍī* and the mufti never [apply the fee] by acting against that [prescription]. They fixed [the fee] at the rate of one fortieth. I did not ask that much. They also said that they reviewed the proceedings [of the division of inheritance]. They lied [*yulghān sūzlār aytībdūrlār*]. They did not even ask me a question at that time; they summoned neither the appellant nor the defendant, Muḥammad Ḥakīm, nor any of the witnesses. The assembly did not even gather officially; [the *qāḍīs*] met somewhere and made a deceitful judgment [*bir yulghān ḥukm khaṭṭ qīlīb*]. On 11 March they sent their decision to the commandant, and they summoned the guardian on the 14th for discovery. But, even if the person who suffered a loss appealed in due time, it is not possible to void [in this way] the only existing decision, which was made according to Islamic law: if, indeed, it violates *sharīʿa*, then it is necessary that it be subjected to judicial review and the truth be ascertained. The judge who issued the decision should be questioned with regard to the rules of Islamic law that he applied, what questions he posed, and what he said; the claimant or her attorney should be summoned and so should the witnesses, and the judicial

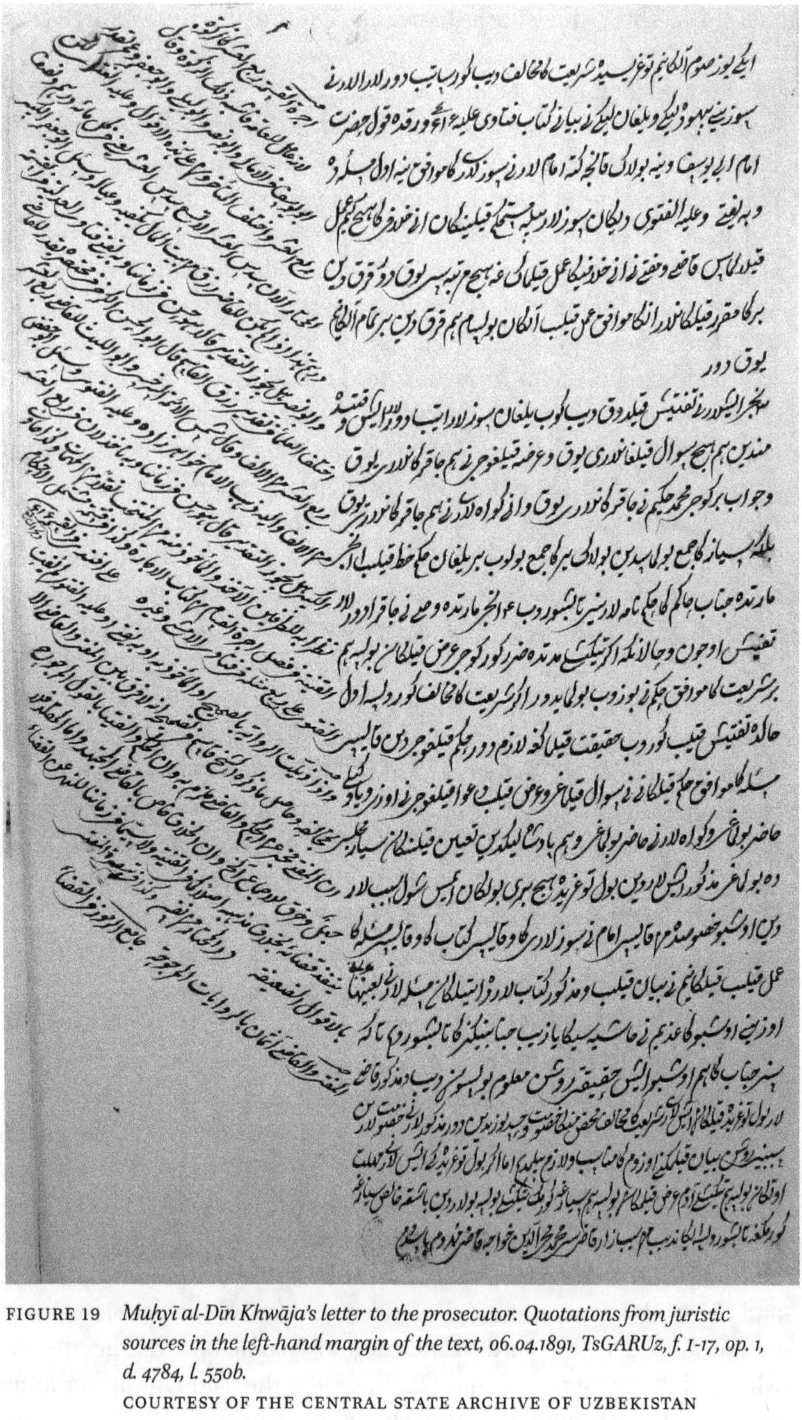

FIGURE 19 *Muḥyī al-Dīn Khwāja's letter to the prosecutor. Quotations from juristic sources in the left-hand margin of the text, 06.04.1891, TsGARUz, f. I-17, op. 1, d. 4784, l. 55ob.*

COURTESY OF THE CENTRAL STATE ARCHIVE OF UZBEKISTAN

> assembly should be convened by a representative of the colonial administration [*pādshāhlīkdīn taʿyīn qīlingān siyāz majlis*]; none of these things occurred. For this reason, I decided to clarify what imams' sayings, books, and opinions I put into practice, and I copied them all from those books here, in the margins of this document. I present all this to you so that the truth about the issue at stake may be ascertained. It is apparent that the conduct of those *qāḍīs* violates Islamic law and is driven by hostility towards me [*manga khuṣūmat*]. I did not consider it necessary to illustrate this animosity. But, even if all these issues were delayed and I did not appeal to the due authority, they should be reviewed by a trustworthy and impartial judicial assembly, different from that one.[184]

This move proved successful for Muḥyī al-Dīn Khwāja. On 9 July 1891, the provincial court voided the decision of the Muslim judicial assessors.[185] After other twists and turns, the case was finally transferred to the provincial prosecutor, who barred it. He argued that 1) native judges could levy a fee according to local customs according to Article 226 of the statute; 2) *sharīʿa* was the customary law of the Turkestanis and had various possible interpretations, none which had the ultimate force of law and all of which could serve as a guideline for native judges; 3) Islamic legal sources indicated that a *qāḍī* could charge a fee of one-fortieth on the entire inheritance; 4) Muḥyī al-Dīn Khwāja levied one sixty-third of the Inheritance; 5) there was no evidence of bribery or of forgery (*net sostava priznakov likhoimstva, kak ravno net sostava priznakov podloga*).[186] Legal action against the *qāḍī* was terminated,[187] and Muḥyī al-Dīn Khwāja was fully acquitted.[188]

Key to the conclusion of the case of Ḥāmida Bībī against Muhyī al-Dīn Khwāja was the expertise of local jurists. Two muftis reviewed the collections of fatwas in order that the judicial inspector of the provincial chancellery might establish some rules on matters regarding fees applicable by *qāḍīs* in cases of inheritance. The muftis reassured the Russian official that their sources represented the most complete possible repertoire of *sharīʿa* law and that they were in use among *qāḍīs*. The inspector also dutifully noted that the muftis based their judgment on the opinion of the great imams, who held that

184 N.d., ibid.: ll. 55–55ob.

185 N.d., ibid.: l. 58ob.

186 31.07.1893, ibid.: l. 73.

187 12.08.1893, ibid.: l 9.

188 06.09.1893, ibid.: l. 75.

"everyone accepts it."[189] One wonders whether the inspector had any way of understanding the subtle juristic idiom in which the muftis spoke. Judging by his obscure transcriptions of the sources provided by the muftis, he probably had little familiarity with such texts. Indeed, the file assembled by the state prosecutor shows that no one among the Russian officials compared this information with all the various fatwas that the Muslim judicial assessors or Muḥyī al-Dīn Khwāja had provided.

Conclusion

The patronage of the Central Asian Muslim dynasties was doubtless an important factor in ensuring that the Hanafi legal doctrine would predominate in the region, but the ability of rulers to establish the specific doctrinal traits of Hanafism remains uncertain. Patronage may well have been more important in politics than in jurisprudence. One could argue instead that Hanafi hegemony was above all a juristic construction. Writing traditions and practices of transmission played a role in creating a discourse on Hanafi authority, which expanded beyond the confines of juristic genres such as fatwas. Court chronicles, mirrors for princes, and poetry are cases in point. But there is another aspect to Hanafi hegemony that should be explored, which pertains to the publicity of law. Publicity is enmeshed in legal practices and legal venues in which people could easily get a sense of their legal entitlements. One such venue was the court, where Hanafi jurists could more forcefully draw the boundaries of their legal doctrine and exercise their interpretive authority. The court was also the place where individuals might approach muftis and solicit legal opinions. Hanafism was, therefore, neither a "dynastic law"[190] (*qānūn*), with which Ottomanists are all too familiar, nor an unequivocal body of rulings, that is, a modern code. It was instead a legal culture that allowed any party to pursue redress by interacting with a juristic authority of her choice and pushing the latter to find the most suitable argument for her cause. Central Asian Hanafism thus differs substantially from its Ottoman counterpart as illustrated

---

189 *i utverdili slovami "Alaliangil fatva" (chto znachit "Vsemi eto odobreno"), Protokol osmotra knigi shariata*, 06.09.1893, ibid.: l. 69ob.

190 I here follow the use of the term "dynastic law" in C.H. Fleischer, *Bureaucrat and Intellectual in the Ottoman Empire: The Historian Mustafa Âli (1541–1600)* (Princeton: Princeton University Press, 1986): 192, 324.

by Guy Burak.[191] The symbol of Hanafism may thus have been the Janus-faced figure of the mufti, who was, on the one hand, the jurisconsult who advised *qāḍī*s and, on the other, a lawyer always willing to satisfy the requests of his clients.

The Russian colonization and the reorganizational changes in judicial institutions did not affect significantly the role of the muftis vis-à-vis the local populace. Muftis (and their scribes) continued to offer the same legal services that were available in the region at least a century before the arrival of the Russians. Muftis were not marginalized and their fatwas lost no legal significance. The appointment of muftis became contingent on the will of a *qāḍī* and the confirmation of Russian administrators, whereas their access to a post had, before the conquest, been dependent on the decision of a local ruler. This change may have affected someone's career, but it did not have a significant impact on the institution itself or on its legal output. There is little evidence that the Islamic traditional knowledge was ever completely displaced. We do not find here the epistemic ruptures that we see in other colonial situations, where the madrasa curriculum underwent significant reorganization.[192]

What changed, then, in the interpretive activity of Muslim jurists in Russian Central Asia? Before colonization, muftis had operated in a well protected domain into which the populace could not intrude. Locals limited themselves to use the services of muftis, i.e. to acquire fatwas mostly when they had to bring them into court. The agency of locals, however, stopped at the ruling of a *qāḍī*, the interpretive authority of other *ʿulamāʾ* in court, or simply the moral suasion of third-party mediators. Under Russian rule, meanwhile, fatwas became for the people the key to the domain of legal hermeneutics and thus to active participation in the definition of *sharīʿa*. Muslims now used them, for example, to cast doubt on the moral standing of their fellow legists. Fatwas became a weapon that could be brandished against native judges and their court personnel, as we have seen in the case of Nāẓira Bībī, the first wife of the deceased Muḥammad Riḍā Bāy. She was willing to support Muḥyī al-Dīn Khwāja's cause and warn the Russians that a false case of malpractice had been concocted against him. A few years later, however, she would stop at nothing to gain access to her underage children's inheritance, which was held in custody by Muḥyī al-Dīn Khwāja. Damning evidence in one of her appeals to the

191 Burak, "The Second Formation of Islamic Law: The Post-Mongol Context of the Ottoman Adoption of a School of Law."

192 M.K. Masud, B. Messick, and D.S. Powers, "Muftis, Fatwas, and Islamic Legal Interpretation." In *Islamic Legal Interpretation: Muftis and Their Fatwas*, ed. M.K. Masud, B. Messick, and D.S. Powers (Cambridge, MA: Harvard University Press, 1996): 26.

Russians was a fatwa issued against Muḥyī al-Dīn Khwāja's powers over the assets of Nāẓira Bībī's underage children.[193] Shrewd moves such as that of Nāẓira Bībī led the Russians to realize that fatwas were a useful resource with which to make local legists answerable, above all, to *sharīʿa*, a domain in the formulation of which Russians too now had a say. It was a strategic alliance between the colonizers and the colonized that paved the way for the birth of a new juristic genre: legal opinions for a non-Muslim state.

The issuance of legal opinions for the Russians followed, in the case of Muḥyī al-Dīn Khwāja, the conventional mode of juristic reasoning and originated from a long-standing hermeneutic practice whose theory was developed in the Hanafi school of law. Clearly, local jurists did not dismiss this practice as irrelevant to their office. Collections of fatwas assembled by Central Asian *ʿulamāʾ* in the colonial period show how just important it was for a mufti to find the correct answer to a question posed by, say, a prosecutor or other Russian official, just as it would been in the precolonial period to deliver the correct opinion on a point of law discussed before a *qāḍī*. Records of such answers found their way into collections of legal opinions. This suggests that such legal texts ranked with fatwas in the minds of those who issued or collected them.[194] From the presence of such texts in fatwa collections one infers that Central Asian jurists viewed the interaction with Russian officials as an opportunity for juristic hermeneutics.

The last observation brings us back to the Bourdieusian notion of juridical field that I used to illuminate the legal system prevailing under the Uzbek khanates. The practices of fatwa-giving in colonial Central Asia show that Russian officials were much more interested in and directly engaged with doctrinal discussions with Muslim jurists than were the khans and the emirs. In doing so, Russian rulers not only acted differently from Muslim rulers but also played a greater, more intrusive role in the shaping of the Islamic juridical field. Muslim rulers no doubt had vested interests in acquiring fatwas that would support their courses of action. There is evidence, for example, that Qunghrat

193 TsGARUz, f. I-17, op. 1, d. 6366, l. 2. More information on this case in P. Sartori, "Constructing Colonial Legality in Russian Central Asian: On Guardianship."

194 See Muḥyī al-Dīn Khwāja's fatwa addressed to the Russian state prosecutor in Tashkent (27.02.1890). The opinion explains the recourse to the exculpatory oath (*qasam*) in judicial contexts, and it is part of a collection of fatwas (*jung*) assembled probably by Muḥyī al-Dīn Khwāja himself. Anon., *Jung*, MS Tashkent, TsVRUz, no. 6102: fols. 315–17. For the attribution of this work, I rely on the notes that Sanjar Ghulomov, a fellow of the al-Beruni Institute in Tashkent, made on the manuscript.

dynasts in Khiva acquired fatwas that ruled in favor of the confiscation of properties belonging to former officeholders found guilty of malpractice.[195] We are also told that Shāh Murād b. Daniyāl Bī, the Manghit ruler of Bukhara (r. 1785–1800), waged war against the Shiʿi Qizilbash on the basis of a fatwa.[196] There were also cases in which Muslim appellants filed a claim with the royal court and produced fatwas as corroborating evidence. Little is known, however, about Central Asian rulers intruding into the affairs of muftis when the latter reviewed legal cases in court. Nor do we know of instances in which emirs or khans entered into conversation with jurists and examined fatwas to sanction or condemn particular behaviors. Russian officials appear, instead, to have believed that fatwas could help them distinguish a correct from an incorrect interpretation of Islamic law. Their administrative practices also demonstrate that Russians viewed fatwas as texts resembling the articles of law codes, which provided a decisive legal basis for the review of disputes, the examination of petitioners' statements, and ruling on claims.

195 Bregel, *Documents from the Khanate of Khiva (17th–19th centuries)*: 53–54.

196 Mīrzā ʿAbd al-ʿAẓīm Sāmī, *Taʾrīkh-i salāṭīn-i manghitīya* (*Istoriia Mangytskikh gosudarei*), ed. L.M. Epifanova (Moscow: Izdatel'stvo Vostochnoi Literatury: 1962): 52.

EPILOGUE

The Legacy: Opportunities from Colonialism

As one story draws to an end, another unfolds. Now that Ḥāmida Bībī failed to achieve what she wanted, it was the turn of Nāẓira Bībī, the first wife of the deceased Muḥammad Riḍā Bāy, to attempt to squeeze money from the *qāḍī* Muḥyī al-Dīn Khwāja. In 1898, Nāẓira Bībī must have been one of the most frequent appellants to the chancellery of the Tashkent city commandant and the military governor of Syr-Darya province. Six times she denounced the supposed malpractices of that *qāḍī* in matters of guardianship. Her story was a common one. After the death of her husband, Nāẓira Bībī was appointed guardian of her underage children, daughter Anzirat Bībī and mentally disabled (*maʿtūh*) son Hāshīm Jān. She was supposed to supervise the wealth they inherited from their deceased father, the considerable sum of more than 28,000 rubles. This sum was deposited in the Tashkent branch of the state bank in 1896. That same year, Nāẓira Bībī's daughter Anzirat Bībī married a certain Mullā ʿAbd al-Wahhāb Iunusbaev, but Anzirat Bībī soon died, and her estate had to be divided between her mother and her husband.

The two parties met half way, agreeing that Iunusbaev was entitled to a share valued at 3,063 rubles. But transferring this money became a problem, because the bank required that the *qāḍī* issue a simple certificate establishing that Iunusbaev was entitled to a share of the estate of which Nāẓira Bībī was the guardian. The judge, Muḥyī al-Dīn Khwāja, refused to issue the certificate, being adamant that Nāẓira Bībī had failed to submit a report about her activity as guardian in the year 1897 and that he would issue no document until he received one. This was the event that triggered all of Nāẓira Bībī's complaints.

A Muslim judicial assembly assessed the conflict and decided that Muḥyī al-Dīn Khwāja must provide the certificate required and Nāẓira Bībī the missing report. Although he gave the woman the documents she needed, the bank would not give her the money, because the certificate she presented did not state from which share the sum should be taken. Nāẓira Bībī's attorney, a Russian by the name of Karacharov, pleaded that the Tashkent city commandant order Muḥyī al-Dīn Khwāja amend the certificate. The *qāḍī* did craft a new document for Iunusbaev, but the commandant found it inappropriate. The Russian officer returned the paper to the Muslim judge with the request that he explain his ill-judged behavior. Muḥyī al-Dīn Khwāja replied to the commandant that the document was sound, because Iunusbaev alone was entitled to receive the money from the bank, whereas the wealth Nāẓira Bībī and her son had inherited had to remain in the bank, at least as long as Nāẓira Bībī failed to provide an account of her activities as guardian in 1897.

Things were getting complicated now, because Nāẓira Bībī's appeals were producing their effect. She approached Russian authorities, depicting the *qāḍī* as displaying personal hostility and inequitable conduct (*nepravil'nye deistviia*).[1] She hammered into the bureaucrats that her relations with the *qāḍī* were inimical (*vrazhdebnye otnosheniia*)[2] and that he was abusing his authority (*prevyshaet svoiu vlast'*).[3] Her appeals finally paid off when she was able to convince Lieutenant Aleksei Fok, assistant to the Tashkent city commandant. On two occasions Fok wrote to the state bank. The first time, he argued the sum in question should be paid to Nāẓira Bībī simply because she was the guardian of the minors' property held in the account. The second time, Fok took a more legalistic tone, referring to the 1897 regulation that stated that native judges should transfer the property of minors to the banks if they were unable to appoint a suitable guardian of the property or lend the money at a profitable rate. Fok wrote:

> This means that the guardian [Nāẓira Bībī] has the full right to take from the bank the minors' money; [this also means] that the refusal of the bank [to pay her...] should be ignored.[4]

Fok was urging the bank to pay out to Nāẓira Bībī, warning that a new refusal would lead him to complain directly to the governor-general. The bank replied that Fok's behavior raised a conflict of jurisdiction:[5] the bank had ignored the new 1897 provision and simply relied on the statutory law, under which native judges oversaw all civil cases among the indigenous population. Were the *qāḍīs* alone to deal with issues of guardianship, or were they not? And, the bank asked, did Fok's notifications have any legal bearing? Fok appeared to be siding with Nāẓira Bībī, and, indeed, he dared to write a note directly to the governor-general charging Muḥyī al-Dīn Khwāja with disobeying his orders to issue the required certification.

1 Nāẓira Bībī to the governor-general, 10.07.1898, TsGARUz, f. I-17, op. 1, d. 6366, l. 36ob.

2 Nāẓira Bībī to the city commandant, 10.04.1898, ibid.: ll. 1, 50b (15.05.1898), and 24ob (25.06.1898); Nāẓira Bībī to the military governor, 19.06.1898, ibid.: l. 23; Nāẓira Bībī to the governor-general, 10.07.1898, ibid.: l. 36.

3 Ibid.: l. 50b.

4 City commandant to the state bank, 17.07.1898, ibid.: ll. 30–30ob.

5 State bank (Tashkent section) to the military govenor, 24.07.1898, ibid.: l. 28.

Fok also tried to bring to the attention of the head of the colonial government the fact that Muḥyī al-Dīn Khwāja had already been investigated several times for malpractice and that the Tashkent city commandant had, on one occasion, requested that he be removed from his post. Fok also emphasized that witnesses had substantiated several accusations against the *qāḍī* but that the provincial chancellery had dropped all the charges against him. In other words, Fok was claiming that, like him, the city chancellery was seeing things that the provincial chancellery had overlooked. Asked to report on the personal initiative he had taken, he explained that he was relying on the judgment of other native judges who agreed that Nāẓira Bībī was entitled to the money. He was also expressing his personal view of the *qāḍī*, which he felt deserved the governor-general's attention, though it diverged substantially from the view of the provincial chancellery.

Though Fok was actively supported by his superior, the city commandant,[6] the pressure exerted by the provincial chancellery proved overwhelming: the bureaucrats of Syr-Darya Province felt that Fok had accused them of covering up the misconduct of the *qāḍī* (*kak by ukryvaet bezzakonnie deistviia kaziia*) and dropping charges against him in the face of clear evidence.[7] Fok was made liable for insubordination due to a turf war between two bureaucratic levels, one trying to bolster its authority by casting a shadow over the activities of the other.

There is, however, a different story here, of continuity in the opinions expressed and of the measures the Tashkent city commandants and their assistants subsequently undertook to restrict the authority of the *qāḍīs* in matters of the guardianship of minors' property. It was Lykoshin who suggested that minors' money be taken from the *qāḍī*s and deposited in banks. This had happened in 1892, when he was instructed to inquire into the claims of embezzlement of minors' money that involved Muḥyī al-Dīn Khwāja. Seven years later, it was Fok who infringed on the activities of the *qāḍī* in matters of guardianship. He sided with Nāẓira Bībī in what he saw as a case of Muslim judicial neglect.

The story of Nāẓira Bībī offers a starting point for recapitulating some of the themes addressed in *Visions of Justi*ce and reflecting on the simplistic nature of the compliance/resistance paradigm that has so far informed our understanding of Central Asian colonial history. Russian rule in the region was based on the purported preservation of traditions that were integral to the regional Islamic legal culture. Russians claimed to have intruded little into the institu-

6 City commandant to the Syr-Darya provincial chancellery, 23.07.1898, TsGARUz, f. I-17, op. 1, d. 6366, l. 33–34ob.

7 Ibid., 40ob.

tions that they found there. They entirely overhauled the local system of justice, according to which the application of *sharīʿa* depended on the Muslim royal court and its representatives (*qāḍīs* included). The Russian policy of the rule of law was designed to draw Muslim subjects nearer to the imperial legal culture so that they would come eventually to prefer Russian law courts to the institutions applying *sharīʿa* and imperial law would replace Islamic law. Russian rule represented a typical colonial enterprise, driven as it was by a civilizing mission. The colonial administration never accomplished the project to shut down the "native courts" in Russian Turkestan, and it was not until the Soviets took power that *sharīʿa* disappeared from the local juridical field, in the 1920s. The deferral of this project, however, did not harm Russian imperialism. Muslim subjects learned to avail themselves of the new institutional arrangements offered by the colony: a constellation of legal venues to which they could bring their affairs and a cohort of bureaucrats eager to listen to and back up Muslims' complaints, actual or ostensible. Involved as they were in everyday conversations with Russian officials, Muslims accustomed themselves to a legal culture in which new institutions and new notions of justice mattered greatly in the pursuit of their own interests. Women like Nāẓira Bībī learned that widows had the right to become the guardians of their underage children and thus dispose of their wealth. This situation would have been unimaginable just a few years before Nāẓira Bībī filed her claims with the colonial administration, because the powers of guardians were the prerogatives of senior male members of the family or of the *qāḍīs*. It is also likely that pastoralists like the residents of Jalayir (whom we encountered in Chapter 3) would come to know that documentation of land ownership was the key to safeguarding their access to pastures. This was another important innovation, because, before Russian rule, local knowledge was enough to avoid or resolve conflicts over land. Hence, the three Uzbek khanates did not develop cadastration, at least not in the way in which we know cadasters in the West. Others, like Mayram Bībī (Chapter 2) and Ḥāmida Bībī (Chapter 5), understood that they could, with a fatwa, gain the trust of the Russian administrators and play it against their enemies in court. It is unlikely that, before Russian colonization, Muslims brandished legal opinions in asking that a royal court uphold a specific point of law.

Did all these historical actors just play along, or did such legal practices ultimately change their understanding of justice, their ideas of right and wrong? Experiences such as those of Nāẓira Bībī and Ḥāmida Bībī must have played an important role in changing perceptions about law. In other words, I am inclined to believe that they and other women must have learned to think that it was right, for example, for them to claim guardianship over their underage children, and they probably understood as wrong and unjust a *qāḍī*'s disposition of the assets of their children. This is crucial to understand, as we consider how a culture changes over time. If Nāẓira Bībī and Ḥāmida Bībī interiorized Russian notions of guardianship, can we still regard what they said about and did with law as anything specific to "Muslim culture" or "Islam"? Or do they exemplify, as I argued in the Introduction, the ordinariness of an experience of cultural change?

A few years ago, I devoted to the notion of "Muslimness" some space in the introduction to a thematic issue of a journal that was dedicated to the study of Islam in the interwar Soviet Union.[8] In it, I called for the adoption of a bottom-up study of the history of Muslim communities in the Soviet Union. Key to my approach was the notion of "Muslimness," which, I suggested, was the category that could best render the conviction that, "by belonging to a religious and ethical community, Soviet Muslims shared a specific cultural experience." At that time I was reading Bruce Privatsky's excellent ethnographic study of Muslim communities in southern Kazakhstan. During his fieldwork in the town of Turkestan, a place famous in Central Asia as home to the shrine of Ahmad Yasawi and important as a hub of Muslim pilgrimage, Privatsky noted the use of the term *musulmanshılıq* among his interviewees to denote, "an ideology and a preference for Muslim life as an experience of the community ... the religious life of the people, including the elders but not excluding anyone except those 'who have gone over to the Russians.'"[9]

In that essay, I outlined my approach to the study of Muslimness by indicating a few ways in which one could disentangle Muslims' "specific cultural experience" from the historical texture and the epistemic embeddedness of the available sources. I pointed to several phenomena in which Muslimness manifested itself: the transmission of traditional patterns of Islamic education that survived the Stalin period; forms of religiosity in the observance of mourning rituals and healing practices; and the cultivation of Islamic ethics through literary gatherings. In advocating this approach, I relied on previous studies that had demonstrated "the reflexive attitudes of Soviet Muslims towards their religion and towards Islam as a culture."[10] In those years, I was an avid reader of the ethnography produced by a group of anthropologists based in Halle

8 P. Sartori, "Towards a History of the Muslims' Soviet Union: A View from Central Asia," *WDI* 50/3–4 (2010): 315–34 (here 322–25).

9 B.G. Privratsky, *Muslim Turkistan: Kazak Religion and Collective Memory* (Richmond, Surrey: Curzon, 2001): 78.

10 J. Rasanayagam, "Introduction."*CAS* 25/3 (2006): 224.

(Germany), who were studying the manifestations of religiosity in post-Soviet Central Asia.

Recently I have come to realize that, in employing this concept of "Muslimness," I was not being as original as I had thought. Several other students of Central Asia have written on the subject, frequently adopting what, at the beginning of this book, I termed an "emic perspective." This would allow me, I thought, to complicate the readily available narratives about Islam in Soviet Central Asia and see aspects of Soviet Muslims' experience and subjectivity that one normally does not see. My belief grew stronger when I noticed that anthropologists Johan Rasanayagam and Sergei Abashin had joined in the same venture, though with a focus on different periods and each with his distinctive approach and style, Rasanayagam writing about Muslim Uzbeks in the post-independence period[11] and Abashin reflecting on the ethnographic notes that he had taken during his early fieldwork in Tajikistan during the Gorbachev era.[12]

While Rasanayagam conceptualizes the emic perspective in terms of morality, Abashin pushes further the reflection on the meaning of Muslimness by analyzing the Soviet public space. He dissects the speeches delivered at rituals called *darveshona* and *xudoy*, in which meals were offered to members of village communities, and reviews the tenor of exchanges between their participants. He reflects on the rhetorical strategies—the "speech acts"—employed by prominent individuals (one a *kolkhoz* brigade leader and one a religious activist) when addressing their audiences. He reaches the conclusion that:

> Muslimness [...] remained the grounding point of their identity and the foundation of their authority and special reputation. This condition gave rise to various techniques of the double game that was supposed to bind the "Soviet" and the "Muslim" together, rather than setting them off against each other.[13]

As I draw this book to an end, and as I pause to reflect on the stories that are assembled therein, I realize that the conception of Muslimness and its underlying implications are not unproblematic. I shall now try to clarify what I mean. What would happen if I were to project the synthesis offered by Abashin onto the material from the tsarist archives on which this book is based? Should I

11 J. Rasanayagam, *Islam in Post-Soviet Uzbekistan: The Morality of Experience* (Cambridge: Cambridge University Press, 2011).

12 "A Prayer for Rain: Practising Being Soviet and Muslim." *JIS* 25/2 (2014): 178–200.

13 Ibid: 197.

conclude that the stories that I have related here show that Central Asians, while being consumers of colonial justice, retained a Muslim cultural core, a Muslimness of sorts? Does it mean that Central Asian Muslims, in petitioning the Russian authorities, disguised their Muslimness and only pretended to submit to the epistemic rules of the empire? No: the material I have examined points to a very different conclusion. The very fact of thinking in terms of "Muslimness," "tsaristness," and "Sovietness" recalls categories employed by the state (the Russian Empire and later the Soviet Union) to conceptualize cultural difference and legitimize the coexistence of multiple jurisdictions. Central Asians did not adopt such categories when they took legal action, attempted to assert their rights, and articulated their moral ideals. They did not need to invoke their "Muslimness" as opposed to the "tsaristness" of the Russian bureaucracy when they pursued redress. Why should one disassemble what existed as a whole, enmeshed as it was in the experience of every legal actor? The challenge that this book has attempted to meet is to render the totality of the experience encountered by Central Asians in the colonial juridical field. It was an experience that reflected a system of signification that was not monolithic and cohesive, but fractured, contradictory, and ambivalent. Though such a system was based on the idea of cultural difference, Central Asian Muslims did not view their behavior, the law, or the moral world in which they lived through the prism of any such epistemic distinction.

Is it possible, to paraphrase Foucault, to live as the subject of a state that produces a discourse on difference and, at the same time—as I argue was the case of Central Asians under Russian rule—to ignore the vocabulary of such a discourse? This is a question for experts in the study of reception. Central Asians did not—every time they took legal action and wrote (or had someone write for them) to the Russian authorities—pause to ponder the fact that they were Muslims addressing a handful of unbelievers. They must have known that this was the way they ought to operate if they wanted to achieve certain purposes. Many of the cases featured in this book illustrate the determination with which Muslims often pursued legal action against such cornerstones of Islamic authority as *qāḍī*s and *waqf*s, seeking either to constrain such entities or to eliminate them. The sources give little indication that legal actors felt any obligation to preserve their "Muslimness" vis-à-vis the Russian officials who listened to their stories. There are too many cases initiated by Central Asian Muslims for us to infer that their primary reason for going to court was *not* to defend Islam and the cultural repertoire that we can call Muslimness. Complaints driven by malice are a case in point. Ultimately, there always was a Qobil Bobo or a Mullā Rustam, rather than just a "Muslim," behind the locals who petitioned the colonial administration.

Another theme that runs through this book is the use of the colonial courts and the consumption of justice. Regardless of their gender and the position they occupied in society, Central Asians made effective use of the legal institutions that the empire created for them. Not only did they do so before the Russian conquest, as I have shown in Chapter 1, but Muslims did so elsewhere in the Islamicate world.[14] People, we are prone to think, tend to regard legal action pragmatically. There is always a utilitarian mind behind a lawsuit, one would say. The work of Daniel Lord Smail encourages us, however, to rethink the way we think of the consumption of justice. Examining material from medieval France, Smail suggests that emotions are an integral part of lawsuits and that, in thirteenth-century Marseille, people went to court to articulate their vision of right and wrong, to express their own moral take on things, regardless of their mere calculations. An altercation might easily turn into a court case simply because a party wanted to air her views, blacken the name of others, and publicize her grievance.[15] A similar impression accrues from many of the cases we have considered in this book. One thinks of the countless cases in which an individual files a complaint for a given amount of money, only to settle for half the sum after an amicable settlement is reached. There is, for example, the case of a homicide in Manghishlaq, in which the brother of the deceased sued three men and claimed blood money. The parties made arrangements for the lawsuit to be heard according to Kazakh customary law. This required the involvement of six arbitrators (*bīs*) who met and required either that the defendants produce four individuals from their own community (chosen by the plaintiff) and have them take an exculpatory oath or that they pay blood money to the plaintiff. The parties met before the Qunghrat governor of Kunya-Urgench, in the Russian protectorate of Khiva. When oath takers declared their willingness to take the exculpatory oath, the plaintiff waived his claim and opted instead for an amicable settlement.

In discussing this case elsewhere,[16] I wondered whether the plaintiff might have been bluffing when be brought his case to the court. I suggested that he may have found himself unable to support his unjustified claim and, facing

14 L. Pierce, *Morality Tales: Law and Gender in the Ottoman Court of Aintab* (Berkeley: University of California Press, 2003).

15 D.L. Smail, *The Consumption of Justice. Emotions, Publicity, and Legal Culture in Marseille, 1264–1423* (Ithaca: Cornell University Press, 2003).

16 P. Sartori, "Murder in Manghishlaq: Notes on an Instance of Application of Qazaq Customary Law in Khiva (1895)." *DI* 88/2 (2012): 217–57.

imminent loss, simply gave up. But there is another possibility: it may have been a deep personal conviction as to the three suspects' guilt that pushed the plaintiff to publicize the homicide and forge ahead blindly with the lawsuit, against all odds. The Manghishlaq murder case reminds us that decisions to take legal action are not always rational but may also reflect a cognitive process informed by a moral imaginary comprising ideals, beliefs, and hopes. By examining Central Asians' consciousness of the law under Russian rule, I have tried to show that such a moral imaginary is always historically situated, because it is immanent in the experience of the self. For Tīnīq Āy, the Kazakh woman whom we encountered in Chapter 2 as she attempted to draw the attention of the Russian authorities to the murder of her baby child, to concoct a false accusation against a native judge would have been an entirely normal course of action. This was what she could, and should, do to be heard by the Russians. Our source does not suggest that, in so doing, she faced any moral dilemma, so I believe that she regarded both petitioning and scapegoating the native judge as legitimate means of publicizing her case and pursuing redress. Changes in consciousness of the law are manifest also in juristic thinking. As he explained the lawfulness of his conduct as a native judge, Muḥyī al-Dīn Khwāja brought fatwa collections into conversation with imperial statutory laws. Each intervention, whether prompted by a Kazakh woman or a Tashkent jurist, reflects a new system of signification and thus a new age of possibilities.

As *Visions of Justice* has addressed the topic of change, we may ask whether Muslims were aware of the cultural change brought about in the Islamic juridical field by colonialism. A half-century or more of examination of colonialism in both imperial history and Islamic studies has produced much scholarship, but it has also yielded many assumptions and narratives about "colonial *sharīʿa*" that must be analyzed and refined. One such narrative propounds that *sharīʿa* underwent, in the nineteenth century, a process of transformation that led ultimately to what many observers have called a rupture. Such a process is usually interpreted as the outcome of modernization, that is, some sort of inevitable evolution in which the West imposed its legal episteme consisting of a new ethos of codification, different institutional arrangements, and altered sensibilities. We are dealing here with a narrative of irreversible decline, in which *sharīʿa* was shattered and could not be reassembled.

While many institutional changes in the law are obvious and require that we reflect on them, their reception among Muslims is, at once, one of the most obscure issues in the history of colonial *sharīʿa* and one of the most important. It is unclear whether Muslims perceived these changes as integral to an experience of total transformation affecting their behavior and morality. It is unclear in part because of the Orientalist view of *sharīʿa* as a jurist's law—which assumes that the evolution of *sharīʿa* should be measured against the juristic models established during the formative period of Islam—and in part because of the anti-Orientalist Muslim critique that propounded a purist view of the law that suggests that everything colonial is contaminated because it comes from the West. The importance of the issue rests not only on the need to understand colonialism, which was so pervasive in many Muslim societies, but above all on the broader benefits that will result from explaining why the transformation of *sharīʿa* encountered mostly muted opposition, especially in the countries in which law codes were introduced. In spite of all the cultural changes mentioned in this work, there is no evidence that Central Asian Muslims resisted such legal changes that accompanied colonization.

As we have seen in Chapter 5, for example, the hermeneutic activity of muftis shows a striking continuity with precolonial practices. We could reach the same conclusion after examining other genres crafted in the conservative Islamic legal vocabulary. Most accommodated small innovations. Deeds of sale notarized in a native court, for example, do not speak "colonial" as much as an endowment deed crafted in the People's Republic of Bukhara cannot speak "Bolshevik."[17] Such continuities allow us to appreciate that Central Asian Muslims probably did not live colonialism as an experience of cultural change, at least when they brought their affairs to native courts. It is true that *qāḍīs*' jurisdiction was substantially restricted and that *qāḍīs* suffered open attacks on their authority, but, in Russian Central Asia, the number of *qāḍī* courts skyrocketed (see Chapter 2). Under Russian rule, there were simply more *qāḍīs* and more muftis, and, ultimately, more cases than had previously been heard "according to *sharīʿa*,"[18] whatever meaning the legists and the laity conferred on that expression. In colonial Central Asia there was transformation coupled with what we might call unwilling *sharʿī*-fication.

Finally, one should contemplate the possibility that there were Central Asian subjects of the Russian Empire who encountered the law only as it was applied by *qāḍīs* and muftis. Their legal consciousness also was the product of exposure to "native courts," themselves a colonial institution. But, in spite of the innovations, Central Asians might regard such courts as perfectly "Islamic," because their output accorded with *sharīʿa*. Muslims clearly lived through times of cultural change, but they probably did not realize the extent to which such changes affected their consciousness of the law.

---

17 P. Reichmuth, "Lost in the Revolution: Bukharan *waqf* and Testimony Documents from the Early Soviet Period." *DWI* 50/3–4 (2010): 362–96.

18 T. Welsford and N. Tashev, *A Catalogue of Arabic-Script Documents from the Samarqand Museum* (Samarqand and Istanbul: IICAS, 2012): docs. 557, 566, 597, 601, 605, 627, 639b.

APPENDIX I

Examples of Diplomas of Appointment to the Office of *Qāḍī*

I here present, in translation, two diplomas of appointment to the office of judge in Wazīr (Khorezm) and Dahbīd (Samarqand Province). A comparison shows the extent to which specific judicial attributes of the *qaḍīs* might differ and the degree to which they depended on the agency of the royal court.

Abū al-Muẓaffar wa al-Manṣūr Abū al-Ghāzī Khwārazmshāh. Our word: On account of his renowned fairness and religiousness, we have bestowed upon Ākhūnd Dāmullā Nūrallāh, [who embodies] the traditions of piety, the vestiges of rectitude and repository of knowledge, the royal favor and the regal benevolence of promoting him [to the office of] *qāḍī* and *ra'is* in the city of Wazīr and all its environs, thus becoming the companion [*sharīk*] of Dāmullā Raḥmān Birdī until he will be suitable to trust. Let him resolve instances of contention, compile deeds and rulings, oversee marriages with or without a guardian [*maʿ al-walī wa bilā walī*],[1] enforce

He [God] is the bestower of benefits. By grace of God the almighty and his divine guidance, we bestowed upon Ākhūnd Mullā Muḥammad Zamān Muftī, [a man] of perfect nature and a companion of tranquility, the refuge of excellence and knowledge, and did him the honor of promoting him to the office of *qāḍī* in Dahbīd and its dependent villages: let the population recognize that said appointee's rule henceforth is in force, refer to his courthouse [*dār al-qaḍā*] for legal matters [*muhimmāt-i sharʿīya*], and obey him. Let the appointee throughout his life make every effort to resolve disputes [*qaṭʿ-i khuṣūmat*], compile deeds and rulings [*kitābat-i ṣukūk*[2]

1 On *walī* as "marriage guardian," see D.S. Powers, *Law, Society, and Culture in the Maghrib, 1300–1500* (Cambridge: Cambridge University Press, 2002): 61; A. Layish, *Sharīʿa and Custom in Libyan Tribal Society. An Annotated Translation of Decisions from the Sharīʿa Courts of Adjābiya and Kufra* (Leiden: Brill, 2005): 19 fn. 29.

2 In translating *ṣakk* as "deed," I follow *Dokumenty k istorii agrarnykh otnoshenii v Bukharskom khanstve*, vol 1, *Akty feodal'noi sobstvennosti na zemliu XVII–XIX vv.* Tashkent: Fan, 1954. ed. and trans. O.D. Chekhovich (Tashkent: Fan, 1954): 67 fn. 7. The formulaic expression *sukūk wa sijillāt* is rendered "documents and registers" in A. Urunbaev, G. Dzhuraeva, and S. Gulomov, *Katalog sredneaziatskikh zhalovannykh gramot iz fonda Instituta vostokovedeniia im. Abu Raikhana Beruni Akademii Nauk Respubliki Uzbekistan* (Halle/Saale: Orientwissenschaftliches Zentrum der Martin-Luther-Universität Halle-Wittenberg,

the division of inheritances, and hold in trust [*muḥāfiẓat*] the possessions of orphans and those of unsound mind. Let him inspect the traders and their affairs, let him teach the Muslims the faith, review [the work of] mullahs, imams, and muezzins, see that the children are educated, and reproach those who do not pray. And let him punish those found in breach of the law. Now, as soon as they are made aware of the content of this royal diploma, let the people of said locality recognize the said appointee as their own *qāḍī-ra'is*, like Dāmullā Raḥman Birdī. Let the people involve both of them in all marriages and pay them the marriage fee. Let the people defer the resolution of legal disputes to them, and let the people not transgress their opinion on points of law. And let the *qāḍīs*, too, behave properly with the people so that, on Judgment Day, they will answer correctly and won't be held *wa sijillāt*] and marriage contracts [*ʿuqūd-i ankaḥā*] with or without guardian [*maʿ al-walī wa bilā walī*], hold in trust [*ḍabṭ*] the properties of orphans and those of unsound mind, appoint guardians, and so forth. When he oversees the testamentary division of estates according to the divine laws of inheritance and issues the [resulting] deeds, let him charge five *tanga*s for every thousand *tanga*s [of transferred property] as a notary fee [*ijrat-i kitābat*]. This is licit; do not let him levy more. When he seizes treasure [*laqaṭa wa baraka*] that belongs to the treasury [*bayt al-māl*], let him hand it over to the latter's proxy [*wakīl*]. For the enforcement of offenses [*ḥudūd*],[3] retaliation [*qiṣāṣ*], and disagreements over compensation for manslaughter [*diyāt-i nafs*], let him refer to the Bukharan *qāḍī* court; let him [administer] the punitive extraction of teeth [*qiṣāṣ-i dandān*] and resolve disputes [involving] the compensation for

2007): 23, 25–26, 43–44, 50, 66–67, and E. Karimov, *Regesty kaziiskikh dokumentov i khanskikh iarlikov Khivinskogo khanstva XVII-nachala XX v.* (Tashkent: Fan, 2007): 34, 94–95, 111. That translation is unfortunate, because there is no proof that Central Asian judges ever kept registers before the Russian conquest.

3 "Thus, those offenses which were regulated—to one extent or another—by the founding texts came to be known as *ḥudūd* (sing. *ḥadd*), literally, the limits prescribed by God, and technically, offenses whose punishments are fixed and are God's right. *Zinā*, wrongful accusation of *zinā* (*qadhf*), drinking alcohol (*shrub al-khamr*), theft (*thariqa*) and highway robbery (*qatʿ al-ṭarīq*) were accepted by all jurists as *ḥudūd* offenses," W.B. Hallaq, *Sharīʿa: Theory, Practice, Transformations* (Cambridge: Cambridge University Press, 2009): 310.

4 IQM, no. 2053.

5 It is unclear why the author uses the term *diya* instead of *arsh*, the latter usually being employed to refer to compensation for injuries. On the difference between *diya* and *arsh*, see R. Peters, *Crime and Punishment in Islamic Law: Theory and Practice from the Sixteenth to the Twenty-First Century* (Cambridge: Cambridge University Press, 2005): s.v.

in breach of their duty. This royal diploma of appointment was written in the year [of Hijra] 1249, in the royal capital of Khiva, may God save it from fire and flood, in the month of Rajab [November–December 1833] corresponding to the year of the Snake.[4]

injuries [*diyāt mā dūn-i nafs*][5] and the miscarriage of fetuses [*ghurra-yi janīn*]. Let him attend weddings that take place among the people or appoint a student [*ṭālib-i ʿilm*] who is knowledgeable in issues concerning marriage. Do not let him solemnize [contracts] by including more than the two stipulations that are sound and known [*maʿrūf wa mashhūr*], and let him prevent anyone from adding a different stipulation.[6] Let him levy the marriage fee [*nikāḥāna*] equivalent to one *ṭilā* for a virgin [*bākira*], should the [parties] be able to pay it; otherwise, let him be tolerant with those who are poverty stricken. Let him not abuse with such orders [*maʿmūrāt*]: they day he abuses, he should be dismissed. When stamped with the royal seal, it should be executed. Month of Shaʿbān 1256 [September–October 1840].[7]

6 The solemnization of marriage contracts was apparently not a duty exclusively of *qāḍīs*: *ra'ise*s and *muḥtasib*s (market superintendents) also were empowered to deal with marriages, TsGARUz, f. I-126, op. 1, d. 6, ll. 14, 15, 23.

7 AMIKINUz, untitled collection of Arabic-script documents: collection series no. 1075; cf. T. Welsford and N. Tashev, *A Catalogue of Arabic-Script Documents from the Samarqand Museum*, with the assistance of M. Ismoilov and H. Aminov (Samarqand and Istanbul: IICAS, 2012): doc. 422. Other diplomas issued in Bukhara repeat these expressions verbatim. See appointment to the office of *qāḍī* in the provinces of Kām, Nūr (1897), and Sarmat (1899), TsGARUz, f. I-126, op. 1, d. 6, ll. 16, 17, 19.

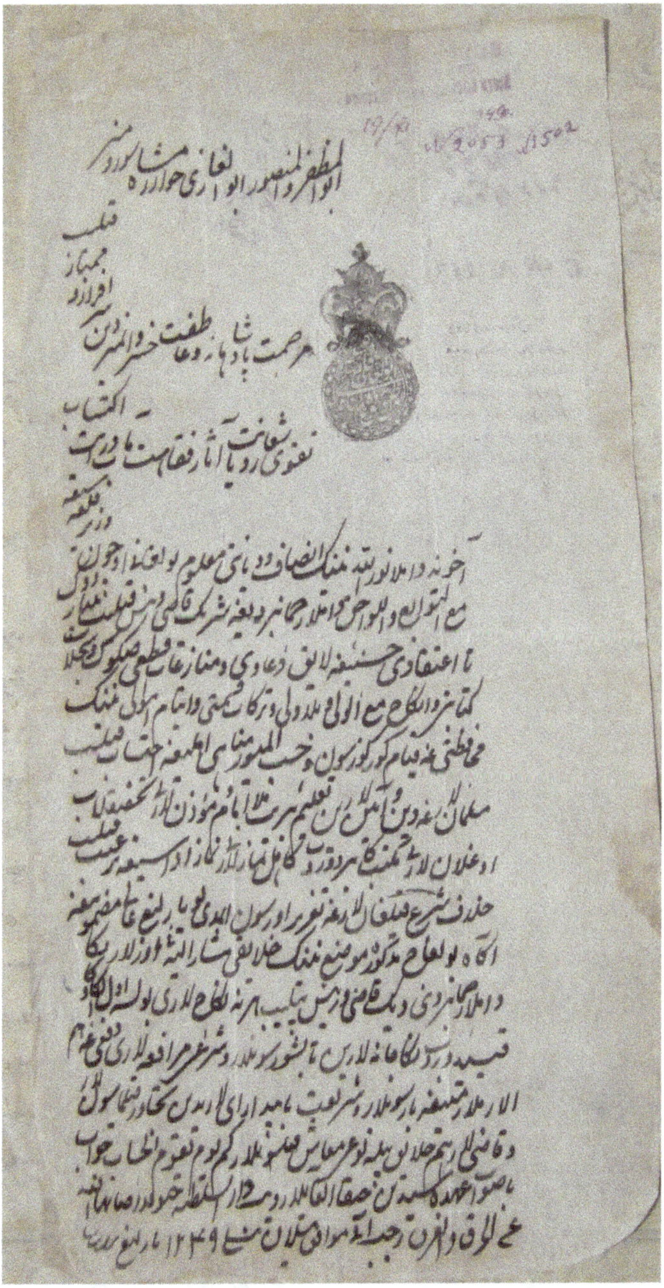

FIGURE 20 *Diploma of appointment to the office of* qāḍī *and* ra'is *in the city of Wazīr, issued by Allāh Qulī Khān, Khiva, November–December 1833.*
COURTESY OF THE ICHAN QAL'A MUSEUM

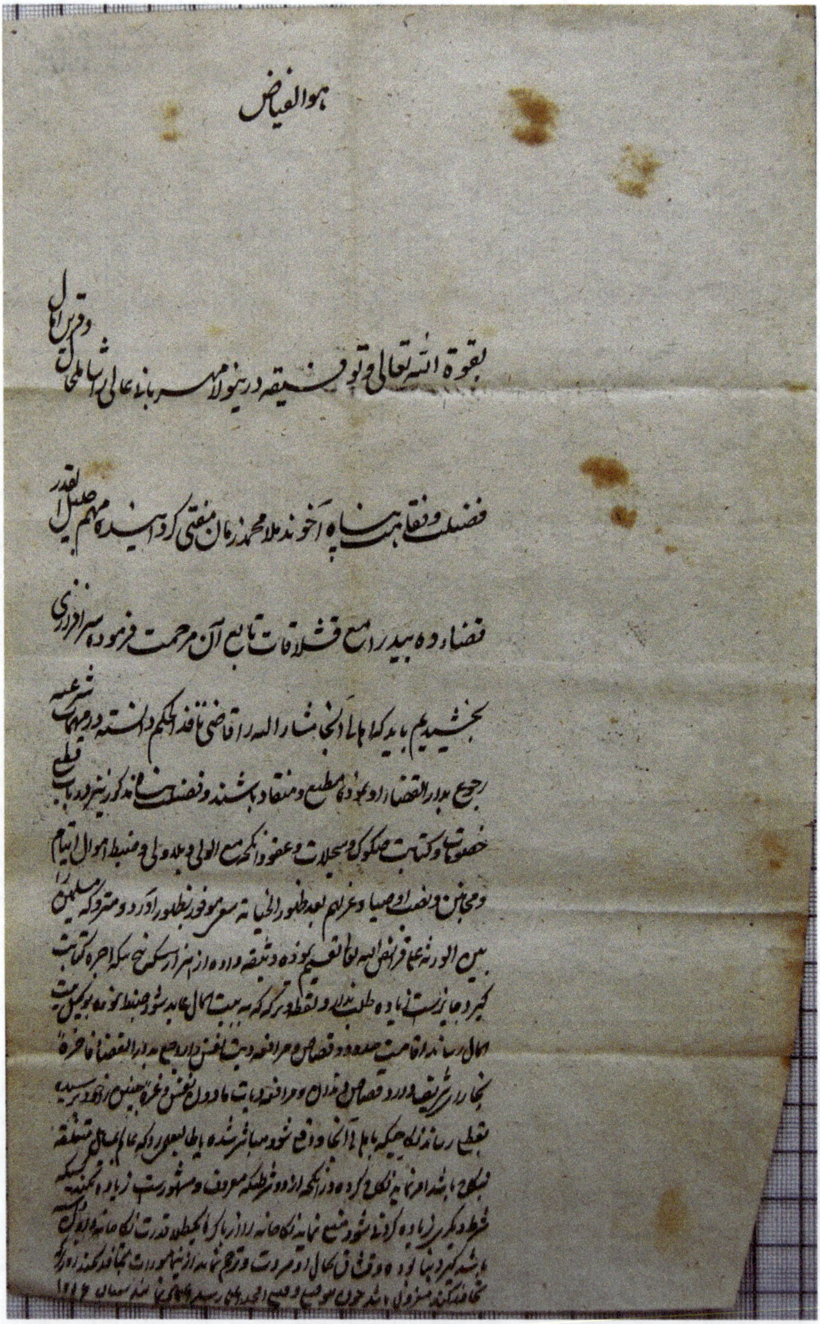

FIGURE 21 *Diploma of appointment to the office of* qāḍī *in the city of Dahbīd, Samarqand, September–October 1840.*
COURTESY OF THOMAS WELSFORD

APPENDIX II

Examples of Sale Deeds of Land in Tashkent, 1856–1883

I compare two sale deeds of land in Tashkent written in the manner of certificates of acknowledgement (*iqrār*), which include all the formulaic phrasings found in documents notarized in Central Asia since the early medieval period.[1] That on the left side is a copy produced in the early 1870s of a deed that was originally notarized in Tahskent in 1856, under the rule of Mīrzā Aḥmad Parvānachī, who was appointed to office by Khudāyār Khān,[2] the ruler of the Khoqand khanate.[3] The deed on the right side was notarized in September–October 1883,[4] nearly twenty years after the Russian takeover and the introduction of new institutional arrangements affecting the *qāḍī* courts:

Description of one plot of land that contains vines and trees, situated in Tashkent, in the Ārqa Kūcha *maḥalla*. The western side partly abuts the estate [*matrūka*] of the deceased Āta Khwāja and partly the property [*milk*]

Description of plots of land suitable for every sort of cultivation, situated in Tashkent, outside the city walls, in the area of Qizil Qurghān and watered by the river [Labzah]. [The plots] have been measured 100 *ṭanābs*.[5] The

1 I have elsewhere compared several formulaic phrases used in legal deeds notarized by *qāḍīs* before and after colonization: "Colonial Legislation Meets *Sharīʿa*": 52–53 and fn. 56. On the adoption of conventional formulae in legal deeds issued by Islamic notaries in Central Asia in the Russian period, see Welsford and Tashev, *A Catalogue of Arabic-Script Documents from the Samarqand Museum*: passim.

2 T.K. Beisembiev, "Vyshchaia administratsiia Tashkenta i iuga Kazakhstana v period Kokandskogo khanstva: 1809–1865 gg. (prosopograficheskii obzor po kokandskim khronikam)." In *Istoriko-kul'turnye vzaimosviazi Irana i Dasht-i Kipchaka v XIII–XVIII vv.* (Almaty: Daik-Press, 2004): 302.

3 TsGARUz, f. I-164, op. 1, d. 6, l. 54. The attribution of the date is made possible by the seals stamped on the document. Muḥammad ʿAẓīm Qāḍī b. Muḥammad Rajab, 1287/1870; Mullā ʿAṭāʾallāh b. Mullā Khān Makhdūm Muftī, 1275/1859; ʿAbd al-Rasūl walad-i Mīr ʿAshūr Muftī-yi Maḥkama-yi Sharʿī, 1279/1862; Maḥmūd Khwāja Qāḍī b. Khān Khwāja Ṣiddīqī, 1275/1859.

4 TsGARUz, f. I-164, op. 1, d. 6, l. 72. Qāḍī-yi Sibzār ʿAzīzlār Khwāja Īshān b. Īshān Āy Khwāja Ḥājjī Shaykh al-Islām, 1300/1883.

5 Lit. "[The plots] have been measured 100 *ṭanābs* in *gaz* known as *sarjīn*". *Gaz* is a unit for land measurements which varied considerably from region to region. Under Russian rule the Tashkent *gaz* was ca. 88 cm. See Davidovich, *Materialy po metrologii srednevekovoi Srednei Azii* (Moscow: Nauka, 1970): 114.

of Badal Mālachī son of [text missing]. The entire northern side abuts the estate of the deceased Īshān Fāḍil Khwāja. The entire eastern side abuts the undivided ancestral property [*milk-i mushtarak*] of Risālat Bībī and ʿĀlīya Bībī, daughters of Mullā Mīr Raḥīm. The entire southern side abuts the property of Ulugh Bībī, daughter of the aforementioned Mullā Mīr Raḥīm. The boundaries are all known. On Jumādī al-Thānī 1272 [February–March 1856] Mastūra Bībī, daughter of Mullā Mīr Raḥīm Ākhūnd, of her own will and in the condition that allows the acknowledgment and the execution of all the usufructs, legally acknowledged the sale of all the described [area] to Īshān Muḥyī al-Dīn Khwāja son of the repository of lordship and the refuge of legal knowledge, the most excellent Īshān Ḥakīm Khwāja Mudarris. [The area in question] is her own property. [The sale of the decribed area] is complete, effective, binding, legal, and definite [and includes] all the abstract rights and material appurtenances, together with everything that is produced inside and outside of [said area]. The price [of the transaction was stipulated at] six *ṭilā*s of Khuqand coinage each of them estimated one legal *mithqāl*.[6] [The transaction occurred] with a sound exchange of two objects of equal value and with the support of the legal guarantee of entire western side abuts the ancestral undivided property [*milk-i mushtarak*] of Sayyid ʿAlīm Khwāja and ʿĀmila Āyim, who are offspring of the deceased Maḥmūd Khwāja Īshān Qāḍī. The eastern side abuts partly the estate [*matrūka*] of the deceased Muḥammad Khwāja Muftī and partly the ancestral undivided property of Sayyida Pāchā Āyim, daughter of the deceased ʿĪsā Khwāja Īshān Qāḍī Kalān, and Āftāb Khān, daughter of the deceased Maḥmūd Khwāja Īshān. The entire northern side abuts the estate of the deceased Shādī Khwāja Īshān. The entire southern side abuts a private road. The boundaries and the attributes are all known. On Dhū al-Qaʿda 1300 [September–October 1883], Zayn al-Dīn Khwāja, known as Tāshkandī, who is the son of the deceased Raḥmatallāh Khwāja Īshān, and belongs to the community of the Qāḍī Kūcha *maḥalla* in Sībzār, came to the court of justice of the same city. Being in the condition that allows the acknowledgment and the execution of all the usufructs legally, he acknowledged the complete, effective, binding, legal, and definite sale of all the described area, which is his own purchased property, with all the abstract rights and material appurtenances, to Īshān Muḥammad Muḥyī al-Dīn Khwāja Qāḍī, who is son of the most excellent deceased Īshān Muḥammad Ḥakīm Khwāja Īshān

6 The *mithqāl* was a unit of weight equivalent to c. 4.8 grams, see ibid.: 94–95.

handover, in absence of fraud or voiding conditions. They confirmed orally and in person what is in the acknowledgement. And all that happened in the presence of just and reliable Muslims.

Qāḍī Kalān. The price [of the transaction was stipulated at] 900 current rubles in banknotes of common usage, each of them estimated five silver current royal *ṭanga*s of 7 *wazn*. [The transaction occurred] with a sound exchange of two objects of equal value and with the support of the legal guarantee, in the absence of fraud or voiding conditions. And all that happened in the presence of just and reliable Muslims.

FIGURE 22 *Sale deed, Tashkent, February–March 1856.*
COURTESY OF THE CENTRAL STATE ARCHIVE OF UZBEKISTAN

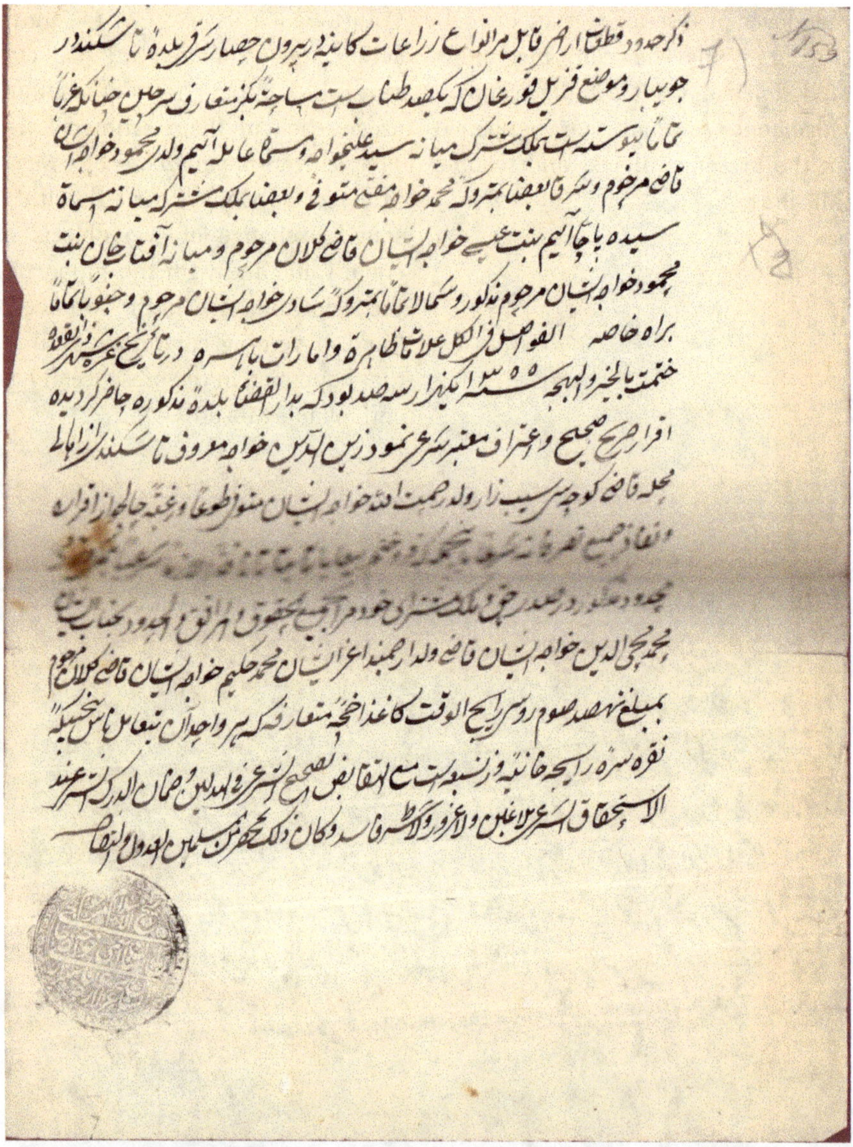

FIGURE 23 *Sale deed, Tashkent, September–October 1883.*
COURTESY OF THE CENTRAL STATE ARCHIVE OF UZBEKISTAN

APPENDIX III

Ṣādiq Jān Ākhūn Jān-ūghlī vs. Muḥyī al-Dīn Khwāja Īshān Qāḍī

I here offer the materials in Russian from the file TsGARUz, f. I-17, op. 1, d. 4887, discussed in Chapter 2. I render names in the form in which they appear in the texts without any attempt at uniformization.

Дело 4887. По обвинению Казия Сибзарской части города Ташкента Мухитдина Ходжи Ташкентским сартом Садыкджаном Уста Ахунджановым в присвоении прав мутавалия над вакуфным имуществом Турабаевой. 1892 год. 74 листов.

[2] Его Превосходительству Господину Военному Губернатору Сыр-Дарьинской Области

Доверенного Ташкентских сартов Садыкджана Ахунджанова и Дада Кузы Нар Кузынова, Антона Глаз

Прошение

На производстве Областного правления Распор. отдел. находится жалоба матери моих доверителей Майрам биби Турабаевой и одного из моих доверителей Садыкджана на действия Мухитдина-Казия, народного судьи Сибзарской части относительно вакуфа Байба Турамбаева. Мои доверители и их [20b.] мать заинтересованы в этом вакуфе, так как они считаются наследниками Бай-баба Турамбаева. Они утверждают, что вакуф вовсе не был учрежден Турамбаевым и что вакуф-наме подложно.

Расследование о действительности и достоверности упомянутого вакуфа производили с одной стороны старший помощник Начальника города, с другой – поземельно-податный Комиссар Благовещенский.

Вакуф Бай баба составляет 6 лавок в Азиатской части города, доходы с коих поступали в пользу Мухитдин-Казия, как мутавалия и мудариса. Дело это тянется уже около 2-х лет. Честь имею покорнейше просить Ваше Превосходительство сделать зависящее распоряжение об ускорении производства по упомянутому делу.

Г. Ташкент, 1891 года Декабря 30 дня. При сем прилагается доверенность.

Антон Глаз

[5] Препровождая настоящее прошение г. Начальнику гор. Ташкента, Областное Правление просит поспешить с доставлением сведений, затребованных Правлением 24 июля 1891 года за № 724/5194.

Г. Ташкент. Февраля 3 дня 1892 г.

Советник [*signature*]

Делопроизводитель [*signature*]

Справка

Из отметок в настольном реестре видно, что при надписи Сыр-Дарьинского Областного Правления от 24 Июля 1891 года за № 724/5194 было препровождено прошение сартянки Майрам биби Турабаевой, для выяснения: а) действительно ли Народный Судья Мухитдин с имущества просительницы собирает доход в свою личную пользу и б) действительно ли отец ее завещал свое имущество вакуфу, а также было ли это дело на рассмотрении суда. Вся эта переписка представлена обратно в Областное Правление при надписи от 27 Июля 1891 года за № 2380, при чем было донесено, что прошение Турабаевой есть повторение жалобы Садыкджана [**5ob.**] Уста Ахунджанова и что вся переписка по этому делу представлена в Областное Правление 4 июля 1891 года за № 1793.

Письмоводитель [*signature*]

[**12**]

Военный Губернатор

6 октября 1892 года

В Канцелярию г. Туркестанского Генерал-губернатора

Вследствие предложения г. Главного Начальника Края от 4 минувшего сентября за № 5541, имею честь уведомить Канцелярию, что донесение по прошению сартянки Турабаевой о наследстве задерживается розыском… (?) бывшего [**12ob.**] Поземельно-податного отделения при С.[ыр]-Д.[арьинском] Обл.[астном] Правлении вакуфного документа на имущество, оспариваемое просительницей Турабаевой и Журнала Общего Присутствия Областного Правления по этому документу. Наведение справок по сему делу усложнилось отсутствием Журнала Обл.[астного] Правлении по Поземельно-податному отделению и некоторых дел, которые взяты означенным отделением в гор. Самарканде.

Подписал: Военный Губернатор [*signature*]

[**16**]

Начальнику города Ташкента

При рассмотрении дела по обвинению сартом Сибзарской части гор. Ташкента Садыкджаном Ахунджановым бывшего Казия той же части Мухетдина Ходжи в подложном составлении вакуфного документа на шесть лавок, оставшихся после смерти дяди названного сарта Байбаба Турабаева, встретилась надобность в нижеследующих сведениях: когда умер Байбаба Турабаев, т.е. в котором году, месяце и которого числа.

Вследствие сего, Областное правление предлагает Вашему Высокоблагородию доставить эти сведения в самом непродолжительном времени.

Подписал Пом. Губернатора Н. Хамутов

Сов. А. Ильинский

Делопроизводитель [*signature*]

Верно: Помощник делопроизводителя [*signature*]

[**22**]

В Сыр-Дарьинское Областное Правление

Ташкентского сарта Сибзарской части, махаля Махсидуз Садыкджана Ахунджанова

Прошение

В дополнение прошения моего, поданного в Областное Правление и подписки, данной управлению Начальника г. Ташкента 16 Ноября минувшего 1892 года, а последним представленной в Областное Правление вместе с делом оного № 172/1887 г. по предписанию за № 877/10383 – 1892 г., о признании мною вакуфного документа, имеющегося в сказанном деле подложным я, в подтверждение заявления моего о подложности вакуфного документа, имею честь доложить следующее: что назначенный по вакуфнаме мутавалием сарт Сибзарской части, махаля Кагата, Закирджан Ахунджанов, умерший 5 лет тому назад, никогда таковым, т.е. мутавалием лавок, назначенных, будто-бы, покойным отцом моим Байбабою в вакуф мечетей квартала Масхидуз – не был, это может подвердить брат его, Хакимджан Ахунбаев, с которым первый, т.е. Закирджан, до самой смерти своей жил вместе и никогда не говорил ему, Хакимджану, о том, что он считается мутавалием вышесказанного вакуфа. Кроме того, я ссылаюсь на целый ряд свидетелей, а именно: сартов Шейхантаурской части махалля Арка-куча – Уста Азима Тапыл- [**22ob.**] дыбаева, Сибзарской части, махаля Казы-куча Надырмета Измаил Ходжинова и Кукчинской части, махаля Кунчилик – Риски Магомет Мирзабаева, Алимджана Рахимджанбаева и Имамджана Мирзабаева, которые могут удостоверить, что покойным отцом моим никакого завещания в вакуф делаемо не было; по поводу этого также необходимо показание, значущегося по вакуфнаме свидетелем сарта Мулла Иманджана Иса Мухаммедбаева. Что же касается другого свидетеля, значущегося в вакуфном документе, мулла Байзака Джансакал Аксакалова, то подобной личности не только что из близких моих знакомых, но и одномахалинцев я не знаю, а также и соседи мои не слыхали подобного имени и фамилии; следовательно, каким же образом он мог попасть в свидетели? В данном деле не безинтересно также и то обстоятельство, что к вакуфному документу приложены неодновременно печати, свидетельствующих оный: Сибзарского казия Мухаммед Мухитдин Ходжа Хаким Ходжа Ишан Казий Ходжинова, муфтия Иса Ходжа Азизляр Ходжа Казиева и агляма Абдурасуля Мулла Мир Ашурова; печати последних двух вырезаны несколькими годами позже составления самого документа.

Докладывая о вышеизложенном Областному Правлению, я вновь имею честь покорнейше просить распоряжения о производстве по сему делу расследования, как и не лишним считаю в подтверждение подложности вакуфного документа.

[**29**] 1892 года Ноября 18 дня я, нижеподписавшийся бывший Народный судья Сибзарской части гор. Ташкента Мухитдин Ходжа, даю сию подписку Управлению Начальника гор. Ташкента в том, что находящийся в деле 172/1887 г. временного поземельно-податного отделения при Сыр-Дарьинском Областном Правлении, приложенном к предписанию того же Правления от 14 сего ноября за № 877/10383 вакуфный документ двух [**29ob.**] мечетей квартала Масхидуз, действительно тот самый, в подложности которого Саиджан Ахунджанов обвиняет меня.

Перевод: Составленный вакуфнаме у меня этот самый есть и при составлении были на нем приложены моя печать и печать агляма Мулла Абдрасуля, но после меня другой казий, назначив на этот вакуф другого мутаваллия – Закирджана, приложил на нем тоже свою печать, а также печать муфтия.

Подпись Мухетдина.

Подписку отбирал Письмоводитель [*signature*]

[**30**] 1892 года Ноября 19 дня я, нижеподписавшийся сарт г. Ташкента Садыкджан Ахунджанов, даю настоящую подписку управлению Начальника города Ташкента в том, что находящийся в деле № 172/1887 г. приложенном к предписанию Сыр-Дарьинского Областного Правления от 14 сего Ноября за № 877/10383 вакуфный документ двух мечетей квартала Махсидуз, действительно есть тот самый документ, в подлинности которого обвиняется бывший казий Мухитдин и назначенный мутавалием к вакуфу Закирджан Ахунджанов. При этом присовокупляю, что если бы мой отец означенные в вакуфнаме лавки назначил в вакуф мечетей, то документы, находящиеся в моих руках на эти недвижимости, не оставил бы мне на владение лавками, а приложил бы к вакуфнаме или по крайней мере объявил бы в вакуфнаме, [**30ob.**] что если на означенные там лавки впоследствии разыщутся какие-либо документы – васики, то их не признавать действительными.

Перевод упоминаемых мною документов, находящихся у меня на руках, в Областное Правление мною уже при прошении представлен.

Перевод: По безграмотству Садыкджана Ахунджанова за него по личной просьбе расписался Садабек Нарбутабеков.

Пер. [*signature*]

Подписку отобрал письмоводитель [*signature*]

[**31**] Его Высокопревосходительству Г. Туркестанскому Генерал Губернатору

Сартянки, г. Ташкента, Сибзарской части, махали Кахабита, Майрам биби Турабаевой

Прошение

Родной мой отец Бай-баба Турабаев назад тому 10 лет помер, оставив после себя имущество, состоящее из пяти лавок в Сибзарской части и одной лавки в Кукчинской части, деньгами 110 руб. и кроме того разного имущества на 300 руб. Всему вышеизложенному имуществу я прихожусь прямой наследницей, но между тем наследство не могу получить до сего времени, по той причине, что будто бы Казий Сибзарской части Мухитдин при смерти отца моего составил документ, что имущество отец мой завещал в вакуф, который документ я считаю вымышленным в силу того, что при совершении документа Казием, отец мой находился не в своей памяти и не в здравом уме, а находился совершенно на одре смертности, чему у меня имеются свидетели, жители одной со мною [**31ob.**] части [personal names follow], если понадобится могу представить многих других.

Казий Мухитдин в течении 7 лет собирал доход с лавок и куда оный он употреблял – я не знаю; но за последнее время в течении трех лет во время казия Азизляр Хана собирал доходы сын мой Закирджан Ахунджанов, но затем по наступлению Казия Мухитдина на должность, этот...(?) собирают доход с моего имущества в свою пользу.

Докладывая о сем Вашему Высокопревосходительству, имею честь покорнейше просить назначить по этому делу дознание и переданное мне по наследству имущество немедленно вернуть мне и взыскать с Казия за 7 лет полученной арендной платы с моего имущества – 840 руб; и Казия привлечь к законной ответственности по общим русским законам на общем основании за злоупотребление. Июня 7 дня [**32**] 1891 года. К сему прошению вместо просительницы неграмотной по просьбе ее подписался Коллежский Асессор [*signature*]

[**Л. 33**] Настоящее прошение по приказанию г. Военного губернатора препровождается г. Начальнику гор. Ташкента для выяснения: а) действительно ли народный судья Мухутдин с имущества просительницы собирал доход в свою личную пользу и б) действительно ли отец просительницы завещал свое имущество вакуфу и в чем ведении состоит оно в настоящее время, а также было ли это дело в рассмотрении подлежащего суда и в утвердительном смысле, какое последовало со стороны суда определение?

Июня 24 дня 1891 года. Город Ташкент.

Советник [*signature*]

[**33ob.**] С представлением настоящей переписки имею честь донести Сыр-Дарьинскому Областному Правлению, что изложенная в прошении Майрам-биби Турабаевой жалоба, есть повторение без всяких изменений жалобы ее двоюродного брата Садыкджана Уста Ахунджанова. Означенный туземец домогается назначения его мутавалием вакуфа, оставленного умершим Байбаба Турабаевым в пользу двух мечетей махалли Максы-дуз Сибзарской части. Между тем прав на это назначение, по содержанию вакуф-наме, Садыкджан никаких не имеет. Прошение Садыкджана Уста Ахунджанова рассматривалось уже Съездом Народных Судей вверенного мне города, восходило на рассмотрение Г. Военного Губернатора Сыр-Дарьинской области и, в последний раз, претензия эта поступила ко мне при предложении Сыр-Дарьинского Областного Правления 6 Апреля сего года за № 439/3072, которым требовалось доставить дополнительные сведения по прошению. Вследствие этого распоряжения мною было поручено Помощнику моему произвести по делу подробное дознание, которое и было представлено со всей перепиской в Сыр-Дарьинское Областное Правление 4 июня сего года за № 1793.

В виду вышеизложенного, по настоящему прошению Майрам биби не представляется возможным доставить каких-либо новых сведений о вакуфе Байбаба Турабаева, не заключающихся в представленном уже по этому делу дознанию Садыкджана Уста Ахунджанова, недобившись ус- [34] пеха. Подавая несколько прошений от своего имени, очевидно, прибегает теперь к уловкам, выставляя в лице двоюродной сестры своей Майрам биби Турабаевой новую претендентку к пожертвованному в вакуф имуществу, состоящему из 6-ти лавок на Азиатском базаре. Июня 27 дня 1891 года.

Начальник города Ташкента,
Артиллерии полковник [*signature*]

[39]

Перевод

Выписка из Шариатских книг

Если подтвердится, что завещание Байбабая относительно отказа своих лавок в вакуфное пользование сделано им на смертном одре, будучи не в здравом уме и памяти, то в таком случае вакуф этот по мусульманскому законоположению должен считаться недействительным и потому отказное имущество подлежит разделу между прямыми наследниками завещателя.

Приложены четыре печати
Перевел Надворный Советник [*signature*]

Справка: Просительница Майрам биби Турабаева, представляя эту выписку его Высокопревосходительству, жаловалась на медленное производство ее дела; из дела же Канцелярии Генерал-губернатора видно, что прошение Турабаевой, согласно резолюции г. Главного Начальника Края, отправлено на заключение г. Военного Губернатора Сыр Дарьинской области 15 Июня 1891 года за № 3602.

Надворный Советник [*signature*]

[**40**]

Представляя настоящую переписку в Сыр Дарьинское Областное Правление, имею честь донести, что по настоящему делу, как выяснилось через опрос заинтересованных сторон, никакого решения съезда народных судей г. Ташкента постановлено не было. Вакуфный документ на недвижимое имущество, заве- [**40ob.**] щанное Турабаевым, по заявлению бывшего народного судьи Мухитдин-Ходжа, находится в Областном Правлении, куда представлен на предмет утверждения.

Гор. Ташкент Сентября 30 дня 1892 года.

Начальник города, полковник [*signature*]

[**41**]

Возвращая настоящую переписку Начальнику города Ташкента, Областное Правление предлагает Его Высокоблагородию донести надписью на сем же: когда и кем были представлены в правление документы на недвижимое имущество, завещанное Турабаевым в вакуфы мечетей Шарафатбая и Ходжа Ахрар Вали.

28 Октября 1892 года.

Помощник Губернатора [*signature*]

Справка: Документ представлен не Начальником города.

Секретарь [*signature*]

[**41ob.**]

1892 г. 2 Ноября бывший Народный судья Мухитдинхан объяснил, что вакуфный документ он сам выдал в Областное правление, куда еще представлял платежное объяснение по этому делу.

Сын умершего мутавалия Ата-Улла-махсума Мулла Хан Махсумова – Махсумхан объяснил, что вакуфный документ представлял в Областное Правление он совместно с родственником вакуфоучредителя Байбабы – Закиром лем 5 тому назад, т.е. тогда же, когда было объявлено о необходимости представления туда всех вакуфных документов.

Сведения эти отбирал Секретарь [*signature*]

[**42**]

АКТ № 69

1891 года июня 3 дня я, Помощник Начальника гор. Ташкента Артиллерии Штабс Капитан Лыкошин, произвел дознание по поводу поданного жителем махалла Махсыдуз Сибзарской части Садыкджана Уста Ахунджановым прошения о присвоении Сибзарским Народным Судьей Мухиддин Ходжа Хакимджановым прав мутаваллия по отношению к вакфу Байбаба Турабаева и о неуплате ему, Садыкджану 110 руб., взятых Народным Судьей при разделе имущества его отца.

По заявлению Садыкджана, его дядя Байбаба Турабаев за несколько дней до смерти призвал его, Садыкджана, и при двух свидетелях объявил, что принадлежащие Турабаеву на большом базаре Азиатской части гор. Ташкента шесть лавок Турабаев намерен пожертвовать в вакф двум мечетям махалли Махсы-Дуз Сибзарской части, но мутаваллием этого вакфа предлагает назначить его – Садыкджана Уста Ахунджанова. По словам Садыкджана, он никогда не читал сам вакф-нама, составленный о пожертвовании 6 лавок, но вполне уверен, что дядя его и распорядился своим имуществом так, как предполагал. Далее Садыкджан говорил, что Сибзарский Народный Судья совершив раздел имения, оставшего- [**420b.**] ся по смерти его отца – Уста Ахунджана, потребовал, чтобы Садыкджан уплатил ему 110 руб., не объясняя за что именно следует эти деньги. Также и с других сонаследников Садыкджана Народный Судья потребовал деньги по своему усмотрению. Садыкджан, как он говорит, из страха пред Народным Судьей, немедленно уплатил 110 руб и до сего времени не получил их обратно. Это было в 1881 году и Садыкджан думает, что при разделе имущества никак не менее 1/10 ЧАСТИ было взято Народным Судьей за совершение раздела.

Для выяснения правильности заявления Садыкджана я отправился лично в Азиатскую часть города, осмотрел вакфные лавки, причем оказалось, что пять из них отремонтированы в этом году, шестая же в местности Купчилик совершенно разрушилась и никакого дохода не приносит. В настоящее время, с Октября 1890 года мутавалием вакфа Байбаба Турабаева состоит по назначению Сибзарского Народного Судьи Махсумхан Атаулла Аглямова. Этот мутаваллий предъявил засвидетельствованную Сибзарским Народным судьей вакф-нама, написанную на персидском языке, из которой видно, что Байбаба Турабаев еще при жизни своей, через особого доверителя – Закирджана Мулла Хакимджанова совершил у Сибзарского Народного судьи акт о пожертвовании шести лавок [**43**] в вакф двум мечетям махалла Махсыдуз Сибзарской части – мечети Шарафатбая и Ходжа Ахрара Вали. Эти две мечети по желанию жертвователя должны пользоваться доходами с лавок и доход этот делить пополам между двумя мечетями. Каждая полученная таким образом сумма должна быть распределена между: 1) мутаваллием, получающим 1/20 всего дохода; 2) Имамом, которому выдавать 5/20 всего дохода; 3) Суфи, получающим 2/20 всего дохода и 4) остальные 2/20 всего дохода должны быть расходуемы на содержание в чистоте самой мечети, приобретение для молящихся плетенок и другие расходы по ремонту и благоустройству мечетей. О том, кто именно должен быть мутаваллием вакфа, в акте не сказано ни слова, не говорится даже о переходе каких-либо прав к потомству (*аулад*) жертвователя, как обыкновенно пишется в вакф-нама, которыми жертвователи, делая богоугодное дело, обеспечивают и свое потомство, завещая всему своему роду право быть распределителем вакфа. Никаких указаний в помянутом акте не заключается, а потому согласно шариата, право назначения мутавалли предоставляется Народному Судье по соглашению или по выбору одномахаллинцев.

Так и делалось, Народный Судья назначал мутаваллиев и наблюдал за распределителем доходов, получаемых с лавок. Между прочими был [**43ob.**] назначен и племянник покойного Турабаева – Закир, но не оправдал доверия, запутал счеты, растратил деньги и за несколько лет с вакфа доходов не получалось. Закир умер и заинтересованным лицам пришлось простить присвоенные им деньги. Этот мутаваллий был назначен бывшим Народным Судьей Азизларханом, когда Закир умер, то махаллинцы не выбирали мутаваллия, а просили Народного Судью собирать и распределять доходы через одного из состоящего при нем мирзы. Так и делал Народный Судья, но в прошлом году назначил мутаваллием имама одной из мечетей махалла Махсы-Дуз – Махсумхана. С тех пор доходы с лавок увеличились почти вдвое, но чистых денег все еще не получается, так как все доходы идут на ремонт лавок. Чистый доход будет получаться с Октября 1891 года и будут делиться между администрацией мечети, как то указано в вакф-нама, хотя впрочем по всей вероятности, с общего согласия, мутаваллию удастся часть денег употребить на ремонт или лучше сказать на постройку заново развалившейся лавки в местности Купчилик, чтобы все шесть лавок приносили доход. Цены за аренду увеличены в 1890 г. и 3 лавки платят по 20 руб. и 2 лавки по 25 руб., всего получается пока 110 руб. в год.

Далее я вызвал всех заинтересованных в получении вакуфного дохода лиц, именно: мутаваллия, [**44**] Имамов и Суфи двух мечетей махалла Махсы-Дуз Сибзарской части Шарафат-бай и Ходжа Ахрар Вали. Все эти лица заявили, что вакфные доходы с шести лавок, оставленных в пользу мечетей Байбаба Турабаевым, получаются и расходуются правильно, что если умерший Закир и растратил доходы за несколько лет, то эту растрату ему простили, так как по бедности, нельзя взыскать деньги с его наследников, а в настоящее время все заинтересованные в получении вакфных доходов лица вполне довольны распоряжениями Народного Судьи по эксплоатации вакфных доходов и к тому претензий не имеют. Претензии же к вакфу Садыкджана Уста Ахунджанова ни на чем не основаны, вполне голословны, на самого же Садыкджана администрация этих двух мечетей имеет претензии – он захватил часть принадлежащей им земли и об этом будет подано прошение. Таким образом, дознанием выяснено, что претензии Садыкджана на то, что его не назначили мутаваллием вакфа Байбаба Турабаева не подтверждаются, судя по копии вакфнама, находящейся в руках мутаваллия Махсумхана, Садыкджан заявил, что копия эта не сходна с подлинным вакфным документом, но сравнить эти два документа я не мог, так как подлинный вакфнама вместе с прочими до- [**44ob.**] кументами находится на рассмотрении в Сыр-Дарьинском Областном Правлении.

Предполагая, что претензии Садыкджана к Народному Судье о 110 руб. настолько же неосновательны, как ранее сего предъявленная Садыкджаном о 90 руб., я предложил жалобщику сначала подтвердить свое голословное заявление какими-либо доказательствами, для представления этих данных мною был назначен срок, к которому Садыкджан не явился, на другой день он привел двух свидетелей, которые не могли с достоверностью сказать за что именно и когда были переданы 110 руб. Народному Судье Мухиддину ходже, но знают, что Народный Судья после раздела 10 лет тому назад получил какие-то деньги; но сколько именно и за что – не знают. Садыкджан еще сослался на многих свидетелей, но когда я попросил его ранее вызова свидетелей сказать – имеют ли эти свидетели возможность подтвердить, что деньги – 110 руб. были взяты Народным Судьей сверх вознаграждения за раздел, принудительно или в виде взятки, то сам Сыдыкджан отозвался, что свидетели им названные знают только, что деньги переданы, а за что именно – сказать тоже не могу. Усматривая из показаний опрошенных мною двух свидетелей Садыкджана, что они долг в 110 руб. считают тот же, о котором в сумме 90 руб. Садыкджан [**45**] уже предъявля иск к Народному Судье, я справился в делах и оказалось, что претензии эти разбирались уже и в иске Садыкджану было отказано. В виду вышеизложенного, я не нашел нужным вызывать свидетелей и закончил производимое мною дознание, находя, что и претензии о 110 руб., также как и претензии на звание мутаваллия Садыкджан Уста Ахунджанов подтвердить не может.

Артиллерии Штабс-Капитан *Н. Лыкошин*

[46]

Сыр-дарьинское Областное Правление

. . . (?) Апреля 1891 года

№ 439/3072

Начальнику города Ташкента

Предписанием от 18 Мая минувшего года за № 459/4306 Областное Правление просило Ваше Высокоблагородие сообщить необходимые сведения по прошению Ташкентского сарта Садыкджана Уста Ахунджанова, который в прошении этом жалуется на то, что Казий Сибзарской части гор. Ташкента Мухитдин Ходжа, присвоив себе звание мутавалия над 6 вакуфными лавками, оставшимися после смер- [46ob.] ти дяди просителя Байбаба Турабаева, пользуется доходами с этих лавок и, что взяв у него – Садыкджана Ахунджанова взаимообразно 110 рублей, Казий не возвращает ему этих денег.

В прошении того же Ахунджанова, поданном г. Военному Губернатору в Сентябре месяце 1889 года и которое Его Превосходительством оставлено без последствий, он, Ахунджанов, обвинял Казия Мухитдина Ходжу в том, что при разделе имущества, оставшегося после смерти отца просителя, между его наследниками, бросил в реку вещи, доставшиеся на долю Садыкджана Ахунджанова и перебрал у него в разное время деньгами 85 руб., не возвратив таковых.

Таким образом, в обоих претензиях Ахунджанова заключаются совершенно [47] разные обвинения Казия Мухитдин Ходжи и подобной жалобы, в которой Ахунджанов заявляет о присвоении Казием прав мутавалия над вакуфным имуществом на рассмотрение г. Военного Губернатора ранее сего не поступало.

Уведомляя об этом Ваше Высокоблагородие с возвращением представленного при надписи Вашей от 18 минувшего марта за № 1793/4064 прошения Садыкджана Уста Ахунджанова, Областное Правление просит Вас сообщить нужные по содержанию этого прошения сведения для доклада г. Военному Губернатору.

Советник [*signature*]

[48]

Его Высокопревосходительству, Господину Туркестанскому Генерал-Губернатору

Ташкентского сарта Сибзарской части, махалли Махсидуз, Садыкджана Уста-Ахунджанова

Прошение

После смерти брата моего Байбаба Турапбаева остались шесть лавок на Ташкентском базаре Азиатской части, что эти лавки вакуфные, согласно вакуф-наме доходами из лавок должен пользоваться я, как наследник вакуфа, но почему-то казий Сибзарской части Мухитдин ходжа, называя себя мутавалием, пользуется доходами вакуфа уже семь лет, отдавая лавки в аренду по двадцать руб. в год, помя- [**48ob.**] нутому казию я отдавал заимообразно сто десять рублей, который их не платил. Вакуф-наме находится у казия Сибзарской части, что названный казий не родственник Турапбаева и он не может быть мутавалием и согласно вакуф-наме мутавалием должен быть я. Относительно этого, я подавал прошение подлежащему начальству, но никакого удовлетворения не получил.

Почтительнейше прошу Ваше Высокопревосходительство поручить это дело кому следует, отобрать лавки и вакуф-нама от казия Мухитдина и взыскать с него 110 руб.

Мая 3 дня 1890 года. [*signature*]

[**49**]

Прошение это представляя в Сыр Дарьинское Областное Правление, имею честь донести на предписание от 18 числа мая 1890 года за № 459/4306, что на подобное уже прошение этого просителя уже донесено было Областному Правлению 6 числа 9 Марта 1889 года за № 4064, которое дало мне знать 5 числа Июля 1890 года за № 1030/6192, что в действиях Казия Сибзарской части о разделе имущества между наследниками Уста Ахунджанова, преступления должности не заключается и жалобы на утрату вещей и незаконное взыскание денег представляются совершенно голословными и дело уже решено окончательно Съездом народных судей, а потому Его Превосходительство Г. Военный Губернатор Сыр Дарьинской Области изволил приказать (резолюцией 4 Июля 1890 года) настоящее дело производством прекратить, что и объявлено тогда же просителю с подпиской.

Марта 18 дня 1891 года.

Начальник г. Ташкента, Артиллерии Полковник [*signature*]

Секретарь [*signature*]

Письмоводитель [*signature*]

[**50**]

Согласно предписания за № 4064 казий Сибзарской части доносит, что в 1881 году, когда еще Байбаба Траббаев был жив, он 6 собственных лавок в Сибзарской части подарил в вакуф двум мечетям, находящимся в этой же части махалле Махсидуз. Согласно шариата составил вакуфный документ так, чтобы доходами с названных шести лавок пользовались следующие лица: 1/10 частью всего дохода Мутавалли обоих мечетей, 5/10 ч. - два Имама обоих мечетей, 3/10 ч. – два Суфия мечетей и остальные 3/10 части – на ремонт мечетей; вакуфный документ был сдан Мутаваллию. В шариате сказано: назначить Му- [**50ob.**] таваллиев не из родных дарителя вакуфа, а из тех того, кого сам даритель вакуфа назначает. После того, в 1883 года было выбрано казием Сибзарской части другое лицо, через три года он, Мухитдин, опять был выбран казием и с того времени, безотрывно заведывает казийским делом Сибзарской части; если он, казий, получал бы сам вакуфные доходы, то служащие в местах заявляли бы о неправильных действиях его, казия. Податель сего прошения Садыкджан не имеет никаких общих дел, касающихся к вышеназванным мечетям, объяснение его в прошении не правильно и это все выясняется при опросе двух имамов мечетей. Такому мошеннику, как податель сего прошения ничего не следует верить. Во время бытности опекуном его родного малолетнего брата более тысячи руб. денег, принадлежащих малолетнему брату им, Садыкджаном, было истрачено, поэтому последовал приговор его, казия, о взыскании с Садыкджана истраченных денег. Приговор этот съездом казиев был отменен. [**51**] После этого он, Садыкджан, желая вредить нарочно казию, предъявил иск на 90 руб., который по просьбе его, казия Мухитдина, Г. Военный губернатором был передан на разбирательство съезда Уездных казиев, а съездом иск Садыкджана был оставлен без последствий. Теперь же он опять начал подавать ложные прошения. Шариат дозволяет казию разобрать дело, а не пользоваться вакуфными доходами.

Печать Казия.

Перевел [*signature*]

[**52**]

Перевод Вакуф-нама по смыслу верен за исключением того, что в этом документе в одном месте сказанно, что назначение вакуфного условия поручено тому казию, который приложит ниже свою печать; также сказано, что две части из двадцати частей получит мутаваллий, назначенный «мянь-лягуль-веляя», т.е. казием.

Переводчик Коллежский секретарь Айдаров

[53]
Описание границ одной мечети, основанной Хазрати Ходжа Ахраром, находящейся в квартале Махси-Дуз в городе Ташкенте.

Граничит: с запада и с юга – общественной дорогой, с востока – дорожкою, ведущею к особому двору, с севера – с землею, оставшеюся [после] Казакбая.

2) Описание границ одной мечети, основанной Шарафитдинбаем в означенном квартале.

Граничит: с запада, востока и юга – общественной дорогой и с севера – частью недвижимостью Абдурасул-касаба Шах Касымова, частью – Имамбахана Мир Дадабаева.

3) Описание границ двух запирающихся досками лавок в означенном же квартале в рядах таккачиян; одна из них длиною с севера к югу 6 арш., шириною 3/2 аршин, другая из них также с севера к югу длиною 3 ½ аршин, а шириною 3 ½ аршин. Граничат: с запада и севера – общественною дорогой, с востока и юга – недвижимостью Байбаба Халифа Трапбаева.

4) Описание границ одной лавки в квартале Купчиян. Граничит: с запада – общественной дорогой, с востока – общественной речкой, с севера – недвижимостью Алибая и с юга – частью наследственной недвижимостью Бай Мухаммадбая, частью таковою же – Шах Каримбая.

5) Описание границ трех запирающихся досками лавок в рядах Чин-фрушан, смежных между собою. Граничат: с запада – частью лавкою Мирхашимбая Нар Мирзабаева и частью лавкою Шарифбая, с севера – лавкою Мулла Ташмухаммада Мухаммед Мусабаева, с востока и юга – общественной дорогой.

Месяц Сафар 1299 года (1881 г. декабря 25 дня) Закирджан Хакимджанов – шариатный общедоверенный, по доверию больного Байбахалифа, доказанного показаниями: Мулла Имамджана Исамухаммедбаева и Мулла Байзака Джан Сакал Аксакалова – оба эти св ... (?) были лица, принятыми по правилу шариата в свидетелях, явившись в камеру казия гор. Ташкента и будучи в здравом рассудке и при всех к тому способностях, из соб- **[530b.]** ственного и чистого имущества поименованного доверителя своего, пожертвовал в вакуф и сделал законное подаяние все недвижимости, значащейся в прописанных выше границах в 3-м и 4-м пунктах, и все постройки, находящиеся на недвижимости сказанной в пятом пункте со всеми их правами и премуществами, находящимися на них и входящими в них правами, в пользу означенных выше в 1-м и 2-м пунктах, мечетей – поровну, для Его только, Великого бога и с целью получить Его благоволение и из страха адского Его мучения, он сделал этот вакуф – вакуфом правильным, законным, обязательным, вечным, доказанным, заключающим в себе все правила шариата, показывающие правильность, обязательность и действительность этого вакуфа и с представлением прав быть назначенным, по входе в законную силу этого документа, мутаваллию владеть оным. Вакуф этот по составлению о нем решения должен считаться обязательным и включающим в себе все условия о правильности его по шариату, так как он совершается мною без всякого упущения всех правил по отношению к решению о вакуфе шариата. Совершающий это решение он, казий, будучи сведующим и понимающим места в области шариата о разногласии и согласии в вопросах шариата основателей его, да будет благословение Бога всем основателям шариата. В виду вышеизложенного, вакуф этот должен считаться правильным, обязательным, законным, вечным, а потому – продавать его, дарить, отдавать в магар или также в вакуфное и унаследовать его, никто не имеет права, ибо Бог должен унаследовать всю землю и все, что находится на ней. Грех тому, который выслушав вышеизложенное, посмеет отменить этот вакуф. Пожертвователем предоставлено мне, казию, приложившему к сему печать ниже, назначить вакуфное условие, а потому определить: что [54] доход этого вакуфа разделить на 20 частей, из коих 2 части выдавать мутаваллию оного вакуфа, назначенному казием; имаму каждой мечети выдавать по 2 части и остальные 4 части употреблять на освещение и подстилку мечетей поровну. Если означенный вакуф не будет нуждаться в ремонте, то остальные, сказанные выше части, выдавать бедным мусульманам. Все пожертвованные выше вакуфные лавки, по показанию поименованного выше доверенного и лиц, пользующихся доверием из жителей означенной махалли, составляют менее одной третьей части остающегося в руках поименованного выше вакуфозавещателя.

Как было обстоятельство данного дела, так и писано, с тем, чтобы оно в случае надобности служило бы пред шариатом доказательством и разъяснило бы прошлое. Документ этот составлен в присуствии сведующих и справедливых лиц. Приложена печать казия Мухаммед Мухитдин Ходжа Хаким Ходжа Ишан Казыкалянова. Ниже сего писано другим почерком нижеследующее: Закирджан Ахунджанов мною назначен мутаваллием на основании того, что назначение мутаваллия Байбабою предоставлено право «мянь-ляхуль-веляя», т.е. казию. Печать казия Сибзарской части Иман Азизляр Ходжа Ишан Афтан Ходжина. Рядом с его печатью следуют еще 2 печати, одна из них муфтия Исаходжи Азизляр Ходжа Казиева, а другая – Агляма Абдурасуля Муин (?) Мир Ашурова.

Перевел [*signature*]

[60]

Журнал Общего Присутствия Сыр-Дарьинского Областного правления 30 Января 1893 года

Слушали: 1). Прошение сарта Сибзарской части гор. Ташкента Садыкджана Уста Ахунджанова от 3-го Мая 1890 года, поданное г. Туркестанскому генерал-губернатору и препровожденное в канцелярию Его Высокопревосходительства на распоряжение г. Военного Губернатора области, коим он жалуется о присвоении Сибзарским казием Мухитдином Ходжей прав мутавалия над имуществом, состоящим из 6-ти лавок, завещанных в вакуф двум мечетям, покойным его дядей Байбаба Турабаевым, мутавалием которого должен быть он, жалобщик, как ближайший родственник завещателя; пользовании доходами, получаемыми с названного вакуфа в сумме 120 руб. в год и о невозврате 110 руб., взятых у него названным казием заимообразно. 2) Препровожденное Канцелярии Туркестанского генерал-губернатора прошение, проживающей в Сибзарской части гор. Ташкента сартянки Майрам Биби Турабаевой от 7-го Июня 1891 года, в коем она заявляет, что после смерти ее отца – Байбаба Турубаева, десять лет тому назад, осталось шесть лавок, 110 руб. денег и на 300 руб. движимого и недвижимого имущества, которые должны перейти в ее распоряжение, как [**Л. 60 об.**] прямой наследницы, но наследство это она не получила, вследствие составленного казием Мухетдином Ходжей вымышленного вакуфного документа на то время, когда отец ее был при смерти, без памяти и не в здравом рассудке. В подтверждении этого обстоятельства, жалобщица указала пять человек свидетелей и заявила, что может представить много других, если то понадобится.

Из представленного названным казием объяснения видно, что покойный Бай баба Турабаев еще при жизни своей в 1881 г. подарил в вакуф двух мечетей Шарафий-бия и Ходжа Ахрара Вали, находящихся в Сибзарской части гор. Ташкента в махалле Махсидуз, 6-ть лавок, о чем и был составлен документ, согласно которому он и распоряжался доходами, что могут подтвердить заинтересованные в том лица. Принесение же на него жалобы Садыкджаном Ахунджановым объясняет враждебным отношением его за сделанное постановление о взыскании растраченных им более 1000 руб. малолетнего брата его в бытность опекуном над ним.

В проведенном по этому делу дознании жалобщик Садыкджан Уста Ахунджанов показал, что покойный дядя его Байбаба Турабаев за несколько дней до смерти объявил ему, в присутствии двух свидетелей, что он намерен пожертвовать в вакуф вышесказанные шесть [61] лавок, мутавалием которого предполагает назначить его, Садыкджана, и он вполне уверен, что дядя распорядился с имуществом, как предполагал. Деньги в сумме 110 руб., по требованию Казия, были даны при разделе имения, оставшегося после смерти отца его, Уста Ахунджанова, которых до сих пор не получил обратно. За раздел же наследства, оставшегося после смерти отца просителя, означенный казий получил десятую часть.

По учреждении вакуфа из имущества дяди просителя первое время был мутавалием племянник жертвователя Закир, который запутал счета, растратил деньги и за несколько лет доходов с вакуфа не получал. По смерти Закира, согласно просьбе общества, казием не назначался мутавалий, а доходы собирались и распределялись им через одного из мирз.

В Октябре месяце 1890 года мутавалием названного вакуфа был назначен казием Максум Хан Атаулла Аглумов, которым была предъявлена помощнику Начальника гор. штабс-капитану Лыкошину, производившему дознание, копия документа вакуф-наме, написанная на персидском языке и засвидетельствованная казием. Из копии этой усмотрено, что названные шесть лавок были завещаны в вакуф двум мечетям Шарафий-бий и Ходжа Ахрара Вали, но о том, кто должен быть назначен мутаваллием в документе [61об] этом завещателем ничего не сказано. При этом жалобщик Садыкджан Уста Ахунджанов заявил, что копия эта с подлинным документом не верна.

ДОПРОШЕННЫЕ: мутавалий, имамы и суфии, состоящие при названных мечетях, заинтересованные в доходах, получаемых с вакуфа, учрежденного Байбаба Турабаевым, показали, что доходы с него получаются и расходуются правильно, что все распоряжениями казия по эксплоатации вакуфных доходов они довольны и никаких претензий не имеют.

Для проверки претензий жалобщика относительно 110 руб. штабс-капитаном Лыкошиным был назначен срок для представления доказательств в присовении казием 110 руб., но он в срок не явился, а привел на другой день двух свидетелей, показавших, что казий, десять лет тому назад, после раздела наследства, оставшегося по смерти отца жалобщика, получил деньги, но сколько именно и за что не знают.

По прошению Майрам Биби Турабаевой, препровожденному Начальнику гор. Ташкента для разъяснений, последний с возвращением переписки, донес, что таковое есть повторение жалобы ее доверенного брата (двоюродного) Садыкджана Уста Ахунджанова, который, не имея успеха в домогательствах своих, относительно назначения его мутаваллием вакуфа, учрежденного Байбаба Турабаевым, очевидно, [62] прибегает теперь к уловке, выставляя в лице доверенной сестры своей Майрам Биби Турабаевой новую претендентку к пожертвованному в вакуф имуществу.

СПРАВКА: 1) Из дела бывшего временно поземельно-податного отделения при Сыр-Дарьинском областном правлении 1877 года за № 172, в коем имеется подлинный вакуфный документе (вакуф-наме) от 25 Декабря 1881 года или 1882 г., в переводе подлинного документа сделана переводчиком Сыр-Дарьинского областного правления, титулярным советником Айдаровым, оговорка, что точно определить год составления документа невозможно по неразборчивости последней цифры года против которого ныне заявлен спор о подлоге, усматривается: а) завещанное Байбаба Турабаевым в вакуф мечетей ходжа Ахрар Вали и Шараф бия имущество состоит из шести лавок в разных кварталах Азиатской части гор. Ташкента;

б) заявление народному судье Сибзарской части гор. Ташкента о пожертвовании Турубаевым упомянутого имущества в вакуф сделано 4 Мая 1881 года, как сказано в самом документе и не самим жертвователем Турабаевым, а по болезни последнего, другим лицом, именно Закирджаном Хакимджановым, который вслед за этим распоряжением сделан был мутавалием, будто бы по доверию Турабаева, данному при двух свидетелях. Совершение же самого документа (вакуф-наме) последовало 25 Декабря 1882 года, т.е. спустя год и семь месяцев после заявления.

[62ob.] в) на документе имеются печати: Казия Мухитдин Ходжи 1286 г. (1869 г.) казия Сибзарской части Ишан Азизляр Ходжи 1300 г. (1883 г.), муфтия Иса Ходжи Азазляр Ходжи Казиева 1300 г. (1883 г.) и агляма Абдурасуля Мулла Мир Ашурова 1282 г. (1865 г.).

2) В Журнале Общего присутствия Областного правления (по поземельно-податному отделению) от 9 Июня 1888 г. сказано: «принимая во внимание, что представленный 1 Июля 1887 года мутавалием Закирджаном Ахунджановым Оглы вакуфный документ составляет собою подлинную вакуф-наме, несодержащую в себе никаких указаний на ее недействительность и, следовательно, неопределяющую основания отнесению ее к числу явно подложенных или утративших силу, Общее присутствие Сыр-Дарьинского областного правления постановило: вакуфный документ на имущество, принадлежащее мечетям квартала Махси-Дуз в гор. Ташкенте признать подлежащим исследованию в установленном для этого порядке и, с этой целью, препроводить его, вместе с делом за № 172 в поземельно-податную комиссию Ташкентского

уезда, для передачи тому из комиссаров, на которого будет впоследствии возложенно исследование вакуфов гор. Ташкента». Так как поземельно-податная комиссия производила поземельно-податные работы исключительно в Ташкентском уезде, но не в самом гор. Ташкенте, а по окончании работ в этом уезде, переведена в минувшем [**63**] 1892 г. в Самаркандскую область, то приведенное выше Журнальное определение осталось неисполненным, а таким образом и вакуф-наме, упомянутый в этом определении, остался неисследованным.

3) В Октябре 1892 г. жалобщик Садыкджан Уста Ахунджанов, в подтверждение подложного составления казием Мухетдином Ходжей вакуфа-наме, представил в областное правления два казийских документа, по коим дядя его Байбаба Турабаев приобрел три лавки, значащиеся в вакуф-наме.

По предъявлении Начальником гор. Ташкента вакуф-наме, согласно предписания Областного правления от 14-го Ноября 1892 г. за № 877/10383, казию Мухетдину Ходже и жалобщику Садыкджану Уста Ахунджанову, оба признали его за тот самый, в подложном составлении которого обвиняется казий. При этом жалобщик добавил, что если бы дядя его завещал означенные лавки в вакуф, то не оставил бы ему документов на право владения таковыми, а приложил бы имеемые у него документы к вакуф-наме или же объяснил бы в нем, что если на завещанные лавки розыщутся какие-либо документы, васихи, то их не признавать действительными.

4) Из донесения Начальника гор. Ташкента от 8 Января сего года за № 86, видно, что Байбаба Турабаев умер, по показанию знавших его, в период времени с 10 декабря 1882 по 7 марта 1883 г.

[**63ob.**] ЗАКОН: 209 и 229 ст. Полож. об упр. Турк. края и 362 ст. Улож. о Наказ. Угол. и испр.

Подписал: и.д. Делопроизводителя [*signature*]

ПРИКАЗАЛИ: Имея в виду: 1) что жалобщица Турабаева категорически заявляет в прошении своем от 7 Июня 1891 года, что вакуфный документ, составленный у казия Мухитдина Ходжи на имущество ее отца, есть вымышленный и что отец ее, во время совершения документа, был на смертном одре не в своей памяти и не в здравом уме, в подтверждении каковаго обстоятельства она указывает 5-ть человек свидетелей и при том заявляет, что если понадобится, может представить много других свидетелей;

2) что жалобщик Ахунджан, как на доказательство подлога указывает на представленные им документы на некоторые из лавок, кои зачислены в вакуф;

3) что время заявления о пожертвовании не совпадает с временем совершения самого вакуфного документа;

4) что приложение печатетей на упомянутом документе в свою очередь произведены, по видимому, в разное время;

5) что подписи или печати Закирджана Хакимджанова на документе вовсе не имеется и, таким образом, факт пожертвования Турабаевым упомянутого имущества в вакуф держится на одном лишь удостоверении бывшего народного судьи Сибзарской части Мухитдина Ходжи, на незаконные действия его и предъявлены жалобы; приложение же к документу "своей [**64**] печати" другим народным судьей уже после совершения не может быть принято во внимание, Общее присутствие Областного правления полагает необходимым в видах выяснения истины, произвести по сему делу формальное следствие.

Что касается 110 руб., отыскиваемых жалобщиком Ахунджановым с бывшего народного судьи Мухитдина Ходжи, то дело это подлежит ведению народного суда на основании 209 ст. Полож. об управ. Турк. края, так как проситель, в прошении своем, заявляет, что дал эти деньги заимообразно; выставленные же им свидетели заявили, что деньги эти были даны десять лет тому назад, но на какой предмет – им неизвестно.

ОПРЕДЕЛИЛИ: 1). По обвинению народного судьи Сибзарской части гор. Ташкента Мухитдина Ходжи Казы Калянова в служебном подлоге, т.е. в преступлении, предусмотренном 362 ст. Улож. о Наказ., произвести формальное следствие чрез помощника мирового судьи гор. Ташкента, которому передать всю по сему делу переписку, а равно и дело бывшего поземельно-податного отделения за № 172; 2) объявить СадыкджануАхунджанову, что 110 руб. он должен искать с упомянутого в предыдущем пункте туземца, бывшего народного судьи Мухитдина Ходжи, в подлежащем народном суде. Журнал представить на утверждение г. Военного Губернатора, а затем препроводить на просмотр г. Областного прокурора.

Подписал: За помощника губ. А. Хлебников

Члены: А. Ильинский и. . . . (?)

Верно: [*signature*]

[65]

Журнал № 44

Соглашаясь с мнением г. Областного прокурора Общее присутствие определяет: дело по обвинению бывшего Сибзарского казия Мухитдина Ходжи Казы Калянова в преступлении, предусмотренном 362 ст. Улож. о нак. дальнейшим производством прекратить за истечением давности на основании 2 п. 7 ст. Всемилостивейшего Манифеста 15 мая 1883 года, представив жалобщикам Садыкджану Ахунджанову и Майрам Биби Турарбаевой оспаривать действительность завещания…(?) Байбаба Турабаева в подлежащем народном суде.

Журнал передать на утверждение г. Военного Губернатора и сообщить на просмотр г. Областного Прокурора.

Подписал помощник губернатора [*signature*] и члены [*signature*].

APPENDIX IV

A *Qāḍī*'s Ruling on a Defamation Case

TsGARUz, f. I-164, op. 1, d. 23, ll. 26–26ob.
35.5 × 22 cm.
35–16 lines, 34.5 × 15.5 cm.

On 3 Jumādī al-Thānī 1307/19 January [1890] I, the *qāḍī* of the Zangī Āta, Jinās, Fūlād, and Maydān Ṭāl *volost*'s, on the basis of order no. 5043 issued by the military governor of Syr-Darya Province, worthy of respect, with regard to the petition [submitted by Muḥammad] Ṣādiq Jān Ākhund Jān-ūghlī, which says that Muḥammad Muḥyī al-Dīn Khwāja Īshān, *qāḍī* of the Sibzar district of Tashkent, extorted 90 rubles that belong to him, I had to question [the parties], ascertain the truth and issue a decision. Therefore, I ordered to summon the aforementioned parties up to three times. The petitioner Ṣādiq Jān and ʿUthmān Khwāja ʿInāyat Khwāja-ūghlī, the attorney of the aforementioned Īshān Qāḍī according to Islamic law appeared at my court. I had them confront one another. I asked Ṣādiq Jān to file the claim of 90 rubles against Muḥammad Muḥyī al-Dīn Khwāja Īshān Qāḍī. Muḥammad Sādiq answered [by asking] to confront the same Īshān Qāḍī, otherwise he does not accept his attorney and that he does not file his claim. I explained to him the rule of Islamic law, and I told him that he should proceed with his claim before an attorney, whoever he is, since, by appointing an attorney, Īshan Qāḍī acted according to Islamic law. He did not accept the rule of Islamic law, he showed contempt, did not file his claim, and left. Finally, according to the order of the aforementioned [governor], worthy of respect, in accordance with the procedures of Islamic law I ruled to dismiss the case. Accordingly, on the basis of a fourth summons, the two parties confronted each other at the chancery of Tashkent District[, i.e. the court of appeals]. When I questioned Ṣādiq Jān with regard to his petition concerning the 90 rubles, he explained orally his plea to the court of appeals. He said that his claim involves the aforementioned *qāḍī* who extorted from him 90 rubles. This money belongs to him, and the *qāḍī* took it illegally. [So] he requested that his money be recovered and returned to him. When I questioned attorney ʿUthmān Khwāja, he declared that Ṣādiq Jān submitted an appeal against his client Īshān Qāḍī illegally and without evidence; according to the procedures of Islamic law, the claim he lodged is not sound, so, given that he did not produce any proof, he should be punished; his claim is based on calumny and falsehood. I questioned Ṣādiq Jān whether he could produce any proof or evidence with regard to the claim of 90 rubles against the *qāḍī*. He declared that his proof is that the aforementioned Īshān Qāḍī had acknowledged his claim of 90 rubles at the presence of the Tashkent *qāḍī*s' assembly, that is, Sharīf Khwāja Īshān, ʿAbdallāh Jān Qāḍī, and Tūra Khān Tūra Qāḍī, but that he had no proof or testimony. I asked him if there was written evidence of the acknowledgment that the *qāḍī* had made before the judicial assembly and, if so, to produce it for his own benefit. Ṣādiq Jān replied that, at present, he has no written evidence issued by the judicial assembly that he could produce for his own benefit. Therefore, I explained to Ṣādiq Jān the [juristic] opinions [that are quoted] at the margin [of this document]. I told him that, acting against a *qāḍī* of Islam with no evidence or proof is, according to the procedures of Islamic law, forbidden and disrespectful, and [such a claim] should be ruled not to be heard. For this reason, it was commanded, recorded, and made in accordance with the court of appeals that the written evidence of the Tashkent judicial assembly, wherever it may be, be brought to the court of appeals. I, the *qāḍī* Īshān Khwāja, affixed my seal. I, the aforementioned attorney, ʿUthmān Khwāja, signed. Because the aforementioned Ṣādiq Jān is illiterate, Khwāja Khān Qāḍī Khwāja-ūghlī signed upon his request.

On the second day of the month of Pisces, that is, 26 Jumādī al-Thānī 1307, upon order [of the Russian authorities], I summoned the aforementioned Muḥammad Ṣādiq and the aforementioned attorney ʿUthmān Khwāja and I made them confront each other in the court of appeals. I questioned the claimant, Ṣādiq, as to whether he had the written evidence of the acknowledgment of Muḥammad Muḥyī al-Dīn Khwāja Īshān Qāḍī issued by the *qāḍī*s' assembly in Tashkent and whether he had any evidence, and, if so, asked that he produce it. Muḥammad Ṣādiq showed a judgment issued by the Tashkent *qāḍī*s' assembly. I scrutinized the judgment from top to bottom, but there was no mention of the acknowledgment made by the Īshān Qāḍī to the benefit of Ṣādiq with regard to the 90 rubles. Instead, he [Ṣādiq] was not permitted to act as guardian of the wealth and the property of his brother who had reached puberty, the 19-year-old Ḥasan Jān. This was the judgment issued by the *qāḍī*s' assembly. Later, the aforementioned Ṣādiq explained to the *qāḍī*s' assembly that he had petitioned [the authorities and declared that] the money belonged to him and not to the *qāḍī* of the Sibzar district. The *qāḍī*s' assembly replied that, without an order [issued by the competent authority], the request would not be accepted. This is written at the end of the judgment. For this reason, because Muḥammad Sādiq did not produce at the aforementioned court of appeals any evidence or proof to the claim for 90 rubles, the [juristic] opinions reported in the margin should be followed; [accordingly,] I ruled that the claim against Īshān Qāḍī should not be heard. Because the claim against a *qāḍī* of Islam in office was groundless and itself a vexation, [it was ruled that] the aforementioned Muḥammad Ṣādiq has no claim against the aforementioned Īshān Qāḍī with regard to the 90 rubles, that the dispute was resolved, and [that the ruling] was conclusive because [the claim] was without proof and warrant. The aforementioned ʿUthmān Khwāja ʿInāyat Khwāja-ūghlī signed as he expressed his satisfaction [with the ruling]. Sayyid ʿAzīz Khwāja signed, as Muḥammad Ṣādiq was dissatisfied [with the ruling]. Khwāja Khān Qāḍī Īshān-ūghlī signed, as he witnessed the event. Ḍiyāʾ al-Dīn Khwāja ʿĪsā Khwāja-ūghlī signed, as he witnessed the event. I, the *qāḍī* of the Zangī Āta, Janās, Fūlād, and Maydān Ṭāl, Īshān Khwāja, signed and affixed my seal.

Seal: Īshān Khwāja Qāḍī b. Maḥmūd Khwāja Īshān Qāḍī ʿAlawī, 1300/1882–83, circular, 4 cm.

Juristic Quotations

1. "If he [the claimant] cannot provide evidence, he is forbidden to submit an appeal," *Ṭaḥṭāwī*.[1]
2. "Simply to claim means nothing," *Niṣāb al-riwāyāt*.[2]
3. "By simply claiming, the truth will not be proved," *Fuṣūl-i ʿImādī*.[3]
4. "Simply to claim is not right according to *sharīʿa*," *Kāfī*.[4]
5. "Nobody has the right to submit an unsupported appeal," *Dhakhīra*.[5]
6. "The claimant is forbidden to submit an [unsupported] appeal," *Fatāwā*.[6]
7. "Adjudications differ according to the different persons, the circumstances, and the times," *Khādimīya*.[7]
8. "It is transmitted from *al-Tabīyīn* that it is obligatory for the *qaḍī* to examine the conditions of the people and act accordingly. Once Abū Yūsuf reflected on this statement after he was appointed to the office of judge and faced the calamity of people's affairs." *Ṭaḥṭāwī*.

---

1 Aḥmad b. Muḥammad b. Ismāʿīl al-Ṭaḥṭawī from Cairo (d. 1816). He was the author of a commentary (*ḥāshiyat*) on al-Ḥaskafī's *Durr al-Mukhtār*.

2 Unidentified work.

3 See Chapter 2 fn. 62.

4 The author of this work is Ḥākim al-Shahīd Muḥammad b. Muḥammad b. Aḥmad b. ʿAbdallāh al-Marwazī (d. 945). It comprises an abbreviated version of the *Ẓāhir al-riwāya* by Muḥammad al-Shaybānī (749–805). See *GAL* SI: 174 (182).

5 See Chapter 5 fn. 45.

6 Unidentified work.

7 Unidentified work.

9. “The claimant has no right to anything unless he supports his claim with testimony,” *Muḥīṭ*,[8] *Dhakhīra*, *Ziyādāt*,[9] *Kāfī*.
10. “If one makes a claim against a knowledgeable or honorable person [before a *qāḍī*] and fails to produce evidence, he should be punished so that he stops such slanderous accusations,” *Mukhtaṣar-i Shāfī*.[10]

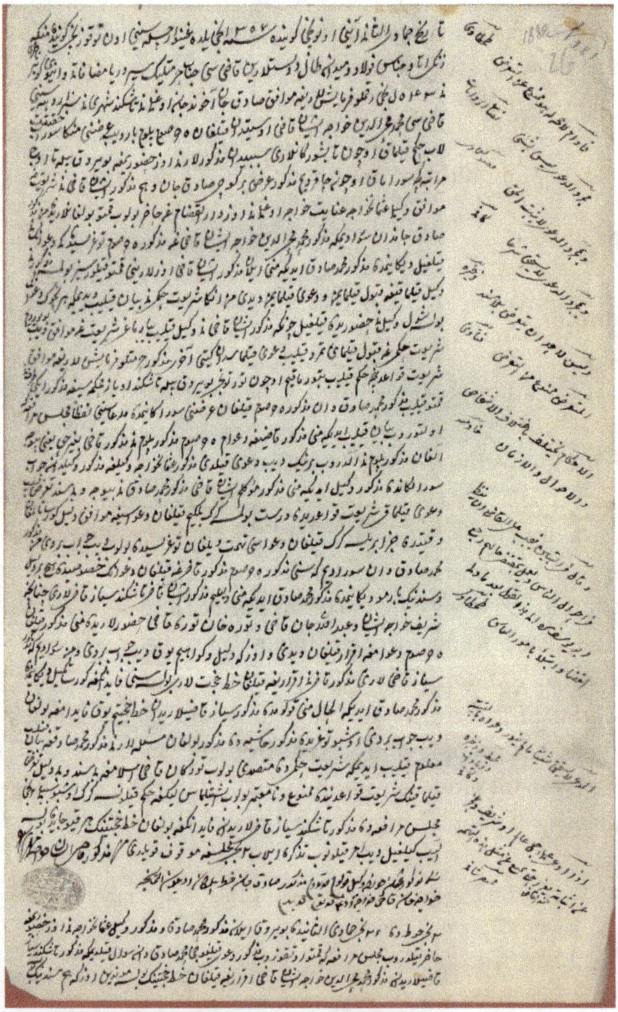

FIGURE 24 *TsGARUz, f. I-164, op. 1, d. 23, l. 26.*
COURTESY OF THE CENTRAL STATE ARCHIVE OF UZBEKISTAN

---

8 See Chapter 5 fn. 44.

9 Unidentified work.

10 Unidentified work.

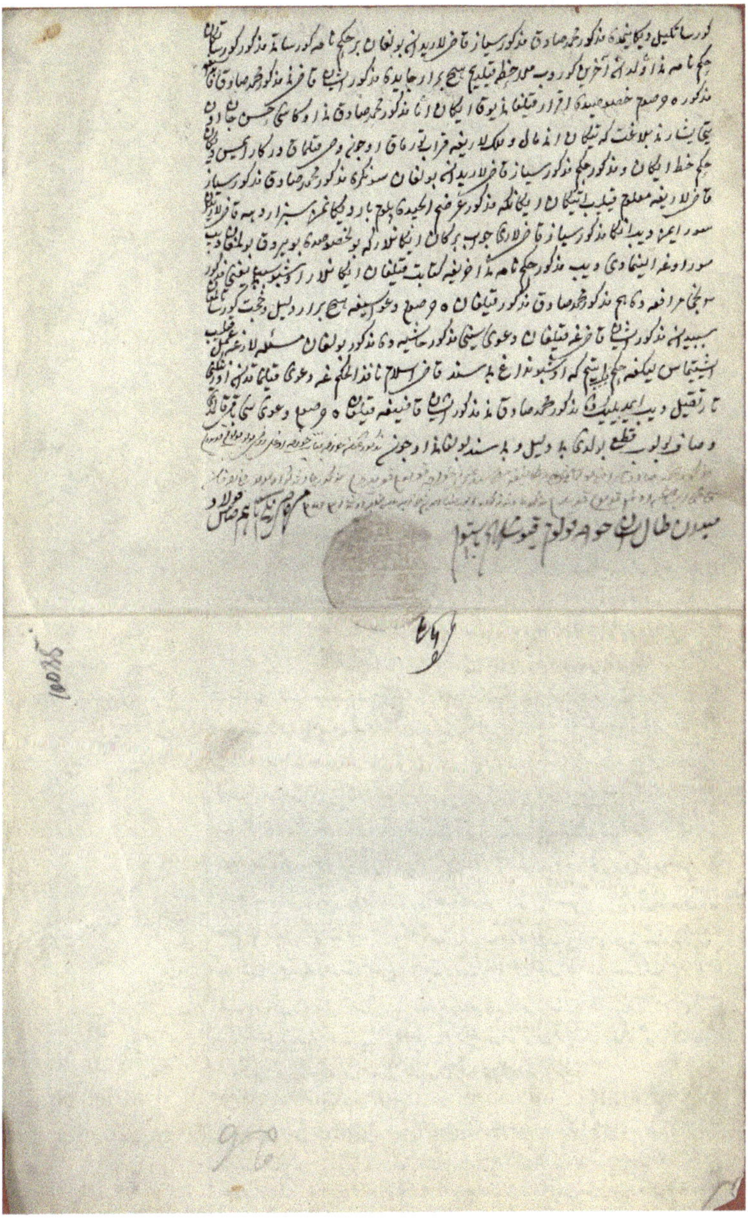

FIGURE 25 *TsGARUz, f. I-164, op. 1, d. 23, l. 260b.*
COURTESY OF THE CENTRAL STATE ARCHIVE OF UZBEKISTAN

Glossary of Islamic Terms

ʿadālat	justice
ʿādat	custom, customary law
aʿlam	senior jurist
ʿamal	practice
amīn	trustee
amlāk	state land under taxation
āqsaqāl	notable, headman of a village or a rural community (lit., white-beard)
arāḍī	land
ʿarḍ	complaint filed with a Muslim royal court (lit., petition)
ark	citadel, royal court
bayyina	witness testimony
bayt al-māl	treasury
bāṭil	null
bāy	notable
bāzyāft	fallow farmland
bī	notable, judge presiding over a tribunal for nomads applying customary law
daʿwā	claim
dafʿ	counterclaim
dargāh	royal court
dhimma	obligation, liability
diyat	blood money (compensation for manslaughter), = *khūn*
dīwān	chancellery
fāsid	void
fatwā	legal opinion
furūʿ al-fiqh	texts of substantive law (lit., the branches of jurisprudence)
gaz	unit of measurement for textiles and land. It varied considerably from region to region (between 60 centimeters and one meter)
gudhar	quarter of a town
guwāh	witness
hadr	manslaughter
ḥākim	governor
ḥawḍ	reservoir
ḥawīlī	courtyard property
ḥukm	ruling

 | DOI 10.1163/9789004330900_013

ibrāʾ	relinquishment of obligation, waiver, cessation of claim
ʿidda	post-divorce waiting period
iqrār	acknowledgment, admission
jāʾiz	valid
jarāḥat	injury
kafīl	guarantor
kharāj	tax on produce (conventionally, one-fifth of the harvest)
khāliṣ [ādam]	impartial actor
khāṣṣa	crown land
khazīna	treasury
khidhmatāna	fee paid to royal court attendants and trustees
khūn	blood money (compensation for manslaughter)
khuṣūmat	dispute, contention, legal disagreement
maḥalla	neighborhood
maḥḍar-i sharʿī	protocol of claim
mahr	dowry
maḥram	trustee
maʿlama	juristic attribute
mamlaka	state land
mamlūk	estate
maraḍ al-mawt	deathbed illness
masʾala	legal case
masmūʿ	admissable
matrūka	estate
mawḍiʿ	rural settlement
mazār	shrine
maẓālim	court of appeals
milk	property (consisting of produce or land)
milk-i ghayr-i ḥurr	taxable property
milk-i ḥurr	tax-exempt property
muddaʿī	plaintiff
muddaʿā ʿalayh	respondent, defendant
mulāzim	attendant
muqirr	one who acknowledges
murāfaʿa	hearing, trial
mushāʿ	jointly owned ancestral undivided property
mushtarak	shared
mushtarī	purchaser
mutawallī	administrator of a *waqf*
nafaqa	post-divorce financial support

nawkar	guard, retainer
pīsh-kash	gift
qāḍī	judge
qaḍī kalān	chief judge
qasam	oath
qaṭʿ	resolution of a dispute
qiṣāṣ	legal relatiation
qishlaq	village
rishwat	bribery
ṣaghīr/ṣaghīra	underage child (masc./fem.)
sahm	share
ṣaḥīḥ	sound, justified
sawgand	oath
shāhid	witness
shufʿa	right of preemption
sijill	copy of a ruling given to parties to a dispute
suknīya	improvement
ṣulḥ	amicable settlement
taḥqīq	inquiry, investigation
tankhwāh	grant of a rent, tax-faming grant
tarīka	inherited estate
tārtīq	gift
tazkīya	test establishing one's credibility (as of a witness)
ṭilā	gold coin
ʿudūl	professional witnesses employed during notarization
ʿushr	tithe (one-tenth of the land's produce)
uskūna	improvement
wakīl	proxy
waqf	charitable endowment (pl., *awqāf*)
wārith	heir
waṣī	guardian for underage children
wathīqa	deed
yārghū	punishment
yasāwul	attendant, trustee
yasāwulbāshī	chamberlain
yir	land
zamīn	land

Archival Files Consulted

Tashkent

TsGARUz, f. I-1 [*Kantseliariia Turkestanskogo General-Gubernatora*], op. 2, d. 1023: *O naznachenii pensii byvshemu Katta-Kurganskomu narodnomu sud'i Mulla-Akhmetu Mulla Adinaevu*, 19.12.1908.

TsGARUz, f. I-1, op. 11, d. 326: *Ob uchrezhdenii komissii dlia obsuzhdeniia voprosa ob ustroistve dukhovnogo upravleniia musul'man i organizatsii vakufnykh uchrezhdenii turkestanskogo kraia*, 1884–5.

TsGARUz, f. I-1, op. 12, d. 44: *Po khodataistvu vakufnogo ustanovleniia Medrese Padshcha Iskander Kukhna v gor. Star. Margelane o prieme v kaznu prinadlezhashchego im uchastka naselennoi vakufnoi zemli ploshchad'iu v 1541 desiatin i voobshche o prave vakufnykh uchrezdenii otchuzhdat' prinadlezhashchie im nedvizhnie imushchestva i o prave vladel'tsev voobshche na otkaz ot prinadlezhashchikh im zemel' posle proizvodstva pozemel'no podatnykh rabot*, 1900–1.

TsGARUz, f. I-1, op. 12, d. 430: *Po prosheniiu Gafurbaia Magdalinova ob uprazdnenii uchrezhdennogo ego ottsom vakufa Magdali-Supi v g. Osh*, 1903–4.

TsGARUz, f. I-1, op. 12, d. 900: *Po prosheniiu doverennogo tuzemtsa Mulla Mir-Umuru Khodzhi Mir Salimova, Mikhaila Ivanovicha Raikova khodataistvuiushchego o nepriznanii vakufom dvukh uchastkov zemli*, 1906.

TsGARUz, f. I-1, op. 14, d. 28: *O vakufnykh i mil'kovykh zemliakh, nakhodiashchikhsia v Zeravshanskom okruge o poriadke raskhodovaniia postupaiushchikh s ėtikh zemel' dokhodov*, 1869–70.

TsGARUz, f. I-1, op. 16, d. 66: *Zhurnaly zasedanii Tashkentskoi organisatsionnoi komissii 1868 g.*

TsGARUz, f. I-1, op. 22, d. 3: *S dokladom komissii po peresmotru i izmeneniiu proekta "Polozheniia ob upravlenii v semirechenskoi obl. i syr-dar'inskoi obl.,"* 1870.

TsGARUz, f. I-1, op. 25, d. 107: *Protokoly zasedaniia komissii uchrezhdennoi prikazom po Turkestanskomu kraiu ot 5 iiunia 1904 za no. 147 po rassmotreniiu voprosov, kasaiushchikhsia postonovki vakufnogo dela v Turkestanskom krae*, 1904.

TsGARUz, f. I-1, op. 27, d. 68: *Ob ustroistve sudebnoi chasti v Turkestanskom krae i ob'iasnitel'naia zapiska o gornom upravlenii v Turkestanskom krae*, 1881.

TsGARUz, f. I-2 [*Diplomaticheskii chinovnik pri Turkestanskom General Gubernatore*] op. 1 d. 314: Nil S. Lykoshin, *Zapiska Amu-Dar'inskogo otdela Polkovnika Lykoshina o sovremennom sostoianii Khivinskogo khanstva*, 1912.

TsGARUz, f. I-17, [*Syr-Dar'inskoe oblastnoe pravlenie*] op. 1, d. 2059: *O naznachenii Kantselarskogo Sluzhitelia Perovskogo Uezdnogo Upravleniia neimeiushchogo china Seita Akbergen o nepravil'nykh deistviiakh nar. sud. eva* [*sic*] *slovesnim perevodchikom Perovskogo Uezdnogo Upravleniia*, 1911.

TsGARUz, f. I-17, op. 1, d. 2850: *Ob opredelenii na Gosudarstvennuiu sluzhbu Mirza Radzhaba Abdudzhabarova*, 1909.

TsGARUz, f. I-17, op. 1, d. 4784: *O khodataistvakh advokatov po delam, razbyraemym po shariatu*, 1886.

TsGARUz, f. I-17, op. 1, d. 4784: *O nepravil'nykh deistviiakh nar. sud. Mukhiddinkhodzha*, 1891.

TsGARUz, f. I-17, op. 1, d. 4887: *Po obvineniiu Kaziia Sibzarskoi chasti goroda Tashkenta Mukhitdina khodzhi Tashkenstkim sartom Sadykdzhanom Usta Akhundzhanovym v prisvoenii prav mutavaliia nad vakufnym imushchestvom Turabaevoi*, 1892.

TsGARUz, f. I-17, op. 1, d. 5387: *Po obvineniiu kaziia Sibzarsoi chasti Mukhiddinkhodzhi*, 1894.

TsGARUz, f. I-17, op. 1, d. 5775: *Po obvineniiu kaziia Sibzarsoi chasti Mukhiddinkhodzhi*, 1896.

TsGARUz, f. I-17, op. 1, d. 6226: *Po obvineniiu kazia Sibzarskoi chasti Mukhiddinkhodzhi i muftiia Sultan Iunusmukhammedova po 362 st.*, 1897.

TsGARUz, f. I-17, op. 1, d. 6366: *Po obvineniiu kaziia Sibzarskoi chasti Mukhiddinkhodzhi o nepravil'nykh deistviiakh*, 1898.

TsGARUz, f. I-17, op. 1, d. 6367: *Po obvineniiu kaziia Sibzarskoi chasti Mukhiddinkhodzhi o nezakonnykh deistviiakh*, 1898.

TsGARUz, f. I-17, op. 1, d. 6468: *Po obvineniiu Mukhitdina Khodzhi po 354 i 352 st.*, 1898.

TsGARUz, f. I-17, op. 1, d. 6469: *Po obvineniiu byv. nar. sud. Sibzarskoi chasti Mukhiddinkhodzhi po sluzhbe*, n.d.

TsGARUz, f. I-17, op. 1, d. 30291/23: *Po voprosu o tom imeiut li silu iuridischeskogo mezhevaniia raboty byvsh. pozemel'no-podatnoi komissii i mogut li byt' premeniaemy i k nim vse ukazaniia mezhevykh zakonov*, n.d.

TsGARUz, f. I-17, op. 1, d. 31916: *Spiski vakufov nakhodiashchikhsia v cherte gorodov*, 1888.

TsGARUz, f. I-17, op. 1, d. 32587: *Po proizvedennomu komissarom 5-go pozemel'no-podatnago uchastka izsledovaniiu dokumentov i imushchestva, otnosiashchikhsia k vakufu medresse "Issa-Khodzha Kazy-Keliana,"* 1892.

TsGARUz, f. I-17, op. 1, d. 32597: *Vakuf mecheti kvartala Kar-Iagdy, v g. Tashkente s vakufnym dokumentom mecheti kvartala Kar Iagdy, predstavlennym mutavaliem Khamra Khodzha Tiura Khodzhinovym*, 1887–8.

TsGARUz, f. I-17, op. 1, d. 32607: *Vakuf dvukh mechetei kvartala Makhsiduz v g. Tashkente. S vakufnymi dokumentami dvukh mechetei kvartala Makhsiduz, predostavlennym mutavaliem Zakirdzhanom Akhundzhanovym*, 1887–88.

TsGARUz, f. I-17, op. 1, d. 32663: *Vakufnye dokumenty medresse nakhodiashchikhsia v gor. Tashkente*, n.d.

TsGARUz, f. I-17, op. 1, d. 35430: *Posluzhnoi spisok pis'mennogo perevodchika pri Upravlenii Nachal'nika goroda Tashkenta, china Shakirdzhana Ishaeva*, 1901.

TsGARUz, f. I-18 [*Samarkandskoe Oblastnoe Pravlenie*], op. 1, d. 139: N. Mordvinov, *Zapiska k proektu o sudebnoi reforme v Turkestanskom krae*, 1891.

TsGARUz, f. I-19 [*Ferganskoe Oblastnoe Pravlenie*], op. 1, d. 3498: untitled.

TsGARUz, f. I-19, op. 1, d. 33346: *Po vozbuzhdennomu upravliaiushchei Turkestanskoiu Kazennoiu Palatoiu voprosu kakoe naznachenie dolzhny poluchit' te vakufnye imushchestva, za kotorymi vakufnoe pravo ne budet priznano*, 1893.

TsGARUz, I-21 [*Upravlenie Nachal'nika Dzhizakskogo Uezda, Samarkandskoi Oblasti*], op. 1, d. 56: *O spore iz-za zemli mezhdu rodami Dzhalair i Turk*, 1888.

TsGARUz, f. I-21, op. 1, d. 59: *Ob iznasilovanii tuzemki Tuganai Suiarkulovoi*, 1888.

TsGARUz, f. I-21, op. 1, d. 75: *O nezakonnykh deistviiakh Narodnogo sud'i no. 2 aula Atu-Kurganskoi volosti Aktana Utenova*, 1889.

TsGARUz, f. I-21, op. 1, d. 108: *Po zhalobam zhitelei Iamskoi volosti o zloupotrebleniiakh sud'i Mulla Khudai Nazara Sarybaeva toi zhe volosti*, 1890–2.

TsGARUz, f. I-21, op. 1, d. 113: *Po zhalobam zhitelei Narkustskoi volosti o vziatochnichestve narodnogo sud'i Bogdanskoi volosti*, 1890.

TsGARUz, f. I-21, op. 1, d. 114: *O vziatochnichestve narodnogo sud'i Magometa Turkebaeva Fistalitausskoi volosti*, 1891–93.

TsGARUz, f. I-21, op. 1, d. 144: *Postanovlenie Samarkandskogo oblastnogo pravleniia po obvineniiu narodonogo sud'i v nepravil'nom sostavlenii resheniia s"ezda narodnykh sudei*, 1891.

TsGARUz, f. I-21, op. 1, d. 202: *O vziatochnichestve narodnogo sud'i no. 1 aula Kizil-Kumskoi volosti Turganbeva*, 1892.

TsGARUz, f. I-21, op. 1, d. 475: [*Materialy o Tuia-Tartarskoi volosti*].

TsGARUz, f. I-21, op. 1, d. 634. *Po razboru spora o zemle mezhdu zhiteliami kishlaka Balgali, Iamskoi volosti, i zhiteliami Dzhalairskogo obshchestva toi zhe volosti*, 1904.

TsGARUz, f. I-21, op. 1, d. 752: *Po zhalobe kirgizki ob ubiistve ee rebenka*, 1911.

TsGARUz, f. I-36 [*Upravlenie Nachal'nika goroda Tashkenta*], op. 1, d. 434: *O reshenii del mezhdu kirgizami podlezhashchikh sudu biev*.

TsGARUz, f. I-36, op. 1, d. 452: *Po prosheniiu kaziev g. Tashkenta ob ostavlenii pri nikh Agliamov i Muftiev na prezhnem osnovanii*, 1868.

TsGARUz, f. I- 36, op. 1, d. 454: untitled.

TsGARUz, f. I-36, op. 1, d. 725: *O smerti Sibzarskogo kaziia i o nazhachenii na ego mesto drugogo litsa*, 1870.

TsGARUz, f. I-36, op. 1, d. 883: *Proshenie zhitelei i svidetel'stva ob izbranii mestnykh dolzhnostnykh lits*, 1873–4.

TsGARUz, f. I-36, op. 1, d. 2049: *Opis' vakufov, medrese, mechetei, mazarov i o dokhodakh s nikh*, n.d.

TsGARUz, f. I-36, op. 1, d. 2170: *Kniga na zapisku reshenii kaziia Bish-agachskoi chasti gor. Tashkenta s 29 Aprelia 1882 goda.*

TsGARUz, f. I-36, op. 1, d. 2273: *Po povodu predstavleniia rivaiata Voennomu Gubernatoru i Tainomu Sovetniku Girsu ob izmenenii poriadka torgovogo sbora i o naznachenii vzamen ego zakiatnogo sbora*, 1883.

TsGARUz, f. I-36, op. 1, d. 2396: *Spiski mull, medrese, prikaz po gorodu, spiski, prosheniia i perepiska o vybore i utverzhdenii muftiev, agliamov, mutavalliev v g. Tashkente*, 1884.

TsGARUz, f. I-36, op. 1, d. 2976: *Perepiska s Syr-Dar'inskim oblastnym pravleniem o dostavlenii dokumentov vsekh vakufov g. Tashkenta v Syr-Dar'inskoe oblastnoe pravlenie*, 1888.

TsGARUz, f. I-36, op. 1, d. 3367: *O prichislenii Sibzarskogo narodnogo sud'i Mukhitdina Khodzhi k otvetstvennosti za upushcheniia po vedeniiu opekunskikh del*, 1887–93.

TsGARUz, f. I-36, op. 1, d. 3494: *Ukaz Pravitel'stvennogo Senata i perepiska o raz'iasnenii prav gorodskikh sudei na sovershenii dokumentov gorozhan na zemliu, nakhodiashchuiusia v Tashkentskom uezde*, 1893.

TsGARUz, f. I-36, op. 1, d. 3587: *Spisok vakufov, raporta, perepiska i vneseniia v komitet blagotvoritel'nogo obshchestva s zemel' vakufa Nazarbiia i o drugikh vakufakh*, 1895.

TsGARUz, f. I-36, op. 1, d. 3708: *Skhema i opis' vakufnykh zemel' Kukel'dash.*

TsGARUz, f. I-36, op. 1, d. 3881: *Reestry razbiraemykh del narodnymi sud'iami, proshenie o nedovol'stve resheniiami narodnykh sudei*, 1898.

TsGARUz, f. I-36, op. 1, d. 4364: *O vakufakh dvukh mechetei, sostoiashchikh v makhaliakh Makhsi-Duz Sibzarskoi chasti*, 1907.

TsGARUz, f. I-36, op. 1, d. 6083: untitled.

TsGARUz, f. I-36, op. 1, d. 6009: *Proekt uprazdneniia narodnykh sudov v Turkestanskom krae*, 1914.

TsGARUz, I-36, op. 1, d. 6487: *S perepiskoi po vakufnym delam o naznachenii mutavalliev, ob iz'iatii uchastkov zemli*, 1914.

TsGARUz, I-36, op. 1, d. 6864: *S perepiskoi, kasaiushcheisia vakufov, prosheniia na nepravil'nye resheniia sudei ob iz'iatii vladenii, o naznachenii novykh mutavalliev i t.p. perepiska*, 1915.

TsGARUz, f. I-125 [*Kantseliaria Khana Khivinskogo*], op. 1, d. 29: *O narushenii nekotorogo punkta torgovogo i mirnogo dogovora Rossii s Khivoi khivinskikh sanovnikami, ob ugone i krazhakh skota, o plennykh turkmen*, 1883–85.

TsGARUz, f. I-125, op. 1, d. 81: *Perepiska ob arenduemykh uchastkah zemli khivinsko i russko poddannymi*, 1900–2.

TsGARUz, f. I-125, op. 1, d. 190: *Perepiska o rassledovanii brachnykh del (neuplata kalyma, uvoz chuzhikh zhen i t.p.) mezhdu khivinsko i russko poddannymi*, 1904–5.

TsGARUz, f. I-125, op. 1, d. 486: *Kaziiskie dokumenty*, 1811–1919.

TsGARUz, f. I-125, op. 1, d. 495: *Obraztsy "fatva" shariatskikh reshenii, /rivoiaty/.*

TsGARUz, f. I-125, op. 1, d. 498: *Zaiavlenie naseleniia na imia iasaul-bashi*, 1909–18.

TsGARUz, f. I-125, op. 1, d. 579: *Instruktsiia kazy i raisu m. Astana Khiv. Khanst. poslannaia vizirem*, 1910.

TsGARUz, f. I-125, op. 2, d. 14: *Iarlik khivinskogo khana Seiid-Mukhammad-Bakhadur-khana o naznachenii Shakh Murada, syna Sarykulia, na dolzhnost' biia v kazakhskom plemeni*, 1279/1862.

TsGARUz, f. I-125, op. 2, d. 633: *Vyzov esaul boshi v rezidentsiiu khana khivinskogo otvetchikov po denezhnomu, dvizhimomu i nedvizhimomu imushchestvu*, 1328/1910.

TsGARUz, f. I-126 [*Upravlenie Kushbegi ėmira bukharskogo*], op. 1, d. 6: *Iarliki bukharskogo ėmira Abd al-Akhada o naznachenii na dolzhnosti kazi, raisov, khakimov v vilaiety Bukharskogo khanstva*, 1884–1910.

TsGARUz, I-126, op. 1, d. 11: *Khodataistva mirshabov pered ėmirom o naznachenii dzharib-bashi v vilaiety Bukharskogo khanstva*, n.d.

TsGARUz, f. I-126, op. 1, d. 20: *Khodataistva bukharskikh chinovnikov pered ėmirom o naznachenii aksakalov i aminov v vilaiety i tumany Bukharskogo khantsva*, n.d.

TsGARUz, I-126, op. 1, d. 22: *Khodataistva bukharskikh chinovnikov pered ėmirom o naznachenii aksakalov i aminov v vilaiety i tumany Bukharskogo khantsva*, n.d.

TsGARUz, f. I-126, op. 1, d. 667: *Ariza kazi koshbegi o postuplenii deneg za arendu vakufnykh zemel' v Bukharskom khanstve*, n.d.

TsGARUz, f. I-126, op. 1, d. 689: *Otchet kazi o postuplenii deneg za sdachu v arendu vakufnoi zemli dakhiaki-amma. Raspiski kazi o poluchenii deneg s arendatorov vakufnykh zemel*, n.d.

TsGARUz, f. I-126, op. 1, d. 746: *Ariza kazi i raisov ėmiru o deiatel'nosti amlakdarov po sboru pozemel'noi podati khissat al-kharadzh v khanstve*, n.d.

TsGARUz, f. I-126, op. 1, d. 754: *Ariza bukharskikh chinovnikov koshbegi o vypolnenii ego ukazaniia po zapresheniiu vzyskaniia khizmatana i farsakh-puli vyshe ustanovlennoi normy*, 1827–1909.

TsGARUz, f. I-126, op. 1, d. 759: *Ariza bukharskikh chinovnikov ėmiru o zhalobakh na amlakdarov i drugikh chinovnikov na nezakonnye deistviia*, n.d.

TsGARUz, f. I-126, op. 1, d. 940: *Mubarakname ėmirov Nasrully, Muzaffara i Abd al-Akhada o razbore konfliktov po vakfu*, 1812–1904.

TsGARUz, f. I-126, op. 1, d. 967: *Ariza bukharskikh chinovnikov koshbegi o vzyskanii s bukharskikh poddannykh gosudarstvennykh dolgov*, 1883–1916.

TsGARUz, f. I-126, op. 1, d. 1003: *Ariza bukharskikh chinovnikov koshbegi po zemel'nym voprosam*, n.d.

TsGARUz, f. I-126, op. 1, d. 1729: *Makhzar i rivaiat, zaverennye v kantseliarii kazi*, n.d.

TsGARUz, f. I-126, op. 1, d. 1761: *Ariza kazi ėmiru o razbore del ob oskorblenii i izbienii v prisutstvii pribyvshego iz rikaba makhrama i vyplate emu khizmatane*, n.d.

TsGARUz, f. I-126, op. 1, d. 1762: *Ariza kazi koshbegi o razbore del ob izbienii i oskorblenii v prisutstvii pribyvshego iz rikaba makhrama i vyplate emu khizmatane*, 1879–1895.

TsGARUz, f. I-126, op. 1, d. 1765: *Ariza kazi koshbegi o razbore del ob izbienii i oskorblenii v prisutstvii pribyvshego iz rikaba makhrama i vyplate emu khizmatane*, n.d.

TsGARUz, f. I-126, op. 1, d. 1796: *Ariza kazi ėmiru ob ustanovlenii blagonadezhnosti lits, vystupaiushchikh na sudebnykh zasedaniiakh v kachestve svidetelei*, n.d.

TsGARUz, f. I-133 [*Prokuror Tashkentskoi sudebnoi palaty, 1899–1918*], op. 1, d. 175: *O Dzhandzhal'skom narodnom sud'e Mulla Abduvali Abdulkasambaev po 216 st. ulozheniia o nakazanii.*

TsGARUz, f. I-133, op. 1, d. 227: *Po delu ob obv. Kokan-Kishlakskogo narodnogo sud'i Tailalbaeva i ego mirza Dzhalial-Bai-Ogli v prestuplenii predusmotrennom 362 st. ul. o nakazanii.*

TsGARUz, f. I-133, op. 1, d. 1020: *Perepiska po protestam na prigovory i razresheniia narodnykh sudov*, 1910.

TsGARUz, f. I-133, op. 1, d. 1325: *Po nabliudeniiu za delom o narodnom sud'e Butitane Narumbetove*, 1913.

TsGARUz, f. I-133, op. 1, d. 1546: *Po obv. narodnogo sud'i osedlogo naseleniia Toi-Tiubinsko i Osman-Atinskoi volosti, Tash. Uezda Mulla-Ali Magomed Khudai Bergenova po 347, 348 i 362 st. ul. o nakazanii*, 1914.

TsGARUz, f. I-133, op. 1, d. 1570: *O protestakh na prigovory i resheniia narodnykh sudov*, 1914.
TsGARUz, f. I-134 [*Prokuror Syr-Dar'inskogo oblastnogo suda*], op. 1, d. 57: *Protesta na resheniia narodnykh sudei*, 1891.
TsGARUz, f. I-134, op. 1, d. 76: *Protesta na resheniia narodnykh sudei*, 1892.
TsGARUz, f. I-134, op. 1, d. 91: *Protesta na resheniia narodnykh sudei*, 1893.
TsGARUz, f. I-134, op. 1, d. 110: *Protesta na resheniia narodnykh sudei*, 1894.
TsGARUz, f. I-134, op. 1, d. 123: *Protesta na resheniia narodnykh sudei*, 1895.
TsGARUz, f. I-134, op. 1, d. 130: *Protesta na resheniia narodnykh sudei*, 1895.
TsGARUz, f. I-134, op. 1, d. 152: *Protesta na resheniia narodnykh sudei*, 1897.
TsGARUz, f. I-134, op. 1, d. 162: *Protesta na resheniia narodnykh sudei*, 1898.
TsGARUz, f. I-134, op. 1, d. 180: *Protesta na resheniia narodnykh sudei*, 1899.
TsGARUz, f. I-164 [*Tashkentskii Kazi-Kalian*], op. 1, d. 1: *Iarliki kokandskogo khana o naznachenii v Tashkente kazi-kalana, alama i dr. dukhovnikh lits*, 1822–61.
TsGARUz, f. I-164, op. 1, d. 3: *Naznachenie generalom Cherniaevym 73 dukhovnykh lits na razlichnye dukhovnye dolzhnosti po khodataistvu kazi-kaliana g. Tashkent*, 1865.
TsGARUz, f. I-164, op. 1, d. 5: *Razlichnye gramoty, svidetel'stva Tashkentskogo kazi-kaliana, poluchennye ot tsarskogo pravitel'stva*, 1865–91.
TsGARUz, f. I-164, op. 1, d. 6: *Lichnye dokumenty kazi Mukhitdina o kupli-prodazhe i prava sobstvennosti*, 1882–92.
TsGARUz, f. I-164, op. 1, d. 7: *Lichnye dokumenty kazi Mukhitdina (prekrashchenie iskovykh del-ibro)*, 1873–1911.
TsGARUz, f. I-164, op. 1, d. 13: *Makhzar i rivoiiat (nachalo sudebnogo deloproizvodstva i stat'i shariata)*, 1822–92.
TsGARUz, f. I-164, op. 1, d. 23: *Resheniia Tashkentskogo kaziia*, 1864–1912.
TsGARUz, f. I-164, op. 1, d. 39: *Zaiavlenie Tura-Khana Tura voennomu general-gubernatoru o naznachenii ego mutavalliem po prinadlezhashchemu pravu po rodu Khodzha-Akhrar*, 1888.
TsGARUz, f. I-164, op. 1, d. 50: *Dokumenty o vybore ėllikbashi*, 1871–1906.
TsGARUz, f. I-164, op. 2, d. 2a: *Biografiia Tashkentskogo uchenogo Seid Mukhammed Khakim Khodzha (Otets Kaziia Mukhitdina)*, n.d.
TsGARUz, f. I-318 [*Tovarish prokuror Tashkentskogo okruzhnogo suda*], op. 1, d. 44: *Perepiska po zhalobam na reshenie nar. sudov*, 1912.
TsGARUz, f. I-318, op. 1, d. 45: *Po prosheniiam ob oprotestovanii reshenii narodnykh sudei*, 1913.
TsGARUz, f. I-318, op. 1, d. 46: *Po prosheniiam ob oprotestovanii reshenii narodnykh sudei*, 1915.
TsGARUz, f. I-318, op. 1, d. 67: *Po prosheniiam ob oprotestovanii reshenii narodnykh sudei*, 1916.

TsGARUz, f. I-318, op. 1, d. 68: *O perepiske po prosheniiam ob otmene reshenii narodnykh sudei*, 1914.

TsGARUz, f. I-318, op. 1, d. 72: *O perepiske po prosheniiam ob otmene reshenii narodnykh sudei*, 1915.

TsGARUz, f. I-318, op. 1, d. 76: *Po prosheniiam ob oprotestovanii reshenii narodnykh sudei*, 1913.

TsGARUz, f. I-318, op. 1, d. 78: *Nariad po prosheniiam ob oprotestovanii reshenii narodnykh sudei*, 1914.

TsGARUz, f. I-318, op. 1, d. 84: *Po obvineniiu narodnykh sudei Saibetova i Balkhatiiarova*, 1899.

TsGARUz, f. I-323 [*Sobranie vakufnykh dokumentov*], op. 1, d. 26: *'Askar Bī Ināq madrasanīng waqfīyasī*, Bukhara 1818.

TsGARUz, f. I-323, op. 1, d. 34: *Waqfīya-yi madrasa-yi Sayyid Amīn Bāy*, Bukhara 1864.

TsGARUz, f. I-323, op. 1, d. 667: *Waqfīya-yi Nazākat Pāchā*, Bukhara 1915.

TsGARUz, f. I-323, op. 2, d. 81: *Saidumukhamat Alikan svoim vysochaishchim ukazom naznachaet* [*text missing*] *Kazy-Kalanom g. Tashkenta*, 1238/1822–23.

TsGARUz, f. I-323, op. 2, d. 87: *Abdul Muzaffar Said Mukhamod Khudaerkhon Bakhodur svoim vysochaishchim ukazom o naznachenii kazy kalanom Tashkentskoi oblasti Said Makmuda Khodzha*, 1263/1847.

TsGARUz, f. I-323, op. 2, d. 88: *Said Amir Mukhamad Khudoer Bakhodir-khon svoim vysochaishim ukazom naznachaet ėshona Makhmud Khodzha nezavisimim Kazy Kalanom Tashkentskoi oblasti*, 1270/1853–54.

TsGARUz, f. I-323, op. 2, d. 89: *Said Mukhammad Malla Khan vysochaishim ukazom naznachaet Makhmud Khodzhu ishana Kazi-Kalanom g. Tashkenta*, 1275/1858–59.

TsGARUz, f. I-336 [*Voennyi Gubernator i komanduiushchii voiskami Turkestanskoi oblasti*], op. 1, d. 14: *Po raznym zhalobam Kirgiz i razbor po ėtomu predmetu*, n.d.

TsGARUz, f. I-365 [*Kazii Sibzarskoi chasti gor. Tashkenta*], op. 1, d. 74: *Kniga na zapisku reshenii kaziia Sibzarskoi chasti gor. Tashkenta 1899 goda.*

TsGARUz, f. I-365, op. 1, d. 85: *Kniga reshenii kaziia Sibzarskoi chasti gor. Tashkenta*, 1910.

TsGARUz, f. I-365, op. 1, d. 94: *Narodnyi sud'ia Sibzarskoi chasti g. Tashkenta. Dukhovnoe zaveshchanie Seid Gazykhana Fatkhullakhana*, 1913–14.

TsGARUz, f. I-717 [*Sovet Turkestanskogo General-Gubernatora*], op. 1, d. 6: *Zhurnaly Soveta Turkestanskogo General-Gubernatora*, 1891.

TsGARUZ, f. R-2773 [*Lichnyi fond M.Z. Massona*], op. 1, d. 1103: *V.L. Viatkin, K voprosam izucheniia Uzbekov v Srednei Azii XVI vek* [*sic*]. Unpublished manuscript, 1932.

TsGARUz, f. R-2678 [*Lichnyi fond O.D. Chekhovich*], op. 1, d. 12: *Iuridischeskie zakliucheniia*, n.d.

TsGARUz, f. R-2678, op. 1, d. 60: *Istoriia razvitiia aktov iuridicheskogo oformleniia feodal'nykh otnoshenii v Srednei Azii XII–XVI vv.* Unpublished manuscript, 1979

TsGARUz, R-2678, op. 1, d. 167: *"Risola-i Khabibiia." (Traktat o zemliakh desiatichnykh i kheradzhnykh). Perevod sochineniia Ibadellakha ibn Khodzha-arifa al-Bukhary s persidskogo iazyka (rukopisi no. 4976 IV Uz). Chernovoi avtograf. Prilozhenie: Faksimile rukopisi no. 4976*, 1963.

TsGARUz, R-2678, op. 1, d. 379: *Vypiski i perevody iz formuliarnika "Mukhtar al'-Ikhtiiara" Ikhtiiara ibn Giiasuddina al Khusaini iz rukopisi no. A-933*, n.d.

TsGARUz, R-2678, op. 1, d. 381: *Vypiska iz raporta Kuna A. s perevodom spiska mulkov Zeravshanskogo okruga ot 20 fevralia 1870 g. Rukopis'. Prilozhenie: Spisok mulkov, sostavlennyi chinovnikom Bukharskogo ėmira Muzaffara*, n.d.

TsGARUz, f. R-2678, op. 1, d. 531: *Pis'ma Davidovich E.A. Chekhovich O.D.*, 1956–81.

TsGARUz, f. R-2678, op. 2, d. 4: *Iuridicheskoe zakliuchenie (rivoiat) musul'manskikh zakonovedov (mufticv) o rezul'tatakh vizual'nogo osmotra tela umershego mal'chika. 1800 (na pechati).*

TsGARUz, f. R-2678, op. 2, d. 17: *Iuridicheskoe zakliuchenie o prioritete cheloveka, obrabatyvaiuschego zemliu v prave rasporiazhatsia eiu. 1904 (na pechati).*

TsGARUz, f. R-2678, op. 2, d. 90: *Kupchaia Astanakula Kushbegi*, n.d.

TsGARUz, f. R-2678, op. 2, d. 126: *Iuridicheskoe zakliuchenie o nevozmozhnosti otkaza ot svoikh prezhnykh pokazanii, sdelannykh v prisutstvii kaziia (sud'i), 1864 g. (na pechati).*

TsGARUz, f. R-2678, op. 2, d. 177: *Kollektsiia aktov Andreeva M.S.*, n.d.

TsGARUz, f. R-2678, op. 2, d. 178: *Kollektsiia aktov Andreeva M.S.*, n.d.

TsGARUz, R- 2678, op. 2, d. 244: *Formuliarnik iuridicheskikh [sic] dokumentatsii XX v. na tadzhikskom iazyke, arabskim shriftom [1910 g.]*

TsGARUz, R-2678, op. 2, d. 251: Qārī Aḥmad, *Tarjuma-yi aḥwāl-i Qāḍī Kalānhā-yi darūn-i Bukhārā*, 1940.

Khiva

IQM, no. 2053: Iarlik Allakuli khana o naznachenii kaziem goroda Vazira Mully Kurully, 1833.

IQM, P-8, kp 3674, ll. 33–33ob, n.d.

Khujand

ObAKh, f. I-145, op. 1, d. 58, ll. 1–20: Kollektsiiai fondi shaxsii Mullomuhammad Sharif ibni Abduzalil [Mullā Muḥammad ʿAẓīm Mullā Muḥammad Sharīf-ūghlī]-qozii volosti Mahram.

Nukus

FBKOANRUz, no. R-90: S.K. Kamalov, *Khoziaistvo karakalpakov XIX v*, notes and documents, n.d.

Samarqand

AMIKINUz, no. 828: M.S. Iusupov, *Sud v Bukhare. Sudoustroistvo i sudoproizvodstvo v Bukharskom emirate v kontse XIX i nachale XX v.v.* Unpublished manuscript, 1941.

AMIKINUz: Untitled collection of Arabic-script documents.

Bibliography

Unpublished Sources

Abū ʿUbaydallāh Khwāja Tāshkandī. *Khulāṣat al-aḥwāl*. MS Tashkent, TsVRUz, no. 2084.

Aḥmad Makhdhūm [Dānish] Muhandis-i Bukhārī, alias Aḥmad-i Kalla. *Tarjimat al-aḥwāl-i amīrān-i Bukhārā-yi sharīf az Amīr-i Dānyāl tā ʿaṣr-i Amīr ʿAbd al-Aḥad*. MS Tashkent, TsVRUz no. 1987.

———. *Nawādir al-waqāyiʿ*. MS Tashkent, TsVRUz inv. no. 4266.

Ākhūnd Mullā Muḥammad Wafā b. Muḥammad Ẓahīr Karmīnagī. *Tuḥfat al-Khānī*. MS Tashkent, TsVRUz, no. 2726/III.

ʿAlā al-Dīn Muḥammad b. Ḥāfiẓ Darwīsh Muḥammad. *Jāmiʿ al-wathāyiq*. MS St. Petersburg, IVRAN, no. A-933.

ʿAlī b. Muḥammad ʿAlī b. ʿAlī b. Maḥmūd al-Mukhtārī al-Khwārazmī al-Kubrawī. *al-Fatāwā al-Shībānīya*. MS Tashkent, TsVRUz, no. 6112/1.

———. *Al-jawāmiʿ al-ʿalīya fī al-wathāʾiq al-sharʿīya wa-l-sijillāt al-marʿīya*. MS Tashkent, TsVRUz, no. 9138.

Amīr Ḥaydar b. Amīr Shāh-Murād. *Al-fawāʾid al-alfīya*. MS Tashkent, TsVRUz, no. 2434/IV.

———. *Maktūbāt-i Amīr Ḥaydar ba Muḥammad Ḥakīm Bī*. MS Tashkent, TsVRUz, no. 2120.

———. *Maktūbāt-i Amīr Ḥaydar*. MS Tashkent, TsVRUz, no. 5412.

Amīr Muẓaffar. *Maktūbāt-i Amīr Muẓaffar ba Sayyid Mīrak wa ʿarāyiḍ-i Sayyid Mīrak*. MS Tashkent, TsVRUz, no. 1740.

Amīr Muẓaffar. *Mubarak-nāmajāt-i Amīr Muẓaffar ba Qāḍī Muḥyī al-Dīn*. MS Tashkent, TsVRUz, no. 407.

Anon. *Jung*. MS Tashkent, TsVRUz, no. 2844/II.

———. *Jung*. MS Tashkent, TsVRUz, no. 6102.

———. *Majmūʿa-yi wathāʾiq*. MS Tashkent, TsVRUz, no. 1386.

———. *Majmūʿa-yi wathāʾiq*. MS Tashkent, TsVRUz 7799.

———. *Majmūʿa-yi wathāʾiq wa murāsalāt*. MS Tashkent, TsVRUz, no. 8958.

———. *Majmūʿa wa taʾrīkh-i Mullā-zāda*. MS Tashkent, TsVRUz, no. 9767.

———. *Wathāʾiq*. MS Tashkent, TsVRUz, no. 4594/II.

———. *Wathāʾiq*. MS Tashkent, TsVRUz, no. 8072.

———. *Wathāʾiq-i mutafarraqa*. MS Tashkent, TsVRUz, no. 6057/1.

Chekhovich, Ol'ga D. 1979. *Istoriia razvitiia aktov iuridicheskogo oformleniia feodal'nykh otnoshenii v Srednei Azii XII–XVI vv.* TsGARUz, f. R-2678, op. 1, d. 60.

[Gippius, A.I.] *Zapiska A.I. Gippiusa o vakufakh*. Tashkent, 1906. MS Tashkent, NBUz, no. 1056.

Ḥamīd Khwāja, *Tanzīl al-imthāl fī dhikr bayān al-aḥwāl*. MS Tashkent, TsVRUz, no. 602.

ʿIbadallāh b. Khwāja ʿArif al-Bukhārī, *Jāmiʿ al-maʿmulāt*. MS Tashkent, TsVRUz, no. 6196/I.

———. *Al-risāla fī taḥqīq arāḍī al-ʿushrīya wa-l-kharājīya = Risāla-yi Ḥabībīya*. MS Tashkent, TsVRUz, no. 6196/II.

Ikhtiyār al-Dīn b. Ghiyāth al-Dīn al-Ḥusaynī. *Mukhtār al-ikhtiyār ʿalā al-madhhab al-mukhtār*. MS Bodleian, Frazer, no. 234, 235, 239.

———. *Mukhtār al-ikhtiyār ʿalā al-madhhab al-mukhtār*. MS Tashkent, TsVRUz no. 5438.

Mīr Ḥabīballāh. *Wāqiʿāt-i dīn-i jalālī*. MS Tashkent, TsVRUz, no. 9019.

Mīr Rabīʿ b. Mīr Niyāz Khwāja al-Ḥusaynī. *Risāla-yi raḥmānīya*. MS Tashkent, TsVRUz, no. 9060/XII.

Mīr Sayyid Muḥyī al-Dīn b. Mīr Sayyid Ḥabīballāh Fatḥābādī. *Khāṭirāt*. MS Tashkent, TsVRUz, no. 328/IV.

Mīrzā ʿĀlim Tashkandī b. Dāmullā Mīrzā. *Ansāb al-ṣalāṭīn wa taʾrīkh al-khawāqīn*. MS Tashkent, TsVRUz, no. 1314/I.

Mīrzā Ṣādiq Munshī Jāndārī. *Munshaʾāt wa manshūrāt*. MS Tashkent, TsVRUz, no. 299/I.

Muḥammad b. Bābāʾ al-Samarqandī. *Al-fatāwā al-samarqandīya*. MS Tashkent, TsVRUz 3132/I.

Mullā Abū al-Qāsim Muftī. *Isāmī-yi kitābhā-yi mawjūda ba dast-i faqīr az manqūlāt-i bahr al-manāfiq*. MS Samarqand, Library of the Historical Museum of Samarqand, no. 4089/9: fol. 3a.

Mullā Kamāl al-Dīn. *Risāla-yi Mullā Kamāl al-Dīn*. MS St. Petersburg, IVRAN, no. S-1690.

Munshaʾāt-i Mirzā Bahādir Khwāja b. Ḥusayn Khwāja Pīrmastī. MS Tashkent, TsVRUz, no. 2667.

Qāḍī ʿAzīzān. *Sīzdah Ganj*. MS Tashkent, TsVRUz, no. 2574/IV.

Qāḍī Muḥammad Wafā Karminagī. *Tuḥfat al-khānī*. MS Tashkent, TsVRUz, no. 16.

Qāḍī Muḥammad Yūsuf Makhdūm Raʾis b. Qādī Khwājam-Birdī Marḥūmī, alias Rājī. *Jung-i Rājī*. MS Tashkent, TsVRUz, no. 7502.

Qārī Aḥmad. *Tarjuma-yi aḥwāl-i Qāḍī Kalānhā-yi darūn-i Bukhārā*. TsGARUz, R-2678, op. 2, d. 251.

Ṣadr-i Ḍiyāʾ. *Tarjuma-yi aḥwāl-i Qāḍī ʿAbd al-Shakūr*. MS Tashkent, TsVRUz, no. 1304/IV.

Safaruf, Bābājān [Babadzhan Safarov]. *Khwārazm taʾrīkhī (1864–1934)*. MS Tashkent, TsVRUz, no. 10231.

Sayyid Amīr Naṣrallah Bahādur Khān. *Majmūʿa-yi maktūbāt-i Sayyid Amīr Naṣrallah Bahādur Khān ba Muḥammad Ḥakīm Bī Kul Qūshbīgī*. MS Tashkent, TsVRUz, no. 1998.

Published Primary Sources

A.Ḥ.D. Mas'ala: Sū'āl – Jawāb. *al-Iṣlāḥ* 5 (1915): 146–9.

Ahmad Makhdumi Donish. *Risola yo mukhtasare az ta'rikhi saltanati khonadoni manghitiia*. Dushanbe: Sarvat, 1992.

Allworth, Edward, ed. *The Personal History of a Bukharan Intellectual. The Diary of Muḥammad-Sharīf-i Ṣadr-i Ziyā*. Trans. from the original manuscript by Rustam Shukurov; with introductory study and commentaries by Muhammadjon Shakuri (Shukurov); project director Shahrbanou Tadjbakhsh; ed., English language edition, Edward A. Allworth. Tashkent and Leiden: Brill, 2004.

Anon. [Maḥmūd Khwāja Bihbūdī]. Qāḍī wa bīlār ḥaqqīnda lāyiḥa. *Āyina* 5 (1913): 106–8.

Anon. Seid-Mukhamed-Rakhim, khivinskii khan, i ego priblizhenie. *Vsemirnaia illustratsiia* n. 243. Repr. *TS* 42 (1873): 118–20.

A.P. Pravo pozemel'noi sobstvennosti v Turkestanskom krae. *TV* 18 (1891): 70.

Arendarenko, G.A. *Dosugi v Turkestane, 1874–1889*. St. Petersburg: Tipografiia M.M. Stasiulevich, 1889.

Bobojon Tarroh-Khodim, *Khorazm shoir va navozandalari*, ed. A. Otamurodova and O. Abdurahimov. Toshkent: Tafakkur qanoti, 2011.

Bregel', Iuri È, ed. *Dokumenty arkhiva khivinskikh khanov po istorii i ètnografii karakalpakov*. Moscow: Nauka, 1967.

Bregel, Yuri. *Documents from the Khanate of Khiva (17th–19th centuries)*. Papers on Inner Asia 40. Bloomington, IN: Research Institute for Inner Asian Studies, 2007.

Chekhovich, Olga D., ed. *Dokumenty k istorii agrarnykh otnoshenii v Bukharskom khanstve*. Vol. 1, *Akty feodal'noi sobstvennosti na zemliu XVII–XIX vv.* Tashkent: Fan, 1954.

———. *Samarkandskie dokumenty XV–XVI vv. (O vladeniiakh Khodzhi Akhrara v Srednei Azii i Afganistane)*. Moscow: Nauka, 1974.

Chīmkintlīk Mullā Īrgash Ṣāliḥ Naẓarūghlī-dan sū'āl. *al-Iṣlāḥ* 16 (1915): 291–2.

Cho'lpon [Abd al-Hamid Sulaymon]. *Kecha va Kunduz*. Tashkent: Sharq, 2000.

[Desmaisons, Jean-Jacques-Pierre, and I.V. Vitkevich]. *Zapiski o Bukharskom khanstve (Otchety P.I. Demezona i I.V. Vitkevicha)*. Trans. V.G. Volvnikov and Z.A. Tsomartova. Moscow: Nauka, 1893.

Dingel'shtedt, N. Odno iz otzhivaiushchikh uchrezhdenii. *ZGUP* 7 (1892): 1–23.

———. Zametki. Sudebnoe preobrazovanie v Turkestane. *ZGUP* 9 (1892): 1–75.

———. Pozemel'nye nedorazumeniia v Turkestane. *Vestnik Evropy* 2 (1892). Repr. *TS* 429 (1908): 36–58.

Ershov. Neskol'ko slov o vyborakh. *TV* 75 (1908): 105–7.

[Fayḍ Muḥammad Kātib Hazāra]. *The History of Afghanistan. Fayẓ Muḥammad Kātib Hazārah's Sirāj al-tawārīkh*. Vol. 1, *The Sādūzā'ī Era 1747–1843*. Trans. and ed. Robert D. McChesney. Leiden: Brill, 2013.

Fedorov, G.P. Moia sluzhba v Turkestane (1870–1910). *Istoricheskii Vestnik* 9 (1913): 809.

Fioletov, N. Sudoproizvodstvo v musul'manskikh sudakh (sudy kaziev) Srednei Azii. *Novii Vostok* 23–24 (1928): 204–17.

Fitrat, R.R., and K.S. Sergeev. *Kaziiskie dokumenty XVI veka*. Tashkent: Komitet Nauk Uzbekistana, 1937.

Frei, A. Zakon 10 iiunia 1900 i primenenie ego k bogarnym zemliam. *TV* 58 (1907). Repr. *TS* 437 (1908): 189–196.

Frideriks, N. Turkestan i ego reform. *Vestnik Evropy* 6 (1869): 691–712.

[Geins, Aleksandr K.]. *Sobranie literaturnykh trudov Aleksandra Konstantinovicha Geinsa*. St. Petersburg: Tipografiya Stasyulevicha, 1898.

Ghiyās al-Dīn b. Himām al-Dīn al-Ḥusaynī, alias Khwāndamīr. *Ta'rīkh-i ḥabīb al-siyar fī akhbār-i afrād-i bashar*, ed. J. Humā'ī. 2nd ed. Tehran: Khayyām, 1353sh/1974–5.

[Girs, Fedor K.] *Otchet revizuiushchego po Vysochaishemu poveleniiu, Turkestanskii krai, Tainogo Sovetnika Girsa*. St. Petersburg: Senatskaia Tipografiia, 1884.

G.[irs, F.K.] K voprosu o zemlevadenii v Turkestanskom krae II. *TV* 26–29 (1885): 62–83.

———. K voprosu o kolonizatsii. *TV* 29 (1885b): 79–83.

Ibrohimov, B., ed. *Vasiqalar to'plami*. (*XVI asrining ikkinchi iarmi Samarkand oblastidagi iuridik dokumentlar*). Tashkent: Fan, 1982.

Iusupov, D.Yu., and R.P. Dzhalilov, ed. *Sobranie vostochnykh rukopisei Akademii Nauk Respubliki Uzbekistan-Istoriia*. Tashkent: Fan, 1998.

Ivanov, P.P. *Khoziaistvo dzhuibarskikh sheikhov. K istorii zemlevladeniia v Srednei Azii v XVI–XVII vv.* Moscow and Leningrad: Izdatel'stvo Akademii Nauk SSR, 1954.

Juvonmardiev, A. *XVI–XIX asrlarda Farghonada er-suv masalalariga doir*. Tashkent: Fan, 1965.

Karimov, Ėlior. *Regesty kaziiskikh dokumentov i khanskikh iarlikov Khivinskogo khanstva XVII-nachala XX v.* Tashkent: Fan, 2007.

Karimov, Ghulom, Paolo Sartori, and Shovosil Ziyodov. *Sebzor dahasi qozisi faoliiatiga oid khujjatlar*. Tashkent: O'zbekiston, 2009.

[Kaufman, Konstantin P.] *Proekt Vsepoddaneishago otcheta General-Ad'iutanta K.P. von Kaufman 1 po grazhdanskomu upravleniu i ustroistvu v oblastiakh Turkestanskogo General-Gubernatorstva. 7 noiabria 1867–25 marta 1881 goda*. St. Petersburg: Voennaia Tip, 1885.

Kazakov, Bahadir. *Bukharan Documents: The Collection in the District Library, Bukhara*. Trans. J. Paul. Berlin: Klaus Schwarz, 2001.

Khalil ibn Ishaq. *Précis de jurisprudence musulmane ou principes de législation musulmane civile et religieuse selon le rite malékite*. Trans. M. Perron. Paris: Imprimerie Nationale: 1848–54.

Khāl Muḥammad Tūra Qūlī. Khujandlī afandī Tūra sū'āllārīna jawāb. *al-Iṣlāḥ* 13 (1 July 1916): 399–403.

Khanykov, N.V. *Opisanie Bukharskogo Khanstva*. St. Petersburg: Tip. Imperatorskoi Akademii Nauk, 1843.

Khondayliqii, Sidqii. *Tanlangan asarlar*, ed. B. Qosimov and R. Javharova. Tashkent: Ma"naviiat, 1998.

Kostenko, I.F. *Sredniaia Aziia i vodvorenie v nei Russkoi Grazhdanstvennosti*. St Petersburg: Tip. B. Bezobrazov, 1871.

Kraft, I.I. *Sbornik uzakonenii o kirgizakh stepnykh oblastei*. Orenburg: Tipo-litografiia P.N. Zharinova, 1898.

———. *Sudebnaia chast' v Turkestanskom krae i v stepnykh oblastiakh*. Orenburg: Tip. N.N. Zharinova, 1898.

Krymskii, A.E. O posobiiakh dlia izucheniia musul'manskogo prava. In *Istoriia musul'manstva. Samostoiatel'nye ocherki, obrabotki i dopol'nennye perevody iz Dozi i Gol'dtsiera*, ed. A.E. Krymskii. St. Petersburg: Tipogr. V. Gattsuk, 1904: part II, 28–38.

Logofet, D.N. *Bukhara: Strana bezspraviia*. St. Petersburg: V. Berezovskii, 1909.

Lykoshin, Nil S. Kazii (Narodnye sud'i): Bytovoi ocherk osedlogo naseleniia Turkestana. In *Russkii Turkestan: Sbornik 1. Prilozhenie k gazete "Russkii Turkestan."* Tashkent: Tipografiia "Russkii Turkestan," 1899: 17–57.

———. *Pol zhizni v Turkestane. Ocherki Byta Tuzemnogo Naseleniia*. Petrograd: V.A. Berezovskii, 1916.

Materialy po kirgizskomu zemlepol'zovaniiu. Syr-Dar'inskaia oblast'. Aulieatinskii uezd. Tashkent: Tipo-Litografiia V.M. Il'ina, 1915.

Materialy po kirgizskomu zemlepol'zovaniiu raiona reki Chu i nizov'ev reki Talasa Cherniaevskogo i Aulieatinskogo uezdov Syr-Dar'inskoi oblasti. Tashkent: Tipo-Litografiia V.M. Il'ina, 1915.

Mīrzā ʿAbd al-ʿAẓīm Būstānī [Sāmī]. *Tuḥfa-yi shāhī*, ed. N. Jalālī. Tehran: Anjuman-i Āthār wa Mafāhir-i Farhangī, 1388sh/2009–10.

Mīrzā ʿAbd al-ʿAẓīm Sāmī. *Ta'rīkh-i salāṭīn-i manghitīya* (*Istoriia Mangytskikh gosudarei*), ed. L.M. Epifanova. Moscow: Izdatel'stvo Vostochnoi Literatury, 1962.

Mīrzā Badīʿ al-Dīvān, *Majmaʿ al-Arqām* (*Predpisaniya Fiska*). (*Priemy dokumentatsii v Bukhare XVIII v.*), ed. A.B. Vil'danova. Moscow: Nauka, 1981.

Muḥammad ʿAlī Bāqir-zāda, ed. *Asnād-i muftīyān-i Bukhārā bar asās-i asnād-i kitābkhāna-yi shakhṣī-yi Sayyid Ṣādir Ḥusaynī Ishkiwarī*. Qum: Mujmaʿ-i Dhakhā'ir-i Islāmī, 1391/1971–72.

Muḥammad Ikrām Muftī, *Risāla dar bayān-i bidʿāt-i mashhūra maʿ ḥikāyāt-i ʿarabīya*. Bukhara: Qārī ʿAbd al-Wāhid Bukhārī, 1330/1911–12.

Muḥammad Riḍā Mīrāb Āgahī. *Jāmiʿ al-wāqiʿāt-i sulṭānī*, ed. N. Tashev. Samarqand and Tashkent: IICAS, 2012.

Mukhamedzhanov, A.R., ed. *Naselennye punkty Bukharskogo émirata (konets XIX-nach. XX vv.). Materialy k istoricheskoi geografii Srednei Azii*. Tashkent: Universitet, 2001.

Mukhtarov, A., ed. *Materialy po istorii Ura-Tiube. Sbornik aktov XVII–XIX vv.* Moscow: Izdatel'stvo Vostochnoi Literatury, 1963.

Munis, Shir Muhammad Mirab, and Muhammad Riza Mirab Agahi. 1999. *Firdaws al-Iqbal (History of Khorezm)*. Trans. Y. Bregel. Leiden: Brill.

Nalivkin, Vladimir P. Polozhenie vakufnogo dela v Turkestanskom krae. *Ezhegodnik Ferganskoi oblasti* 3 (1904): 1–56.

Namangāndan Niẓām al-Dīn Khwāja Sayf al-Dīn Khwāja-ūghlī ṭarafindan sū'āllār. *al-Iṣlāh* 5 (1916): 152–53.

Naẓrallāh Bāy b. Qāyil Bāy and Mullā Sulṭān b. Mullā Ṣābir. *Jung-i fatāwā wa maḥḍarāt*. Bukhara: 1325/1907–8.

Niẓām al-Dīn 'Abd al-Wāsi' Niẓāmī [Bakharzī]. *Manshā' al-inshā'*, ed. Rukn al-Dīn Ḥumāyūn-Farrukh. Vol. 1. Tehran: Intishārāt-i dānishgāh-i millī-yi Īrān, 1357sh/1978–79.

Ostroumov, Nikolai P. *Sarty. Ėtnograficheskie materialy (obshchii ocherk)*. 3rd ed. Tashkent: Tip. Gazety "Sredneaziatskaia Zhizn'," 1908.

———. *Islamovedenie. 4. Shariat po shkole (mazkhab) Abu-Khanify*. Tashkent: Tip. Pri Kants. Turk. Gen.-Gub: 1912.

[Pahlen, Konstantin K.] *Otchet po revizii Turkestanskogo kraia po Vysochaishemu poveleniiu Senatorom Gofmeisterom Grafom K.K. Palenom. Narodnye Sudy Turkestanskogo Kraia*. St. Petersburg: Senatskaia Tipografiia, 1909.

Polozhenie ob upravlenii Turkestanskogo kraia (2 iiunia 1886 g). In *Materialy po istorii politicheskogo stroia Kazakhstana (so vremeni prisoedineniia Kazakhstana k Rossii do Velikoi Oktiabr'skoi sotsialisticheskoi revoliutsii)*. Vol. 1, ed. M.G. Masevich. Alma-Ata: Izdatel'stvo Akademii Nauk Kazakhskoi SSR, 1960.

Polozhenie ob upravlenii Turkestanskogo kraia s izmenieniiami i dopolneniiami po 1-e ianvaria 1901 g. Tashkent: Tip. Porcevykh, 1901.

Proekt polozheniia ob upravlenii semirechenskoi i syr-dar'ynskoi oblastei. In *Materialy po istorii politicheskogo stroia Kazakhstana k Rossii do Velikoi Oktiabr'skoi sotsialisticheskoi revoliutsii*. Vol. 1, ed. M.G. Masevich. Alma-Ata: Izdatel'stvo Akademii Nauk Kazakhskoi SSR, 1960.

Qahhor, Abdulla. *Asarlar (6 tomlik)*. Tashkent: Ghofur Ghulom Nashriyoti, 1967.

Qandīya wa Samarīya. Dū risāla dar ta'rīkh-i mazārāt wa jughrāfiyā-yi Samarqand, ed. Īraj Afshār. Tehran: Mu'assasa-yi Farhangī-yi Jahāngīrī, 1367/1948.

Rostislavov, M.N. *Ocherk vidov zemel'noi sobstvennosti i pozemel'nyi vopros v Turkestanskom krae*. St. Petersburg: Tip. Brat. Panteleevykh, 1879.

Ṣadr al-Dīn 'Aynī. *Yāddāshthā*, ed. Ja'faruf. Stalinabad: Matba'a-yi Wizārat-i Madaniyat RSS Tājikistān, 1959.

———. *Bukhārā inqilābīning ta'rīkhī*, ed. Shizuo Shimada and Sharifa Tosheva. Tokyo: Dept. of Islamic Area Studies, Center for Evolving Humanities, Graduate School of Humanities and Sociology, University of Tokyo, 2010.

Sarimsoqov, B., I. Haqqulov, A. Musaqulov, and R. Zarifov. *O'zbek khalq maqollari*. Tashkent: Fan: 1978.

Schuyler, Eugene. *Turkistan: Notes of a Journey in Russian Turkistan, Khokand, Bukhara, and Kuldja*. 2 vols. London: Sampson & Lowe, 1876.

Semenov, Aleksander. *Ocherk pozemel'no-podatnogo i nalogogo ustroistva b. Bukharskogo khantsva*. Tashkent: Izd. Sredne-Aziatskogo Gosudarstvennogo Universiteta: 1929.

———. *Ocherk ustroistva tsentral'nogo administrativnogo upravleniia Bukharskogo khantsva pozdneishego vremeni*. Stalinabad: Izdatel'stvo Akademii Nauk Tadzhikskoi SSR: 1954.

Semenov, Aleksander, et al., ed. *Sobranie vostochnykh rukopisei Akademii Nauk Uzbekskoi SSR*. 10 vols. Tashkent: Fan, 1962–87.

Shakhnazarov, A.I. *Sel'skoe khoziaistvo v Turkestanskom krae*. St. Petersburg: V.F. Kirshbaum, 1908.

Shaykh Muhammad Sodiq Muhammad Yusuf. *Ikhtiloflar, sabablar, yechimlar*. Tashkent: Sharq, 2011.

———. *Zikr ahlidan so'rang 1*. Tashkent: Sharq, 2011.

Tornau, Baron. *Musul'manskoe pravo*. St. Petersburg: Tip. Vtorago otdeleniia sobstvennoi E.I.V. Kantseliarii, 1866.

Turkistān wilāyatīdaghī ḍabt wa rabṭ qīlmaq ya'nī bāshqārmāghīnīng niẓāmī. Tashkent: Tip. Portsevikh, 1901.

Urunbaev, Assom, Galiba Dzhuraeva, and Sanjar Gulomov. *Katalog sredneaziatskikh zhalovannykh gramot iz fonda Instituta vostokovedeniia im. Abu Raikhana Beruni Akademii Nauk Respubliki Uzbekistan*. Halle/Saale: Orientwissenschaftliches Zentrum der Martin-Luther-Universität Halle-Wittenberg, 2007.

Urunbaev, Assom, et. al. *Katalog Khivinskikh kaziiskikh dokumentov (XIX-nach. XX vv.)*. Tashkent and Tokyo: Department of Islamic Area Studies, 2011.

Vámbéry, Arminius. *Travels in Central Asia: Being an Account of a Journey from Teheran Across the Turkoman Desert of the Eastern Shore of the Caspian to Khiva, Bokhara, and Samarcand*. London: John Murray, 1864.

Welsford, Thomas, and Nouryaghdi Tashev, with the assistance of M. Ismoilov and H. Aminov. *A Catalogue of Arabic-Script Documents from the Samarqand Museum*. Samarqand and Istanbul: IICAS, 2012.

Wood, William. *A Collection of Tarkhan Yarlïqs from the Khanate of Khiva*. Papers on Inner Asia 38. Bloomington: Indiana University Research Institute for Inner Asian Studies, 2005.

Zagriazhskii, G. O narodnom sude u kochevago naseleniia Turkestanskago kraia, po obychnomu pravu (*zan'*). In *Materialy dlia statistiki Turkestanskago kraia: Ezhegodnik*, ed. N.A. Maev. Vol. 4. St. Petersburg: Tip. Transhelia, 1876.
Zuev, A. Kirgizskii narodnyi sud. *Zhurnal ministerstva iustitsii* 12 (1907): 161–208.

Secondary Literature

Abashin, Sergei et al., ed. *Tsentral'naia Aziia v sostave Rossiiskoi Imperii*. Moscow: Novoe Literaturnoe Obozrenie, 2008.
———. A Prayer for Rain: Practising Being Soviet and Muslim. *JIS* 25/2 (2014): 178–200.
Abduraimov, M.A. O nekotorykh kategoriiakh feodal'nogo zemlevladeniia i polozhenii krest'ian v Bukharskom khanstve v XVI-nachale XIX veka. *ONU* (1963/7): 32–44.
———. *Ocherki agrarnykh otnoshenii v Bukharskom khanstve*. Tashkent: Fan, 1970.
Abdurasulov, Ulfatbek. Ol'ga Chekhovich: Two Facets of a Soviet Academic. *IS* 48/5 (2015): 785–804.
———. Pravovaia i fiskal'naia dinamika zemlevladeniia v Khorezme (XIX-nachalo XX v.). *Vostok-Oriens* 4 (2015): 32–46.
Agamben, Giorgio. *State of Exception*. Trans. K. Attell. Chicago: University of Chicago Press, 2005.
Agmon, Iris, and Ido Shahar. Shifting Perspectives in the Study of *Sharīʿa* Courts: Methodologies and Paradigms. *ILS* 15/1 (2009): 1–19.
Akramova, K., and N. Akramov. *Vostokoved Mikhail Stepanovich Andreev* (*nauchno-biograficheskii ocherk*). Dushanbe: Irfon, 1973.
Alam, Muzaffar. Trade, State Policy and Regional Change: Aspects of Mughal-Uzbek Commercial Relations, c. 1550–1750. *JESHO* 37/3 (1994): 202–27.
———. *Shariʿa* and Governance in the Indo-Islamic Context. In *Beyond Turk and Hindu: Rethinking Religious Identities in Islamicate South Asia*, ed. David Gilmartin and Bruce B. Lawrence. Gainesville: University Press of Florida, 2000: 216–45.
———. *The Languages of Political Islam: India, 1200–1800*. Chicago: University of Chicago Press, 2004.
Arendarenko, G. *Bukhara i Afganistan v nachale 80-kh godov XIX veka*. Moscow: Glavnaia Redaktsiia Vostochnoi Literatury, 1974.
Astanova, G.Iu. Dokumenty iz arkhivov Uzbekistana po istorii Tadzhikistana XIX-nachala XX veka. *ONU* (1991/8): 55–60.
Azad, Arezou, and Olga Yastrebova, Reflections on an Orientalist: Aleksandr Kuhn (1840–88), the Man and His Legacy. *IS* 48/5 (2015): 675–94.
Azadaev, F. *Tashkent vo vtoroi polovine XIX veka. Ocherki sotsial'no-ekonomicheskoi i politicheskoi istorii*. Tashkent: Izdatel'stvo Akademii Nauk Uzbekskoi SSR, 1959.

Babadzhanov, Bakhtiiar M. Dukchi Ishan i Andizhanskoe vosstanie 1898 g. In *Podvizhniki islama: kul't sviatykh i sufism v Srednei Azii i na Kavkaze*, ed. S.N. Abashin and V.O. Bobrovnikov. Moscow: RAN, 2003: 241–77.

———. Russian Colonial Power in Central Asia as Seen by Local Muslim Intellectuals. In *Looking at the Coloniser: Cross-Cultural Perceptions in Central Asia and the Caucasus, Bengal, and Related Areas*, ed. Beate Eschment and Hans Harder. Berlin: Ergon, 2004: 75–90.

———. *Kokandskoe Khanstvo: Vlast', Politika, Religiia*. Tokyo and Tashkent: NIHU Program Islamic Area Studies Center at the University of Tokyo/Institut Vostokovedeniia Akademii Nauk Respubliki Uzbekistan, 2010.

Babajanov, Bakhtiyar. "How Will We Appear in the Eyes of *Inovertsy* and *Inorodtsy*?" Nikolai Ostroumov on the Image and Function of Russian Power. *CAS* 33/2 (2014): 270–88.

Baberowski, Jörg. Law, the Judicial System, and the Legal Profession. *The Cambridge History of Russia*. Vol. 2, *Imperial Russia, 1689–1917*, ed. Dominic Lieven. Cambridge: Cambridge University Press, 2006.

Balachandran, Gopalan. Claiming Histories beyond Nations: Situating Global History. *IESHR* 49/2 (2012): 242–72.

Barth, Fredrik. An Anthropology of Knowledge. *Current Anthropology* 43/1 (2002): 1–18.

Bayly, Christopher A. *The Birth of the Modern World, 1780–1914: Global Connections and Comparisons*. Malden, MA: Blackwell, 2004.

Beisembiev, Timur K. Vyshchaia administratsiia Tashkenta i iuga Kazakhstana v period Kokandskogo khanstva: 1809–1865 gg. (prosopograficheskii obzor po kokandskim khronikam). In *Istoriko-kul'turnye vzaimosviazi Irana i Dasht-i Kipchaka v XIII–XVIII vv.* Almaty: Daik-Press, 2004: 97–114.

———. *Annotated Indices to the Kokand Chronicles* (Tokyo: Research Institute for Languages and Cultures of Asia and Africa, 2008).

von Benda-Beckmann, Keebet. Forum Shopping and Shopping Forums: Dispute Processing in a Minangkabau Village. *JLP* 19 (1981): 117–59.

Ben-Bassat, Yuval. *Petitioning the Sultan: Protesters and Justice in Late Ottoman Palestine*. London: I.B. Tauris, 2013.

Benton, Lauren. *Law and Colonial Cultures: Legal Regimes in World History: 1400–1900*. Cambridge: Cambridge University Press, 2002.

———. Not Just a Concept: Institutions and the "Rule of Law." *JAS* 68/1 (2009): 117–22.

———. Law and Empire in Global Perspective: Introduction. *AHR* 117/4 (2012): 1092–100.

Benton, Lauren, and Richard J. Ross. Empires and Legal Pluralism: Jurisdiction, Sovereignty, and Political Imagination in the Early Modern World. In *Legal Pluralism and Empires, 1500–1850*, ed. Laurent Benton and Richard J. Ross. New York: New York University Press, 2013: 1–17.

van Berkel, Maaike. Embezzlement and Reimbursement. Disciplining Officials in ʿAbbasid Baghdad (8th–10th Centuries AD). *International Journal of Public Administration* 34 (2011): 712–19.

Binbaş, İlker Evrim. The Anatomy of a Regicide Attempt: Shāhrukh, the *Ḥurūfīs*, and the Timurid Intellectuals in 830/1426–27. *JRAS* 23/2 (2013): 391–428.

Blichner, L. Ch., and A. Molander. Mapping Juridification. *European Law Journal* 14/1 (2008): 36–54.

Bobrovnikov, Vladimir O. *Musul'mane Severnogo Kavkaza: Obychai, pravo, nasilie.* Moscow: Vostochnaia Literatura, 2002.

Bourdieu, Pierre. The Force of Law: Toward a Sociology of the Juridical Field. *HLJ* 38 (1986–7): 805–53.

Bregel, Yuri. *The Administration of Bukhara under the Manghits and Some Tashkent Manuscripts*. Papers on Inner Asia 34. Bloomington, IN: Research Institute for Inner Asian Studies, 2000.

———. Historiography xii: Central Asia. *Encyclopædia Iranica*, ed. Ehsan Yarshater. New York: Encyclopædia Iranica Foundation, 2004: XII: 395–402.

Brockelmann, Carl. *Geschichte der arabischen Literatur*. Leiden: Brill, 1996 [1st ed. 1943], 5 vols (vols. G.I–II and S.I–III).

Brown, Nathan J. *Shariʿa* and State in the Modern Muslim Middle East. *IJMES* 29:3 (1997): 359–76.

Burak, Guy. The Second Formation of Islamic Law: The Post-Mongol Context of the Ottoman Adoption of a School of Law. *CSSH* 55/3 (2013): 579–602.

———. Evidentiary Truth Claims, Imperial Registers, and the Ottoman Archive: Contending Legal Views of Archival and Record-Keeping Practices in Ottoman Greater Syria (Seventeenth–Nineteenth Centuries). *BSOAS* 79/2 (2016): 233–54.

Burbank, Jane. An Imperial Rights Regime: Law and Citizenship in the Russian Empire. *Kritika* 7/3 (2006): 397–431.

Burke, Peter. *A Social History of Knowledge: From Gutenberg to Diderot*. Cambridge: Blackwell Publishers, 2000.

Buskens, Léon. Sharia and the Colonial State. In *The Ashgate Research Companion to Islamic Law*, ed. R. Peters and P. Bearman. Farnham, Surrey: Ashgate, 2014: 209–21.

Cahen, Claude. K͟harād͟j. In *The Encyclopaedia of Islam*, ed. P. Bearman et al. 2nd ed. Leiden: Brill, 1997: IV: 1030–4.

Calero Secall, M. Isabel. Ruler and *Qāḍīs*: Their Relationship during the Naṣrīd Kingdom. *ILS* 7/2 (2000): 235–55.

Campbell, Ian W. Settlement Promoted, Settlement Contested: The Shcherbina Expedition of 1896–1903. *CAS* 30/3–4 (2011): 423–36.

Chatterjee, Nandini. Law, Culture and History. Amir Ali's Interpretation of Islamic Tradition. In *Legal Histories of the British Empire: Laws, Engagements and Legacies*, ed. S. Dorsett and J. McLaren. London: Routledge, 2014: 23–46.

———. Muslim or Christian? Family Quarrels and Religious Diagnosis in a Colonial Court. *AHR* 117/4 (2012): 1101–22.

Chekhovich, Ol'ga D. O razmere kheradzha v Bukhare XIX veka. *ONU* (1961/3): 38–44.

———. K probleme zemel'noi sobstvennosti v feodal'noi Srednei Azii. *ONU* (1976/11): 36–44.

Christelow, Allen. Islamic Law and Judicial Practice in Nigeria: An Historical Perspective. *JMMA* 22/1 (2010): 185–204.

Cohn, Bernard S. The Command of Language and the Language of Command. In *Writings on South Asian History and Society*, ed. Ranajit Guha, Subaltern Studies 4. Delhi: Oxford University Press, 1985: 276–329.

Comaroff, John L. Colonialism, Culture, and the Law: A Foreword. *LSI* 26 (2011): 305–14.

Comaroff, Jean, and John Comaroff. *Of Revelation and Revolution: Christianity, Colonialism, and Consciousness in South Africa.* Chicago: University of Chicago Press, 1991.

Cooper, Barbara M. *Marriage in Maradi: Gender and Culture in a Hausa Society in Niger, 1900–1989*. Portsmouth, NH: Heinemann, 1997.

———. Injudicious Intrusions: Chiefly Authority and Islamic Judicial Practice in Maradi, Niger. In *Muslim Family Law in Sub-Saharan Africa: Colonial Legacies and Post-Colonial Challenges*, ed. S. Jeppie, E. Moosa, and R. Roberts. Amsterdam: Amsterdam University Press, 2010: 183–218.

Crews, Robert D. Empire and the Confessional State: Islam and Religious Politics in Nineteenth-Century Russia. *AHR* 108/1 (2003): 50–83.

———. *For Prophet and Tsar: Islam and Empire in Russia and Central Asia.* Cambridge, MA: Harvard University Press, 2006.

Dagyeli, Jeanine E. By Grace of Descent: A Conflict between an *Īšān* and Craftsmen over Donations. *DI* 88 (2012): 279–307.

Dale, Stephen. The Later Timurids c. 1450–1526. In *The Cambridge History of Inner Asia: The Chinggisid Age*, ed. Nicola di Cosmo, Allen J. Frank, and Peter B. Golden. Cambridge: Cambridge University Press, 2009: 199–217.

Davidovich, Elena A. Usilenie feodal'noi razdroblennosti. Zhizn' tadzhikov v Bukharskom khanstve v XVII i pervoi polovine XVIII v. In *Istoriia tadzhikskogo naroda*. Vol. 2, *Pozdnyi feodalizm (XVII v.–1917 g.)*, ed. B.I. Iskandarov and A.M. Mukhtarov. Moscow: Nauka, 1963–65: 21–56.

———. *Materialy po metrologii srednevekovoi Srednei Azii.* Moscow: Nauka, 1970.

———. Feodal'nyi zemel'nyi milk v Srednei Azii XV–XVIII vv.: Sushchnost' i transformatsiia. In *Formy feodal'noi zemel'noi sobstvennosti i vladeniia na Blizhnem i Srednem Vostoke. Bartol'dovskie chtenia 1975 g.*, ed. B.G. Gafurov, G.F. Girs, and E.A. Davidovich. Moscow: Nauka, 1979: 39–62.

Dmitrieva, L.V., and S.N. Muratov. *Opisanie tiurkskikh rukopisei instituta vostokovedeniia*. Vol 2. Moscow: Nauka, 1975.

Dresch, Paul. Legalism, Anthropology, and History: A View from Part of Anthropology. In *Legalism: Anthropology and History*, ed. Paul Dresch and Hannah Skoda. Oxford: Oxford University Press, 2012: 1–37.

Dudoignon, Stéphane A. “La question scolaire a Boukhara et au Turkestan russe, du “premier renouveau” a la sovietisation (fin du XVIIIe siecle-1937).” CMR 37/1–2 (1996): 133–210.

———. Les “tribulations” du juge Ziyā. Histoire et mémoire du clientélisme politique à Boukhara (1868–1929). AHSS 59/5–6 (2004): 1095–135.

[Editors.] The Imperial Turn. *Kritika* 7/4 (2006): 705–12.

Ergene, Boğaç A. *Local Court, Provincial Society and Justice in the Ottoman Empire: Legal Practice and Dispute Resolution in Çankırı and Kastamonu (1652–1744)*. Leiden: Brill, 2003.

———. Evidence in Ottoman Courts: Oral and Written Documentation in Early-Modern Courts of Islamic Law. JAOS 124/3 (2004): 471–91.

Ėrkinov, A., N. Polvonov, and H. Aminov. *Muhammad Rahimkhon II Feruz Kutubkhonasi Fehristi (Khorazmda kitobat va kutubkhonachilik tarikhidan)*. Tashkent: Yangi Asr Avlodi, 2008.

Esposito, John L. *Women in Muslim Family Law*. 2nd ed. Syracuse: Syracuse University Press, 2001.

Ewick, Patricia, and Susan S. Silbey. *The Common Place of Law: Stories from Everyday Life*. Chicago: University of Chicago Press, 1998.

Fadel, Mohammad. The Social Logic of *Taqlīd* and the Rise of the *Mukhataṣar*. ILS 3/2 (1996): 193–233.

Fleischer, Cornell H. *Bureaucrat and Intellectual in the Ottoman Empire: the Historian Mustafa Âli (1541–1600)*. Princeton: Princeton University Press, 1986.

Frank, Allen J. *Bukhara and the Muslims of Russia: Sufism, Education, and the Paradox of Islamic Prestige*. Leiden: Brill, 2012.

———. A Month among the Qazaqs in the Emirate of Bukhara: Observations on Islamic Knowledge in a Nomadic Environment. In *Explorations in the Social History of Modern Central Asia (19th- Early 20th Century)*, ed. Paolo Sartori. Leiden: Brill, 2013: 247–66.

Gazzini, Claudia. When Jurisprudence Becomes Law: How Italian Colonial Judges in Libya Turned Islamic Law and Customary Practice into Binding Legal Precedent. JESHO 55/4–5 (2012): 746–70.

Gerber, Haim. *State, Society and Law in Islam: Ottoman Law in Comparative Perspective*. Albany: State University of New York Press, 1994.

———. *Islamic Law and Culture, 1600–1840*. Leiden, Boston, Köln: Brill, 1999.

Ghosh, Durba. Another Set of Imperial Turns? AHR 118/3 (2012): 772–93.

Giunchi, Elisa. The Reinvention of *Sharīʿa* under the British Raj: In Search of Authenticity and Certainty. JAS 69/4 (2010): 1119–42.

Guerin, Adam. Racial Myth, Colonial Reform, and the Invention of Customary Law in Morocco, 1912–1930. *The Journal of North African Studies* 16/3 (2011): 361–80.

Gulomov, Sandzhar. O nekotorykh podlinnykh dokumentakh iz kollektsii rukopisnykh proizvedenii fonda IVANRUz. In *History and Culture of Central Asia*, ed. B. Babadjanov and K. Yayoi. Tokyo: TIAS: Department of Islamic Area Studies Centre for Evolving Humanities Graduate School of Humanities and Sociology, 2012: 135–70.

Hallaq, Wael B. The *Qāḍī*'s *Dīwān* (*Sijill*) before the Ottomans. *BSOAS* 61/3 (1998): 415–36.

———. *An Introduction to Islamic Law*. Cambridge: Cambridge University Press, 2009.

———. *Sharīʿa: Theory, Practice, Transformations*. Cambridge: Cambridge University Press, 2009.

———. Islamic Law: History and Transformation. In *The New Cambridge History of Islam*. Vol. 4, *Islamic Cultures and Societies to the End of the Eighteenth Century*, ed. Robert Irwin. Cambridge: Cambridge University Press, 2010: 142–83.

———. On Orientalism, Self-Consciousness and History. *ILS* 18/3–4 (2011): 387–439.

Hann, Christopher. Introduction: The Embeddedness of Property. In *Property Relations: Renewing the Anthropological Tradition*, ed. C. Hann. Cambridge: Cambridge University Press, 2008: 1–47.

Heffening, W. [J. Schacht]. Ḥanafiyya. In *Encyclopaedia of Islam*. 2nd ed., ed. P. Bearman et al. Leiden: Brill, 1986: III: 162–4.

Hennigan, Peter C. *The Birth of a Legal Institution: The Formation of the Waqf in Third-Century A.H. Ḥanafī Legal Discourse*. Leiden: Brill, 2004.

Heyd, Uriel. Some Aspects of the Ottoman Fetvā. *BSOAS* 32/1 (1969): 35–56.

Hilgers, Irene. *Why do Uzbeks Have to Be Muslims? Exploring Religiosity in the Ferghana Valley*. Berlin: Lit, 2008.

Hoexter, Miriam. *Waqf* Studies in the Twentieth Century: The State of the Art. *JESHO* 41/4 (1998): 474–95.

———. The *Waqf* and the Public Sphere. In *The Public Sphere in Muslim Societies*, ed. Miriam Hoexter, Shmuel Eisenstadt, and Nehemia Levtzion. Albany: State University of New York Press, 2002: 119–38.

Holzwarth, Wolfgang. The Uzbek State as Reflected in Eighteenth Century Bukharan Sources. *AS* 60/2 (2006): 321–53.

Hussin, Iza. The Pursuit of the Perak Regalia: Law and the Making of the Colonial State. *LSI* 32/3 (2007): 759–88.

Idrisov, Abdusalim, Ashirbek Muminov, and Maria Szuppe. *Manuscrits en écriture arabe du Musée regional de Nukus (République autonome du Karakalpakstan, Ouzbékistan). Fonds arabe, persan, turkī et Karakalpak*. Rome: Istituto per l'Oriente C.A. Nallino, 2007.

Il'iasov, S.I. *Zemel'nye otnoshenii v Kirgizii v kontse XIX-nachale XX vv.* Frunze: Izdatel'stvo Akademii Nauk Kirgizskoi SSR, 1963.

Irvin, Robert G. What the Partridge Told the Eagle: A Neglected Arabic Source on Chinggis Khan and the Early History of the Mongols. In *The Mongol Empire and Its Legacy*, ed. R. Amitai-Press and D. Morgan. Leiden: Brill, 1999: 5–11.

Isogai, Ken'ichi. A Commentary on the Closing Formula in the Central Asian Waqf Documents. In *Persian Documents*, ed. Nobuaki Kondo. London: RoutledgeCurzon, 2003: 3–12.

———. Seven Fatwa Documents from Early 20th Century Samarqand: The Function of the Mufti in the Judicial Proceedings Adopted at Central Asian Islamic Court. *Annals of Japan Association of Middle East Studies* 27 (2011): 259–82.

Iusupov, D.Iu., and R.P. Dzhalilov. *Sobranie vostochnykh rukopisei Akademii Nauk Uzbekistan. Istoriia*. Tashkent: Fan, 1998.

Ivermee, Robert. *Shari'at* and Muslim Community in Colonial Punjab, 1865–1885. *MAS* 47/5 (2013): 1–28.

Jeppie, Shamil, Ebrahim Moosa, and Richard Roberts. *Muslim Family Law in Sub-Saharan Africa: Colonial Legacies and Post-Colonial Challenges*. Amsterdam: Amsterdam University Press, 2010.

Jersild, Austin. *Orientalism and Empire: North Caucasus Mountain Peoples and the Georgian Frontier*. Montreal: McGill-Queen's University Press, 2002.

Johansen, Baber. *The Islamic Law on Land Tax and Rent: The Peasants' Loss of Property Rights as Interpreted in the Hanafite Literature of the Mamluk and Ottoman Period.* London and New York: Croom Helm, 1998.

———. Signs as Evidence: The Doctrine of Ibn Taymiyya (1263–1328) and Ibn Qayyim al-Jawziyya (d. 1351) on Proof. *ILS* 9/2 (2002): 168–93.

Jurdi Abisaab, R. *Converting Persia: Religion and Power in the Safavid Empire*. London: I.B. Tauris, 2004.

Kaiumova, Khurshida A. *Narodnaia metrologiia i khronologiia Tadzhikov Karategina, Darvaza i Zapadnogo Pamira XIX—nachala XX vv.* Avtoreferat dissertatsii na soiskanie uchenoi stepeni kandidata istoricheskikh nauk. Khojand, 2009.

Kamalov, Sabir Kamalovich. *Karakalpaki v XVIII–XIX vekakh: K istorii vzaimootnoshenii s Rossiei i sredneaziatskimi khanstvami.* Tashkent: Fan, 1968.

Karev, Yuri. From Tents to City. The Royal Court of the Western Qarakhanids between Bukhara and Samarqand. In *Turko-Mongol Rulers, Cities and City Life*, ed. David Durand-Guédy. Leiden: Brill, 2013: 99–147.

Karimov, Ghulom K. *O'zbek adabiioti tarikhi. Uchinchi kitob* (*XIX asrning iqqinchi iarmidan XX asr boshlarigacha*). Tashkent: O'qituvchi, 1975.

Kawahara, Yayoi. *Private Archives on a Makhdūmzāda Family in Marghilan*. Tokyo: Department of Islamic Area Studies, Center for Evolving Humanities, Graduate School of Humanities and Sociology, University of Tokyo, 2012.

Kehl-Bodrogi, Krisztina. *"Religion Is Not So Strong Here": Muslim Religious Life in Khorezm after Socialism*. Berlin: Lit, 2008.

Kemper, Michael. *Herrschaft, Recht und Islam in Daghestan: Von den Khanaten und Gemeindebünden zum ǧihād-Staat.* Wiesbaden: Harrassowitz, 2005.

———, and Maurus Reinkowski. Einleitung: Gewohnheitsrecht zwischen Staat und Gesellschaft. In *Rechtspluralismus in der Islamischen Welt. Gewohnheitsrecht zwischen Staat und Gesellschaft*, ed. M. Kemper and M. Reinkowski. Berlin and New York: De Gruyter, 2005: 1–16.

Khalfin, N.A. *Rossiia i khantsva Srednei Azii (pervaia polovina XIX veka).* Moscow: Nauka, 1974.

Khalfoui, Mouez. Together but Separate: How Muslim Scholars Conceived of Religious Plurality in South Asia in the Seventeenth Century. *BSOAS* 74/1 (2011): 87–96.

Khalid, Adeeb. *The Politics of Muslim Cultural Reform: Jadidism in Central Asia.* Berkeley: University of California Press, 1998.

———. Society and Politics in Bukhara, 1868–1920. *CAS* 19/3–4 (2000): 367–96.

———. *Islam after Communism: Religion and Politics in Central Asia.* Berkeley: University of California Press, 2007.

———. *Making Uzbekistan: Nation, Empire, and Revolution in the Early USSR.* Ithaca and London: Cornell University Press, 2015.

Kisliakov, Nikolai A. *Patriarkhal'no-feodal'nye otnosheniia sredi osedlogo naseleniia Bukharskogo ėmirata v kontse XIX-nachale XX vv.* Moscow: Nauka, 1962.

Koch, Ebba. *Dara Shikoh Shooting Nilgais: Hunt and Landscape in Mughal Painting.* Occasional Papers 1. Washington, DC: Freer Gallery of Art, Arthur M. Sackler Gallery, Smithsonian Institution, 1998.

Kolsky, Elizabeth. Introduction. *LHR* 28/4 (2010): 973–8.

Komatsu, Hisao. *Dār al-Islām* under Russian Rule as Understood by Turkestani Muslim Intellectuals. In *Empire, Islam, and Politics in Central Eurasia*, ed. Tomohiko Uyama. Tokyo: Slavic Research Center, 2007: 3–21.

———. From Holy War to Autonomy: *Dār al-Islām* Imagined by Turkestani Muslim Intellectuals. *Cahiers d'Asie centrale* 17–18 (2009): 449–75.

Kostin, B.A. *Mikhail Dimitrovich Skobelev.* Moscow: Moladaia Gvardia, 2000.

Kozlowski, Gregory C. *Muslim Endowments and Society in British India.* Cambridge: Cambridge University Press, 1985.

Krsmárik, Johann. Das Waḳfrecht vom Standpunkte des Śarîʿarechtes nach der ḥanefitischen Schule: Ein Beitrag zum Studium des Islamischen Rechtes. *ZDMG* 45 (1891): 511–76.

von Kügelgen, Anke. *Die Legitimierung der mittelasiatischen Mangitendynastie in den Werken ihrer Historiker, 18.–19. Jahrhundert.* Istanbul: Ergon, 2002.

Kuran, Timur. *The Long Divergence: How Islamic Law Held Back the Middle East.* Princeton: Princeton University Press, 2011.

Lambton, Ann S. *Landlord and Peasant in Persia: A Study of Land Tenure and Land Revenue Administration.* London: Oxford University Press, 1953.

———. Justice in the Medieval Persian Theory of Government. *Studia Islamica* 5 (1956): 91–119.

———. Islamic Mirror for Princes. In *Atti del covegno internazionale sul tema, La Persia nel Medioevo (Roma, 31 marzo–5 aprile 1970)*. Rome: Accademia Nazionale dei Lincei, 1971: 419–42.

Layish, Aharon. The Mālikī Family *waqf* According to Wills and *waqfiyyāt*. BSOAS 46/1 (1983): 1–32.

———. The Family *Waqf* and the *Sharīʿa* Law of Succession in Modern Times. *Journal of International Law* 4/3 (1997): 352–88.

———. The Transformation of the *Sharīʿa* from Jurists' Law to Statutory Law in the Contemporary Muslim World. *WDI* 44/1 (2004): 85–113.

———. Sharīʿa *and Custom in Libyan Tribal Society. An Annotated Translation of Decisions from the* Sharīʿa *Courts of Adjābiya and Kufra*. Leiden: Brill, 2005.

———. *Shahādat al-naql* in the Judicial Practice in Modern Libya. In *Dispensing Justice in Islam: Qadis and Their Judgements*, ed. M. Kh. Masud, R. Peters and D.S. Powers Brill, 2006: 495–516.

———. *Waqfs* of Awlād al-Nās in Aleppo in the Mamluk Period as Reflected in a Family Archive. *JESHO* 51/2 (2008): 287–326.

———. *Legal Documents from the Judean Desert: The Impact of the Shariʿa on Bedouin Customary Law*. Leiden: Brill, 2011.

Lewis, Eric Beverley. Frontier as Resource: Law, Crime, and Sovereignty on the Margins of Empire. *CSSH* 55/2 (2013): 241–72.

Litvinskii, B.A., and N.M. Akramov. *Aleksandr Aleksandrovich Semenov (nauchno-bibliograficheskii ocherk)*. Moscow: Nauka, 1971.

Lydon, Ghislaine. Droit islamique et droits de la femme d'après les registres du Tribunal Musulman de Ndar (Saint-Louis du Sénégal). *Canadian Journal of African Studies* 41/2 (2007): 289–307.

Makinde, Abdul-Fatah 'Kola, and Philip Ostien. Legal Pluralism in Colonial Lagos: The 1894 Petition of the Lagos Muslims to their British Colonial Masters. *WDI* 52/1 (2012): 51–68.

Manz, Beatrice Forbes. *Power, Politics and Religion in Timurid Iran*. Cambridge: Cambridge University Press, 2007.

Martin, Virginia. *Law and Custom in the Steppe: The Kazakhs of the Middle Horde and Russian Colonialism*. Richmond, UK: Curzon, 2001.

———. Kazakh Oath-Taking in Colonial Courtrooms: Legal Culture and Russian Empire-Bulding. *Kritika* 5/3 (2004): 483–514.

Masud, Muhammad Khalid, Brinckley Messick, and David S. Powers. Muftis, Fatwas, and Islamic Legal Interpretation. In *Islamic Legal Interpretation: Muftis and Their*

Fatwas, ed. M.K. Masud, B. Messick, and D.S. Powers. Cambridge, MA: Harvard University Press, 1996: 1–32.

Masud, Muhammad Khalid, Rudolph Peters, and David S. Powers. *Qāḍīs* and Their Courts: An Historical Survey. In *Dispensing Justice in Islam: Qadis and Their Judgments*, ed. M.K. Masud, R. Peters, and D.S. Powers. Leiden: Brill, 2006: 1–44.

Matthee, Rudi. Was Safavid Iran an Empire? *JESHO* 53/1–2 (2010): 233–65.

Maurer, Bill. The Cultural Power of Law? Conjunctive Readings. *LHR* 38/4 (2004): 843–50.

McChesney, Robert D. *Waqf in Central Asia: Four Hundred Years in the History of a Muslim Shrine, 1480–1889*. Princeton: Princeton University Press, 1991.

———. Central Asia xi. Economy from the Timurids until the 12th/18th Century. In *Encyclopædia Iranica*, ed. Ehsan Yarshater. Costa Mesa, CA.: Mazda, 1992: V: 216–21.

———. *Central Asia: Foundations of Change*. Princeton: Darwin Press, 1996.

———. Shībānī Khān and Shībānids. In *Encyclopaedia of Islam*. 2nd ed., ed. P. Bearman et al. Leiden: Brill, 1997: IX: 426–31.

———. Waḳf. V. In Central Asia. *Encyclopaedia of Islam*. 2nd ed., ed. CE Bosworth et al. Leiden: Brill, 2002: XI: 92.

Meier, Astrid. Für immer und ewig? Befristete Formen islamischer Stiftungen in osmanischer Zeit. In *Islamische Stiftungen zwischen juristischer Norm und sozialer Praxis*, ed. Astrid Meier, Johannes Pahlitzsch, and Lucian Reinfandt. Berlin: Akademie Verlag, 2009: 191–212.

Merry, Sally Engle. *Colonizing Hawai'i: The Cultural Power of Law*. Princeton: Princeton University Press, 2000.

———. Comments on Comments. *LSR* 38/4 (2004): 861–6.

Messick, Brinkley. *The Calligraphic State: Textual Domination and History in a Muslim Society*. Berkeley: University of California Press, 1993.

Miklukho-Maklai, N.D., ed. *Opisanie tadzhikskikh i persidskikh rukopisei Instituta narodov Azii*. Vol. 1. Moscow: Izdatelst'stvo Vostochnoi Literatury, 1964.

Mommsen, Wolfgang, and Jaap de Moor, eds. *European Expansion and Law: The Encounter of European and Indigenous Law in 19th and 20th Century Africa and Asia*. Oxford and New York: Berg, 1992.

Moore, Sally Falk. Certainties Undone: Fifty Turbulent Years of Legal Anthropology, 1949–1999. *JRAI* 7/1 (2001): 95–116.

Morgan, David. The "Great Yasa" of Chinggis Khan Revisited. In *Mongols, Turks, and Others: Eurasian Nomads and the Sedentary World*, ed. R. Amitai and M. Biran. Leiden and Boston: Brill, 2005: 291–308.

Morrison, Alexander S. *Russian Rule in Samarkand, 1868–1910: A Comparison with British India*. Oxford: Oxford University Press, 2008.

———. Metropole, Colony, and Imperial Citizenship in the Russian Empire. *Kritika* 13/2 (2012): 327–64.

———. Sufism, Pan-Islamism and Information Panic: Nil Sergeevich Lykoshin and the Aftermath of the Andijan Uprising. *PP* 214 (2012): 255–304.

———. *Amlākdārs*, *Khwājas* and *Mulk* Land in the Zarafshan Valley after the Russian Conquest. In *Explorations in the Social History of Modern Central Asia (19th–20th Century)*, ed. Paolo Sartori. Leiden: Brill, 2013: 23–64.

———. Creating a Colonial Shari'a for Russian Turkestan: Count Pahlen, the Hidaya and the Anglo-Muhammadan Law. In *Imperial Cooperation and Transfer, 1870–1930: Empires and Encounters*, ed. Volker Barth and Roland Cvetkovski. London: Bloomsbury, 2015: 127–49.

Mottahedeh, Roy P. *Loyalty and Leadership in an Early Islamic Society*. 2nd ed. London and New York: I.B. Tauris, 2001.

Mukminova, Roziia G. *K istorii agrarnykh otnoshenii v Uzbekistane XVI v. (po materialam "Vakfname")*. Tashkent: Nauka, 1966.

———. *Sotsialnaia differentsiatsia naseleniia gorodov Uzbekistana v XV–XVI vv.* Tashkent: Fan, 1985.

Muminov, Ashirbek, N. Abdulahatov, and Y. Kawahara, ed. *Mazar Documents from Xinjang and Ferghana (Facsimile)*, vol. 3. Tokyo: Research Institute for Languages and Cultures of Asia and Africa, Tokyo University of Foreign Studies, 2007.

Mundy, Martha, and Richard Saumarez Smith. *Governing Property, Making the Modern State: Law, Administration and Production in Ottoman Syria.* London: I.B. Tauris, 2007.

Murphey, Rhoads. Mustafa Safi's Version of the Kingly Virtues as Presented in His *Zübdet'ül Tevarih*, or Annals of Sultan Ahmed, 1012–1023 A.H./1603–1614 AD. In *Frontiers of Ottoman Studies,* vol. 1, ed. Colin Imber and Keiko Kiyotaki. London: I.B. Tauris, 2005: 5–24.

Nabiev, R.N. *Iz istorii kokandskogo khanstva (Feodal'noe kkhoziaistvo Khudoiar-Khana)*. Tashkent: Fan, 1973.

Newbigi, Eleanor, Leigh Denault, and Rohit De. Introduction: Personal Law, Identity Politics and Civil Society in Colonial South Asia. *IESHR* 46/1 (2009): 1–4.

Northrop, Douglas. *Veiled Empire: Gender and Power in Stalinist Central Asia*. Ithaca: Cornell University Press, 2013.

Oberauer, Norbert. Early Doctrines on *Waqf* Revisited: The Evolution of Islamic Endowment Law in the 2nd Century AH. *ILS* 20/1–2 (2013): 1–47.

Parker, Kunal M. The Historiography of Difference. *LHR* 23/3 (2005): 685–95.

Paul, Jürgen. *Die politische und soziale Bedeutung der Naqšbandiyya in Mittleasien im 15. Jahrhundert*. Berlin and New York: Walter de Gruyter, 1991.

———. Recent Monographs on the Social History of Central Asia. *CAS* 29/1 (2010): 119–30.

———. *Zentralasien.* Frankfurt am Main: Fischer, 2012.

Penati, Beatrice. Swamps, Sorghum, and Saxauls: Marginal Lands and the Fate of Russian Turkestan. *CAS* 29/1 (2010): 61–78.

———. Notes on the Birth of Russian Turkestan's Fiscal System: A View from the Fergana Oblast'. *JESHO* 53/5 (2010): 679–711.

———. Beyond Technicalities: On Land Assessment and Land-Tax in Russian Turkestan. *JFGO* 59/1 (2011): 1–27.

———. The Cotton Boom and the Land Tax in Russian Turkestan (1880s–1915). *Kritika* 14/4 (2013): 741–74.

———. Managing Rural Landscapes in Colonial Turkestan: A View from the Margins. In *Explorations into the Social History of Modern Central Asia (19th–20th century)*, ed. Paolo Sartori. Leiden Brill, 2013: 65–109.

Peters, Ruud. *Crime and Punishment in Islamic Law: Theory and Practice from the Sixteenth to the Twenty-First Century.* Cambridge: Cambridge University Press, 2005.

———. What Does It Mean to Be an Official Madhhab? Hanafism and the Ottoman Empire. In *The Islamic School of Law: Evolution, Devolution, and Progress*, ed. P. Bearman, R. Peters, and F.E. Vogel. Cambridge MA: Harvard University Press, 2006: 147–58.

Peterson, Derek R. Morality Plays: Marriage, Church Courts, and Colonial Agency in Central Tanganyika, ca. 1876–1928. *AHR* 111/4 (2006): 983–1010.

Pianciola, Niccolò and Paolo Sartori. *Waqf* in Turkestan: The Colonial Legacy and the Fate of an Islamic Institution in Early Soviet Central Asia (1917–1924). *CAS* 26/4 (2007): 475–98.

Pierce, Leslie. *Morality Tales: Law and Gender in the Ottoman Court of Aintab.* Berkeley: University of California Press, 2003.

Pirie, Fernanda. Legal Autonomy as Political Engagement: The Ladakhi Village in the Wider World. *LSR* 40/1 (2006): 77–103.

———. *The Anthropology of Law.* Oxford: Oxford University Press, 2013.

Powers, David S. Orientalism, Colonialism, and Legal History: The Attack on Muslim Family Endowments in Algeria. *CSSH* 31/3 (1989): 535–71.

———. The Islamic Inheritance System: A Socio-Historical Approach. In *Islamic Family Law*, ed. Chibli Mallat and Jane Connors. London, Dordrecht, and Boston: Graham & Trotman, 1990: 11–29.

———. The Maliki Family Endowment: Legal Norms and Social Practices. *IJMES* 25 (1993): 379–406.

———. *Law, Society, and Culture in the Maghrib, 1300–1500.* Cambridge: Cambridge University Press, 2002.

Pravilova, Ekaterina. The Property of Empire. Islamic Law and Russian Agrarian Policy in Transcaucasia and Turkestan. *Kritika* 12/2 (2011): 353–86.

Prior, Daniel G. High Rank and Power among the Northern Kirghiz: Terms and Their Problems, 1845–1864. In *Explorations in the Social History of Modern Central Asia (19th–20th Century)*, ed. Paolo Sartori. Leiden: Brill, 2013: 137–79.

Privratsky, Bruce G. *Muslim Turkistan: Kazak Religion and Collective Memory*. Richmond, Surrey: Curzon, 2001.

Rao, Velcheru Narayana, David Shulman, and Sanjay Subrahmanyam. *Textures of Time: Writing History in South India 1600–1800*. New York: Other Press, 2003.

Rapoport, Yossef. Royal Justice and Religious Law: *Siyāsah* and *Sharīʿah* under the Mamluks. *MSR* 16 (2012): 71–102.

Rasanayagam, Johan. Introduction. *CAS* 25/3 (2006): 219–33.

———. *Islam in Post-Soviet Uzbekistan: The Morality of Experience*. Cambridge: Cambridge University Press, 2011.

Rebstock, Ulrich. A *Qāḍī*'s Errors. *ILS* 6/1 (1999): 1–37.

Reichmuth, Philipp "Lost in the Revolution": Bukharan *Waqf* and Testimony Documents from the Early Soviet Period. *WDI* 50/3–4 (2010): 362–96.

Renucci, Florence. Le juge et la connaissance du droit indigène. Eléments de comparaison entre l'Algérie et la Libye aux premiers temps de la colonization. In *Le juge et l'Outremer*. Vol. 3, *Médée ou les impératifs du choix*, ed. B. Durand and E. Gasparini. Lille: CHJ, 2007: 211-26.

Reynolds, Michael A. Muslim Mobilization in Imperial Russia's Caucasus. In *Islam and the European Empires*, ed. D. Motadel. Oxford: Oxford University Press, 2014: 187–212.

Riles, Annalise. Law as Object. In *Law and Empire in the Pacific: Fiji and Hawai'i*, ed. S.E. Merry and D. Brenneis. Santa Fe, NM: School of American Research Press, 2004: 187–212.

Roberts, Richard, and Kristin Mann. Law in Colonial Africa. In *Law in Colonial Africa*, ed. K. Mann and R. Roberts. Portsmouth, NH: Heinemann, 1991.

Ro'i, Yaacov. *Islam in the Soviet Union: From the Second World War to Gorbachev*. New York: Columbia University Press, 2000.

Rosen, Lawrence. *The Anthropology of Justice: Law as Culture in Islamic Society*. Cambridge: Cambridge University Press, 1989.

Rubin, Avi. *Ottoman Nizamiye Courts: Land and Modernity*. New York: Palgrave MacMillan, 2011.

Sachs, Jeffrey Adam. "Native Courts" and the Limits of the Law in Colonial Sudan: Ambiguity as Strategy. *LSI* 38/4 (2013): 973–92.

Saha, Jonathan. A Mockery of Justice? Colonial Law, the Everyday State and Village Politics in the Burma Delta, c. 1890–1910. *PP* 217 (2012): 187–212.

Sahadeo, Jeff. *Russian Colonial Society in Tashkent, 1863–1923*. Bloomington: Indiana University Press: 2007.

Sartori, Paolo. Judicial Elections as a Colonial Reform: The Qadis and Biys in Tashkent, 1868–1886. *CMR* 49/1 (2008): 79–100.

———. Il *waqf* nel Turkestan russo tra legislazione e pratica amministrativa coloniale. *Quaderni Storici* 132/3 (2009): 802.

———. Colonial Legislation Meets *Sharīʿa*: Muslims' Land Rights in Russian Turkestan. *CAS* 29/1 (2010): 43–60.

———. Towards a History of the Muslims' Soviet Union: A View from Central Asia. *WDI* 50/3–4 (2010): 315–34.

———. The Evolution of Third-Party Mediation in *Sharīʿa* Courts in 19th- and Early 20th-Century Central Asia. *JESHO* 54/3 (2011): 311–52.

———. The Birth of a Custom: Nomads, *Sharīʿa* Courts and Established Practices in the Tashkent Province, ca. 1868–1919. *ILS* 18/4 (2011): 293–326.

———. Authorized Lies: Colonial Agency and Legal Hybrids in Tashkent, c. 1881–1893. *JESHO* 55/4–5 (2012): 688–717.

———. Murder in Manghishlaq: Notes on an Instance of Application of Qazaq Customary Law in Khiva (1895). *DI* 88/2 (2012): 217–57.

———. Constructing Colonial Legality in Russian Central Asia: On Guardianship. *CSSH* 56/2 (2014): 419–47.

———. *Ijtihād* in Bukhara: Central Asian Jadidism and Local Genealogies of Cultural Change. *JESHO* 59/1–2 (2016): 193–236.

———. Seeing like a Khanate: On Archives, Cultures of Documentation, and 19th-Century Khorezm. *JPS* 8/2 (2016): 228–57.

———, and Ido Shahar. Legal Pluralism in Muslim-Majority Colonies: Mapping the Terrain. *JESHO* 55/4–5 (2012): 637–63.

Savitskii, A.P. *Pozemel'nyi vopros v Turkestane (v proektakh i zakone 1867–1886)*. Tashkent: Izdatel'stvo SamGU, 1963.

Schacht. Joseph. *Introduction to Islamic Law*. Oxford: Clarendon Press, 1965.

Scheele, Judith. A Taste for Law: Rule Making in Kabylia (Algeria). *CSSH* 50/4 (2008): 895–919.

———. Councils without Customs, Qadis without State: Property and Community in the Algerian Touat. *ILS* 17/3 (2010): 350–74.

———. *Smugglers and Saints of the Sahara: Regional Connectivity in the Twentieth Century*. Cambridge: Cambridge University Press, 2012.

———. Rightful Measures: Irrigation, Land, and the *Sharīʿah* in the Algerian Touat. In *Legalism: Anthropology and History*, ed. Paul Dresch and Hannah Skoda. Oxford: Oxford University Press, 2012.

Schwarz, Florian. Bargeldstiftungen im Chanat von Chiva, 1840–1922. *DI* 80/1 (2003): 86–87.

———. Contested Grounds: Ambiguities and Disputes over the Legal and Fiscal Status of Land in the Manghit Emirate of Bukhara. CAS 29/1 (2010): 33–42.

Shaham, Ron. *Family and the Courts in Modern Egypt: A Study Based on Decisions by the Sharīʿa Courts 1900–1955*. Leiden: Brill, 1997.

———. *The Expert Witness in Islamic Courts: Medicine and Crafts in the Service of Law*. Chicago: University of Chicago Press, 2010.

Shaniiazov, K. Ob osnovnykh vidakh zemel'noi sobstvennosti i razmerakh kharadzha v Bukharskom khanstve v kontse XIX-nachale XX veka (po ėtnograficheskim dannym). ONU (1962/3): 51–6.

Sharafi, Mitra. The Marital Patchwork of Colonial South Asia: Forum Shopping from Britain to Baroda. LHR 28/4 (2010): 979–1009.

Shereikis, Rebecca. From Law to Custom: The Shifting Legal Status of Muslim *Originaires* in Kayes and Medine, 1903–13. *Journal of African Studies* 42 (2001): 261–83.

Silbey, Susan. Legal Consciousness. In *New Oxford Companion to Law*, ed. P. Cane and J. Conaghan. Oxford: Oxford University Press, 2008: 695–6.

———. After Legal Consciousness. *Annual Review of Law and Social Sciences* 1 (2005): 323–68.

Singha, Radhika. *A Despotism of Law: Crime and Justice in Early Colonial India*. New Delhi: Oxford University Press, 1998.

Skinner, Quentin. *Vision of Politics*. Vol. 1, *Regarding Method*. Cambridge: Cambridge University Press, 2002.

Smail, Daniel Lord. *The Consumption of Justice: Emotions, Publicity, and Legal Culture in Marseille, 1264–1423*. Ithaca NY: Cornell University Press, 2003.

Smith, Jay M. Between Discourse and Experience: Agency and Ideas in the French Pre-Revolution. *History and Theory* 40 (2001): 116–42.

Soares, Benjamin. The Attempt to Reform Family Law in Mali. WDI 49/3–4 (2009): 398–428.

Stewart, Frank H. Customary Law among the Bedouin of the Middle East and North Africa. In *Nomadic Societies in the Middle East and North Africa: Entering the 21st Century*, ed. Dawn Chatty. Leiden: Brill, 2005: 239–79.

———. False Friends: Overlapping Terminology in Arab Customary Law and in Islamic Law. Paper delivered at the 6th Conference of the International Society for Islamic Legal Studies, Exeter, 13 July 2009.

Stoler, Ann Laura. "In Cold Blood": Hierarchies of Credibility and the Politics of Colonial Narratives. *Representations* 37 (1992): 151–89.

———. *Along the Archival Grain: Epistemic Anxieties and Colonial Commonsense*. Princeton: Princeton University Press, 2010.

Strawson, John. Revisiting Islamic Law: Marginal Notes from Colonial History. *GLR* 12/3 (2003): 362–83.

Subrahmanyam, Sanjay. Between a Rock and a Hard Place. Some Afterthoughts. In *The Brokered World: Go-Betweens and Global Intelligence, 1770–1820*, ed. S. Schaffer, L. Roberts, K. Raj, and J. Delbourgo. Sagamore Beach, MA: Science History Publications, 2009: 429–40.

———. *Courtly Encounters: Translating Courtliness and Violence in Early Modern Eurasia*. Cambridge, MA: Harvard University Press, 2012.

Subtelny, Maria Eva. The Sunni Revival under Shāh-Rukh and Its Promoters: A Study of the Connection between Ideology and Higher Learning in Timurid Iran. *Proceedings of the 27th Meeting of Haneda Memorial Hall Symposium on Central Asia and Iran August 30, 1993*. Kyoto: Institute of Inner Asian Studies, 1993: 16–21.

———. A Late Medieval Persian Summa on Ethics: Kashifi's *Akhlāq-i Muḥsinī*. *IS* 36/4 (2003): 601–14.

———. *Timurids in Transition: Turko-Persian Politics and Acculturation in Medieval Iran*. Leiden: Brill, 2007.

Sugawara, Jun, and Yayoi Kawahara, ed. *Mazar Documents from Xinjang and Ferghana (Facsimile)*, vol. 1. Tokyo: Research Institute for Languages and Cultures of Asia and Africa, Tokyo University of Foreign Studies, 2006.

Tamanaha, Brian Z. Understanding Legal Pluralism: Past to Present, Local to Global. *SLR* 29 (2007): 374–411.

Tamdoğan, Işık. *Ṣulḥ* and the 18th Century Ottoman Courts of Uskudar and Adana. *ILS* 15/1 (2008): 55–83.

Togan, İsenbike. Uluğbek zamanında Yasa ve Şeriat Tartışmaları. *Tarih Çevresi* 1 (1994): 9–16.

Travers, Robert. *Ideology and Empire in Eighteenth-Century India: The British Bengal*. Cambridge: Cambridge University Press, 2007.

Vallerani, Massimo. *Medieval Public Justice*, trans. Sarah Rubin Blanshei. Washington, DC: Catholic University of America Press, 2012.

Walsh, J.R. Fatwā ii: Ottoman Empire. In *The Encyclopaedia of Islam*. 2nd ed., ed. P. Bearman et al. Leiden: Brill, 1991: II: 866–7.

Welsford, Thomas. *Four Types of Loyalty in Early Modern Central Asia: The Tūqāy-Tīmūrid Takeover of Greater Mā warā al-Nahr, 1598–1605*. Leiden: Brill, 2012.

———. Fathers and Sons: Re-Readings in a Samarqandi Private Archive. In *Explorations in the Social History of Modern Central Asia (19th–20th Century)*, ed. Paolo Sartori. Leiden: Brill, 2013: 299–323.

Werth, Paul. Changing Conceptions of Difference, Assimilation, and Faith in the Volga-Kama Region, 1740–1870. In *Russian Empire: Space, People, Power, 1700–1930*, ed.

J. Burbank, M. von Hagen, and A. Remnev. Bloomington: Indiana University Press, 2007: 169–214.

Wilde, Andreas. Creating the Façade of a Despotic State: On *Āqsaqāls* in Late 19th-Century Bukhara. In *Explorations in the Social History of Modern Central Asia (19th–Early 20th Centuries)*, ed. Paolo Sartori. Leiden: Brill, 2013: 267–98.

———. *What is Beyond the River? Power, Authority and Social Order in Transoxiana*, 18th–19th Centuries. Vienna: Verlag der Österreichischen Akademie der Wissenschaften, 2016.

Index